RAND McNALLY

the road atlas

and TRAVEL GUIDE | BEST EATS EDITION

WHAT'S INSIDE

Best Eats

Northeast: pages BE 2–BE 7
South: pages BE 8–BE 13
Midwest: pages BE 14–BE 19
Rocky Mountains/Plains: pages BE 20–BE 25
West/Southwest: pages BE 26–BE 31
Food Festivals: page BE 32

Maps

Maps: pages 4–140
Legend: page 3
Index: pages 141–148

Travel Guide

State-by-state trip ideas; border crossing info;
hotel, rental car, and cell phone emergency numbers.

Pages 149–255

Mileage Chart

Driving distances between 90 North American cities and national parks.

Page 256

Mileage and Driving Times Map

Distances and driving times between hundreds of North American cities and national parks.

Inside back cover

Photo acknowledgements
(t) = top, (c) = center, (b) = bottom,
(l) left, (r) right.
Cover: Joseph Sohm/Digital Vision/Punchstock.
Page 1 (1 of 5) ©Alison Miksch/FoodPix/Jupiter
Images, (3 of 5) ©Photodisc, (4 of 5) ©Photodisc,
(5 of 5) ©Photodisc; 2 ©Hussenot/photocuisine/
Corbis; 3 (t) ©Alison Miksch/FoodPix/Jupiter Im-
ages, (bl) ©David H. Wells/Aurora/Getty Images,
(br) ©Ron Gladkowski; 4 (t) ©Joe Sohm/Visions
of America, LLC/Alamy, (bl) ©John Blais/Food-
Pix/Jupiter Images, (br) ©Edward Savara,Jr./
Courtesy Philadelphia CVB; 5 (t) ©Ellen
Isaacs/Alamy, (b) ©Christopher Martin/Quahog.
org; 6 (t) ©D. Hurst/Alamy, (c) ©Stephen Saks
Photography/Alamy, (b) ©Ted Morrison/Food-
Pix/Jupiter Images; 7 (t) ©Megapress/Alamy,
(b) ©Jeremy Hoare/Alamy; 8 ©Kelly-Mooney
Photography/Corbis; 9 (t) ©Paul Poplis/Food-
Pix/Jupiter Images, (bl) ©Steve Skjold/Alamy,
(br) ©Jesse Goldstein; 10 (tl) ©Brigette Sullivan,
(tr) ©Carl Purcell/New Orleans MCVB, (b)
©Carl Purcell/New Orleans MCVB; 11 (t) ©Lew
Roberston/FoodPix/Jupiter Images, (b) ©Bon
Appetit/Alamy; 12 (t) ©Creative Expression/
Alamy, (c) ©Susan C. Bourgoin/FoodPix/Jupi-
ter Images, (b) ©Todd Wilson; 13 (tl) ©Lewis
Jackson/Alamy, (tr) ©Pinehurst, Southern Pines,
Aberdeen Area CVB, (b) ©Natchitoches Area
CVB; 14 © Steven Widoff/Alamy; 15 (t) ©Bruce
James/FoodPix/Jupiter Images, (c) ©Photodisc,
(b) ©Brigette Sullivan; 16 (t) ©Todd Wilson, (c)
©Michael Stern/Roadfood.com, (b) ©Richard
Levine/Alamy; 17 (t) ©Brigette Sullivan, (b)
©foodfolio/Alamy, 18 (t) ©Kim Karpeles, (c)
©Jeff Greenberg/Alamy, (b) ©Jeff Greenberg/
Alamy; 19 (tl) ©Skyline Chili, (tr) Courtesy
Superdawg, (bl) Courtesy Glier's Goetta Co.,
(br) ©Brigette Sullivan; 20 ©William Joseph
Boch/StockFood Creative/Getty Images; 21 (t)
©Alison Miksch/FoodPix/Jupiter Images, (bl)
©Somos Images/Corbis, (br) Courtesy Sooner's
Legends; 22 (t) ©Richard Cummins/Superstock,
(cl) ©Terry Tuck/Courtesy Spud Fudge, (cr)
©Daniel Templeton/Alamy, (b) ©Todd Wilson; 23
(t) ©Burke/Triolo Productions/Jupiter Images, (c)
©South Dakota Tourism, (b) ©Photodisc/Punch-
stock; 24 (t) ©M L Pearson/Alamy, (c) ©Cliff
Keeler/Alamy, (b) Courtesy Runza National, Inc.;
25 (t) ©Eddie Lin, (b) ©Todd Wilson; 26 ©Dave
G. Houser/Corbis; 27 (t) ©Photodisc/Punchstock,
(bl) ©Jeff Greenberg/PhotoEdit, Inc., (br)
Courtesy The Joel Palmer House Restaurant; 28
(tl) ©Brigette Sullivan, (tr) ©Todd Wilson, (b)
©Photodisc; 29 (t) ©Tim Hill/Alamy, (c) ©Todd
Wilson, (b) Courtesy Jelly Belly Candy Company;
30 (t) ©Susan C. Bourgoin/FoodPix/Jupiter
Images, (c) ©Allison Day/sushiday.com, (b)
©Photodisc; 31(t) ©Shiyana Thenabadu/Alamy,
(c) ©John Burwell/FoodPix/Jupiter Images, (b)
©Steve Lewis, Santa Fe CVB; 32 (tl) ©Image
Source/Punchstock, (tr) ©Jane Grushow/Alamy,
(c) ©Photodisc, (b) ©Photodisc.

Copyright ©2009 by Rand McNally
& Company. All rights reserved.

Library of Congress Catalog
Number: 92-060588

For licensing information and
copyright permissions, contact us at licensing@
randmcnally.com.

If you have a comment, suggestion,
or even a compliment, please visit
us at go.randmcnally.com/contact
or e-mail us at
consumeraffairs@randmcnally.com.

or write to:
Rand McNally Consumer Affairs
P.O. Box 7600
Chicago, Illinois 60680-9915

Published in U.S.A.
Printed in China

1 2 3 LE 09 08

Peanut butter and jelly sandwiches, ice cream cones, chocolate chip cookies: none of these culinary standards has been around for much more than a century. Yet along with fast-food cheeseburgers and chicken nuggets, they make up the kind of cuisine that many of us automatically associate with the term "American food." Pity. Not that we're slamming a good pb and j, but American dishes deserve more credit than they often get.

The sheer size of our country means that just about every corner of it has had the chance to develop its own tasty quirk, from kringle to coffee milk. So in your travels, why not seek out some of the regional specialties profiled on the pages ahead? You'll also meet a handful of fun and fascinating American cooks—not cable-TV celebrichefs, but regular Joes and Janes dedicated to keeping the art of eating alive. Pull your chair up to the table; you'll find plenty to chew on.

Northeast

The Pilgrims who landed in the New World in 1620 probably thought of eels, swans, and seals as dishes on a dinner table, not animals in a zoo. Who knows what they'd make of the regional foods for which New England and the rest of the Northeast are known today? Especially since colonial-era favorites like pease pottage and hasty pudding have long since given way to foods inspired by other cultures, such as New York-style pizza (brought here by the Neapolitans) and scrapple (invented by the Germans known as Pennsylvania Dutch).

Some modern Northeast favorites are known throughout the country, such as Philly cheese steaks and Atlantic City salt-water taffy, but a surprising number of dishes remain known only to locals—and to the persevering foodies who seek them out. Rhode Islanders have been gulping down the java-flavored beverage called coffee milk since at least the 1930s, but few out-of-staters have even heard of it. And while Americans everywhere, even in the land-locked Midwest, eat lobster, most of them never eat it at home out of hand atop a toasted hot dog bun, as in Maine. Although the Northeast is by far the smallest U.S. region, its potential for new culinary experiences is large.

> *"My secret ingredient is nutmeg"*
> —*Barb Hummel*

PERSONALITY PROFILE

Barb Hummel, who owns Skyland Farm Gallery and Café with her husband in Hector, N.Y., keeps quite busy assisting the visitors who come to buy local arts and crafts, wander through the garden, and have a bite to eat. But somehow, each fall, she finds the time to bake dozens of grape pies for the café. Made from her neighbors' Concord grapes, the **double-crust pies— a regional specialty**— feature a jam-like filling. "My secret ingredient is nutmeg," Hummel says.

Summer brings a different treat: eggs from the farm's chickens, which lead happy chicken lives, "eating green grass and running around outside," she says. The eggs are ingredients in several café offerings, such as the lemon meringue pie. Summer visitors may also try any of the 25 flavors of gelato, including **apricot chardonnay and hazelnut biscotti.** (Hummel notes, "What's funny is, we don't have vanilla. And nobody misses it.") And in the winter, marshmallows sit in a jar on the café counter, waiting to be added to one of the 11 available types of hot chocolate served in a mug that Hummel made.

The gallery and café are open late June through Dec. 24 only, seven miles north of the town of Watkins Glen on NY 414. Hummel's generally there whenever it's open, so say hello when you hit the café for a treat.

It came from... **Burlington, Vermont**

Ben and Jerry's

Three dollars and a sweet tooth are all that's required to tour Ben and Jerry's ice cream factory (in Waterbury, Vt.; exit 10 from I-89), which includes free samples, *a "mooooovie" about the company's origins,* and a chance to visit the "Flavor Graveyard," an outdoor mock cemetery of discontinued flavors. (Lemon Peppermint Carob Chip, anyone?) The half-hour tours fill up fast, especially on weekdays, when visitors can actually see the ice cream being produced.

In 1978, friends Ben Cohen and Jerry Greenfield began making and selling ice cream out of a renovated gas station in Burlington, Vt., and the years that followed brought flavors that still top the company's best-seller list—among them cherry-and-fudge *Cherry Garcia®* (1987), banana-walnut-fudge Chunky Monkey® (1988), and the self-explanatory Chocolate Chip Cookie Dough (1991).

Cohen and Greenfield sold the company in 2000, but their influence remains, particularly in the company's refusal to use milk from cows that have been treated with recombinant bovine growth hormone, its new line of organic ice cream, and the annual *Free Cone Day* each spring, when patrons of Ben and Jerry's Scoop Shops get free ice cream cones in celebration of the company's founding.

After the tour, factory visitors can hit the gift shop for souvenirs, including pints of 30 ice cream flavors and a T-shirt that proclaims "Body by Ben and Jerry's."

Pepperoni roll

Wrap some vaguely sweet dough around some pepperoni, bake it, and you've got yourself a pepperoni roll. You can split it open and stick some cheese on it if you want to, but if you leave the roll uncut, *you can eat it one-handed* (useful if you're holding a shopping bag at the same time). West Virginians love their pepperoni rolls so much that several years ago, state senator John D. Rockefeller IV stepped in to prevent the USDA from potentially putting the small, family-owned bakeries that make them out of business. When a senator saves a snack food, something serious is going on.

Pepperoni rolls were reportedly invented in Fairmont, W. Va., a town in the north central part of the state off I-79, at the intersection of US 19 and US 250. The Country Club Bakery (1211 Country Club Rd.) sells them fresh for 90 cents every day but Wednesday and Sunday. For a larger version with peppers, cheese, and sauce, head to Colasessano's (506 Pennsylvania Ave.). Bakeries in Clarksburg, which lies southwest of Fairmont at the intersection of US 50 and US 19, offer them too, such as the nearly century-old Tomaro's Bakery (411 N. 4th St.).

Cheese steak

The proper components of a Philadelphia cheese steak are the subject of intense controversy. *Is Cheez Whiz preferable to provolone?* Should the steak be sliced thinly or chopped up altogether? The only thing everyone seems to agree on: the roll must be from Amoroso's Baking Company, which has been supplying Philadelphia with crusty Italian bread since 1904.

Pat's King of Steaks (1237 E. Passyunk Ave.), opened by Pat Olivieri in 1930, claims to be cheese steak ground zero. So why did Joe Vento decide to open up rival Geno's Steaks (1219 South 9th St.) right across the street in 1966? "You want to sell cheese steaks, you go where they eat cheese steaks," he told a reporter. Hard to argue. Elsewhere in town, Jim's Steaks has four locations, but locals favor the one at 400 South St. Here the steak comes chopped into hash form, and the cheese goes under the meat instead of over it.

Whichever place you choose, be ready to give your order the right way—state your cheese choice first ("Whiz," provolone, or American), and say "with" or "without" to indicate your onion preference. And if you bend forward a little bit while you eat, you'll minimize your chances of ending up with grease on your pants or shirt.

FiZZ FACTS

Moxie

The Northeast is home to several quirky regional sodas, such as Yup (New Hampshire) and Manhattan Special (New York). But you'll find only one of them in the dictionary: Moxie.

More than 125 years ago, Moxie started out as a patent medicine in Massachusetts, peddled as a "nerve food" purported to cure "nervous exhaustion," "loss of manhood," and "softening of the brain." In 1884, it turned into a carbonated soda—America's first mass-produced soft drink. Despite Moxie's strong taste, it became so popular that its name entered the English language as a synonym for "spunky" or "peppy." Everyone from baseball great Ted Williams to legendary *Charlotte's Web* author E.B. White to President Calvin Coolidge was a fan. But the rise of Coca-Cola reduced Moxie to a regional favorite, albeit one with its own festival (held each year in Lisbon Falls, Maine) and fan club (the New England Moxie Congress).

Moxie drinkers in the rest of the country often have to resort to ordering the brew online, but in New England, it's everywhere. Stop & Shops, Big Y, Price Chopper, and Market Basket supermarkets are among the chains that often carry it; while you're on the road, keep an eye out for the orange can in restaurants and mom-and-pop stores, too.

Coffee milk

There are coffee drinkers who think putting anything in their brew besides a spoon is a sign of weakness. And at the other end of the spectrum, there are coffee drinkers who stop dumping in the cream and sugar only when what's in their cups tastes like melted coffee ice cream. Judging by their serious coffee milk habit, Rhode Islanders seem to lean toward the latter.

Coffee milk is simply milk with coffee-flavored syrup added, *sort of like chocolate milk for grown-ups* (though kids drink it, too). It's all over the place in this state, from diners to grocery stores. In 1993, it even beat out another locally beloved beverage, Del's Lemonade, to become the official state drink.

At Gray's Ice Cream (16 East Rd.) in Tiverton (in the eastern part of the state, off RI 24), visitors can try a variation—coffee cabinet, which is coffee milk with ice cream added. In Providence, the Haven Brothers diner-on-wheels parks in front of City Hall (25 Dorrance St.) every night after 5 p.m.; the workers will hand over a coffee milk for just $1. North of Providence in North Smithfield, try it at Coffee and Cream (1065 Eddie Dowling Hwy., a.k.a. RI 146), which boasts a coffee-pot-shaped fountain outside.

Saltwater taffy

Atlantic City was promoted in the 1800s as a resort for convalescents—a place where the salty sea breezes were reputed to cure everything from consumption to insanity. Now the city's reputation as the home of sticky-sweet saltwater taffy makes any health claims a little harder to justify. Fralinger's Original Salt Water Taffy (two locations including 1325 Boardwalk) was founded more than 100 years ago by Joseph Fralinger, a former fish merchant who came to style himself *"The Salt Water Taffy King."* The original flavors—chocolate, vanilla, and molasses—are still available, along with others such as peppermint, root beer, and lime.

James' Candy Company (the Boardwalk at New York Avenue), a contemporary of Fralinger's, distinguished itself by cutting its taffy into bite-sized rectangular pieces instead of logs, making it easier to eat. James' taffy purportedly doesn't stick to candy wrappers (or teeth). Flavors such as cinnamon and coconut can be purchased packaged in a retro souvenir barrel that doubles as a coin bank. More oddball flavors include bay breeze, sea breeze, and mimosa. Both companies offer gift packages featuring saltwater taffy alongside other treats such as macaroons, peanut butter chews, and creamy after-dinner mints.

Pizza

About a hundred years ago, a Neapolitan immigrant named Gennaro Lombardi started selling pizza out of his grocery store in Little Italy, and the New York-style pie was born. The key components of a classic slice: a thin, crispy crust topped with fresh mozzarella and straightforward additions such as pepperoni, olives, and fresh garlic (no barbecue sauce, no shrimp, no arugula).

Lombardi's (32 Spring Street, Manhattan) still fires pizzas in a coal-burning oven; the granddaddy of all New York pizza parlors, it often features lines around the block. At Brooklyn's DiFara Pizzeria (1424 Avenue J), artisanal pizza baker Dominic DeMarco refuses to rush his craft. Despite the crowds, he's the only one who makes the pies here, and *he dusts each one with parmesan* before presenting it to the customer. Totonno Pizzeria Napolitana (four locations including the original at 1524 Neptune Ave., Coney Island) is so proud of the freshness of its dough that it reportedly makes just enough for the day—if any's left over, it's thrown out. Veggie lovers who don't mind departing from tradition enjoy slices from Viva Herbal Pizzeria (179 2nd Ave., Manhattan), a vegan/vegetarian spot where toppings include tofu, shitake mushrooms, and pesto.

Lobster roll

Lazy seafood lovers, take heart: here in Maine, the lobster roll, a toasted bun filled with lobster meat *drizzled with mayonnaise or butter*, lets you savor lobster without going to all the trouble of cracking apart your own crustacean. But be prepared to pay labor costs and then some; these sandwiches sometimes go for $16.95, depending on the market price for lobsters. While lobster rolls can be found as far afield as Connecticut and New York, Maine still holds the biggest claim to them.

The place for lobster rolls is Red's Eats (41 Water St., Wiscasset), a roadside stand (open summers) near the intersection of ME 27 and US 1 that has been around since 1938. Each roll, they'll tell you here, holds at least a pound of lobster meat. Red's serves the condiments on the side, but Alisson's Restaurant, further down the coast in Kennebunkport (11 Dock Square) simplifies things by mixing the mayo with the lobster before it ever hits your table. And at Harraseeket Lobster in Freeport (Town Landing), diners can chase their lobster rolls with another favorite Maine dish, homemade whoopie pies, which consist of two palm-sized chocolate cakes sandwiched together with fluffy white frosting.

Stuffed ham

The *New York Times* once described the taste of southern Maryland stuffed ham as "pleasantly disturbing." Even more disturbing: the instructions in some old cookbooks to tie the ham in an old pillowcase before simmering it on the stove. But to locals, this is a *well-loved traditional dish* that dates back to the time of George Calvert, founder of Maryland and the first Lord Baltimore. The recipe calls for cutting slits into a corned ham, then stuffing them with a mixture of blanched kale, cabbage, and onions that has been heavily seasoned with both ground and crushed red pepper.

Traditionally served in homes at Thanksgiving, Christmas, and Easter, stuffed ham can be found in several restaurants in Maryland's St. Mary's County, such as St. Mary's Landing (Rt. 5, Charlotte Hall), which has even been known to offer it for breakfast. If you'd rather take an entire stuffed ham home as a souvenir, try Raley's Town & Country Market (Route 5, Ridge) or Chaptico Market and Deli (25466 Maddox Rd., Chaptico).

Scrapple

In their thriftiness, the Pennsylvania Dutch saved the bits and pieces that were left over at hog butchering time. (What kind of bits and pieces, exactly? Well, one recipe calls for "cooked pork head meats, skins, [and] tongue." You get the idea.) They mixed the scraps with cornmeal and flour, and formed loaves to cut into slices and fry until crusty. And lo: scrapple was born.

Usually a breakfast dish, often served alongside eggs and topped with maple syrup or ketchup, scrapple isn't hard to find in Pennsylvania, particularly in Lancaster County. The People's Restaurant in New Holland (140 W. Main St.) serves it, along with local Lancaster County sausage. Or you can try it at the Green Dragon Farmers Market in Ephrata (955 North State St.), which *overflows with Amish and Pennsylvania Dutch atmosphere.* The market's open Fridays only, so if that doesn't fit into your travel plans and you're in serious scrapple pursuit, head to the Reading Terminal Market in Philadelphia (12th and Arch Sts.), where every day except Sunday, vendors such as Dutch Country Meats sell shoppers scrapple to take home and cook, and others such as the Dutch Eating Place will set you up with some to eat on the spot.

Sugar-on-Snow

Fans of Laura Ingalls Wilder's Little House books might remember their descriptions of a special wintertime treat: the candy that forms when you pour hot maple syrup onto fresh, white, fluffy snow. Canadians call it maple taffee or tire d'érable, but in New England it's known as sugar-on-snow. For reasons lost to history, it's traditional to accompany sugar-on-snow with pickles and plain doughnuts or saltine crackers. The process is a little trickier than it sounds; syrup that hasn't been boiled properly will run instead of harden.

If you have neither a) your own grove of maple trees nor b) access to nonpolluted snow, some sugar houses in Vermont and elsewhere offer sugar-on-snow events, like Dakin Farm in Ferrisburgh (5797 US 7). During its annual sugar-on-snow weekend parties, visitors can not only try the sticky treat, but also see maple syrup being made, tour the farm's smokehouse, and *dive into a pancake breakfast.* Dates change yearly, though, so check www.dakinfarm.com well before your trip. Bragg Farm Sugarhouse & Gift Shop in East Montpelier (off VT 14 N, about five miles east of Montpelier) offers sugar-on-snow on March and April weekend afternoons, along with a walking trail and ice cream parlor with maple milk shakes.

South

So you think you know Southern food? Sweet potato pie, boiled peanuts, okra, grits, and fried green tomatoes—they're not hard to find down here (and nobody's going to try to talk you out of them). But when's the last time you cracked open a Cheerwine? What goes in a hot brown sandwich? Which tiny central North Carolina town is just about the only place in the country to eat dewberries? And what's a dewberry, anyway? The full range of Southern cuisine stretches from overexposed (if tasty) dishes to more esoteric finds like benne seed wafers and Natchitoches meat pies.

A trip to Dixie offers the chance to eat mass-produced treats such as Moon Pies in their native habitat. And you can find out why you'll never come across Spanish bean soup in Madrid or Barcelona, or show your support for post-Katrina New Orleans by biting into a beignet. This is where to learn how Vidalia onions got sweet enough for some folks to eat 'em like apples, and—if you're lucky—try a slice of Lane cake, reputed to be the most pain-in-the-neck recipe ever to come out of Alabama. Dig in.

> *"I just put a tweak in it"*
> —*"Biscuit Lady"*

PERSONALITY PROFILE

Does Carol Fay Ellison, a.k.a. the "Biscuit Lady," ever give away her secret recipe? "Ohhhh, no. Ohhhhh, no," she says. All she'll say is that when she started cooking at the famed Loveless Cafe in Nashville, Tenn. (8400 TN 100), "they had a recipe already, and I just put a tweak in it." Now, more than 25 years later, her biscuits have landed her a spot on Ellen DeGeneres' talk show, as well as the admiration of celebrities from Al Gore and Britain's Princess Anne to Minnie Pearl and Martha Stewart (who called her Loveless meal "the best breakfast I've ever had").

Ellison makes more than biscuits, though—she's also responsible for the **sausage gravy and homemade strawberry, peach, or blackberry preserves**

to eat them with. She estimates her daily biscuit output in the thousands, both those that customers eat on site and those they order to go. "They'd have 'em shipped, if we shipped 'em," she says. No such luck, but you can buy her biscuit mix, along with the preserves and the cafe's country ham, in the on-site Hams and Jams store. "We have a lot of ham and biscuits going out of here," she says. "Oh, yes, honey."

FiZZ FACTS

Cheerwine

Many sodas have borrowed the names of the alcoholic drinks they resemble: root "beer," ginger "ale," and that Southern favorite, Cheerwine. This dark red, cherry-flavored pop, which has been around since 1917, has more cherry flavor than cherry colas; in fact, its maker, Carolina Beverage Corp., calls it "the original cherry-flavored soda." For its first 65 years, however, it was available only in North Carolina. Scratch that—only in *western* North Carolina. Not until the early 1980s was it for sale in other (mostly Southern) states.

These days the company has expanded its Cheerwine repertoire to include diet Cheerwine, Cheerwine ice cream, and a cane sugar-sweetened version in the original glass bottles. Still, even today it's hard to find this soda outside the South, with the exception of a few pockets in the Midwest and—for some unknown reason—Norway.

Any Southern diner, barbecue joint, ice cream shop, or gas station worth its salt carries Cheerwine: try Bridges Barbecue Lodge in Shelby, N.C. (2000 E. Dixon Blvd., a.k.a. US 74). It's also widely available in the region's grocery stores, particularly the Food Lion chain. In downtown Salisbury, N.C., home of the Carolina Beverage Corp., ask the waitstaff at Spanky's Homemade Ice Cream and Deli (101 N. Main St.) to pour some of the soda over vanilla ice cream for a Cheerwine float.

Beignets

Two reasons to leave the sophisticated black wardrobe at home when visiting New Orleans: one, it's often too hot; two, the powdered sugar fallout from beignets (pronounced "ben-YAYs") becomes all too obvious.

Locals and visitors alike love these *sweet, puffy, powdery squares of fried dough* so much that when the original Café du Monde (800 Decatur St.; six additional locations) reopened two months after Hurricane Katrina and began serving them again, it made national news. Now that the café has returned to its regular hours—24 hours a day, 7 days a week, except for Christmas—diners can sit inside or in the courtyard to enjoy their beignets with café au lait. Also in the city, Café Beignet (locations include 334-B Royal St.) serves not only beignets, but also the rest of its breakfast menu, all day long.

West of New Orleans, outside Lafayette off I-10, Café des Amis (140 E. Bridge St. in the town of Breaux Bridge) offers beignets for breakfast Fridays, Saturdays, and Sundays. And on Saturday mornings from 8:30 to 11:30, there's a *"Zydeco Breakfast,"* complete with live music and dancing.

Lane cake

Invented by Emma Rylander Lane of Clayton, Ala., who included it in her 1898 cookbook Some Good Things to Eat, Lane cake has almost disappeared over the years. This white or yellow cake *made with bourbon, custard, coconut, and pecans* requires at least three layers (some say four) and about eight eggs. The occasional Lane cake recipe pops up now and then in magazines like Food and Wine, but actually finding the cake itself in a restaurant or bakery is rare. In your Southern travels, keep an eye out, and maybe you'll be lucky enough to spot this culinary obscurity.

Hot browns

In 1923, chef Fred Schmidt of the Brown Hotel in Louisville, Ky., got tired of making the same old ham and eggs in the wee hours of the morning for patrons who needed sustenance after the hotel's nightly dinner-dance. So he created the hot brown, an open-faced turkey sandwich with *bacon and a creamy parmesan cheese sauce.* The Brown Hotel still serves the classic hot brown in its J. Graham's Café (335 W. Broadway), but it's also available in various incarnations at other restaurants around town (and around the state). No matter where you try it, though, be warned that this is a sandwich in name only—i.e., you're going to need a knife and fork.

The quirkily furnished Lynn's Paradise Café (984 Barret Ave., Louisville) serves its rendition, the "Paradise Hot Brown," with a slice of cheddar on top. While patrons wait for their orders here, they can survey the mural made out of beer caps. Northeast of Louisville, the Hofbräuhaus Newport in Newport (200 E. 3rd St.) might not, at first glance, seem like a likely hot brown venue. But this German spot does indeed serve it, albeit with Teutonic ingredients: Bavarian ham, shredded pork, and a cheese sauce made with Hofbräu beer.

Moon Pies

If a soda and a chocolate-covered marshmallow graham cracker sandwich sound like lunch to you, well, you'd probably enjoy that *Southern noontime staple: an RC cola and a Moon Pie.* No one knows quite how the combination came about, but it might have something to do with the fact that decades ago, it cost all of 10 cents. It's a surprisingly filling combo, too.

The Chattanooga Bakery of Chattanooga, Tenn., has made Moon Pies since 1917, when an employee named Earl Mitchell Sr. supposedly asked some coal miners what kind of snacks they'd like. As the story goes, one of them framed the rising moon with his hands and said he wanted a filling treat about that big. Mitchell returned to the bakery, where he noticed some workers snacking on graham crackers that they'd dipped into hot marshmallow and then allowed to cool. The rest is history.

You can hardly walk into a supermarket, convenience store, or general store in the South without falling over a case of the original Moon Pies and/or its offspring—the Double Decker Moon Pie and Mini Moon Pie, which, like the original, are now available in chocolate, vanilla, banana, and orange. Microwaved for a few seconds, they turn into delightfully gooey, s'more-like confections.

BEST EATS   South

It came from...   Avery Island, Louisiana

Tabasco Sauce

It's been carried into space to spice up astronauts' bland rations, toted along by the archaeologist who discovered King Tut's tomb, and featured in films like *Apocalypse Now* and *The Spy Who Loved Me.* It's Tabasco sauce, and though it's hardly the only hot sauce in the world, it's certainly the most well known. The peppers that produce this spicy red condiment have been grown on Louisiana's Avery Island since 1868. (Although these days the bulk of the crop comes from Central and South America, some of the peppers still grow on the island.)

During free 15- to 20-minute tours of the Tabasco bottling plant, visitors can watch the sauce being packaged for consumption. Many are surprised to learn that Tabasco takes three and a half years to make; the peppers are picked by hand and pureed before being barrel-aged. A glass wall protects onlookers from the intense pepper fumes, which would otherwise trigger burning eyes and coughing fits.

To get there, take US 90 west from New Orleans, then head south on LA 329, which dead-ends into the island. A $1 toll gets you across the bridge. In addition to the Tabasco plant, the island also hosts a bird sanctuary with snowy egrets, blue herons, and other fascinating fowl.

Vidalia onions

No matter how sweet an onion is, if it's from, say, Ohio, it's not a Vidalia. To earn that designation, it has to be grown in a specific 20-county area in east-central Georgia that encompasses the town of Vidalia, where farmer Mose Coleman *accidentally invented them* in 1931. (What did the trick? The area's mild climate and the low sulfur content of its soil.)

In the spring, visitors can contact the Vidalia Convention and Visitor Bureau at (912) 538-8687 to arrange a tour of a working Vidalia onion farm; the bureau itself also houses the Vidalia Onion Museum (100 Vidalia Sweet Onion Dr.), with displays on the onion's history and cultivation. Meanwhile, the Vidalia Onion Factory and Gift Shop (3309 E. First St.) sells the onions May through December (assuming the supply holds out). But even if the fresh onions are gone before you get there, you can still buy 'em in *pickled, relish, salsa, salad dressing, mustard, and even jelly form.*

Each year on the last weekend in April, the Vidalia Onion Festival offers a cook-off, rodeo, Miss Vidalia Onion competition, 10K race, carnival rides, and the "World Famous Onion Eating Contest." It also attracts celebrity chefs such as Jeffrey Buben, owner of the Washington, D.C. Vidalia Restaurant, proving that love for the sweet onion ranges far and wide.

Spanish bean soup

Trying to order Spanish bean soup in Spain will get you nowhere, even if you ask nicely ("Sopa con garbanzos, por favor"). This dish, made with garbanzo beans, ham and beef bones, salt pork, chorizo, and potatoes, is generally available only in Florida, specifically Tampa, where it was invented at the Columbia Restaurant (seven locations including the original at 2117 East 7th Ave.) around 1910. As the story goes, the restaurant's founder, Casimiro Hernandez, Sr., took a *Spanish dish called cocido madrileno* that was traditionally served in two courses (first the broth; then the meat, beans, and potatoes) and decided to simplify matters by stirring all the ingredients together. Enjoy a bowl while taking in a flamenco show.

Like the Columbia, other good Tampa soup spots lie in the historic Ybor City neighborhood. Carmine's Seventh Avenue (1802 E. 7th Ave.) offers it with half a sandwich on the side—its house specialty, the Cuban sandwich, is a good bet. La Tropicana Café, just down the street (1822 E. 7th Ave.), serves its version with a piece of crusty, buttery Cuban bread.

Benne seed wafers

When slaves from West Africa arrived in Charleston, S.C., in the early 1700s, so did benne seeds, now more commonly known as sesame seeds. Benne seed wafers (a.k.a. benne seed cookies), now a local tradition, can be bought from many vendors in the downtown open-air shopping area known as the Market (Market St. between Meeting St. and E. Bay St.). The wafers have become part of the African American holiday Kwanzaa, celebrated annually from Dec. 26th to Jan. 1st, but they're available year-round.

One of the biggest purveyors of the treats: the Olde Colony Bakery (1391 B Stuart Engalls Blvd.) in nearby Mount Pleasant, which claims that its recipe is more than 100 years old.

To take some of the wafers back home, stop by the Charleston Cooks! kitchen store (194 E. Bay St.) for a bagful. Depending on the day, you may be lucky enough to sit in on a "Taste of the Lowcountry" cooking demonstration, too. (Check www.charlestoncooks.com for a class schedule.)

Dewberries

What's the difference between a blackberry and a dewberry? Dewberries are smaller and scarcer; unless you grew up in the South, *you've probably never tasted one.* Remedy that in North Carolina's central Piedmont region, specifically in the town of Cameron, once considered the dewberry capital of the world for its large-scale farming of the tart-sweet fruit. Because of the plants' many prickles, dewberries are something of a pain to pick, so it's just as well to let someone else do it for you. Dewberry season: June and July.

These days Cameron—southwest of Raleigh at the intersection of US 1 and NC 24—is a tiny town mostly made up of antiques stores, *but visitors can still dig into dewberry pie* at a few places in its downtown area, which is on the National Register of Historic Places. At Miss Belle's Tea Room & Antique (562 Carthage St.), a cast-iron stove keeps diners warm in winter, and the menu features dewberry-inspired desserts as well as more substantial fare such as soup and sandwiches. Down the block, the first floor of the Old Hardware hosts the Dewberry Deli and Soda Fountain (485 Carthage St.), which serves dewberries over cheesecake.

Meat pies

The small Louisiana town of Natchitoches (say: NACK-ih-tush), about an hour and a half south of Shreveport off I-49, is famous for two things. First, it appeared in the film *Steel Magnolias.* Second, it's the home of meat pies—individual, half-moon-shaped fried pie shells filled with seasoned ground beef and pork (they may have been introduced to the region by Cajuns in the 1700s).

Lasyone's Meat Pie Kitchen (622 Second St.), the self-dubbed "Home of the Meat Pie," has been featured everywhere from *Gourmet* to *Good Morning America.* Opened in 1967, it's still run by the daughters of the man who founded it, James Lasyone. *Hard-core meat pie fans eat them for breakfast,* but they're usually considered lunch or dinner fare.

Meanwhile, The Landing Restaurant (530 Front St.) serves miniature meat pies as an appetizer, along with other regional delicacies such as fried crawfish tails and spicy "voodoo" oysters. And the annual Meat Pie Festival, held in the town every fall, features a meat pie-eating contest and the "Meat Pie Tri" triathlon, along with a beauty pageant in which one lucky young woman is crowned Miss Natchitoches Meat Pie Festival.

Midwest

Maybe because of the Midwest's dual reputation as America's breadbasket and the country's beef and pork supplier, the words "Midwestern cuisine" tend to conjure up images of mystery meat hot dishes, white bread, Jell-O™ salad, and chicken-fried steak. After all, working the land takes a lot of calories; consider the 19th-century farmers who sometimes ate apple pie for breakfast, often with a wedge of cheese thrown in for good measure. Soy sausages and Egg Beaters™ wouldn't get the fields plowed, after all.

While it's true that many regional Midwestern dishes aren't known for their experimental seasonings or airy textures, that doesn't mean that dinner in these states is all meat and potatoes. Top chefs prize Indiana's shagbark syrup, made from the bark of shagbark hickory trees. Chicago hot dogs have gone upscale with new varieties made from wild boar and Thai chicken sausage. Sweet-tooth foodies in particular are in luck, with choices such as elegantly shaped kringle pastries from Racine, Wisc.; fresh-made frozen custard; and many varieties of St. Louis gooey butter cake. Hold out for hot dish and white bread if you must, but with all this culinary bounty, why would you want to?

> *"I'm just trying to do a couple things really really well"*
> —James Ventrella

PERSONALITY PROFILE

"I'm not trying to create magic; I'm just trying to do a couple things really, really well," says James Ventrella. A second-generation Italian American, he owns Ventrella's Caffe on Chicago's north side, which **features a small but elegant menu** of gourmet panini, Italian pastries, and gelato. This is as Italian American as it gets—two of Ventrella's aunts make many of the pastries, the coffee is Italy's famed Lavazza brand, and most of the furnishings came from now-shuttered establishments in Chicago's historically Italian neighborhoods. Ventrella even keeps copies of Italian periodical *La Gazzetta dello Sport* out for perusal.

Because he's not only the owner but also the only full-time employee, Ventrella is generally on hand to chat with patrons and explain flavors to gelato neophytes. (For the record, stracciatella is "sort of the Italian version of a chocolate chip, but **the chocolate is 75 percent cocoa**, so it's not like a waxy chocolate.") Some panini, such as prosciutto with provolone and green apple, are always available; others, like the gorgonzola-and-pear and banana-and-Nutella versions, are less predictably on the menu.

It's been a major career switch for Ventrella, who opened the café after being laid off from his TV producer job. Scary? Not really. "I can work hard, and I'm just gonna work," he says. Stop by to enjoy the fruits of his labor at 4947 N. Damen.

Loose meat sandwich

To scoop up all the stray bits of tastiness that fall out of a loose meat sandwich—a.k.a. a Maid-Rite, after the Iowa-based chain that popularized it—*you just have to use a spoon.* Sort of a tidier, sauce-less version of the sloppy joe, a loose meat sandwich consists of rice-sized bits of ground meat, spiced and served on a bun with onions, mustard (not ketchup), and, of course, a utensil.

The most famous Maid-Rite franchise lies off IA 14 in Marshalltown, Iowa: Taylor's Maid-Rite (106 S. 3rd Ave.), which has sold them for nearly 80 years. If you get hooked, Taylor's will ship sandwiches anywhere in the United States. In the state's northwest corner, north of Sioux City on US 75 S in Le Mars, the loosemeats at Bob's Drive-Inn are called "taverns," and indecisive diners can get a "Bob dog"— loosemeat sandwich filling spooned over a hot dog. In Sioux City at Tastee Inn & Out (2610 Gordon Dr.), loosemeat assumes yet another alias: the Tastee sandwich. Perhaps for better ease of eating while on the road, Tastee serves its sandwiches wrapped in paper to catch the inevitable fallout.

Gooey butter cake

Turning a mistake into a tasty new dish is a well-known culinary tradition. Just ask the anonymous St. Louis baker who, in the 1930s, supposedly got the quantities of his cake ingredients mixed up. What emerged from the oven was a yellow cake with a sticky, oozy, gooey, deliciously runny top. *Some eat it for breakfast like a coffee cake,* others have it as a dessert. Either way, one slice of this very rich cake, accompanied by a cup of coffee or tea, is usually enough for most.

Try it at bakeries and coffee shops including Kaldi's Coffeehouse (four locations including 120 S. Kirkwood Rd. in Kirkwood, Mo.), the fifty-some-year-old McArthur's Bakery (four locations including 3055 Lemay Ferry Rd.), and Federhofer's Bakery (9005 Gravois Rd.), which sports a charming retro neon sign boasting "QUALITY-VARIETY." Meanwhile, Park Avenue Coffee (1919 Park Ave.) makes dozens of varieties, from mint chocolate chip to seasonal flavors such as gingerbread and eggnog.

Formal restaurants serve it too, sometimes with an upscale spin. To wit: Moxy Contemporary Bistro (4584 Laclede Ave.), which offers a blueberry version with mango sorbet and port wine reduction.

It came from... Battle Creek, Michigan

Corn Flakes

Given the growing concern about an American diet high in refined sugar, many breakfast cereal manufacturers have rushed to introduce lower-sugar versions of old favorites. It's a beyond-the-grave victory of sorts for John Harvey Kellogg, who invented what we now know as Corn Flakes with his brother in 1894. Twelve years after he and his brother, Will Keith Kellogg, first served plain toasted grain flakes to the patients at the Battle Creek Sanitarium in Battle Creek, Mich., the brothers parted ways. Will wanted to add sugar to the flakes to make them more popular with consumers; John didn't. Will established the Battle Creek Toasted Corn Flake Company (later renamed the Kellogg Company), and before long, the introduction of pasteurized milk made cereal even more popular as an American breakfast food.

More than 100 years later, Kellogg's cereals have gone everywhere from the South Pole to outer space. Some have fallen by the wayside—"Kellogg's Raisins, Rice & Rye" didn't stick around—but many more have become household names: Rice Krispies, Frosted Mini-Wheats, Raisin Bran, Froot Loops.

FIZZ FACTS

Green River

When Prohibition came along, one could argue our country gained in soft drinks what it lost in hard liquor. Rather than go out of business, many breweries and wineries turned to making soda, leading *Time* magazine to observe in 1925: "In the last few years there has been almost an epidemic of temperance-drink companies, following in the highly successful wake of Coco Cola of Atlanta."

One of them was Chicago's Schoenhofen Brewery, which began in 1919 to manufacture Green River, a very sweet, lime-flavored, violently green soft drink originally available at soda fountains. After nearly going extinct over the decades, Green River was brought back to life by Clover Club Bottling Co., who bought the brand and widened its distribution. Now those bright green bottles show up in many ice cream parlors and sandwich shops in the Midwest.

If you'd like to try Green River in its city of origin, a good bet is downtown Chicago's Eleven City Diner (1112 S. Wabash St.), which serves it in a Green River ice cream float. Near the city, you can drink Green River straight up at Uncle Harry's of Wisconsin (1453 W. Lake St., Addison) or at the railroad-themed The Depot Restaurant in Winnetka (749 Elm St.).

Pasty

We have the copper and iron deposits of Michigan's Upper Peninsula to thank for the small, tasty meat-and-vegetable pies known as pasties (pronounced PASS-tees). Without them, miners from the United Kingdom's County Cornwall wouldn't have flocked to the U.P. in the mid-1800s, *bringing their savory hand-held lunches.* As the story goes, pasties made a perfect meal in the mines because they were portable, easy to heat up over a candle flame, and could be gripped by their crimped crusts so that the dirt from a miner's hands wouldn't contaminate his lunch. (Bonus: the miners could then leave the crusts behind to appease the tommy-knockers—the mischievous spirits that haunted mines.)

Traditionally, pasties were filled with beef, potatoes, onions, and possibly rutabaga, but these days variations are common. In addition to a beef version, Dobber's Pasties (1402 S. Stephenson Ave., Iron Mountain, Mich., and 827 N. Lincoln Rd., Escanaba, Mich.), makes chicken and vegetable-only pasties (and even a pasty-shaped candy bar). And The Pasty Oven (7270 US 2, Quinnesec, Mich.) goes so far as to make a pizza pasty with sausage or pepperoni and a breakfast pasty with eggs, potatoes, cheese, and ham, sausage, or bacon.

Shagbark syrup

When Gordon Jones and his wife Sherrie Yarling bought their land in Trafalgar, Indiana, they had no intention of becoming the country's only source of shagbark syrup—*a smoky-sweet elixir* made from the bark of the shagbark hickory trees on the property. But after a man who stopped by to ask for firewood told them how his great-great-grandmother once made syrup from the trees' bark, they started experimenting. Now several years later, their business, Hickoryworks (3615 Peoga Rd.), has supplied shagbark syrup to chefs from Julia Child to Rick Bayless. In *Gourmet*'s view, it's "shagadelic."

Though there's only one shagbark syrup supplier, there are plenty of ways to try it. The easy way: *buy a bottle yourself and pour it over pancakes.* But to really experience its versatility, hit one of Indiana's upscale restaurants, such as Carmel's Glass Chimney (12901 Old Meridian St.), where the chef has been known to mix it with bourbon as a marinade for pork, and Indianapolis's Oceanaire Seafood Room (30 S. Meridian St.), where the menu has featured a peaches and Bibb lettuce salad with hickory syrup. But really, shagbark syrup can show up anywhere that sugar or maple syrup would, so if you're dining in the Indianapolis area, keep an eye out. It might even appear on drink and dessert menus.

Frozen custard

Frozen custard may have originated on Coney Island around 1919, but these days the Milwaukee area reportedly sells more of the icy treat than anyplace else (though it's found throughout the rest of the Midwest, too). Three things distinguish frozen custard from ice cream: it has a smaller amount of air whipped into it, it contains more egg yolk, and it's made fresh daily.

A German immigrant named Elsa Kopp started Kopp's Frozen Custard (three locations including 5373 N. Port Washington Rd., Glendale, Wisc.) in 1950. The tradition is carried on by her son, who offers flavors such as mocha chip and cherry amaretto cheesecake. There's something about frozen custard that requires a 1950s atmosphere—Kitts Frozen Custard Drive-In (7000 W. Capitol Dr., Milwaukee) uses vintage custard machines and sports a huge retro neon sign, while Leon's Frozen Custard (3131 S. 27th

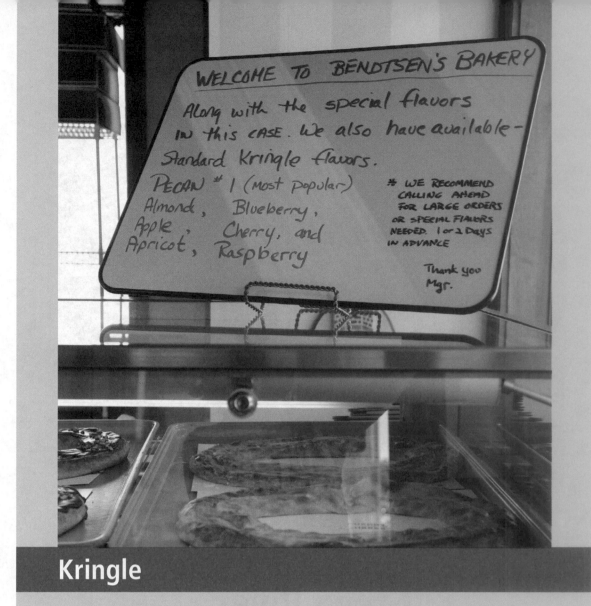

Kringle

Danish immigrants brought the fruit- or nut-filled coffee cake known as kringle to Racine, Wisc., in the 1800s. Racine still has a lot of Danes, and—fortunately for the rest of the country—it still makes a lot of kringle. Though Danes in the old country form their kringles to look like pretzels, somewhere along the way the American version took on a simpler ring shape. *No matter, it's still tasty—and it still takes three days to make* (for one thing, the dough has to rest overnight).

Happily, Racine brims with bakeries that will do the work for you. The O&H Danish Bakery (1841 Douglas Ave. and 4006 Durand Ave.) is *a kringle addict's delight*—not only can you buy the pastry on site, you can also sign up for the Kringle-of-the-Month Club.

Other pastry enablers include Larsen's Bakery (3311 Washington Ave.); Lehmann's Bakery (4900 Spring St.), which offers a banana-split version by special order; and Racine Danish Kringles (2529 Golf Ave.), home of "gourmet" kringles like key lime and chocolate éclair. A bastion of tradition, Bendtsen's Bakery (3200 Washington Ave.), which at 70 years and counting calls itself the oldest family-owned bakery in town, still uses the recipes that founder Lauritz Bendtsen brought from Odense, Denmark, in 1934.

St., Milwaukee) supposedly inspired Arnold's snack shop on the TV show *Happy Days*.

Another Midwestern custard legend, Ted Drewes Frozen Custard, lies in St. Louis, Mo. (4224 S. Grand Blvd. and 6726 Chippewa). The "concretes" (super-thick milkshakes) here are so dense that the servers hand them to you upside down.

For those who take their custard very, very seriously, www.custardlist.com lists flavors-of-the-day for many stands—a quick online visit might mean you'll never miss "Raspberry Cordial" or "Toffee Crunch" day again.

Chili

It's said that Cincinnati has more chili parlors than it does McDonald's.

Most of those are outposts of two chains—Gold Star and Skyline, which both have their fans—but plenty of others thrive as well. At Empress Chili (locations include 8340 Vine St.), you can try the original recipe. This is where, in 1922, Tom Kiradjieff, a Macedonian immigrant, invented Cincinnati-style chili-spiced ground beef in tomato sauce ladled over spaghetti. He's also the one who started the custom of ordering it "two-way" (with spaghetti only), "three-way" (spaghetti and grated cheese), "four-way" (spaghetti, grated cheese, and chopped onions), or "five-way" (spaghetti, grated cheese, chopped onions, and kidney beans).

For a spicier version and 24-hour service, head to Camp Washington Chili (3005 Colerain Ave.), which won a Regional Classics Award from the James Beard Foundation a few years ago. On the city's west side, Price Hill Chili (4920 Glenway Ave.) reigns; locals often gather here after high school football games to celebrate (or mourn) with a plate of coneys—small hot dogs topped with chili, onions, mustard, and cheese. And if a mere bowlful at Blue Ash Chili (9565 Kenwood Rd., Blue Ash) doesn't meet your chili needs, get a gallon to go for $25.

Hot dog

You can put a lot of things on a Chicago hot dog—onions, tomatoes, sport peppers, celery salt, and neon-green sweet relish—*but ketchup is not one of them,* says Rich Bowen, author of the classic (and, unfortunately, out-of-print) *Hot Dog Chicago: A Native's Dining Guide.* "It's too sweet," he says. "Plus you're adding a vinegar note that you don't really want."

He favors Byron's Hot Dog Haus (three locations including 1017 W. Irving Park Rd., near Wrigley Field), where patrons can nosh at sidewalk tables or take their paper-wrapped dogs and fries to go. The Wiener's Circle (2622 N. Clark St.), meanwhile, is known for entertainingly sarcastic service and occasionally rowdy clientele (especially after midnight).

Superdawg (6363 N. Milwaukee Ave.) is a bit of a drive from downtown, but you can't miss it—it's the drive-in with the two 12-foot hot dog statues on the roof (their names are Maurie and Flaurie). Still run by the couple who founded it in 1948, it's been featured on *Emeril Live* and the *Today* show. And at the other end of the tradition spectrum, Hot Doug's Sausage Superstore and Encased Meat Emporium (3324 N. California Ave.) draws devotees who line up for tasty oddities like corned beef sausage with horseradish mustard and chicken liver mousse.

Goetta

Somewhere along the way, the culinary gods granted Cincinnati not one but two signature foods (see: chili). While no one's proposing a taste-off, goetta—pronounced "GEH-tuh"—is probably the more versatile. *It's a breakfast food! It's a side dish! It's a sandwich filling!* And yes, some people really do call it "Cincinnati caviar." But what is it?

A dish of German origin, goetta is a mixture of spiced ground meat (usually pork and beef), onions, and steel-cut oats that's formed into

loaves, sliced into squares, and fried. Originally intended as a means of stretching expensive meat over several meals, *it's now considered a specialty in its own right.* Price Hill Chili (4920 Glenway Ave.) serves it morning, noon, and night; you can even get a goetta omelet. And in nearby Erlanger, Ky., the Colonial Cottage (3140 Dixie Hwy.) has been known to serve goetta stuffing around Thanksgiving.

At the supermarket, the first name in goetta is Glier's, which has been manufacturing it for decades. Bowing to changing tastes, it now offers low-fat and no-pork versions, in addition to an all-goetta cookbook. The company even sponsors the annual Glier's Goettafest (see www.goettafest.com for dates), where visitors can try goetta reubens, goetta calzones, and goetta-stuffed mushrooms. Where will it end?

Rocky Mountains/Plains

When it comes to cuisine, the Rocky Mountains and Plains states don't get nearly as much respect as the rest of the country. Say "Rocky Mountain," and most foodies will think "oyster." Say "Plains" and you might—*might*—get "fry bread," the sweet Native American snack often found in South Dakota and neighboring states. But that's about it.

The regional desserts often overlooked are enough to fill a menu all by themselves, from the classic chocolate-and-marshmallow Idaho Spud candy bar to the huckleberries of northwestern Montana and the fruit-and-custard-topped German cake known as kuchen in South Dakota. Meanwhile, barbecue fans who've declared their allegiance to the Memphis and North Carolina versions may find their loyalties challenged once they try Kansas City's and Oklahoma's takes on it.

Then there are the less easily categorized runza—a baked, meat-filled bun that's considered fast food in these parts—and the cheese frenchee, a deep-fried cheese sandwich mostly found between Omaha and Lincoln, Neb. Visitors who'd rather stick to the familiar can fall back on the Denver omelet (found everywhere these days, but best enjoyed in its hometown) and wash it down with a Dr Pepper, one of the most famous products of Waco, Tex.

PERSONALITY PROFILE

"We get real acquainted with everybody"
—Valerie Kennon

Out-of-towners who stop to eat at the restaurant in Sooner Legends Inn and Suites in Norman, Okla. (1200 24th Ave. SW), don't stay strangers for long. "I can tell you who was sitting at almost every table in the restaurant last night," says Valerie Kennon, who oversees the kitchen and, with her brother Doug and her sister Sharlyn, owns the hotel itself. "We get real acquainted with everybody. You just know everybody and hug everybody, and it's like a big ol' family."

The restaurant is famous both for its pork ribs, which are cooked over a 22-foot open barbecue pit, and for its red velvet cake with cream cheese icing, dubbed "crimson and cream cake" after the colors of the local Oklahoma Sooners college football team. Kennon based the cake on her grandma's recipe. "She had an old café on Route 66 years ago. It only had some barstools and one table. She'd always make fresh homemade pies and cakes, and oh, could she cook," she says. Come hungry—the cake is served not so much by the slice as by the slab: "I have one lady who comes in and takes a piece home, and she says she eats on it for four days."

It came from... **Waco, Texas**

Dr Pepper

Nowadays, if you asked your pharmacist to mix up a soda, you might get a strange look. But in the 19th century, *many pharmacists added soda water and fruit syrups to medicines* to make them go down easier. Those bubbly drinks eventually turned into the sodas we know today—the oldest major brand

of which is Dr Pepper, first whipped up at Morrison's Old Corner Drug Store in Waco in 1885 and introduced to masses of Americans at the 1904 World's Fair in St. Louis, Mo. (the same fair at which ice cream cones and hot dog buns first appeared).

At Waco's Dr Pepper Museum (300 South 5th St.), visitors can see old Dr Pepper commercials, wander the Soft Drink Hall of Fame, learn about the *ill-fated soda made especially for Lyndon B. Johnson*, have a Dr Pepper float in the

replica old-time soda fountain, and hit the gift shop for "I'm A Pepper" T-shirts. To round out a Dr Pepper road trip, head northeast on TX 6 to Dublin, home of the only Dr Pepper bottler that still uses cane sugar instead of high-fructose corn syrup, the Dublin Bottling Works (105 E. Elm). The works has its own museum and soda shop, as well as a gift shop with items like *Dr Pepper cake mix.*

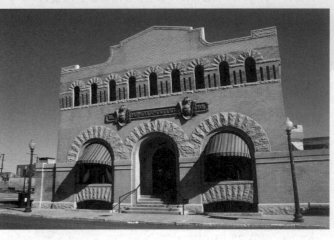

Idaho Spud & Spud Fudge

Considering the unhealthy things done to potatoes to these days—frying, salting, drenching in butter and sour cream—you might as well just snarf down a spud-shaped candy bar and be done with it. The Idaho Spud, a potato-shaped lump of cocoa-flavored marshmallow wrapped in a cocoa coating and dusted with coconut, was the *brainchild of a door-to-door chocolate salesman* in the early 1900s. Eventually he formed the Idaho Candy Company in Boise (412 S. 8th St.), which still uses some machinery from 1915. You can get your own Idaho Spud right at the factory, in most Idaho grocery stores, or in one of these specialty shops: Made in Idaho (350 North Milwaukee St.) or downtown's Taters (249 S. 8th St.), which sells them individually or, for the serious Spud fan, in cases of 24.

Northeast of Boise, at the junction of ID 28 and US 93, Sandee's Candees of Salmon produces Spud Fudge, hunks of fudge that not only look like baked potatoes (complete with chocolate "sour cream" and wrapped in aluminum foil), but also contain potatoes. Sandee Tuck uses potatoes in her fudge to produce a lower-sugar product with a creamier texture. Eat one at Kay's Hallmark (516 Main St.) or take some home as gifts; just don't try to plant them.

Huckleberry sundae

With a short growing season and a distaste for domestic cultivation, huckleberries can be hard to come by. They grow very well in the mountain forests of northwest Montana, and many locals make a yearly ritual of picking them in July and August. But unless you're prepared to spend hours in the forest with a bucket and a sharp eye out for bears, a huckleberry sundae in a restaurant or soda shop is probably the easiest way to sample the sweet-tart fruit.

Off I-91 west of Billings in the town of Big Timber, Cole Drug (136 McLeod) serves huckleberry syrup poured over vanilla ice cream at its old-fashioned soda fountain. In Fishtail, off I-90 closer to Billings, Montana Hanna's Trout Hole Restaurant (1383 Nye Rd.) ups the huckleberry factor a notch with brandied berries over huckleberry ice cream.

Huckleberry shakes, cheesecake with huckleberry sauce, and chocolate cake with huckleberry frosting await at the Montana City Grill in Montana City (take I-15 to exit 187), outside Helena. If you miss huckleberry season, *take consolation in a bottle of huckleberry syrup* or a jar of huckleberry jam from Montana-based Cream of the West (creamofthewest.com) to pour on your ice cream or waffles back home.

Denver omelet

Denver omelet, Denver sandwich, Denver skillet—as long as it contains eggs, green bell peppers, cheese, ham, and onions, no one's picky. Sure, you can get a Denver *(also known as a Western)* omelet everywhere from Poughkeepsie to Portland these days, but there's something particularly satisfying about eating one in its eponymous city. For one thing, you have a built-in excuse to order a side of hash browns with it: some say carbohydrates help prevent altitude sickness.

Try the Denver omelet at Dozens (236 W. 13th Ave.), where the menu focuses on eggs and the kitchen will make them any way you like. Racine's (650 Sherman St.) serves its version skillet-style, with white cheddar cheese on top and a biscuit alongside. At Dixon's Downtown Grill (16th and Wazee), carnivores can try the traditional version while their vegetarian buddies go for the veggie equivalent, made with tomatoes and zucchini instead of ham. Pete's University Park Café (2345 E. Evans Ave.) lets diners choose the cheese (American, Swiss, or cheddar) for their Denver omelets, which are accompanied by hash browns. This is one dish that's easy to adapt at home; for the ham some people substitute bacon or even—yes—Spam®.

FiZZ FACTS

Micro root beers

Late 19th-century America was a soda pop breeding ground.

Not only did Dr Pepper and Coca Cola first make their appearances (in 1885 and 1886, respectively), but so did the first commercial root beer, Hires, first sold to the public in bottles in 1893. Before then, root beer was mostly a medicinal, mildly alcoholic drink made by housewives from ingredients such as cherry tree bark, licorice root, sarsaparilla root, sassafras, birch bark, and dandelion root.

In addition to the widely available root beer brands like Barq's and A&W, dozens of smaller, artisanal brands are made across the country, often by microbreweries as a nonalcoholic alternative to their other products. With its plethora of breweries, microbreweries, and brew pubs, Colorado in particular is excellent root beer hunting ground. And since the ingredients in root beer vary widely, trying different varieties is guaranteed to provide a taste of the unexpected.

In Idaho Springs, Colo. (about 25 miles west of Denver off I-70), at the Tommyknocker Brewpub (1401 Miner St.), house-made root beer is available on draft as well as in bottles. In Denver, the Wynkoop Brewing Co. (1634 18th St.) serves Tiger Root Beer, made with honey. Meanwhile, Durango's Carver Brewing Company (1022 Main Ave.) makes a strong version available in half-gallon jugs as well as by the glass.

Kuchen

At about 40 percent of the population, German is by far the largest ancestry group in South Dakota, and kuchen (German for "cake") pays tribute to that heritage. *A custard-topped dessert made with sweet-roll dough and finished with fruit and cinnamon,* it's traditionally made with apples, peaches, rhubarb, or prunes, but you can also find it in varieties such as strawberry or even peanut butter. The town of Eureka, at the intersection of SD 10 and SD 47, is the kuchen epicenter of the country.

The Eureka Kuchen Factory (1407 J Ave.) sells a four-inch single-serving version, as well as low-sugar apple, peach, apricot, and cherry kuchen made with Splenda®. On the other end of the caloric spectrum? Cinnamon chip, double chocolate, chocolate chip with peanut-butter streusel, and more.

Fry bread

After being forced onto reservations in the 1800s, Native Americans no longer had access to their traditional foods, and had to make do with the bread and lard the government rationed out to them. The result—fry bread—has morphed over the years into a puffy, crispy, Frisbee-sized round often topped with honey or powdered sugar, or else piled with chili and cheese and called an "Indian taco." *By now it's considered a part of Native American culture,* and while it pops up at fairs, dances, powwows, and other events in many areas, only in South Dakota is it the official state bread.

In the town of Interior, just outside Badlands National Park off SD 44, Wooden Knife Manufacturing ships fry bread through its website, www.woodenknife.com. In the park itself, the Cedar Pass Lodge Restaurant (20681 SD 240) adds a note of authenticity by using buffalo meat in its version of the Indian taco; it also offers great views of the park and its rock formations.

From the park, a few hours' drive northwest brings you to Tatanka: Story of the Bison (one mile north of Deadwood off SD 85), a small museum dedicated to the American buffalo. Here you can buy locally made fry bread in the museum gift shop.

Cheese frenchie

If there's one lesson to be learned from a survey of American food, it's this: *People can—and will—deep-fry anything.* Twinkies, candy bars, Oreos, ice cream, and even Coke are all fair game these days, especially at the cholesterol festivals known as state fairs. ("Fried Coke," by the way, means Coca Cola syrup mixed into a batter, shaped into balls, deep-fried, and topped with more syrup. Oh, and whipped cream.)

But before any of those, there was the cheese frenchie *(also "frenchee"),* the deep-fried cheese sandwich first popularized by the now-shuttered King's Food Host chain. Take a cheese sandwich, cut it into wedges, spread it with mayo, roll it in crushed cornflakes, throw it in the deep fryer, and you're pretty much done.

Between Omaha and Lincoln, Neb., another chain, Don & Millie's, has stepped in to fill the void that King's left (locations include 14321 Harrison St. in Omaha and 5200 S. 56th St. in Lincoln). Also in Omaha, Wheat Field's Eatery and Bakery (1224 S. 103rd St.) serves its frenchies with fries. And at the Woodhouse Restaurant in Bismarck (1825 N. 13th St.), you can get a frenchee with ham.

Runza

In the hallowed culinary tradition of wrapping dough around meat—a practice that we have to thank for pepperoni rolls, meat pies, and pasties, not to mention pierogis, empanadas, and most recently, Hot Pockets®—comes the runza (also known as a bierock). Baked dough pockets filled with beef, cabbage, or sauerkraut and *brought to the New World by German-Russian immigrants,* they hail from both Nebraska, where they're shaped like rectangles, and Kansas, where they're shaped like ovals.

They are so popular in these parts that there's even a Runza Restaurant fast-food chain, based out of Lincoln, Neb., with 70-some locations. Omaha boasts 15 of them (including 13236 Arbor Plaza); the 14 Lincoln locations include 1240 West O St. The chain serves the classic runza as well barbecue/bacon, Swiss cheese/mushroom, and other variations.

In the most technical sense, the only place you can have a runza is at the Runza chain, which has trademarked the word. But *keep an eye out for suspiciously runza-like sandwiches* (sometimes called "bunzas" or "Nebraska buns") in other establishments on your Nebraska travels. Watch for them, too, at football games, county or state fairs, and (should you be so lucky) in the home of someone's Nebraskan grandmother.

Barbecue

The famed Kansas City Stockyards may have shut down in 1991, but this is still a meat-eating town—and it owes its reputation for barbecue to a man named Henry Perry, who in 1907 began *selling barbecued ribs wrapped in newspaper* out of a pushcart. Eventually he set up shop in an old trolley barn, declared himself "Barbecue King," and drew crowds demanding his spicy, sweet, tomato-based sauce.

Perry died in 1940, but one of his former employees has carried on his legacy at Arthur Bryant's (locations include 1727 Brooklyn), declared "the single best restaurant in the world" by writer and Kansas City native Calvin Trillin. Taste the fare of another contender for the barbecue throne, George Gates, at Gates and Sons Bar-B-Q (six locations, including 1325 East Emanuel Cleaver Blvd and 3205 Main). It's known not only for its sauce (available in original, extra hot, and sweet and mild versions) but for its rigorous employee training—all of its workers attend the Gates College of Bar-B-Que Knowledge, a.k.a. Rib Tech.

Less well-known but just as authentic is Rosedale Barbecue (600 Southwest Blvd., Kansas City, Kansas), where the sauce is thinner and hotter than most in town. Wherever you go, to pass as a local, ask for the blackened, *crispy pieces of brisket known as "burnt ends."*

Rocky Mountain oysters

Known by an entertaining variety of other euphemisms—prairie oysters, calf fries, cowboy caviar, swinging beef—Rocky Mountain oysters have nothing to do with the ocean, and everything to do with the part of the male calf that, um, gets cut off so he becomes a steer instead of a bull. They're usually skinned, sliced, floured, and deep-fried, and you either love them, hate them, or get dared into eating them.

The birthplace of the Rocky Mountain oyster: the now-shuttered Bruce's Bar in Severance, Colo., *a favorite of motorcylists* that began serving the "oysters" as far back as 1959 (motto: "Where the geese fly and the bulls cry"). These days, Denver's oldest restaurant, the Buckhorn Exchange (1000 Osage St.), serves them with horseradish dipping sauce.

In Oklahoma City, the legendary Cattlemen's Steakhouse (a favorite of diners such as Gene Autry and George Bush, Sr.; 1309 S. Agnew) serves the lamb version, called "lamb fries." In case you need to get up the nerve to try them (and aren't driving), Cattlemen's also makes its own beer, the 22-ounce Double Deuce.

Pig sandwich

When it comes to barbecue, Oklahoma is somewhat of a melting pot. In general, Oklahomans favor the sweet, tomato-based, Kansas City-style sauce (see left), and occasionally the vinegar-based, North Carolina-style sauce makes an appearance. But *there's one barbecue innovation Oklahoma can call its own:* the pig sandwich, pulled pork topped with pickle relish and served on a bun. (Unless you believe the Texans who say they invented it, but that's another story.)

The Van's Pig Stand franchise (four locations including 717 East Highland in Shawnee) has served pig sandwiches for decades. Van's uses homemade relish and goes the tomato-based barbecue sauce route when dressing its pulled pork. At 70-plus years old and counting, the Shawnee location is the oldest family-operated barbecue joint in Oklahoma.

In the small town of Pauls Valley, off US 77 north of Norman, lies Bob's Pig Shop (829 North Ash). Back in 1933, its owners couldn't afford to join the Van's franchise, so they called their business a "pig shop" instead of a "pig stand." The pig sandwich here is a little different than Van's, too—it arrives at the table dressed in a vinegar sauce, and diners can choose to top it or not with the separate, tomato-based sauce that awaits in bottles on each table.

Best Eats West/Southwest

West/Southwest

An 1850s guide for the westward-bound recommended the following supplies per adult: 150 lb. flour, 20 lb. cornmeal, 50 lb. bacon, 40 lb. sugar, 10 lb. coffee, 15 lb. dried fruit, 5 lb. salt, 1/2 lb. baking soda, 2 lb. tea, 5 lb. rice, and 15 lb. beans. "To the above may be added as many nicknacks as you see fit," the guide assured.

Considering the culinary bounty the West and Southwest offer nowadays, visitors may want to pack light—and save space for "nicknacks" such as bottles of fry sauce (a ketchup-mayonnaise concoction) and Apple Beer (Utah's favorite soda). Fans of Spam musubi, the sushi-like snack of Hawaii, can snag a "musubi maker" for home use. And while a San Francisco burrito might not survive the entire drive home, its foil wrapping means you can at least wolf down one warm one en route.

Alas, other regional treats don't travel so well: shave ice, Hawaii's answer to sno-cones; Frito pie, the taco eaten out of a bag; sloppy, colorful green chile cheeseburgers; gâteau basque, a custard-filled cake; and avocado pie, a surprisingly sweet innovation. As for the fish and shellfish stew called cioppino, well, you'll need a bib and some serious utensils, which pretty much rules it out as road food. All the more reason to eat hearty while you're there.

> *"I've been hunting mushrooms all my life"*
> —Jack Czarnecki

PERSONALITY PROFILE

Attention fungus fans: The Joel Palmer House restaurant in Dayton, Ore. (600 Ferry St.), is for you. Chef Jack Czarnecki (author of *A Cook's Book of Mushrooms*) has dedicated the menu to wild mushrooms and truffles, which he gathers himself from west-central Oregon's plentiful bounty. In fact, they're the reason he moved here from Pennsylvania: "There's more wild mushrooms harvested in Oregon than in all the rest of the states combined," he says.

It takes a lot of mushroom hunting to supply an entire restaurant. "I'm out three or four times a week," Czarnecki says. Of the mushrooms he gathers, "some we dry, some we put away and freeze for the winter." The rest he serves in soups and tarts, over filet mignon and venison, alongside beef stroganoff, and stirred into pasta with cream sauce. He's even been known to use them in desserts, such as  truffle ice cream—made with actual truffles, not the chocolate variety—that he says has "a natural pineapply, earthy characteristic, a smell and a taste that will send you to the moon."

Though he's a bacteriologist by training and a chef by trade, Czarnecki sums up his career this way: "I've been hunting mushrooms all my life. It's my hobby, it's my life, it's everything that I do."

FiZZ FACTS

Apple Beer

First things first: just because the carbonated, amber- or choco-late-colored beverage in that bottle on the shelf isn't alcoholic, that doesn't mean it's not beer. According to the Random House dictionary, one definition of beer is "any of various beverages, whether alcoholic or not, made from roots, molasses or sugar, yeast, etc." Strictly speaking, that means root beer and ginger beer qualify. So does that Western-region specialty, Apple Beer.

Because Apple Beer contains neither alcohol nor caffeine, it's a favorite in Utah, where 60 percent of the residents belong to the Church of Jesus Christ of Latter-Day Saints, which eschews both substances. But just about anyone can enjoy the sparkling drink, manufactured in Salt Lake City since the 1960s. Apple Beer is actually a variant of the traditional German drink fassbrause. Like beer, it has an amber color and a foamy head.

In Provo near the Brigham Young University campus, diners at the Brick Oven Restaurant (111 E. 800 N) can order Apple Beer on draft with their pizza. Salt Lake City's Skybox sports restaurant (4 S. Rio Grande St.) serves it with stick-to-your-ribs classics like chicken-fried steak and cheese fries. South of Salt Lake City, off I-215 in West Jordan, a less macho environment awaits at Sweet Afton's candy shop (1100 W. 7800 South), which sells Apple Beer in bottles.

Avocado pie/avocado ice cream

At first, the custardy light-green dessert calls up memories of Key limes, or possibly that crème-de-menthe concoction, grasshopper pie. *The rich, smooth texture of this pie,* however, comes not from sweetened condensed milk or marshmallow fluff, but from the natural creaminess of the . . . avocado?

Avocado pie. For many people, it may take some time for that concept to sink in. But devotees swear to its deliciousness, and home chefs say it's amazingly easy to make. Because California grows 95 percent of the country's avocados, and because the no-bake recipe is ideal in hot weather, avocado pie is most frequently found in the West and Southwest. Orlando's New Mexican Café in Taos, N.M., (1114 Don Juan Valdez Lane) serves a frozen version of the sweet dessert dish.

In San Francisco, Mitchell's Ice Cream (688 San Jose Ave.) takes *the avocado dessert concept* in another direction with avocado ice cream. (Whether that's more or less of a taste adventure than the purple yam ice cream here is difficult to say.) Mitchell's doesn't franchise and doesn't ship, so eat up while you can. Meanwhile, fans of Mr. Baguette, a Vietnamese eatery in the Los Angeles area (8702 Valley Blvd., Rosemead), say the avocado smoothies here are surprisingly light.

Gâteau basque

Around 1850, some of the Basque—a people who have lived for thousands of years in a small area on the Spanish/French border—migrated to the American West to establish themselves as sheepherders. Many of them settled in Nevada, where they founded boardinghouses and restaurants, some of which remain to this day.

Basque cuisine is characterized by family-style service (often at communal tables), plentiful use of garlic, and Spanish- and French-influenced dishes such as chorizo (pork sausage), lamb stew, and jambon de bayonne (cured ham). Gâteau basque, a cake filled with almond-flavored custard, often rounds out the meal. Look for it in downtown Elko, Nev., where Silver Street overflows with Basque restaurants—the Nevada Dinner House (351 Silver St.), the Biltoki (405 Silver St.), and the dining room of the Star Hotel (246 Silver St.), to name a few.

About 300 miles southwest in Reno, the deceptively named Santa Fe Hotel (235 Lake St.) serves gâteau basque in its restaurant, along with other traditional Basque desserts such as flan. And at Louis' Basque Corner (301 E. 4th St), voted best Basque restaurant in the state by *Nevada Magazine,* the waitstaff wear traditional Basque outfits—berets and cummerbunds on the men, head-kerchiefs, bodices, and full skirts on the women—for extra atmosphere.

Sourdough

Considering that San Francisco already lays claim to burritos and cioppino (see pp. BE 30 and BE 31), it seems downright greedy for it to try to snatch up sourdough, too. After all, Alaska has just as much claim. In the late 19th century, the Klondike Gold Rush brought a flood of prospectors to the Alaska Territory. With little or no access to commercial yeast, they relied on sourdough starter to leaven their bread. It's said that some miners even slept with their precious starter so it wouldn't freeze. To this day, a hardcore Alaskan—particularly a solitary, old-timer bachelor type—is called a "sourdough."

In Fairbanks, Sam's Sourdough Café (3702 Cameron St.) serves even hamburgers on sourdough bread; it also offers breakfast all day, including sourdough pancakes. Climbers with their sights on Mt. McKinley often stop in the tiny town of Talkeetna (off AK 3, south of Denali National Park) for overnight lodging at the Talkeetna Roadhouse, where breakfast includes not only sourdough toast, but also sourdough muffins. Driving south on AK 3, then north on AK 1 will lead you to the town of Gakona and the Sourdough Roadhouse (open May-September; Mile 147.5 Richardson Hwy.), with a restaurant that claims to use a sourdough starter from 1896.

It came from... | **Los Angeles, California**

Jelly Bellies

Before the late 1970s, jelly beans were, if you believe former L.A. candy distributor and Jelly Belly inventor David Klein, kind of boring. Every bean usually featured the same plain white interior with a limited variety of flavors—cherry, orange, lemon, and the like. With the help of the company then known as Herman Goelitz Candy, in 1976 Klein came up with a smaller jelly bean made with actual fruit juice, featuring a flavored center, and available in offbeat flavors like cream soda and tangerine.

Once President Ronald Reagan started keeping a stash of them in the Oval Office and on Air Force One, the candy's popularity soared. Today the original eight flavors have expanded to 50, from buttered popcorn to strawberry cheesecake. (Jelly Belly also makes a Harry Potter-inspired line of Bertie Bott's Every Flavor Beans, which include such taste treats as "booger," "rotten egg," and "dirt.")

In the company's Fairfield, Calif., facility about an hour north of San Francisco (1 Jelly Belly Lane), visitors can take a 40-minute walking tour to watch Jelly Bellies being made, try every flavor at the sampling bar, and (because that sugar buzz won't last forever) nosh on a jelly-bean-shaped hamburger or pizza in the Jelly Belly Café.

Spam musubi

We have World War II to thank for Spam®—sort of. Though first introduced in 1937, it wasn't until its maker, Hormel Foods, provided troops with more than 100 million pounds of the canned spiced ham that the world really got acquainted with it.

These days, many in the U.S. disdain it—but not, for some reason, the Hawaiians, who eat more Spam than any other state. A dish called Spam musubi, a sushi-like snack featuring seaweed wrapped around a small block of Spam-topped rice, has become part and parcel of Hawaiian culture. You can buy it just about everywhere on the islands, including in delis and gas stations; Hawaiian kitchen shops sell musubi makers for home use, too.

The ABC chain of convenience stores, found all over the islands, carries Spam musubi as a carry-out snack. On the north shore of Oahu, Ted's Bakery (59-024 Kamehameha Hwy.) may be famous for its pies, but its Spam musubi deserves recognition as well.

Green chile cheeseburger

At the 50-some-year-old Bert's Burger Bowl (235 N. Guadalupe St.) in Santa Fe, N.M., diners who down six half-pound cheeseburgers in half an hour get them free. Less ambitious patrons might want to relish just one item: the green chile cheeseburger, purportedly invented here and now a staple of chile-happy New Mexican cuisine. *It's pretty much what it sounds like*—a cheeseburger laden with chopped hot green chiles in addition to the more usual condiments. Unlike some other places, Bert's puts the chiles on top of the cheese instead of underneath, making for a messier (but more colorful) sandwich.

A few miles outside of Santa Fe, patrons write their names on a chalkboard to get a seat at the small Bobcat Bite (420 Old Las Vegas Hwy.), which lies on the former Route 66. Downtown at Dave's Not Here (1115 Hickox St.), Dave is in fact no longer in residence, but the green chile cheeseburgers still are. The chile here comes in a cup on the side, so diners can add as much or as little as they want. Meanwhile, San Antonio, N.M., boasts the Owl Bar and Cafe (77 US 380, off I-25 at exit 139), which serves green chile cheeseburgers all day, even at breakfast.

Burritos

Burritos are everywhere, but those in San Francisco's Mission District have two particularly endearing characteristics. Number one, they're huge. The dozens upon dozens of taquerias here steam their flour tortillas, so they'll stretch further and *won't break when stuffed to capacity and wrapped in foil.* And number two, they're cheap for what you get. A "super burrito" with meat, rice, beans, cheese, sour cream, guacamole, lettuce, tomato, and salsa makes an extremely filling meal (or even two) and will set you back less than $8.

With its late-night hours, El Farolito (4817 Mission St.) is popular with bar-goers who need a bite before heading home. Pancho Villa Taqueria (3071 16th St.), though often crowded, is worth a trip—it's even been featured in *Bon Appetit*. Taqueria Cancun (2288 Mission St.) wins favor with vegetarians for its lard-free tortillas, *but it has lots to offer carnivores as well,* such as the burrito mojado with al pastor (marinated pork).

Mission burritos tend to pack a calorific punch, so visitors worrying about their vacation waistline might want to try Papalote Mexican Grill (3409 24th St.). Papalote's abundant vegetarian options and lean cuts of meat give it a reputation for healthfulness.

Shave ice

To the uninitiated, the snowy treat known as shave ice in Honolulu and its environs sounds a lot like a plain old sno-cone. But islanders (and savvy visitors) know that shave ice has a much smoother texture because it's shaved off a block of ice—not crushed. You're not chomping on ice crystals but lapping up a mouthful of icy fluff. Many places *also offer extras in the bottom of the cup,* such as a miniature scoop of vanilla ice cream.

In Honolulu, try Waiola Bakery and Shave Ice (525 Kapahulu Ave.), which features more than 40 flavors including lychee, coconut, and pickled plum, along with toppings such as Hershey's syrup and condensed milk. Many Hawaiians enjoy adding sweet red azuki beans to their shave ice, too.

An hour-long, very pretty drive from Honolulu to Hale'iwa brings you to Matsumoto's Shave Ice (66-087 Kamehameha Hwy.), which has been in business for more than 50 years. The shave ice here is reputedly sweeter and chunkier than Waiola's, and is available in three-flavor combos including the Rainbow (strawberry, pineapple, and lemon). Also in Hale'iwa, Aoki's Shave Ice (66-117 Kamehameha Hwy.), which offers sugar-free syrups, is still run by the great-grand-daughter of the first couple to serve shave ice on the North Shore.

Fry sauce

It's rare that a fast food chain not only carries a city-specific food, but also invents one. Such is the case with the Salt Lake City-based Arctic Circle burger franchise (five area locations including 135 E. 900 South and 3408 E. 7800 South), which claims to have originated the condiment called fry sauce, a ketchup-mayonnaise combination with various seasonings, in the 1940s. *Some suspect it's really Thousand Island dressing in disguise,* but Arctic Circle—which makes vague references to using "tomato concentrate, lemon juice, eggs, and a whole bunch of other ingredients" in its version—isn't talking. Utahns take their fry sauce so seriously that during the 2002 Winter Olympics in Salt Lake City, it was featured on a commemorative souvenir pin.

Plenty of other Salt Lake City joints carry their own fry sauce variations, such as Apollo Burgers (1625 W. North Temple) and Hires Big H (425 S. 700 East). At Provo's Burgers Supreme (1796 N University Pkwy.), hard-core fry sauce fans dip their onion rings in it, too. You can buy fry sauce in Utah grocery stores under the Some Dude's Fry Sauce brand, which claims to contain garlic and Santa Fe chiles.

Cioppino

Cioppino (say chih-PEEN-oh), a fish and tomato stew, is said to have its origins in the early-1900s Italian fishing community of San Francisco. Many cioppino recipes call for bass, crab or lobster, clams or mussels, and shrimp, though some throw anchovies and/or octopus in there, too. The shellfish arrive shells-on, so eating cioppino is a labor-intensive and messy, if tasty, process.

In San Francisco, try it at Cioppino's on Fisherman's Wharf (400 Jefferson St.), which serves it with grilled sourdough toast, or Scoma's (Pier 47 on Al Scoma Way), where you can have it with either a half or a whole crab. At the Tadich Grill (240 California St.)—open since 1849—diners can order a bowl of the house cioppino while sitting in the semi-private booths.

South of San Francisco off CA 1 in Moss Landing, Phil's Fish Market and Eatery (7600 Sandholdt Rd.) sells cioppino by the gallon, in *$70 buckets that hold enough to feed four to six people.* But truly indolent foodies should head north to Newport, Ore.'s Sharks Seafood Bar and Steamer Co. (852 SW Bay Bl.), which serves a "lazy man's cioppino" (with all shells removed) and sells cioppino sauce by the liter for home use.

Frito pie

Two separate cities lay claim to inventing the Frito pie—Santa Fe, N.M., and San Antonio, Tex.—and in the interest of culinary fairness, you should probably try one in each city on your next Southwestern jaunt.

Styles vary: Some people spread Fritos in a baking dish, then top them with chili, cheese, and onions (occasionally even fancying it up with lettuce and tomato), while others *just snip open a snack-size Fritos bag* and pour the toppings directly in.

In Santa Fe, the Frito pie hot spot is the Five and Dime General Store (58 E. San Francisco St.), where $4 gets you a bag of Fritos into which New Mexico chili and grated cheese (and, at your request, onions and jalapenos) have been ladled. Grab a plastic fork and dig into your "walking taco" as you stroll around Santa Fe's historic Plaza. In San Antonio, try one at Casbeers (1719 Blanco Rd.) while listening to live country music, or the family-friendly Longhorn Café (17625 Blanco Rd.).

Eat your way across the U.S.A.

Savor time-honored recipes and share in the wonderful world
of delicious—and sometimes wacky—things to eat at a food festival. From chiles to chocolate, swamp cabbage to shrimp, persimmons to pumpkins, down-home food celebrations are diverse enough to please any palate. To plan a stop, read on.

Spring

World Catfish Festival
First or second Saturday in April
Belzoni, Mississippi
Sample a genuine Southern mid-day dinner of fried catfish, hush puppies, and coleslaw.
(800) 408-4838,
www.catfishcapitalonline.com

Chocolate Festival
Third weekend in April
Washington, Kentucky
Rivers of sweet chocolate flow through shops, and a fudge contest brings out chocolate creativity.
(606) 759-7423, www.washingtonky.com

Vidalia Onion Festival
Last weekend in April
Vidalia, Georgia
Munching on raw onions is common practice here; there's also an onion cook-off and an onion-eating contest.
(912) 538-8687, www.vidaliaonionfestival.com

Stockton Asparagus Festival
Last full weekend in April
Stockton, California
Stockton has asparagus to spare: Nearly 20 tons are cooked during this weekend extravaganza.
(209) 644-3740, www.asparagusfest.com

Vermont Maple Festival
Last weekend in April
St. Albans, Vermont
Start each morning at the festival with fresh-made pancakes topped with maple syrup.
(802) 524-5800, www.vtmaplefestival.org

San Marcos Fair
Second week in April to first week of May
Aguascalientes, Mexico
This "fair of fairs" is an enormous national event. Treats include scrumptious turkey in rich chocolate mole sauce.
(800) 446-3942, www.visitmexico.com

Summer

Great Wisconsin Cheese Festival
First weekend in June
Little Chute, Wisconsin
Sample more than 30 types of cheese, including Wisconsin's native Colby. Don't miss the cheese-carving demos.
(920) 788-7390, www.littlechutewi.org/calendar_events/cheesefest.html

International Horseradish Festival
Second weekend in June
Collinsville, Illinois
This annual celebration features a Root Toss, a recipe contest, and Root Golf, played with balls carved from horseradish.
(618) 344-2884, www.horseradishfestival.com

Pink Tomato Festival
First full week of June
Warren, Arkansas
This is one tomato that's supposed to be pink. Taste it for yourself at this festival, which features a tomato-eating contest and an all-tomato luncheon.
(870) 226-5225, www.bradleypinktomato.com

Olathe Sweet Corn Festival
First Saturday in August
Olathe, Colorado
Nothing says summer like corn-on-the-cob, and they've got plenty to give away on festival day (more than 70,000 free ears!).
(866) 363-2676, www.olathesweetcornfest.com

National Lentil Festival
Third Friday and Saturday in August
Pullman, Washington
Festival highlights include a parade led by mascot Tase T. Lentil, a lentil cook-off, and 250 gallons of free lentil chili.
(800) 365-6948, www.lentilfest.com

Shrimp and Petroleum Festival
Labor Day weekend
Morgan City, Louisiana
Have no fear: Cajun Country's two most important resources are kept separate at all times at this festival.
(985) 385-0703, www.shrimp-petrofest.org

Paella y Vino Festival
First Sunday in June
Tijuana, Mexico
Listen to Mexican music, watch folk dancers, and discover for yourself why paella (a rice dish) is considered the food of kings.
(888) 775-2417, www.seetijuana.com

Fish, Fun & Folk Festival
Last weekend in July
Twillingate, Newfoundland
Festivalgoers head to the dining hall for traditional Newfoundland meals of cod, salmon, and lobster.
(709) 884-2678, www.fishfunfolkfestival.com

Hatch Chile Festival
Labor Day weekend
Hatch, New Mexico
The "Chile Capital of the World" celebrates the harvest with chile eggplant parmesan, chile chocolate cake, and more.
(505) 267-5050, www.hatchchilefest.com

Blackberry Festival
Mid-August
Powell River, British Columbia
Enjoy a street party, music, clowns, and, of course, lots of blackberries.
(604) 458-4701, www.discoverpowellriver.com/visitors/Blackberry.htm

Fall

McClure Bean Soup Festival
Second week of September
McClure, Pennsylvania
Fireworks, parades, and Civil War reenactments top off this annual celebration.
(800) 338-7389, www.mcclurebeansoup.com

Texas Gator Fest
Weekend following September 10
Anahuac, Texas
Does alligator really taste like chicken? Find out at this three-day celebration in the Alligator Capital of Texas
(409) 267-4190, www.texasgatorfest.com

Okrafest
Second Saturday of September
Checotah, Oklahoma
Sample free fried okra. Antique tractors, an open car show, live music, and vendors round out the fest.
(918) 473-4178

AppleJack Festival
Third weekend in September
Nebraska City, Nebraska
Try all sorts of apple-based goodies, including apple fritters, caramel apples, and apple cider.
(402) 873-6654, www.nebraskacity.com/ajack.html

Idaho Spud Day
Third Saturday in September
Shelley, Idaho
Spud Day isn't for couch potatoes. The Great Potato Games feature the World Spud-Picking Championships as well as a kids' parade.
(208) 529-9619

Persimmon Festival
Last full week of September
Mitchell, Indiana
If you've never eaten a persimmon, you can make up for lost time with persimmon fudge, bread, cookies, cake, and ice cream.
(812) 849-4441, www.mitchellpersimmonfestival.org

Barnesville Pumpkin Festival
Last full weekend in September
Barnesville, Ohio
Treat yourself to pumpkin pancakes, pumpkin fudge, or maybe even a pumpkin shake.
(740) 425-2593, www.barnesvillepumpkinfestival.com

Norsk Høstfest
Tuesday through Saturday after the first full weekend in October
Minot, North Dakota
For those who can't stomach lutefisk (cod soaked in lye and then boiled), there are other Scandinavian specialties like Swedish meatballs.
(701) 852-2368, www.hostfest.com

Boggy Bayou Mullet Festival
Third weekend in October
Niceville, Florida
If smoked or fried mullet doesn't tempt your taste buds, try other local specialties like crawfish bread, boiled peanuts, and alligator-on-a-stick.
(850) 729-4008, www.mulletfestival.com

Chatworth Cranberry Festival
Third full weekend in October
Chatsworth, New Jersey
Strap on your waders and jump into one of the dozens of cranberry bogs at the third-largest U.S. cranberry harvest.
(609) 726-9237, www.cranfest.org

Barbecue Festival
One of last two Saturdays in October
Lexington, North Carolina
Festival-goers make tracks for pork shoulder cooked over hickory coals and basted with a ketchup and vinegar sauce.
(336) 956-1880, www.barbecuefestival.com

Winter

Kona Coffee Cultural Festival
10-day festival starts first Friday in November
Kailua Kona, Hawaii
Watch as local growers brew their best coffee, then try your hand harvesting beans in the Kona-picking competition.
(808) 326-7820, www.konacoffeefest.com

Chitlin' Strut
Saturday after Thanksgiving
Salley, South Carolina
"Chitlin'" is Southern slang for "chitterling," a cleaned pig intestine floured and deep-fried in peanut oil. More than 20,000 lb. are devoured on festival day.
(803) 258-3485, www.chitlinstrut.com

Swamp Cabbage Festival
Last full weekend in February
La Belle, Florida
Enjoy music, armadillo races, and lots of swamp cabbage (a.k.a. heart of palm), served raw, stewed, or frittered.
(863) 675-2995, www.swampcabbagefestival.org

✹RAND McNALLY

the road
atlas
& TRAVEL GUIDE

CONTENTS

Locator Map
Find regional, state, vicinity, city, and national park maps

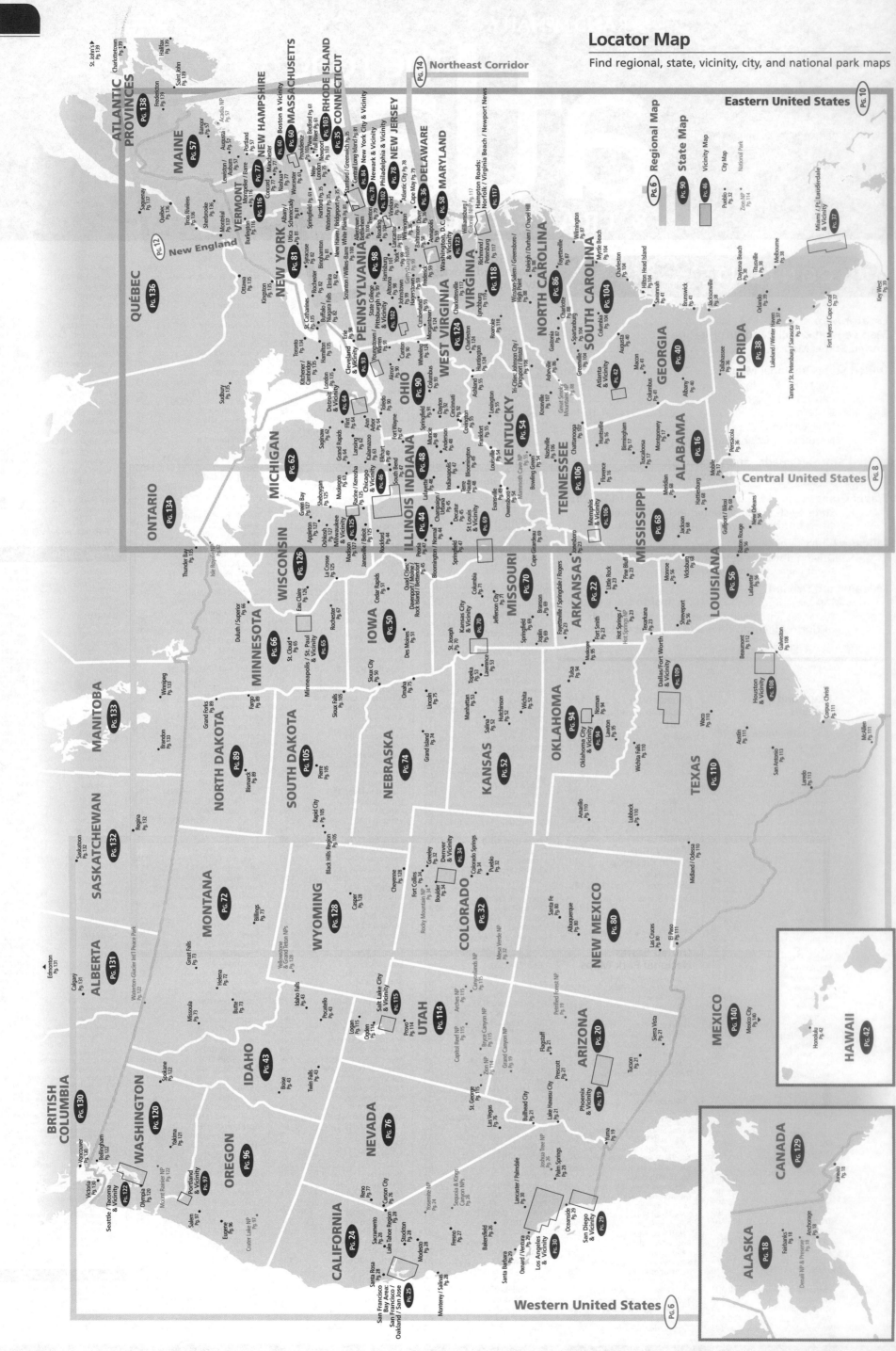

Toll Roads

State	Name		Location (Start point to end point)	Miles	Price
Alabama	Foley Beach Expressway		AL 59 north of Foley to AL 180 in Orange Beach	15.0	$3.00
California	Eastern Trans. Corridor	CA 133 section	I-5 to Foothill Transportation Corridor	4.3	$2.50
		CA 241 section	CA 91 to Foothill Transportation Corridor	12.2	$2.75
		CA 261 section	Jamboree Rd. to CA 241	6.0	$1.75
	Foothill Transportation Corridor (CA 241)		Eastern Transportation Corridor to Oso Pkwy.	9.5	$3.50
	San Joaquin Hills Trans. Corridor (CA 73)		MacArthur Blvd. to I-5	17.7	$5.00
Colorado	E-470		I-25 N to I-25 S	46.1	$9.75
	I-25 Express Lanes		HOV lanes in I-25 to/from downtown Denver to US 36	7.0	$3.25
	Northwest Parkway		I-25 N and US 36	10.0	$2.00
Delaware	DE 1		S. Dover to Delaware City	32.9	$2.00
	John F. Kennedy Memorial Highway		Maryland state line to jct DE 141	11.0	$4.00
Florida	Airport Expressway (FL 112)		Miami International Airport to I-95	4.1	$1.25
	Beachline Expressway (FL 528)		I-4 to FL 520	31.0	$2.75
	Central Florida Greenway (FL 417)		I-4S to Seminole county line	38.0	$4.50
		Southern Connector	I-4 to the Central Florida Greenway	3.9	$0.75
	Crosstown Expressway		Gandy Blvd (US 92) to I-75	13.9	$2.25
	Dolphin Expressway (FL 836)		Florida's Turnpike's Homestead Extension to I-95	11.8	$1.25
	Don Shula Expressway (FL 874)		Florida's Tpk. Homestead Ext. to the Palmetto Expressway	7.2	$1.25
	East-West Expressway (FL 408)		Colonial Dr. (east) to Florida's Turnpike	22.0	$2.50
	Everglades Parkway (Alligator Alley)		Naples to Andytown	78.0	$2.50
	Florida's Turnpike	Mainline Ticket System	South of St. Cloud, FL to jct with FL 804 near Greenacres	143.0	$13.70
		Homestead Extension	Miramar to Florida City	47.0	$3.75
		Northern Coin System	I-75 to Three Lakes Toll Plaza (start of ticket system)	84.0	$3.75
		Southern Coin System	Lantana Toll Plaza to Miami	39.0	$2.75
	Gratigny Parkway (FL 924)		Palmetto Expwy. to NW 32nd Ave.	5.4	$1.25
	Osceola Parkway (FL 522)		Florida's Turnpike to Walt Disney World Drive	12.4	$1.50
	Polk Parkway (FL 570)		I-4 near Clark Rd. to I-4 near Mt. Olive Rd.	25.1	$3.00
	Sanibel Causeway		Connecting Sanibel Island to the mainland	3.0	$6.00
	Sawgrass Expressway (FL 869)		I-75 to I-95	23.0	$2.00
	Seminole Expressway (FL 417)		I-4 near FL 46 to Seminole county line	18.0	$2.00
	Snapper Creek Expressway (FL 878)		US 1 to FL 874 (Don Shula Expressway)	2.7	$1.25
	Suncoast Parkway (FL 589)		Veterans Expwy. to US 98	42.0	$3.25
	Veterans Expressway (FL 589)		Dale Mabry Hwy. to Courtney Campbell Causeway	15.0	$1.75
	Western Expressway (FL 429)		US 192 to US 441 (FL 429)	25.0	$2.50
Georgia	GA 400		Lenox Rd. to I-285	3.6	$0.50
Illinois	Chicago Skyway (I-90)		I-94 to Indiana state line	7.8	$2.50
	Veterans Memorial Tollway (I-355)		I-290, Addison, to I-80	30.0	$4.00
	Jane Addams Memorial Tollway (I-90)		Des Plaines to South Beloit	76.0	$5.80
	Ronald Reagan Memorial Tollway (I-88)		I-294 to Rock Falls	97.0	$5.40
	Tri-State Tollway	northbound (I-294 & I-94)	I-94 / IL 394 to Wisconsin state line	83.0	$4.90
		southbound (I-94 & I-294)	Wisconsin state line to I-94 / IL 394	83.0	$4.70
Indiana	Indiana Toll Road	barrier portion (I-90)	Illinois state line to LaPorte ticket plaza	24.0	$0.50
		ticket portion (I-80/90)	LaPorte, IN to Ohio state line	133.0	$4.15
Kansas	Kansas Turnpike (I-70 & I-35 & I-335)		Kansas City to Oklahoma state line	236.0	$9.25
Maine	Maine Turnpike		York to Augusta	100.0	$4.00
Maryland	John F. Kennedy Memorial Highway		Toll bridge between Havre de Grace and Perryville	50.0	$5.00
Massachusetts	Massachusetts Turnpike (westbound only)		East Boston to New York state line	138.0	$7.60
New Hampshire	Blue Star Turnpike		Portsmouth to Seabrook	15.0	$1.00
	F.E. Everett Turnpike		Nashua to Concord	44.7	$1.50
	Spaulding Turnpike		Portsmouth to Milton, NH	33.2	$1.00
New Jersey	Atlantic City Expressway		Turnersville to Atlantic City	44.0	$2.50
	Garden State Parkway (southbound only)		Montvale to Cape May	173.0	$4.20
	New Jersey Turnpike		Delaware Memorial Bridge to US 46	148.0	$6.45
New York	New York Thruway	eastbound	Pennsylvania state line to New York City	496.0	$22.50
		westbound	New York City to Pennsylvania state line	496.0	$18.50
		Berkshire section	Selkirk to Massachusetts Turnpike	15.0	$1.50
		New England section	New York City to Connecticut state line	15.0	$1.25*
		Niagara section	Buffalo to Niagara Falls	21.0	$0.75
Ohio	J.W. Shocknessy Ohio Turnpike		Pennsylvania state line to Indiana state line	241.2	$10.25
Oklahoma	Cherokee Turnpike		East of US 69 to east of US 59	32.8	$2.25
	Chickasaw Turnpike		Ada to Sulphur	27.1	$0.55
	Cimarron Turnpike		I-35 to Tulsa	59.2	$2.50
	Creek Turnpike		Turner Turnpike to Will Rogers Turnpike	33.2	$2.45
	H.E. Bailey Turnpike		Oklahoma City to Texas state line	86.4	$4.00
	Indian Nation Turnpike		Henryetta to Hugo	105.2	$4.75
	John Kilpatrick Turnpike		I-40 to I-35/44	25.3	$2.00
	Muskogee Turnpike		Tulsa to Webbers Falls	53.1	$2.50
	Turner Turnpike		Oklahoma City to Tulsa	86.0	$3.50
	Will Rogers Turnpike		Tulsa to Missouri state line	88.5	$3.50
Pennsylvania	Amos K. Hutchinson Bypass (PA 66)		US 119 to US 22	13.2	$1.00
	James E. Ross Hwy (PA 60)	northbound	Beaver Falls to New Castle	16.5	$1.00
		southbound	New Castle to Beaver Falls	16.5	$0.50
	Mon/Fayette Expressway	northern section (PA 43)	PA 51 to US 40	24.0	$1.75
		southern section (PA 43)	Uniontown to WV state line	28.0	$0.75
		Findlay Connector (PA 576)	US 22 to PA 60	4.2	$0.50
	Pennsylvania Turnpike	Main section (eastbound)	Ohio state line to New Jersey state line	359.0	$22.75
		Main section (westbound)	New Jersey state line to Ohio state line	359.0	$19.75
		Northeast section	Norristown to Scranton	110.0	$6.25
Texas	TX 1		TX 45 to Parmer Lane	4.0	$0.75
	TX 45		TX 183A to TX 130	8.0	$1.50
	TX 121		Bus. TX 121 to Old Denton Rd	8.2	$1.60
	TX 130		I-35 to US 183	36.0	$6.00
	TX 183A		TX 45 to US 183	9.0	$1.50
	Camino Colombia Toll Road		I-35 to Mexican border	22.0	$2.00
	Dallas North Tollway		I-35 E to US 380	22.0	$4.05
	Fort Bend Parkway		TX 6 to Alt US 90	9.0	$1.00
	Hardy Toll Road		I-610 to I-45	21.6	$3.00
	President George Bush Turnpike		TX 161 to TX 78	29.2	$5.00
	Sam Houston Tollway			61.3	
		East	I-45 to I-10		$3.50
		North	US 290 to I-45		$1.50
		South	US 59 to I-45		$3.00
		West	US 59 to US 290		$3.00
	Westpark Tollway		I-610 to TX 99		$2.50
Utah	Adams Av. Parkway		I-84 to US 89	1.0	$1.00
Virginia	Chesapeake Expressway (VA 168)		I-64 to the North Carolina border	16.0	$2.00
	Downtown Expressway		I-195 to I-95	2.5	$0.50
	Dulles Greenway		VA 28 to Leesburg	14.3	$3.20
	Dulles Toll Road		VA 123 to VA 28	14.0	$0.75
	Pocahontas Parkway		I-95 connecting to I-295	7.5	$2.25
	Powhite Parkway Extension		VA 150 to Old Hundred Rd	12.5	$0.75
West Virginia	West Virginia Turnpike		Charleston to Princeton	88.0	$3.75

NOTE: Cash price is rate for automobiles for full toll route length during weekday peak hours.   **Eastbound only*

Map Legend

Roads and related symbols

	Free limited-access highway
	Toll limited-access highway
	New road (under construction as of press time)
	Other multilane highway
	Principal highway
	Other through highway
	Other road (conditions vary — local inquiry suggested)
	Unpaved road (conditions vary — local inquiry suggested)
	Ramp; one way route
	Ferry
96 / BR 96	Interstate highway; Interstate highway business route
31 / BR 31	U.S. highway; U.S. highway business route
	Trans-Canada highway; Autoroute
1	Mexican highway or Central American highway
18	State or provincial highway
147	Secondary state, secondary provincial, or county highway
NM	County trunk highway
	Construction site or construction zone
	Scenic route
	Best of the Road™ route
TOLL	Service area; toll booth or fee booth
	Tunnel; mountain pass
2 8 10	Interchanges and exit numbers (For most states, the mileage between interchanges may be determined by subtracting one number from the other.)
9 / 4 3 2	Highway distances (segments of one mile or less not shown): Cumulative miles (red): the distance between arrows Intermediate miles (black): the distance between intersections Comparative distance 1 mile = 1.609 kilometers 1 kilometer = 0.621 mile

Cities & towns (size of type on map indicates relative population)

⊛ ⊛	National capital; state or provincial capital
⊙	County seat or independent city
● ○	City, town, or recognized place; neighborhood
	Urbanized area
	Separate cities within metropolitan area

Parks, recreation areas, & points of interest

	U.S. or Canadian national park
	U.S. or Canadian national monument, other National Park Service facility, state/provincial park or recreation area
♣ ♠	Park with camping facilities; park without camping facilities
▲ ⛱	Campsite; wayside or roadside park
	National forest, national grassland, or city park
	Wilderness area; wildlife refuge
▪ □	Point of interest, historic site or monument
✈	Airport
	Building
	Foot trail
⚐	Golf course or country club
H	Hospital or medical center
	Indian reservation
?	Information center or Tourist Information Center (T.I.C.)
✈	Military or governmental installation; military airport
	Rest area with toilets; rest area without toilets

Physical features

	Dam
△ ▲	Mountain peak; highest point in state/province
	Lake; intermittent lake; dry lake
	River; intermittent river
	Desert; glacier
	Swamp or mangrove swamp

Other symbols

	Area shown in greater detail on inset map
52	Inset map page indicator (if not on same page)
✿	Great River Road
	Port of entry
	Intracoastal waterway
	Railroad
COOK	County or parish boundary and name
	State or provincial boundary
	National boundary
	Continental divide
	Time zone boundary
33°00′ 95°00′	Latitude; longitude

Population figures are from the latest available census or are Census Bureau or Rand McNally estimates.

For a complete list of abbreviations that appear on the maps, visit go.randmcnally.com/ABBR.

©2009 Rand McNally

Land area: 3,537,438 sq. mi.
Population: 296,410,404
Largest city: New York City, 8,143,197

INDEX OF CITIES PG. 141

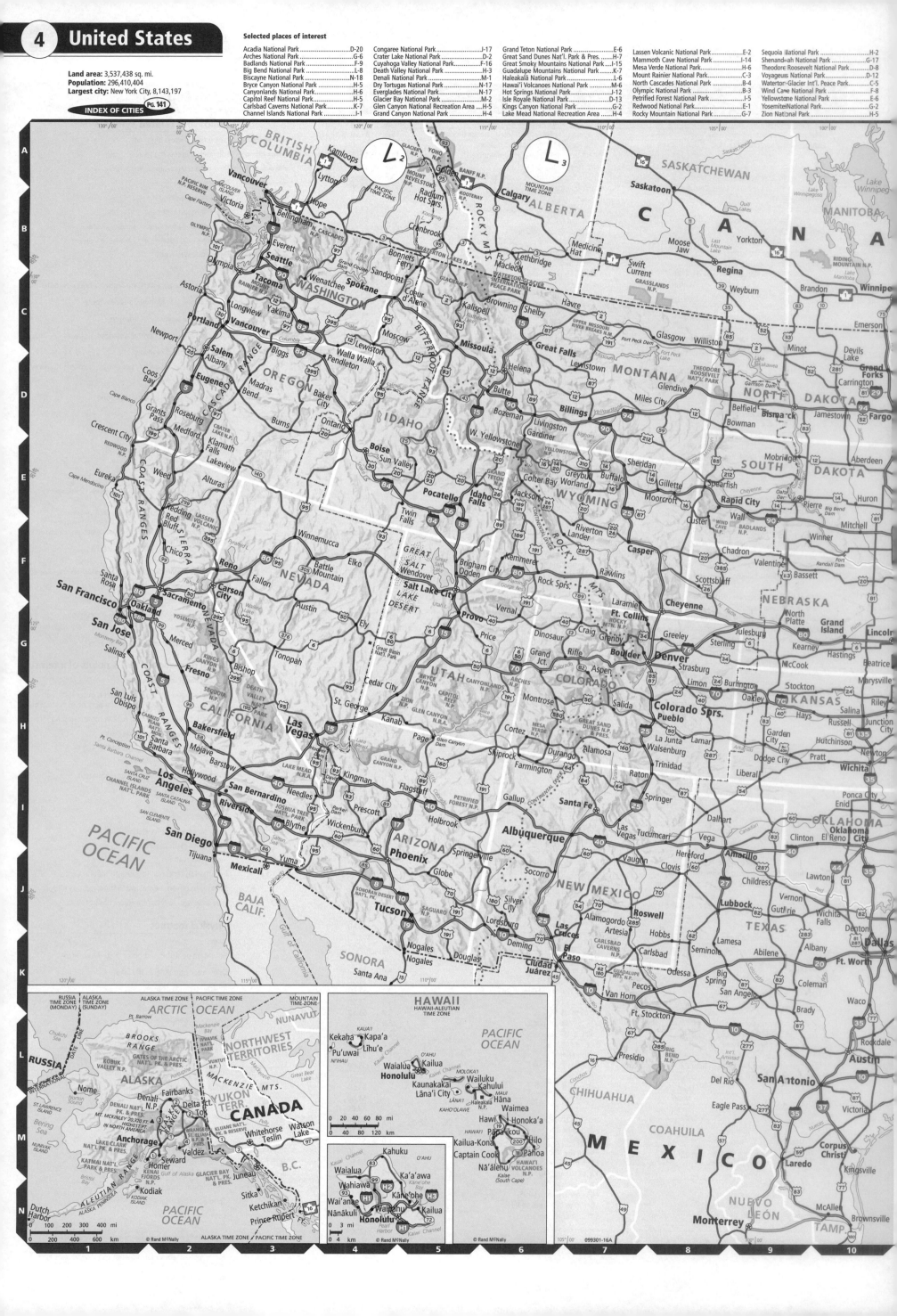

Explore
randmcnally.com

6 United States/Western

Includes:

- Arizona
- California
- Colorado
- Idaho
- Montana
- Nevada
- New Mexico
- Oregon
- Utah
- Washington
- Wyoming

Mileage between cities

	Albuquerque, NM	Billings, MT	Boise, ID	Colorado Sprs, CO	Denver, CO	El Paso, TX	Eugene, OR	Flagstaff, AZ	Great Falls, MT	Las Vegas, NV	Los Angeles, CA	Phoenix, AZ	Regina, SK	Salt Lake City, UT	San Diego, CA	San Francisco, CA	Seattle, WA	Spokane, WA	Vancouver, BC
ALBUQUERQUE, NM		994	719	372	439	267	1490	327	1216	576	799	463	1282	605	816	1097	1434	1327	1572
BILLINGS, MT	994		620	622	555	1261	1001	1071	222	967	1240	1207	475	552	1300	1183	820	539	958
DENVER, CO	439	555	830	67		706	1256	766	777	749	1022	902	843	529	1082	1276	1320	1096	1458
LOS ANGELES, CA	799	1240	846	1087	1022	806	860	472	1262	275		370	1717	689	124	381	1142	1215	1285
PHOENIX, AZ	463	1207	922	835	902	436	1301	530	1229	290	370		1684	656	353	751	1412	1378	1550
SALT LAKE CITY, UT	605	552	340	596	529	868	766	574	530	416	689	656	1029		749	747	830	723	968
SAN FRANCISCO, CA	1097	1183	648	1343	1187		529	770	1205	573	381	751	660	747	505		811	885	954
SEATTLE, WA	1434	820	495	1097	1326	1697	285	1349	647	1122	1142	1062	753	830	1266	811		281	143

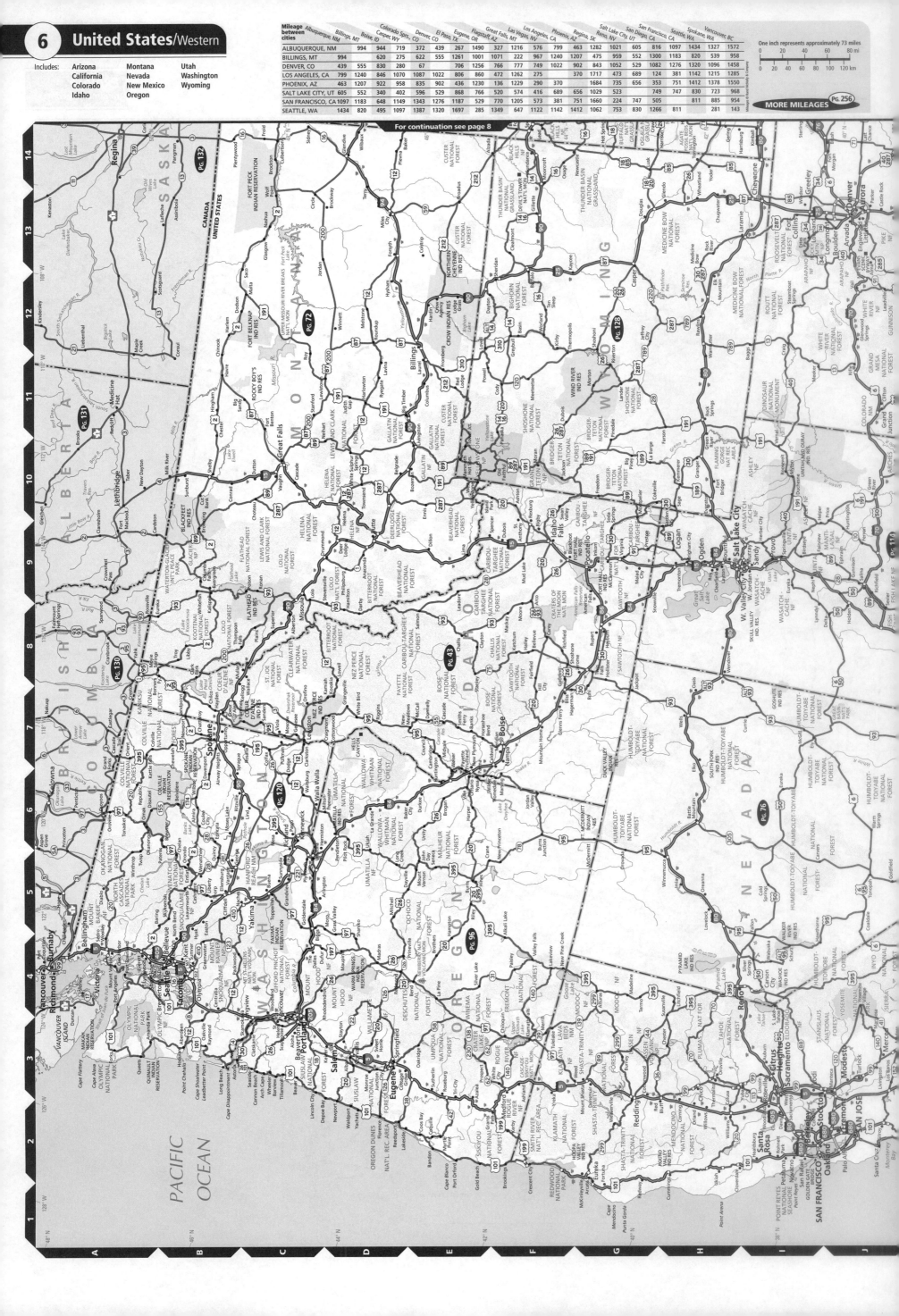

One inch represents approximately 73 miles

For continuation see page 8

MORE MILEAGES — Pg. 256

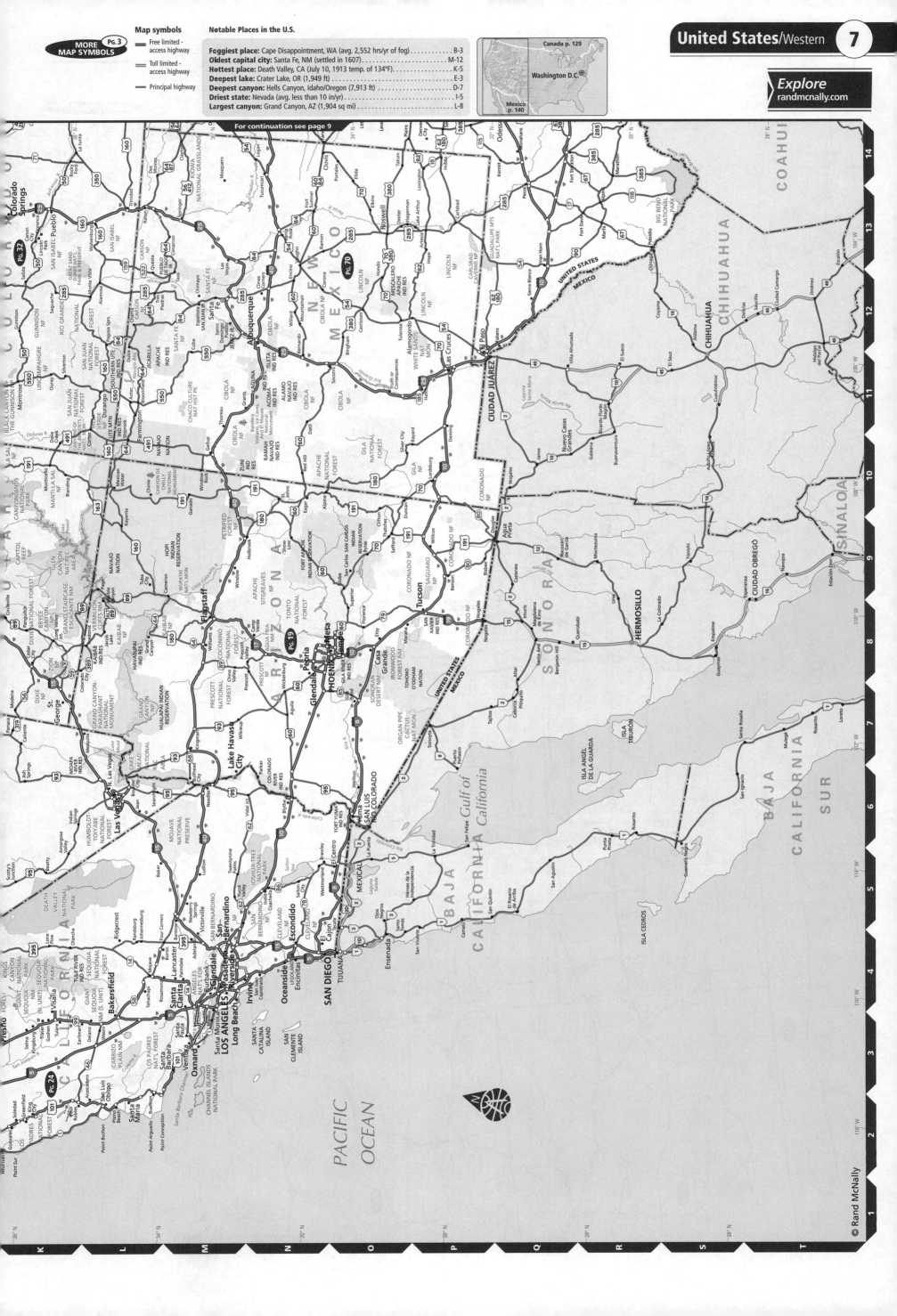

Explore
randmcnally.com

MORE MAP SYMBOLS PG. 3

Map symbols
— Free limited - access highway
= Toll limited - access highway
— Principal highway

Notable Places in the U.S.
Foggiest place: Cape Disappointment, WA (avg. 2,552 hrs/yr of fog) B-3
Oldest capital city: Santa Fe, NM (settled in 1607). M-12
Hottest place: Death Valley, CA (July 10, 1913 temp. of 134°F). K-5
Deepest lake: Crater Lake, OR (1,949 ft) E-3
Deepest canyon: Hells Canyon, Idaho/Oregon (7,913 ft) D-7
Driest state: Nevada (avg. less than 10 in/yr) I-5
Largest canyon: Grand Canyon, AZ (1,904 sq mi) L-8

Canada p. 129
Washington D.C. ⊗
Mexico p. 140

For continuation see page 9

© Rand McNally

Includes:

Arkansas	Minnesota	Oklahoma
Illinois	Mississippi	South Dakota
Iowa	Missouri	Texas
Kansas	Nebraska	Wisconsin
Louisiana	North Dakota	

Mileage between cities	Albuquerque, NM	Bismarck, ND	Brownsville, TX	Chicago, IL	Dallas, TX	Denver, CO	El Paso, TX	Green Bay, WI	Jackson, MS	Kansas City, MO	Little Rock, AR	Memphis, TN	Minneapolis, MN	New Orleans, LA	Oklahoma City, OK	Omaha, NE	Rapid City, SD	San Antonio, TX	St. Louis, MO	Thunder Bay, ON	Wichita, KS
ALBUQUERQUE, NM		1140	993	1343	647	439	267	1448	1055	783	881	1014	1222	1173	544	869	839	715	1043	1564	593
CHICAGO, IL	1343	833	1480		933	1011	1490	209	747	529	655	536	406	927	798	473	909	1210	300	652	719
DENVER, CO	439	701	1220	1011	882		706	1147	1226	608	964	1097	921	1407	674	542	400	942	864	1263	517
KANSAS CITY, MO	783	789	1036	529	489	608	930	665	664		383	453	439	844	344	188	707	766	256	781	190
MEMPHIS, TN	1014	1242	927	536	454	1097	1087	743	212	453	139		851	392	470	641	1160	731	284	1153	580
MINNEAPOLIS, MN	1222	430	1475	406	928	921	1369	287	1062	439	821	851		1242	783	383	609	1205	578	345	629
NEW ORLEANS, LA	1173	1633	706	927	526	1407	1100	1134	180	844	423	392	1242		733	1032	1551	546	675	1544	890
SAN ANTONIO, TX	715	1433	278	1210	277	942	558	1410	637	766	592	731	1205	546	473	937	1334		910	1547	630

One inch represents approximately 73 miles

0 20 40 60 80 mi

0 20 40 60 80 100 120 km

MORE MILEAGES — PG. 256

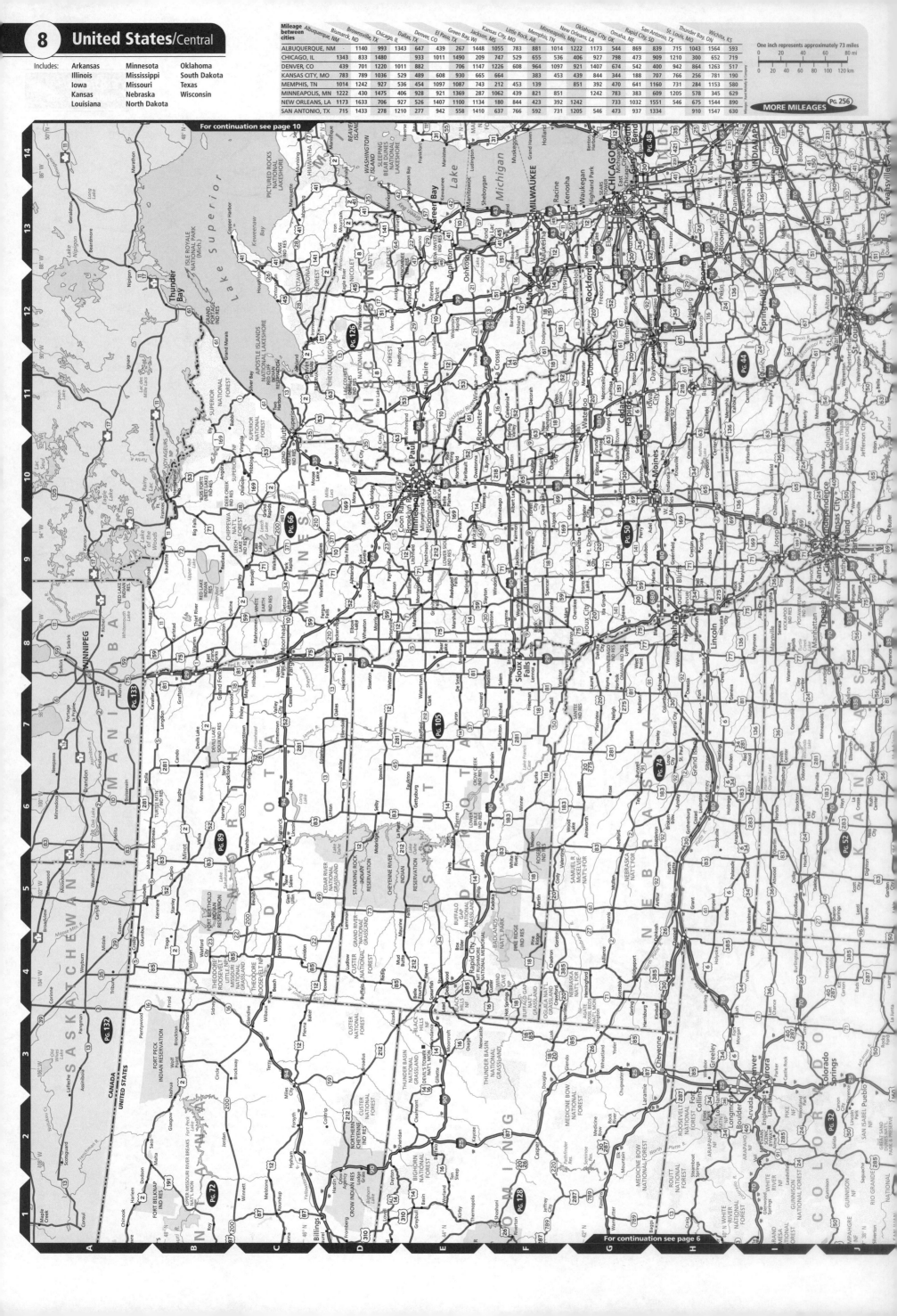

For continuation see page 10

For continuation see page 6

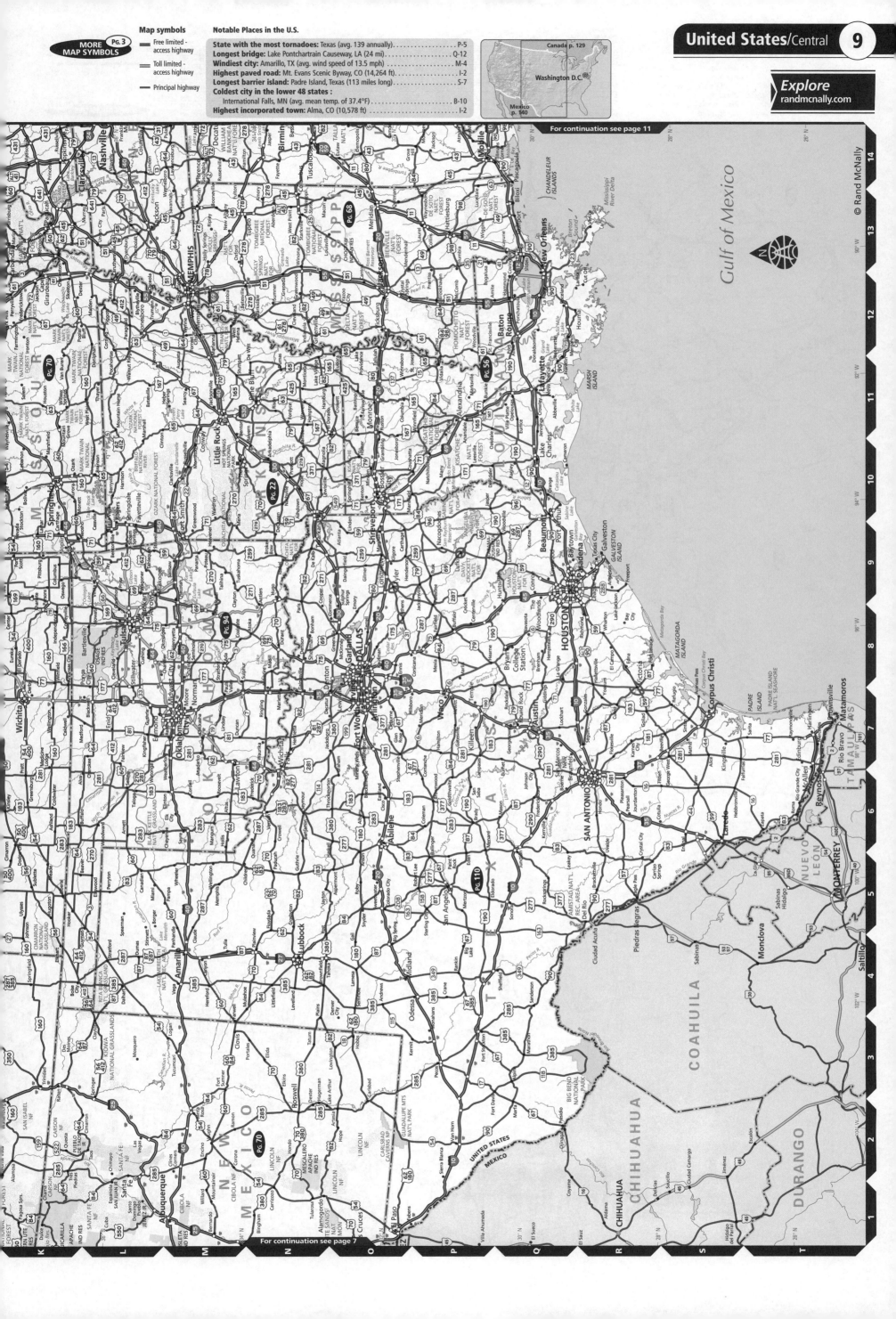

For continuation see page 11

For continuation see page 7

Map symbols

Free limited - access highway

Toll limited - access highway

Principal highway

MORE MAP SYMBOLS Pg. 3

Notable Places in the U.S.

State with the most tornadoes: Texas (avg. 139 annually) P-5
Longest bridge: Lake Pontchartrain Causeway, LA (24 mi) Q-12
Windiest city: Amarillo, TX (avg. wind speed of 13.5 mph) M-4
Highest paved road: Mt. Evans Scenic Byway, CO (14,264 ft) I-2
Longest barrier island: Padre Island, Texas (113 miles long) S-7
Coldest city in the lower 48 states :
    International Falls, MN (avg. mean temp. of 37.4°F) B-10
Highest incorporated town: Alma, CO (10,578 ft) I-2

Canada p. 129
Washington D.C
Mexico p. 140

Explore
randmcnally.com

© Rand McNally

Gulf of Mexico

Includes:

Alabama	Kentucky	New Jersey	South Carolina
Connecticut	Maine	New York	Tennessee
Delaware	Maryland	North Carolina	Vermont
Florida	Massachusetts	Ohio	Virginia
Georgia	Michigan	Pennsylvania	West Virginia
Indiana	New Hampshire	Rhode Island	

Mileage between cities	Atlanta, GA	Boston, MA	Charlotte, NC	Chicago, IL	Columbus, OH	Detroit, MI	Indianapolis, IN	Jacksonville, FL	Lexington, KY	Memphis, TN	Miami, FL	Milwaukee, WI	Montgomery, AL	Montpelier, VT	Montréal, QC	New Orleans, LA	New York, NY	Philadelphia, PA	Syracuse, NY	Toronto, ON	Washington, DC
ATLANTA, GA		1098	244	713	575	726	528	346	387	391	661	812	160	1180	1222	468	873	772	966	958	636
BOSTON, MA	1098		836	984	781	812	953	1139	933	1314	1482	1085	1258	187	324	1524	208	310	311	564	438
CHICAGO, IL	713	984	771		350	278	181	1059	372	536	1374	92	751	949	844	927	811	762	679	511	706
COLUMBUS, OH	575	781	432	350		202	173	814	191	597	1157	449	668	746	724	916	554	473	476	438	417
MIAMI, FL	661	1482	727	1374	1157	1189	1343	1048	691	1587		1473	691	1587	1640	861	1281	1180	1416	1493	1044
MEMPHIS, TN	391	1314	618	536	597	748	472	709	422		1024	626	333	1396	1313	392	1113	1016	1072	980	874
NEW ORLEANS, LA	468	1524	712	927	916	1067	814	546	741	392	861	1017	308	1606	1648		1323	1226	1392	1299	1084
WASHINGTON, DC	636	438	398	706	417	534	593	701	543	874	1044	807	796	543	596	1084	237	136	374	499	

One inch represents approximately 73 miles

0 20 40 60 80 mi

0 20 40 60 80 100 120 km

MORE MILEAGES Pg.256

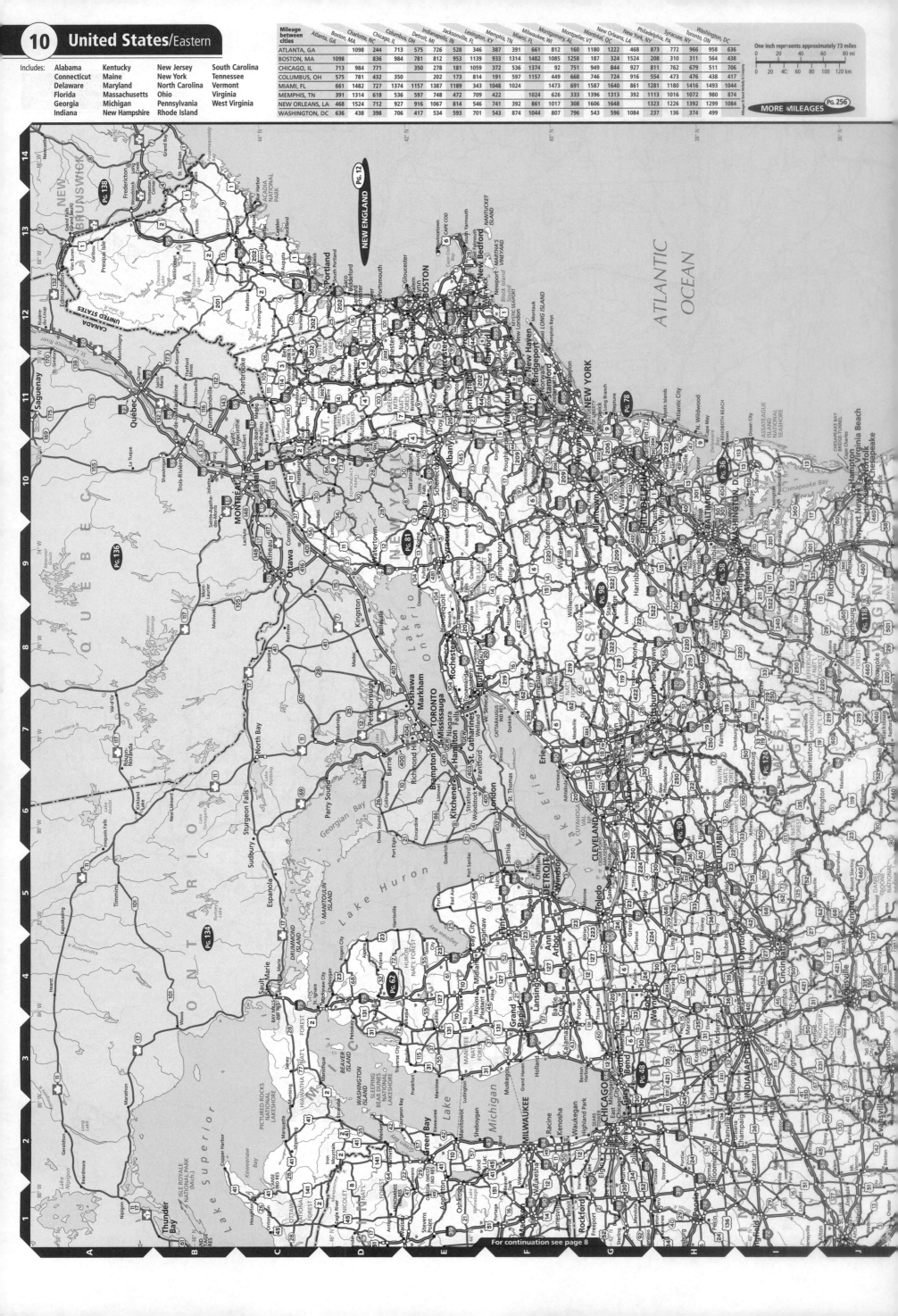

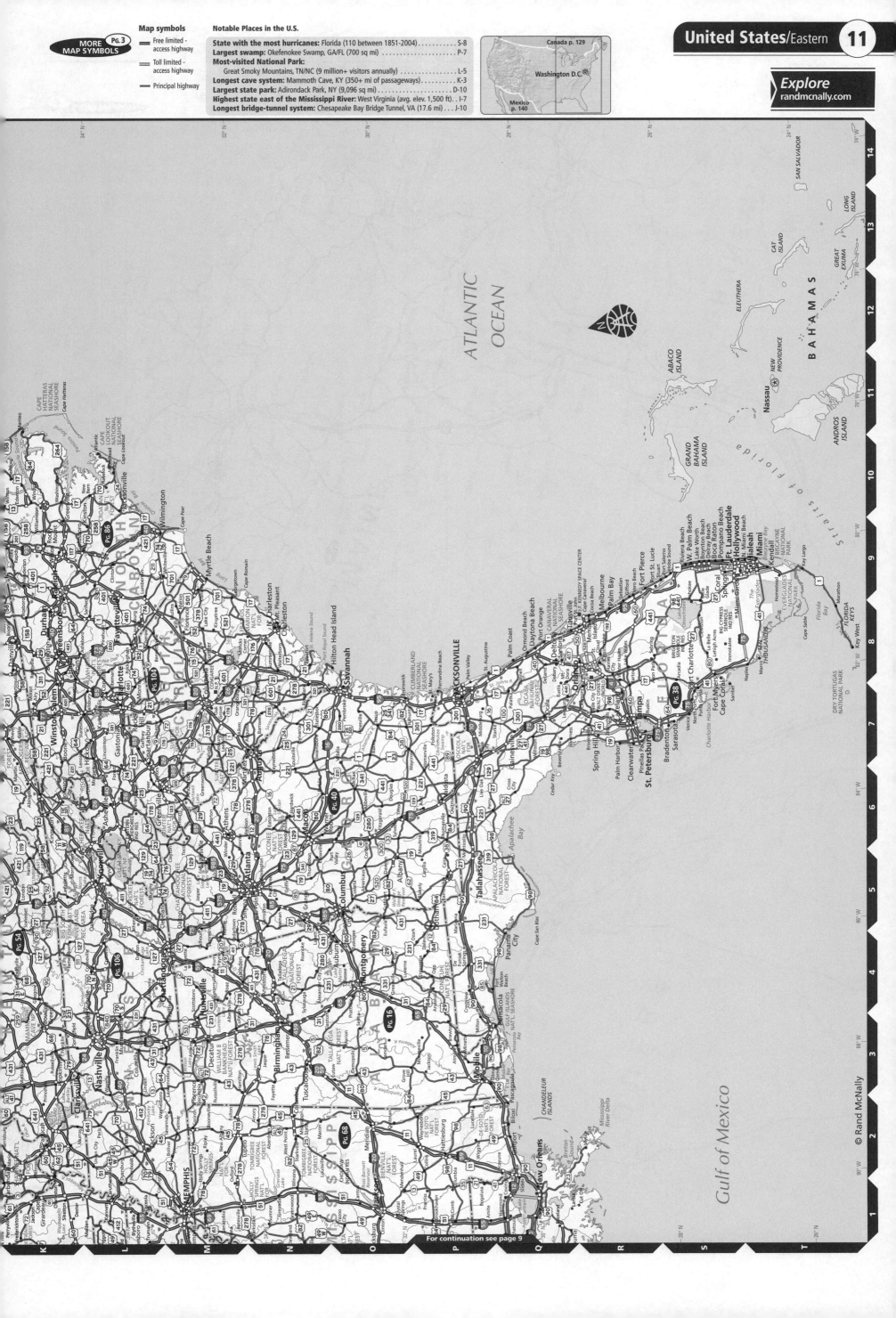

MORE MAP SYMBOLS Pg. 3

Map symbols
- Free limited - access highway
- Toll limited - access highway
- Principal highway

Notable Places in the U.S.
- **State with the most hurricanes:** Florida (110 between 1851-2004) S-8
- **Largest swamp:** Okefenokee Swamp, GA/FL (700 sq mi) P-7
- **Most-visited National Park:**
  Great Smoky Mountains, TN/NC (9 million+ visitors annually) L-5
- **Longest cave system:** Mammoth Cave, KY (350+ mi of passageways) K-3
- **Largest state park:** Adirondack Park, NY (9,096 sq mi) D-10
- **Highest state east of the Mississippi River:** West Virginia (avg. elev. 1,500 ft) . . . I-7
- **Longest bridge-tunnel system:** Chesapeake Bay Bridge Tunnel, VA (17.6 mi) . . . J-10

Canada p. 129
Washington D.C.
Mexico p. 140

Explore randmcnally.com

© Rand McNally

For continuation see page 9

Includes:
Connecticut
Maine
Massachusetts
New Hampshire
Rhode Island
Vermont

Mileage between cities	Albany, NY	Augusta, ME	Bar Harbor, ME	Bennington, VT	Berlin, NH	Boston, MA	Bridgeport, CT	Chatham, MA	Concord, NH	Fredericton, NB	Hartford, CT	Jackman, ME	Montpelier, VT	Montréal, QC	New York, NY	Plattsburgh, NY	Portsmouth, NH	Presque Isle, ME	Providence, RI	Québec, QC	Springfield, MA
ALBANY, NY		323	448	40	260	164	136	247	149	592	109	436	169	226	159	161	217	558	162	373	83
AUGUSTA, ME	323		127	263	92	173	313	266	152	271	259	115	176	253	367	299	106	237	224	222	247
BOSTON, MA	164	173	298	169	187		154	93	73	442	100	286	187	324	208	306	67	408	50	403	88
CONCORD, NH	149	152	277	109	113	73	204	166		421	150	264	115	252	258	234	46	387	124	329	138
HARTFORD, CT	109	259	384	114	264	100	57	183	150	528		372	202	335	111	270	153	494	88	430	26
MONTPELIER, VT	169	176	298	122	94	187	259	280	115	442	202	246		139	313	121	163	408	238	259	176
NEW YORK, NY	159	367	492	199	372	208	54	278	258	636	111	480	313	384		319	261	602	179	531	137
PROVIDENCE, RI	162	224	349	167	238	50	125	99	124	493	88	337	238	375	179	323	118	459		454	86

MORE MILEAGES Pg.256

One inch represents approximately 23 miles

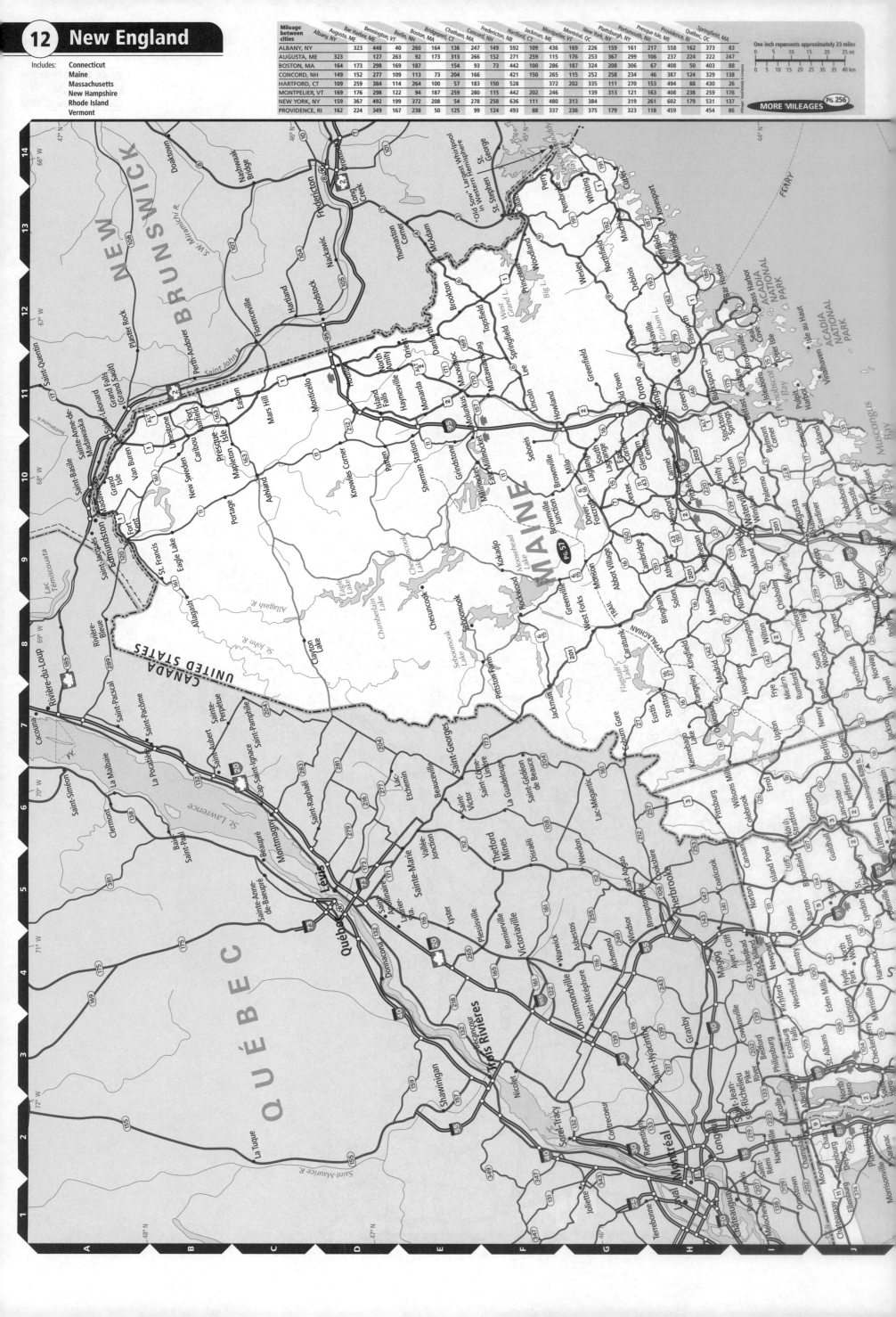

Map symbols

MORE MAP SYMBOLS PG. 3

Free limited - access highway
Toll limited - access highway
Principal highway

Notable Places in the U.S.

Windiest place: Mt. Washington, NH (April 12, 1934 wind speed of 231 mph) J-6
Highest tides: Passamaquoddy Bay, ME (up to 28 ft) F-14
Smallest state capital: Montpelier, VT (population 8,035) K-4
Coastal state with the shortest coastline: New Hampshire (13 mi) M-8
Longest mountain trail: Appalachian Trail, Maine to Georgia (2,175 mi) M-4
Largest whirlpool:
   "Old Sow," between Deer Island, New Brunswick and Eastport, Maine F-14

Canada p. 129
Washington D.C.
Mexico p. 140

© Rand McNally

Explore
randmcnally.com

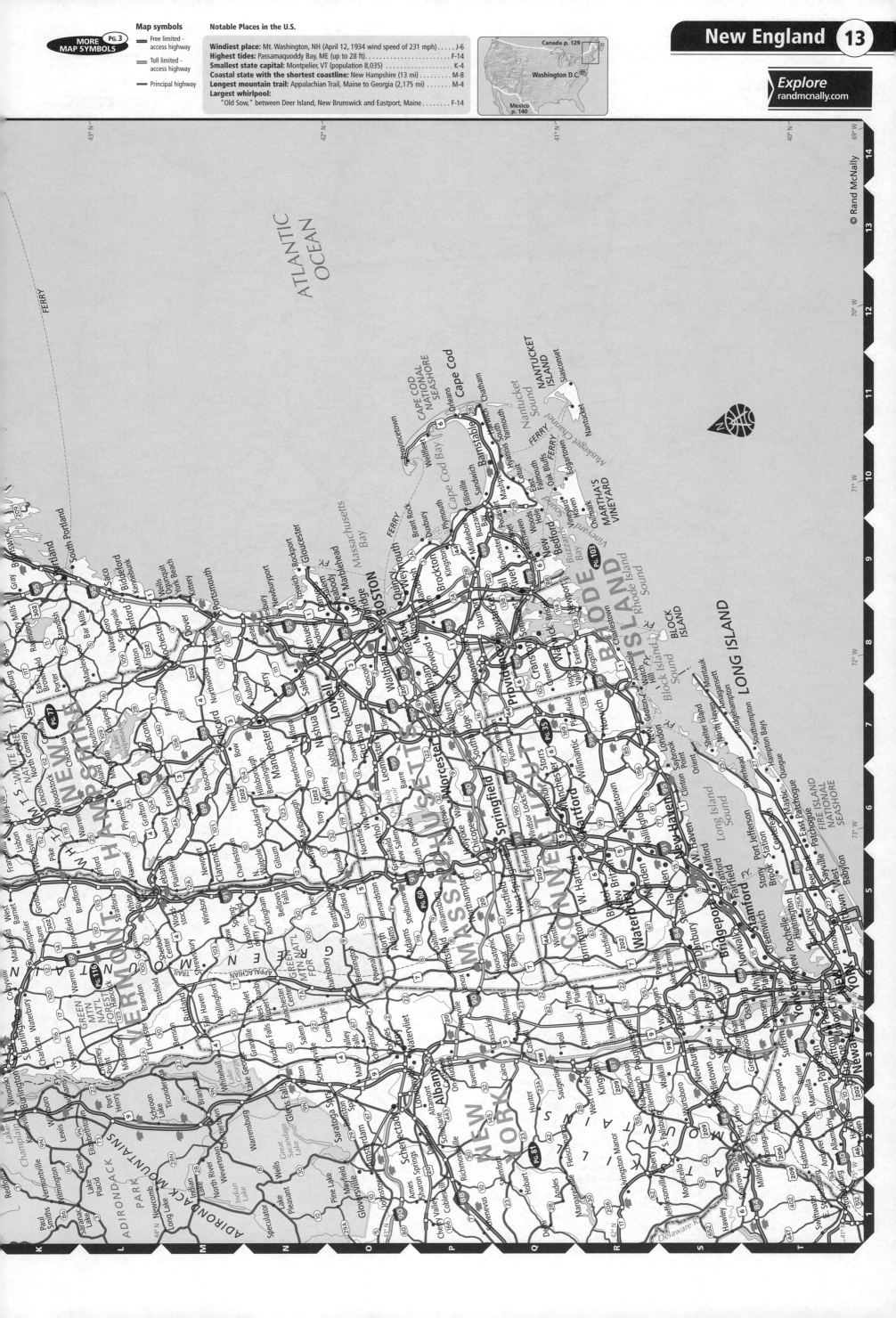

Includes: **Connecticut**   **New Jersey**   **Rhode Island**

And portions of: **Delaware**   **New York**   **West Virginia**
Maryland   **Pennsylvania**
Massachusetts   **Virginia**

Mileage between cities	Allentown, PA	Atlantic City, NJ	Baltimore, MD	Barnstable, MA	Boston, MA	Dover, DE	Elmira, NY	Hagerstown, MD	Hampton Bays, NY	Harrisburg, PA	Hartford, CT	New Bedford, MA	New Haven, CT	New York, NY	Philadelphia, PA	Poughkeepsie, NY	Providence, RI	Scranton, PA	Springfield, MA	Washington, DC	Wilmington, DE
BALTIMORE, MD	150	152		453	404	104	248	74	279	82	307	407	269	203	102	274	375	198	333	38	69
BOSTON, MA	310	344	404	72		384	356	461	280	390	100	58	137	208	310	203	50	298	88	438	343
HARTFORD, CT	213	247	307	162	100	287	301	364	183	293		135	40	111	213	103	88	198	26	341	246
NEW YORK, NY	109	141	203	257	208	183	252	260	79	189	111	211	73		90	87	179	124	137	237	142
PHILADELPHIA, PA	66	62	102	359	310	86	241	181	185	111	213	313	175	109		180	281	146	239	136	35
PROVIDENCE, RI	281	315	375	78	50	355	354	432	112	361	88	32	106	179	281	181		276	86	409	314
WASHINGTON, DC	184	186	38	487	438	93	286	75	313	120	341	441	303	237	136	308	409	236	367		103
WILMINGTON, DE	83	86	69	392	343	49	258	146	218	102	246	346	208	142	35	213	314	143	272	103	

One inch represents approximately 19 miles

MORE MILEAGES — Pg. 256

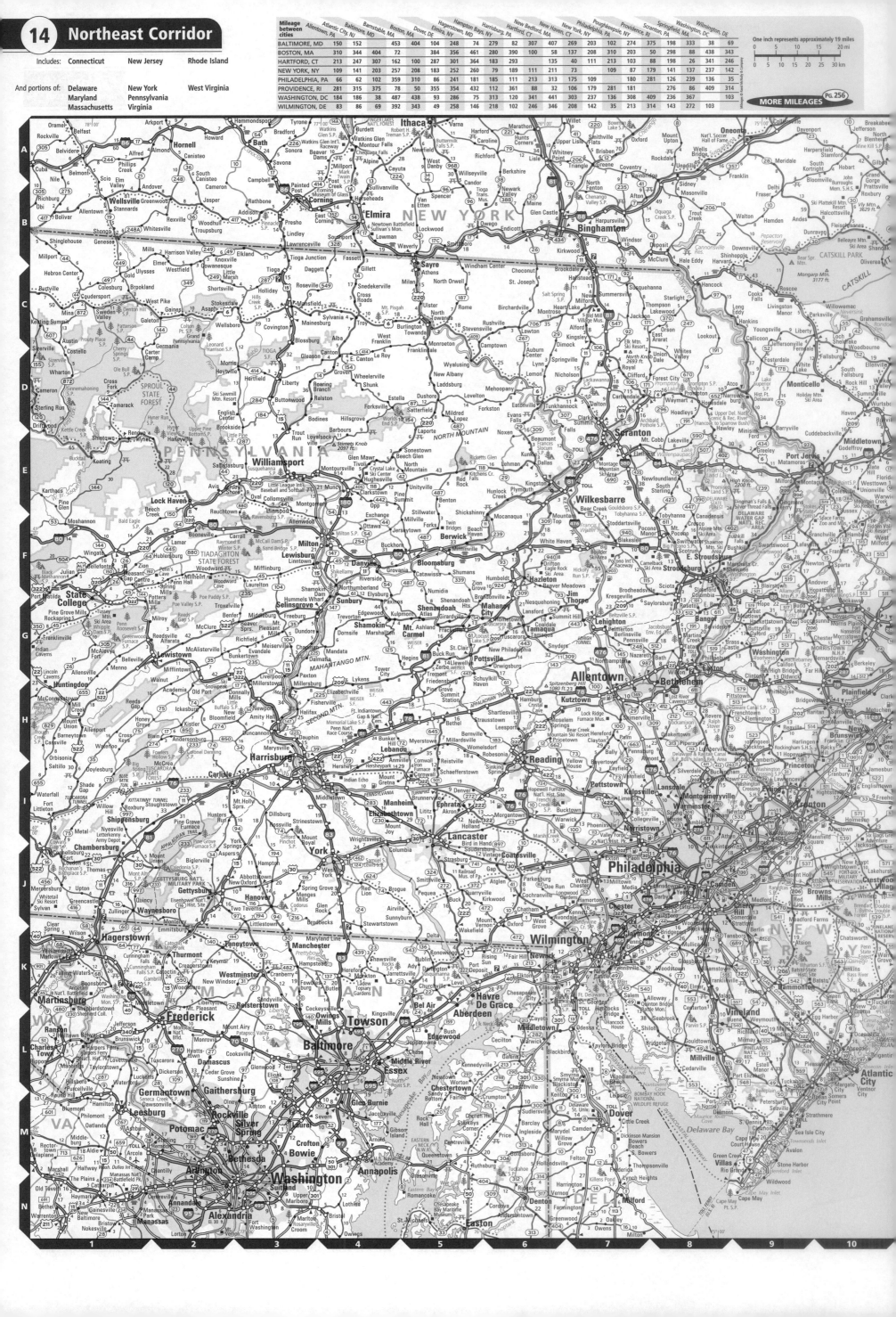

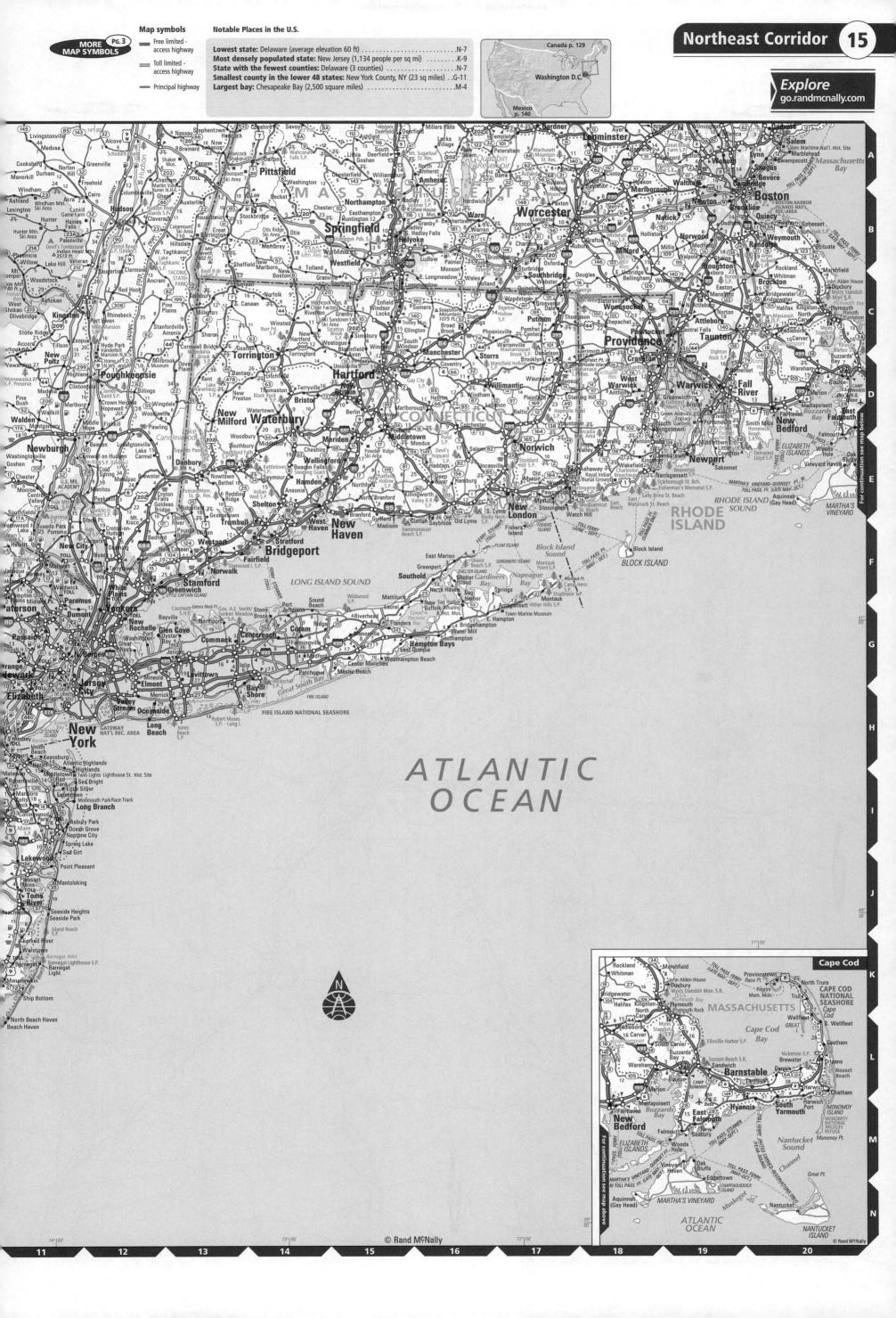

Nickname: The Heart of Dixie
Land area: 50,744 sq. mi. (rank: 28th)
Population: 4,557,808 (rank: 23rd)
Largest city: Birmingham, 231,483

INDEX OF CITIES Pg. 141

Mileage between cities	Andalusia	Anniston	Atlanta, GA	Auburn	Birmingham	Chattanooga, TN	Decatur	Dothan	Eufaula	Florence	Gadsden	Huntsville	Jasper	Meridian, MS	Mobile	Montgomery	Pensacola, FL	Phenix City	Selma	Troy	Tuscaloosa
ATLANTA, GA	249	90		106	148	115	227	202	151	275	120	193	188	290	329	165	319	105	210	193	203
BIRMINGHAM	181	66	148	111		143	80	199	182	128	61	98	41	188	261	92	251	141	94	142	59
CHATTANOOGA, TN	319	116	115	218	143		130	314	263	179	86	105	183	289	399	230	389	217	232	280	202
DOTHAN	75	210	202	124	199	314	277		51	325	255	295	238	253	201	107	156	97	151	57	212
HUNTSVILLE	277	103	193	244	98	105	26	295	278	67	73		90	240	357	188	347	276	190	238	153
MOBILE	125	282	329	225	261	399	339	201	255	387	317	357	300	134		169	65	257	193	173	206
MONTGOMERY	89	113	160	56	92	230	170	107	90	218	148	188	131	152	169		159	88	50	50	105
TUSCALOOSA	194	121	203	161	59	202	135	212	195	122	120	153	56	93	206	105	261	193	75	155	

Total mileage through Alabama

10 — 66 miles   59 — 241 miles
20 — 215 miles   65 — 367 miles

MORE MILEAGES Pg. 256

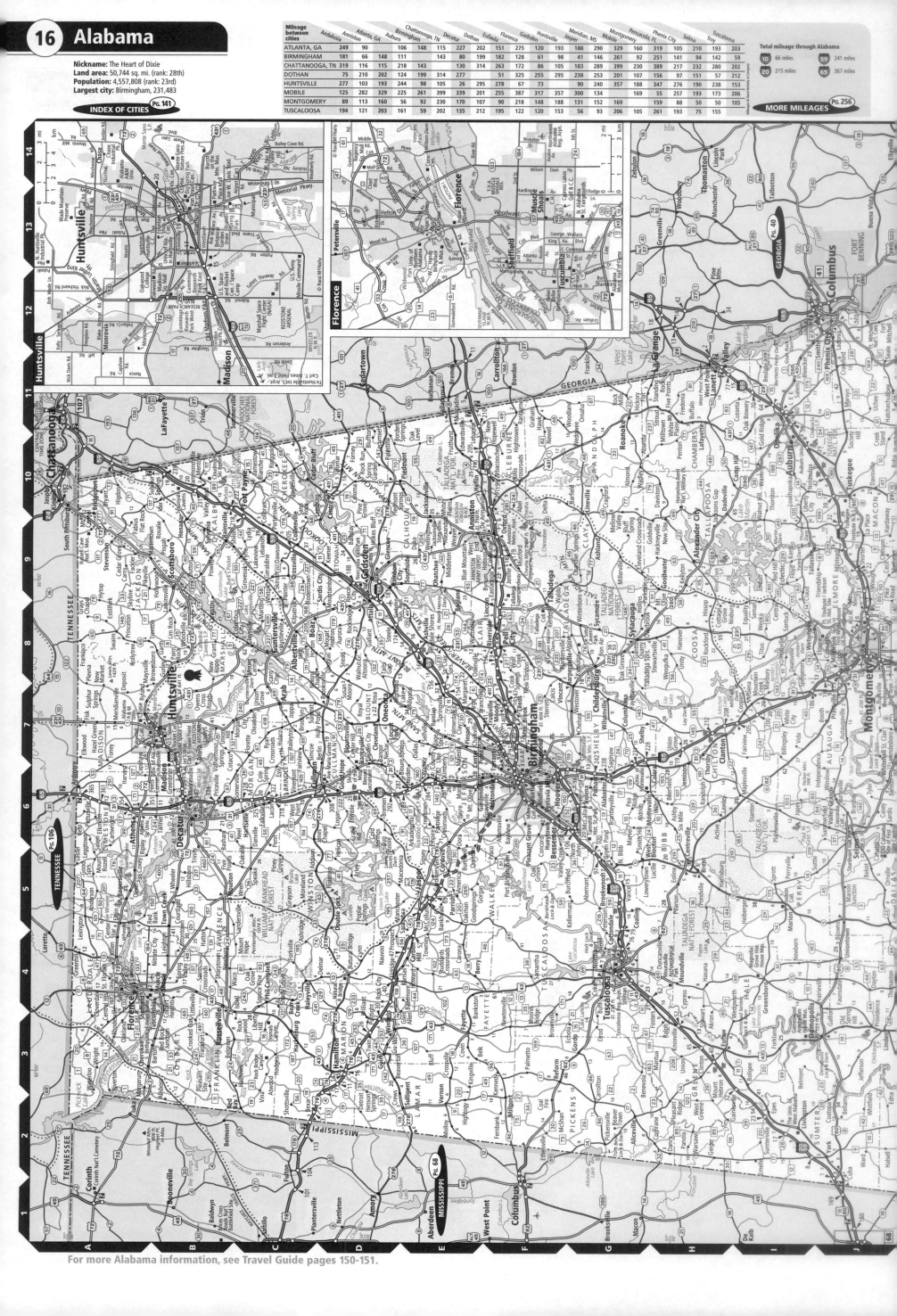

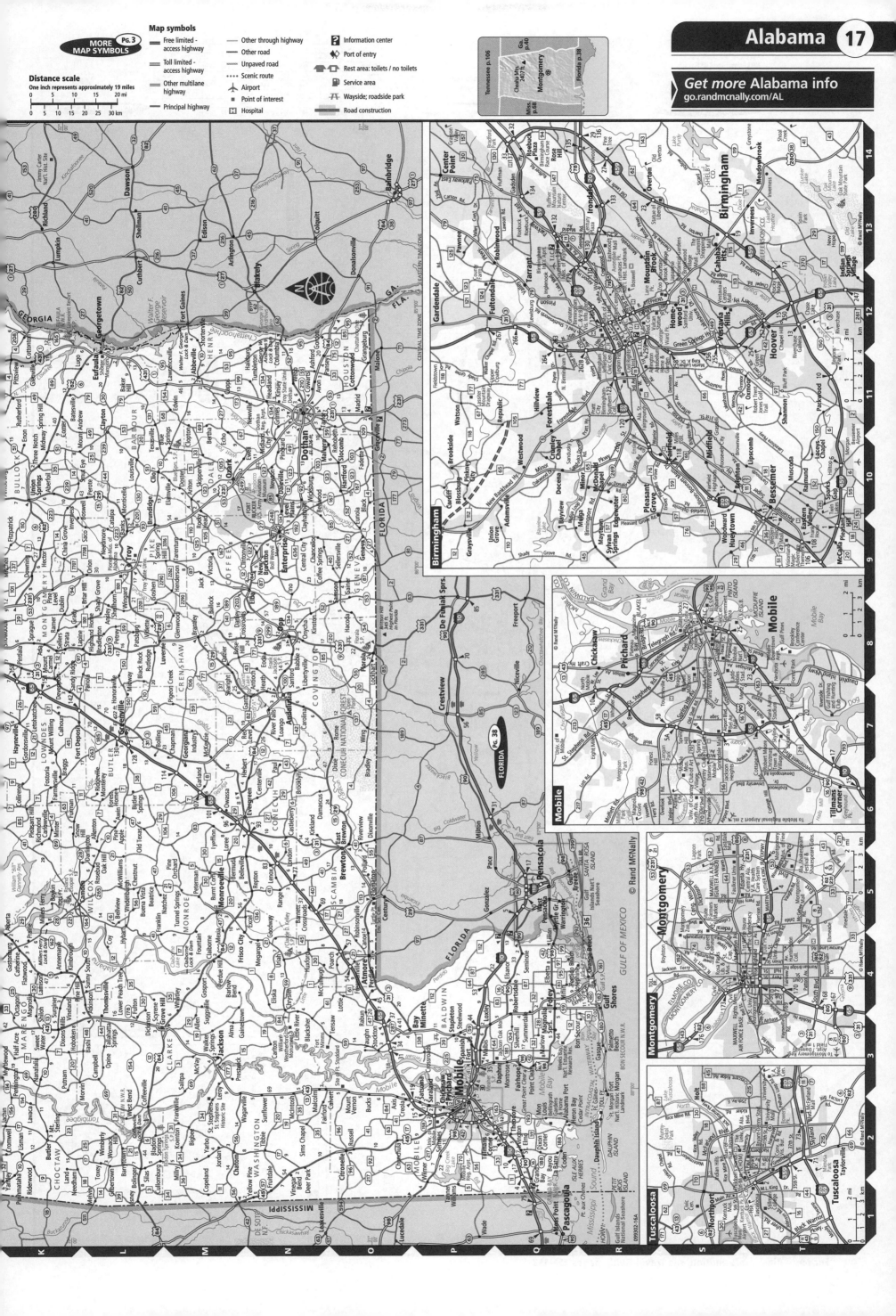

Get more Alabama info
go.randmcnally.com/AL

Map symbols

MORE MAP SYMBOLS PG. 3

Free limited - access highway
Toll limited - access highway
Other multilane highway
Principal highway
Other through highway
Other road
Unpaved road
Scenic route

Information center
Port of entry
Rest area: toilets / no toilets
Service area
Wayside; roadside park
Road construction

Airport
Point of interest
Hospital

Distance scale
One inch represents approximately 19 miles
0 5 10 15 20 mi
0 5 10 15 20 25 30 km

Tennessee p. 106
Ga. p.40
Cheaha Mtn. 2407 ft.
Montgomery
Miss. p.68
Florida p.38

Plan a trip
go.randmcnally.com/AK

Nickname: The Last Frontier
Land area: 571,951 sq. mi. (rank: 1st)
Population: 663,661 (rank: 47th)
Largest city: Anchorage, 275,043

INDEX OF CITIES Pg. 141

Mileage between cities	Anchorage	Fairbanks	Glennallen	Haines	Homer	Kenai	Seward	Tok	Valdez
ANCHORAGE		360	187	782	225	158	127	325	304
FAIRBANKS	360		253	665	585	518	487	208	366
HAINES	782	665	595		1007	940	909	457	708
HOMER	225	585	412	1007		89	174	550	529
KENAI	158	518	345	940	89		107	483	462
SEWARD	127	487	314	909	174	107		452	431
TOK	325	208	138	457	550	483	452		251
VALDEZ	304	366	117	708	529	462	431	251	

Distance scale
One inch represents approximately 134 miles

Total mileage through Alaska
① 408 miles ③ 325 miles
② 202 miles

MORE MILEAGES PG. 256

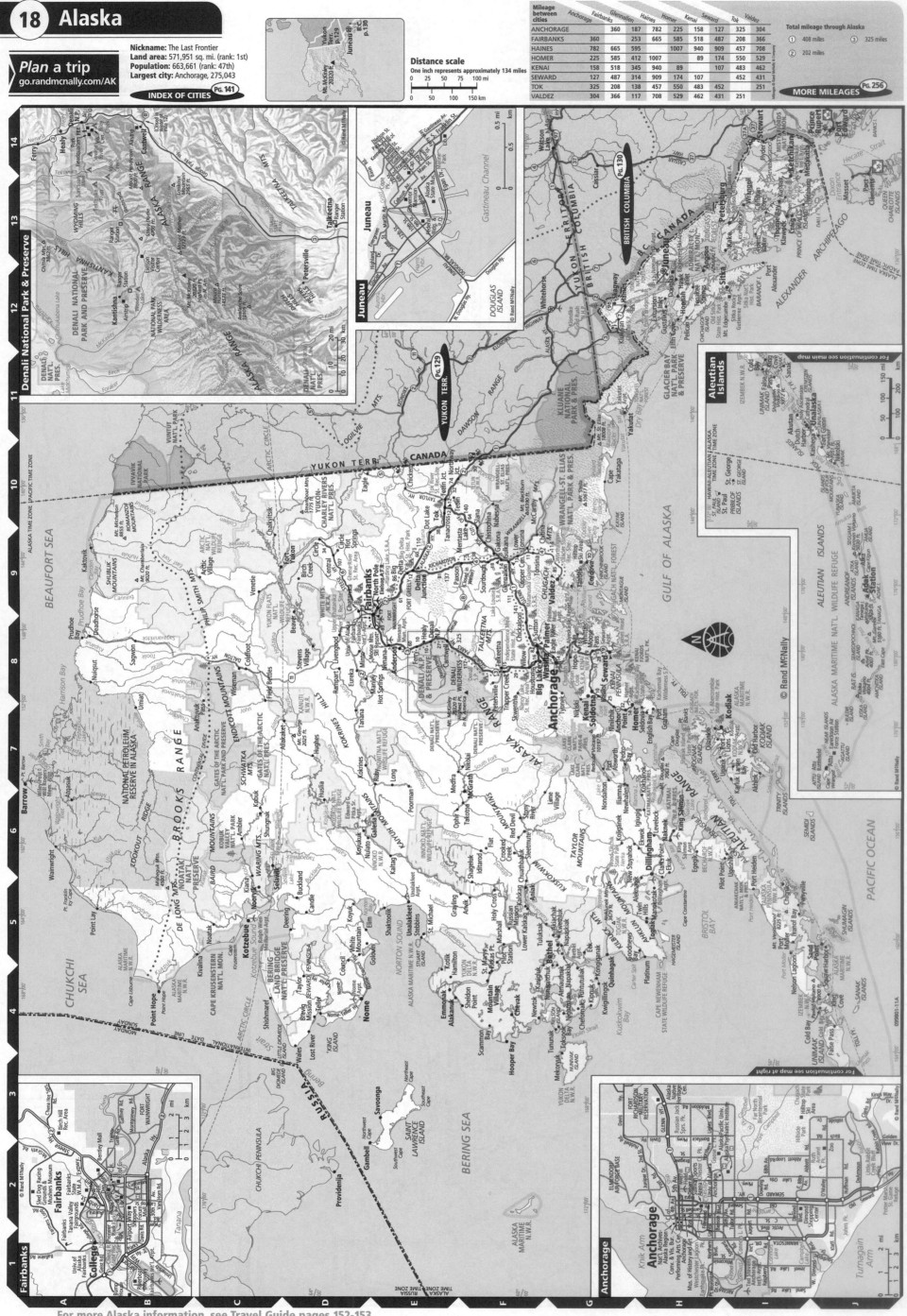

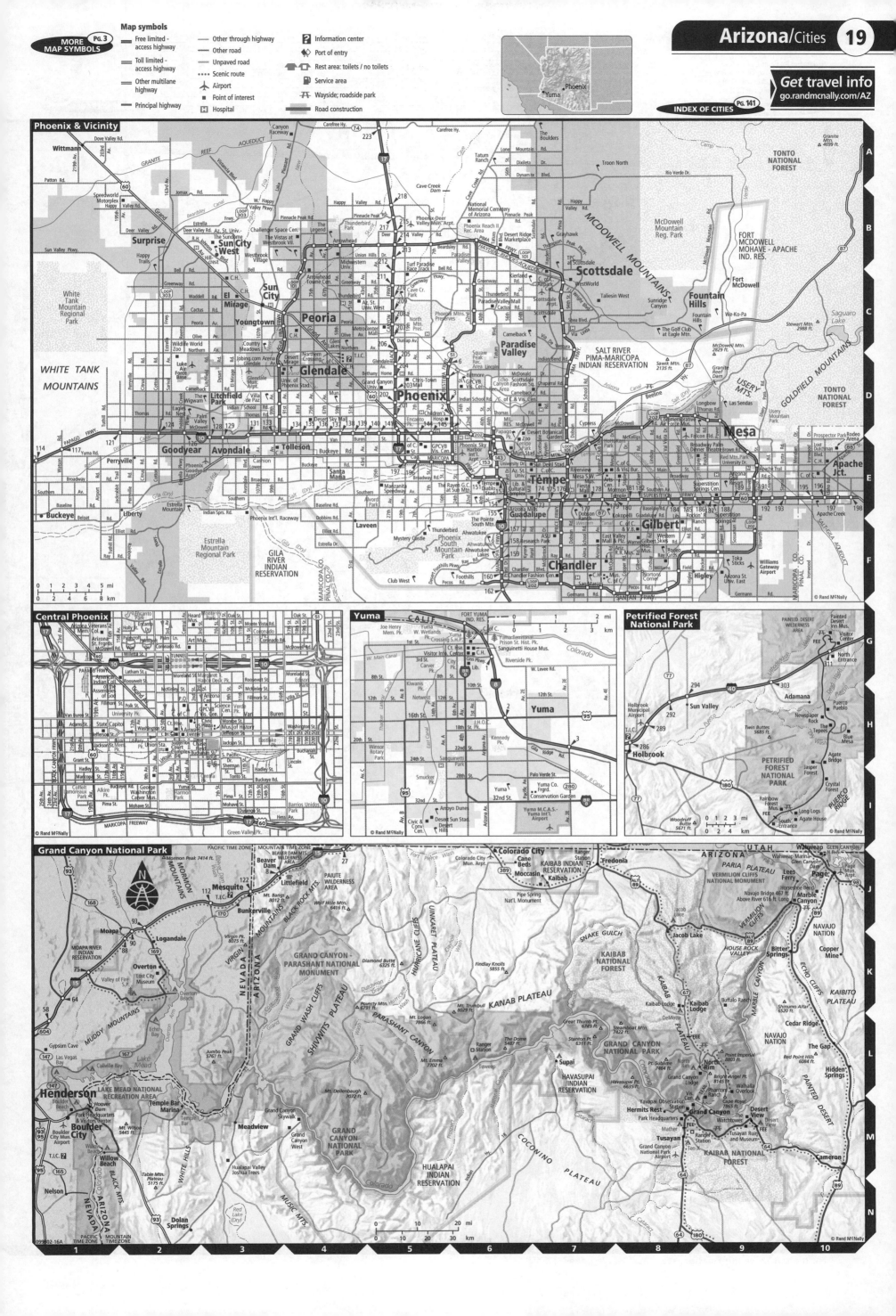

MORE MAP SYMBOLS Pg. 3
INDEX OF CITIES Pg. 141

Get travel info
go.randmcnally.com/AZ

Map symbols

Free limited-access highway
Toll limited-access highway
Other multilane highway
Principal highway
Other through highway
Other road
Unpaved road
Scenic route
Airport
Point of interest
Hospital

Information center
Port of entry
Rest area: toilets / no toilets
Service area
Wayside; roadside park
Road construction

Phoenix & Vicinity

Central Phoenix

Yuma

Petrified Forest National Park

Grand Canyon National Park

© Rand McNally

Nickname: The Grand Canyon State
Land area: 113,635 sq. mi. (rank: 6th)
Population: 5,939,292 (rank: 17th)
Largest city: Phoenix, 1,461,575

INDEX OF CITIES — PG. 141

Mileage between cities	Blythe CA	Casa Grande	Eagar	Flagstaff	Gallup, NM	Grand Canyon	Holbrook	Kingman	Lake Havasu City	Las Vegas, NV	Lordsburg, NM	Nogales	Page	Phoenix	Shiprock, NM	Tucson	Yuma
CASA GRANDE	197		221	187	318	268	221	236	249	341	224	131	324	51	145	411	67	172
FLAGSTAFF	282	187	179		188	81	92	144	204	249	410	317	137	136	93	281	253	318
HOLBROOK	374	221	87	92	97	169		236	296	341	305	217	228	185	190	241	410
KINGMAN	157	236	323	144	332	167	236		60	105	459	366	279	185	146	425	302	215
PHOENIX	146	51	225	136	324	217	228	185	198	290	274	181	273		94	417	117	182
PRESCOTT	155	145	272	93	281	123	185	146	206	251	368	275	230	94		374	211	214
TUCSON	263	67	241	253	338	334	241	302	315	407	157	64	390	117	211		237
YUMA	103	172	397	318	506	337	410	215	296	394	301	455	182	214	431	237	

Total mileage through Arizona
- 8 — 178 miles
- 17 — 146 miles
- 10 — 392 miles
- 40 — 359 miles

MORE MILEAGES — PG. 256

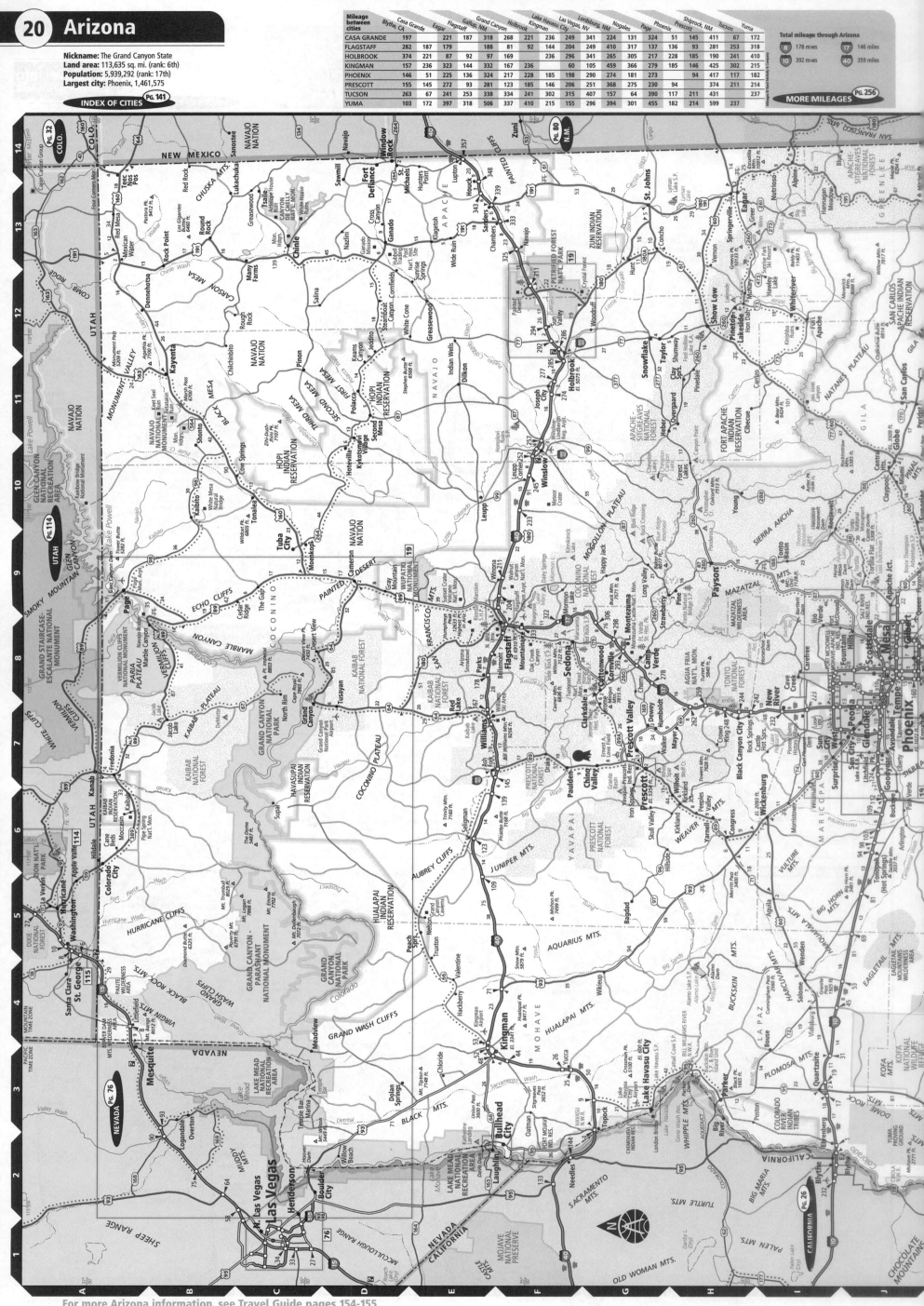

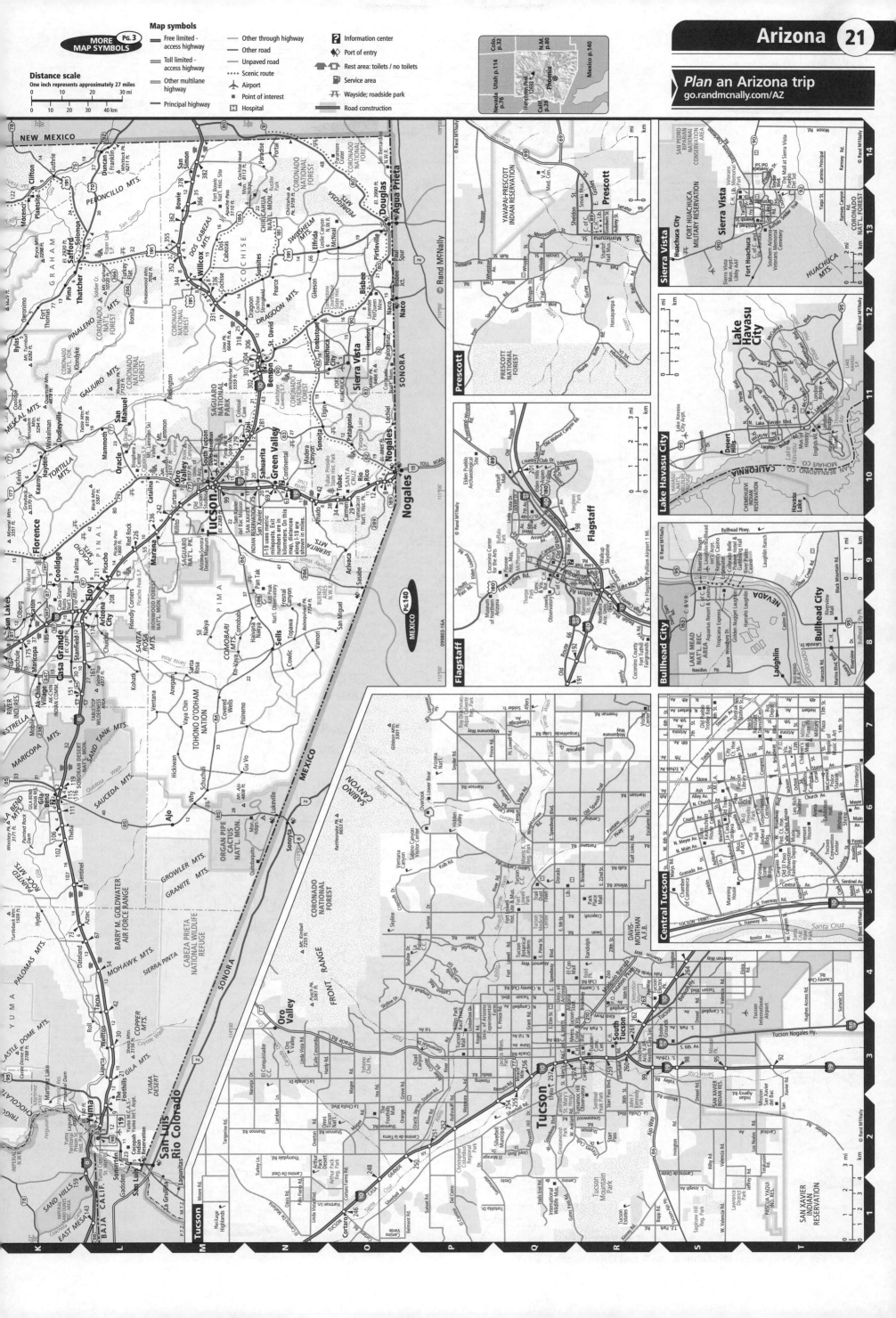

Plan an Arizona trip
go.randmcnally.com/AZ

Map symbols

MORE MAP SYMBOLS Pg.3

Free limited-access highway
Toll limited-access highway
Other multilane highway
Principal highway
Other through highway
Other road
Unpaved road
Scenic route
Airport
Point of interest
Hospital

Information center
Port of entry
Rest area: toilets / no toilets
Service area
Wayside; roadside park
Road construction

Distance scale
One inch represents approximately 27 miles

Prescott
Flagstaff
Bullhead City
Sierra Vista
Lake Havasu City
Central Tucson
Tucson

Nickname: The Natural State
Land area: 52,068 sq. mi. (rank: 27th)
Population: 2,779,154 (rank: 32nd)
Largest city: Little Rock, 184,564

INDEX OF CITIES   PG. 141

Mileage between cities	Batesville	DeQueen	El Dorado	Fayetteville	Fort Smith	Greenville, MS	Harrison	Hot Springs	Jonesboro	Little Rock	Monticello	Pine Bluff	Russellville	Texarkana	West Memphis
EL DORADO	212	141		306	275	110	255	128	250	117	69	91	326	191	90	244
FAYETTEVILLE	254	183	306		57	335	78	183	292	189	279	231	24	116	235	312
FORT SMITH	223	128	275	57		304	135	128	261	158	248	200	77	85	180	281
HARRISON	116	261	255	78	135	284		184	172	138	228	180	78	87	272	261
JONESBORO	69	281	250	292	261	217	172	187		135	223	175	250	177	275	63
LITTLE ROCK	97	146	117	189	158	146	138	52	135		90	42	209	74	140	129
TEXARKANA	237	54	90	235	180	199	272	147	275	140	153	151	255	208		269
WEST MEMPHIS	127	275	244	312	281	155	261	181	63	129	189	144	332	197	269	

Total mileage through Arkansas		
30	143 miles	55	72 miles
40	284 miles	65	309 miles

MORE MILEAGES   PG. 256

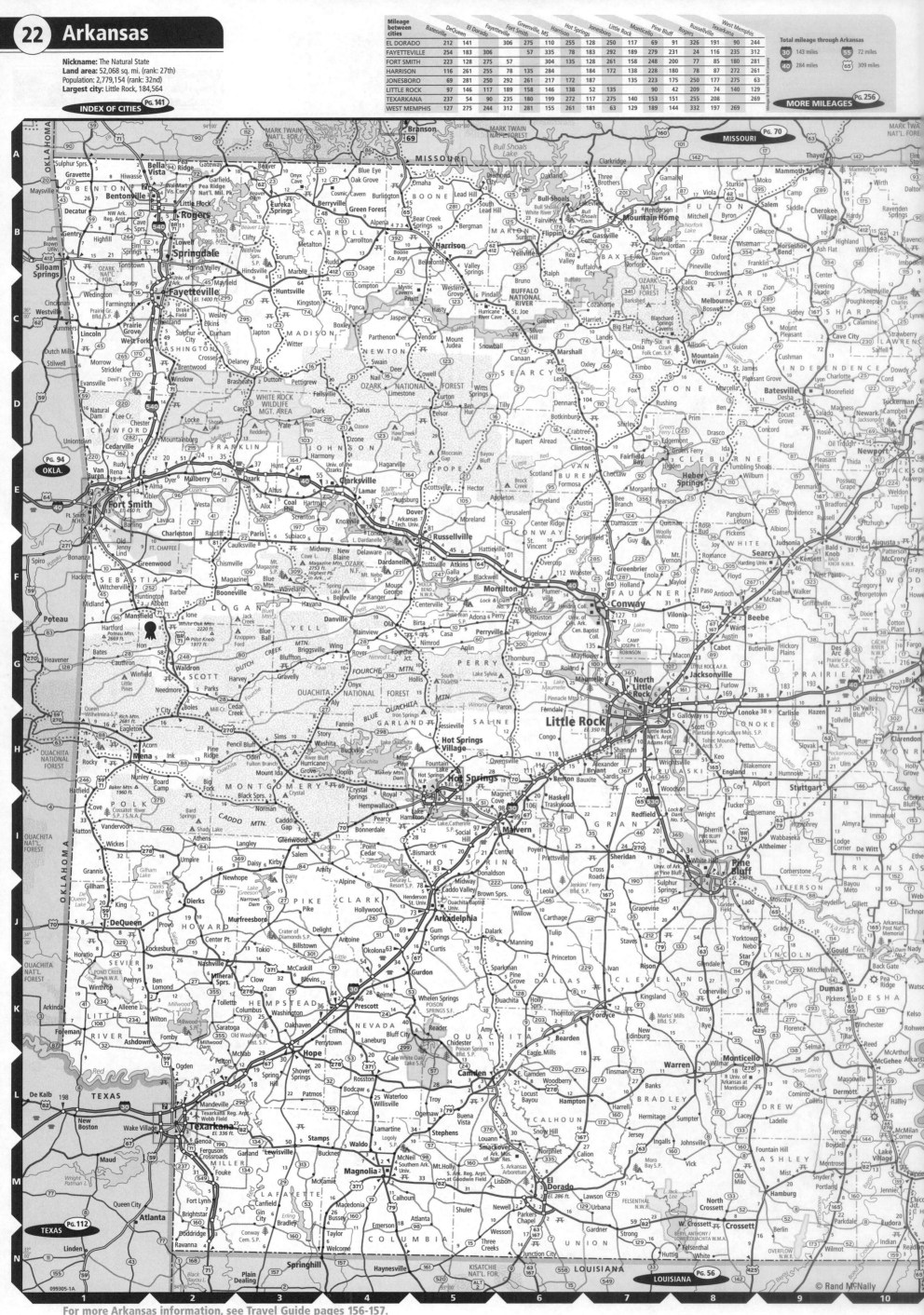

For more Arkansas information, see Travel Guide pages 156-157.

099305-1A   © Rand McNally

MORE MAP SYMBOLS PG. 3

Map symbols

Free limited - access highway
Toll limited - access highway
Other multilane highway
Principal highway
Other through highway
Other road
Unpaved road
Scenic route
Airport
Point of interest
Hospital

Information center
Port of entry
Rest area: toilets / no toilets
Service area
Wayside; roadside park
Road construction

Distance scale
One inch represents approximately 19 miles

Jonesboro

Fayetteville / Springdale / Rogers

Hot Springs / Hot Springs National Park

Pine Bluff

Fort Smith

Little Rock

Texarkana

MISSISSIPPI

TENNESSEE

MISSOURI

Nickname: The Golden State
Land area: 155,959 sq. mi. (rank: 3rd)
Population: 36,132,147 (rank: 1st)
Largest city: Los Angeles, 3,844,829

INDEX OF CITIES PG. 141

PG. 256 MORE MILEAGES

Mileage between cities	Alturas	Bishop	Crescent City	Eureka	Oakland	Oroville	Redding	Sacramento	San Francisco	San Jose	Santa Rosa	South Lake Tahoe	Stockton	Susanville	Ukiah	Yosemite NP	Yreka
BISHOP	385		623	556	289	333	402	273	297	286	347	180	237	288	421	298	139	458
EUREKA	300	556	82		281	233	154	296	281	324	223	398	342	268	162	264	463	214
REDDING	146	402	217	154	209	98		165	217	246	226	267	211	114	189	189	336	97
SACRAMENTO	307	273	378	296	83	72	165		91	116	100	102	47	197	148	63	171	260
SAN FRANCISCO	359	297	363	281	8	149	217	91		44	58	193	80	269	119	32	190	312
SAN JOSE	388	286	406	324	43	194	246	116	44		101	218	69	298	163	52	179	341
S. LAKE TAHOE	239	180	477	398	185	155	267	102	193	218	202		149	142	250	165	187	312
VALLEJO	331	298	346	264	24	121	189	63	32	63	52	165	68	241	102		191	284

Total mileage through California
5 797 miles 101 791 miles
80 199 miles

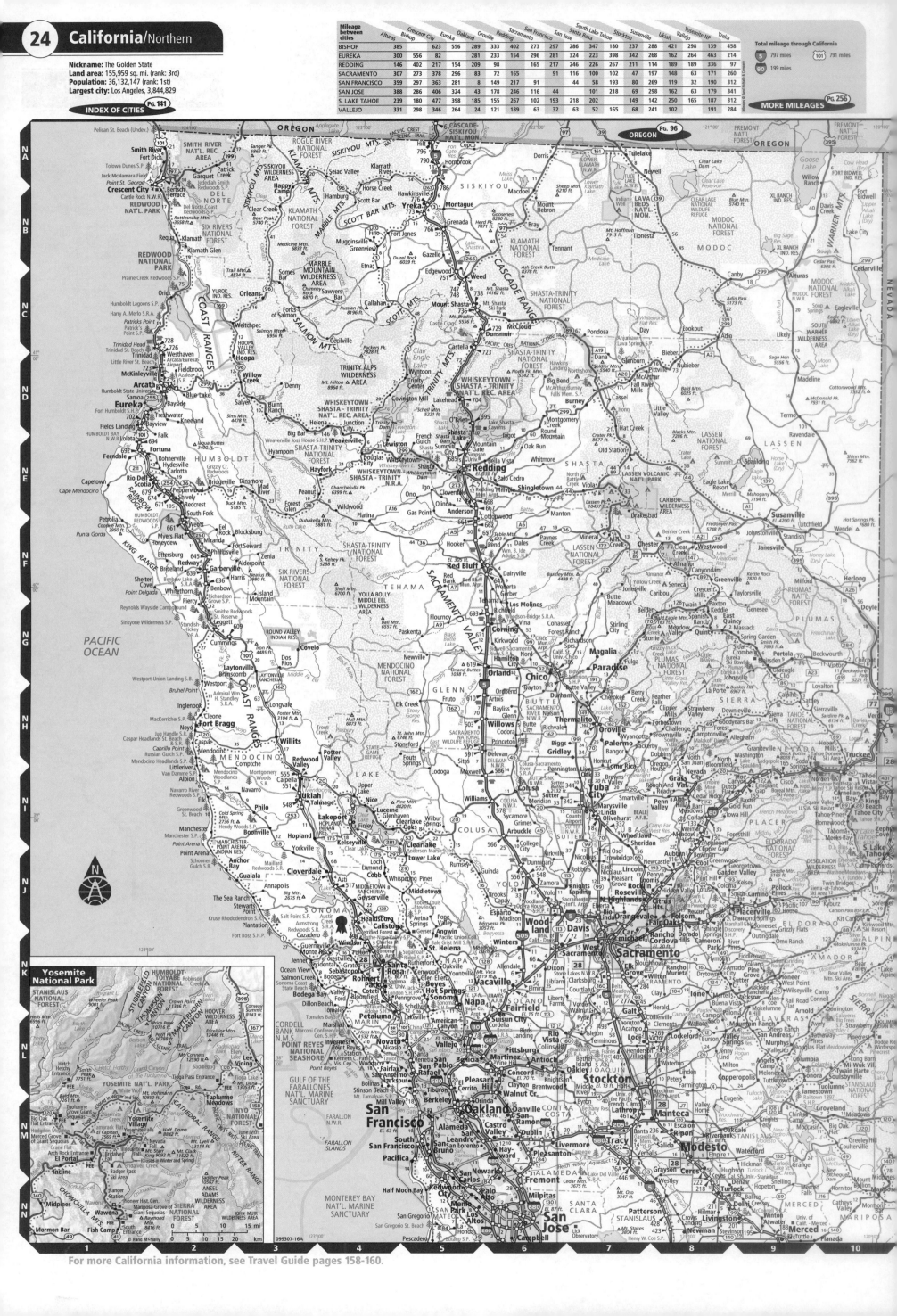

For more California information, see Travel Guide pages 158-160.

099307-16A

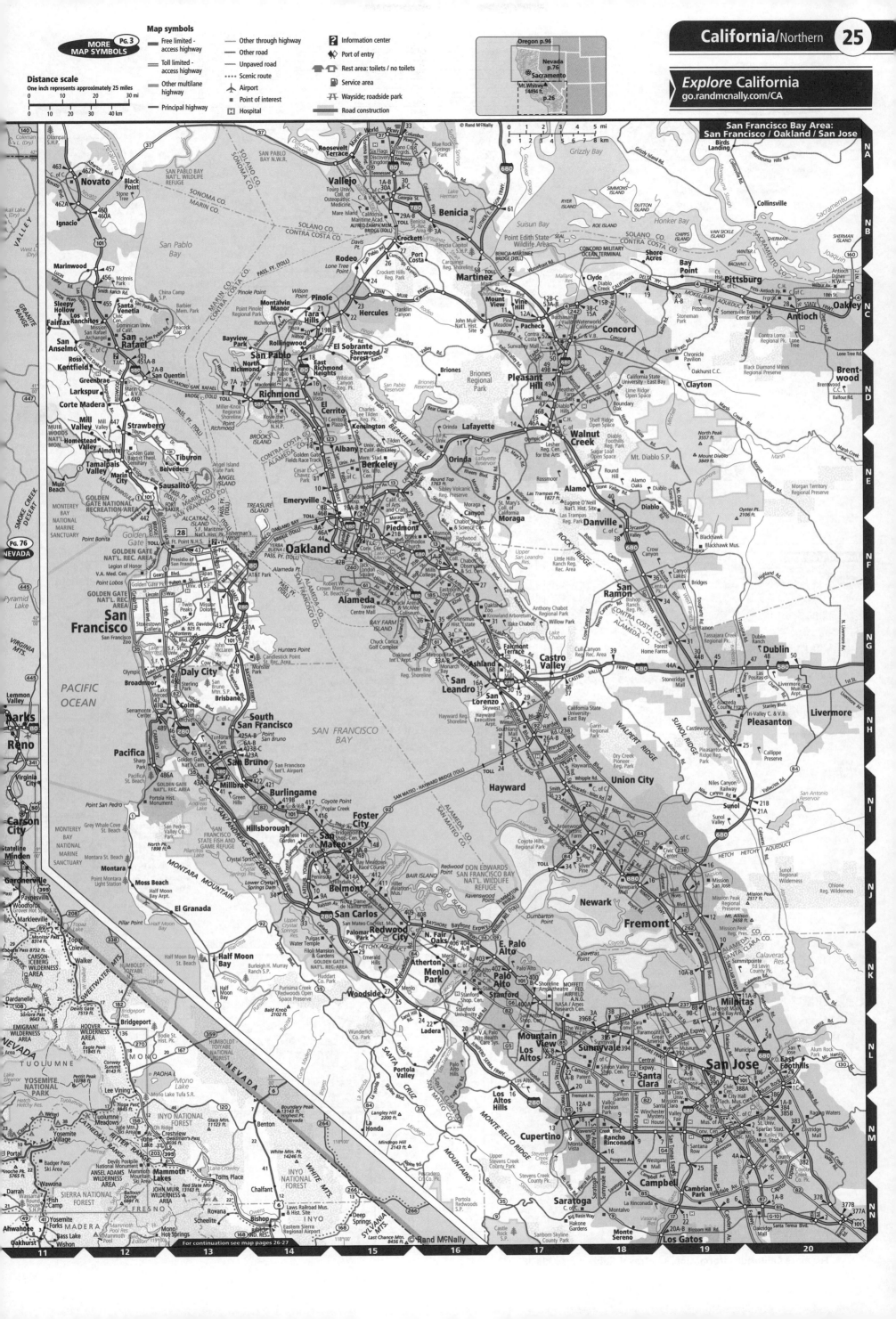

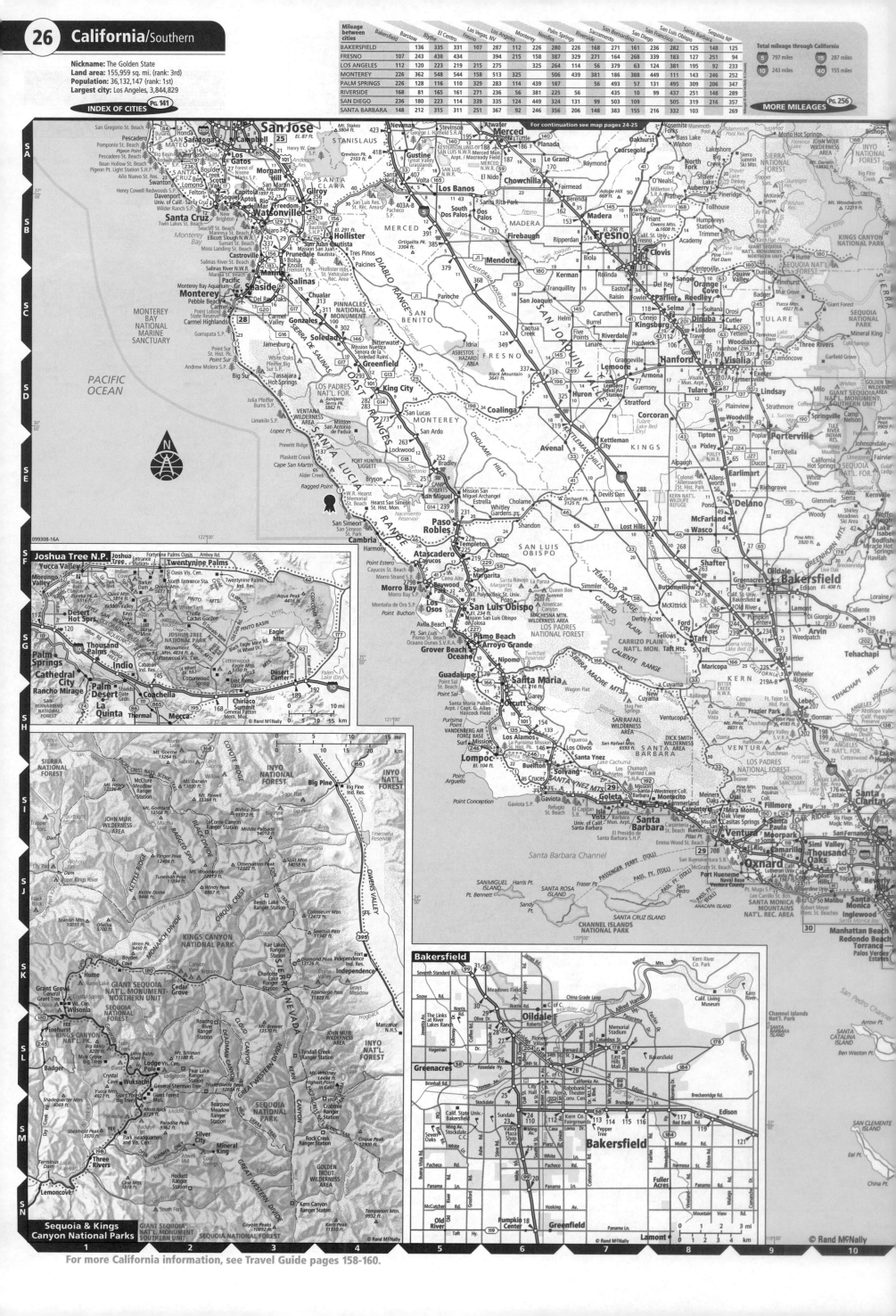

Nickname: The Golden State
Land area: 155,959 sq. mi. (rank: 3rd)
Population: 36,132,147 (rank: 1st)
Largest city: Los Angeles, 3,844,829

INDEX OF CITIES Pg. 141

Mileage between cities	Bakersfield	Barstow	El Centro	Las Vegas, NV	Los Angeles	Monterey	Palm Springs	Riverside	Sacramento	San Bernardino	San Diego	San Francisco	San Luis Obispo	Santa Barbara	Sequoia NP
BAKERSFIELD		136	335	331	107	287	112	226	280	226	168	271	161	236	282	125	148	125
FRESNO	107	243	438	434		394	215	158	387	329	271	164	268	339	183	127	251	94
LOS ANGELES	112	120	223	219	215	275		325	264	114	56	379	63	124	181	195	92	233
MONTEREY	226	362	548	544	158	513	325		506	439	381	186	388	449	111	143	246	252
PALM SPRINGS	226	128	116	110	329	283	114	439	187		56	493	57	131	495	309	206	347
RIVERSIDE	168	81	165	161	271	236	56	381	225	56		435	10	99	437	251	148	289
SAN DIEGO	236	180	223	114	339	371	124	449	324	131	99	503	109		505	319	216	357
SANTA BARBARA	148	212	315	311	251	367	92	246	356	206	148	383	155	216	332	103		269

Total mileage through California
- 5 · 797 miles
- 15 · 287 miles
- 10 · 243 miles
- 40 · 155 miles

MORE MILEAGES Pg. 256

PACIFIC OCEAN

Joshua Tree N.P.

Bakersfield

Sequoia & Kings Canyon National Parks

© Rand McNally

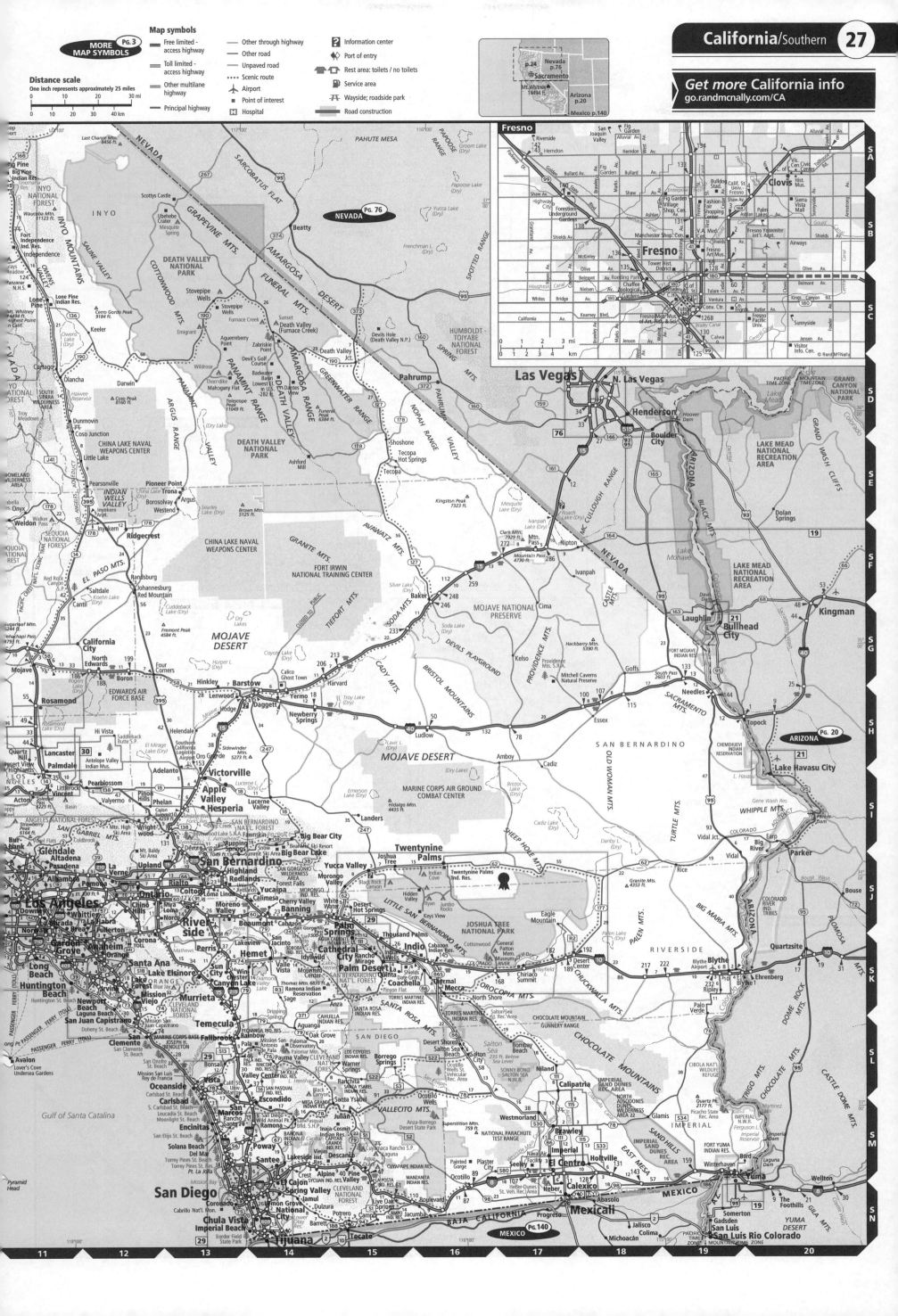

Get travel info
go.randmcnally.com/CA
INDEX OF CITIES PG. 141

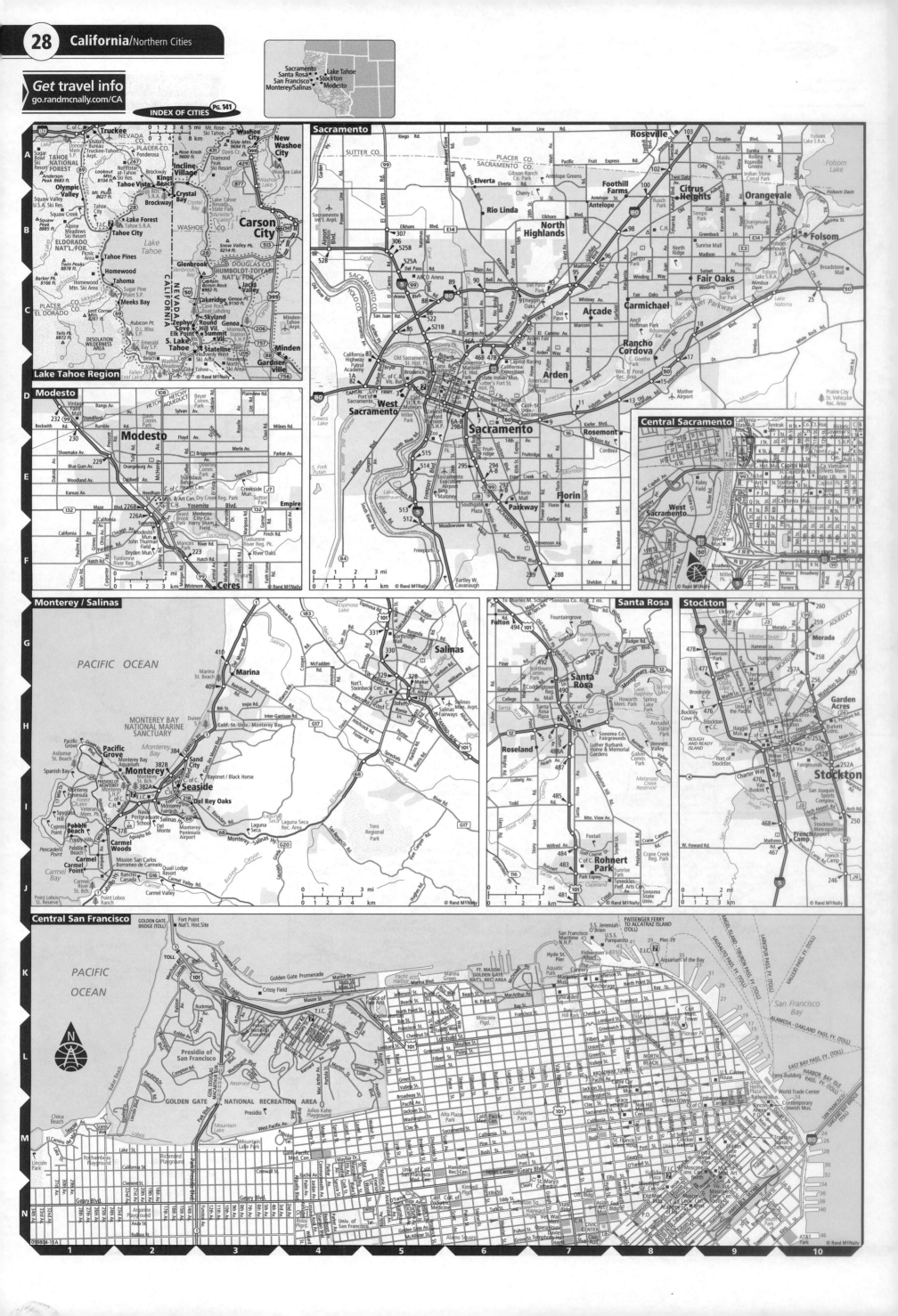

Lake Tahoe Region

Sacramento

Central Sacramento

Modesto

Monterey / Salinas

PACIFIC OCEAN

Santa Rosa

Stockton

Central San Francisco

PACIFIC OCEAN

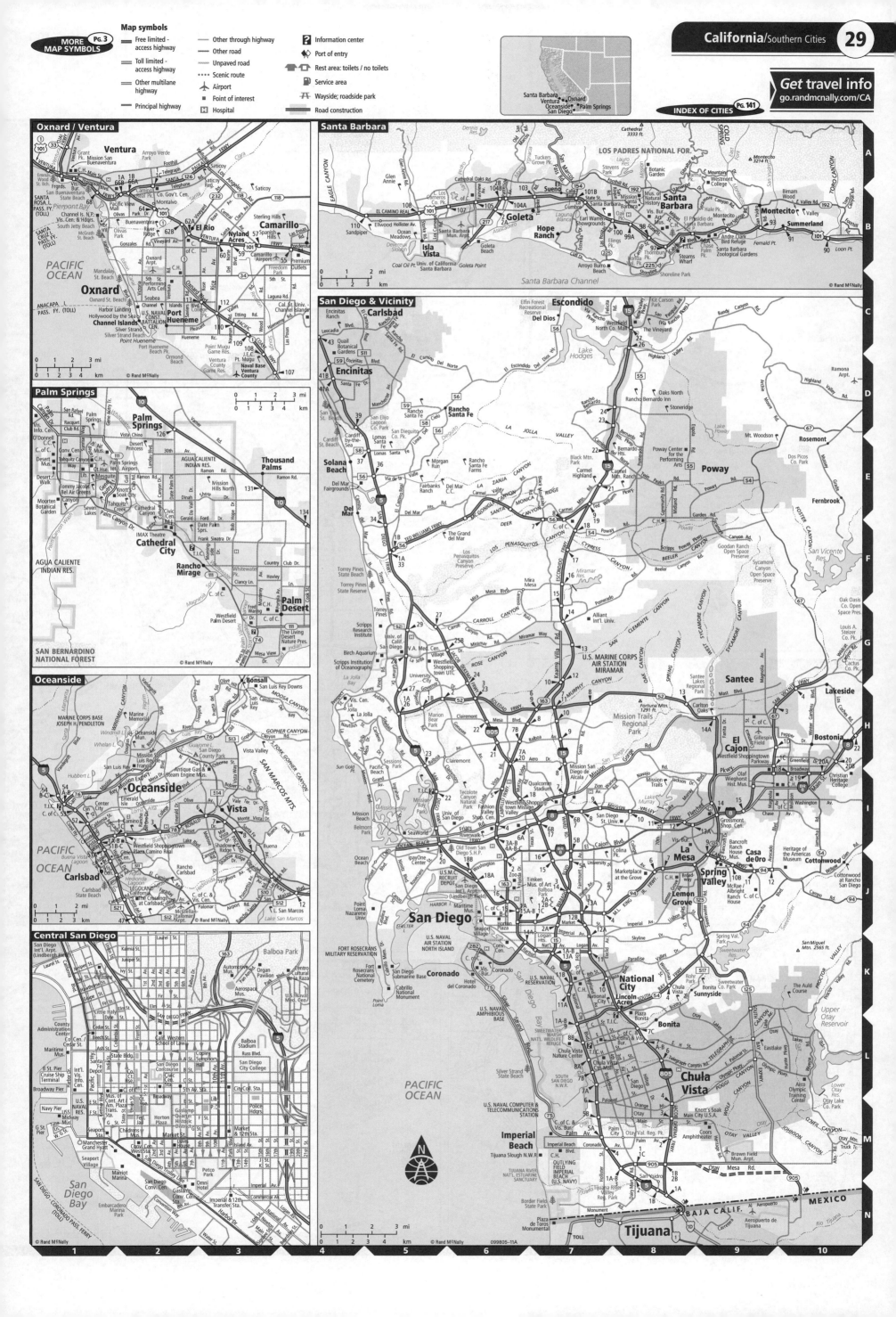

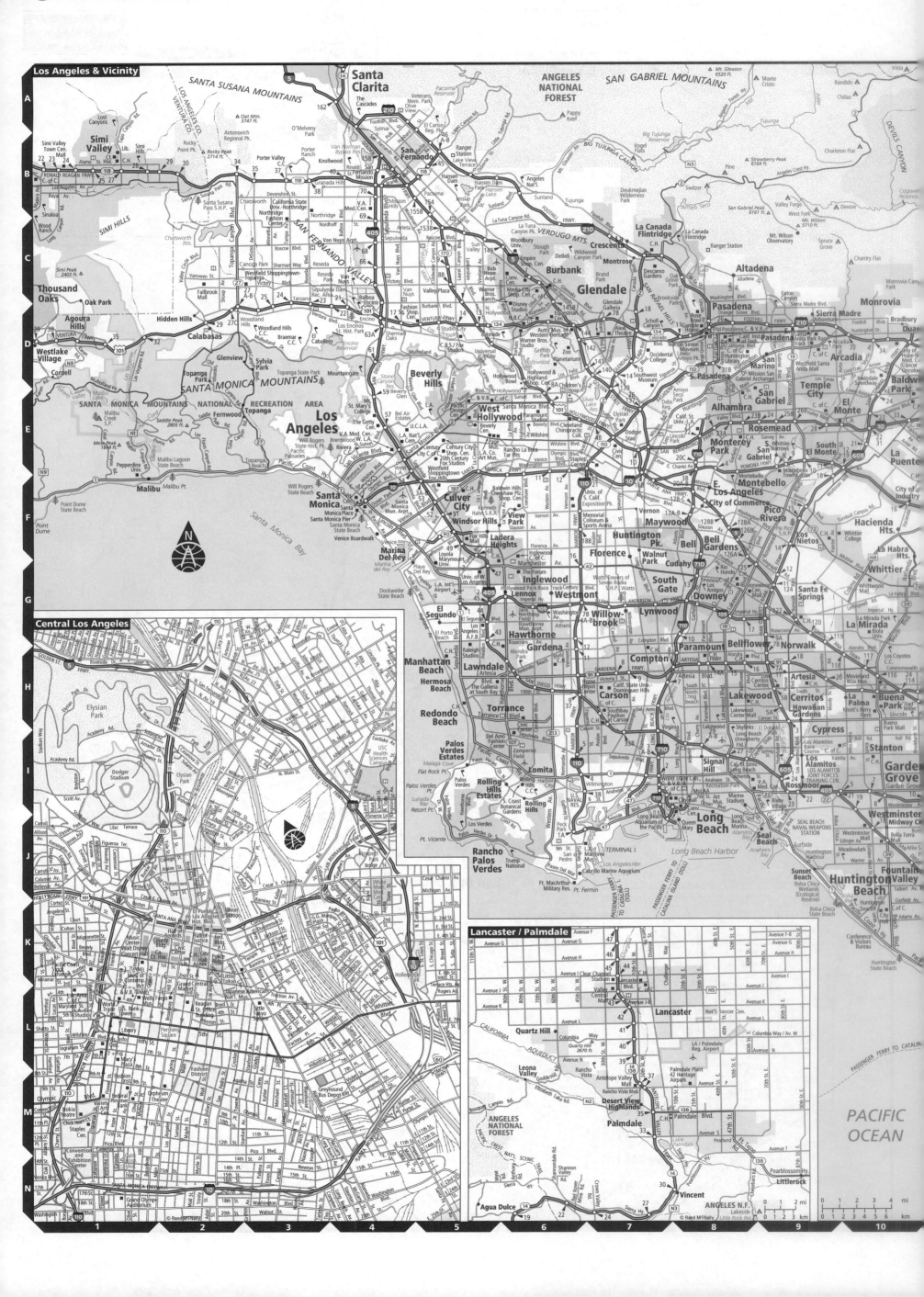

Map symbols

- Free limited-access highway
- Toll limited-access highway
- Other multilane highway
- Principal highway
- Other through highway
- Other road
- Unpaved road
- Scenic route
- Airport
- Point of interest
- Hospital
- Information center
- Port of entry
- Rest area: toilets / no toilets
- Service area
- Wayside; roadside park
- Road construction

MORE MAP SYMBOLS Pg. 3

Nickname: The Centennial State
Land area: 103,718 sq. mi. (rank: 8th)
Population: 4,665,177 (rank: 22nd)
Largest city: Denver, 557,917

INDEX OF CITIES   PG. 141

MORE MILEAGES   PG.256

Mileage between cities	Alamosa	Aspen	Boulder	Burlington	Colorado Springs	Craig	Denver	Durango	Estes Park	Fort Collins	Glenwood Springs	Grand Junction	Gunnison	Lamar	Leadville	Pueblo	Sterling	Trinidad
BURLINGTON	304	308	181		151	361	163	455	218	217	319	408	311	109	265	185	142	243
COLORADO SPRINGS	161	157	93	151		264	67	312	130	129	222	311	166	162	128	42	194	126
DENVER	228	162	26	163	67	199		379	63	62	157	246	233	208	103	109	127	193
DURANGO	151	250	405	455	312	317	379		442	441	253	170	174	353	256	270	506	260
FORT COLLINS	290	221	56	217	129	201	62	441	42		216	305	295	262	162	171	102	255
GRAND JCT.	248	131	256	408	311	153	246	170	285	305	89		126	453	175	285	370	345
LEADVILLE	138	59	113	265	128	161	103	256	149	162	86	175	119	275		155	227	215
PUEBLO	119	184	135	185	42	306	109	270	172	171	264	285	159	122	155		236	84

Total mileage through Colorado
25	300 miles	75	185 miles
70	451 miles	50	467 miles

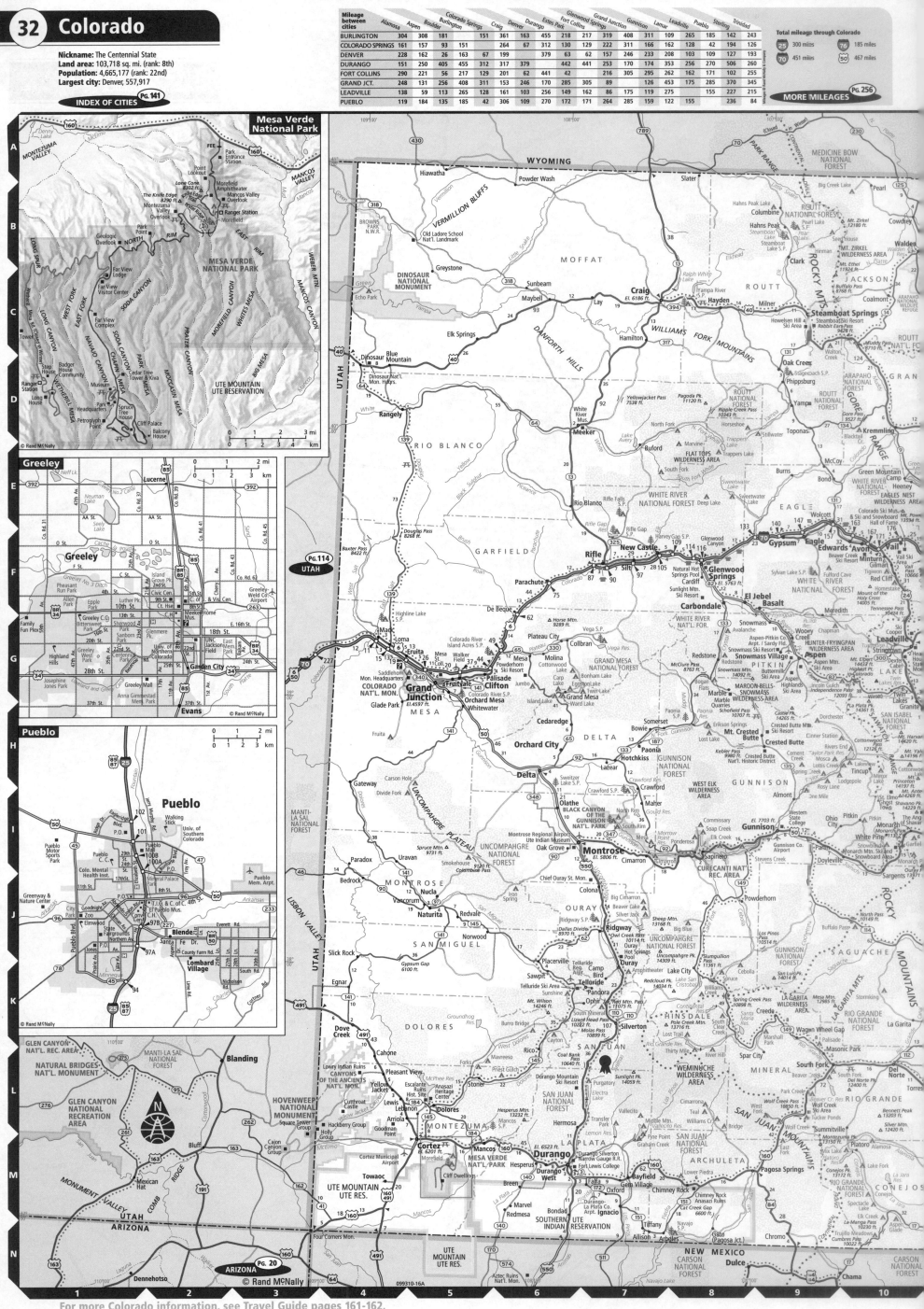

Mesa Verde National Park

Greeley

Pueblo

PG.114 UTAH

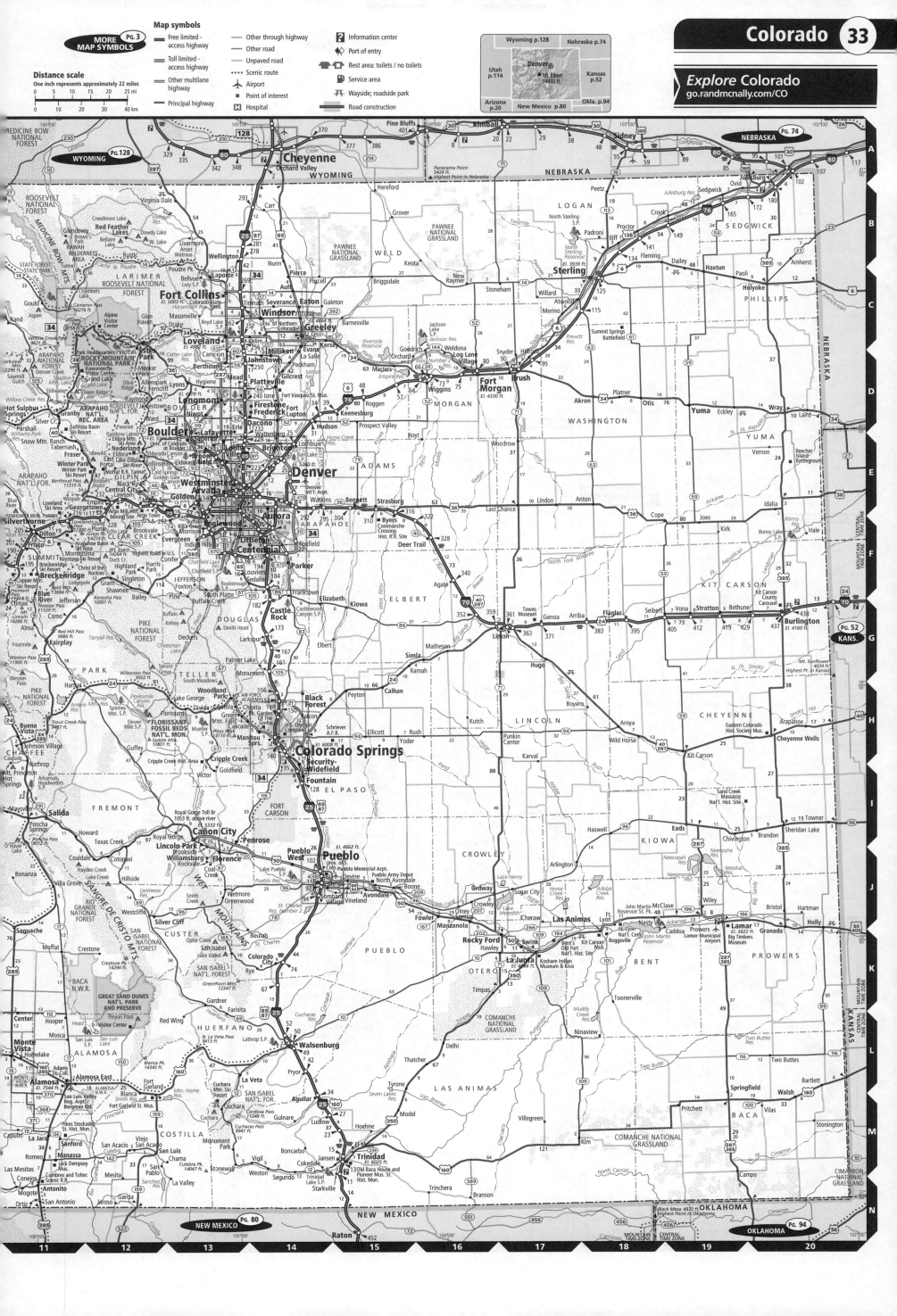

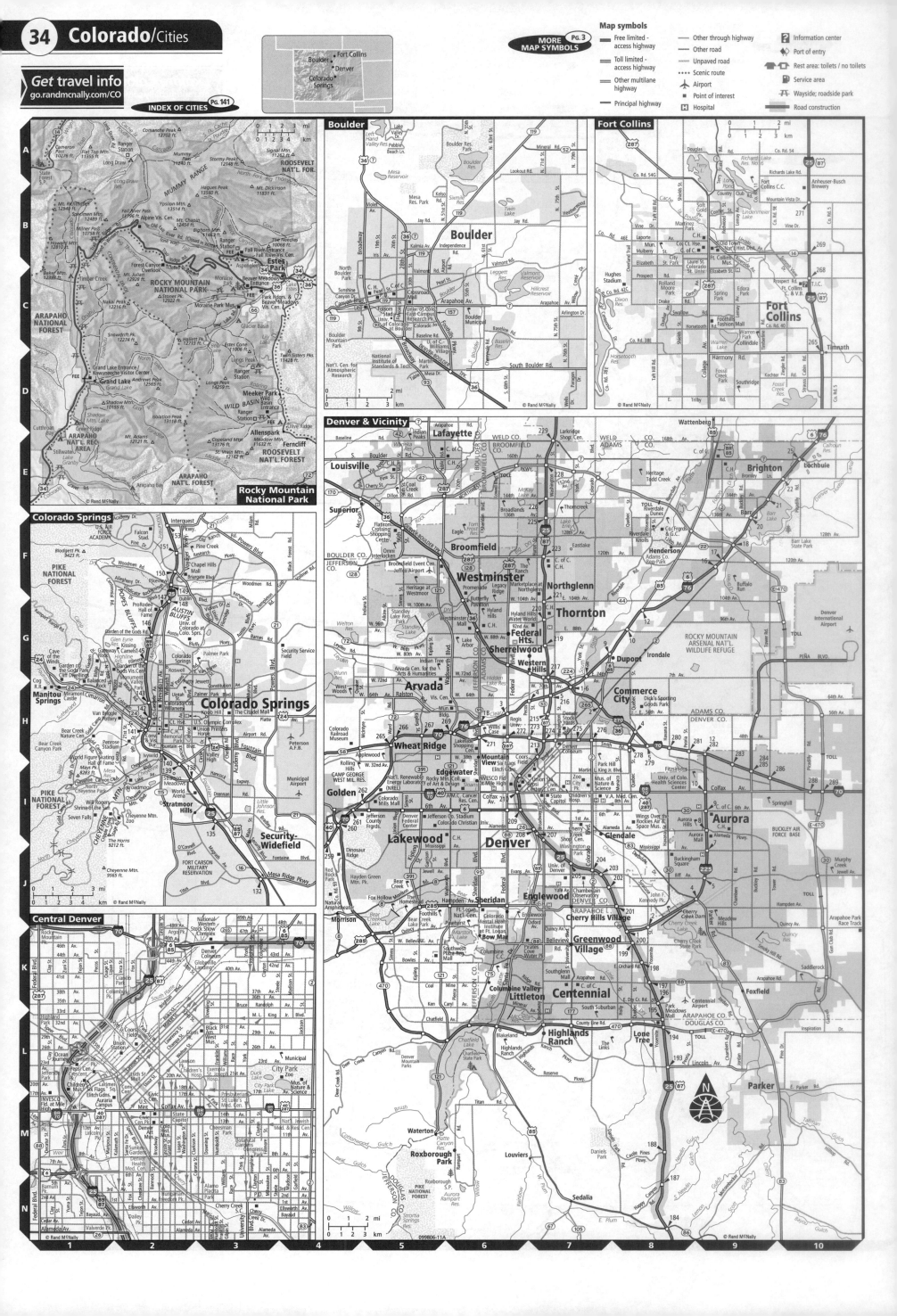

Get travel info
go.randmcnally.com/CO

INDEX OF CITIES PG. 141

MORE MAP SYMBOLS Pg.3

Map symbols
— Free limited-access highway
— Toll limited-access highway
— Other multilane highway
— Principal highway
— Other through highway
— Other road
— Unpaved road
•••• Scenic route
✈ Airport
■ Point of interest
Ⓗ Hospital
? Information center
Port of entry
Rest area: toilets / no toilets
Service area
Wayside; roadside park
Road construction

Boulder

Fort Collins

Denver & Vicinity

Colorado Springs

Rocky Mountain National Park

Central Denver

© Rand McNally

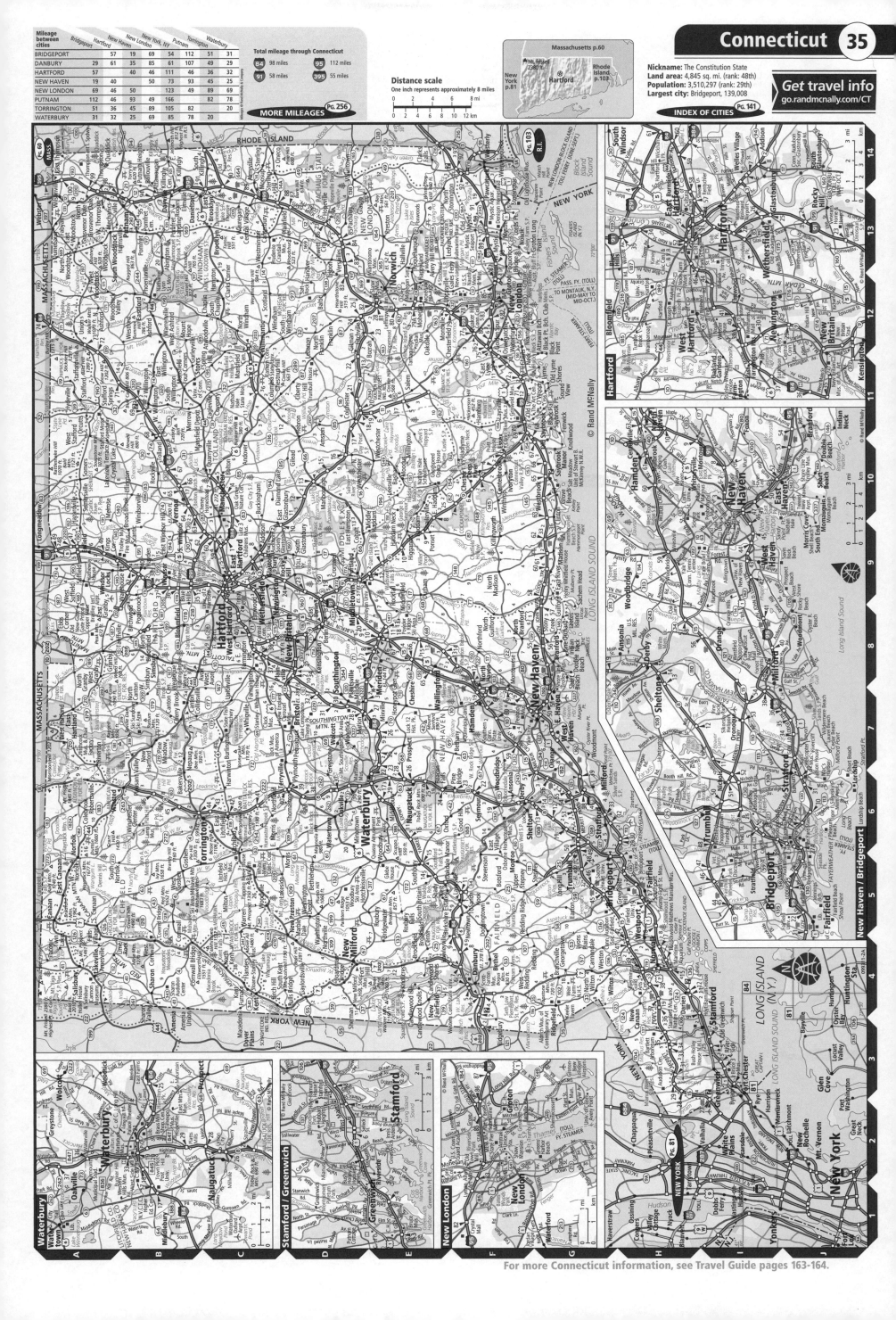

Mileage between cities	Bridgeport	Hartford	New Haven	New London	New York, NY	Putnam	Torrington	Waterbury
BRIDGEPORT		57	19	69	54	112	51	31
DANBURY	29	61	35	85	61	107	49	29
HARTFORD	57		40	46	111	46	36	32
NEW HAVEN	19	40		50	73	93	45	25
NEW LONDON	69	46	50		123	49	89	69
PUTNAM	112	46	93	49	166		82	78
TORRINGTON	51	36	45	89	105	82		20
WATERBURY	31	32	25	69	85	78	20	

Total mileage through Connecticut

84 — 98 miles   95 — 112 miles
91 — 58 miles   395 — 55 miles

MORE MILEAGES Pg. 256

Distance scale
One inch represents approximately 8 miles

Massachusetts p.60
Mt. Frissell 2380 ft.
New York p.81
Hartford
Rhode Island p.103

INDEX OF CITIES Pg. 141

Nickname: The Constitution State
Land area: 4,845 sq. mi. (rank: 48th)
Population: 3,510,297 (rank: 29th)
Largest city: Bridgeport, 139,008

Get travel info
go.randmcnally.com/CT

For more Connecticut information, see Travel Guide pages 163-164.

© Rand McNally

Plan a trip
go.randmcnally.com/DE

Nickname: The First State
Land area: 1,954 sq. mi. (rank: 49th)
Population: 843,524 (rank: 45th)
Largest city: Wilmington, 72,786

INDEX OF CITIES Pg. 141

Pennsylvania p.100
New Castle County p.448 ft.
N.J. p.78
Maryland p.58
Dover
Virginia p.118

Distance scale
One inch represents approximately 9 miles
0   5 mi
0   5 km

Mileage between cities	Dover	Georgetown	Lewes	Milford	Newark	Salisbury, MD	Selbyville	Wilmington
DOVER		35	38	19	46	56	55	47
GEORGETOWN	35		14	16	83	27	21	84
LEWES	38	14		20	86	41	33	87
MILFORD	19	16	20		67	42	36	68
NEWARK	46	83	86	67		104	103	13
SALISBURY, MD	56	27	41	42	104		24	105
SELBYVILLE	55	21	33	36	103	24		104
WILMINGTON	47	84	87	68	13	105	104	

Total mileage through Delaware
95 23 miles   1 104 miles
13 108 miles

MORE MILEAGES Pg. 256

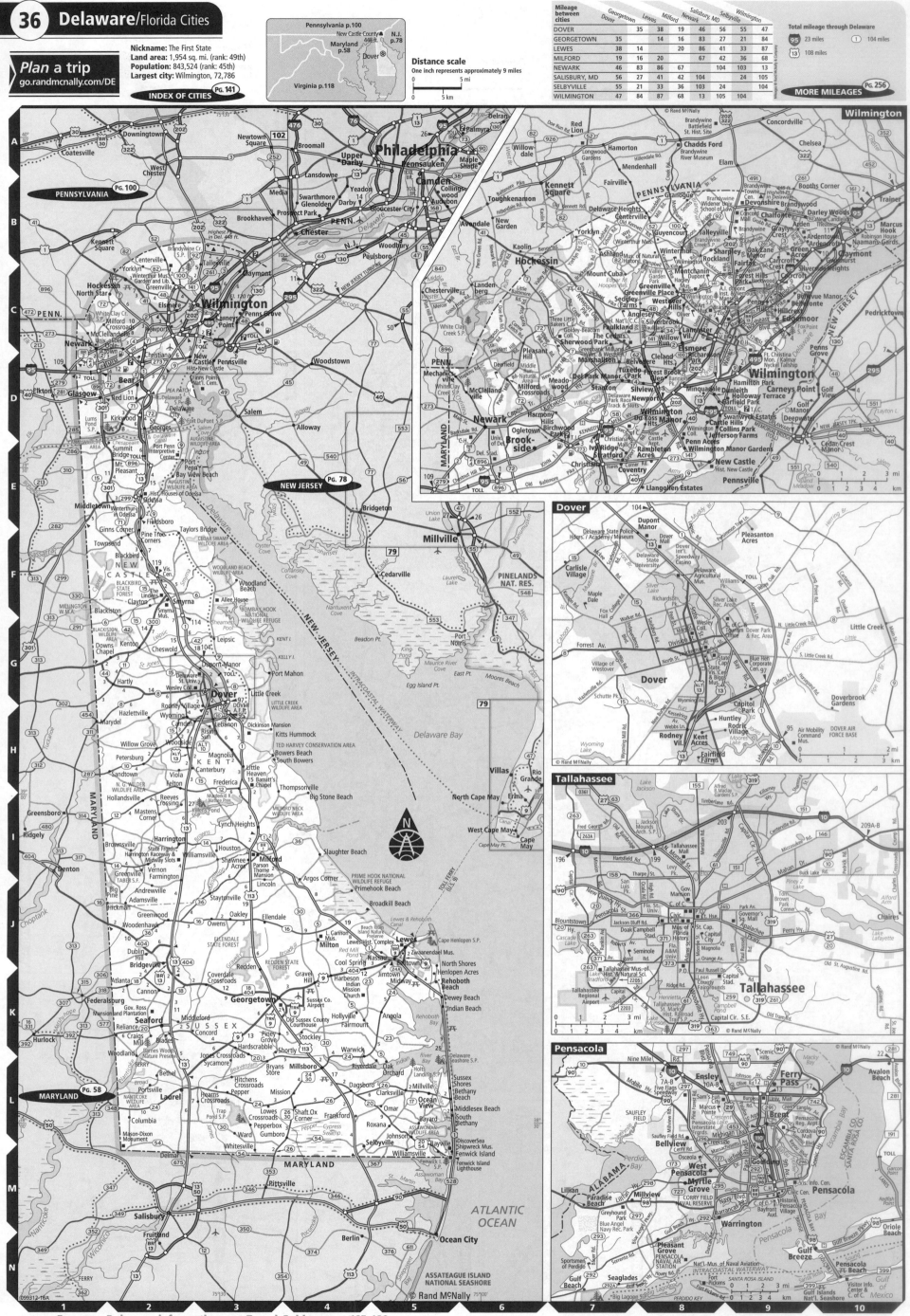

For more Delaware information, see Travel Guide pages 165-166.

© Rand McNally

Map symbols

- Free limited-access highway
- Toll limited-access highway
- Other multilane highway
- Principal highway
- Other through highway
- Other road
- Unpaved road
- Scenic route
- Airport
- Point of interest
- Hospital
- ? Information center
- Port of entry
- Rest area: toilets / no toilets
- Service area
- Wayside; roadside park
- Road construction

Tampa / St. Petersburg / Sarasota

Miami / Fort Lauderdale & Vicinity

Lakeland / Winter Haven

Fort Myers / Cape Coral

Central Miami

Nickname: The Sunshine State
Land area: 53,927 sq. mi. (rank: 26th)
Population: 17,789,864 (rank: 4th)
Largest city: Jacksonville, 782,623

INDEX OF CITIES Pg. 142

Mileage between cities	Atlanta GA	Daytona Beach	Fort Lauderdale	Fort Myers	Fort Pierce	Gainesville	Jacksonville	Key West	Lakeland	Melbourne	Miami	Orlando	Panama City	Pensacola	St. Petersburg	Sarasota	Tallahassee	Tampa	Titusville	West Palm Beach
FORT MYERS	581	212	141		128	253	298	289	111	172	152	170	517	593	261	116	78	189	195	129
JACKSONVILLE	346	90	318	298	223	73		503	196	176	341	140	282	358	41	219	175	202	133	278
MIAMI	661	446	650	593	152	126	333	341	164	223		229	597	673	304	260	222	478	273	212	66
ORLANDO	440	56	206	156	119	112	142	391	54	72	229		376	452	105	108	128	257	84	39	166
PENSACOLA	319	446	650	593	566	344	358	835	467	519	673	452	103		397	494	520	196	479	480	610
TALLAHASSEE	270	251	455	398	371	149	163	640	272	324	478	257	98	196	299	325		275	294	415
TAMPA	458	140	262	129	151	130	202	410	33	130	273	84	394	470	189	24	56	275		123	202
WEST PALM BEACH	598	190	43	129	57	270	278	230	173	107	66	166	534	610	241	226	197	415	202	149	

Total mileage through Florida	
4 132 miles	75 471 miles
10 362 miles	95 382 miles

MORE MILEAGES Pg. 256

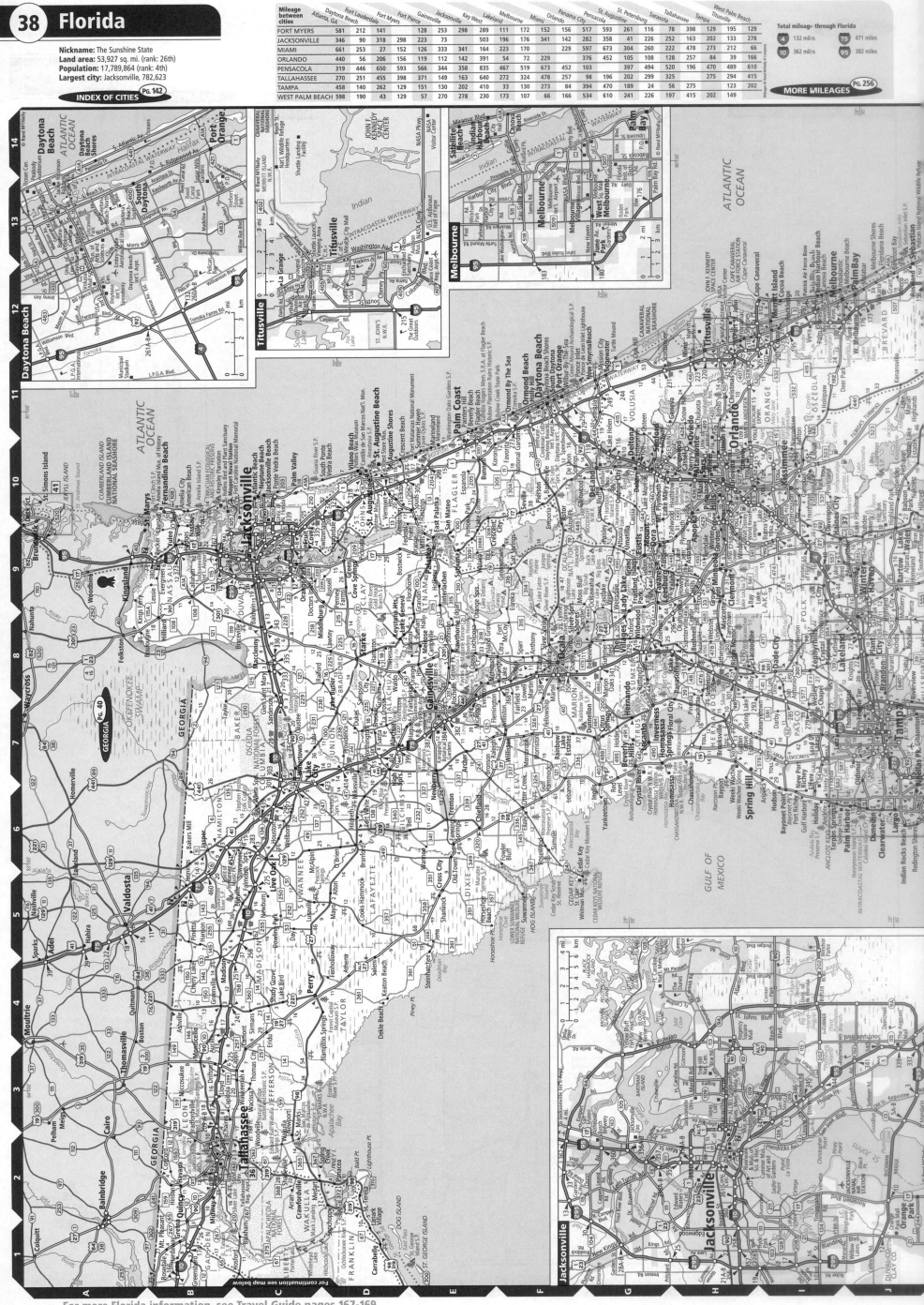

For more Florida information, see Travel Guide pages 167-169.

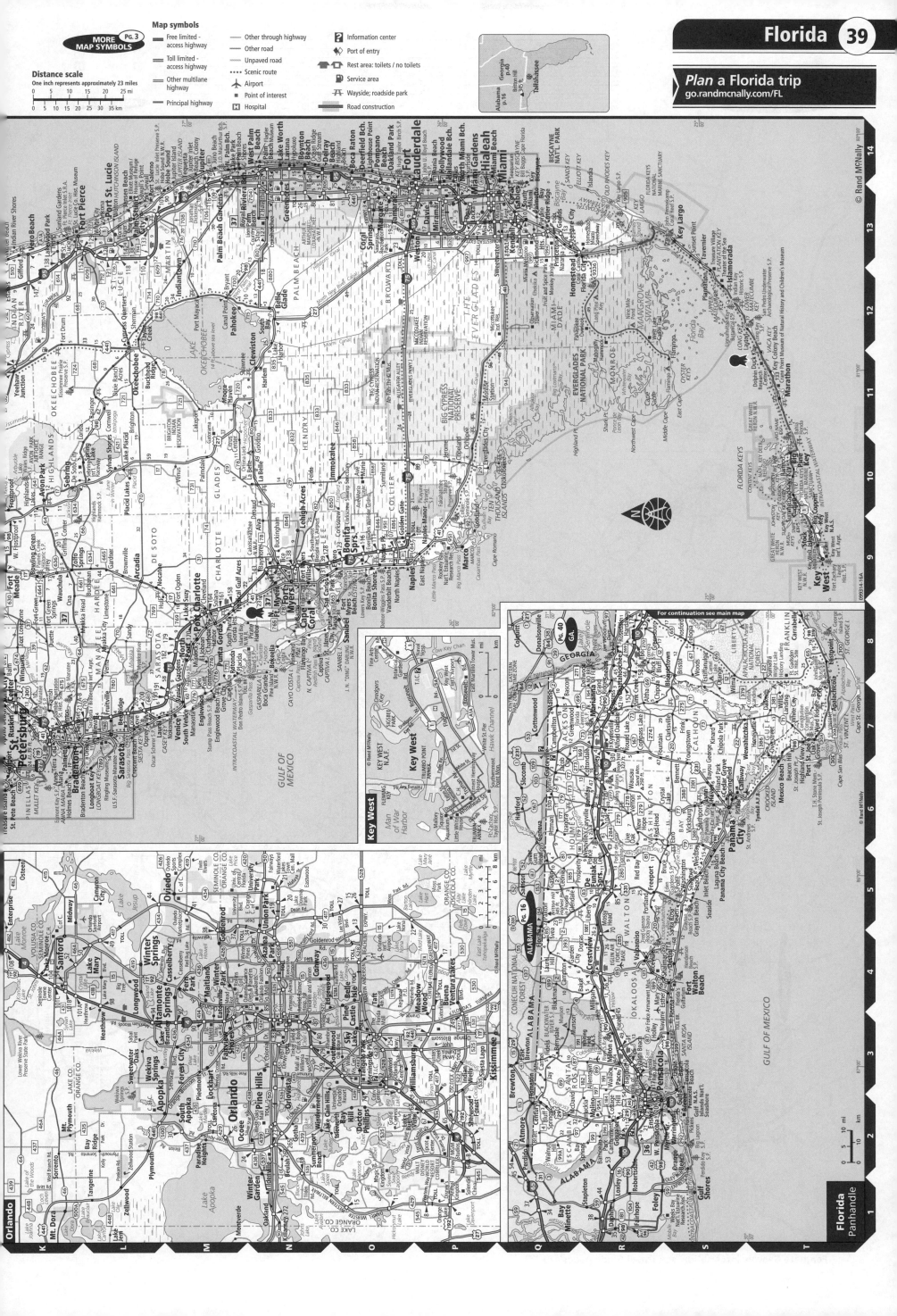

Plan a Florida trip
go.randmcnally.com/FL

Map symbols

MORE MAP SYMBOLS PG. 3

Distance scale
One inch represents approximately 23 miles

	Free limited-access highway
	Toll limited-access highway
	Other multilane highway
	Principal highway
	Other through highway
	Other road
	Unpaved road
	Scenic route
✈	Airport
	Point of interest
H	Hospital

?	Information center
	Port of entry
	Rest area: toilets / no toilets
	Service area
	Wayside; roadside park
	Road construction

Nickname: The Peach State
Land area: 57,906 sq. mi. (rank: 21st)
Population: 9,072,576 (rank: 9th)
Largest city: Atlanta, 470,688

INDEX OF CITIES — PG. 142

Mileage between cities	Albany	Americus	Athens	Atlanta	Augusta	Bainbridge	Brunswick	Chattanooga, TN	Columbus	Gainesville	Greenville, FL	Jacksonville, FL	La Grange	Macon	Rome	Savannah	Toccoa	Valdosta	Warner Robins	Waycross
ATLANTA	182	129	67		150	240	310	115	104	51	142	346	65	81	66	252	90	229	177	98	254
AUGUSTA	229	197	97	150		287	198	265	249	138	115	260	210	124	140	130	223	97	141	188
CHATTANOOGA, TN	297	244	168	115	265		355	425		216	128	243	461	177	196	68	367	191	344	292	213	369
COLUMBUS	89	62	171	104	249	129	262	216		155	246	295	45	97	148	268	194	178	193	90	204
JACKSONVILLE, FL	207	238	342	346	260	203	71	461	295	393	390		340	269	412	140	432	120	164	260	79
MACON	105	73	90	81	124	163	229	196	97	128	219	269	112		147	171	167	152	96	17	162
SAVANNAH	231	210	222	252	140	250	78	367	268	299	256	140	283	171	318		264	168	95	166	106
VALDOSTA	90	121	242	229	223	82	120	344	178	276	367	120	223	152	295	168	315		112	143	62

Total mileage through Georgia
20 — 203 miles 85 — 180 miles
75 — 355 miles 95 — 112 miles

MORE MILEAGES — PG. 256

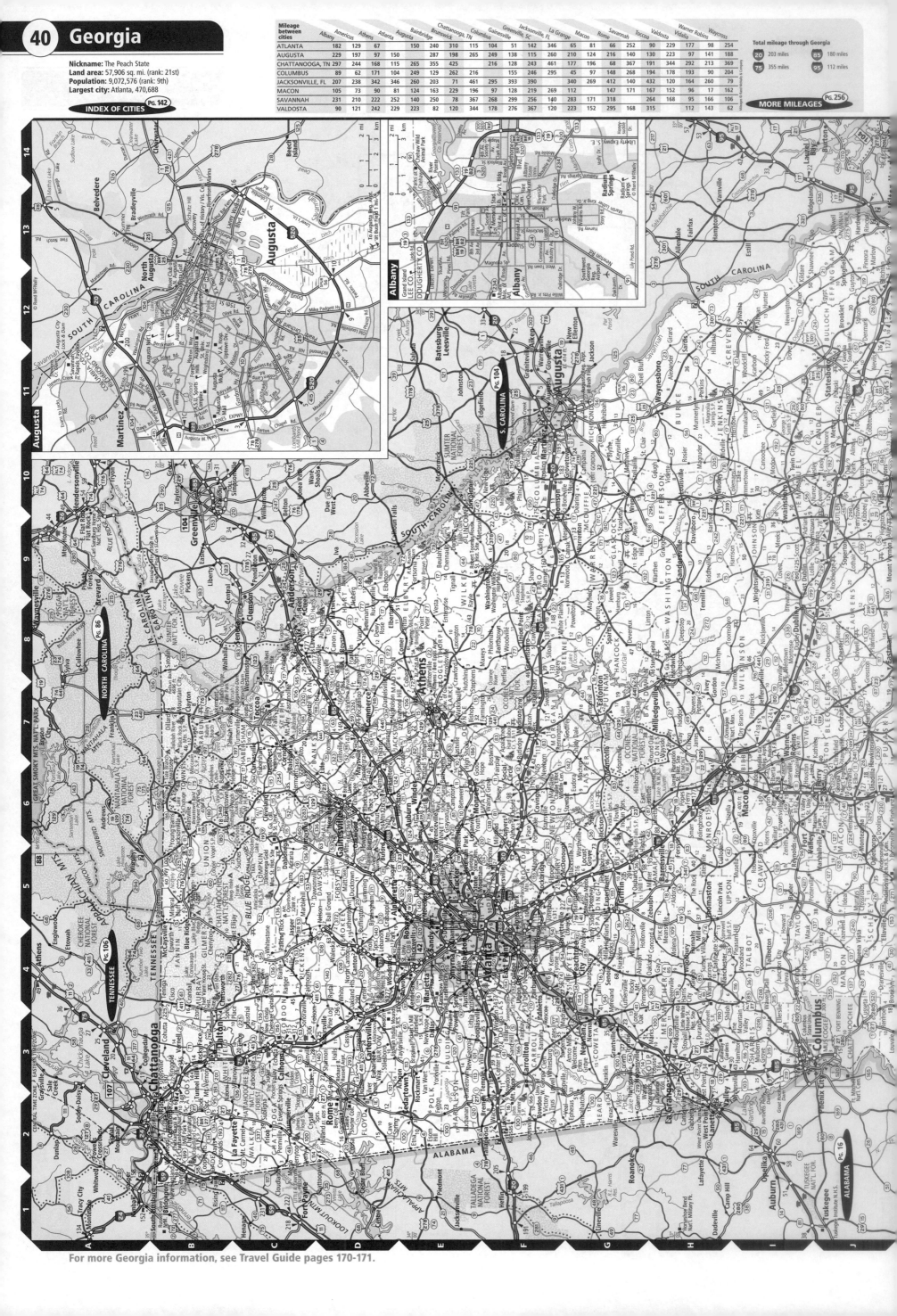

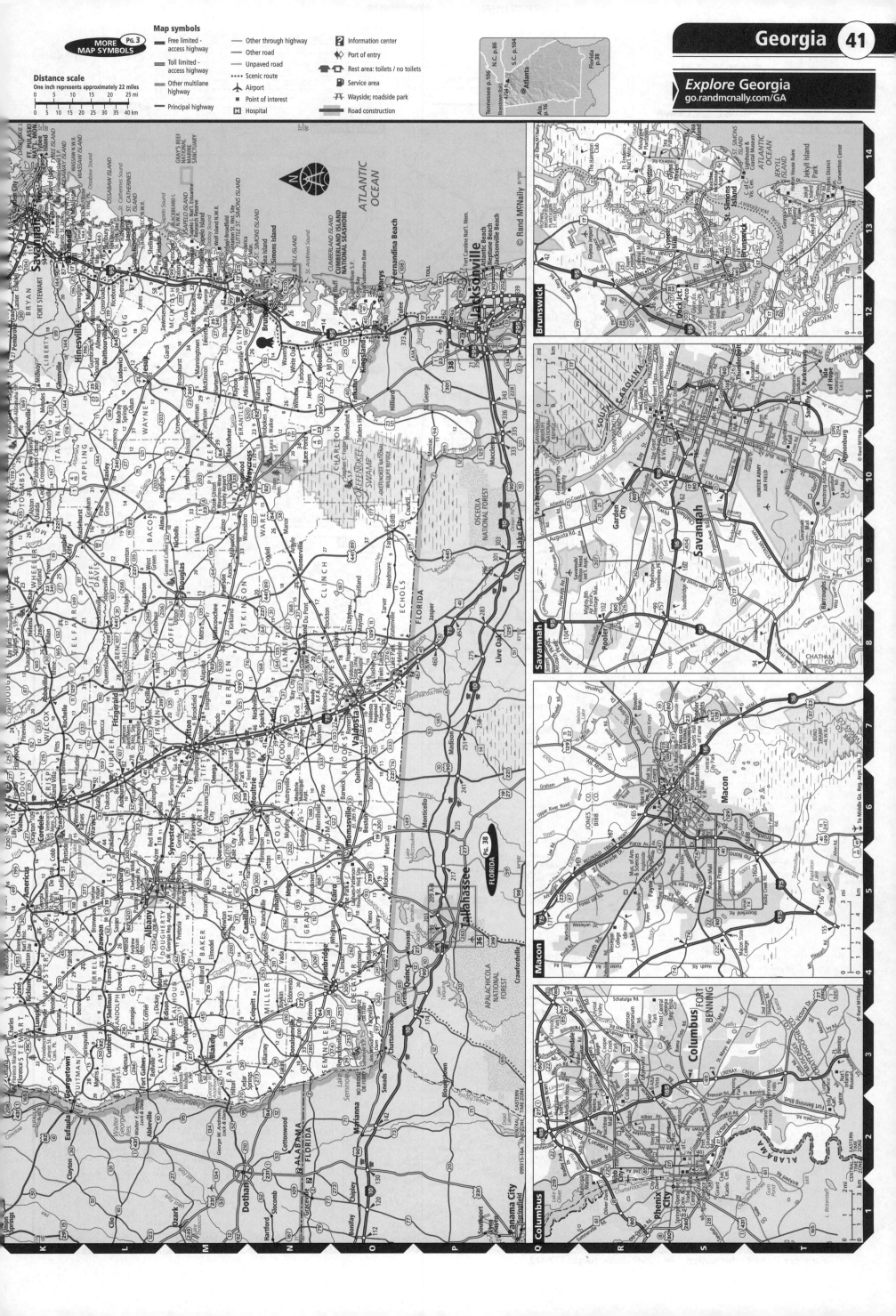

MORE MAP SYMBOLS Pg. 3

Explore Georgia
go.randmcnally.com/GA

Plan a trip
go.randmcnally.com/HI

Nickname: The Aloha State
Land area: 6,423 sq. mi. (rank: 47th)
Population: 1,275,194 (rank: 42nd)
Largest city: Honolulu, 377,379

INDEX OF CITIES Pg. 142

Honolulu

Distance scale
One inch represents approximately 39 miles

Mileage between cities	Hilo	Honolulu	Kahului	Kailua	Kailua Kona	Kapa'a	Lahaina	Maunaloa	*Via Air
HILO		221*	123*	234*	87	320*	146*	179*	237*
HONOLULU	221*		105*	12	196*	115*	128*	66*	20
KAHULUI	123*	105*		118*	118*	213*	23	58*	121*
KAILUA KONA	234*	12	118*		209*	128	141*	79*	31
KAPA'A	87	196*	118*	209*		305*	174*	212*	
LAHAINA	320*	115*	213*	128*	305*		236*	131	
WAHIAWĀ	146*	128*	23	141*	141*	236*		81*	144*
	237*	20	121*	31	212*	131*	144*	82*	

Total mileage through Hawaii
H1 27 miles H3 15 miles
H2 8 miles

MORE MILEAGES Pg. 256

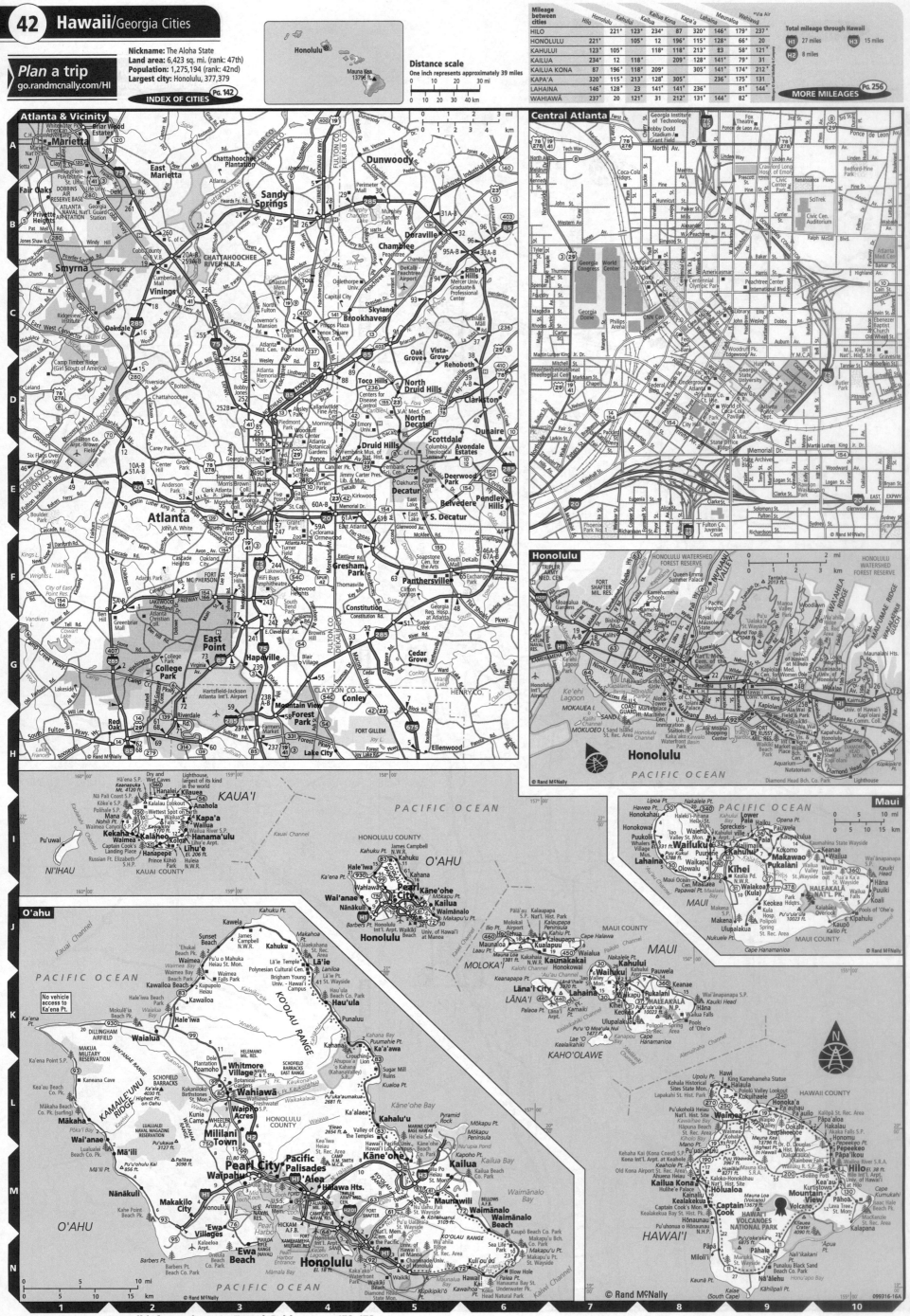

Nickname: The Gem State
Land area: 82,747 sq. mi. (rank: 11th)
Population: 1,429,096 (rank: 39th)
Largest city: Boise, 193,161

Get travel info
go.randmcnally.com/ID

Mileage between cities	Boise	Coeur d'Alene	Lewiston	Missoula, MT	Mountain Home	Pocatello	Salmon	Twin Falls
BOISE		454	276	371	45	237	255	130
COEUR D'ALENE	454		119	168	494	528	308	579
LEWISTON	276	119		218	325	517	337	410
MISSOULA, MT	371	168	218		420	360	143	471
MOUNTAIN HOME	45	494	325	420		193	294	86
POCATELLO	237	528	517	360	193		212	115
SALMON	255	308	337	143	294	212		247
TWIN FALLS	130	579	410	471	86	115	247	

Total mileage through Idaho
15 196 miles   86 63 miles
84 276 miles   90 74 miles

MORE MILEAGES Pg.256

Distance scale
One inch represents approximately 39 miles

B.C. p.130
Washington p.120
Montana p.72
Oregon p.96   Boise
                 Wyoming p.128
Nev. p.76 Utah p.114

INDEX OF CITIES Pg.142

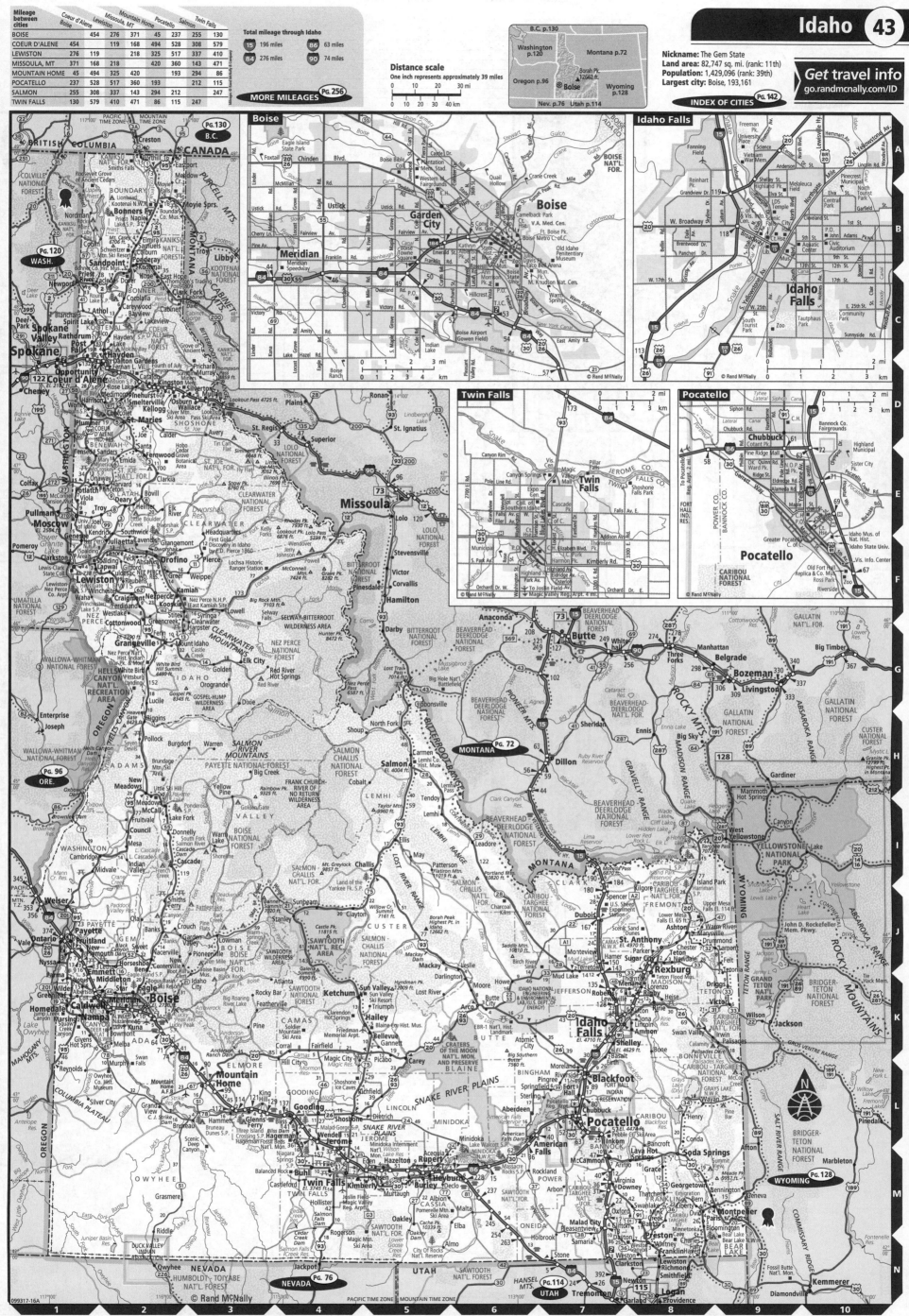

For more Idaho information, see Travel Guide pages 174-175.

© Rand McNally
099317-16A

Nickname: Land of Lincoln
Land area: 55,584 sq. mi. (rank: 24th)
Population: 12,763,371 (rank: 5th)
Largest city: Chicago, 2,842,518

PG. 142

INDEX OF CITIES

Mileage between cities	Bloomington	Carbondale	Cairo	Champaign	Chicago	Decatur	De Kalb	Dubuque, IA	Effingham	Elgin	Galesburg	Kankakee	Lawrenceville	Moline	Mt. Vernon	Peoria	Quincy	Rockford	St. Louis, MO	Springfield	Waukegan
CARBONDALE	249		59	202	333	185	370	415	124	369	297	274	149	340	58	248	231	384	108	178	377
CHAMPAIGN	51	244	202		135	47	172	257	78	171	139	76	127	182	148	90	195	186	182	85	179
CHICAGO	136	375	333	135		178	66	175	209	38	198	56	250	165	279	170	310	84	300	200	40
MOLINE	132	410	340	182	165	169	103	74	256	152	48	153	305		314	92	147	117	262	162	189
PEORIA	40	318	248	90	170	77	129	167	164	153	49	121	213	92	222		130	143	170	70	198
ROCKFORD	136	426	384	186	84	179	44	91	260	48	150	121	309	117	330	143	267		296	196	71
ST. LOUIS, MO	164	109	100	182	300	118	282	337	104	307	219	254	147	262	82	170	133	296		100	328
SPRINGFIELD	64	248	178	85	200	38	182	237	89	207	119	157	154	162	152	70	110	196	100		228

Total mileage through Illinois			
55	313 miles	80	164 miles
70	136 miles	90	124 miles

MORE MILEAGES
PG. 256

For more Illinois information, see Travel Guide pages 176-177.

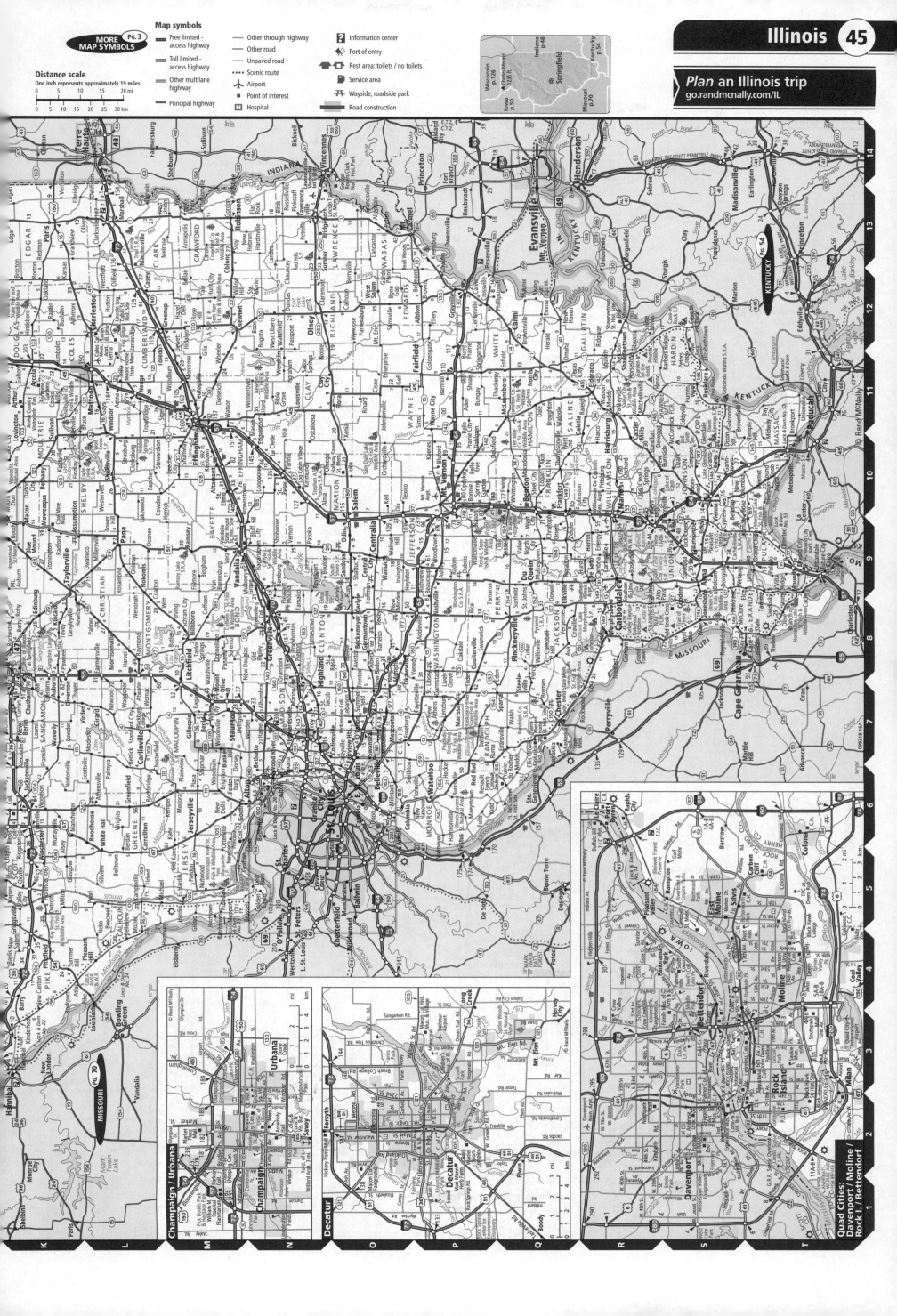

MORE MAP SYMBOLS PG. 3

Map symbols

Free limited-access highway
Toll limited-access highway
Other multilane highway
Principal highway
Other through highway
Other road
Unpaved road
Scenic route
Airport
Point of interest
Hospital
Information center
Port of entry
Rest area: toilets / no toilets
Service area
Wayside; roadside park
Road construction

Distance scale
One inch represents approximately 19 miles

Quad Cities:
Davenport / Moline /
Rock I. / Bettendorf

INDEX OF CITIES   Pg. 142

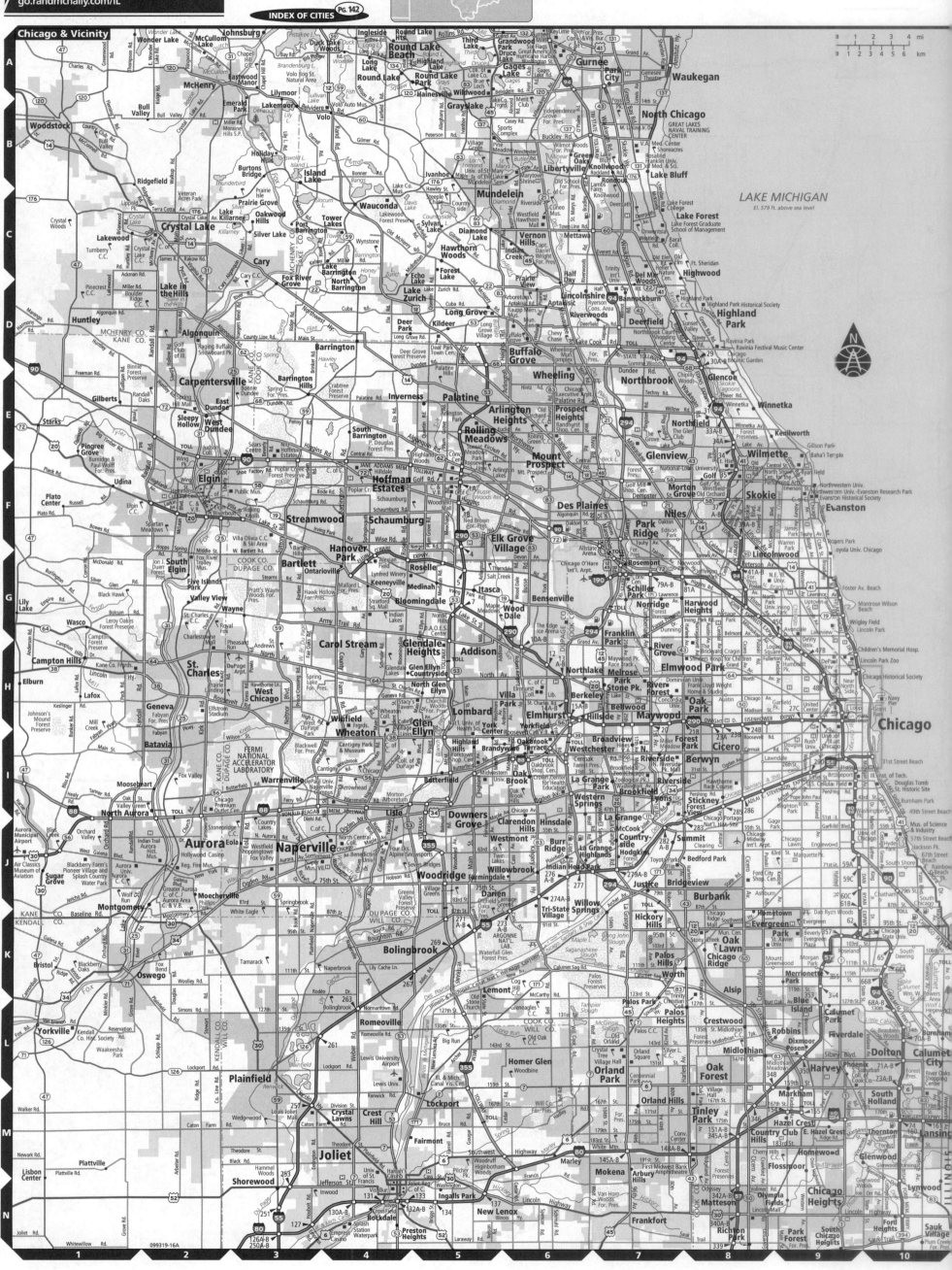

Chicago & Vicinity

LAKE MICHIGAN
El. 579 ft. above sea level

Nickname: The Hoosier State
Land area: 35,867 sq. mi. (rank: 38th)
Population: 6,271,973 (rank: 15th)
Largest city: Indianapolis, 784,118

INDEX OF CITIES PG. 142

Mileage between cities	Anderson	Angola	Bloomington	Chicago, IL	Crawfordsville	Danville, IL	Evansville	Fort Wayne	Gary	Greensburg	Indianapolis	Kokomo	Lafayette	Michigan City	Muncie	New Albany	Richmond	South Bend	Terre Haute	Vincennes
EVANSVILLE	234	353	134	294	179	178		169	319	278	198	239	203	298	228	111	259	326	112	54
FORT WAYNE	89	42	180	164	175	168	208	319		135	152	133	90	120	118	85	242	95	92	211	265
GARY	182	135	199	28	202	130	278	135		202	150	136	92	26	196	269	221	58	186	224
INDIANAPOLIS	48	167	50	179	48	56	96	133	150	50		53	62	170	62	115	73	140	78	132
NEW ALBANY	157	276	49	298	71	166	206	111	242	269	90	115	172	181	289	171		182	259	188	137
RICHMOND	59	140	120	250	115	129	169	259	95	221	67	73	104	133	241	43		182	191	151	205
SOUTH BEND	142	76	198	87	192	133	173	326	92	58	186	140	91	107	34	141	259	191		218	272
TERRE HAUTE	126	245	57	182	121	57	57	112	211	166	123	78	131	92	186	140	188	151	218		58

Total mileage through Indiana

65 261 miles	**74** 172 miles
70 157 miles	**90** 156 miles

MORE MILEAGES PG. 256

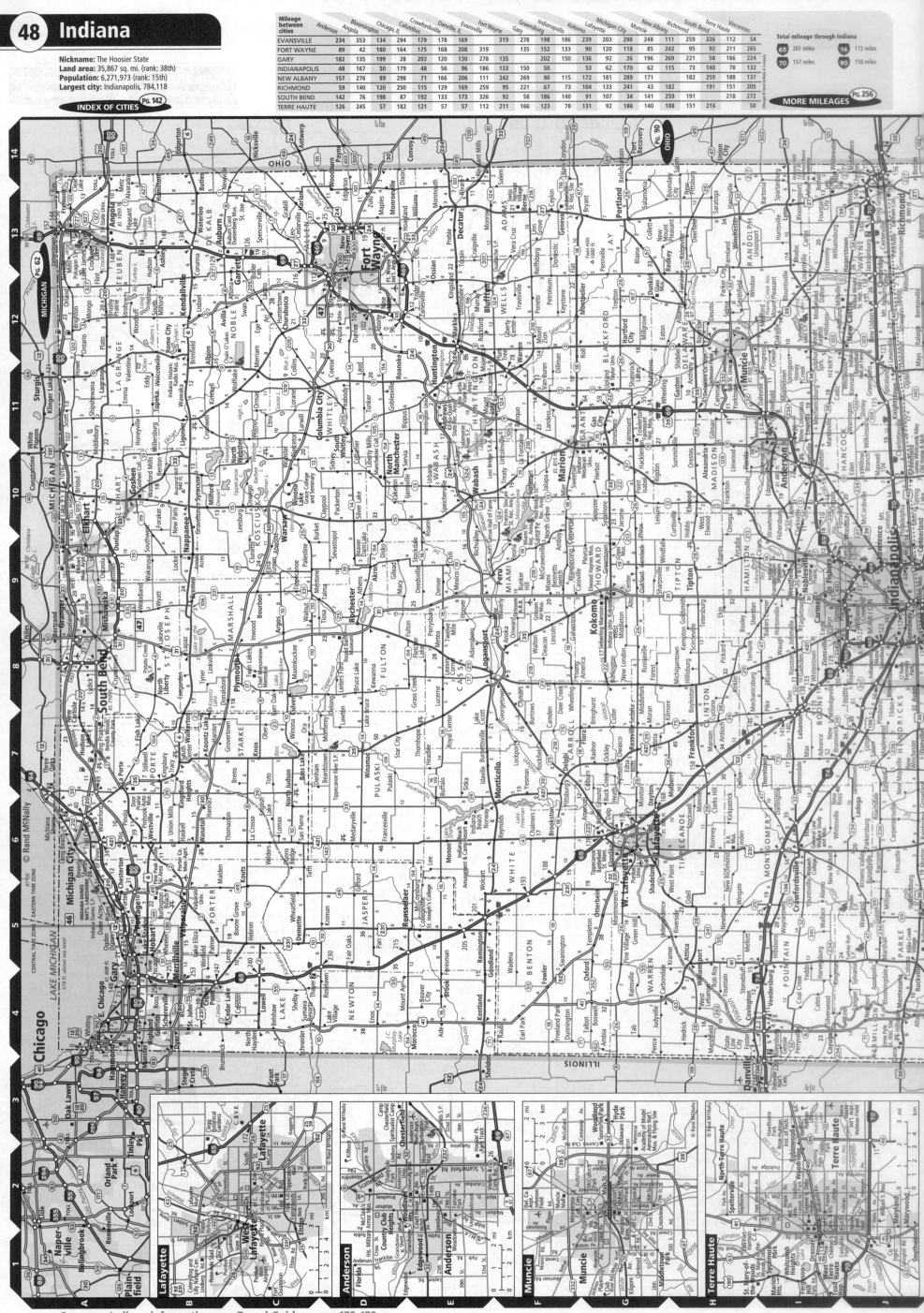

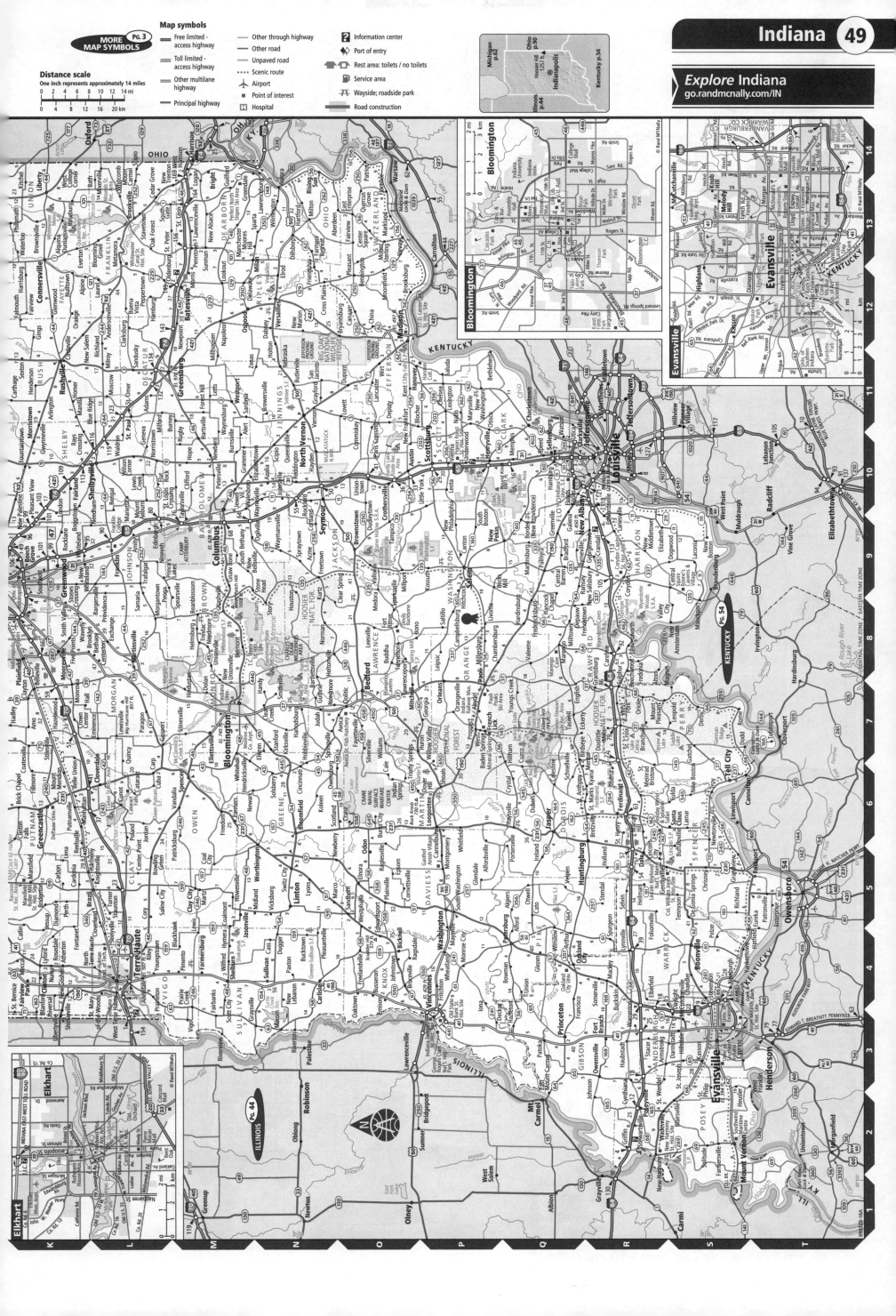

Nickname: The Hawkeye State
Land area: 55,869 sq. mi. (rank: 23rd)
Population: 2,966,334 (rank: 30th)
Largest city: Des Moines, 194,163

INDEX OF CITIES PG. 143

Mileage between cities	Ames	Burlington	Cedar Rapids	Council Bluffs	Davenport	Decorah	Des Moines	Dubuque	Fort Dodge	Iowa City	Keokuk	Mason City	Ottumwa	Sioux City	Sioux Falls, SD	Spirit Lake	Storm Lake	Waterloo
BURLINGTON	208		100	314	79	210	185	151	273	77	42	239	77	386	471	376	331	158
CEDAR RAPIDS	106	100		256	82	110	127	72	174	26	118	139	113	328	360	262	231	58
COUNCIL BLUFFS	162	314	256		296	337	127	329	158	240	332	250	217	95	180	186	128	237
DAVENPORT	190	79	82	296		175	167	70	255	57	121	221	129	368	453	358	313	140
DES MOINES	33	185	127	127	167	208		200	98	111	203	121	90	199	284	201	156	108
DUBUQUE	187	151	72	329	70	105	200		209	85	191	174	188	325	395	297	266	93
SIOUX CITY	176	386	328	95	368	309	199	325	123	312	404	213	289		85	110	75	230
WATERLOO	99	158	58	237	140	79	108	93	114	84	176	81	131	230	302	204	173	

Total mileage through Iowa
- 29: 155 miles
- 35: 218 miles
- 80: 303 miles
- 218: 257 miles

MORE MILEAGES PG. 256

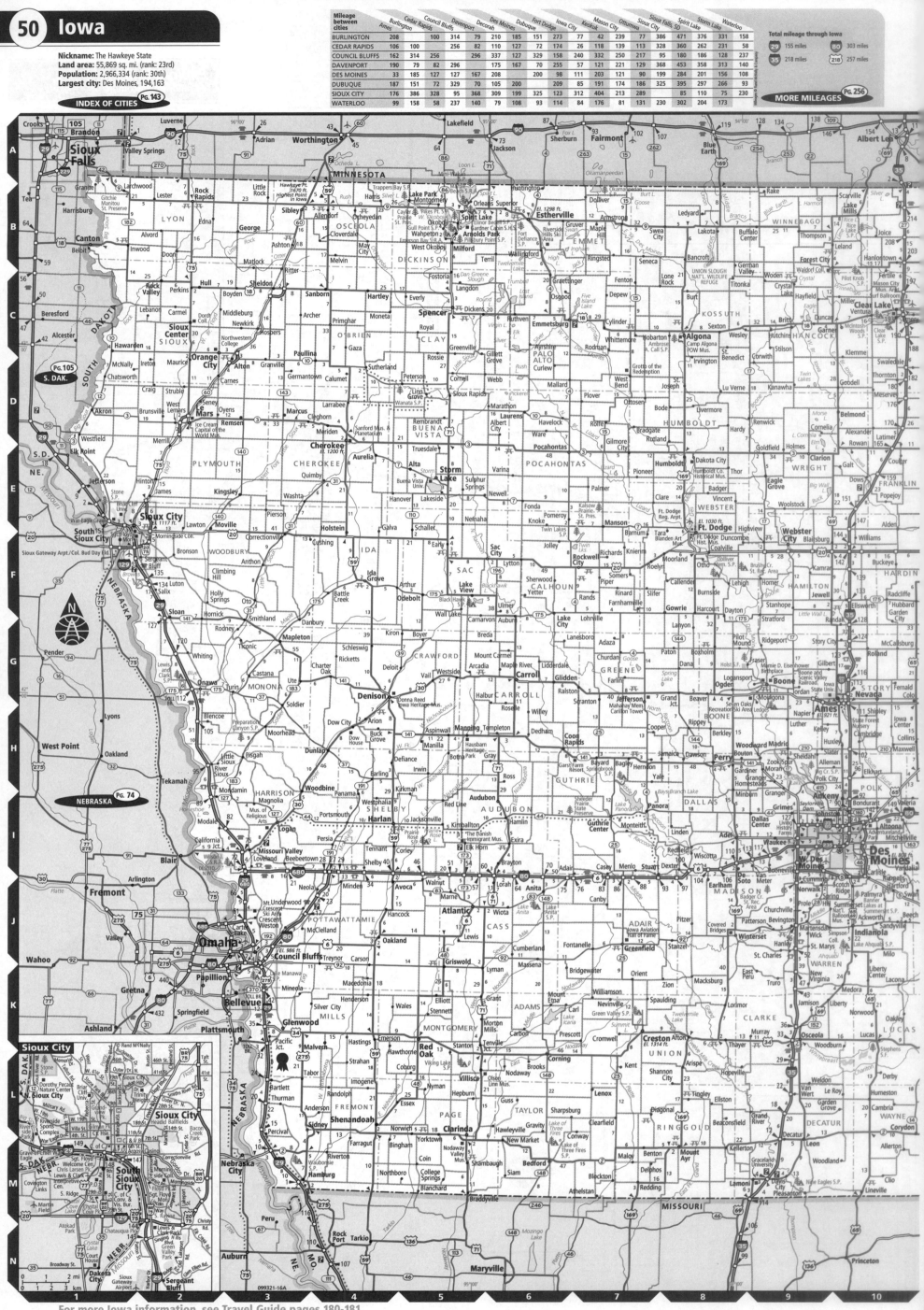

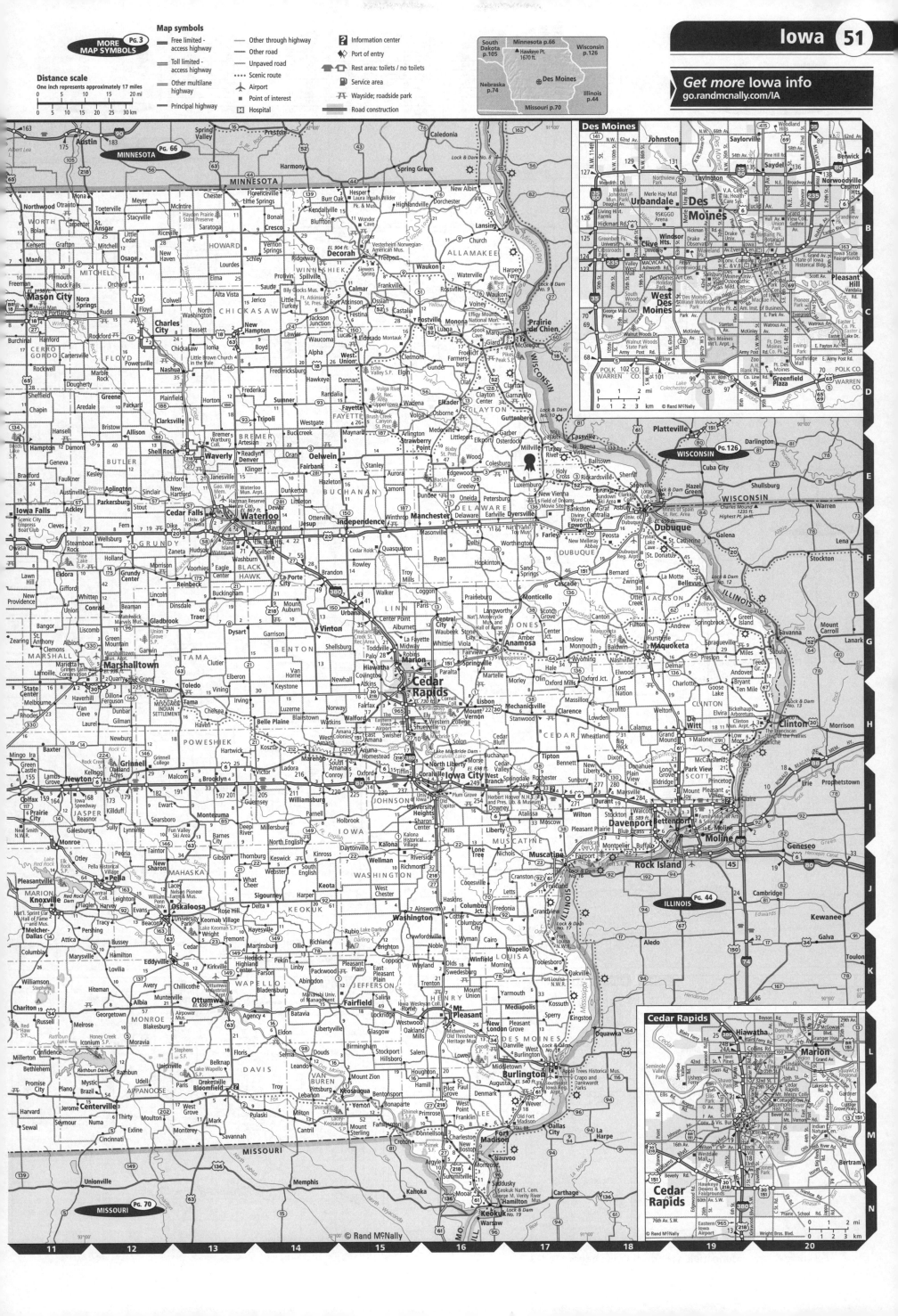

MORE MAP SYMBOLS PG. 3

Map symbols

Free limited - access highway
Toll limited - access highway
Other multilane highway
Principal highway
Other through highway
Other road
Unpaved road
Scenic route
Airport
Point of interest
Hospital

Information center
Port of entry
Rest area: toilets / no toilets
Service area
Wayside; roadside park
Road construction

Distance scale
One inch represents approximately 17 miles
0 5 10 15 20 mi
0 5 10 15 20 25 30 km

Des Moines

Cedar Rapids

© Rand McNally

Nickname: The Sunflower State
Land area: 81,815 sq. mi. (rank: 13th)
Population: 2,744,687 (rank: 33rd)
Largest city: Wichita, 354,865

INDEX OF CITIES   PG. 143

Mileage between cities	Arkansas City	Atchison	Coffeyville	Dodge City	Emporia	Fort Scott	Goodland	Great Bend	Hays	Hutchinson	Joplin, MO	Kansas City	Liberal	Manhattan	Oakley	Salina	Topeka	Wichita
DODGE CITY	211	328	300		239	306	193	86	104	125	338	83	231	134	166	277	154
GOODLAND	385	398	459	193	349	481		207	145	268	512	408	208	301	59	236	347	324
HUTCHINSON	120	235	194	125	109	205	268	63	127		247	212	192	138	211	73	184	59
JOPLIN, MO	157	196	68	345	175	34	512	307	371	247		148	434	251	455	280	193	191
KANSAS CITY	225	54	171	338	103	89	408	253	267	212	148		401	119	351	172	61	188
SALINA	153	162	227	166	117	245	236	81	95	73	280	172	226	619	175		111	92
TOPEKA	177	52	158	277	61	134	347	192	206	184	193	61	353	58	290	111		140
WICHITA	61	192	138	154	85	152	324	119	183	59	191	188	213	129	267	92	140	

Total mileage through Kansas
🛣35 235 miles   🛣56 464 miles
🛣70 424 miles   🛣81 220 miles

MORE MILEAGES   PG. 256

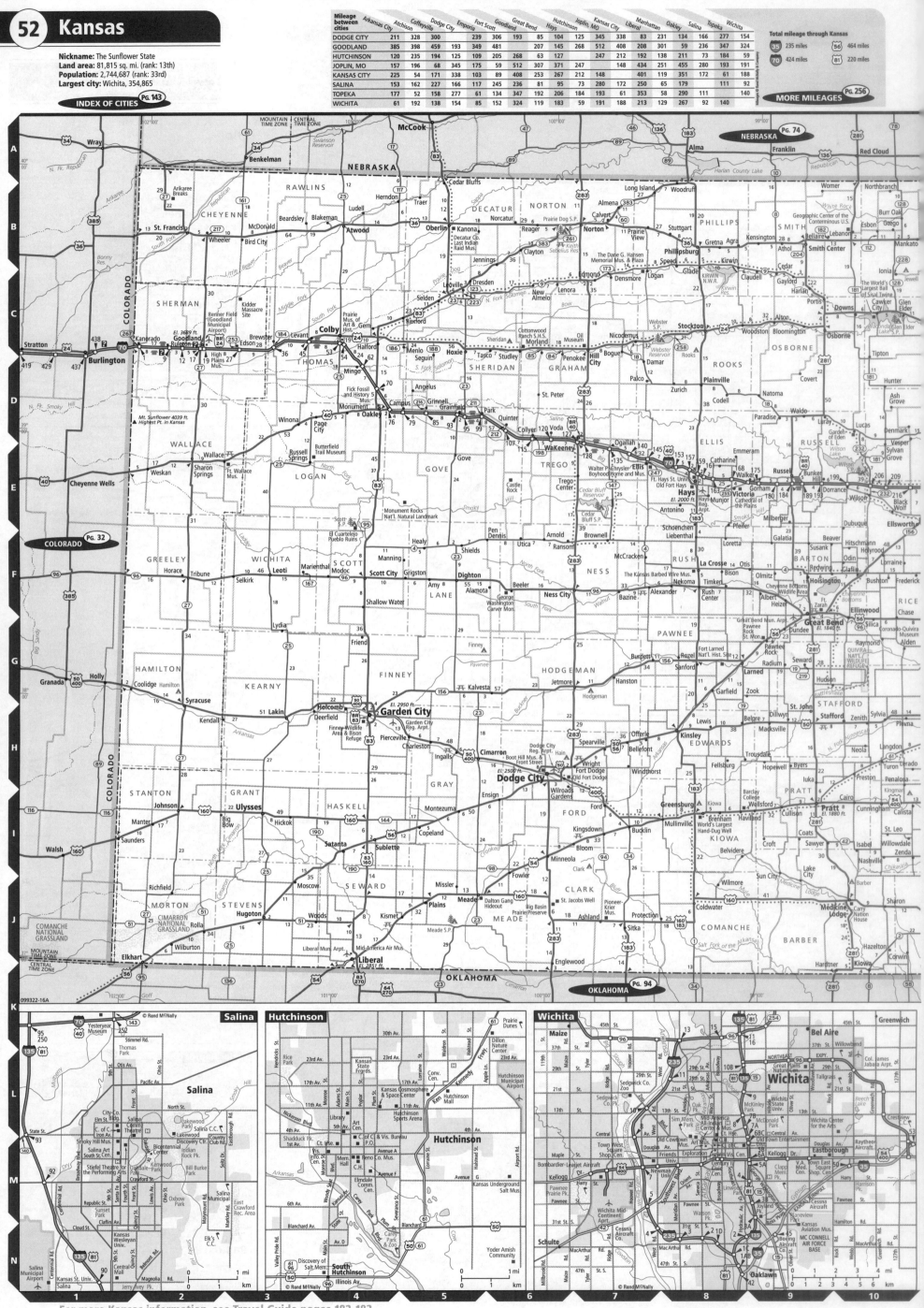

099322-16A

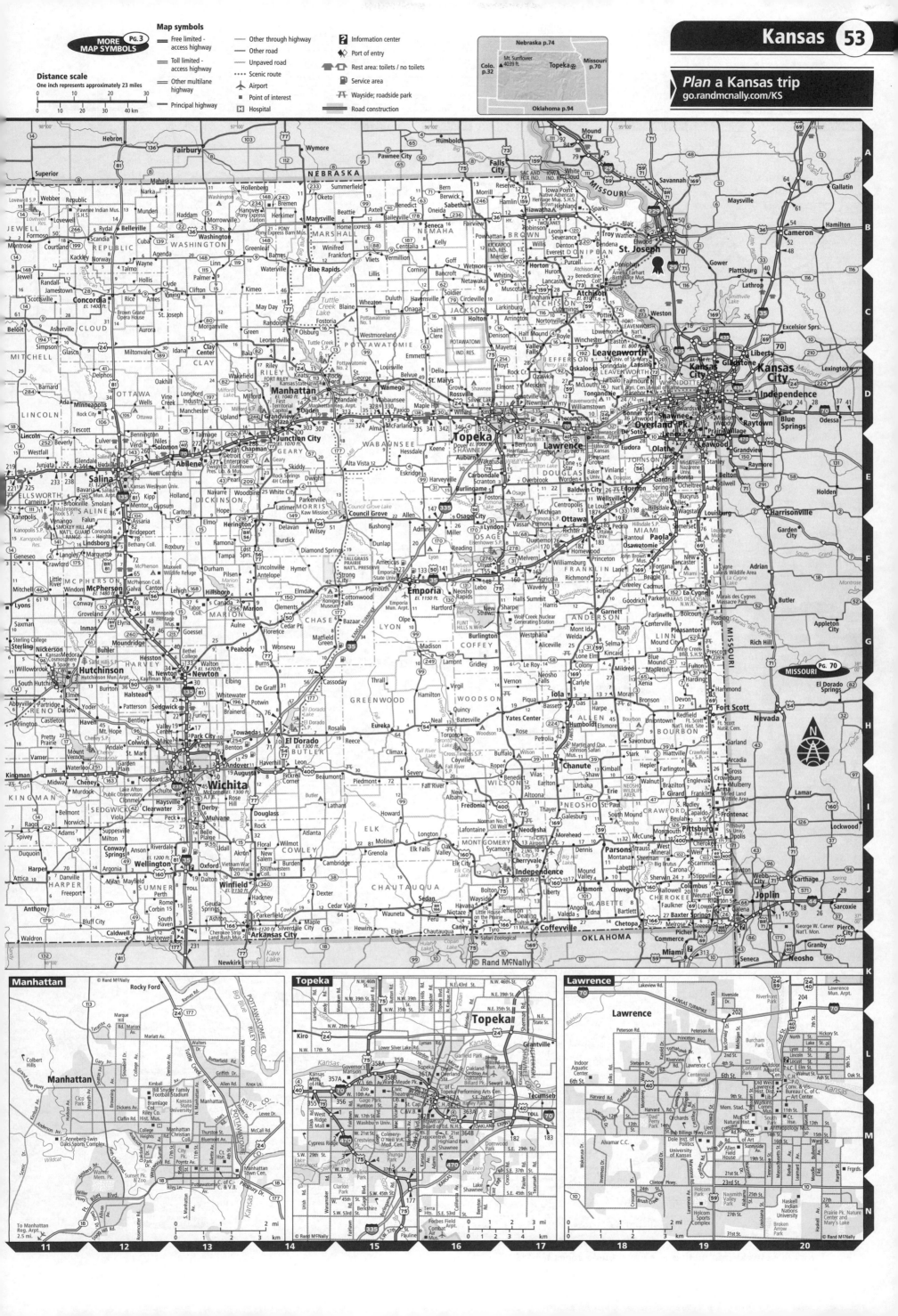

Plan a Kansas trip
go.randmcnally.com/KS

Nickname: The Bluegrass State
Land area: 39,728 sq. mi. (rank: 36th)
Population: 4,173,405 (rank: 26th)
Largest city: Louisville, 556,429

INDEX OF CITIES PG. 143

Mileage between cities	Ashland	Bardstown	Bowling Green	Cave City	Covington	Elizabethtown	Frankfort	Hopkinsville	Huntington, WV	Lexington	London	Louisville	Mayfield	Maysville	Owensboro	Paducah	Pikeville	Somerset
ASHLAND		183	278	250	135	209	146	334	18	123	176	197	394	80	303	385	100	179
BOWLING GREEN	278	95		30	218	71	145	63	282	155	145	116	162	227	71	153	263	111
COVINGTON	135	137	218	190		147	89	274	139	82	154	102	334	53	208	325	218	157
HOPKINSVILLE	334	151	63	97	274	127	201		338	211	212	172	85	283	99	76	353	178
LEXINGTON	123	60	155	127	82	86	23	211	127		78	74	271	66	180	262	142	81
LOUISVILLE	197	40	116	88	102	45	52	172	201	74	172		232	135	106	223	216	134
OWENSBORO	303	120	71	108	208	96	170	99	307	180	223	106	159	252		150	322	189
PADUCAH	385	202	153	190	325	178	252	76	389	262	76	223	24	334	150		404	271

Total mileage through Kentucky
| 54 | 185 miles | 71 | 97 miles |
| 65 | 137 miles | 75 | 192 miles |

MORE MILEAGES PG. 256

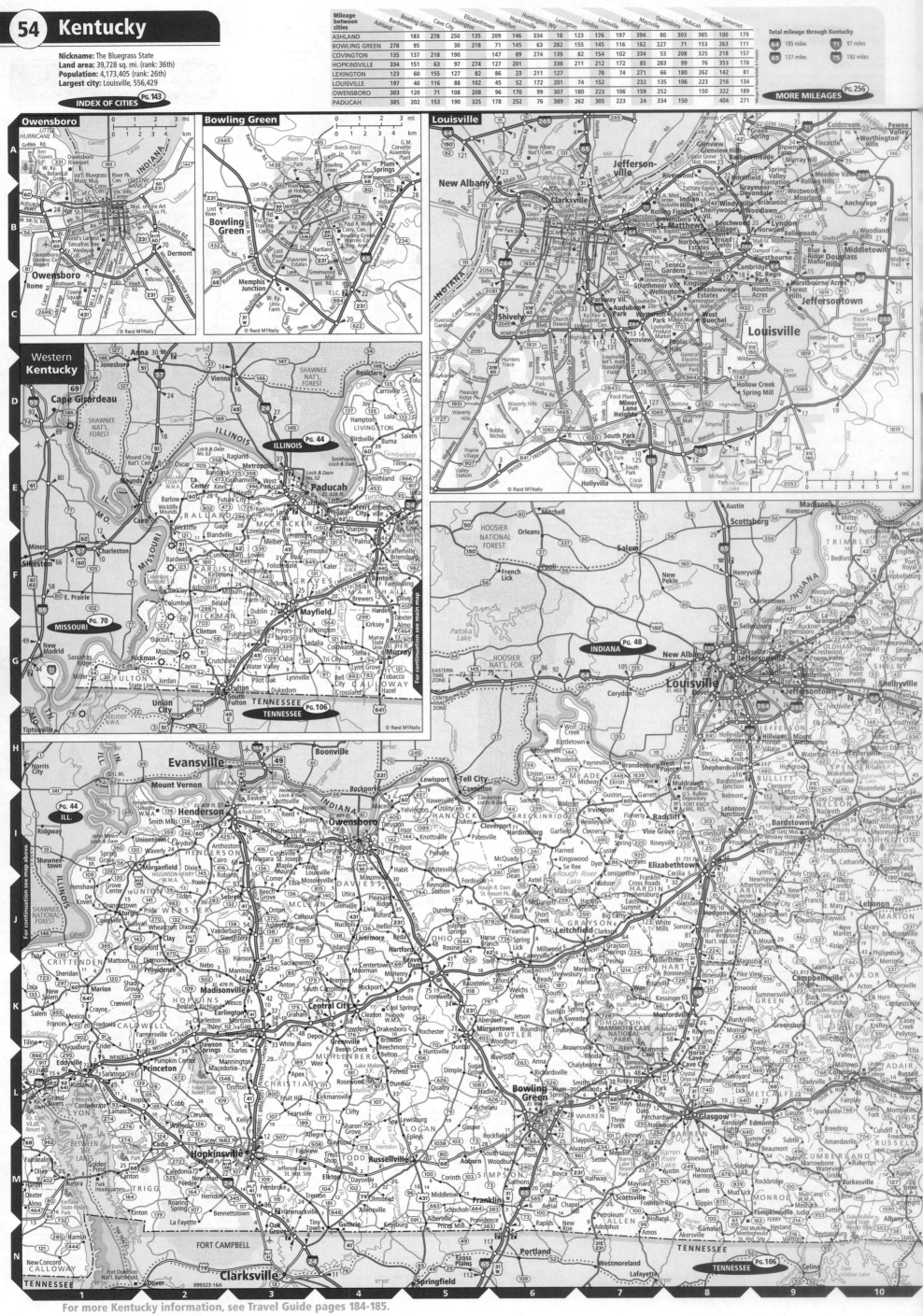

For more Kentucky information, see Travel Guide pages 184-185.

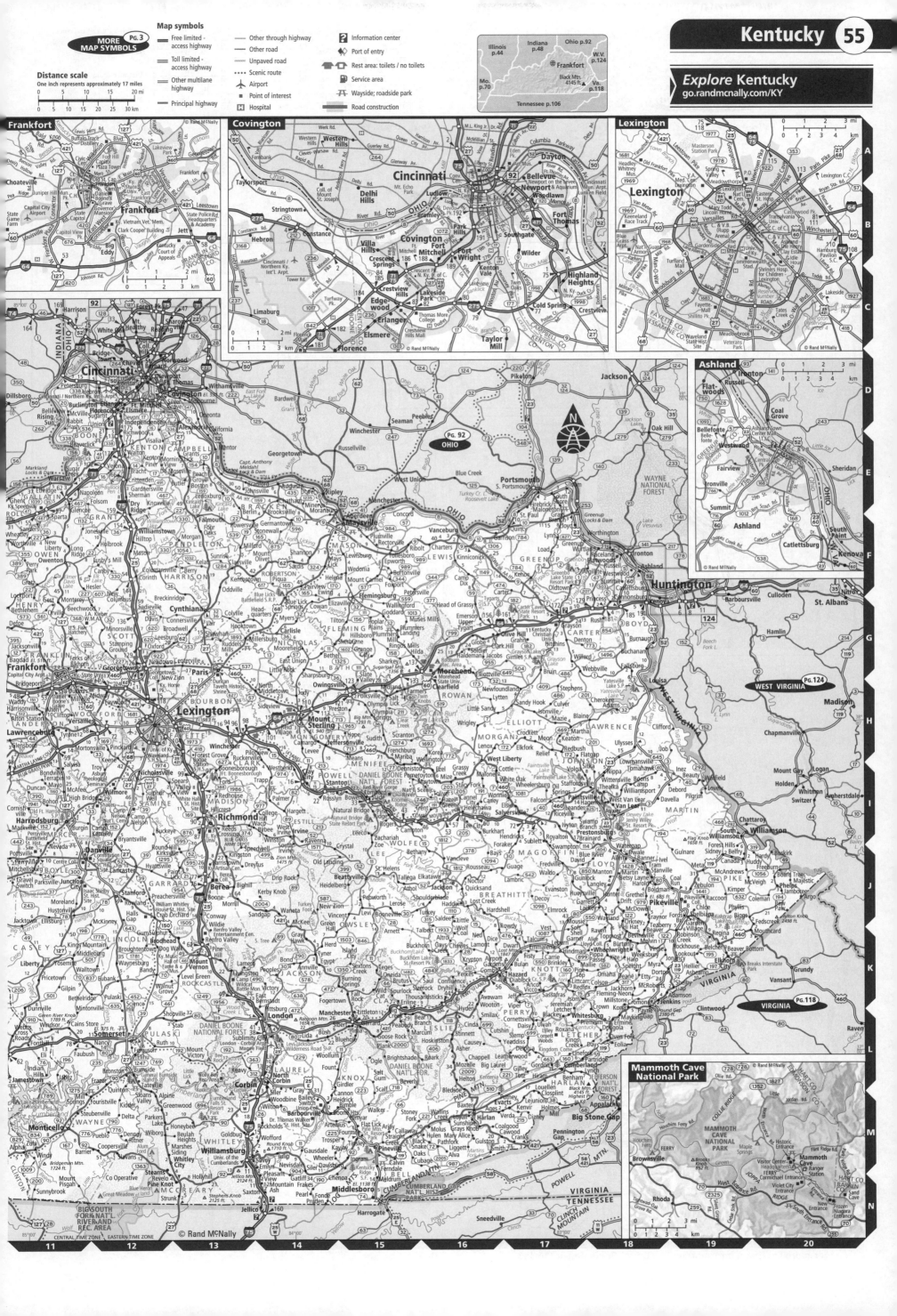

Get travel info
go.randmcnally.com/LA

Nickname: The Pelican State
Land area: 43,562 sq. mi. (rank: 33rd)
Population: 4,523,628 (rank: 24th)
Largest city: New Orleans, 454,863

INDEX OF CITIES **PG. 143**

Mileage between cities	Baton Rouge	Beaumont, TX	Bogalusa	De Ridder	El Dorado, AR	Gulfport, MS	Houma	Natchitoches	New Iberia	New Orleans	Shreveport	Tallulah	Vicksburg, MS
ALEXANDRIA	144	160	243	72	147	65	277	204	60	115	223	126	139	156
BATON ROUGE		184	99	168	253	100	133	87	202	67	79	258	162	159
GULFPORT, MS	133	317	68	301	346	223		131	335	200	76	401	225	204
LAKE CHARLES	54	134	153	118	241	131	187	110	152	71	133	218	193	213
LAFAYETTE	126	58	225	48	249	165	259	186	123	97	205	182	239	256
NEW ORLEANS	79	263	69	247	367	186	76	58	281	146		347	246	225
SHREVEPORT	268	195	357	134	95	188	401	328	76	239	347		160	177
VICKSBURG, MS	159	314	180	226	142	79	204	255	171	226	225	177	21	

Total mileage through Louisiana

10	274 miles
20	190 miles
49	208 miles
55	66 miles

Distance scale
One inch represents approximately 29 mi
0 10 20 30 40 km

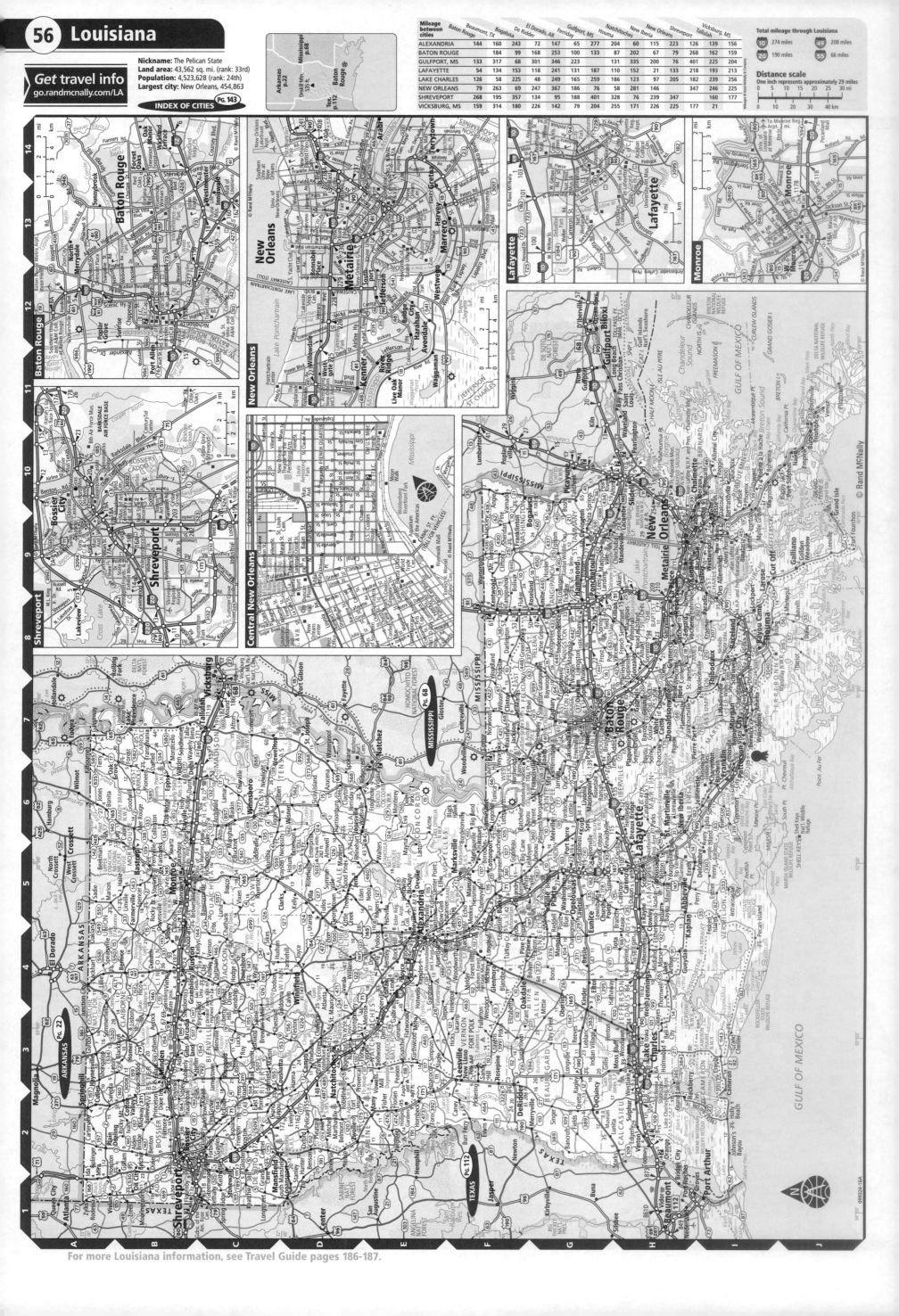

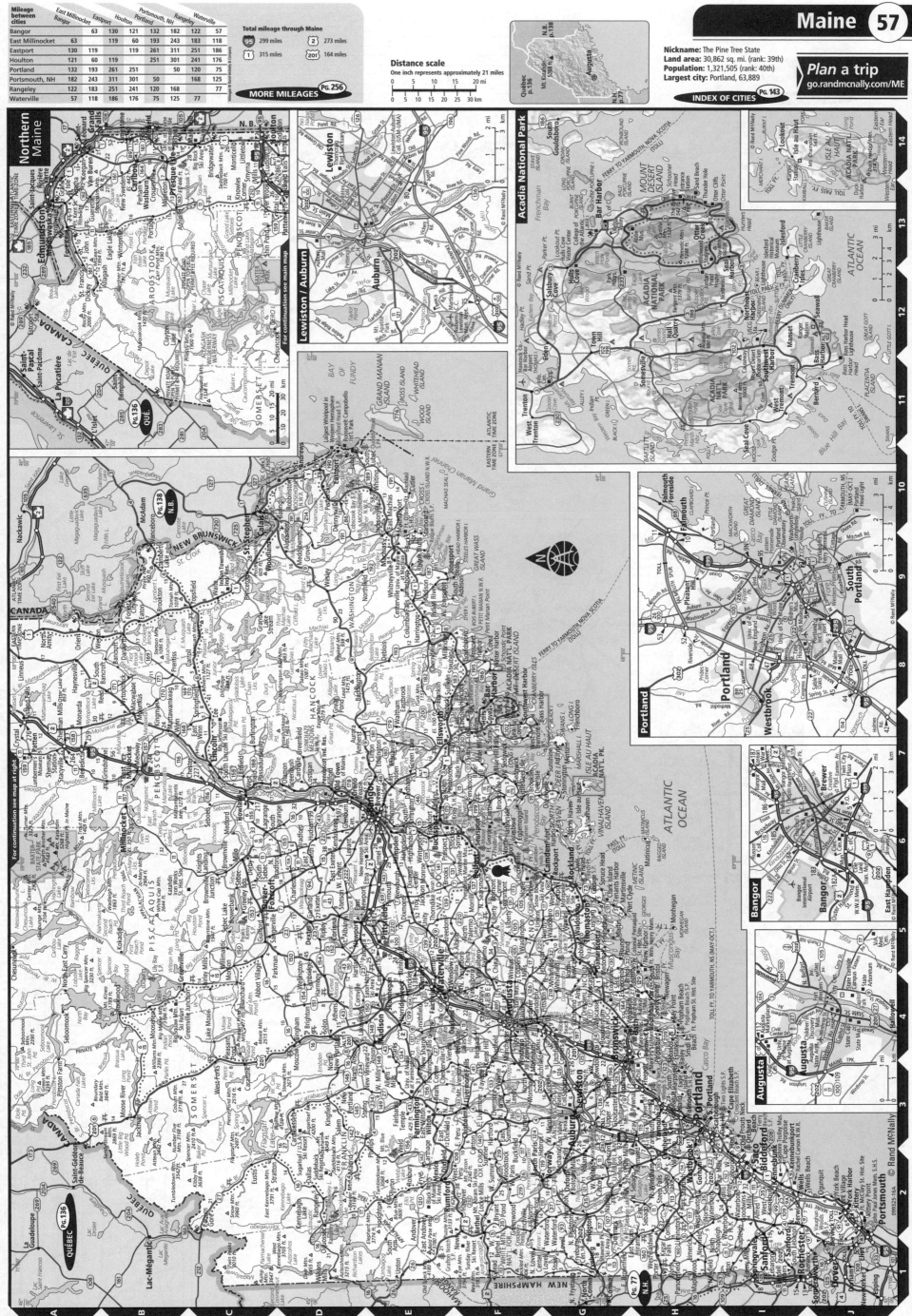

Mileage between cities	Bangor	East Millinocket	Eastport	Houlton	Portland	Portsmouth, NH	Rangeley	Waterville
Bangor		63	130	121	132	182	122	57
East Millinocket	63		119	60	193	243	183	118
Eastport	130	119		119	261	311	251	186
Houlton	121	60	119		251	301	241	176
Portland	132	193	261	251		50	120	75
Portsmouth, NH	182	243	311	301	50		168	125
Rangeley	122	183	251	241	120	168		77
Waterville	57	118	186	176	75	125	77	

Total mileage through Maine
95 — 299 miles   2 — 273 miles
1 — 315 miles   201 — 164 miles

MORE MILEAGES Pg. 256

Distance scale
One inch represents approximately 21 miles

Nickname: The Pine Tree State
Land area: 30,862 sq. mi. (rank: 39th)
Population: 1,321,505 (rank: 40th)
Largest city: Portland, 63,889

Plan a trip
go.randmcnally.com/ME

INDEX OF CITIES Pg. 143

For more Maine information, see Travel Guide pages 188-189.

Nickname: The Old Line State
Land area: 9,774 sq. mi. (rank: 42nd)
Population: 5,600,388 (rank: 19th)
Largest city: Baltimore, 635,815

INDEX OF CITIES Pg. 143

Mileage between cities	Aberdeen	Annapolis	Baltimore	Cambridge	Chestertown	Cumberland	Edgewood	Frederick	Harrisburg, PA	Lexington Park	Ocean City	Pocomoke City	Rockville	St. Charles	Salisbury	Washington, DC	Wilmington, DE
ABERDEEN		56	30	113	65	175	11	83	107	107	113	134	149	73	86	121	64	41
ANNAPOLIS	56		28	58	48	163	48	71	95	122	72	111	115	39	43	89	28	95
BALTIMORE	30	28		85	75	142	22	50	74	88	85	138	142	43	60	116	38	69
CUMBERLAND	175	163	142	220	210		167	93	70	143	210	273	277	121	176	251	143	214
HAGERSTOWN	107	95	74	152	142	70	99	25		75	142	205	209	53	108	183	75	146
LEXINGTON PARK	113	72	85	129	119	210	105	118	142	179		182	186	86	42	160	67	152
SALISBURY	121	89	116	33	85	251	141	159	183	212	160	29	26	127	131		116	105
WASHINGTON, DC	64	28	38	85	75	143	56	51	75	126	67	139	142	22	33	116		103

Total mileage through Maryland

68	81 miles	81	12 miles
70	94 miles	95	110 miles

MORE MILEAGES Pg. 256

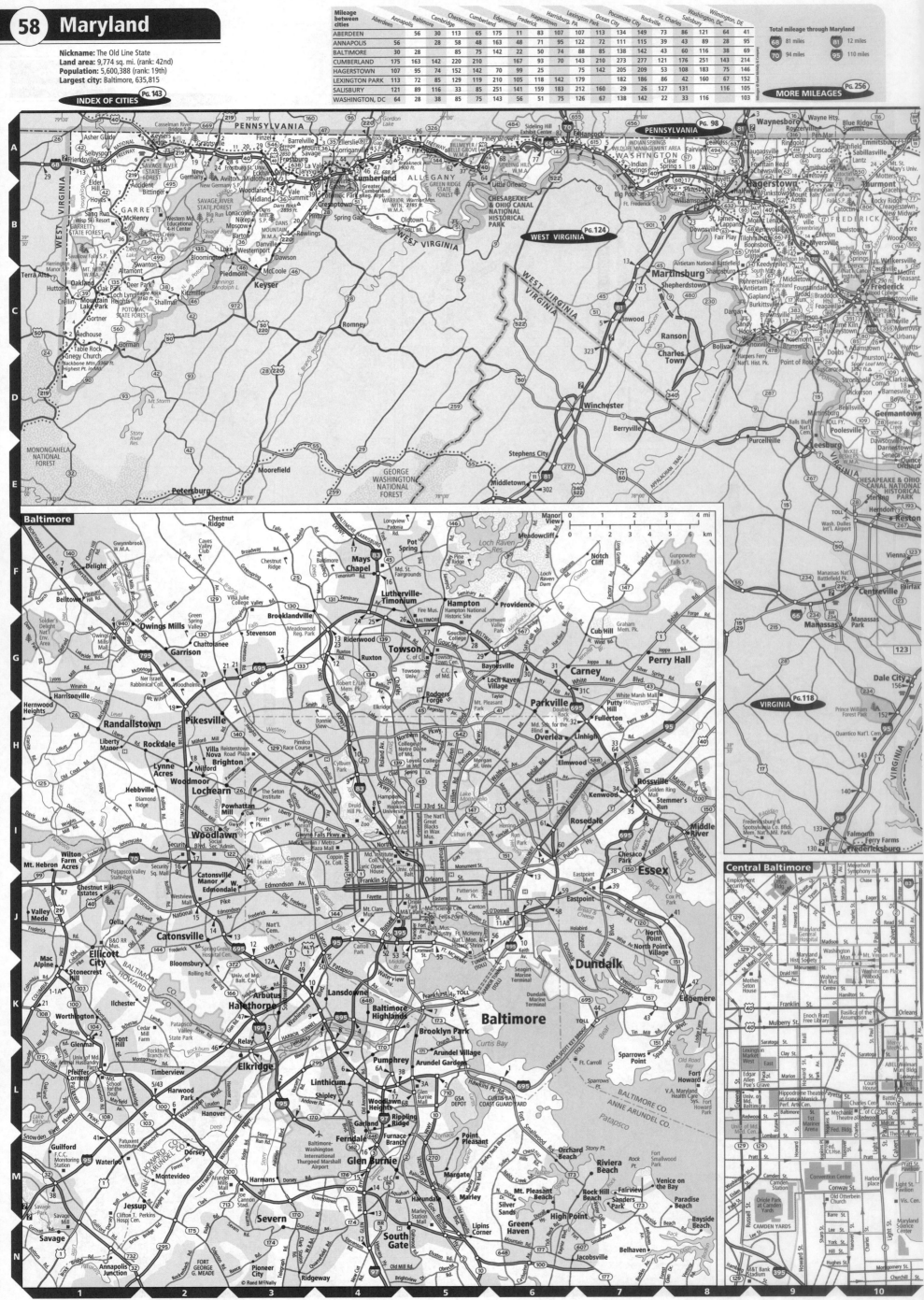

For more Maryland information, see Travel Guide pages 190-191.

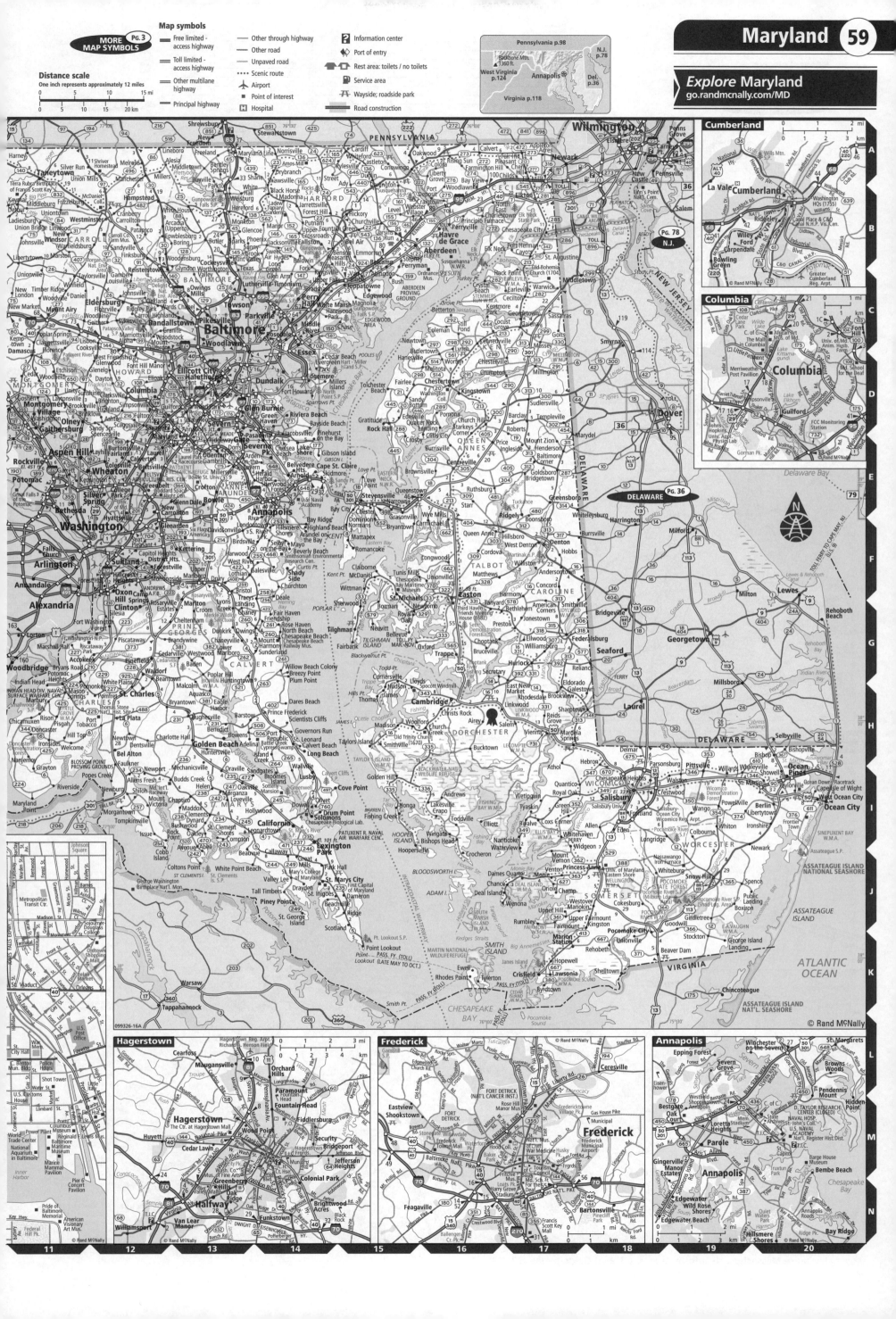

Explore Maryland
go.randmcnally.com/MD

Nickname: The Bay State
Land area: 7,840 sq. mi. (rank: 45th)
Population: 6,398,743 (rank: 13th)
Largest city: Boston, 559,034

INDEX OF CITIES PG. 143

Mileage between cities	Albany, NY	Boston	Brockton	Falmouth	Fitchburg	Gloucester	Greenfield	Hartford, CT	New Bedford	North Adams	Northampton	Pittsfield	Plymouth	Providence, RI	Provincetown	Springfield	Worcester
BOSTON	166		24	71	51	43	99	102	32	58	163	102	134	40	50	117	90	48
GLOUCESTER	201	43	67	114	77		125	137	49	101	164	137	169	83	93	160	125	85
LOWELL	168	32	51	104	33	49	81	104		85	120	104	136	72	71	149	92	41
NEW BEDFORD	199	58	37	40	93	101	154	119	85		196	135	167	45	32	92	123	84
PLYMOUTH	197	40	24	35	89	83	137	133	72	45	194	133	165		53	81	121	82
SPRINGFIELD	83	90	105	142	78	125	38	26	92	123	80	19	51	121	87		194	51
WORCESTER	127	48	63	103	27	85	82	63	41	84	124	63	95	82	43	155	51	

Total mileage through Massachusetts			
90	136 miles	**93**	47 miles
91	55 miles	**95**	92 miles

MORE MILEAGES PG. 256

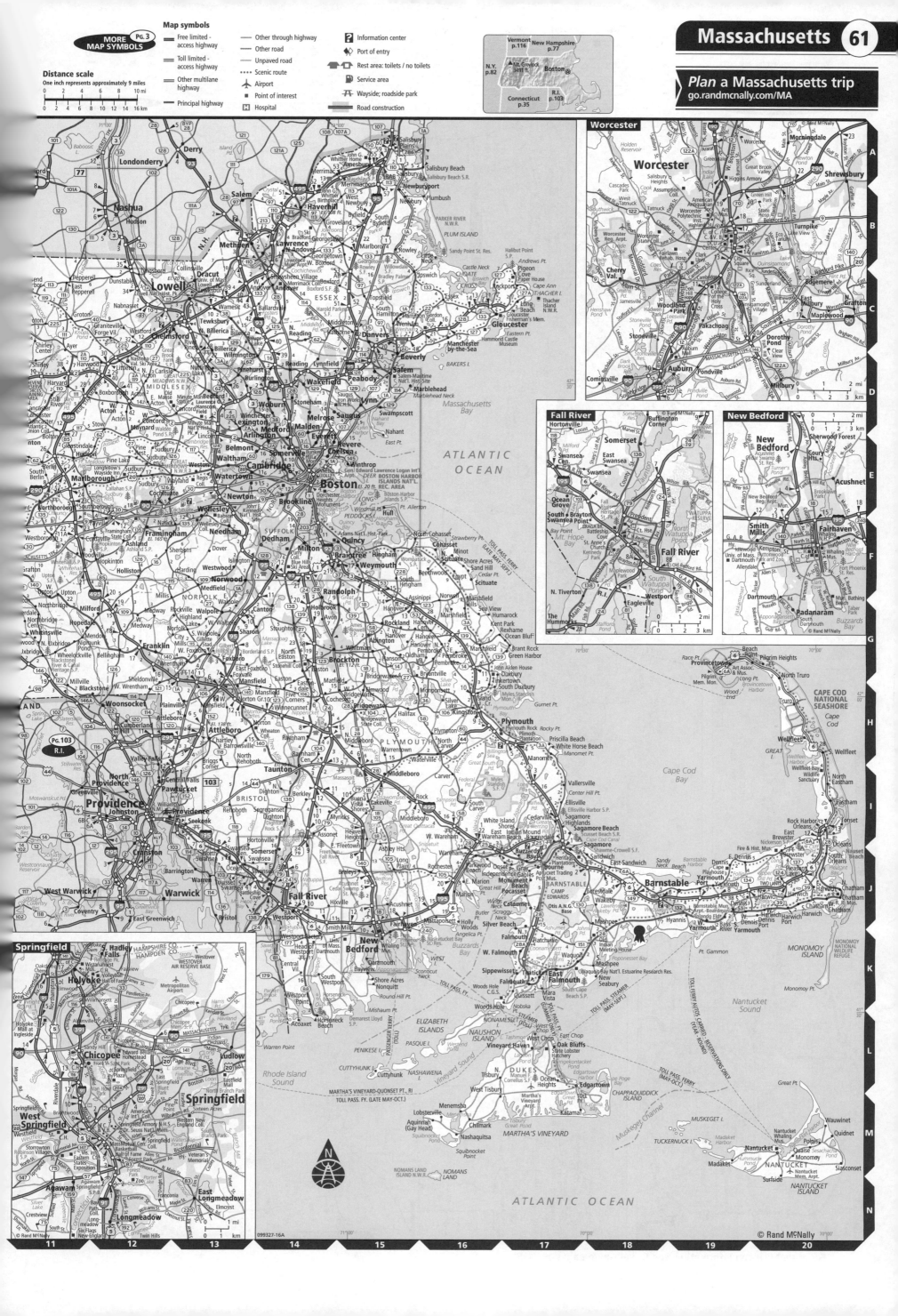

Plan a Massachusetts trip
go.randmcnally.com/MA

Nickname: The Wolverine State
Land area: 56,804 sq. mi. (rank: 22nd)
Population: 10,120,860 (rank: 8th)
Largest city: Detroit, 886,671

INDEX OF CITIES Pg. 144

Mileage between cities	Alpena	Ann Arbor	Benton Harbor	Chicago, IL	Detroit	Flint	Grand Rapids	Houghton	Ironwood	Jackson	Kalamazoo	Lansing	Mackinaw City	Menominee	Muskegon	Pontiac	Port Huron	Sault Ste. Marie	Toledo, OH	Traverse City
ANN ARBOR	231		145	236	41	53	131	547	591	35	92	63	175	479	167	46	98	87	334	54	239
CHICAGO, IL	425	236	94		278	269	175	418	408	204	140	215	394	266	183	283	339	303	450	239	315
DETROIT	245	41	187	278		64	156	561	605	77	139	88	292	493	192	31	60	101	348	62	253
FLINT	182	53	178	269	64		114	498	542	89	130	54	229	430	150	32	70	38	285	108	190
GRAND RAPIDS	250	131	81	175	156	114		488	592	107	51	68	219	243	39	143	184	114	275	186	140
KALAMAZOO	300	97	49	140	139	130	51	539	557	65		76	270	415	90	144	200	164	326	151	191
LANSING	232	63	124	215	88	54	68	495	539	39	76		226	427	104	71	124	88	282	118	178
MACKINAW CITY	94	278	300	394	292	229	219	269	313	261	270	226		201	234	260	299	192	56	333	106

MORE MILEAGES Pg. 256

Total mileage through Michigan
- 69: 199 miles
- 75: 396 miles
- 94: 275 miles
- 96: 192 miles

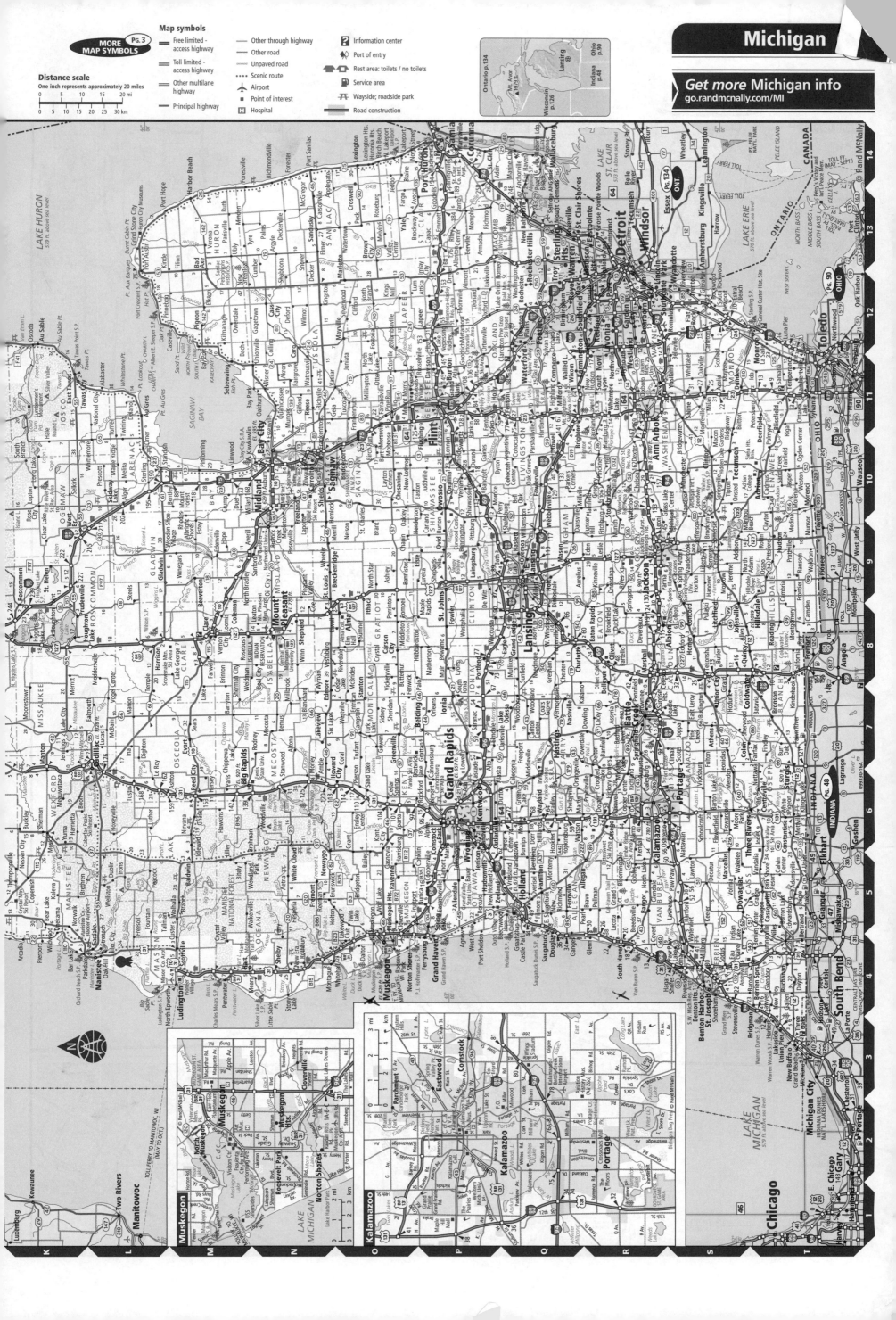

Plan a trip
go.randmcnally.com/MI

INDEX OF CITIES PG. 144

Grand
Rapids
Flint
Detroit
Ann Arbor

Grand Rapids

Three Mile Rd.

Blandford
Nature Center

Comstock Riverside

Michigan Vet. Facility

Cornerstone University

Frederik Meijer Gardens

Walker

O'Brien St.

Grand Rapids

Kendall Coll. of Art & Design

Van Andel Arena

DeVos Pl.
Highland Park

H.C. of C.

Calvin Theo. Sem.

Aquinas Coll.

East Grand Rapids

Calvin Coll.

Gerald R. Ford Int'l. Airport

Forest Hills

Ada

Cascade

Indian Trails

Woodland Shop. Cen.

Grandville

Wyoming

Kentwood

Maple Hill
The Pines

Battle

Cutlerville

Dutton

Alaska

© Rand McNally

Ann Arbor

Barton Hills

Dhu Varren

Dixboro

Leslie

Univ. of Mich. Glazier

Gerald R. Ford Pres. Lib.

U. of M. Botanical Gardens

Amtrak Sta.
Conv. & Vis. Bur.

Huron St.

Univ. of Mich.

Gallup

V.A. Med. Cen.

Concordia Univ.

Radrick Farms

Burns Park

Huron Hills

Scio Church Rd.

Michigan Stad. & Crisler Arena

Univ. of Mich.

Eisenhower Pkwy.

Buhr Pk.

Arboretum

Ann Arbor

Briarwood Mall

Waters Rd.

Lake Forest

Ellsworth Rd.

Stonebridge

Ann Arbor - Saline

Morgan Rd.

Pittsfield

© Rand McNally

Flint

Coldwater Rd.

Beecher

Hasselbring

Stepping Stone Falls

Carpenter Rd.

Kelly Rd.

Flushing

Pierson Rd.

Davenport University

Flushing Valley

Winter Green

Potter

Flint

Univ. of Mich.-Flint

Kettering Univ.

C. of C. & V.B.

For-Mar Nature Preserve

Bassett Park

Corunna Rd.

Genesee Valley Shop. Cen.

Burton

Bishop Int'l. Airport

Swartz Creek

Hill Rd.

Grand Blanc

© Rand McNally

Detroit & Vicinity

Rose Center

Davisburg

Andersonville Rd.

Pine Knob Ski Resort

Voorheis Lake

Bald Mtn. St. Rec. Area

Stony Creek Metropark

Ray Center

New Haven

Clarkston

White Lake

Indian Springs Metropark

Lake Oakland

Waterford

Drayton Plains

Oakland Co. Int'l. Arpt.

Palace of Auburn Hills

Great Lakes Crossing Shop. Cen.

Rochester Hills

Goodison

Washington

Davis

Chesterfield

Clyde

Duck Lake

Alpine Valley Ski Area

Pontiac

Oakland Univ.

Auburn Hills

Rochester

Cherry Creek

Disco

Macomb

Meade

New Baltimore

Highland

Highland State Rec. Area

Oxbow Lake

White Lakes Oak

Summit Place Mall

Pontiac Silverdome

Walter P. Chrysler Mus.

Rochester Coll.

Rochester-Utica State Rec. Area

Utica

Shelby

Waldenburg

Bellow Woods

Selfridge Air Nat'l. Guard Base

Anchor Bay

Brentwood

Union Lake

Dodge No. 4 St. Pk.

Cass L.

Sylvan Lake

Keego Harbor

Bloomfield Hills

Sterling Hts.

Clinton

Mt. Clemens

Harrison

Milford

Proud Lake St. Rec. Area

Wolverine

Upper Straits L.

Orchard Lake

Cranbrook Institute of Science & Art Mus.

Troy

Troy Sports Center

Central Macomb C.

Metropolitan Pkwy.

Metro Beach Metropark

Kensington Metropark

Commerce

Lower Str. L.

W. Bloomfield

Knollwood

Bloomfield

The Somerset Collection

Oakland Mall

G.M. Tech. Cen.

Fraser

Wolverine Lake

Walled Lake

Franklin Hills C.C.

Birmingham

Clawson

Macomb Mall

Warren

St. Clair Shores

Wixom

Lyon Oaks

New Hudson

Lakeshore Pk.

Twelve Oaks Mall

Glen Oaks

Franklin

Beverly Hills

Holocaust Mem. Cen.

Bingham Farms

Madison Hts.

C. of C.

Roseville

St. Clair Shores

Metro East

Edsel & Eleanor Ford House

Reuther Heritage Mus.

Lathrup Village

P.O.

Berkley

Detroit Zoological

Royal Oak

Hazel Park Raceway

Center Line

Metro Beach

Novi

Rock Financial Showplace

Farmington Hills

C. of C.

Twelve Mile

Huntington Woods

Pleasant Ridge

Hazel Pk.

Eastpointe

Northville

Northville Downs

Farmington

Lawrence Tech. Univ.

Oak Park

Northland Shop. Cen.

Ferndale

State Frgrds.

Grosse Pointe Woods

Harper Woods

Grosse Pointe Shores

Maybury S.P.

7 Mile Rd.

Laurel Park Place Mall

Southfield

Marygrove Coll.

Univ. of Detroit Mercy

McNichols Rd.

Eastland Cen.

Grosse Pointe Farms

Salem

Livonia

Livonia Mall

Redford

Highland Park

Coleman A. Young Muni. Arpt.

Grosse Pte.

U. S. CANADA

Plymouth

Madonna Univ.

C. of C.H.

River Rouge Park

Detroit

Motown Hist. Mus.

Wayne St. Univ.

The New Detroit Science Center

Grosse Pointe Park

BELLE ISLE

PECHE ISLAND

Westland

Garden City

Dearborn Hts.

Univ. of Mich.-Dearborn

Arab American Mus.

Motor City Casino Field

Comerica Park

Canton

Inkster

Henry Ford Mus.

Dearborn

Greenfield Village

The Henry Ford

Fairlane Town Cen.

Univ. of Windsor

Windsor

Tecumseh

Elmstead

Ypsilanti

Eastern Michigan Univ.

C. of C.

Denton

Wayne

Willow Run Airport

Yankee Air Force Mus.

Romulus

Taylor Meadows

Goddard

Melvindale

River Rouge

Allen Park

Lincoln Park

Ecorse

FIGHTING ISLAND

La Salle

Windsor Raceway & Slots

MAC DONALD-CARTIER FRWY.

Belleville

Taylor

Southland Shop. Cen.

Wyandotte

Southgate

ONTARIO MICHIGAN

Seven Lakes

Willis

New Boston

Detroit Metro. Wayne Co. Airport

Lower Huron Metropark

Riverview

Whittaker

Brownstown

Trenton

Woodhaven

Grosse Ile

Grosse Ile Mun. Arpt.

Amherstburg

Fort Malden Nat'l. Hist. Park

GROSSE ILE

Waltz

Flat Rock

Gibraltar

Lake Erie Metropark

WAYNE CO.
MONROE CO.

Oakville-Waltz Rd.

Carleton

Central Detroit

Fox Theatre

Comerica Park

Greektown Casino

MGM Grand Casino

Greyhound Bus Terminal

Joe Louis Arena

Terminal for Detroit-Windsor Tunnel

© Rand McNally

090211-7A

Map symbols

Free limited - access highway	Other through highway	Information center	
Toll limited - access highway	Other road	Port of entry	
Other multilane highway	Unpaved road	Rest area: toilets / no toilets	
	Scenic route	Service area	
	Airport	Wayside; roadside park	
Principal highway	Point of interest	Road construction	
	Hospital		

I-35W between 3rd St. and 4th St. S.E. exits in Minneapolis is closed for bridge reconstruction until further notice.

Get travel info go.randmcnally.com/MN

INDEX OF CITIES Pg. 144

Minneapolis / St. Paul & Vicinity

Central Minneapolis

Central St. Paul

Nickname: The North Star State
Land area: 79,610 sq. mi. (rank: 14th)
Population: 5,132,799 (rank: 21st)
Largest city: Minneapolis, 372,811

INDEX OF CITIES Pg. 144

Mileage between cities	Albert Lea	Austin	Bemidji	Brainerd	Duluth	Fairmont	Fergus Falls	Grand Forks, ND	Hibbing	International Falls	La Crosse, WI	Mankato	Marshall	Minneapolis	Moorhead	Red Wing	Rochester	St. Cloud	Sioux Falls, SD	Willmar
BEMIDJI	315	319		99	153	296	141	113	108	116	389	272	261	222	142	280	315	150	231	384	194
DULUTH	251	255	153	114		306	211	264	76	164	239	237	276	157	254	198	235	143	151	423	209
MINNEAPOLIS	97	101	222	133	157	152	184	318	196	299	164	80	155		237	60	94	72	10	269	96
MOORHEAD	330	334	142	140	254	357	55	80	216	256	400	283	202	237		295	330	173	246	244	174
ROCHESTER	64	39	315	226	235	119	277	411	274	377	72	82	193	94	330	49		165	84	236	186
ST. CLOUD	165	169	150	61	143	146	120	254	178	250	235	122	133	72	173	130	165		81	221	66
ST. PAUL	100	104	231	142	151	155	193	327	190	293	154	86	161	10	246	50	84	81		272	106
SIOUX FALLS, SD	175	197	384	274	423	121	236	318	462	498	297	155	90	269	244	283	236	221	272		156

Total mileage through Minnesota
- 35 260 miles
- 94 260 miles
- 90 276 miles
- 2 255 miles

MORE MILEAGES Pg. 256

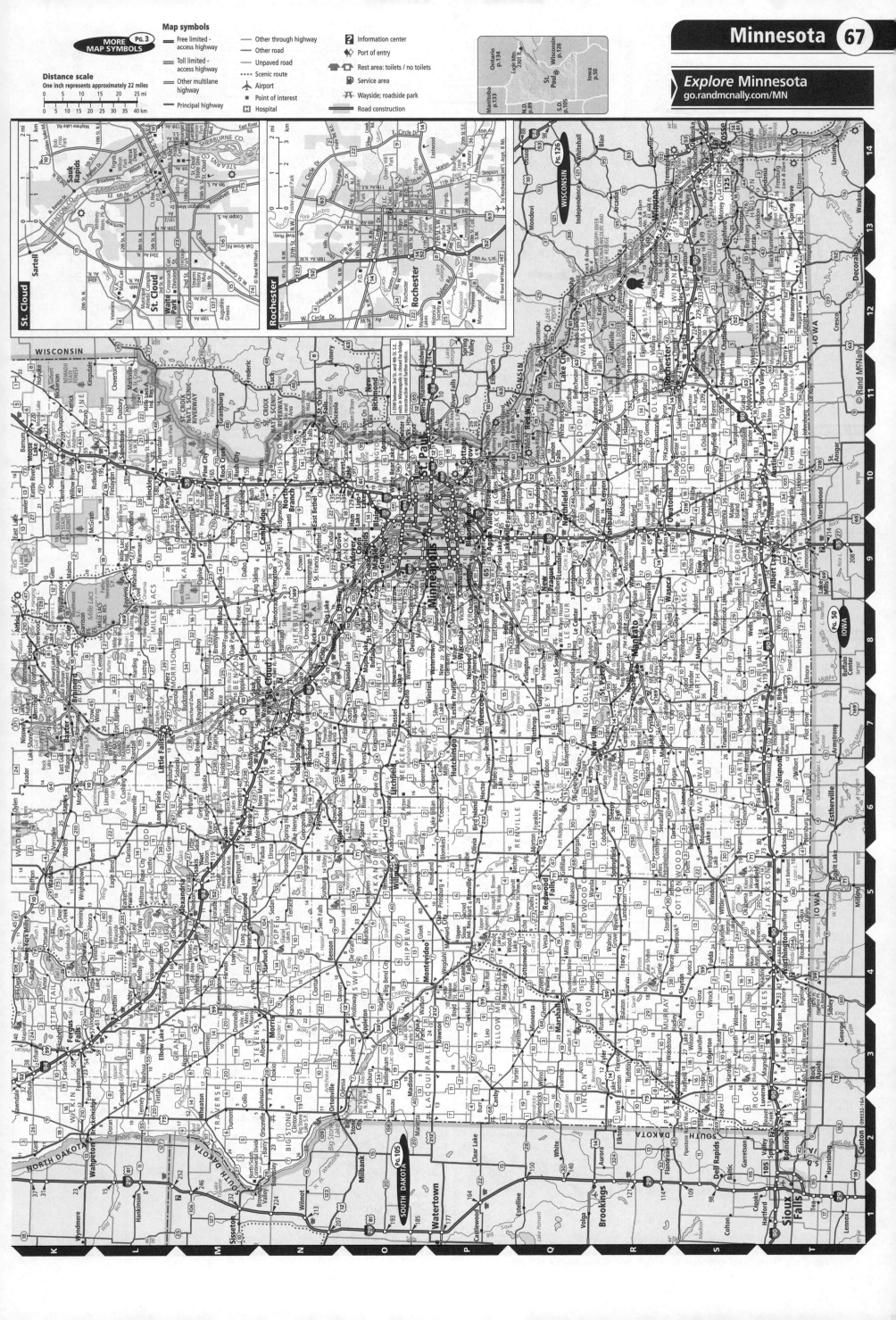

Map symbols

MORE MAP SYMBOLS Pg. 3

Free limited-access highway
Toll limited-access highway
Other multilane highway
Principal highway

Other through highway
Other road
Unpaved road
Scenic route
Airport
Point of interest
Hospital

Information center
Port of entry
Rest area: toilets / no toilets
Service area
Wayside; roadside park
Road construction

Distance scale
One inch represents approximately 22 miles

0 5 10 15 20 25 mi
0 5 10 15 20 25 35 40 km

Ontario p.134
Eagle Mtn. 2301 ft.
St. Paul
Wisconsin p.126
Manitoba p.133
N.D. p.88
Iowa p.50
S.D. p.105

St. Cloud

Sauk Rapids
Sartell

Rochester

© Rand McNally

Plan a trip
go.randmcnally.com/MS

Nickname: The Magnolia State
Land area: 46,907 sq. mi. (rank: 31st)
Population: 2,921,088 (rank: 31st)
Largest city: Jackson, 177,977

INDEX OF CITIES PG. 144

Distance scale
One inch represents approximately 27 miles

Mileage between cities	Biloxi	Greenville	Jackson	Memphis, TN	Meridian	New Orleans, LA	Tupelo	Vicksburg
BILOXI		290	170	378	168	223	87	312	215
GREENVILLE	290		120	147	192	153	300	193	101
JACKSON	170	120		212	93	114	180	225	45
MEMPHIS, TN	378	147	212		230	326	392	107	254
MERIDIAN	168	192	93	230		207	196	144	138
NEW ORLEANS, LA	87	300	180	392	196		175	340	225
TUPELO	312	193	225	107	144	339		340	267
VICKSBURG	215	101	45	254	138	74	225	267	

Total mileage through Mississippi
10 77 miles   55 290 miles
20 169 miles 59 172 miles

MORE MILEAGES PG. 256

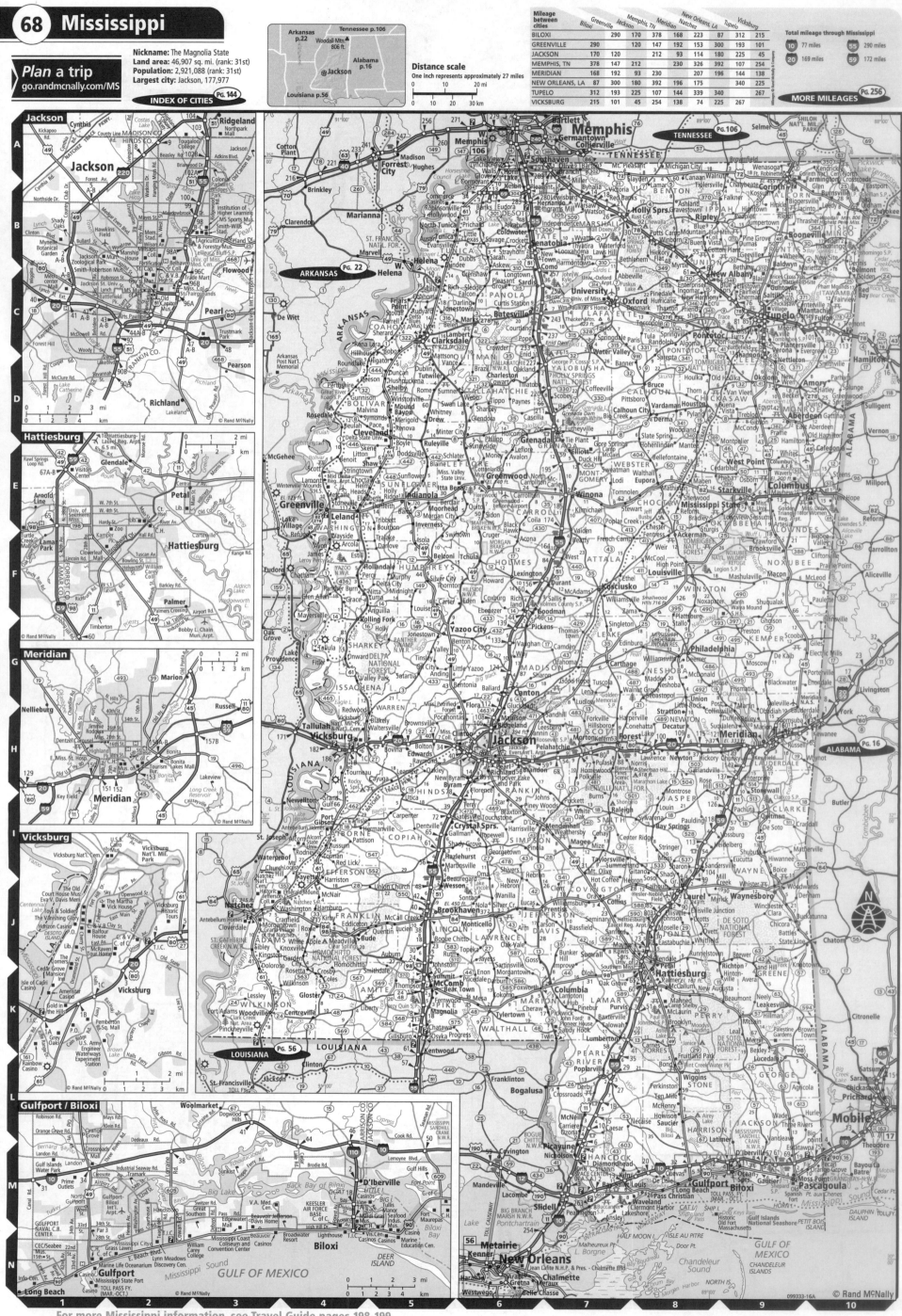

© Rand McNally

099333-16A

Nickname: The Show Me State
Land area: 68,886 sq. mi. (rank: 18th)
Population: 5,800,310 (rank: 18th)
Largest city: Kansas City, 444,965

INDEX OF CITIES Pg. 144

Mileage between cities	Branson	Cape Girardeau	Brookfield	Columbia	Hannibal	Jefferson City	Joplin	Kansas City	Kirksville	Maryville	Osage Beach	Poplar Bluff	Rolla	St. Joseph	St. Louis	Springfield	West Plains
CAPE GIRARDEAU	342		320	227	219	81	236	374	356	320	452	257	197	412	114	304	186
COLUMBIA	205	97		227	97	31	237	129	97	225	76	264	93	185	124	167	192
JOPLIN	112	274		374	312	326	206	150	315	242	161	263	178	202	282	72	180
KANSAS CITY	211	356		129	213	433	160	150	158	94	173	393	222	54	253	169	279
POPLAR BLUFF	219	357		84	264	206	63	222	263	393	357	489	230	170	449	151	193
ST. JOSEPH	265	100		412	185	196	489	216	202	54	141	42	229	449	278	309	223
ST. LOUIS	250	217		114	124	116	131	133	282	253	217	349	165	151	105	309	212
SPRINGFIELD	42	200		304	167	242	256	136	72	169	260	263	95	193	108	223	212

Total mileage through Missouri

35	115 miles	55	210 miles
44	290 miles	70	252 miles

MORE MILEAGES Pg. 256

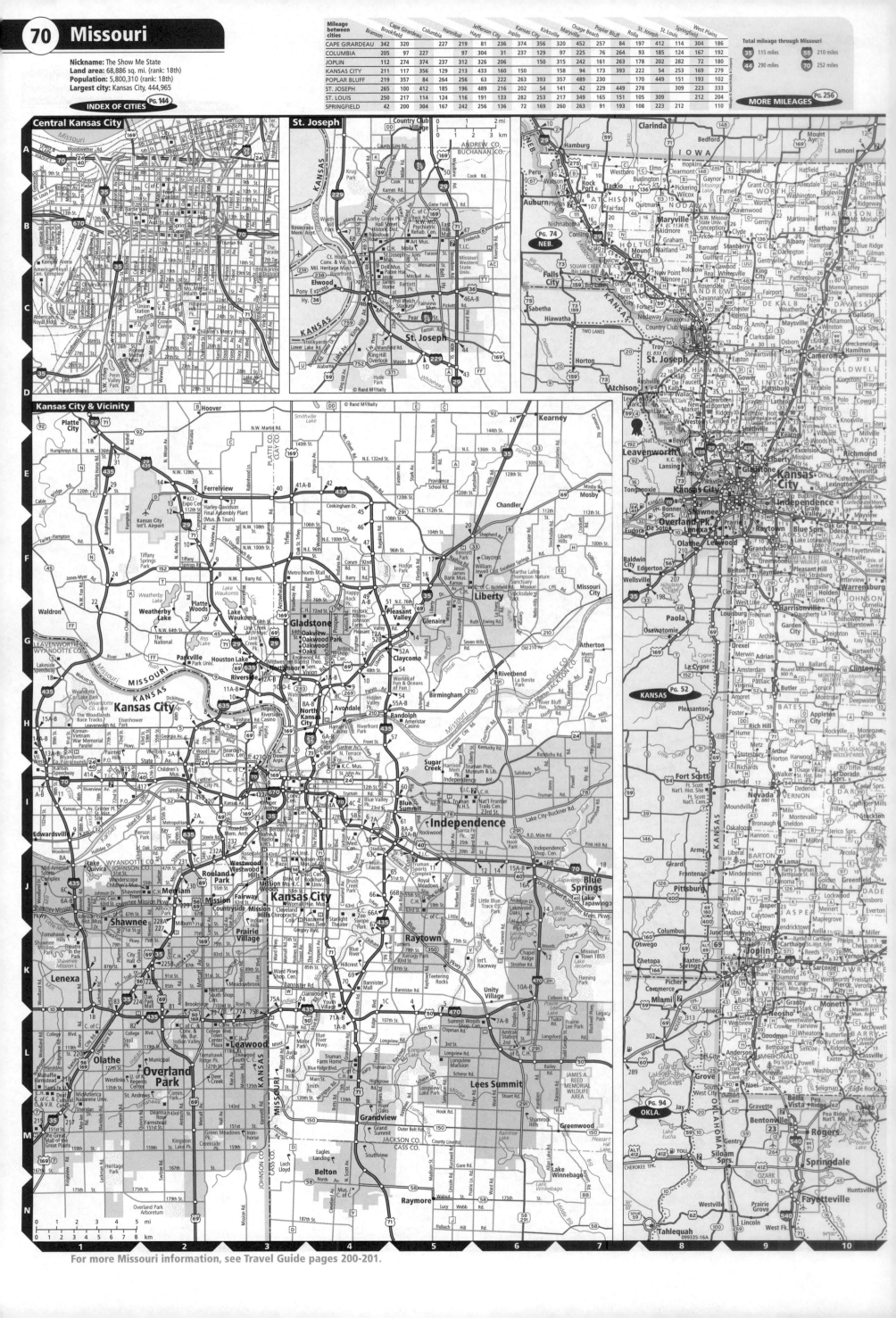

For more Missouri information, see Travel Guide pages 200-201.

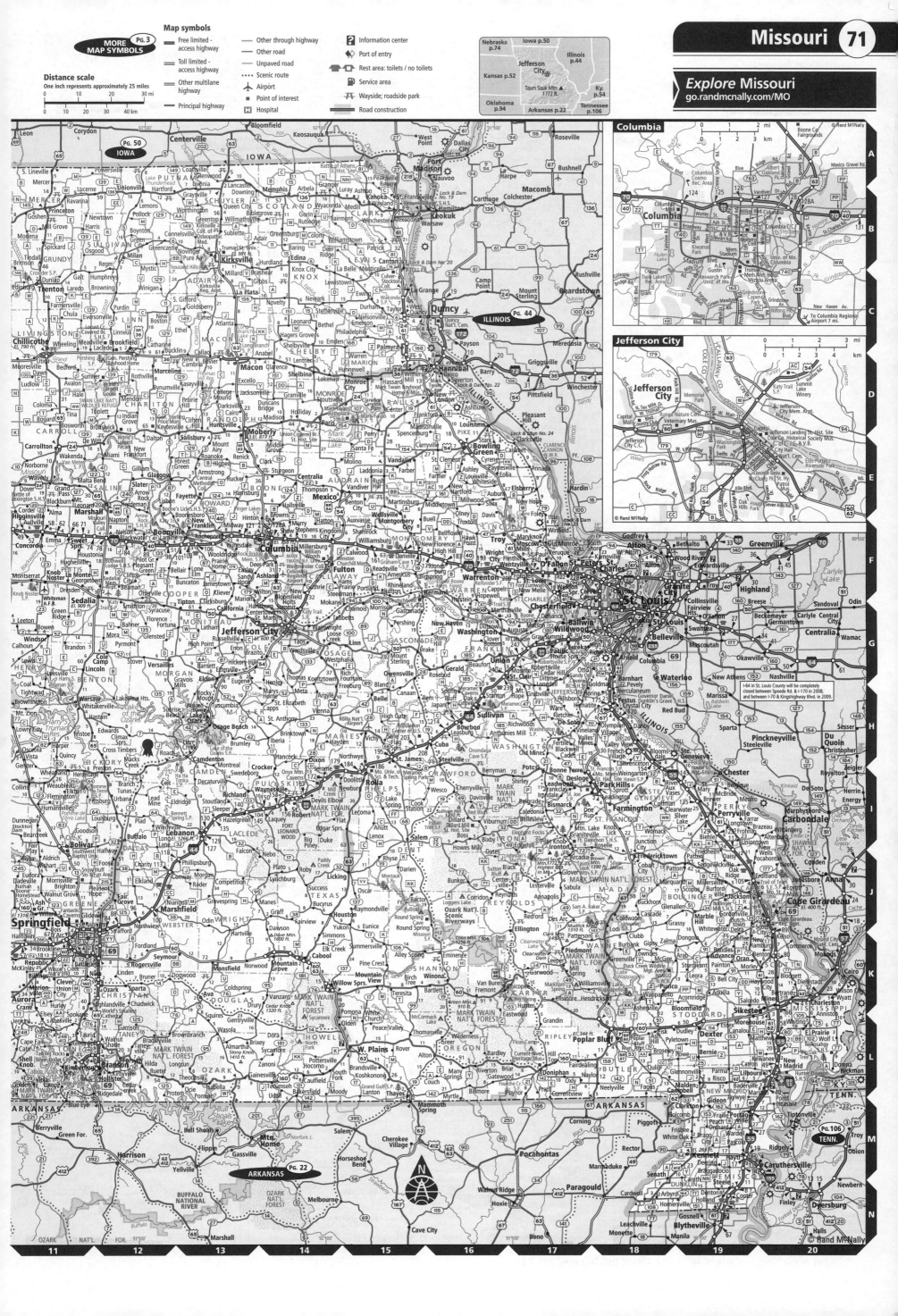

Explore Missouri
go.randmcnally.com/MO

Nickname: The Treasure State
Land area: 145,552 sq. mi. (rank: 4th)
Population: 935,670 (rank: 44th)
Largest city: Billings, 98,721

INDEX OF CITIES   PG. 144

MORE MILEAGES   Pg. 256

Mileage between cities	Billings	Bozeman	Butte	Dillon	Glasgow	Great Falls	Havre	Helena	Kalispell	Lewistown	Miles City	Missoula	St. Mary	Sheridan, WY	West Yellowstone Sidney
BILLINGS		140	221	254	278	222	249	239	463	126	532	144	340	387	309	127	271	229
BOZEMAN	140		82	115	367	190	305	100	324	162	393	286	201	306	271	269	413	89
BUTTE	221	82		67	431	155	270	65	242	243	311	367	119	271	236	350	494	148
GREAT FALLS	222	190	155	222	276		115	91	233	106	324	327	167	164	86	349	379	269
HELENA	239	100	65	132	367	91	206		198	195	289	385	111	207	172	368	512	179
KALISPELL	463	324	242	295	425	233	264	198		340	91	606	123	86	160	592	565	390
MILES CITY	144	286	367	400	222	327	344	385	609	221	678		486	492	414	201	129	375
MISSOULA	340	201	119	172	443	167	282	111	123	274	192	486		209	227	469	613	267

Total mileage through Montana
15 396 miles   94 249 miles
90 552 miles

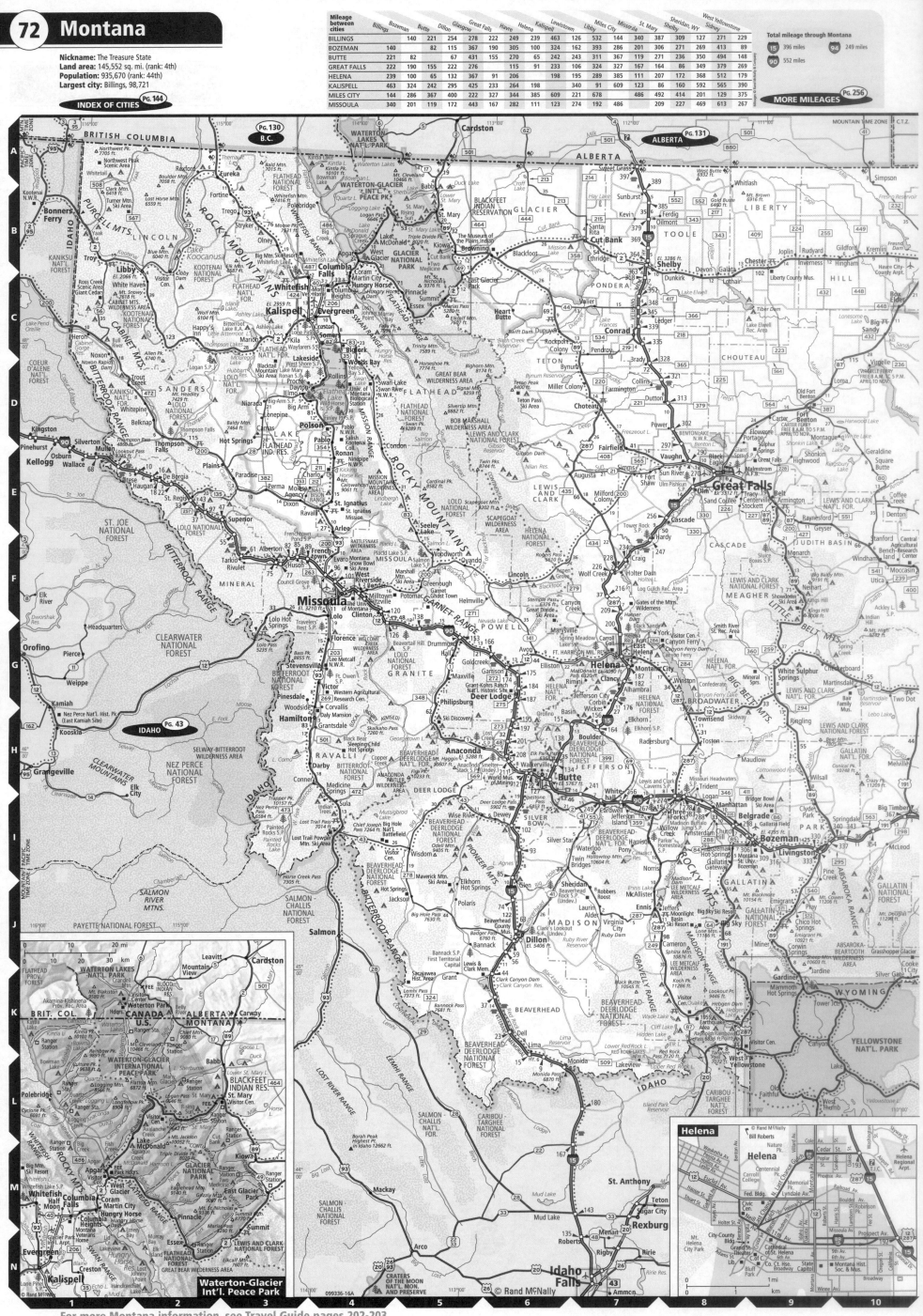

© Rand McNally

099336-16A

For more Montana information, see Travel Guide pages 202-203.

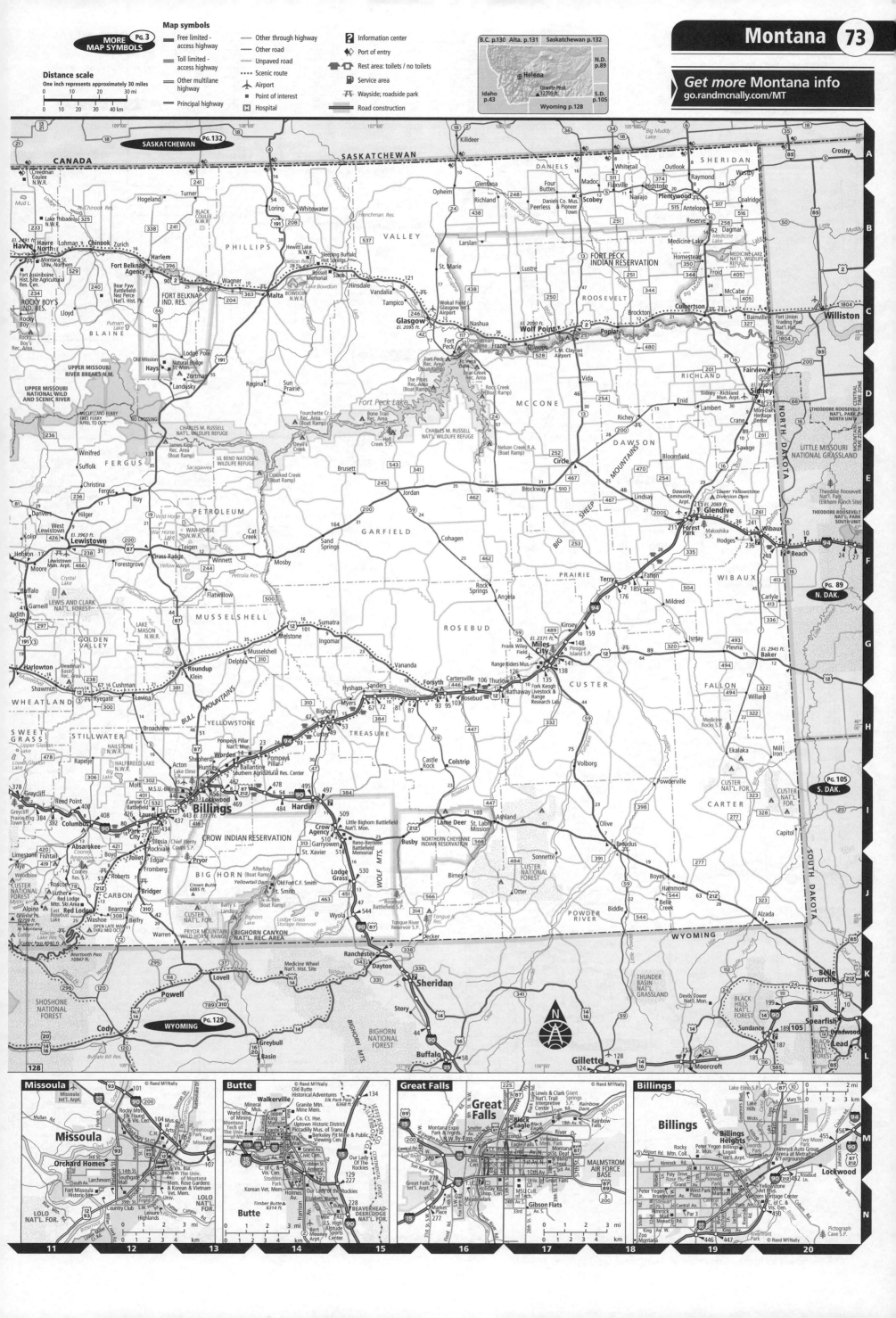

Nickname: The Cornhusker State
Land area: 76,872 sq. mi. (rank: 15th)
Population: 1,758,787 (rank: 38th)
Largest city: Omaha, 414,521

INDEX OF CITIES PG. 144

Mileage between cities	Alliance	Beatrice	Chadron	Cheyenne, WY	Columbus	Grand Island	Kearney	Lincoln	McCook	Nebraska City	Norfolk	North Platte	Ogallala	Omaha	O'Neill	Scottsbluff	Sioux City, IA	Valentine
GRAND ISLAND	321	134	379	365	63		51	97	155	145	109	147	198	152	111	320	179	211
LINCOLN	400	40	458	444	78	97	130		234	49	124	226	277	58	207	399	155	306
NORFOLK	329	161	324	474	46	109	160	124	264	154		256	307	112	75	429	74	186
NORTH PLATTE	177	263	235	221	210	147	100	234	68	274	256		54	281	194	176	378	131
OGALLALA	123	314	181	169	261	198	151	277	118	325	307	54		332	248	122	429	185
OMAHA	455	98	513	499	88	152	185	58	289	44	112	281	332		188	454	98	299
SCOTTSBLUFF	57	436	99	109	383	320	273	399	240	447	429	176	122	454	329		453	218
VALENTINE	164	343	138	352	232	211	195	306	199	354	186	131	185	299	111	218	235	

Total mileage through Nebraska

	miles		miles
80	455	83	226
81	219	20	436

MORE MILEAGES PG. 256

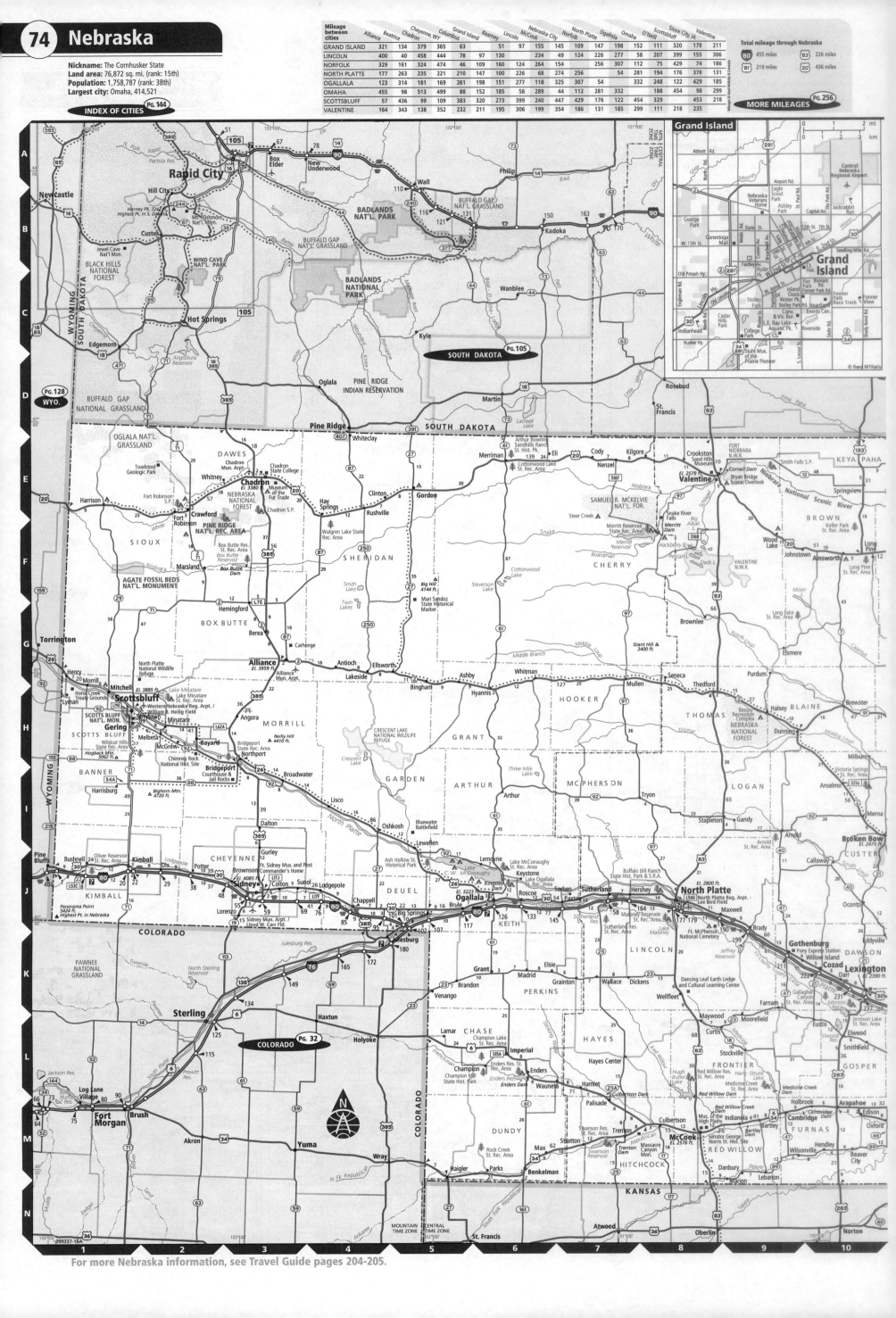

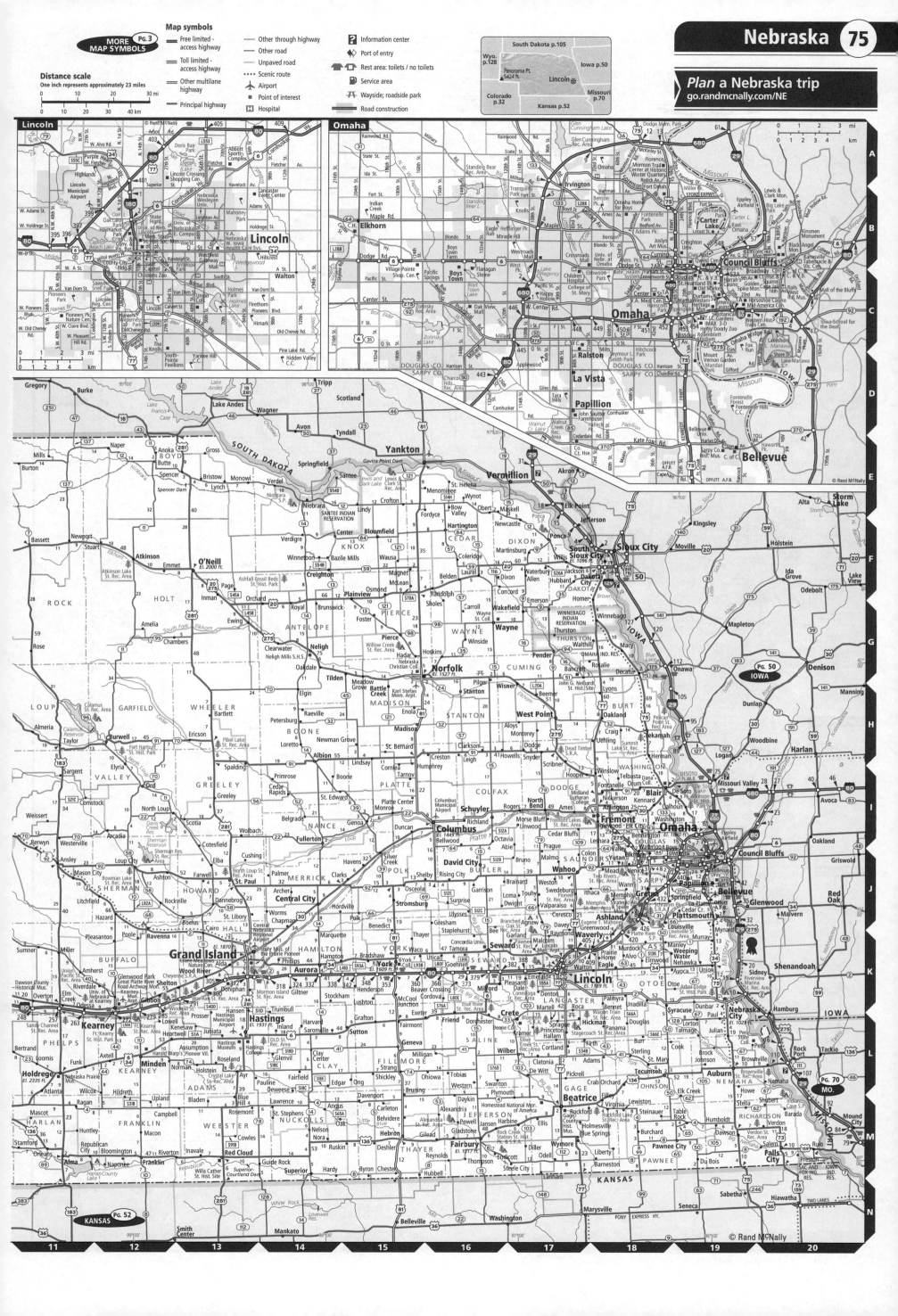

Get travel info
go.randmcnally.com/NV

Nickname: The Silver State
Land area: 109,826 sq. mi. (rank: 7th)
Population: 2,414,807 (rank: 35th)
Largest city: Las Vegas, 545,147

INDEX OF CITIES Pg. 144

Oregon p.96   Idaho p.43
Carson City
California p.24   Boundary Pk. (13143 ft.)   Utah p.114
Arizona p.20

Mileage between cities	Austin	Battle Mountain	Beatty	Boulder City	Carson City	Elko	Ely	Fallon	Hawthorne	Jackpot	Las Vegas	McDermitt	Panaca	Reno	Tonopah	Winnemucca
ELKO	160	71	368	462	306		190	253	325	119	436	199	307	289	276	125
ELY	146	217	259	273	318	190		256	271	207	245	345	120	317	167	271
LAS VEGAS	324	413	116	26	435	436	245	384	312	453		540	165	445	208	466
RENO	171	217	329	473	32	289	317	61	133	408	445	238	437		237	164
S. LAKE TAHOE, CA	200	262	326	468	28	334	346	90	136	453	442	283	444	60	240	209
TONOPAH	116	205	92	234	227	276	167	176	104	395	208	332	204	237		258
WENDOVER, UT	271	182	381	393	417	111	121	364	436	187	367	310	238	409	289	236
WINNEMUCCA	142	53	350	492	181	125	271	128	200	244	466	74	391	164	258	

Total mileage through Nevada
15 — 124 miles   6 — 307 miles
80 — 411 miles   95 — 652 miles

Distance scale
One inch represents approximately 38 miles
0 10 20 30 mi
0 10 20 30 40 km

Mileage between cities	Berlin	Boston, MA	Concord	Keene	Lebanon	Littleton	Manchester	Nashua	Portsmouth
BERLIN		187	113	166	119	41	131	150	117
CONCORD	113		73		51	57	83	17	36	46
KEENE	166	90	51		68	138	58	52	111
LEBANON	119	129	57	68		80	73	92	117
LITTLETON	41	157	83	138	80		101	120	127
MANCHESTER	131	58	17	58	73	101		19	52
NASHUA	150	47	36	52	92	120	19		60
PORTSMOUTH	117	67	46	111	117	127	52	60	

Total mileage through New Hampshire
89 61 miles **95** 16 miles
93 132 miles **U.S. 2** 36 miles

Distance scale
One inch represents approximately 14 mi

MORE MILEAGES Pg. 256

Québec p.136
Maine p.57
Vermont p.116 Mt. Washington 6288 ft.
Concord
Mass. p.60

INDEX OF CITIES Pg. 144

Nickname: The Granite State
Land area: 8,968 sq. mi. (rank: 44th)
Population: 1,309,940 (rank: 41st)
Largest city: Manchester, 109,691

Plan a trip
go.randmcnally.com/NH

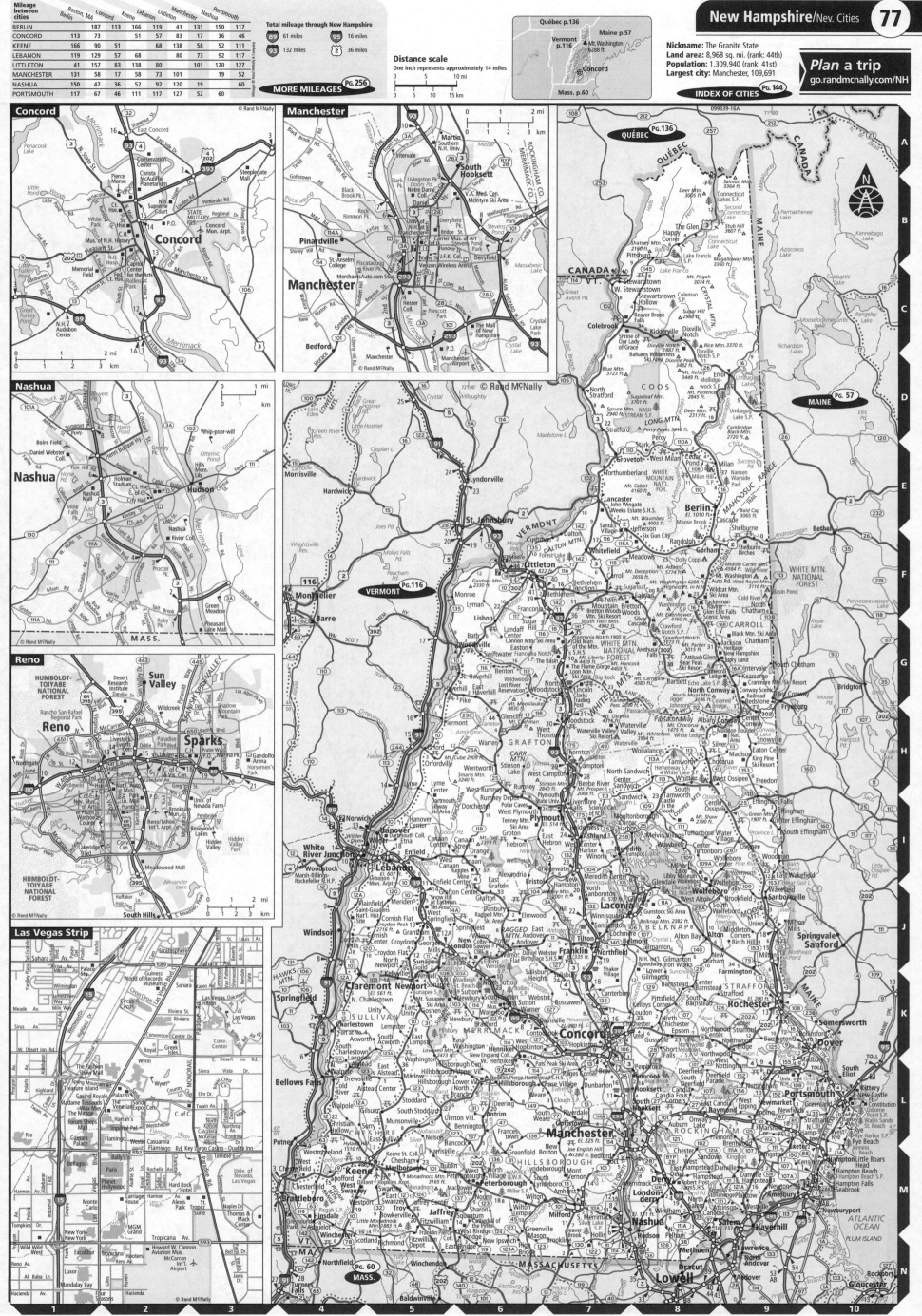

Nickname: The Garden State
Land area: 7,417 sq. mi. (rank: 46th)
Population: 8,717,925 (rank: 10th)
Largest city: Newark, 280,666

INDEX OF CITIES PG. 144

Mileage between cities	Atlantic City	Camden	Cape May	Cherry Hill	Elizabeth	Jersey City	Long Branch	New Brunswick Newark	New York NY	Paterson	Phillipsburg	Point Pleasant	Port Jervis, NY	Princeton	Somerville	Toms River	Trenton	Vineland	Wilmington, DE
ATLANTIC CITY		60	49	55	114	122	81	117	95	140	129	145	64	182	93	119	51	81	37	70	86
CAMDEN	60		93	6	79	87	77	82	63	97	94	85	71	147	48	70	55	37	38	14	36
NEWARK	117	82	151	78	5		46		25	15	19	63	56	75	41	34	66	55	115	68	117
NEW BRUNSWICK	95	63	129	59	22	30	33	25		40	37	52	38	90	18	14	44	36	96	49	98
PATERSON	129	94	163	90	22	15	58	19	37	31		66	54	58	41	78	67	127	80	129
PHILLIPSBURG	145	85	178	91	63	68	86	63	52	78	66		96	76	56	39	106	57	123	70	100
TRENTON	81	37	114	33	52	60	50	55	36	70	67	57	44	107	12	31	46		70	26	68
WILMINGTON, DE	86	36	63	42	83	114	122	112	117	98	132	129	100	106	162	79	101	88	68	44	51

Total mileage through New Jersey		
78	68 miles	
95	98 miles	
80	68 miles	

MORE MILEAGES PG. 256

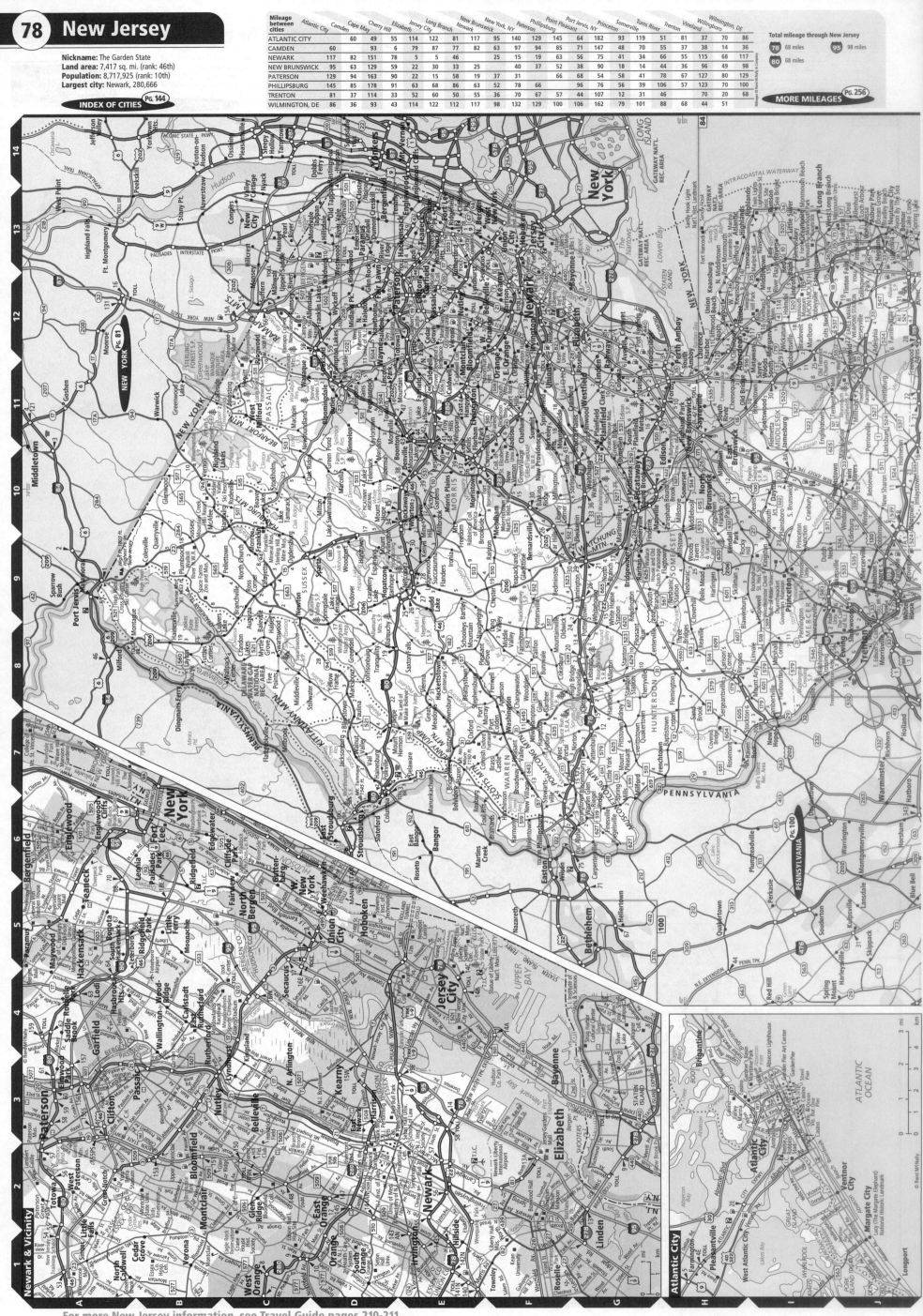

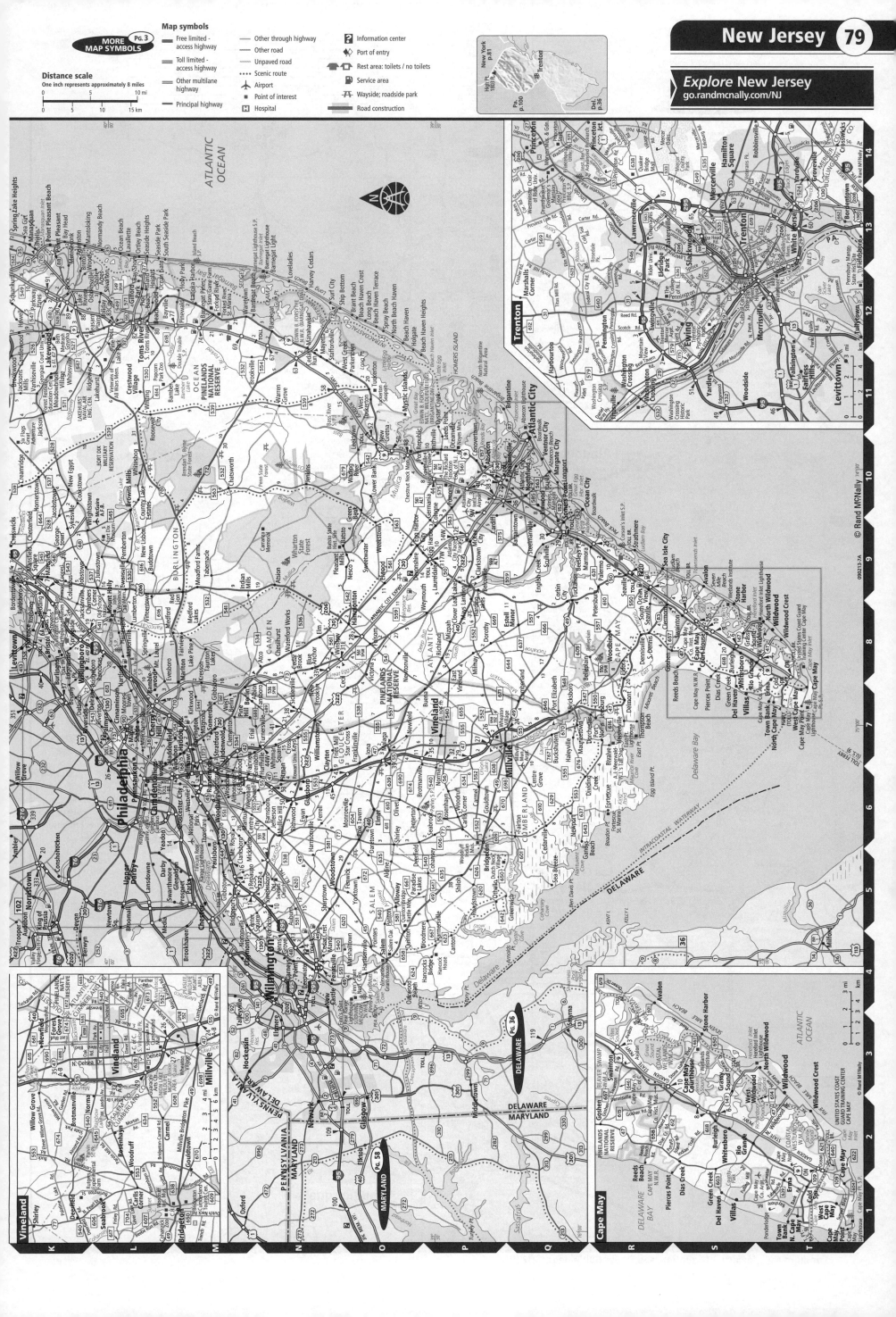

Nickname: Land of Enchantment
Land area: 121,356 sq. mi. (rank: 5th)
Population: 1,928,384 (rank: 36th)
Largest city: Albuquerque, 494,236

INDEX OF CITIES Pg. 145

Mileage between cities	Alamogordo	Albuquerque	Carlsbad	Clovis	El Paso, TX	Grants	Las Cruces	Las Vegas	Lordsburg	Raton	Santa Fe	Socorro	Truth or Consequences	Tucumcari
ALBUQUERQUE	210		275	217	267	79	315	224	118	294	224	58	78	126	150	174
CARLSBAD	146	275		179	165	354	70	208	253	334	359	267	240	328	280	242
CLOVIS	229	217	179		314	296	127	298	165	416	233	209	246	240	318	82
GALLUP	324	139	414	356	381	61	454	338	257	303	363	197	192	265	264	313
LAS CRUCES	69	224	70	298	46	278	257		342	118	448	282	146	350	75	305
SANTA FE	217	58	267	209	325	137	307	282	63	352	169		136	69	208	166
TRINIDAD, CO	345	246	381	255	430	325	382	470	128	542	22	191	324	118	396	199
TUCUMCARI	236	174	242	82	321	253	200	305	122	468	177	166	252	197	324	

Total mileage through New Mexico
10 164 miles 40 374 miles
25 462 miles

Distance scale
One inch represents approximately 38 miles

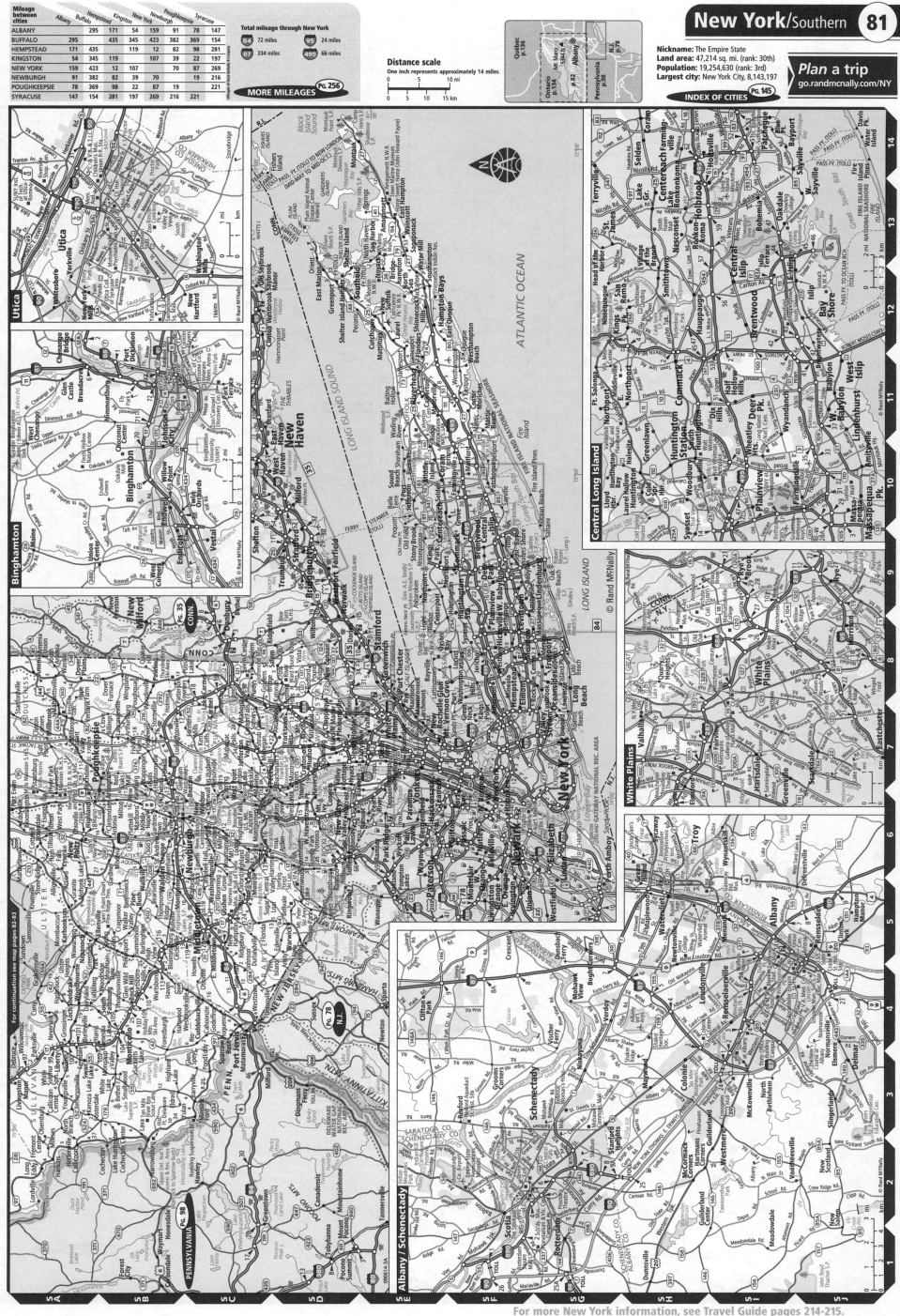

Nickname: The Empire State
Land area: 47,214 sq. mi. (rank: 30th)
Population: 19,254,630 (rank: 3rd)
Largest city: New York City, 8,143,197

Plan a trip
go.randmcnally.com/NY

INDEX OF CITIES   PG. 145

Mileage between cities	Albany	Buffalo	Hempstead	Kingston	New York	Newburgh	Poughkeepsie	Syracuse
ALBANY		295	171	54	159	91	78	147
BUFFALO	295		435	345	423	382	369	154
HEMPSTEAD	171	435		119	12	82	98	281
KINGSTON	54	345	119		107	39	22	197
NEW YORK	159	423	12	107		70	87	269
NEWBURGH	91	382	82	39	70		19	216
POUGHKEEPSIE	78	369	98	22	87	19		221
SYRACUSE	147	154	281	197	269	216	221	

Total mileage through New York
84 — 72 miles
87 — 334 miles
95 — 24 miles
495 — 66 miles

MORE MILEAGES PG. 256

Distance scale
One inch represents approximately 14 miles

Nickname: The Empire State
Land area: 47,214 sq. mi. (rank: 30th)
Population: 19,254,630 (rank: 3rd)
Largest city: New York City, 8,143,197

INDEX OF CITIES   Pg. 145

Mileage between cities	Albany	Auburn	Binghamton	Buffalo	Elmira	Glens Falls	Ithaca	Jamestown	Kingston	Lake Placid	Massena	New York	Niagara Falls	Olean	Oneonta	Oswego	Plattsburgh	Rochester	Syracuse	Utica	Watertown
ALBANY		176	134	295	192	58	176	357	54	142	221	159	309	304	80	176	161	231	147	95	208
BINGHAMTON	134	90		230	59	179	51	224	263	342	195	244	171	56	116	282	766	76	93	148
BUFFALO	295	128	230		148	313	154	71	345	347	312	417	22	77	277	159	378	78	154	204	218
JAMESTOWN	357	193	224	71		166	402	191		356	412	377	93	56	279	224	505	143	219	269	283
PLATTSBURGH	161	259	282	378	342	110	287	505	214	49	87	319	392	452	228	259		314	230	188	170
ROCHESTER	231	64	166	78	121	249	90	143	281	283	248	198	18	213	77	314		90	140	154
SYRACUSE	147	27	76	154	93	165	58	219	197	201	166	269	188	191	123	40	230	90		56	72
UTICA	95	85	93	204	147	113	113	269	145	164	161	250	218	241	62	85	188	140	56		84

MORE MILEAGES   Pg. 256

Total mileage through New York		
81	184 miles	87	334 miles
86	176 miles	90	385 miles

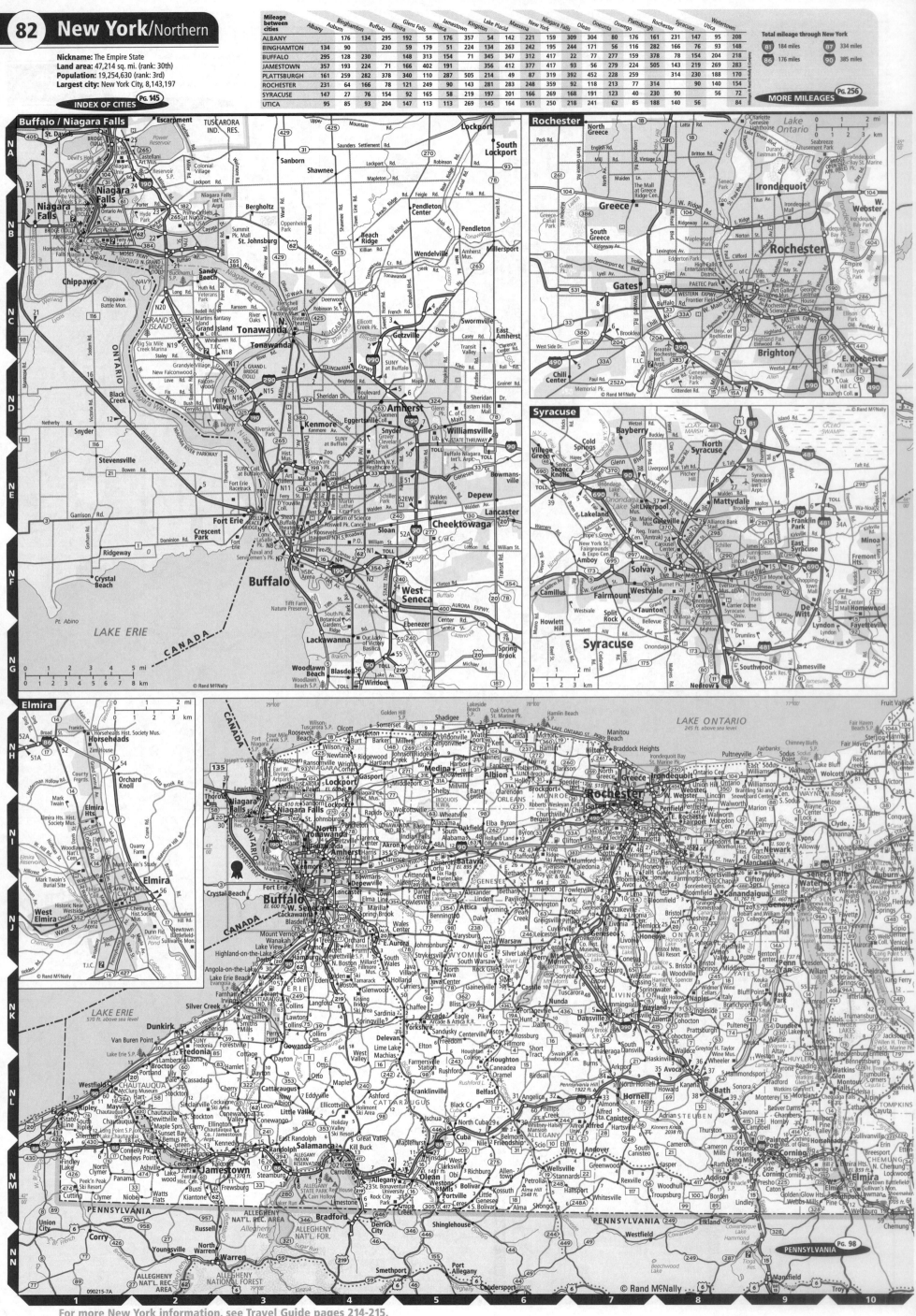

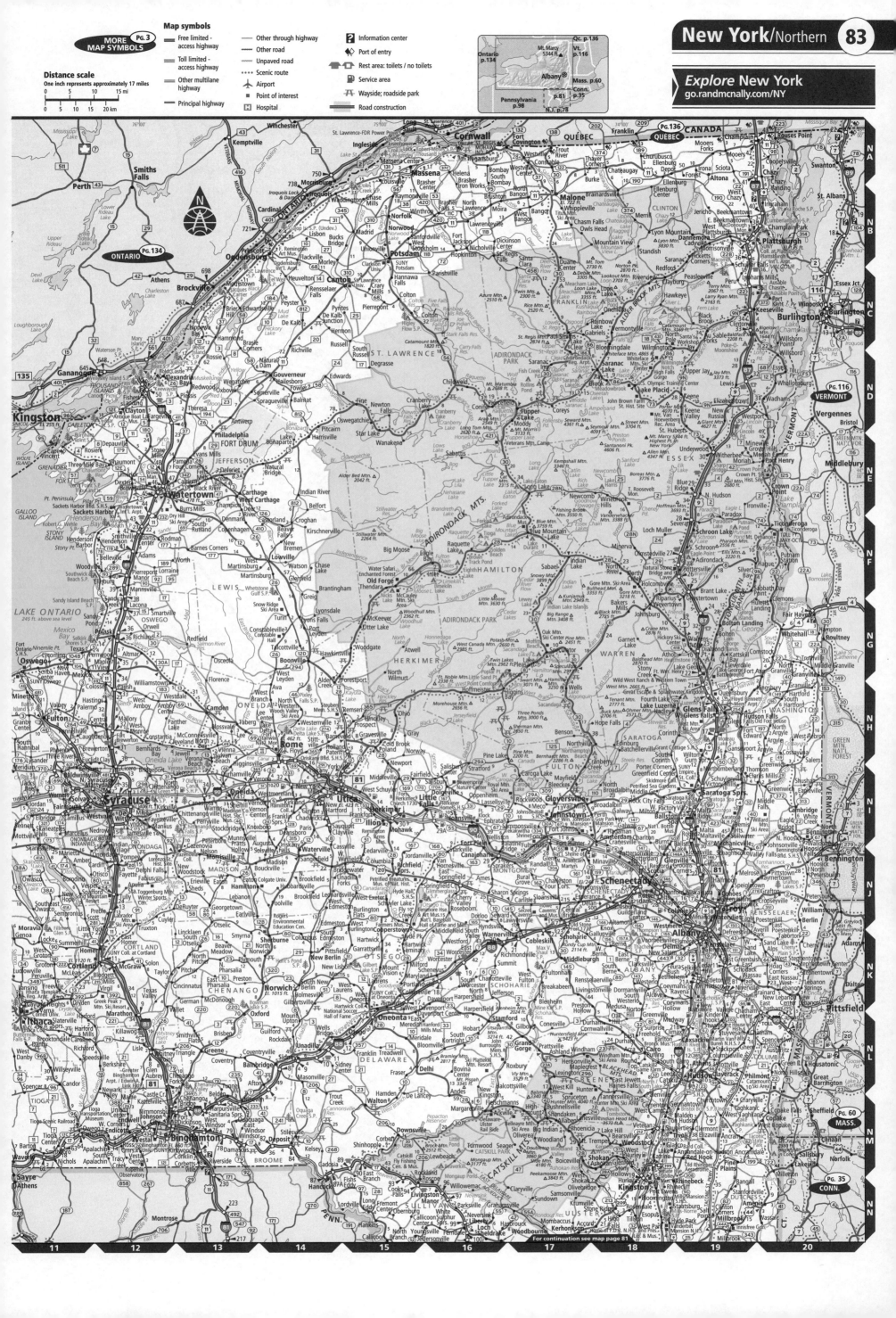

For continuation see map page 81

Nickname: The Tar Heel State
Land area: 48,711 sq. mi. (rank: 29th)
Population: 8,683,242 (rank: 11th)
Largest city: Charlotte, 610,949

INDEX OF CITIES Pg. 145

Mileage between cities	Asheville	Boone	Charlotte	Durham	Elizabeth City	Fayetteville	Greensboro	Greenville	Hickory	Knoxville, TN	Nags Head	New Bern	Roanoke Rapids Raleigh	Rockingham	Rocky Mt.	Wilmington	Winston-Salem
ASHEVILLE		85	126	221	409	261	168	325	73	115	444	358	247	306	199	299	328	144
CHARLOTTE	126	118		143	331	139	97	247	63	229	366	280	169	228	75	221	204	83
FAYETTEVILLE	261	206	139	92	206		98	109	192	373	241	130	66	128	64	96	118	121
GREENSBORO	168	113	97	53	241	98		157	99	280	276	190	79	138	90	131	208	28
GREENVILLE	325	270	247	105	96	109	157		256	437	131	46	80	174	38	137	185	
RALEIGH	247	192	169	27	164	66	79	80	174	359	199	112		86	97	54	130	107
WILMINGTON	328	321	204	156	213	118	208	137	307	431	239	90	181	192	129	160		236
WINSTON-SALEM	144	89	83	81	269	121	28	185	75	256	304	218	107	166	109	159	236	

Total mileage through North Carolina

40	419 miles	**85**	233 miles
77	102 miles	**95**	182 miles

MORE MILEAGES Pg. 256

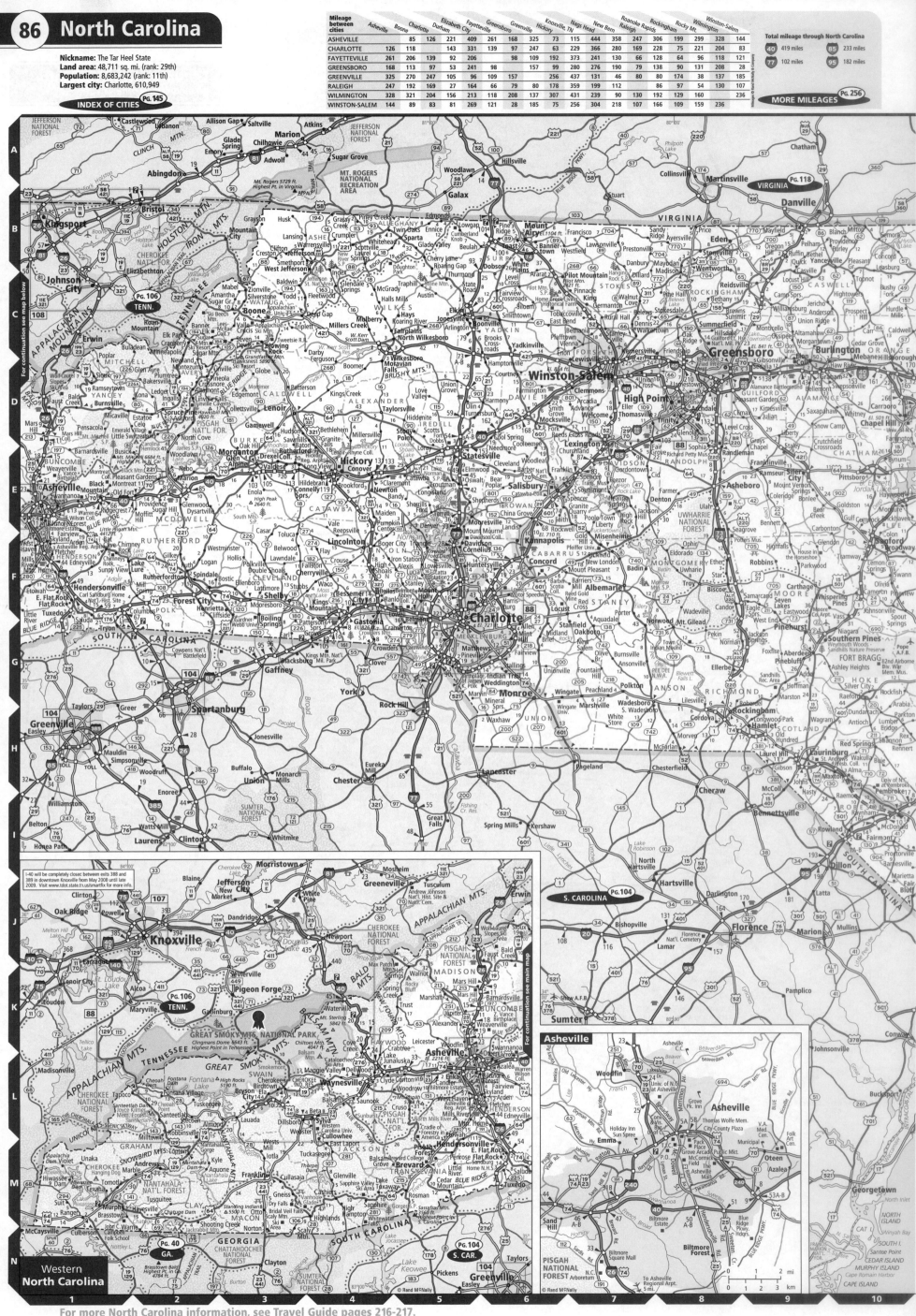

Western North Carolina

I-40 will be completely closed between exits 388 and 389 in downtown Knoxville from May 2008 until late 2009. Visit www.tdot.state.tn.us/smartfix for more info.

For more North Carolina information, see Travel Guide pages 216-217.

© Rand McNally

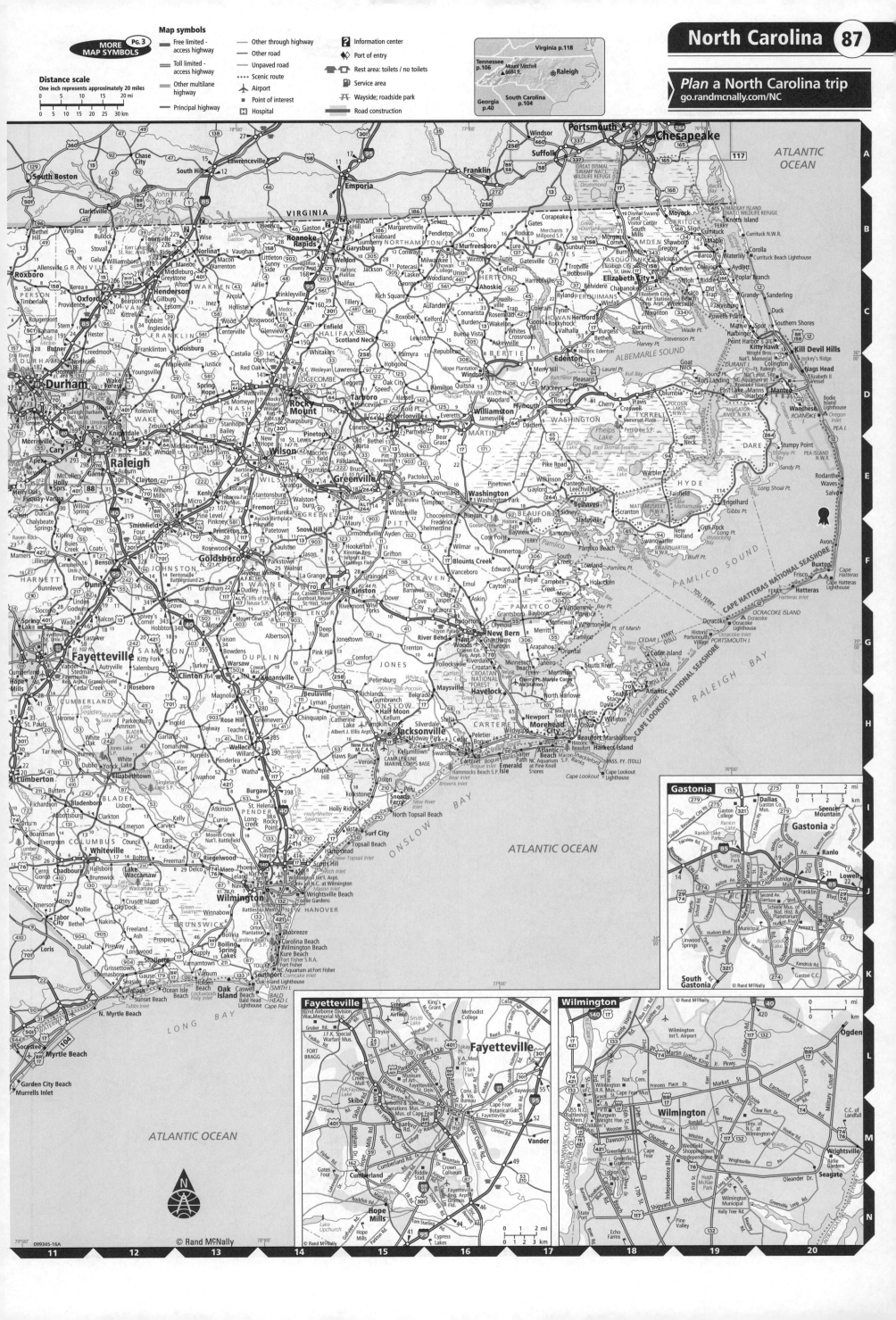

Plan a North Carolina trip
go.randmcnally.com/NC

Get travel info
go.randmcnally.com/NC

INDEX OF CITIES **PG. 145**

MORE **PG. 3** MAP SYMBOLS

Map symbols

- Free limited - access highway
- Toll limited - access highway
- Other multilane highway
- Principal highway
- Other through highway
- Other road
- Unpaved road
- Scenic route
- ✈ Airport
- ■ Point of interest
- Ⓗ Hospital
- ? Information center
- Port of entry
- Rest area: toilets / no toilets
- Service area
- Wayside; roadside park
- Road construction

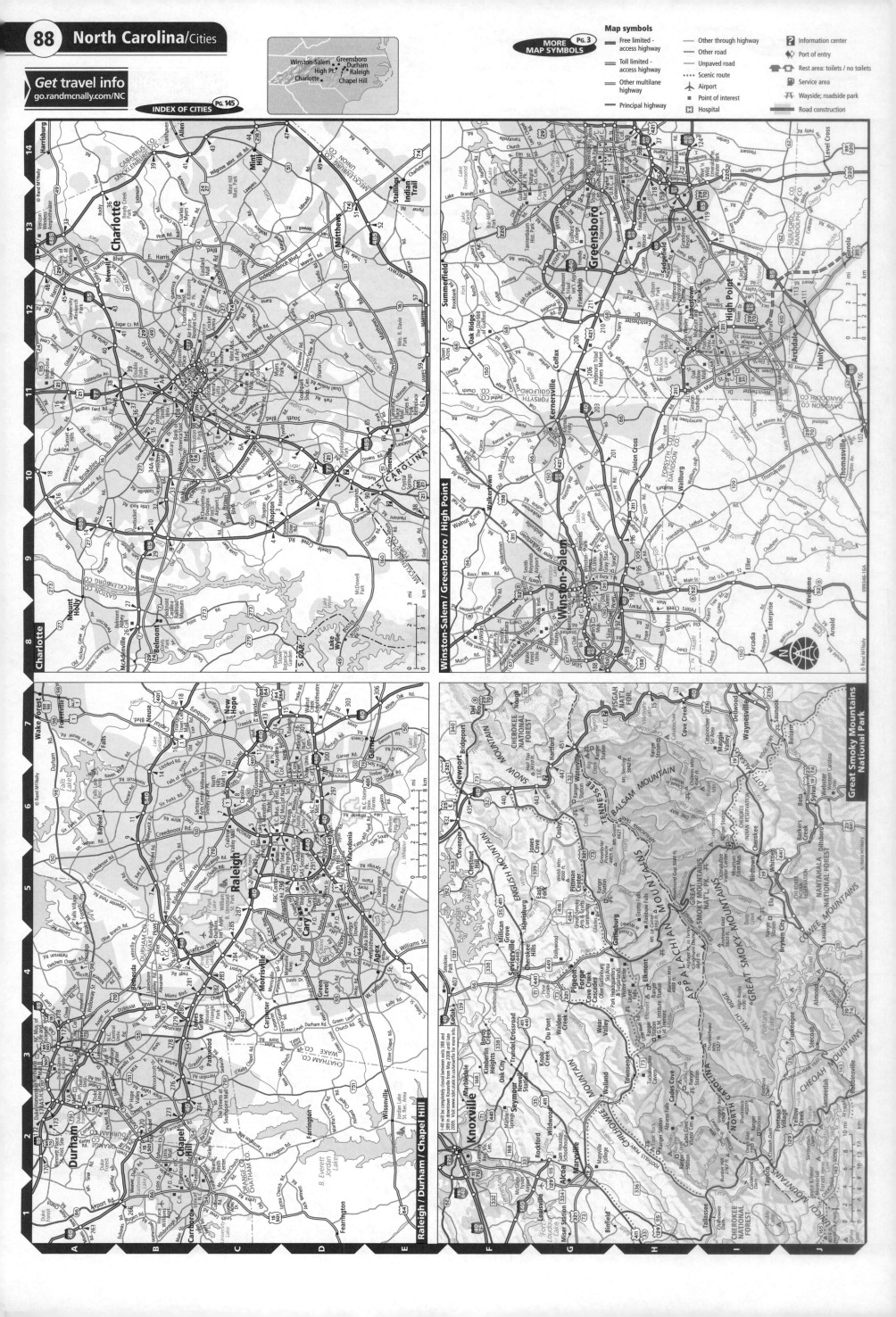

Charlotte

Winston-Salem / Greensboro / High Point

Raleigh / Durham / Chapel Hill

Great Smoky Mountains National Park

Nickname: The Peace Garden State
Land area: 68,976 sq. mi. (rank: 17th)
Population: 636,677 (rank: 48th)
Largest city: Fargo, 90,672

Plan a trip
go.randmcnally.com/ND

INDEX OF CITIES PG. 145

Mileage between cities	Bismarck	Devils Lake	Dickinson	Fargo	Garrison	Grand Forks	Minot	Williston
BISMARCK		179	99	193	76	269	111	230
DEVILS LAKE	179		275	163	168	89	121	249
DICKINSON	99	275		289	148	365	183	131
FARGO	193	163	289		266	78	263	420
GARRISON	76	168	148	266		257	47	141
GRAND FORKS	269	89	365	78	257		210	338
MINOT	111	121	183	263	47	210		126
WILLISTON	230	249	131	420	141	338	126	

Total mileage through North Dakota
29 218 miles   **2** 359 miles
94 352 miles   **83** 265 miles

MORE MILEAGES Pg. 256

Distance scale
One inch represents approximately 30 miles

For more North Dakota information, see Travel Guide pages 218-219.

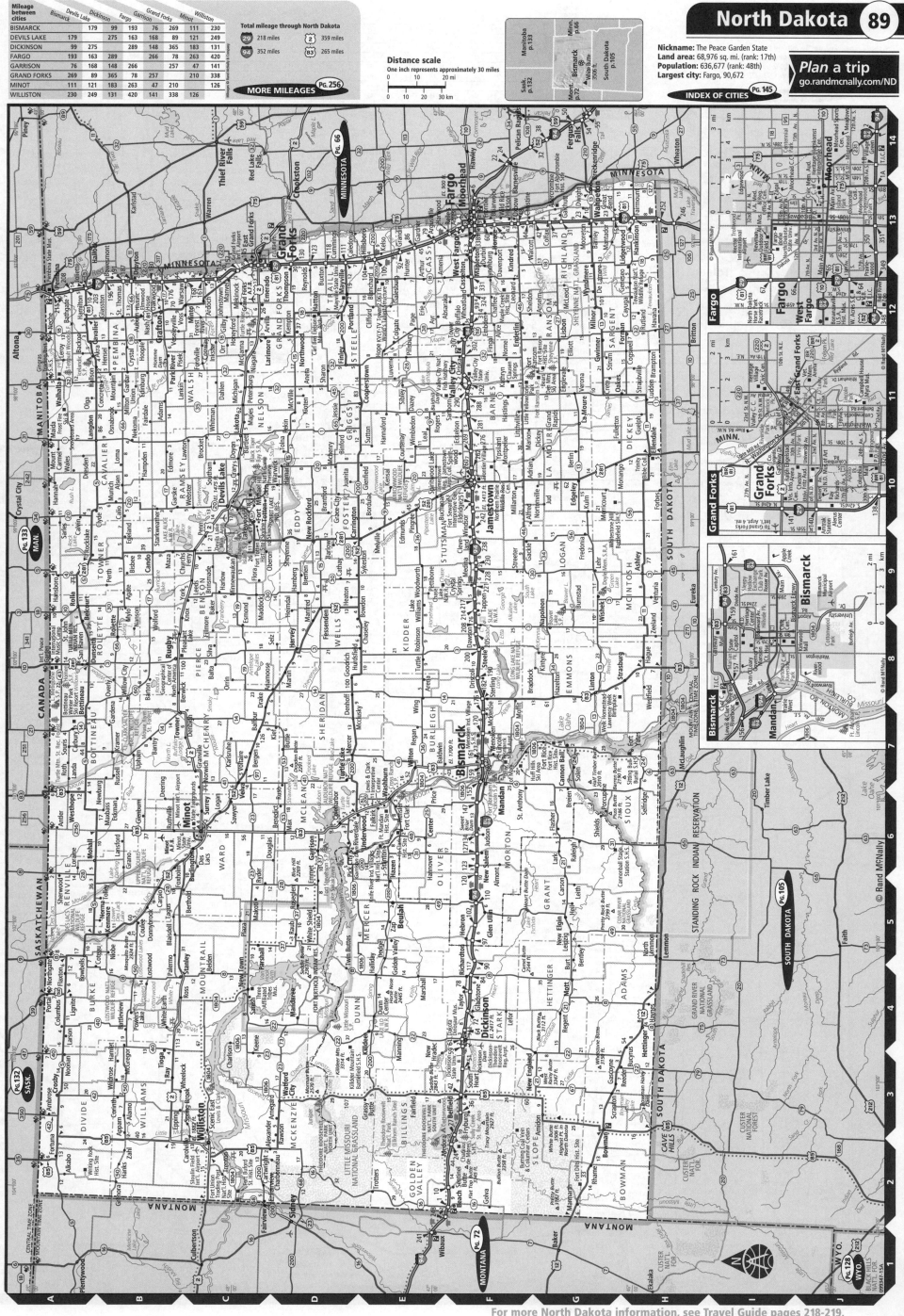

Nickname: The Buckeye State
Land area: 40,948 sq. mi. (rank: 35th)
Population: 11,464,042 (rank: 7th)
Largest city: Columbus, 730,657

INDEX OF CITIES PG. 145

Mileage between cities	Akron	Ashtabula	Canton	Cincinnati	Cleveland	Columbus	Defiance	Findlay	Lima	Mansfield	New Philadelphia	Marion	Pittsburgh, PA	Sandusky	Steubenville	Toledo	Wheeling, WV	Youngstown
AKRON		84	20	238	39	128	184	133	152	66	104	45	107	85	78	137	101	48
CLEVELAND	39	59	58	252		142	162	124	157	80	118	83	135	62	132	115	139	76
COLUMBUS	128	198	127	111	142		150	98	93	66	118	51	120	183	113	150	142	176
FINDLAY	133	183	132	157	124	98	51		33	69	48	138	240	63	192	43	194	181
LIMA	152	216	151	126	157	93	42	33		88	54	75	259	96	211	74	219	200
MANSFIELD	66	126	65	176	80	66	121	69	88		40	71	173	54	125	103	127	114
TOLEDO	137	174	156	198	115	142	43	74	103	92	157	233	60	230		213	174
YOUNGSTOWN	48	59	68	286	76	176	221	181	200	114	152	93	70	122	96	174	97

Total mileage through Ohio

| 71 | 248 miles | 80 | 237 miles |
| 75 | 211 miles | 90 | 245 miles |

MORE MILEAGES PG. 256

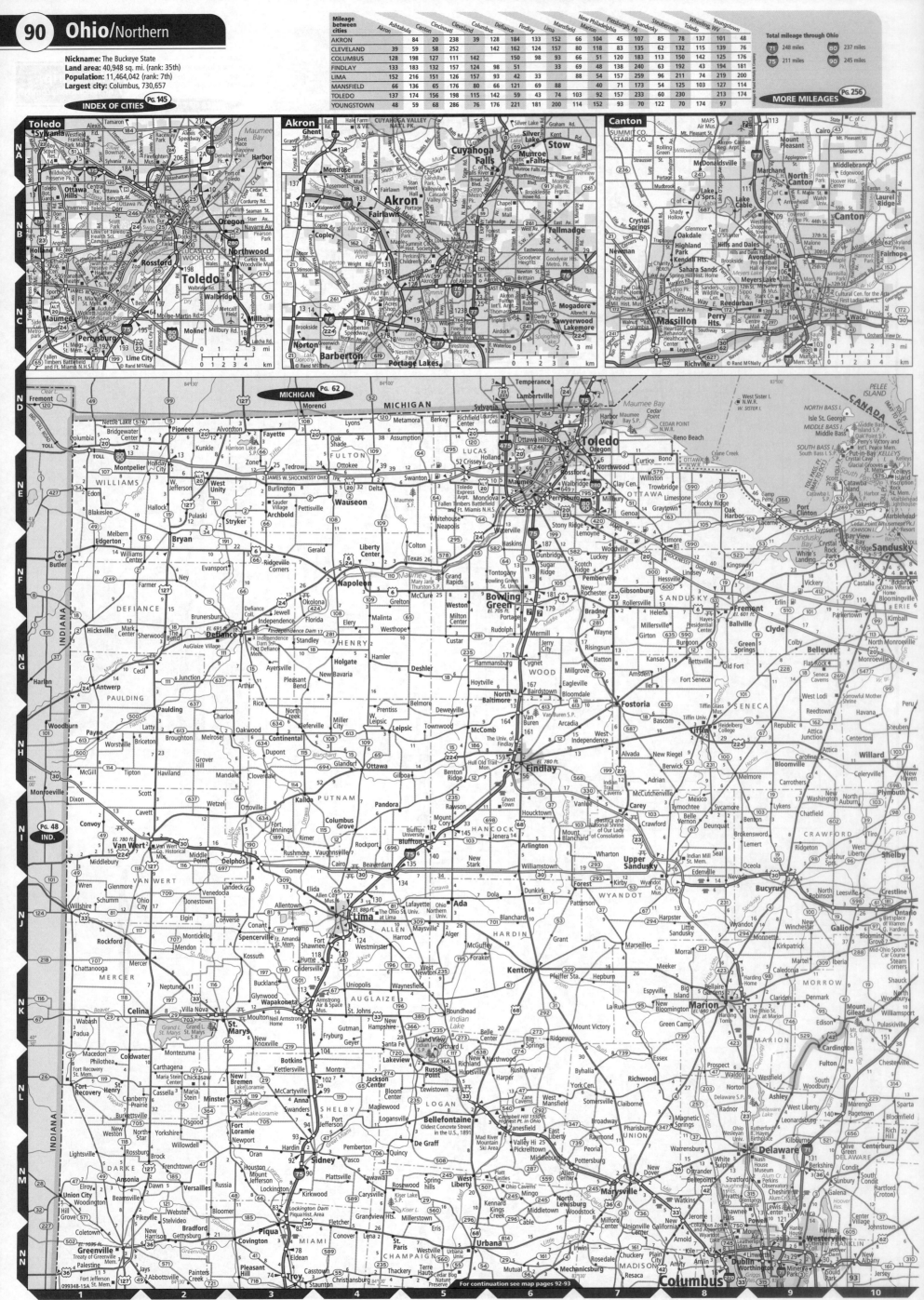

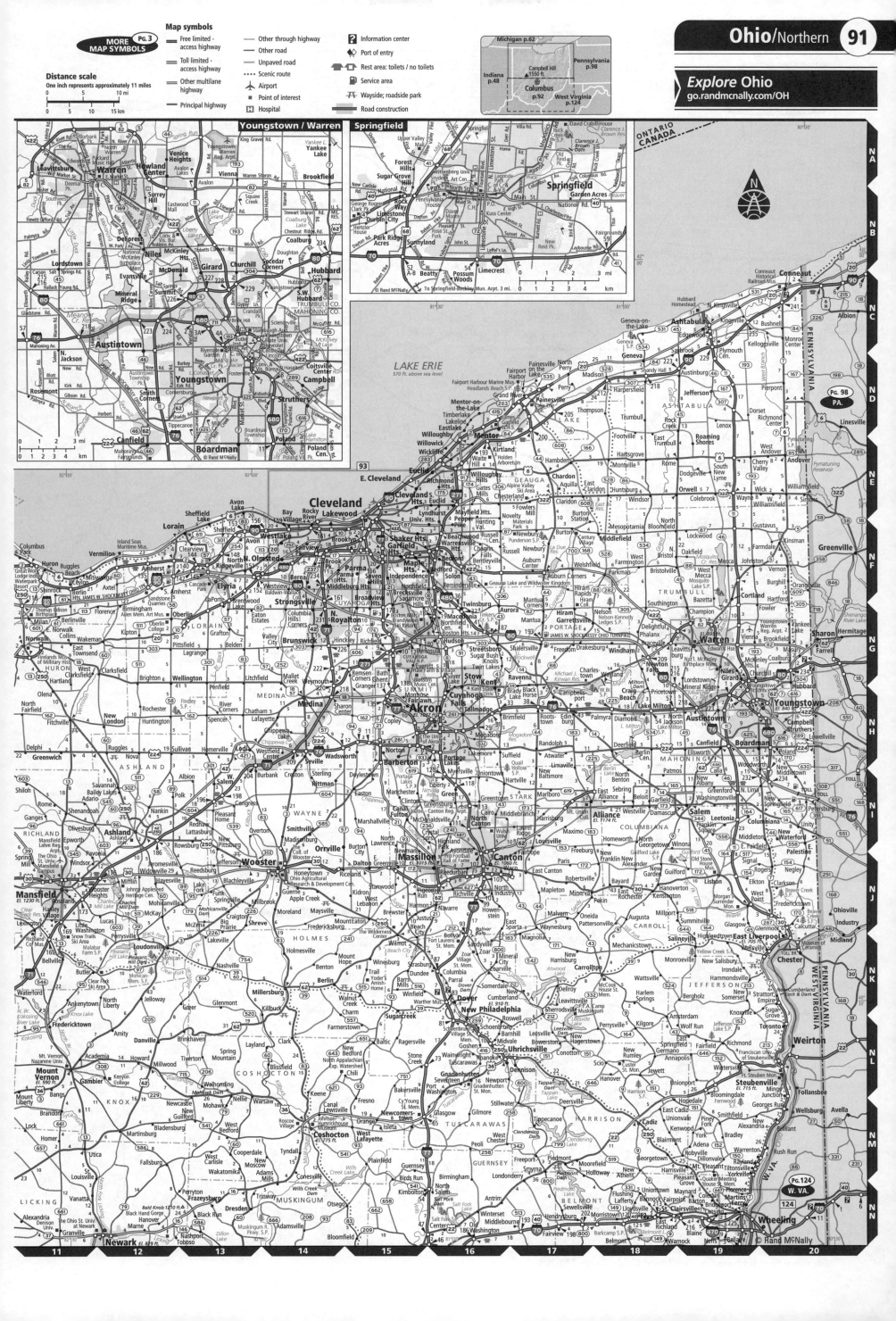

Nickname: The Buckeye State
Land area: 40,948 sq. mi. (rank: 35th)
Population: 11,464,042 (rank: 7th)
Largest city: Columbus, 730,657

INDEX OF CITIES PG. 145

Mileage between cities	Athens	Cambridge	Chillicothe	Cincinnati	Cleveland	Columbus	Dayton	Gallipolis	Huntington, WV	Jackson	Lancaster	Marietta	Portsmouth	Springfield	Washington C.H.	Wheeling	Wilmington	Zanesville
CINCINNATI	164	185	112		252	111	52	154	141	124	135	232	121	80	81	232	54	162
COLUMBUS	74	78	48	111	142		73	108	138	77	30	125	91	45	41	125	64	55
DAYTON	148	152	82	52	214	73		144	174	113	104	199	127	28	51	199	37	129
GALLIPOLIS	48	121	63	154	249	108	144		36	32	85	70	54	148	95	163	115	106
MARIETTA	44	50	106	232	166	125	199	74	137	86	83		131	171	138	92	185	70
PORTSMOUTH	87	161	43	121	232	91	127	54	47	47	86	131		131	78	208	98	138
SPRINGFIELD	120	124	74	80	186	45	28	148	178	117	76	171	131		43	171	39	101
ZANESVILLE	58	23	95	162	144	55	129	106	205	89	45	70	138	101	92	70	115	

Total mileage through Ohio

70	225 miles	75	211 miles
71	248 miles	77	160 miles

MORE MILEAGES Pg. 256

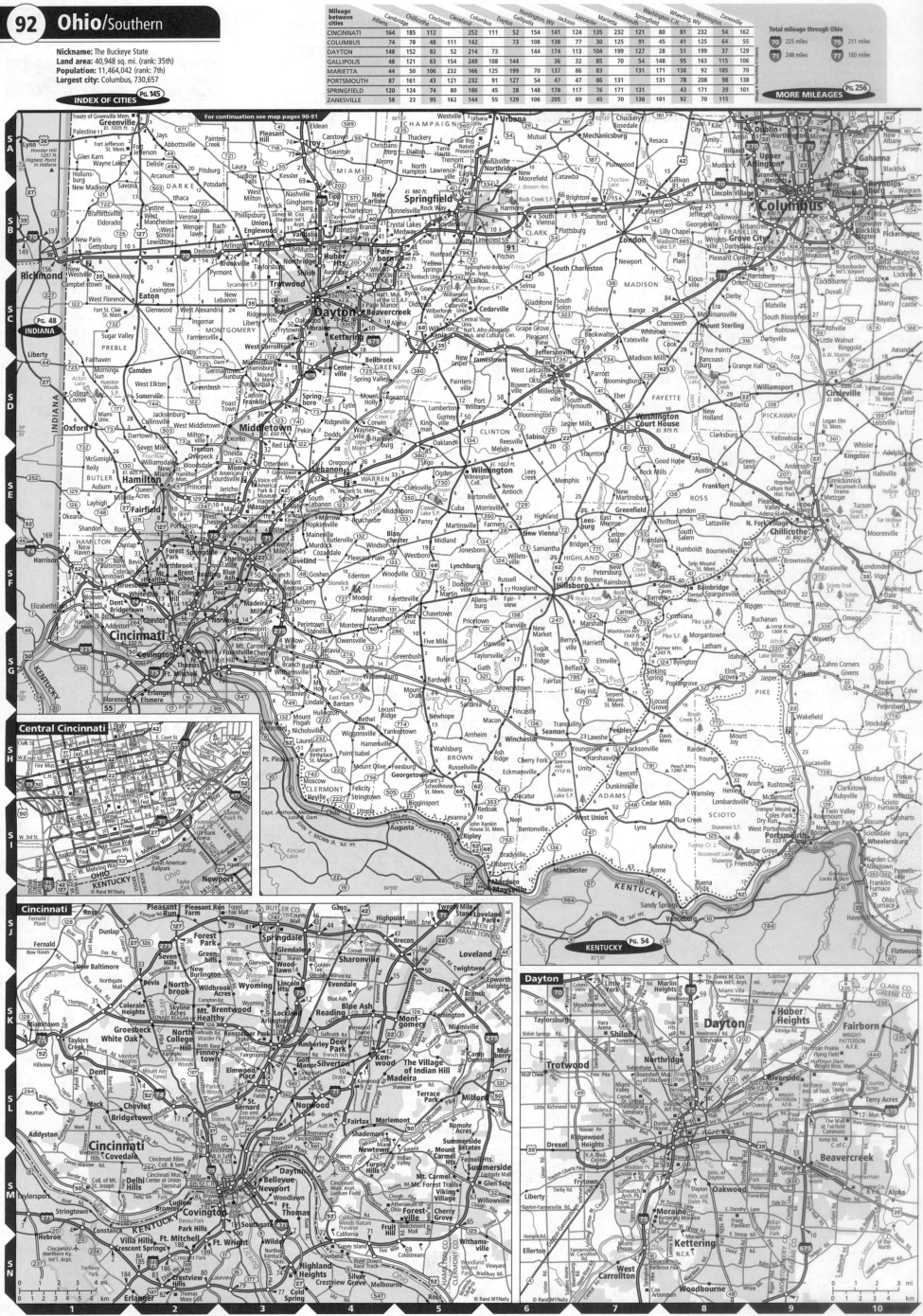

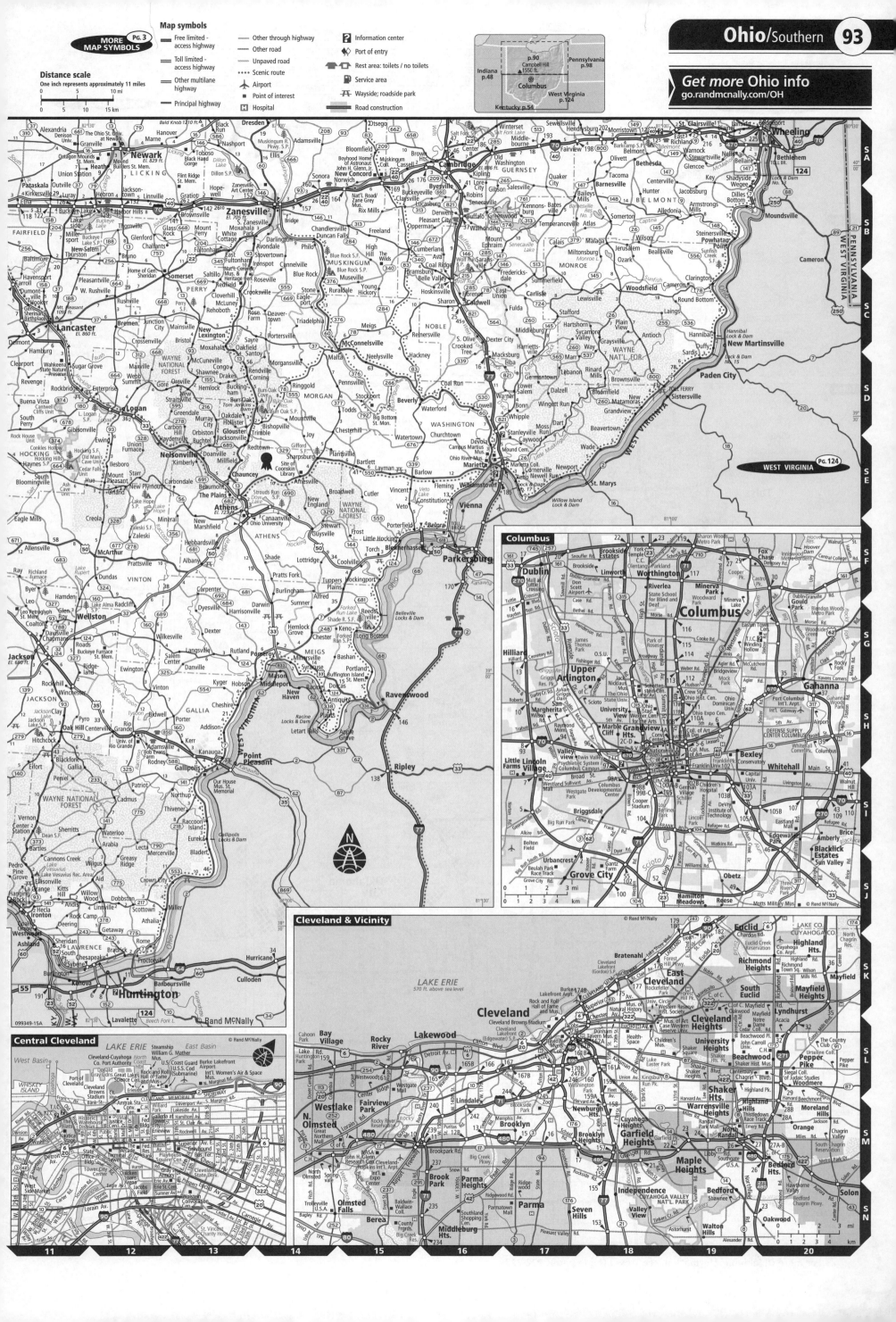

Get more Ohio info
go.randmcnally.com/OH

Nickname: The Sooner State
Land area: 68,667 sq. mi. (rank: 19th)
Population: 3,547,884 (rank: 28th)
Largest city: Oklahoma City, 531,324

INDEX OF CITIES Pg. 146

Mileage between cities	Altus	Ardmore	Bartlesville	Dallas TX	Elk City	Enid	Ft. Smith, AR	Guymon	Joplin, MO	Lawton	McAlester	Muskogee	Oklahoma City	Ponca City	Stillwater	Tulsa	Wichita Falls, TX	Woodward
ARDMORE	160		248	112	210	196	233	362	315	106	120	191	98	203	163	203	91	236
ELK CITY	59	210		263	320	151	292	185	330	108	240	250	112	218	178	218	144	79
ENID	195	196	132	306	151		231	213	229	145	204	164	98	69	65	115	198	87
LAWTON	55	106	238	187	108	145	263	297	305		211	221	87	193	153	193	53	171
MUSKOGEE	274	191	91	238	250	164	71	377	119	221	67		138	141	120	49	274	251
OKLAHOMA CITY	140	98	150	208	112	98	180	264	217	87	128	138		105	65	105	140	138
TULSA	246	203	45	262	218	115	116	328	114	193	93	49	105	92	71		246	202
WICHITA FALLS, TX	85	91	291	134	144	198	316	317	358	53	264	274	140	246	206	246		224

Total mileage through Oklahoma
35	236 miles	44	329 miles
40	331 miles	75	227 miles

MORE MILEAGES Pg. 256

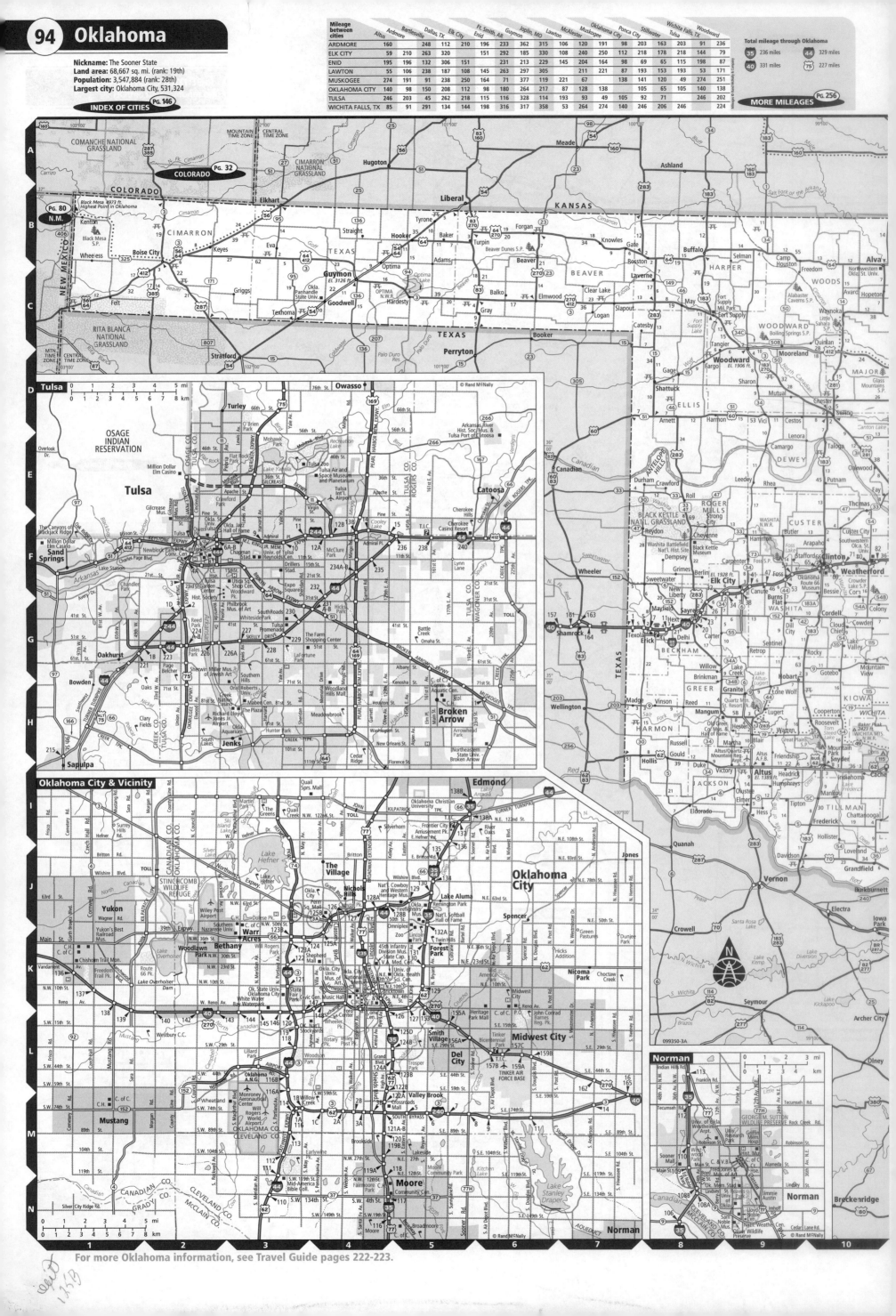

For more Oklahoma information, see Travel Guide pages 222-223.

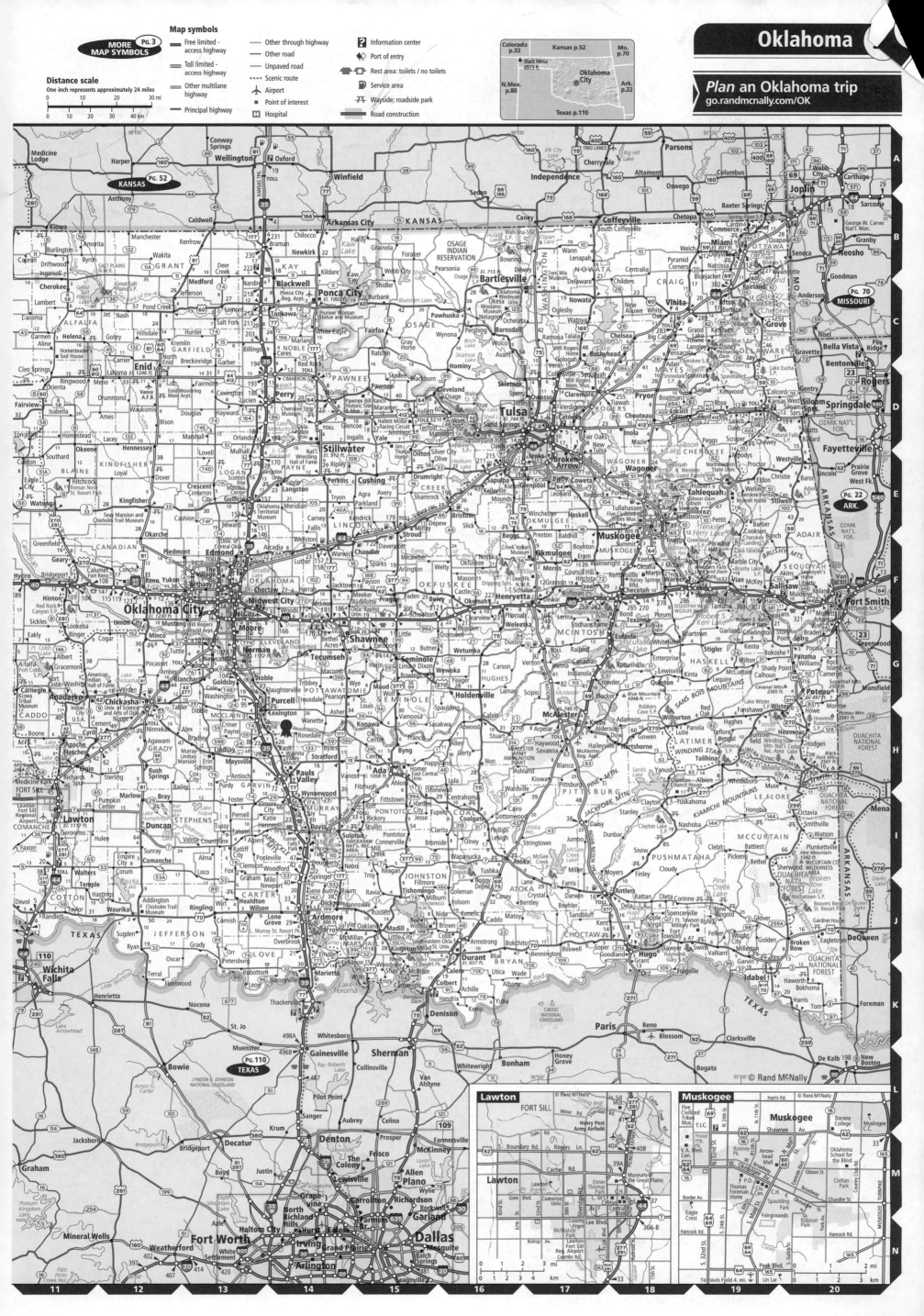

Nickname: The Beaver State
Land area: 95,997 sq. mi. (rank: 10th)
Population: 3,641,056 (rank: 27th)
Largest city: Portland, 533,427

INDEX OF CITIES — PG. 146

Mileage between cities	Astoria	Bend	Brookings	Burns	Coos Bay	Corvallis	Crater Lake NP	Eugene	Grants Pass	John Day	Klamath Falls	Lakeview	Medford	Ontario	Pendleton	Portland	Salem	The Dalles
BEND	257		296	130	222	128	106	115	194	153	139	175	175	261	243	161	132	133
BURNS	387	130	426		352	258	236	245	324	70	236	140	305	131	199	291	262	263
CORVALLIS	177	128	227	258	120		183	45	182	263	216	303	208	389	288	81	36	165
EUGENE	205	115	214	245	107	45	142		141	250	175	263	167	376	316	109	64	193
MEDFORD	368	175	129	305	170	208	79	167	27	328	78	172		436	418	272	227	356
ONTARIO	466	261	557	131	483	389	367	376	455	133	367	271	436		164	371	418	287
PENDLETON	302	243	515	199	408	288	349	316	421	129	382	339	418	164		207	254	123
PORTLAND	100	161	308	291	201	81	247	109	246	265	281	200	336	272	371		47	84

Total mileage through Oregon
- (5) 308 miles
- (84) 375 miles
- (82) 11 miles
- (101) 348 miles

MORE MILEAGES — PG. 256

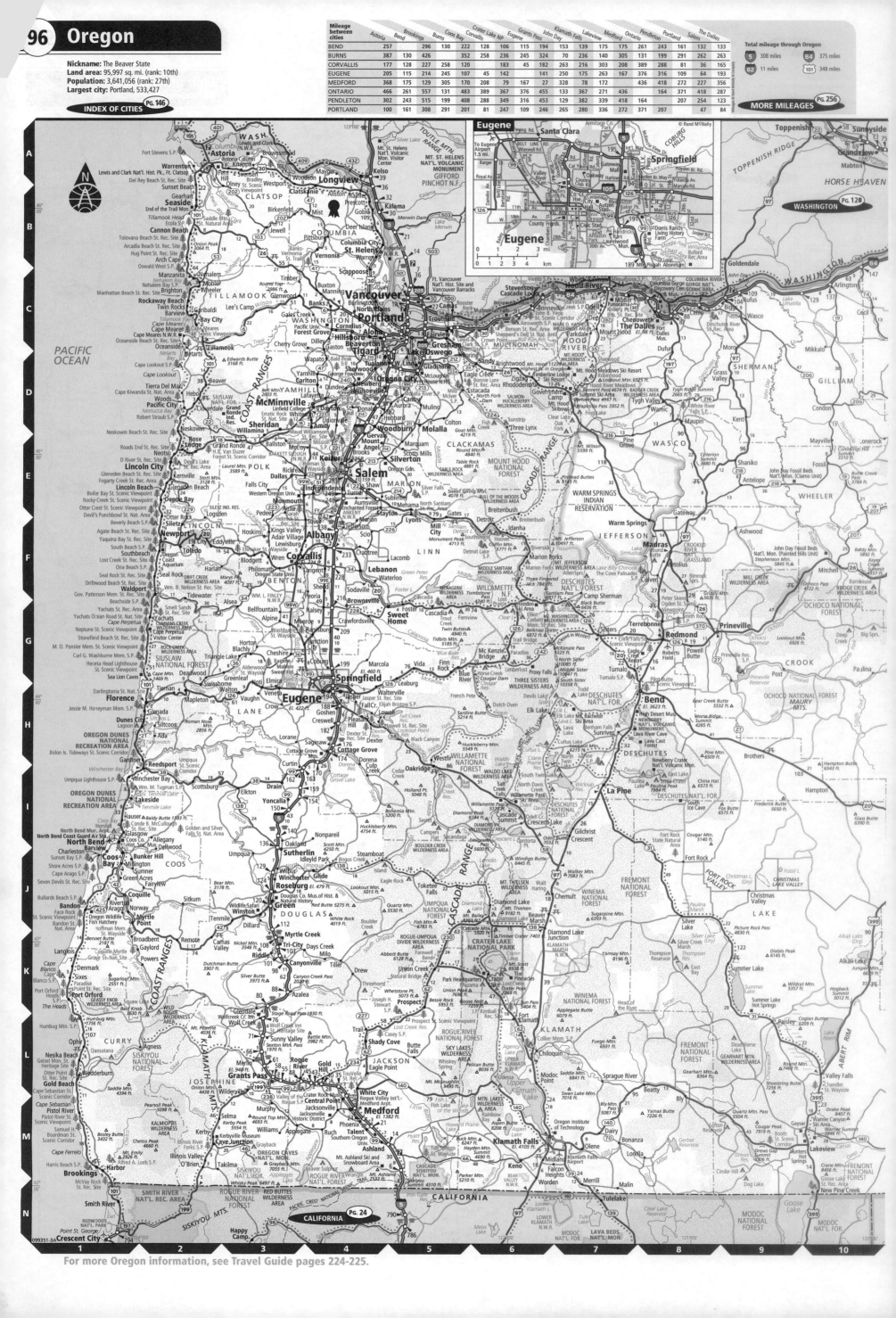

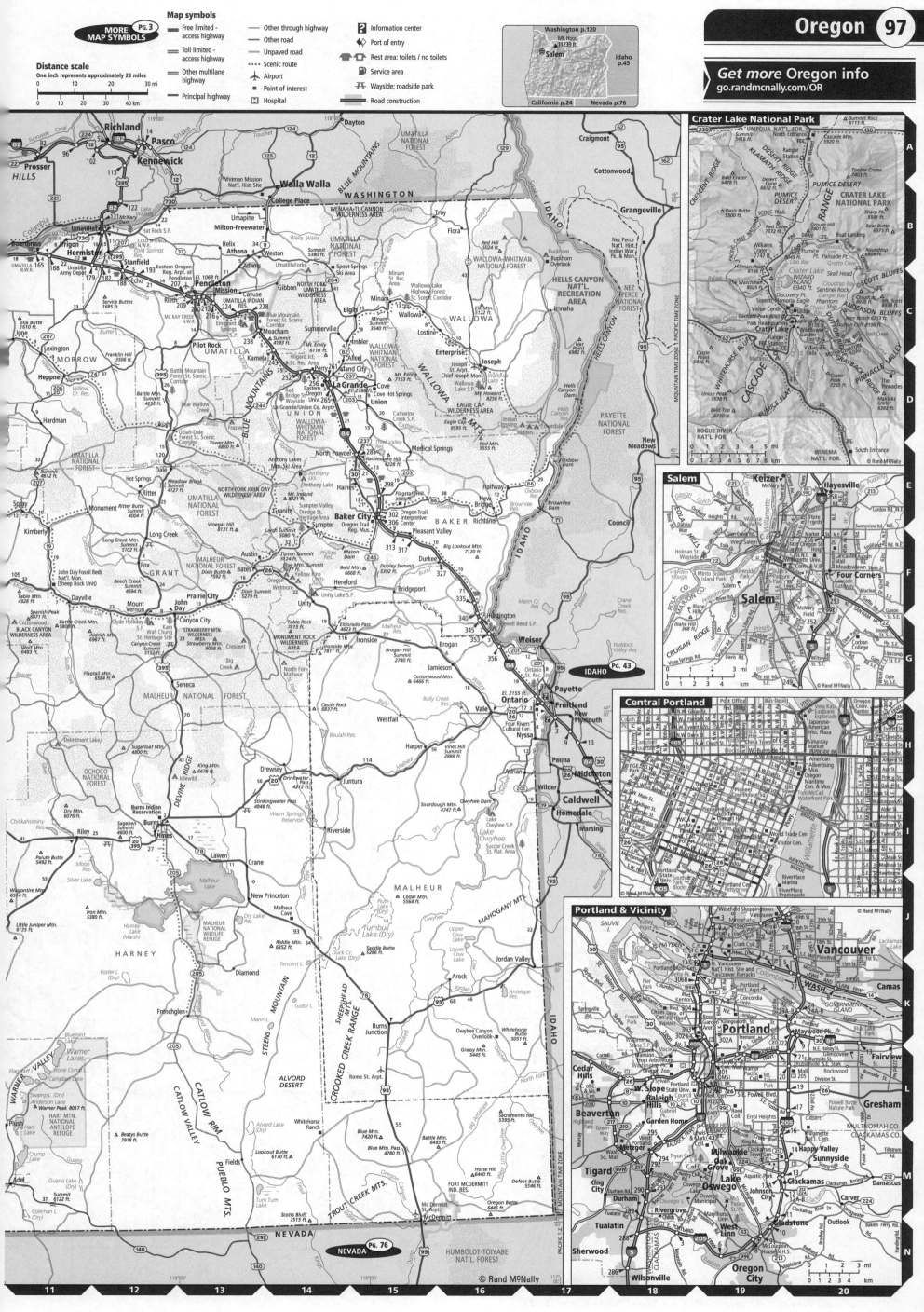

Nickname: The Keystone State
Land area: 44,817 sq. mi. (rank: 32nd)
Population: 12,429,616 (rank: 6th)
Largest city: Philadelphia, 1,463,281

INDEX OF CITIES Pg. 146

Mileage between cities	Altoona	Beaver Falls	Bedford	Chambersburg	Du Bois	Greensburg	Erie	Harrisburg	Indiana	Johnstown	Kittanning	Meadville	New Castle	Philadelphia	Pittsburgh	State College	Uniontown	Warren	Washington	Williamsport	Youngstown, OH
ALTOONA		132	35	92	73	203	73	134	57	45	78	168	144	238	95	43	112	133	127	105	160
ERIE	203	117	230	283	150		156	300	156	191	123	43	98	426	127	209	184	69	150	261	100
HARRISBURG	134	239	105	54	151	300		181		178	140	204	265	251	114	204	89	185	211	212	89	267
JOHNSTOWN	45	105	41	93	87	191	46	140	29		55	156	117	244	68	87	81	157	108	149	133
NEW CASTLE	144	22	156	209	110	98	82	251	82	117	51	63		355	54	169	110	118	74	221	16
PITTSBURGH	95	40	109	162	105	127	33	204	60	68	42	92	54	308		137	47	147	29	199	70
STATE COLLEGE	43	174	77	135	60	209	115	89	94	87	120	174	169	199	137		159	137	156	66	171
WILLIAMSPORT	105	240	139	135	112	261	175	89	156	149	172	226	221	184	199	66	216	172	231		223

Total mileage through Pennsylvania

70	168 miles	79	183 miles
80	311 miles	90	46 miles

MORE MILEAGES Pg. 256

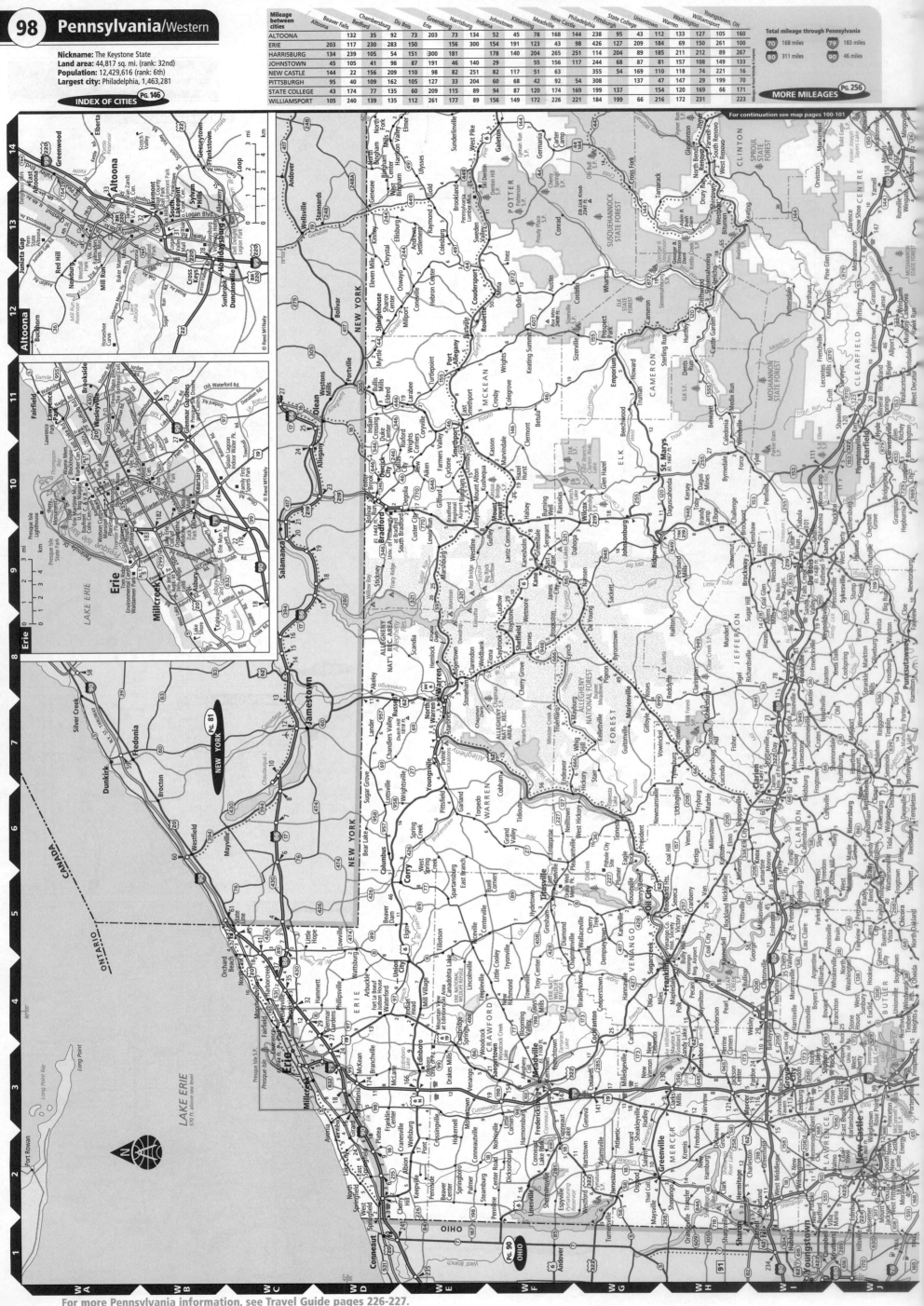

For continuation see map pages 100-101

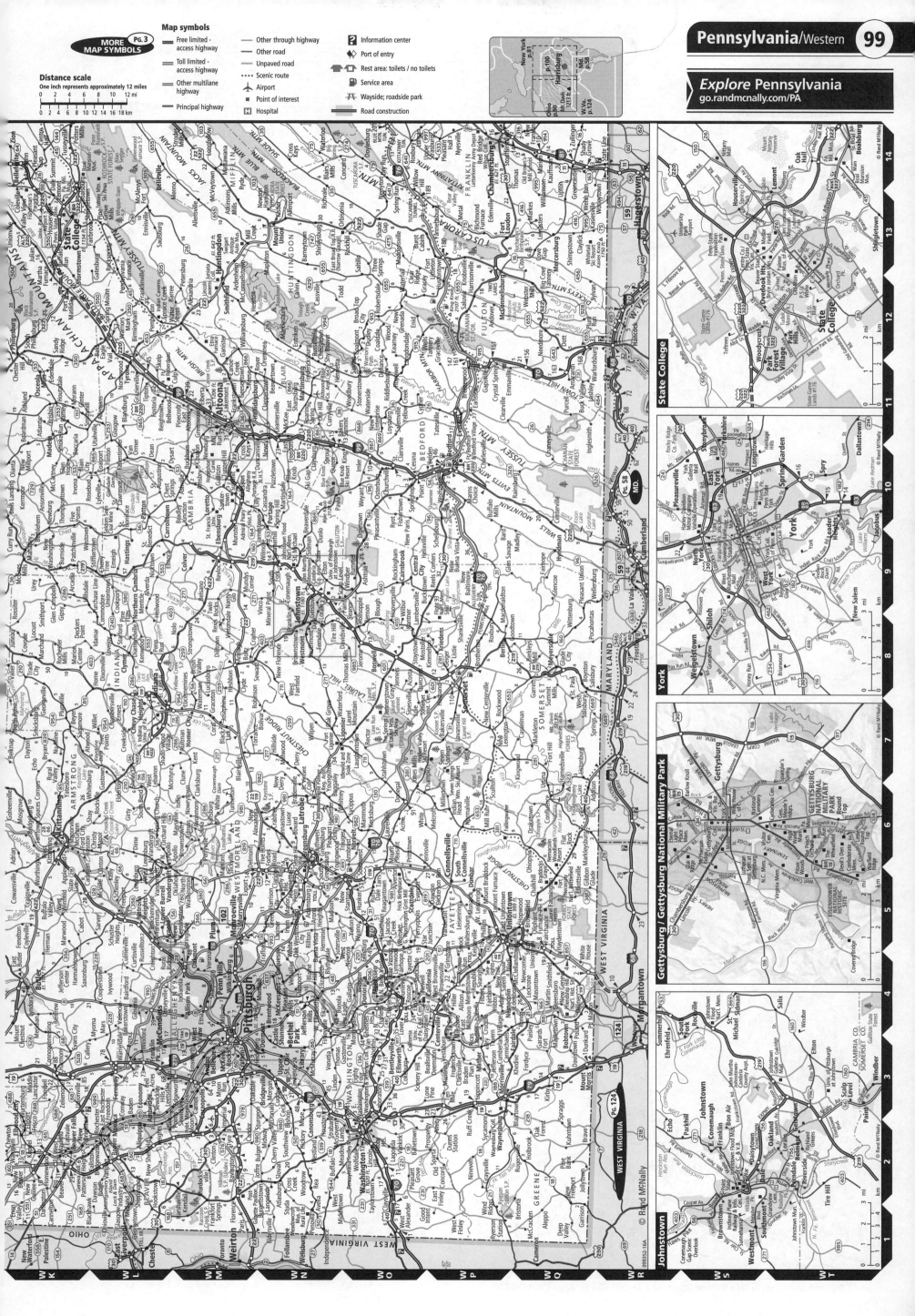

Nickname: The Keystone State
Land area: 44,817 sq. mi. (rank: 32nd)
Population: 12,429,616 (rank: 6th)
Largest city: Philadelphia, 1,463,281

INDEX OF CITIES — Pg. 146

Mileage between cities	Allentown	Altoona	Baltimore, MD	Binghamton, NY	Chambersburg	Easton	Gettysburg	Harrisburg	Hazleton	Lancaster	Mansfield	Philadelphia	Pittsburgh	Port Jervis, NY	Reading	Scranton	State College	Trenton, NJ	Wilkes-Barre	Williamsport	York
ALLENTOWN		214	162	134	134	19	123	84	49	72	183	66	284	83	34	76	169	78	62	134	110
CHAMBERSBURG	134	92	97	234		149	25	54	129	88	184	158	162	231	111	170	135	177	156	135	71
HARRISBURG	84	134	88	184	54	99	39		79	44	138	104	204	181	67	120	89	133	106	89	36
PHILADELPHIA	66	238	102	184	158	81	143	114	99	83	233		308	145	65	120	199	35	112	184	109
READING	34	191	100	158	111	53	90	67	53	34	163	65	261	119		100	152	84	86	114	60
SCRANTON	76	192	198	59	170	68	159	120	47	154	104	126	286	61	100		153	138	16	106	146
STATE COLLEGE	169	43	173	217	135	190	126	89	128	129	111	199	137	214	152	153		218	139	66	121
WILLIAMSPORT	134	105	173	125	135	143	126	89	81	129	49	184	199	167	114	106	66	196	70		121

Total mileage through Pennsylvania
76 — 350 miles 81 — 232 miles
80 — 311 miles 95 — 51 miles

MORE MILEAGES — Pg. 256

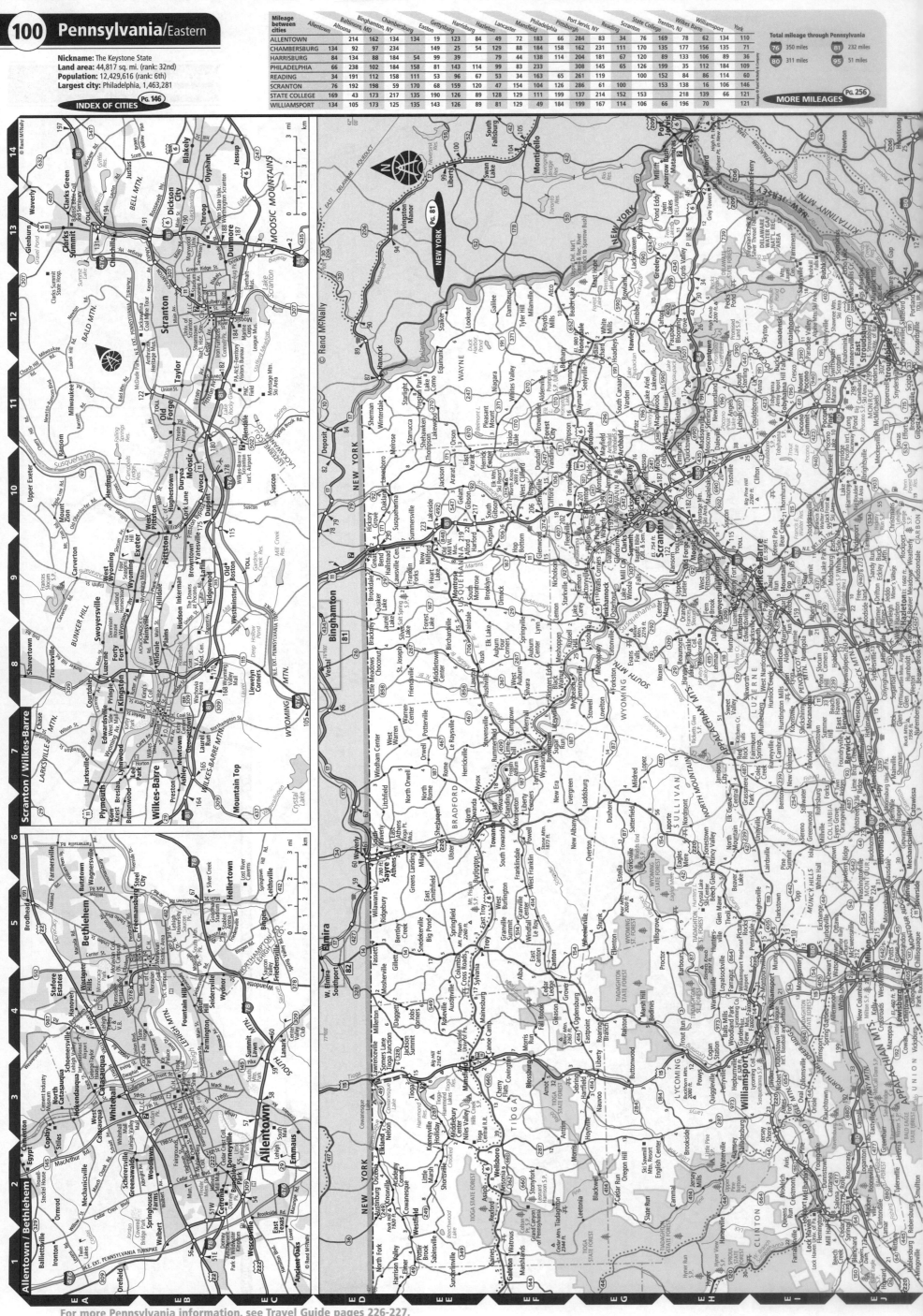

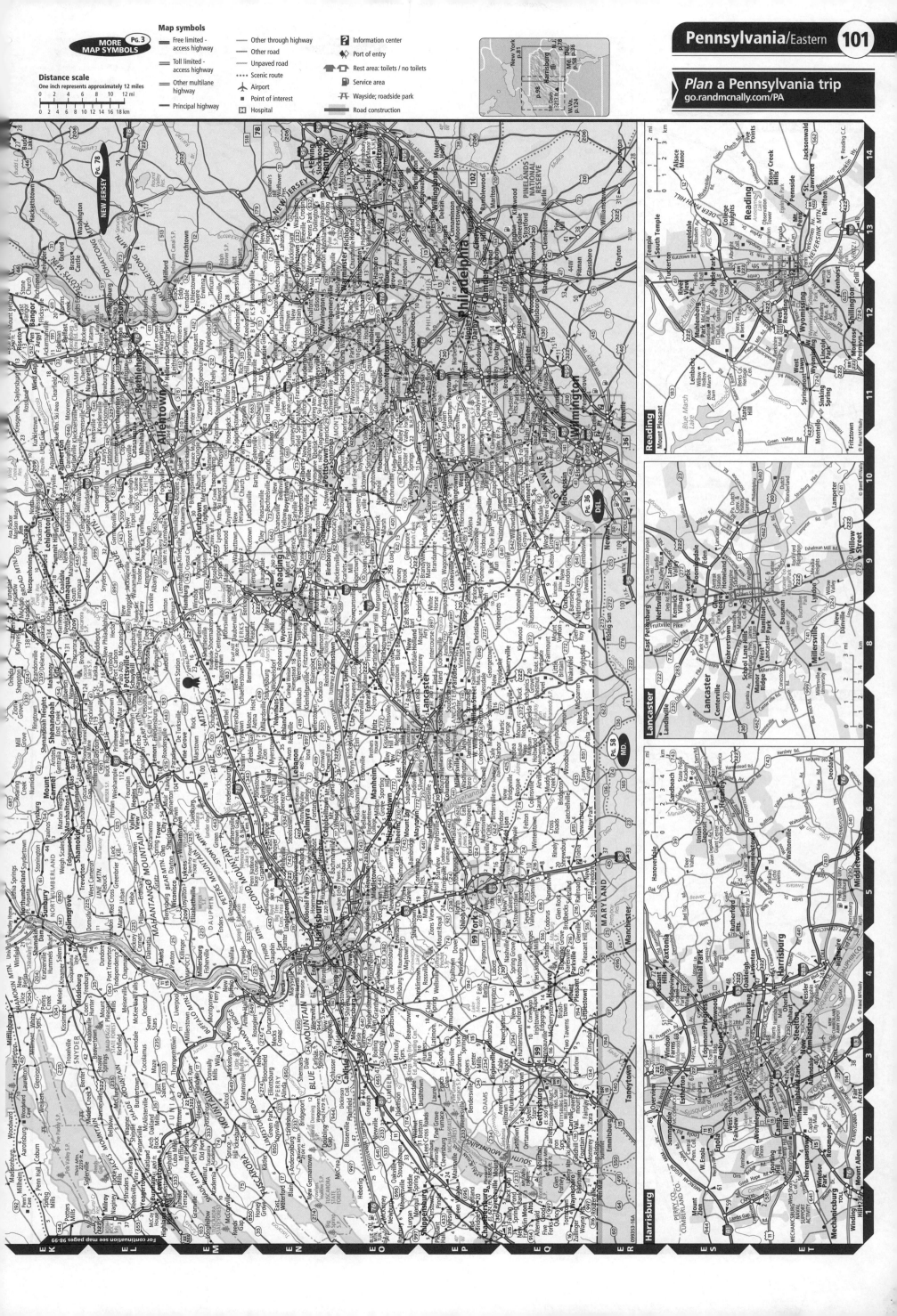

Map symbols

MORE MAP SYMBOLS   PG. 3

Distance scale
One inch represents approximately 12 miles

Free limited - access highway
Toll limited - access highway
Other multilane highway
Principal highway
Other through highway
Other road
Unpaved road
Scenic route
Airport
Point of interest
Hospital

Information center
Port of entry
Rest area: toilets / no toilets
Service area
Wayside; roadside park
Road construction

Reading

Mount Pleasant

Lancaster

Harrisburg

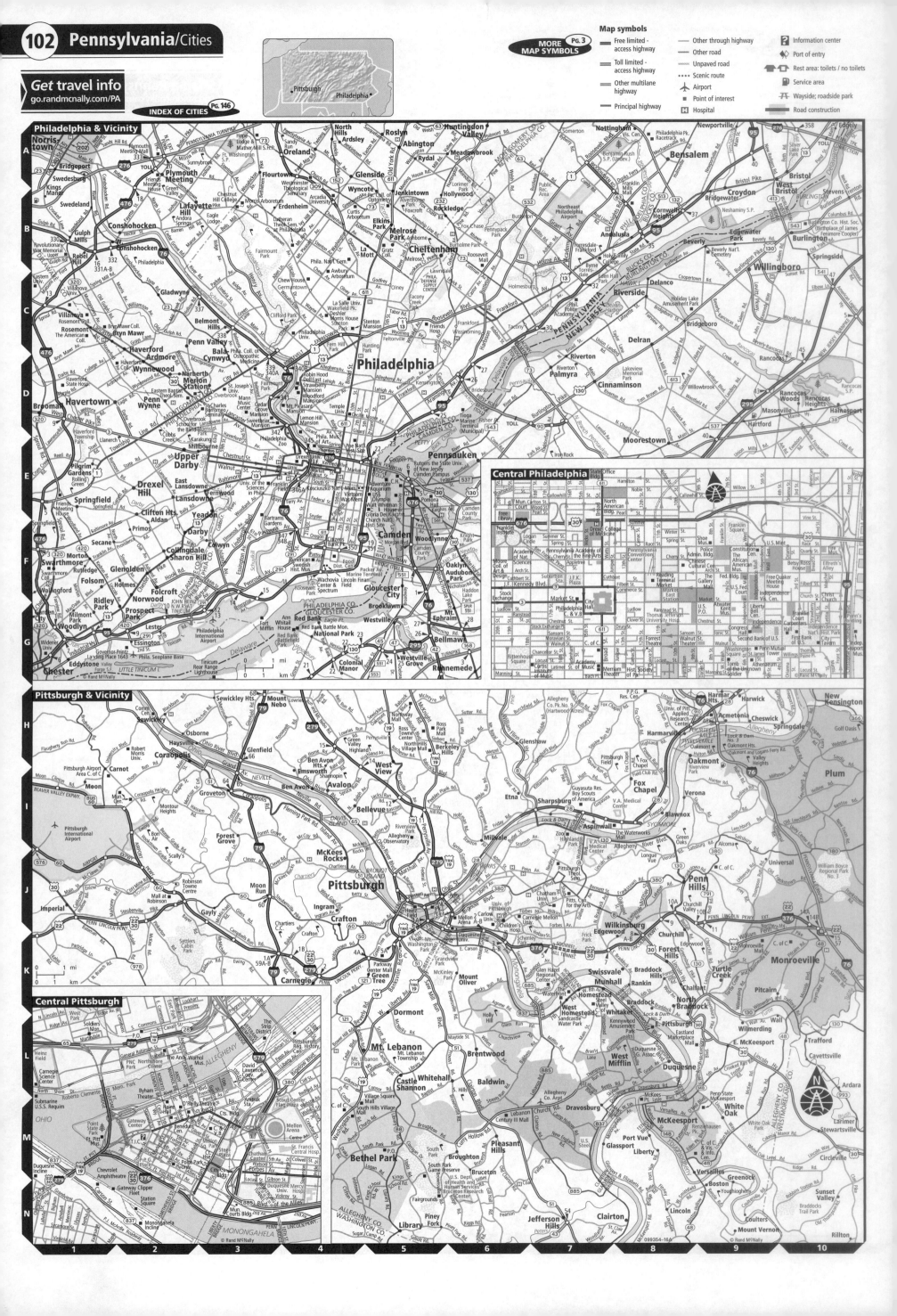

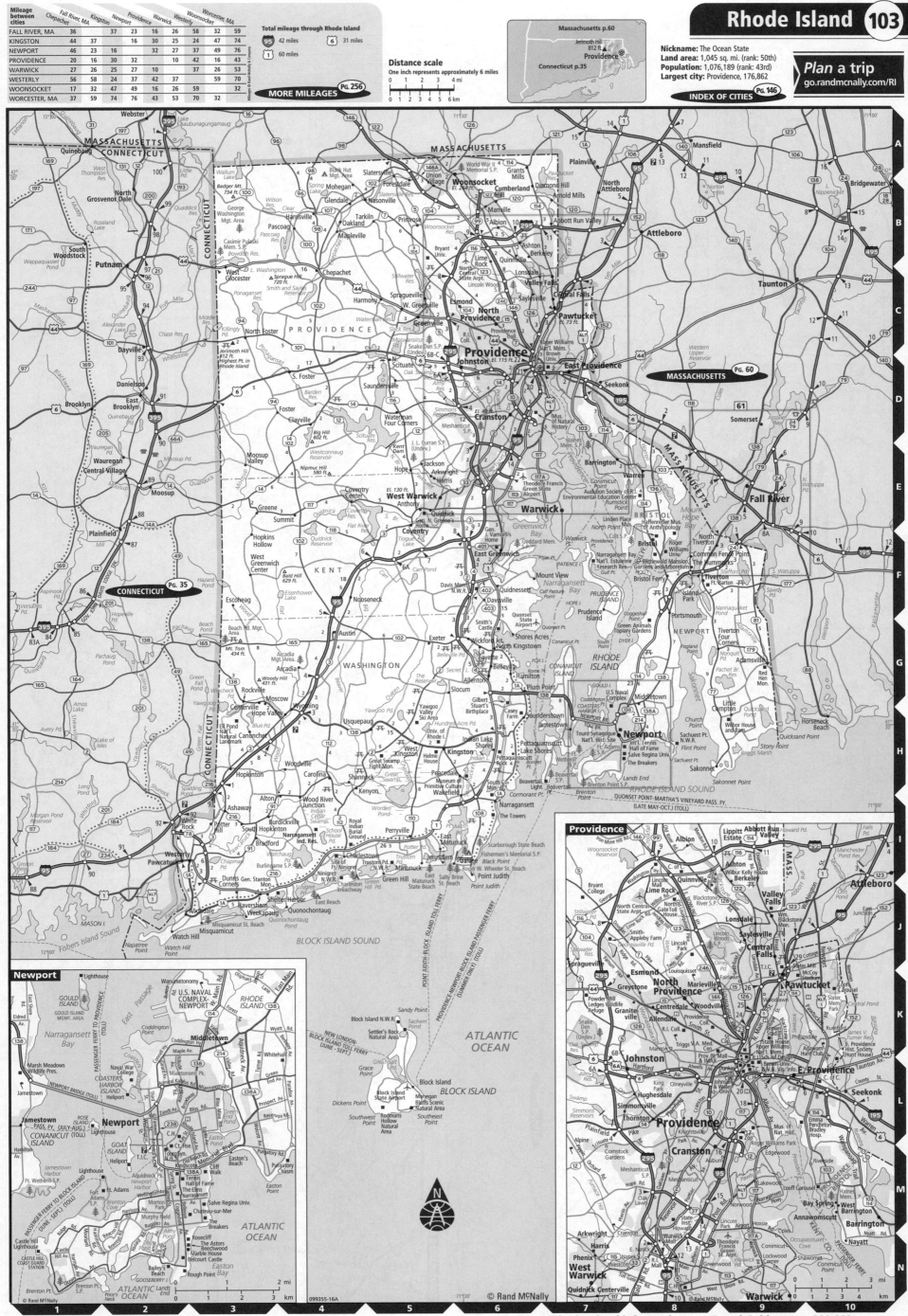

Nickname: The Ocean State
Land area: 1,045 sq. mi. (rank: 50th)
Population: 1,076,189 (rank: 43rd)
Largest city: Providence, 176,862

Plan a trip
go.randmcnally.com/RI

INDEX OF CITIES PG. 146

Mileage between cities	Chepachet	Fall River, MA	Kingston	Newport	Providence	Warwick	Westerly	Woonsocket	Worcester, MA
FALL RIVER, MA	36		37	23	16	26	58	32	59
KINGSTON	44	37		16	30	25	24	47	74
NEWPORT	46	23	16		32	27	37	49	76
PROVIDENCE	20	16	30	32		10	42	16	43
WARWICK	27	26	25	27	10		37	26	53
WESTERLY	56	58	24	37	42	37		59	70
WOONSOCKET	17	32	47	49	16	26	59		32
WORCESTER, MA	37	59	74	76	43	53	70	32	

Total mileage through Rhode Island
95 42 miles   6 31 miles
1 60 miles

Distance scale
One inch represents approximately 6 mi
0 1 2 3 4 mi
0 1 2 3 4 5 6 km

MORE MILEAGES PG. 256

Massachusetts p.60
Jerimoth Hill 812 ft.
Providence
Connecticut p.35

Get **travel info**
go.randmcnally.com/SC

Nickname: The Palmetto State
Land area: 30,109 sq. mi. (rank: 40th)
Population: 4,255,083 (rank: 25th)
Largest city: Columbia, 117,088

INDEX OF CITIES PG. 146

Mileage between cities	Anderson	Augusta, GA	Beaufort	Charleston	Charlotte, NC	Columbia	Fayetteville, NC	Georgetown	Greenwood	Myrtle Beach	Orangeburg	Savannah, GA	Spartanburg	Sumter
AUGUSTA, GA	104		122	176	158	68	233	212	59	214	85	140	120	116
CHARLESTON	223	176	69		207	113	217	99	196	95	77	105	202	99
CHARLOTTE, NC	134	158	229	207		91	139	190	123	173	136	249	75	115
COLUMBIA	114	68	135	113	91		166	128	87	147	42	155	93	44
FLORENCE	189	146	152	110	105	79	91	85	162	68	172	168	45
MYRTLE BEACH	257	214	170	95	173	147	127	36	230		144	206	236	97
SAVANNAH, GA	265	140	39	105	249	155	259	170	204	206	119		244	141
SPARTANBURG	60	120	224	202	75	93	255	238	64	236	131	244		137

Total mileage through South Carolina
20 142 miles   **85** 106 miles
26 221 miles   **95** 199 miles

Distance scale
One inch represents approximately 23 miles

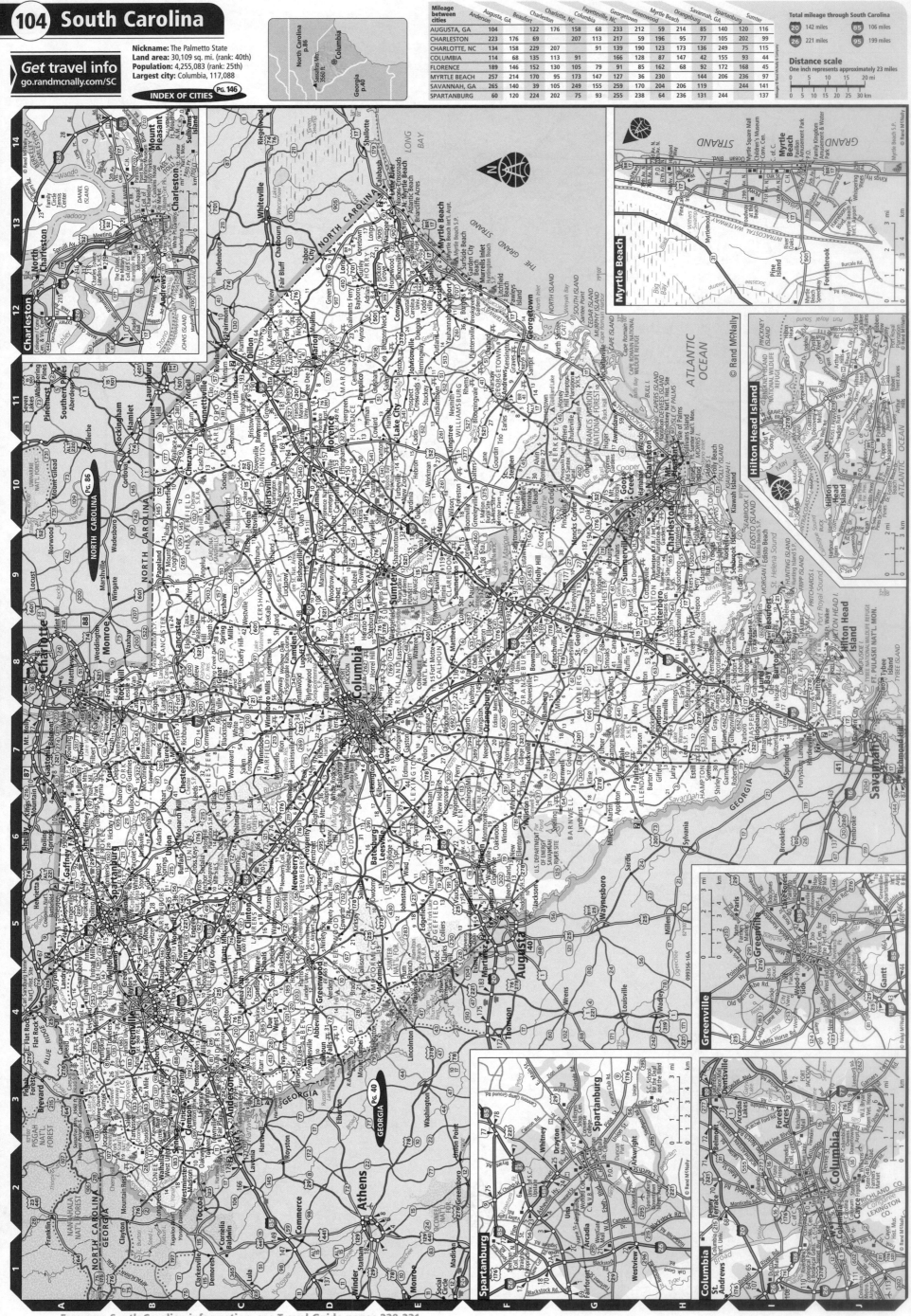

Nickname: The Mount Rushmore State
Land area: 75,885 sq. mi. (rank: 16th)
Population: 775,933 (rank: 46th)
Largest city: Sioux Falls, 139,517

Plan a trip
go.randmcnally.com/SD

INDEX OF CITIES   Pg. 146

Mileage between cities	Aberdeen	Belle Fourche	Mobridge	Pierre	Rapid City	Sioux City, IA	Sioux Falls	Watertown
ABERDEEN		312	100	159	350	285	204	105
BELLE FOURCHE	312		213	247	60	485	404	365
MOBRIDGE	100	213		109	241	385	304	205
PIERRE	159	247	109		191	306	225	190
RAPID CITY	350	60	241	191		429	348	406
SIOUX CITY, IA	285	485	385	306	429		85	185
SIOUX FALLS	204	404	304	225	348	85		104
WATERTOWN	105	365	205	190	406	185	104	

Total mileage through South Dakota
29 — 253 miles   12 — 317 miles
90 — 413 miles   83 — 242 miles

MORE MILEAGES   Pg. 256

Distance scale
One inch represents approximately 33 miles

For more South Dakota information, see Travel Guide pages 232-233.

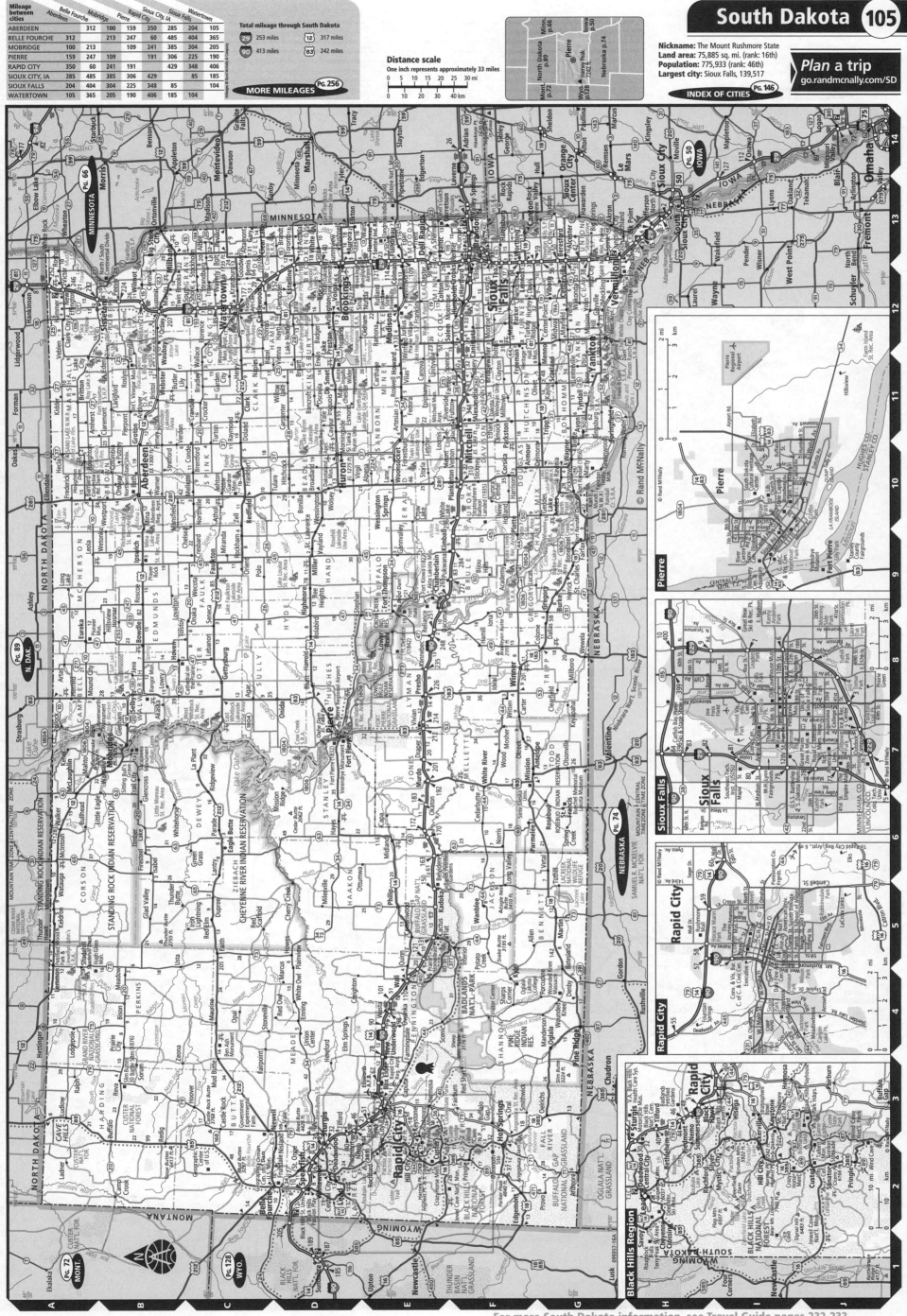

Nickname: The Volunteer State
Land area: 41,217 sq. mi. (rank: 34th)
Population: 5,962,959 (rank: 16th)
Largest city: Memphis, 672,277

INDEX OF CITIES PG. 146

MORE MILEAGES PG. 256

Mileage between cities	Atlanta, GA	Bristol	Chattanooga	Clarksville	Cookeville	Dyersburg	Fayetteville	Gatlinburg	Jackson	Johnson City	Kingsport	Knoxville	La Follette	Memphis	Morristown	Nashville	Oak Ridge	Union City
CHATTANOOGA	115	227		172	100	297	97	154	255	221	213	114	151	335	161	127	114	310
CLARKSVILLE	287	336	172		124	174	137	263	132	330	322	223	260	212	270	47	207	139
DYERSBURG	412	463	297	174	251		242	390	49	457	449	350	387	76	397	173	334	35
FAYETTEVILLE	212	324	97	137	109	242		251	200	318	310	211	248	252	258	90	190	232
JOHNSON CITY	268	25	221	330	210	457	318	415			24	107	44	495	72	285	132	468
KNOXVILLE	215	113	114	223	103	350	211	40	308	107	99		39	388	47	178	25	361
MEMPHIS	393	501	335	212	289	76	252	428	87	495	487	388	425		435	211	372	113
NASHVILLE	242	291	127	47	79	173	90	291	131	285	277	178	215	211	225		162	185

Total mileage through Tennessee

40	455 miles	75	161 miles
65	121 miles	81	76 miles

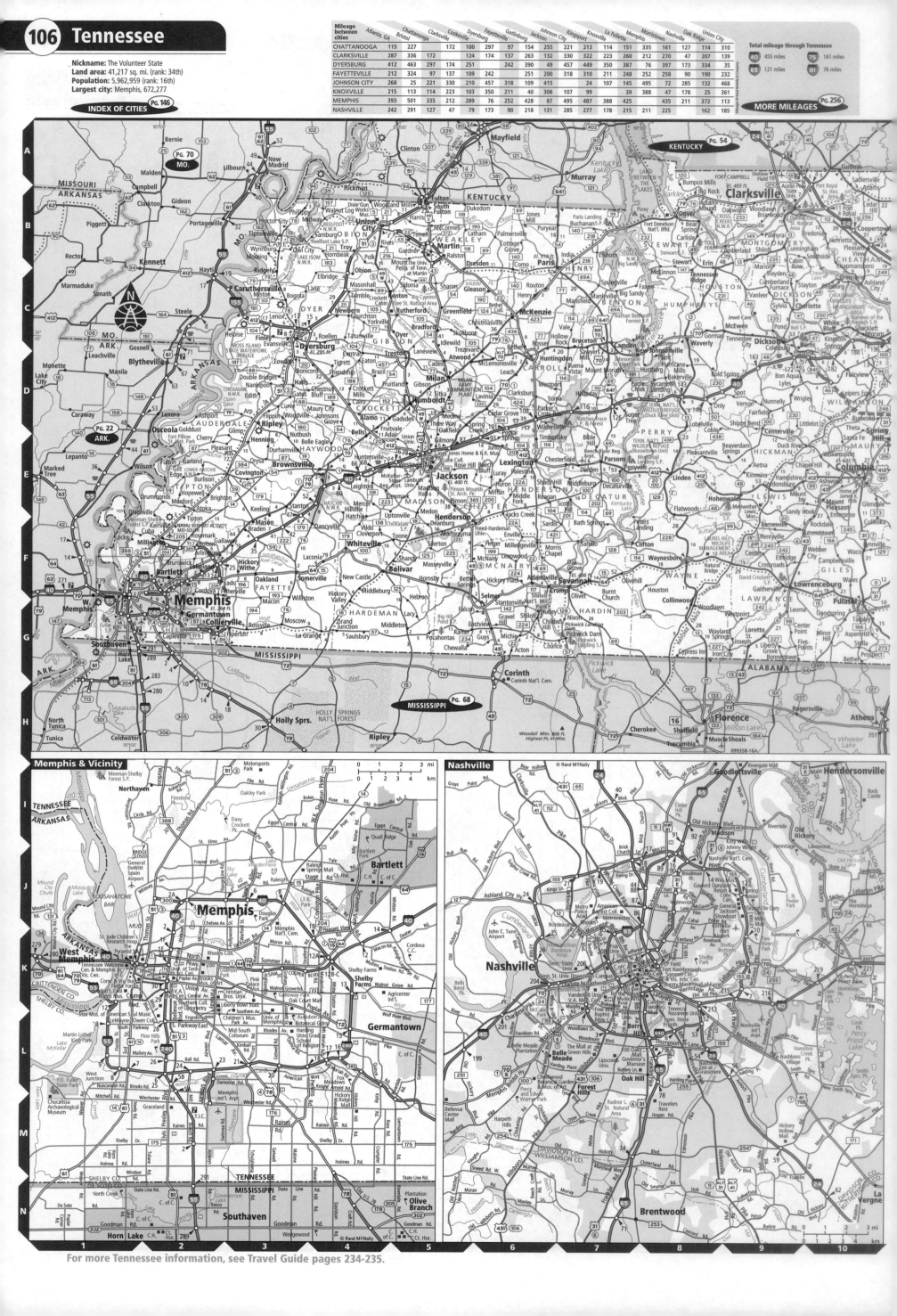

Memphis & Vicinity

Nashville

For more Tennessee information, see Travel Guide pages 234-235.

© Rand McNally

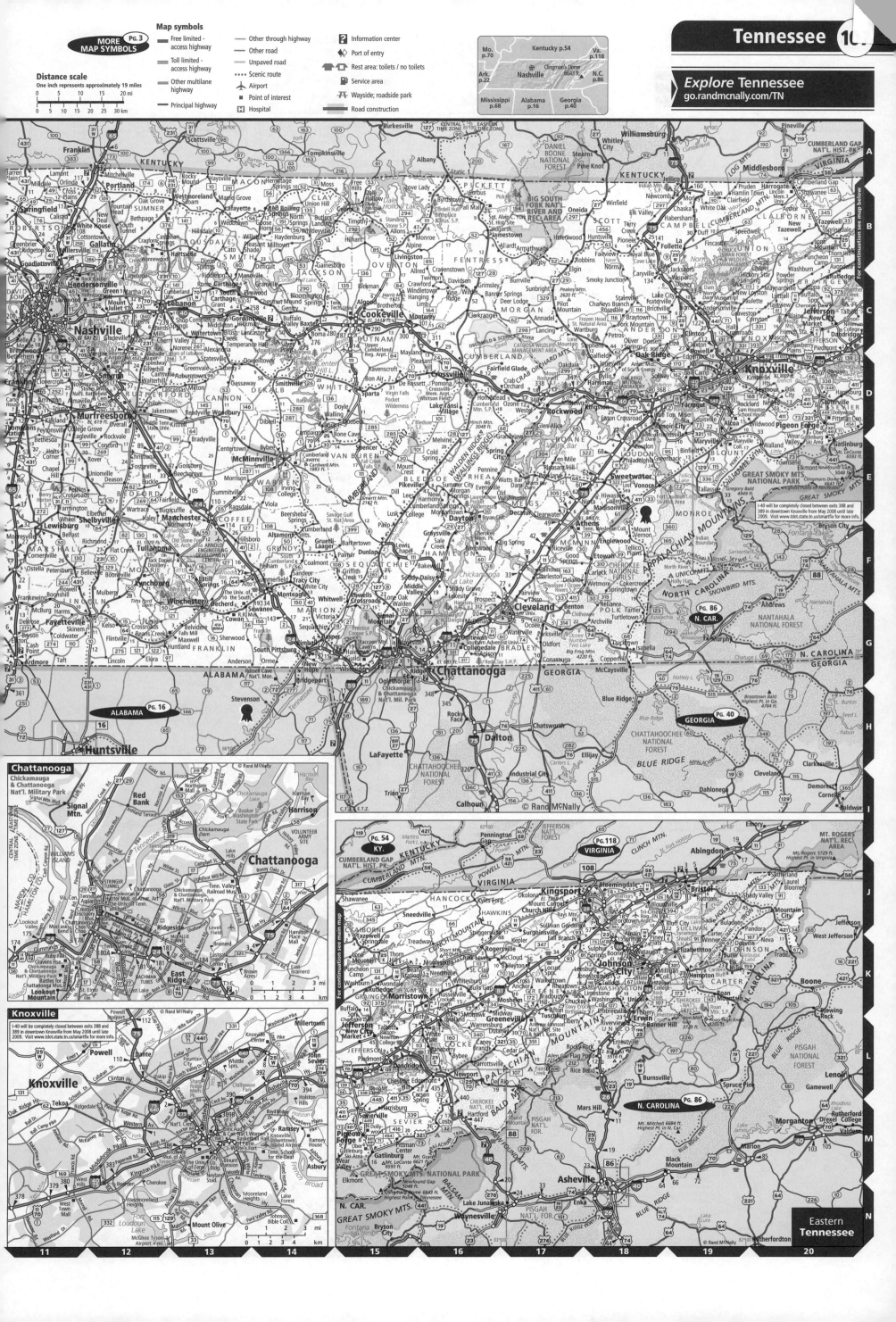

Eastern
Tennessee

Plan a trip
go.randmcnally.com/TN

Get travel info
go.randmcnally.com/TX

INDEX OF CITIES PG. 147

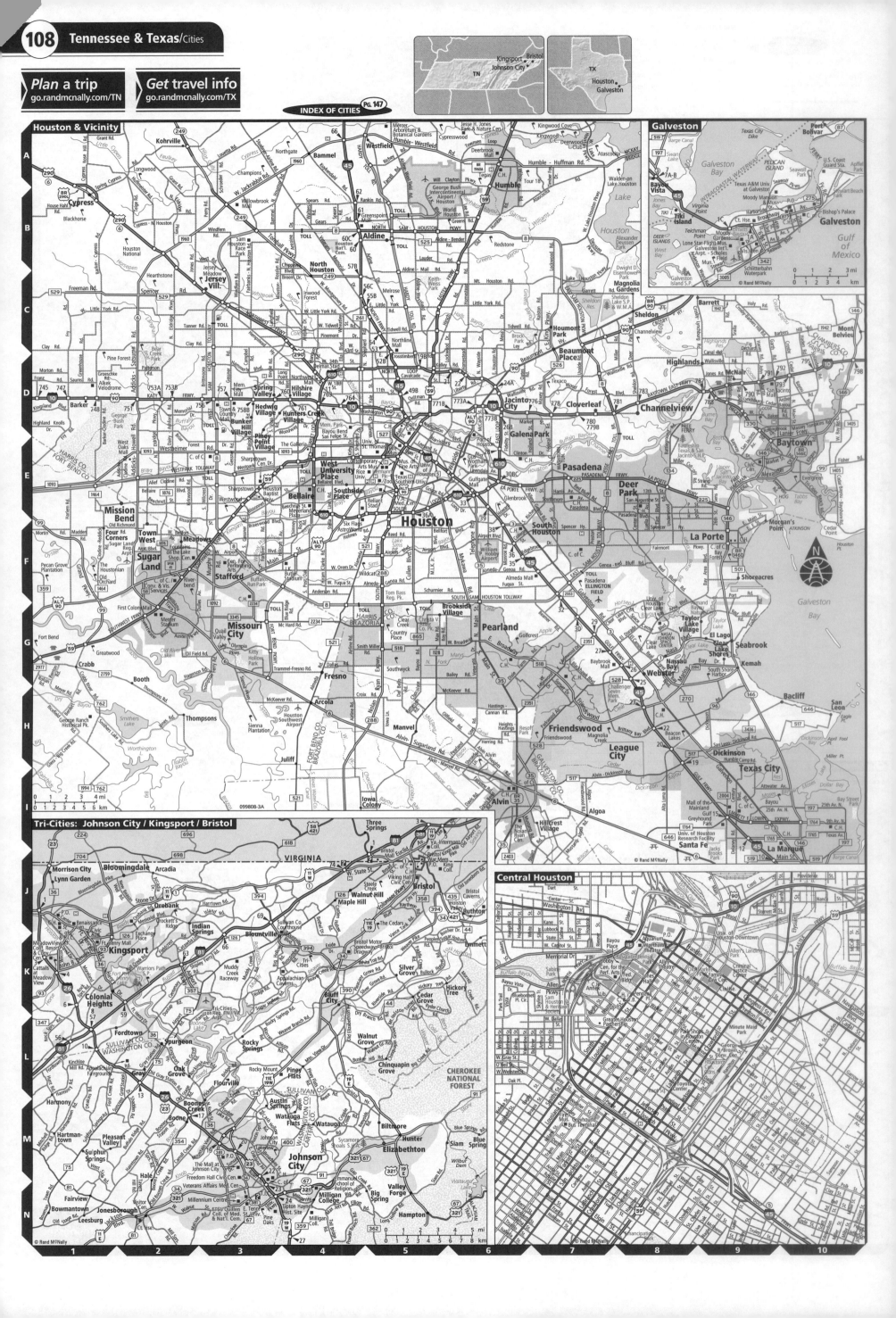

Houston & Vicinity

Galveston

Central Houston

Tri-Cities: Johnson City / Kingsport / Bristol

© Rand McNally

MORE MAP SYMBOLS PG. 3

Map symbols

- Free limited-access highway
- Toll limited-access highway
- Other multilane highway
- Principal highway
- Other through highway
- Other road
- Unpaved road
- •••• Scenic route
- ✈ Airport
- ■ Point of interest
- Ⓗ Hospital
- ? Information center
- ◆ Port of entry
- Rest area: toilets / no toilets
- Service area
- Wayside; roadside park
- Road construction

Plan a trip
go.randmcnally.com/TX

INDEX OF CITIES PG. 147

Dallas / Fort Worth & Vicinity

Central Dallas

Central Fort Worth

© Rand McNally

Nickname: The Lone Star State
Land area: 261,797 sq. mi. (rank: 2nd)
Population: 22,859,968 (rank: 2nd)
Largest city: Houston, 2,016,582

INDEX OF CITIES Pg. 147

Mileage between cities	Abilene	Amarillo	Big Bend NP	Big Spring	Carlsbad, NM	Childress	Clovis, NM	Dallas	Del Rio	Eagle Pass	El Paso	Fort Stockton	Houston	Lubbock	Midland	Odessa	Pecos	Perryton	San Angelo	San Antonio	Van Horn
ABILENE		283	379	108	276	155	269	185	247	302	447	252	347	165	147	168	242	307	92	261	328
AMARILLO	283		469	225	296	117	103	359	449	504	432	342	605	118	235	258	332	121	300	512	418
DALLAS	185	359		565	294	462	242	455		425	416	633	438	247	351	333	334	396	262	277	514
EL PASO	447	432	324	340	165	556	314	633				238	753	344	301	284	207	524	402	558	119
LUBBOCK	165	118	351	61	179	147	104	351	331	386	344	224	519		117	140	214	239	182	394	300
ODESSA	168	258	213	61	139	277	203	354	250	305	281	86	546	140		22	76	379	131	351	162
SAN ANGELO	92	300	290	86	255	286	262	155	210	402	163	363	182	111	205	378				213	283
SAN ANTONIO	261	512	446	299	458	417	498	277	151	139	558	319	199	394	331	351	374	569	213		439

Total mileage through Texas
- 10 — 881 miles
- 40 — 177 miles
- 20 — 636 miles

MORE MILEAGES Pg. 256

For more Texas information, see Travel Guide pages 236-238.

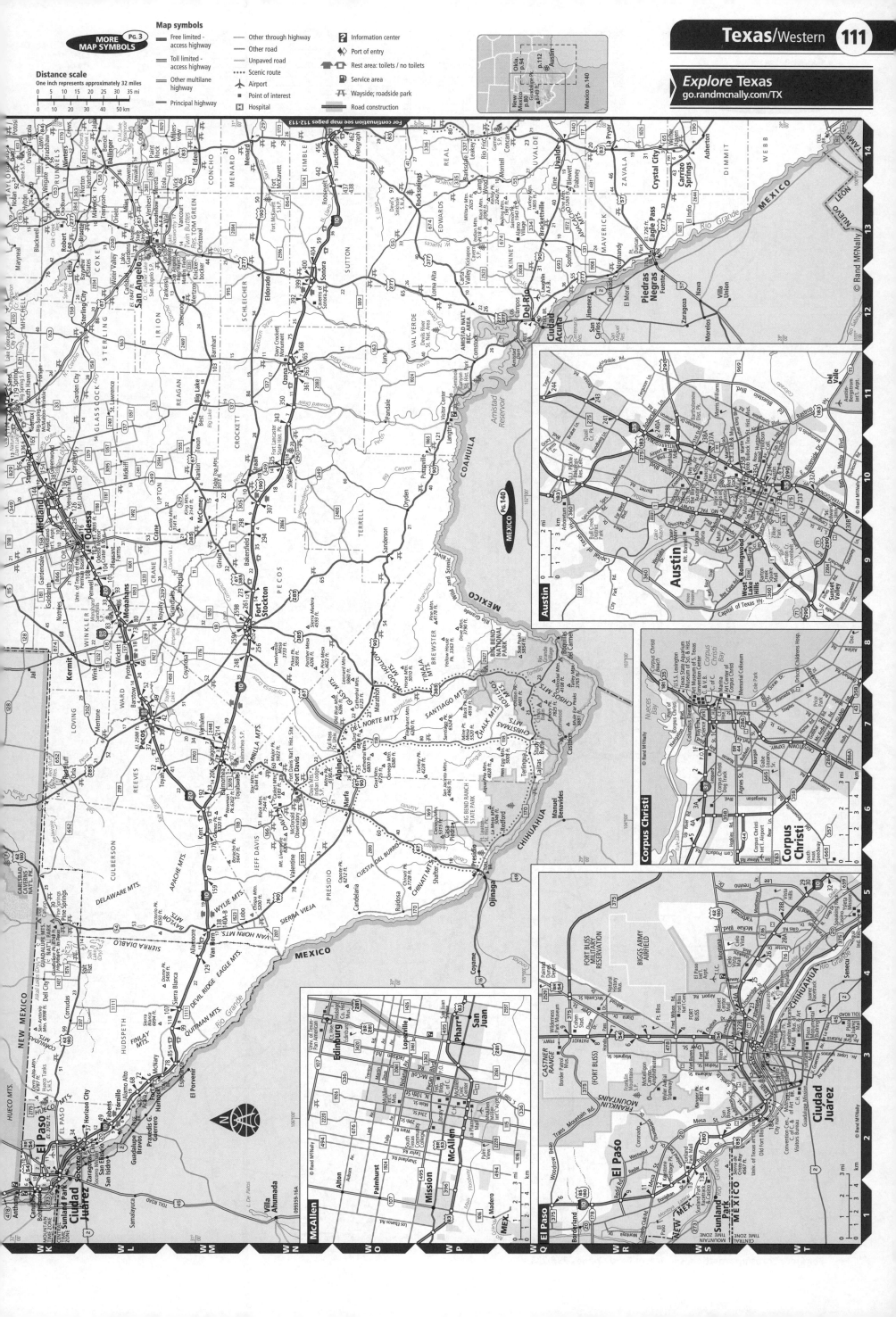

Nickname: The Lone Star State
Land area: 261,797 sq. mi. (rank: 2nd)
Population: 22,859,968 (rank: 2nd)
Largest city: Houston, 2,016,582

INDEX OF CITIES — Pg. 147

Mileage between cities	Abilene	Austin	Beaumont	Brownsville	Corpus Christi	Dallas	Fort Worth	Galveston	Houston	Laredo	Lufkin	McAllen	Paris	San Angelo	San Antonio	Shreveport, LA	Texarkana	Tyler	Victoria	Waco	Wichita Falls
ABILENE		230	467	539	405	185	155	394	347	409	359	497	294	92	261	373	362	285	352	191	141
AUSTIN	230		246	352	218	195	190	209	162	232	222	310	304	206	82	327	372	228	124	99	303
BROWNSVILLE	539	352		443	159	547	542	386	355	203	473	63	656	491	278	655	580	231	451	553	
CORPUS CHRISTI	405	218	303	159		413	408	232	215	141	333	152	522	357	144	453	506	446	94	317	521
DALLAS	185	195	294	547	413		30	294	247	427	182	505	109	262	277	186	177	98	307	96	134
HOUSTON	347	162	88	355	215	247	267	47		349	119	348	310	363	199	239	292	206	127	188	380
SAN ANTONIO	261	82	283	278	144	277	272	246	199	150	313	236	386	213		409	454	310	117	181	385
SHREVEPORT, LA	373	327	195	593	453	186	216	286	239	559	119	586	150	450	409		71	99	365	228	320

MORE MILEAGES — Pg. 256

Total mileage through Texas

10	811 miles	30	223 miles
20	636 miles	35	504 miles

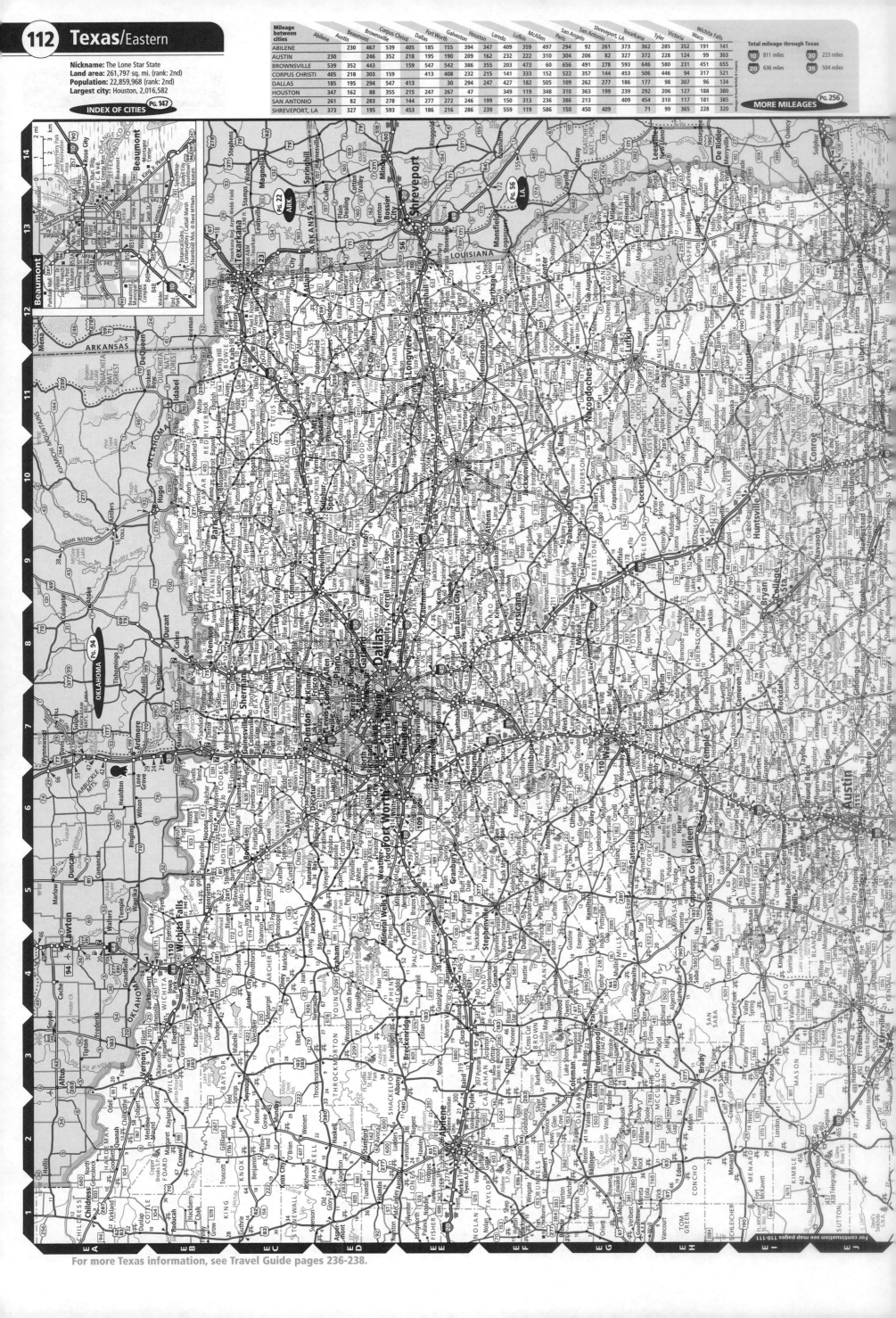

For more Texas information, see Travel Guide pages 236-238.

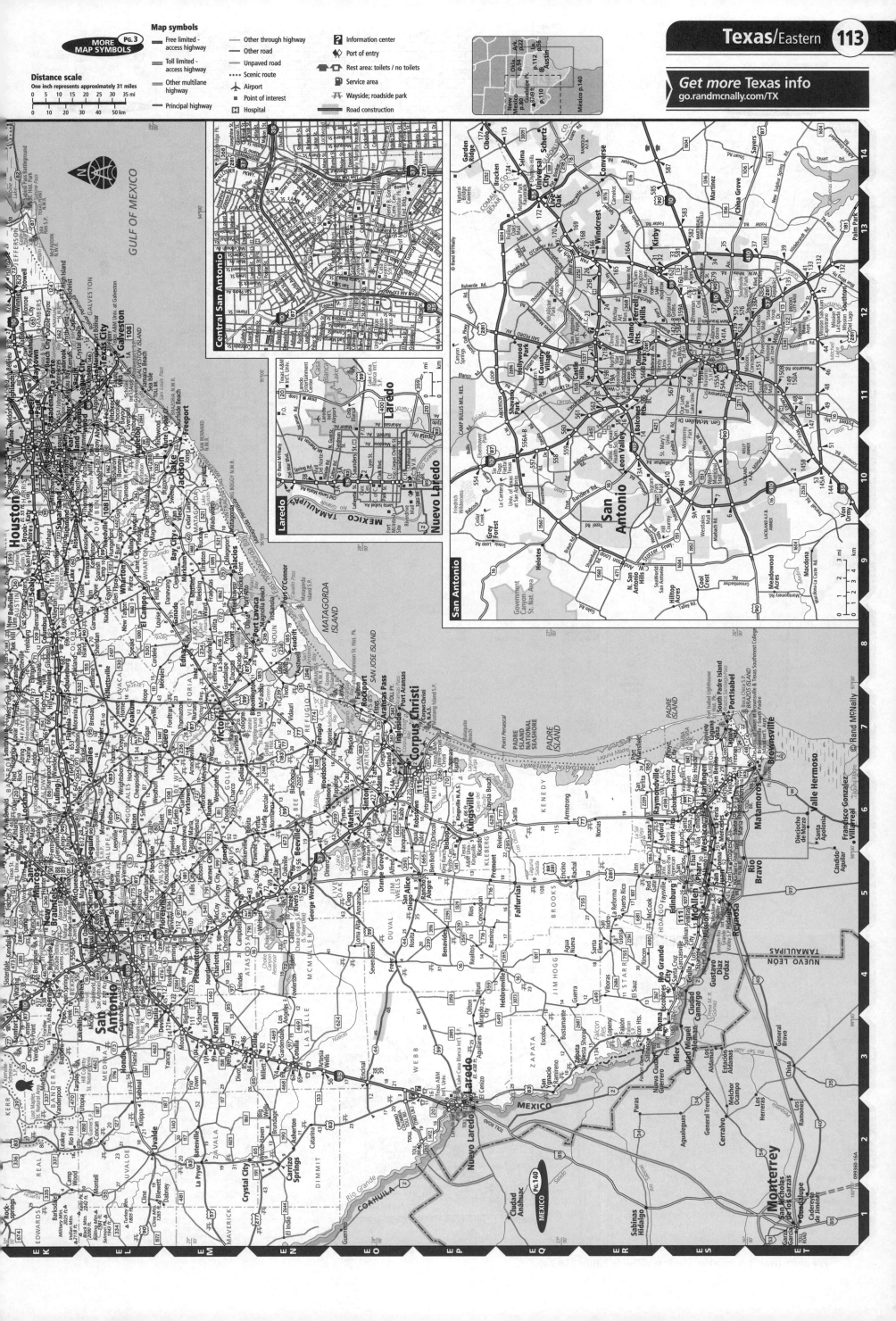

Get more Texas info
go.randmcnally.com/TX

Map symbols

MORE MAP SYMBOLS — PG. 3

- Free limited-access highway
- Toll limited-access highway
- Other multilane highway
- Principal highway
- Other through highway
- Other road
- Unpaved road
- Scenic route
- ✈ Airport
- ■ Point of interest
- ⊞ Hospital
- 🛈 Information center
- ◆ Port of entry
- Rest area: toilets / no toilets
- Service area
- Wayside; roadside park
- Road construction

Distance scale

One inch represents approximately 31 miles

0 5 10 15 20 25 30 35 mi
0 10 20 30 40 50 km

Central San Antonio

Laredo
Nuevo Laredo
MEXICO TAMAULIPAS

San Antonio

Nickname: The Beehive State
Land area: 82,144 sq. mi. (rank: 12th)
Population: 2,469,585 (rank: 34th)
Largest city: Salt Lake City, 178,097

INDEX OF CITIES PG. 147

Mileage between cities	Bicknell	Blanding	Cedar City	Evanston, WY	Grand Jct., CO	Las Vegas, NV	Logan	Moab	Ogden	Page, AZ	Park City	Price	Provo	Richfield	Salt Lake City	Vernal	Wendover
GRAND JCT., CO	217	186	332	287		505	361	112	321	375	288	165	243	224	385	286	141	403
LOGAN	274	387	318	115	361	491		313	42	458	110	197	118	232	371	74	249	192
MOAB	169	74	284	295	112	457	313		273	263	240	117	195	176	332	238	223	355
OGDEN	234	347	278	75	321	451	42	273		418	70	157	78	192	331	34	209	152
PROVO	156	269	200	101	243	373	118	195	78	340	46	79		114	253	43	157	160
ST. GEORGE	199	345	54	353	345	121	371	337	331	156	298	280	253	162		296	409	413
SALT LAKE CITY	199	312	243	78	286	416	74	238	34	383	28	122	43	157	296		170	122
VERNAL	226	297	356	146	141	529	249	223	209	453	147	115	157	233	409	170		293

Total mileage through Utah

15	401 miles
70	232 miles
80	196 miles
84	119 miles

MORE MILEAGES PG. 256

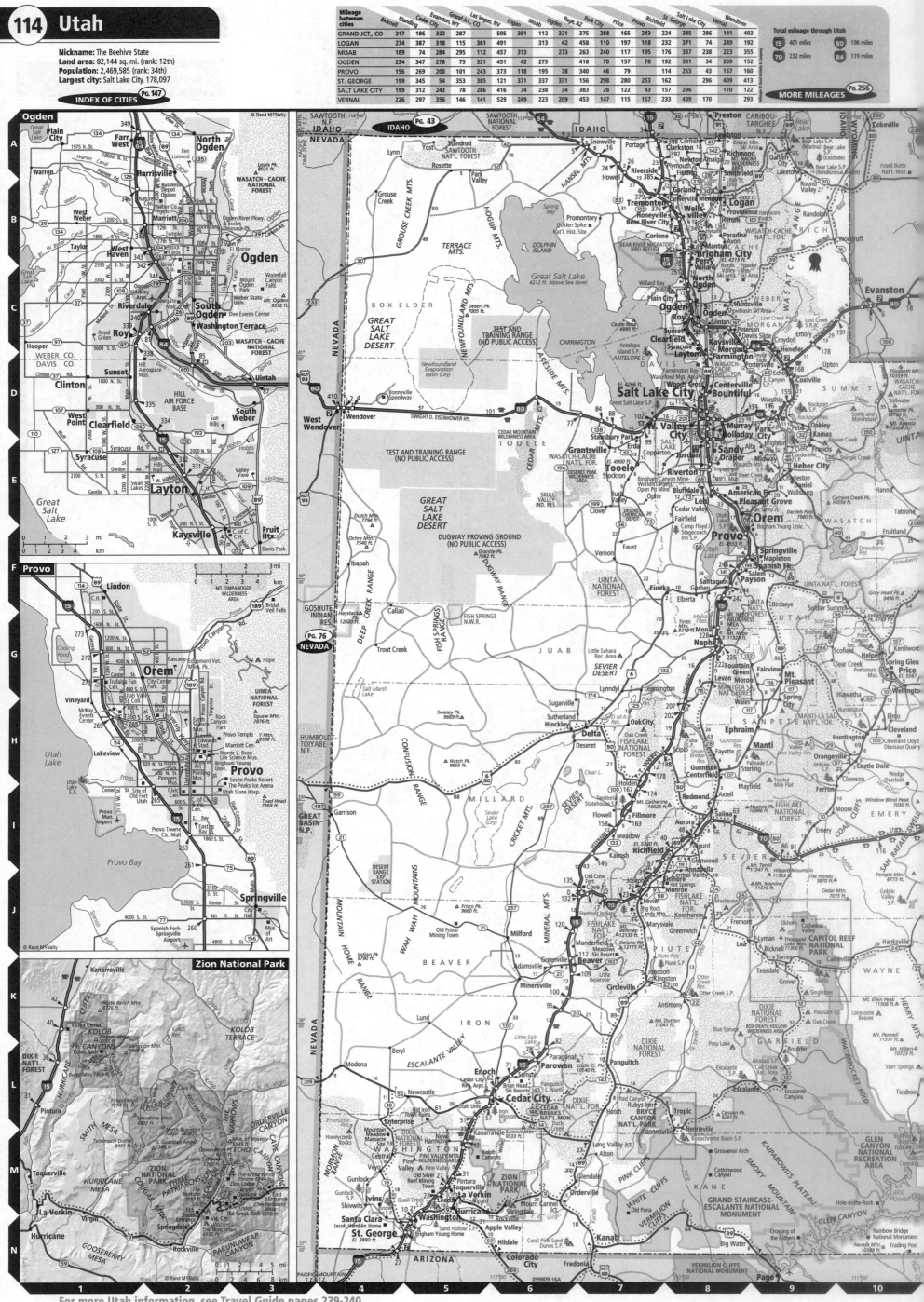

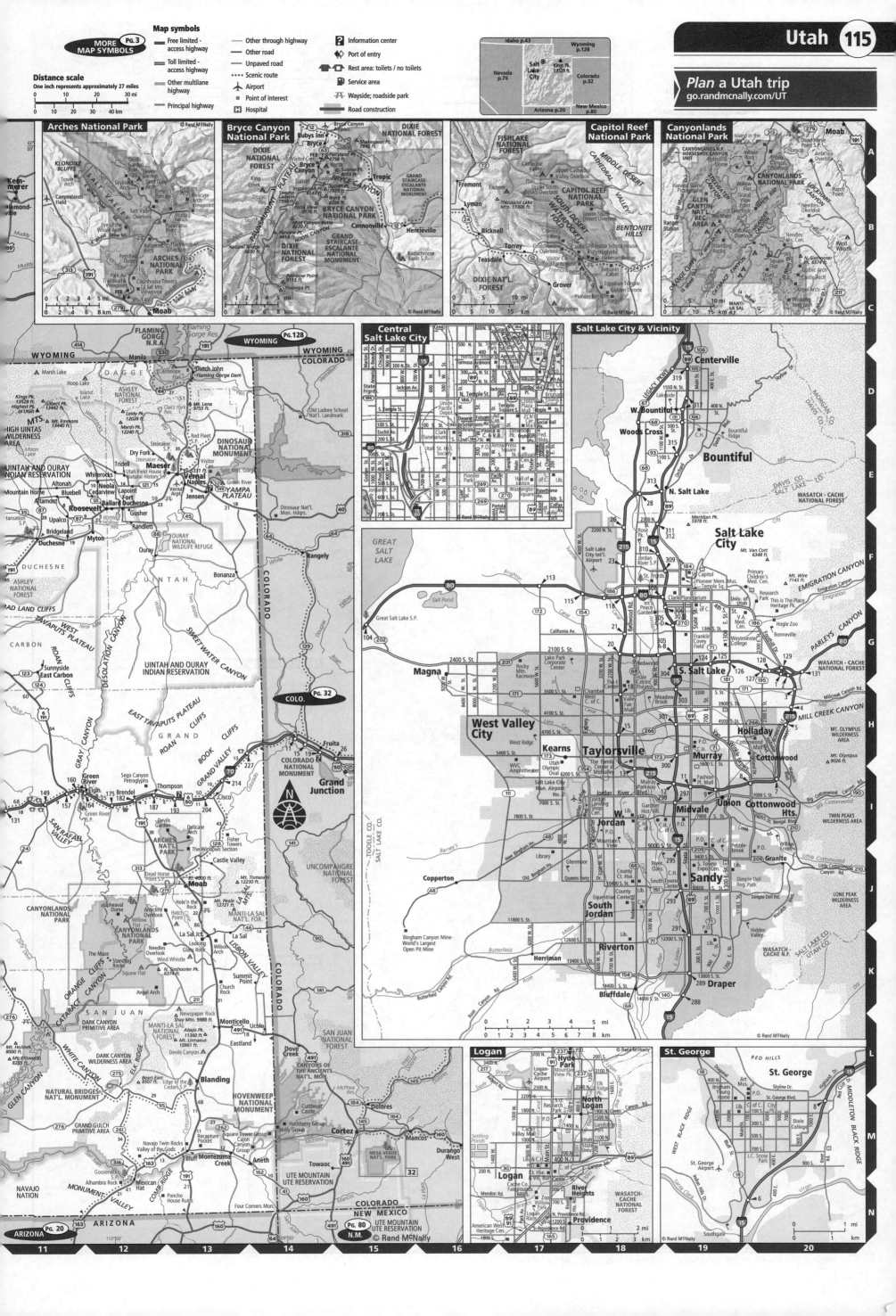

Nickname: The Green Mountain State
Land area: 9,250 sq. mi. (rank: 43rd)
Population: 623,050 (rank: 49th)
Largest city: Burlington, 38,531

Get travel info
go.randmcnally.com/VT

INDEX OF CITIES   Pg. 147

Distance scale
One inch represents approximately 14 miles

MORE MILEAGES   Pg. 256

Mileage between cities	Albany, NY	Brattleboro	Burlington	Montpelier	Newport	Rutland	St. Johnsbury	White River Jct.
ALBANY, NY		81	152	162	246	96	202	145
BRATTLEBORO	81		154	117	166	77	122	65
BURLINGTON	152	154		39	75	67	77	91
MONTPELIER	162	117	39		80	66	38	54
NEWPORT	246	166	75	80		146	44	101
RUTLAND	96	77	67	66	146		102	45
ST. JOHNSBURY	202	122	77	38	44	102		57
WHITE RIVER JCT.	145	65	91	54	101	45	57	

Total mileage through Vermont
89 — 130 miles   93 — 11 miles
91 — 177 miles   4 — 64 miles

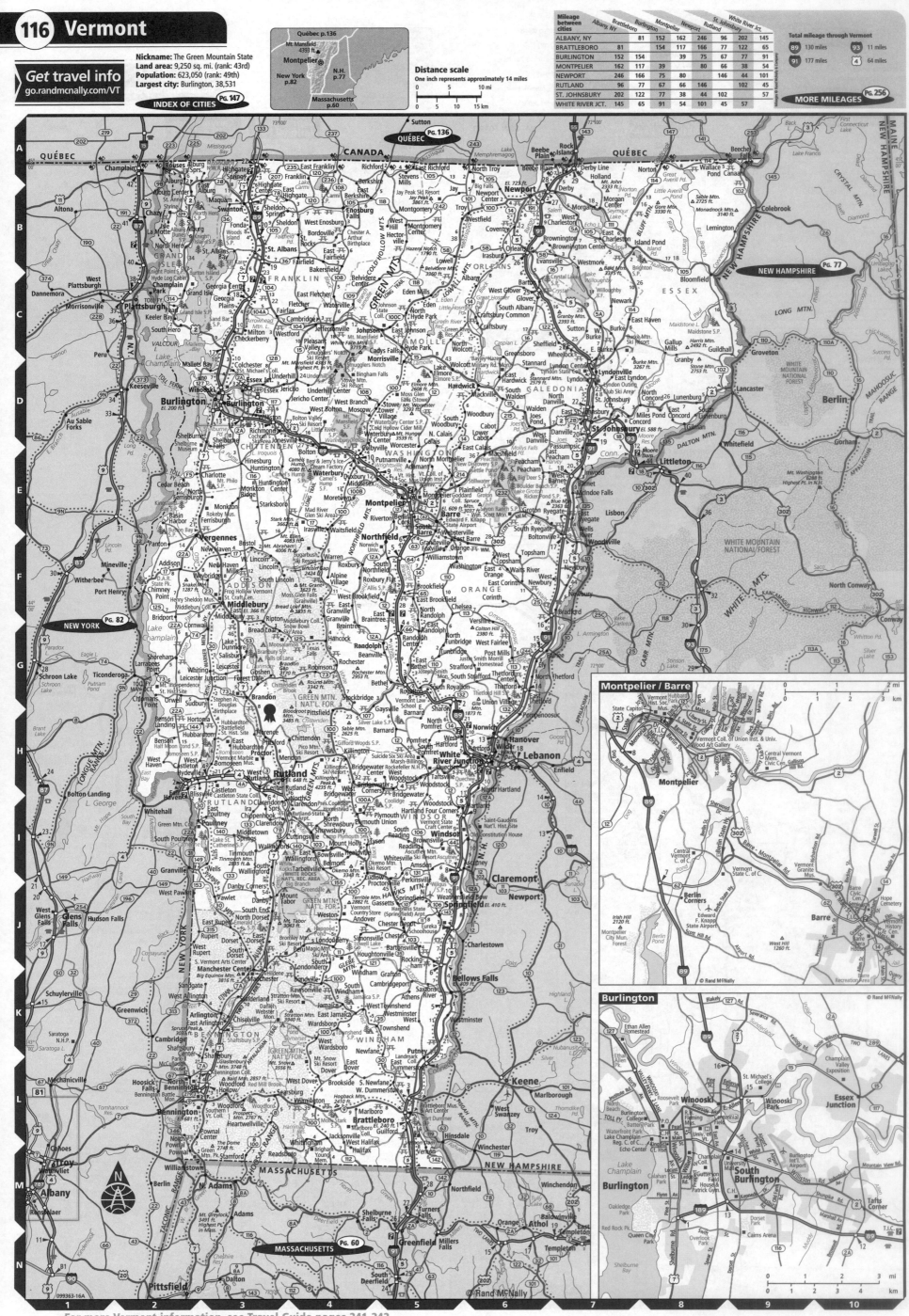

For more Vermont information, see Travel Guide pages 241-242.

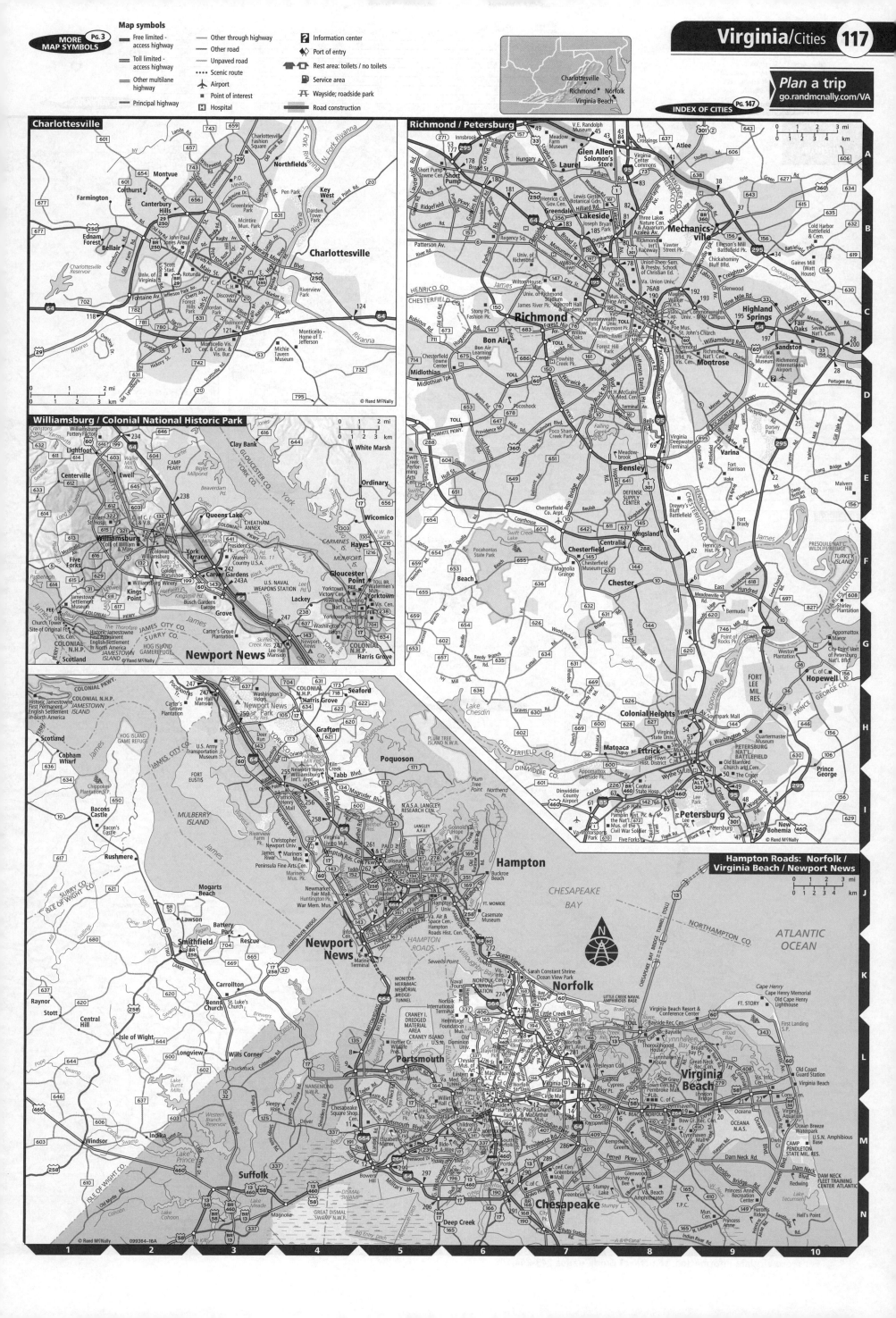

Nickname: Old Dominion
Land area: 39,594 sq. mi. (rank: 37th)
Population: 7,567,465 (rank: 12th)
Largest city: Virginia Beach, 438,415

INDEX OF CITIES PG. 147

Mileage between cities	Bristol	Charlottesville	Chincoteague	Danville	Fredericksburg Emporia	Hagerstown, MD	Harrisonburg	Lynchburg	Manassas	Norfolk	Richmond	Roanoke	Virginia Beach	Washington, DC	Williamsburg	Winchester	Wytheville
CHARLOTTESVILLE	252		261	126	138	80	167	59	63	95	168	74	180	122	126	125	182
EMPORIA	341	138		180	113		119	235	195	127	156	74	64	178	88	170	106	198	271
NORFOLK	418	168	105	186	74	145	261	225	194	182		93	280	17	196	46	224	348
RICHMOND	324	74	186	149	64	55	171	131	118	92	93		186	105	106	51	134	254
ROANOKE	146	114	373	82	178	194	217	109	54	209	280	186		292	236	238	175	76
WASHINGTON, DC	374	122	161	250	17	190	54	75	129	185	37	196	106		236	208	154	304
WINCHESTER	313	125	242	220	198	82	42	68	157	53	224	134	175	236	77		182	243
WYTHEVILLE	69	182	441	120	271	262	285	177	132	277	348	254	76	360	304	306	243	

Total mileage through Virginia
64: 298 miles
81: 325 miles
85: 69 miles
95: 179 miles

MORE MILEAGES PG. 256

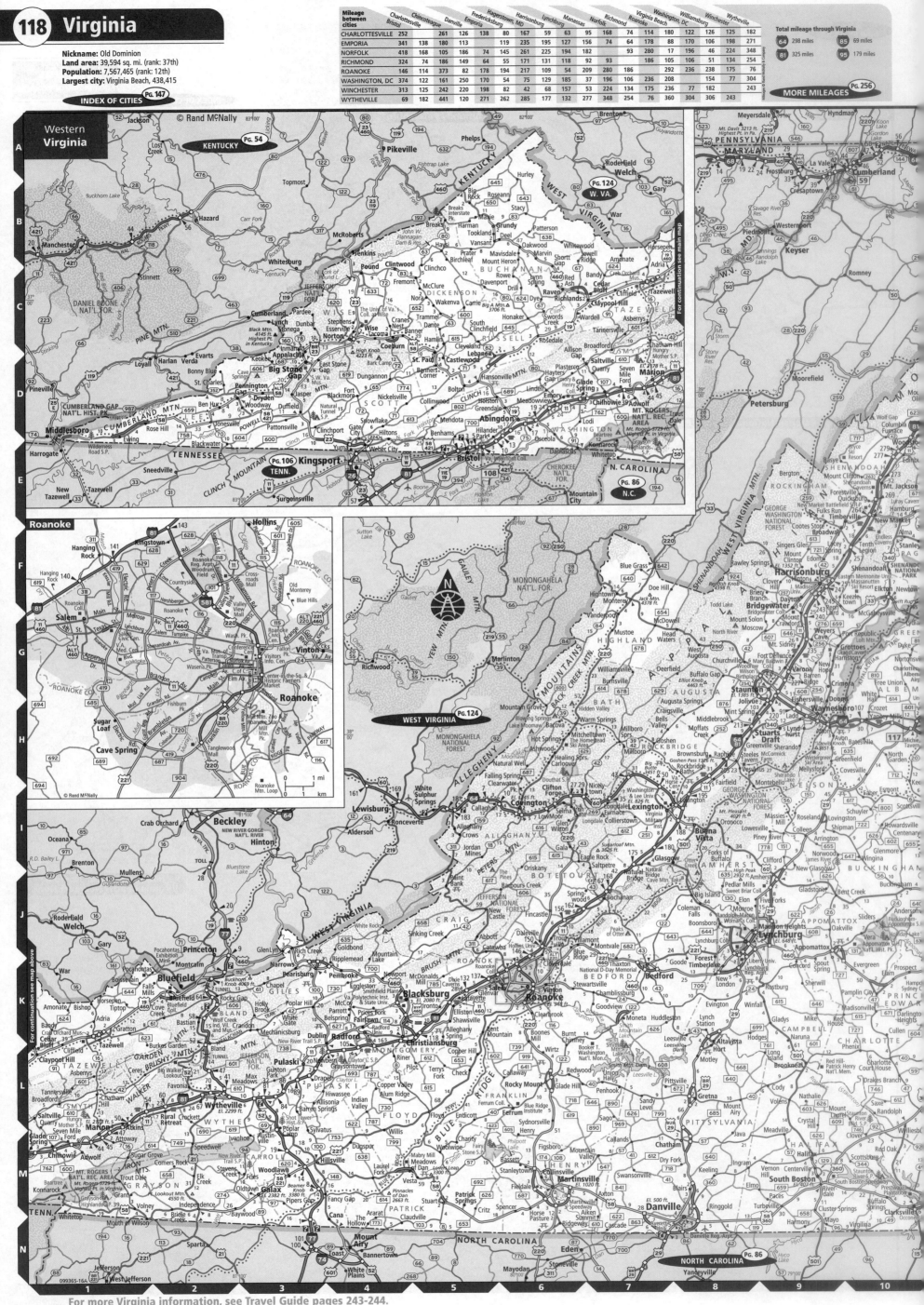

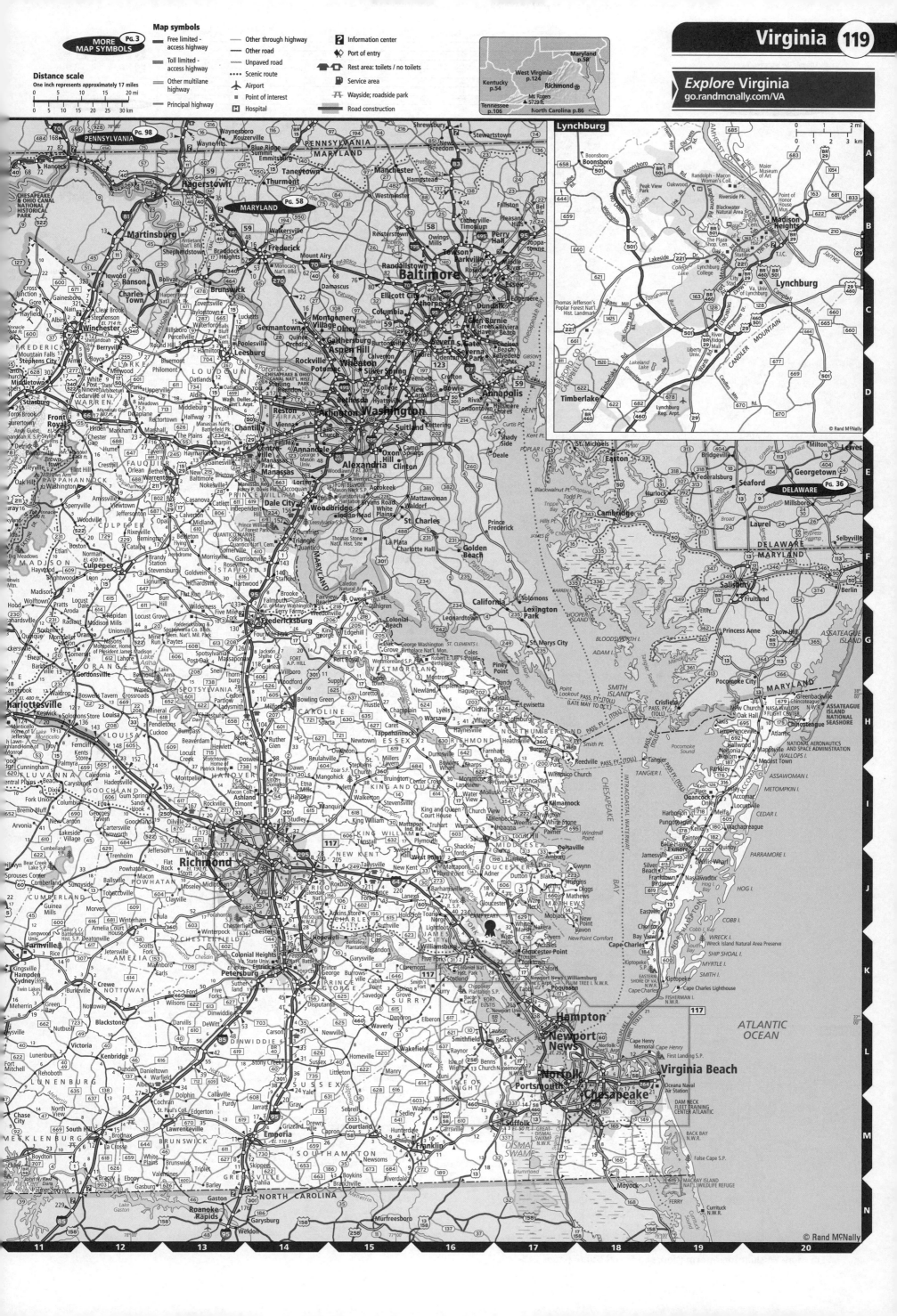

Nickname: The Evergreen State
Land area: 66,544 sq. mi. (rank: 20th)
Population: 6,287,759 (rank: 14th)
Largest city: Seattle, 573,911

INDEX OF CITIES **PG. 147**

Mileage between cities	Aberdeen	Bellingham	Bremerton	Colville	Kennewick	Lewiston, ID	Longview	Olympia	Omak	Port Angeles	Portland, OR	Seattle	Spokane	Tacoma	The Dalles, OR	Vancouver, BC	Wenatchee	*Via Ferry Yakima
BELLINGHAM	197		152*	326	302	397	217	147	208	124*	262	88	365	119	324	55	185	223
KENNEWICK	286	302	265*	210		122	255	260	189	338	213	219	139	232	219	357	140	79
PORTLAND, OR	145	262	174	423	213	334	49	115	377	232		174	352	143	84	317	291	185
SEATTLE	109	88	64*	353	219	314	129	59	241	82*	174		282	31	241	143	153	140
SPOKANE	373	365	328*	71	139	365	371	323	138	401*	352	282		295	268	420	172	202
TACOMA	78	119	33	366	232	327	98	28	254	106*	143	31	295		220	174	166	153
THE DALLES, OR	222	324	251	339	129	250	126	192	293	309	84	241	268	220		378	207	101
YAKIMA	207	223	186*	273	79	200	169	181	192	259*	185	140	202	153	101	378	106	

Total mileage through Washington

5	277 miles	90	297 miles
82	133 miles	101	373 miles

MORE MILEAGES **PG. 256**

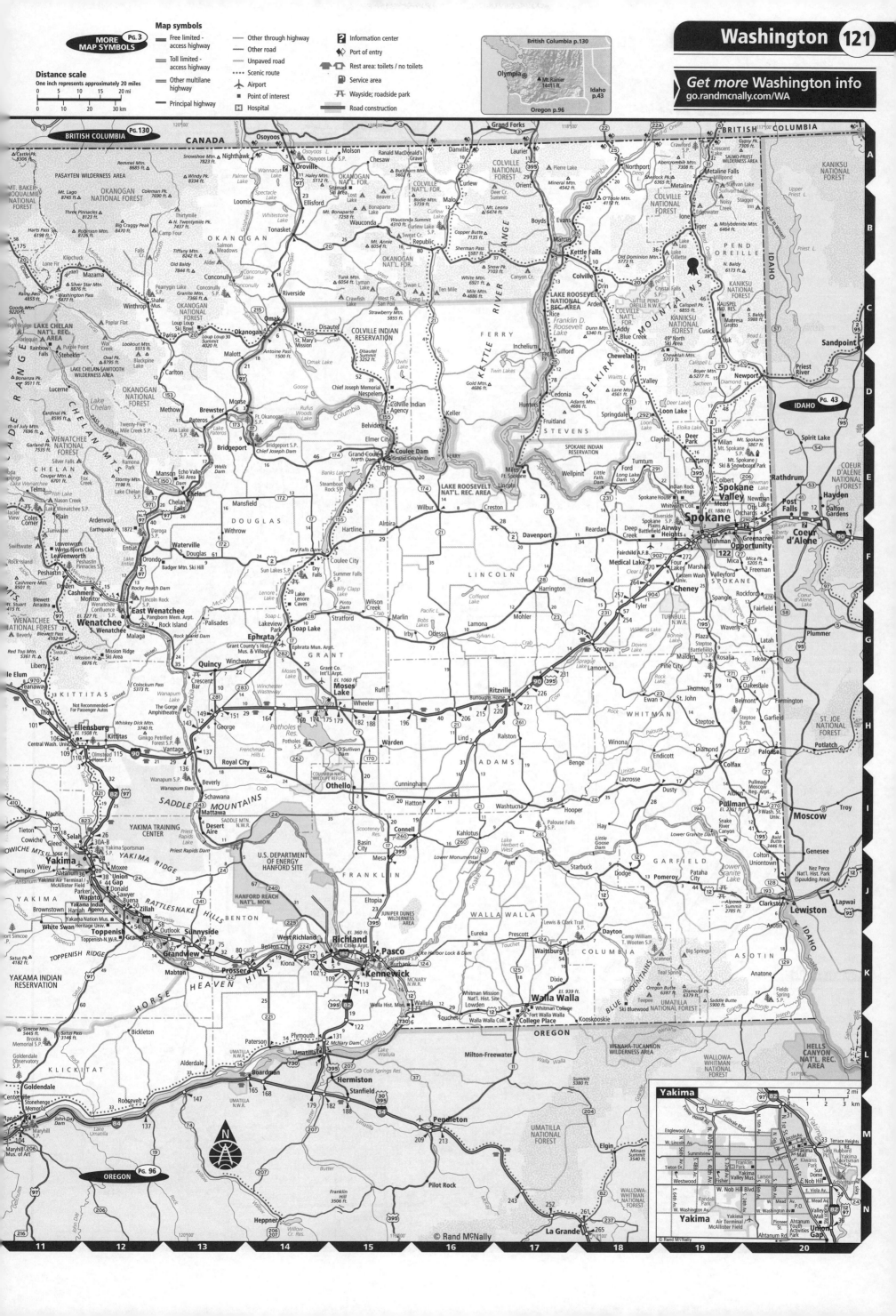

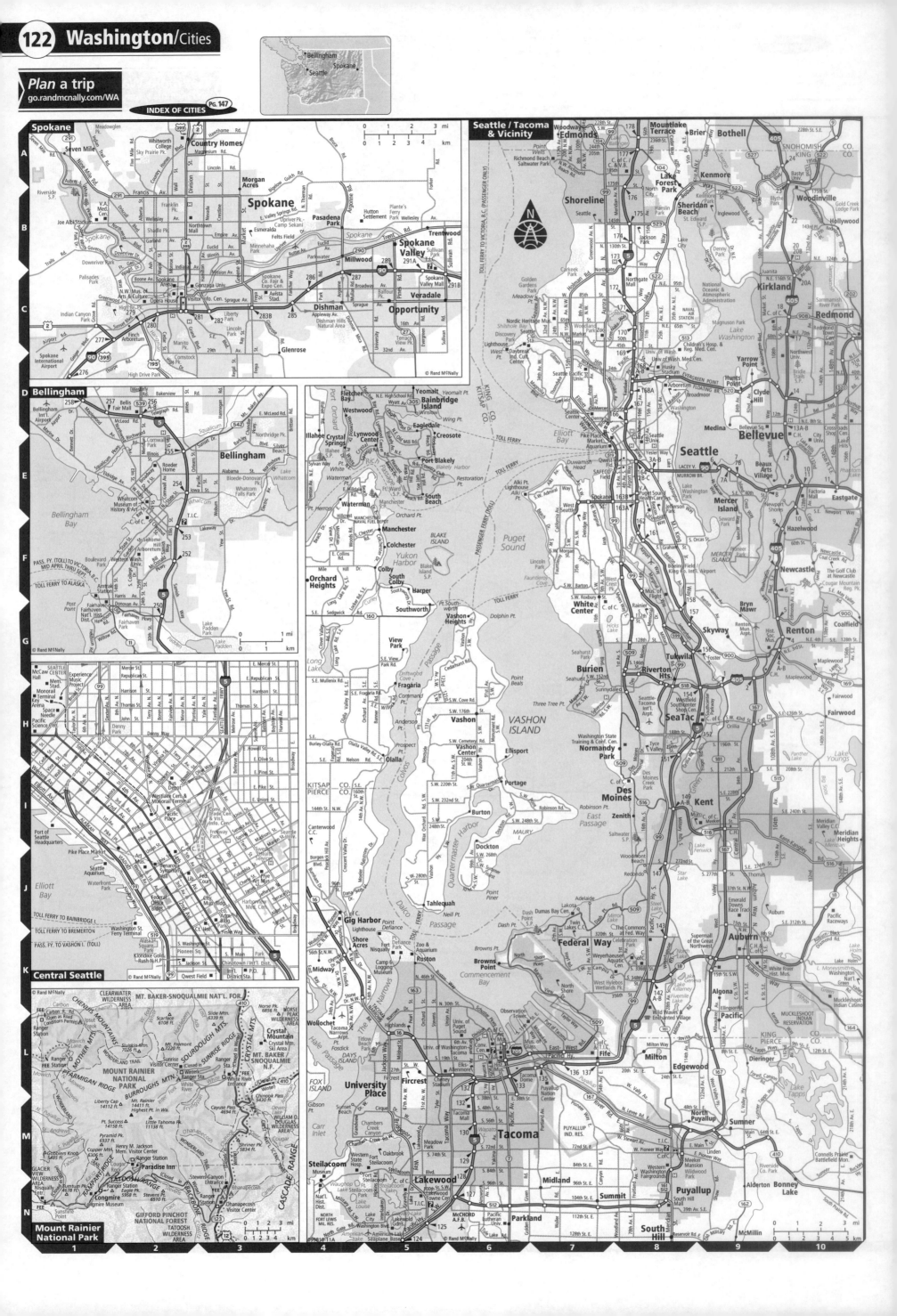

Map symbols

— Free limited-access highway
— Toll limited-access highway
— Other multilane highway
— Principal highway
— Other through highway
— Other road
— Unpaved road
•••• Scenic route
✈ Airport
■ Point of interest
Ⓗ Hospital

? Information center
◆ Port of entry
Ⓡ Rest area: toilets / no toilets
Service area
Ⓦ Wayside; roadside park
Road construction

Maryland
Virginia
Washington D.C.

Land area: 61 sq. mi.
Population: 550,521

INDEX OF CITIES PG. 142

Get travel info
go.randmcnally.com/DC

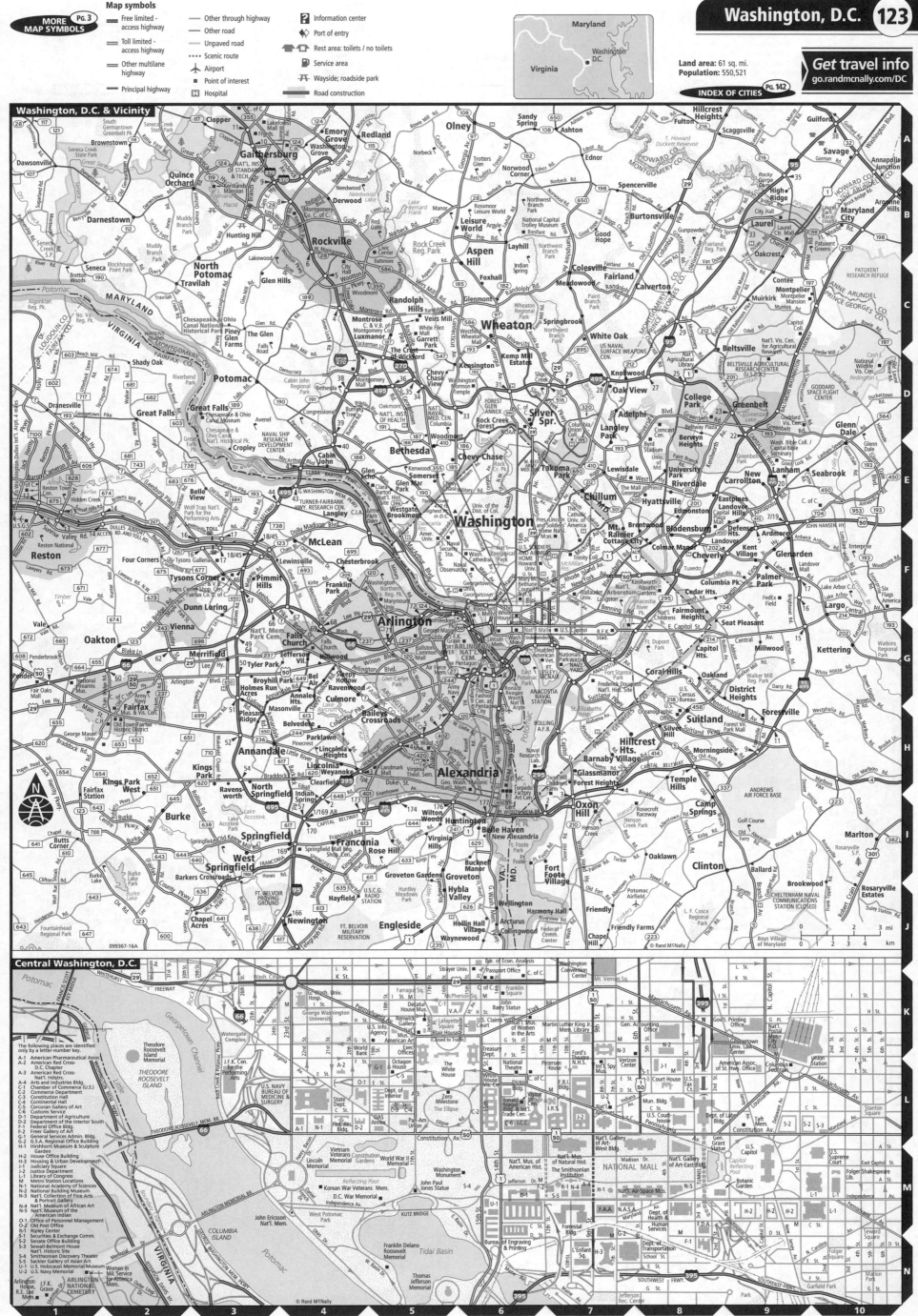

Washington, D.C. & Vicinity

Central Washington, D.C.

The following places are identified only by a letter-number key.

A-1 American Pharmaceutical Assoc.
A-2 American Red Cross-D.C. Chapter
A-3 American Red Cross-Nat'l. Hdqtrs.
B-1 Arts and Industries Bldg.
C-1 Chamber of Commerce (U.S.)
C-2 Commerce Department
C-3 Constitution Hall
C-4 Continental Hall
C-5 Corcoran Gallery of Art
C-6 Customs Service
D-1 Department of Agriculture
D-2 Department of the Interior South
E-1 Executive Office Bldg.
F-1 Federal Office Bldg.
F-2 Freer Gallery of Art
G-1 General Services Admin. Bldg.
G-2 G.S.A. Regional Office Building
G-3 Hirshhorn Museum & Sculpture Garden
H-1 House Office Building
H-2 Housing & Urban Development
J-1 Judiciary Square
J-2 Justice Department
L-1 Library of Congress
M Metro Station Locations
N-1 National Academy of Sciences
N-2 National Archives
N-3 Nat'l. Collection of Fine Arts & Portrait Gallery
N-4 Nat'l. Museum of African Art
N-5 Nat'l. Museum of the American Indian
O-1 Office of Personnel Management
O-2 Old Post Office
R-1 Ripley Center
S-1 Securities & Exchange Comm.
S-2 Senate Office Building
S-3 Sewall-Belmont House Nat'l. Historic Site
S-4 Smithsonian Discovery Theater
S-5 Sackler Gallery of Asian Art
U-1 U.S. Holocaust Memorial Museum
U-2 U.S. Navy Memorial

Plan a trip
go.randmcnally.com/WV

Nickname: The Mountain State
Land area: 24,078 sq. mi. (rank: 41st)
Population: 1,816,856 (rank: 37th)
Largest city: Charleston, 51,176

INDEX OF CITIES PG. 147

Distance scale
One inch represents approximately 20 miles

Mileage between cities	Beckley	Charleston	Cumberland, MD	Huntington	Morgantown	Parkersburg	Wheeling	Wh. Sulphur Springs
BECKLEY		60	241	111	169	135	236	60
CHARLESTON	60		227	51	155	75	176	125
CUMBERLAND, MD	241	227		278	72	181	146	193
HUNTINGTON	111	51	278		206	126	227	176
MORGANTOWN	169	155	72	206		109	74	201
PARKERSBURG	135	75	181	126	109		105	200
WHEELING	236	176	146	227	74	105		301
WH. SULPHUR SPRS.	60	125	193	176	201	200	301	

Total mileage through West Virginia

64	189 miles	77	187 miles
70	14 miles	79	161 miles

MORE MILEAGES PG. 256

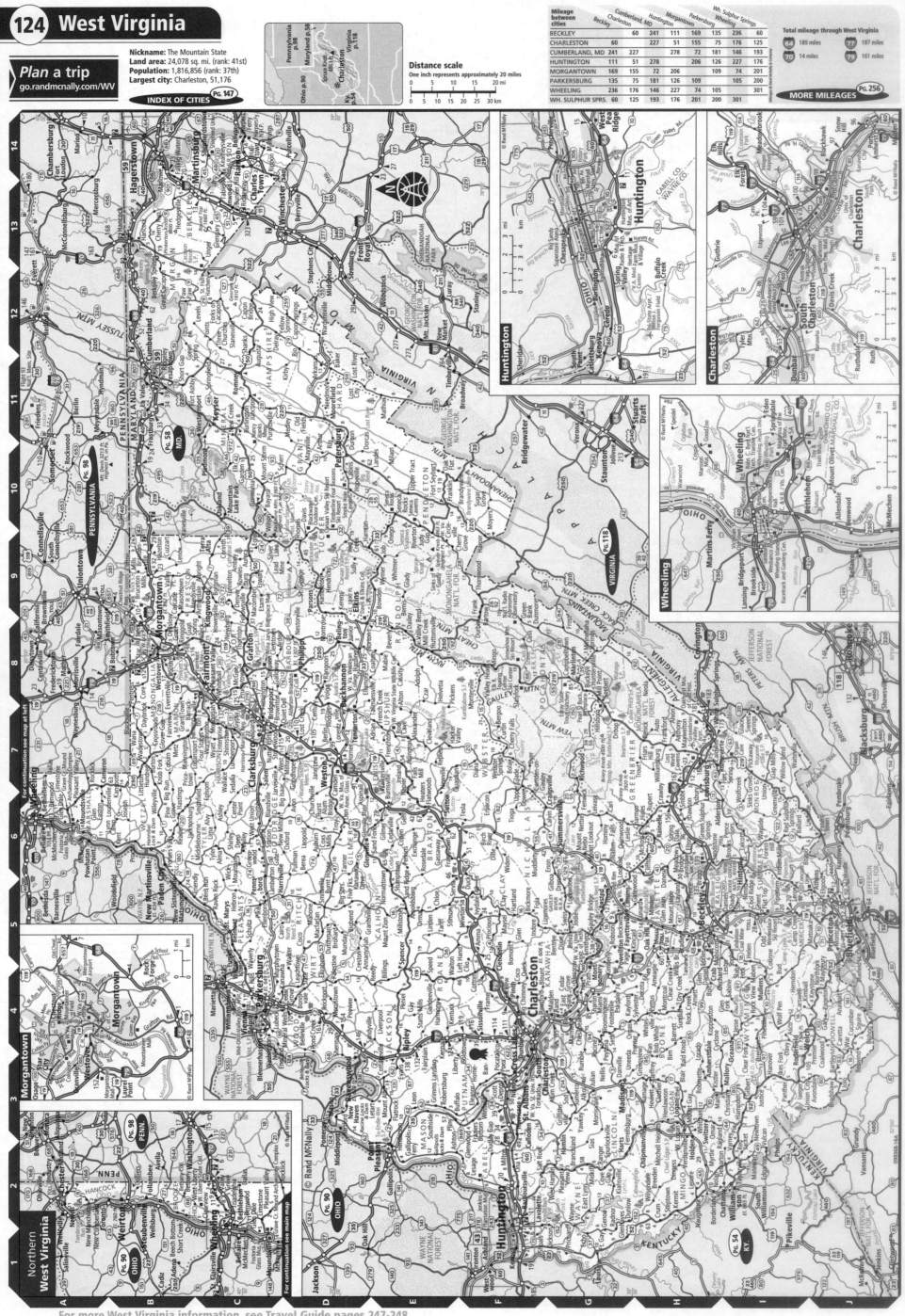

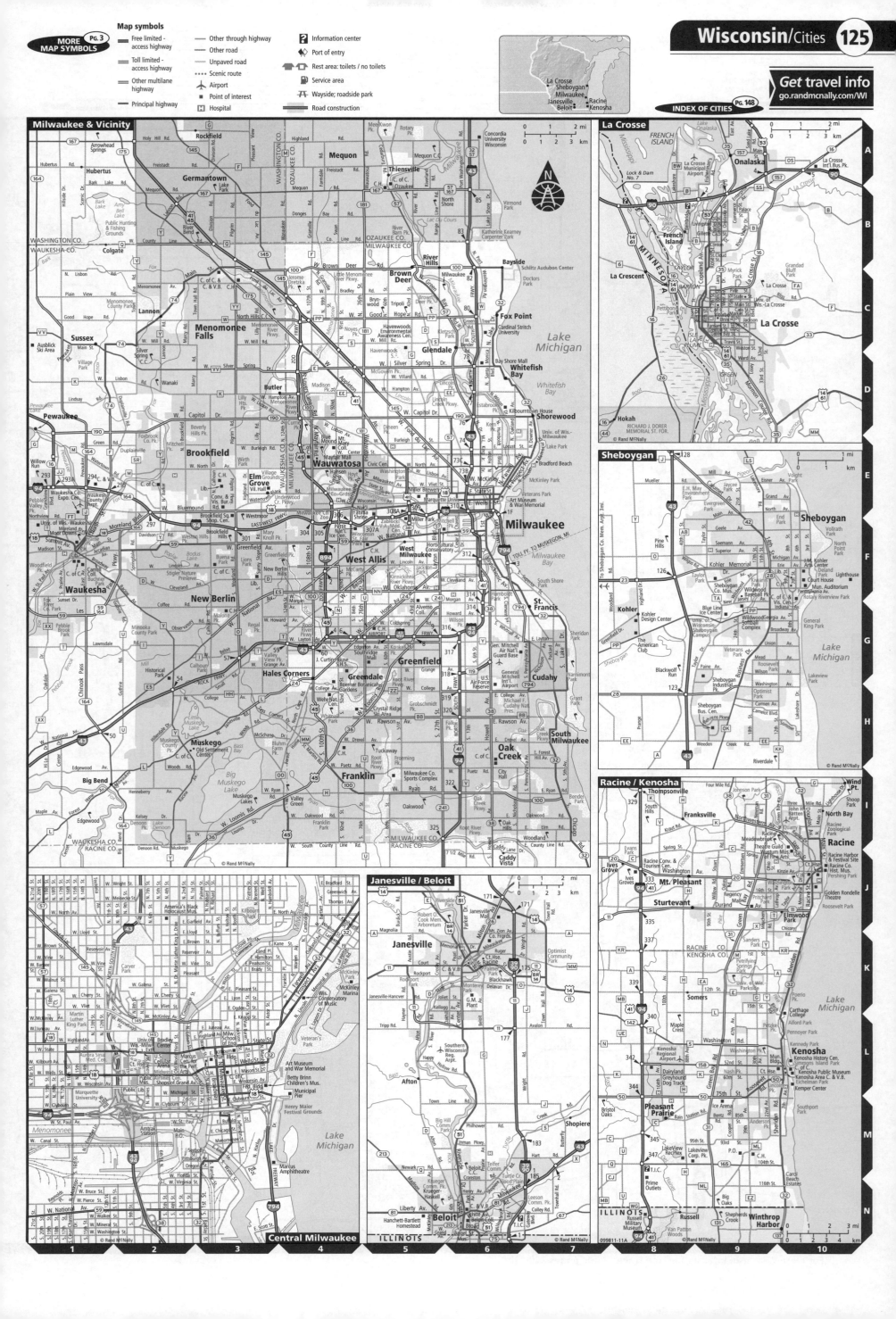

Nickname: The Badger State
Land area: 54,310 sq. mi. (rank: 25th)
Population: 5,536,201 (rank: 20th)
Largest city: Milwaukee, 578,887

INDEX OF CITIES Pg. 148

Mileage between cities	Ashland	Beloit	Chicago, IL	Dubuque, IA	Eau Claire	Green Bay	Hayward	Kenosha	La Crosse	Madison	Manitowoc	Marinette	Milwaukee	Oshkosh	Rhinelander	Sheboygan	Stevens Point	Sturgeon Bay	Superior	Wisconsin Dells	Wausau
CHICAGO, IL	446	96		175	312	209	419	64	278	146	176	264	92	177	342	148	246	247	460	282	192
EAU CLAIRE	165	220	312	198		198	107	279	87	175	239	225	241	178	161	229	124	64	148	101	122
GREEN BAY	246	191	209	232	198		286	156	206	138	39	55	117	53	129	64	96	42	327	97	133
LA CROSSE	252	186	278	126	87	206	194	245		141	209	257	207	153	204	195	117	250	236	144	88
MADISON	309	54	146	94	175	138	282	115	141		128	189	77	85	205	133	109	182	323	45	155
MILWAUKEE	375	74	92	173	241	117	348	39	207	77	84	172		86	271	56	175	185	389	211	121
SUPERIOR	66	368	460	346	148	327	70	427	235	323	368	300	389	326	185	377	263	371		230	270
WAUSAU	167	190	282	239	101	97	189	249	144	145	138	124	211	103	63	163	37	181	230	114	

Total mileage through Wisconsin

39	182 miles
43	192 miles
90	189 miles
94	341 miles

MORE MILEAGES Pg. 256

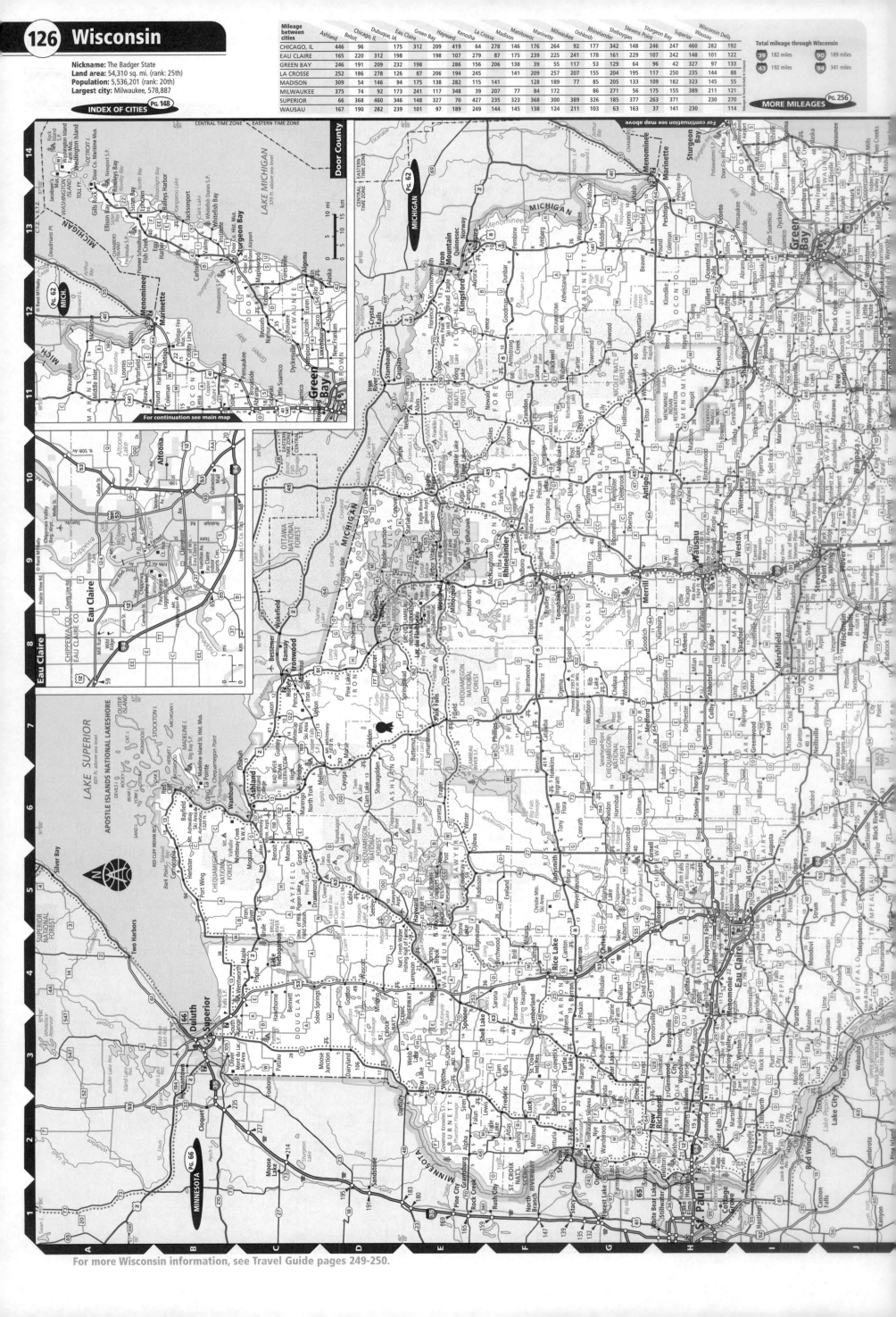

For more Wisconsin information, see Travel Guide pages 249-250.

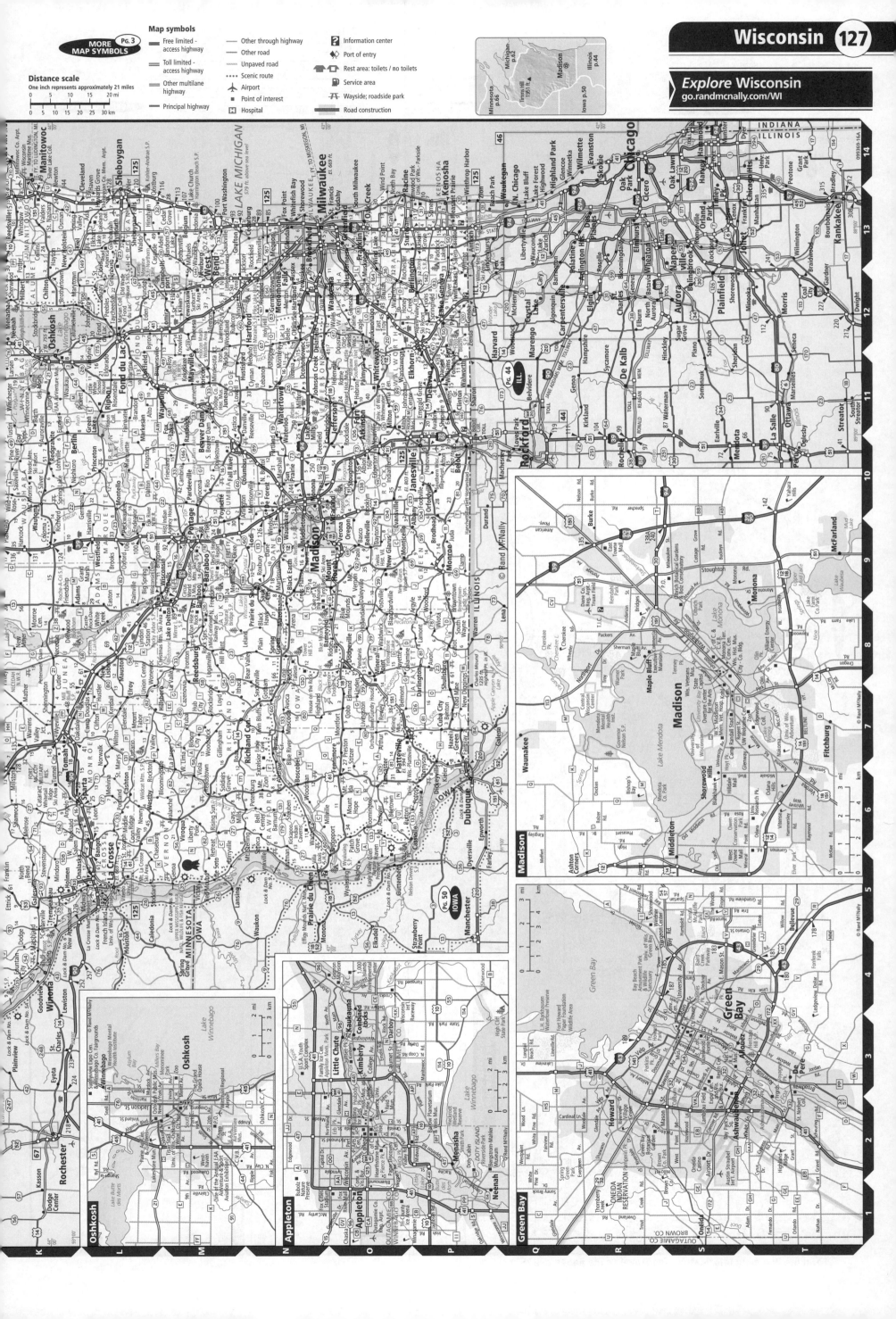

MORE MAP SYMBOLS Pg. 3

Distance scale
One inch represents approximately 21 miles
0 5 10 15 20 mi
0 5 10 15 20 25 30 km

Map symbols

Free limited-access highway
Toll limited-access highway
Other multilane highway
Principal highway

Other through highway
Other road
Unpaved road
Scenic route
Airport
Point of interest
Hospital

Information center
Port of entry
Rest area: toilets / no toilets
Service area
Wayside; roadside park
Road construction

Michigan p.62
Minnesota p.66
Iowa p.50
Illinois p.44
Madison p.50
Timms Hill 1951 ft.

Plan a trip
go.randmcnally.com/WY

Nicknames: The Equality State
Land area: 97,100 sq. mi. (rank: 9th)
Population: 509,294 (rank: 50th)
Largest city: Cheyenne, 55,731

INDEX OF CITIES **Pg. 148**

Distance scale
One inch represents approximately 38 miles

Mileage between cities	Casper	Cheyenne	Cody	Jackson	Riverton	Rock Springs	Sheridan	Spearfish, SD
CASPER		180	214	282	119	226	152	223
CHEYENNE	180		395	436	275	258	329	295
CODY	214	395		178	139	282	148	346
JACKSON	282	436	178		166	178	326	509
RIVERTON	119	275	139	166		143	217	346
ROCK SPRINGS	226	258	282	178	143		378	449
SHERIDAN	152	329	148	326	217	378		199
SPEARFISH, SD	223	295	346	509	346	449	199	

Total mileage through Wyoming

25	301 miles	90	209 miles
80	403 miles	20	505 miles

MORE MILEAGES **Pg. 256**

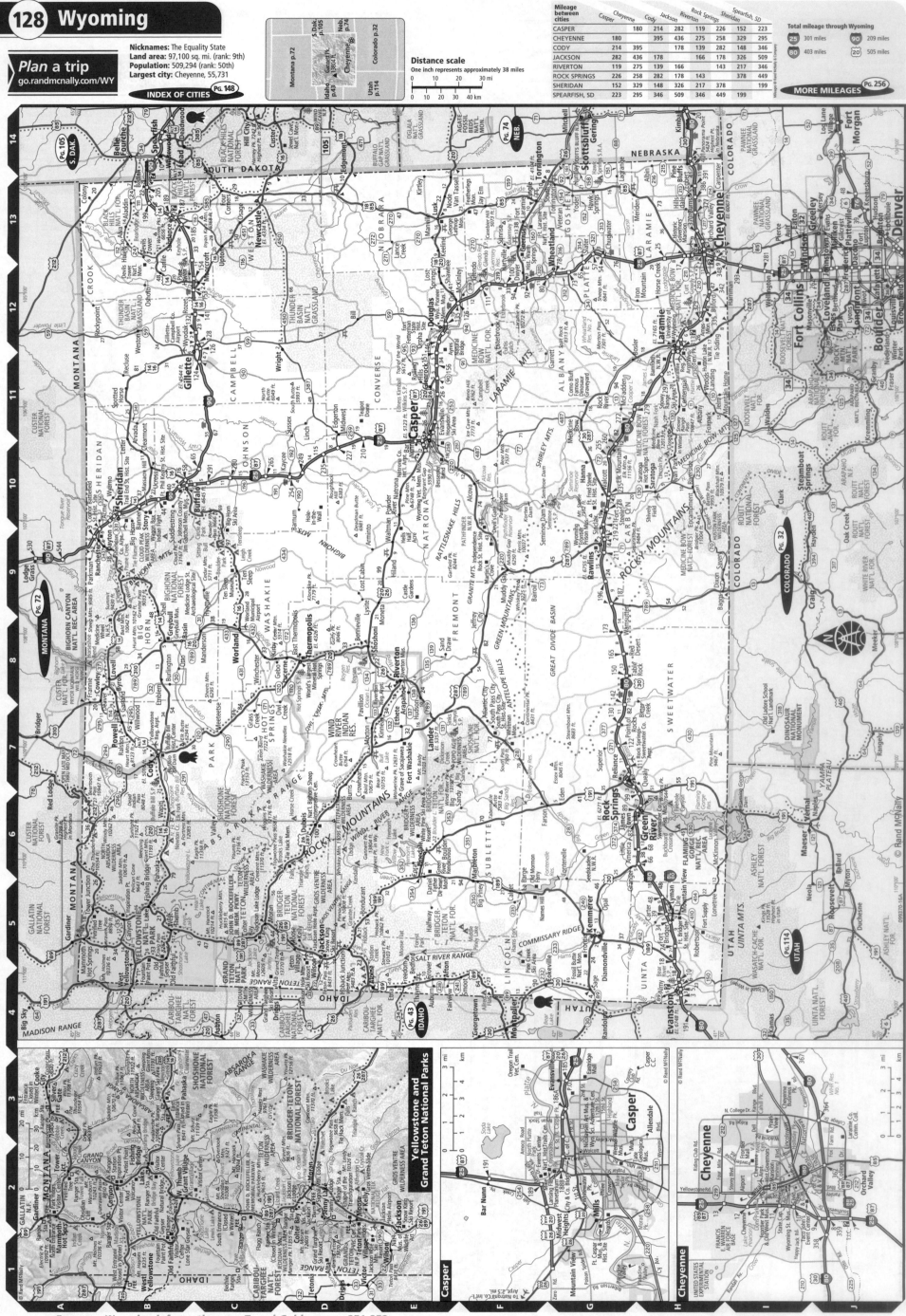

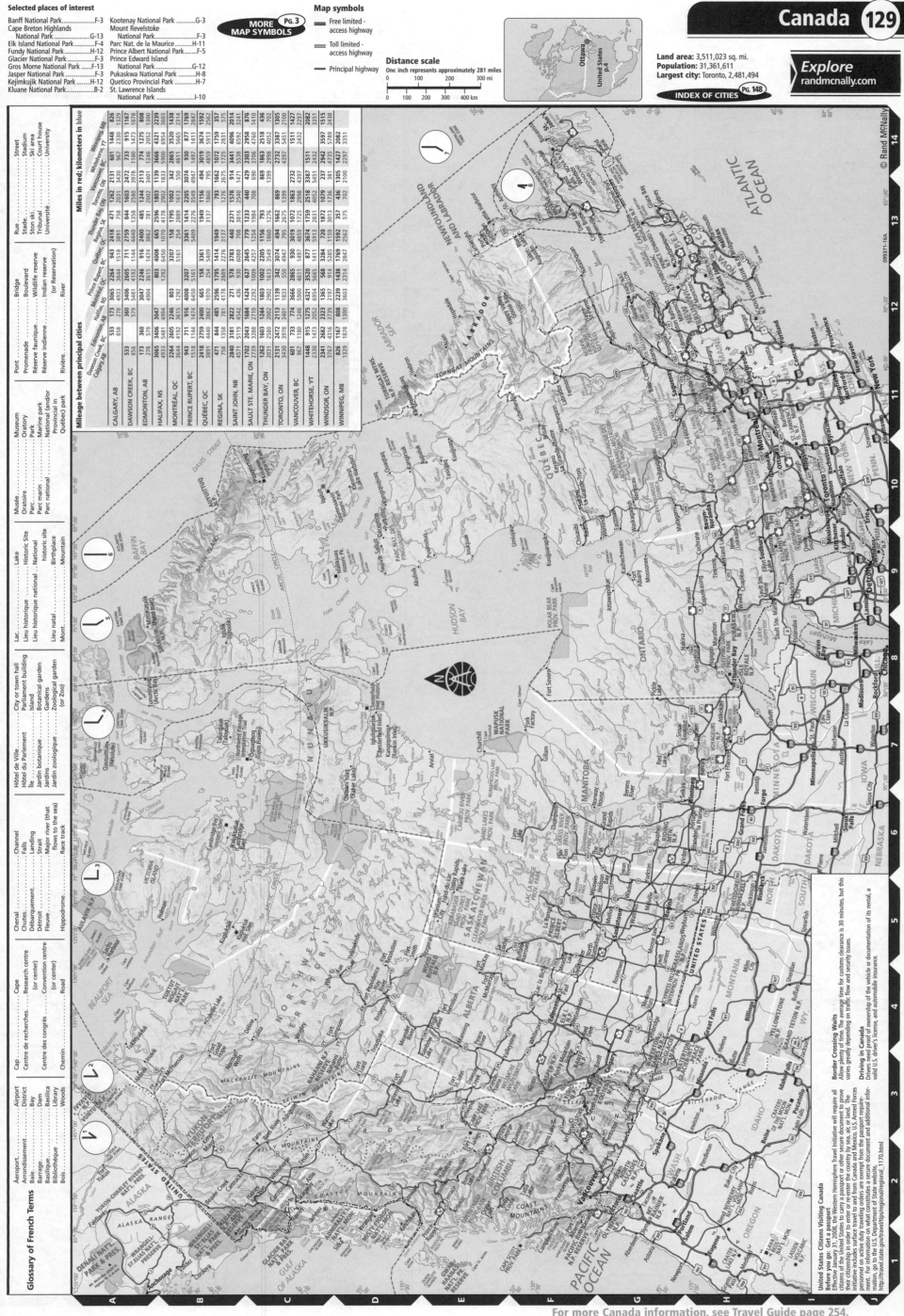

Selected places of interest

Banff National Park F-3
Cape Breton Highlands National Park G-13
Elk Island National Park F-4
Fundy National Park H-12
Glacier National Park F-3
Gros Morne National Park F-13
Jasper National Park F-3
Kejimkujik National Park H-12
Kluane National Park B-2
Kootenay National Park G-3
Mount Revelstoke National Park F-3
Parc Nat. de la Maurice H-11
Prince Albert National Park F-5
Prince Edward Island National Park G-12
Pukaskwa National Park H-8
Quetico Provincial Park H-7
St. Lawrence Islands National Park I-10

MORE MAP SYMBOLS Pg. 3

Map symbols

Free limited - access highway
Toll limited - access highway
Principal highway

Distance scale
One inch represents approximately 281 miles
0 100 200 300 mi
0 100 200 300 400 km

INDEX OF CITIES Pg. 148

Land area: 3,511,023 sq. mi.
Population: 31,361,611
Largest city: Toronto, 2,481,494

Explore randmcnally.com

Glossary of French Terms

Aeroport .... Airport
Arrondissement .... District
Baie .... Bay
Barrage .... Dam
Basilique .... Basilica
Bibliothèque .... Library
Bois .... Woods
Cap .... Cape
Centre de recherches .... Research centre (or center)
Centre des congrès .... Convention centre (or center)
Chemin .... Road
Chenal .... Channel
Chutes .... Falls
Débarquement .... Landing
Détroit .... Strait
Fleuve .... Major river (that flows to the sea)
Hippodrome .... Race track
Hôtel de Ville .... City or town hall
Hôtel du Parlement .... Parliament building
Île .... Island
Jardin botanique .... Botanical garden
Jardins .... Gardens
Jardin zoologique .... Zoological garden (or Zoo)
Lac .... Lake
Lieu historique .... Historic Site
Lieu historique national .... National historic site
Lieu natal .... Birthplace
Mont .... Mountain
Musée .... Museum
Oratoire .... Oratory
Parc .... Park
Parc marin .... Marine park
Parc national .... National (and/or Provincial in Quebec) park
Point .... Point
Promenade .... Promenade
Réserve faunique .... Wildlife reserve
Réserve indienne .... Indian reserve (or Reservation)
Rivière .... River
Rue .... Street
Stade .... Stadium
Ston ski .... Ski area
Tribunal .... Court house
Universite .... University

Miles in red; kilometers in blue

Mileage between principal cities

For more Canada information, see Travel Guide page 254.

© Rand McNally

Get travel info
go.randmcnally.com/BC

British Columbia
Land area: 357,216 sq. mi. (rank: 4th)
Population: 4,114,981 (rank: 3rd)
Largest city: Vancouver, 545,671
INDEX OF CITIES Pg. 148

Distance scale
One inch represents approximately 45 miles

0 10 20 30 40 mi
0 10 20 30 40 50 60 km

MORE MILEAGES PG. 256

Mileage between cities	Banff AB	Cranbrook	Dawson Creek	Hope	Jasper, AB	Nanaimo	Nelson	Port Alberni	Port Hardy	Revelstoke	Vancouver	Whitehorse, YT	Williams Lake	*Via Ferry
BANFF, AB		169	501	427	173	563*	314	614*	811*	175	520	638*	1443	485
CRANBROOK	169		638	428	310	564*	145	615*	810*	249	521	639*	1553	552
DAWSON CREEK	501	638		647	328	731	783	782*	979*	610	733	806	915	401
KAMLOOPS	304	378	575	123	290	259*	285	310*	510	129	216	334*	1353	174
KELOWNA	299	318	681	149	394	285*	206	336*	533*	124	360	1459	280	
PRINCE GEORGE	406	543	255	385	233	521*	605	572*	767*	449	478	596*	1037	146
PRINCE RUPERT	862	999	711	844	689	928*	1086	979*	299*	908	930	1003	877	598
VANCOUVER	520	521	733	93	506	44*	426	95*	290*	345		119*	1511	332

Total mileage through British Columbia
⓱ 538 miles in BC– N. Vancouver to AB line
⓰ 658 miles in BC– Prince Rupert to AB line

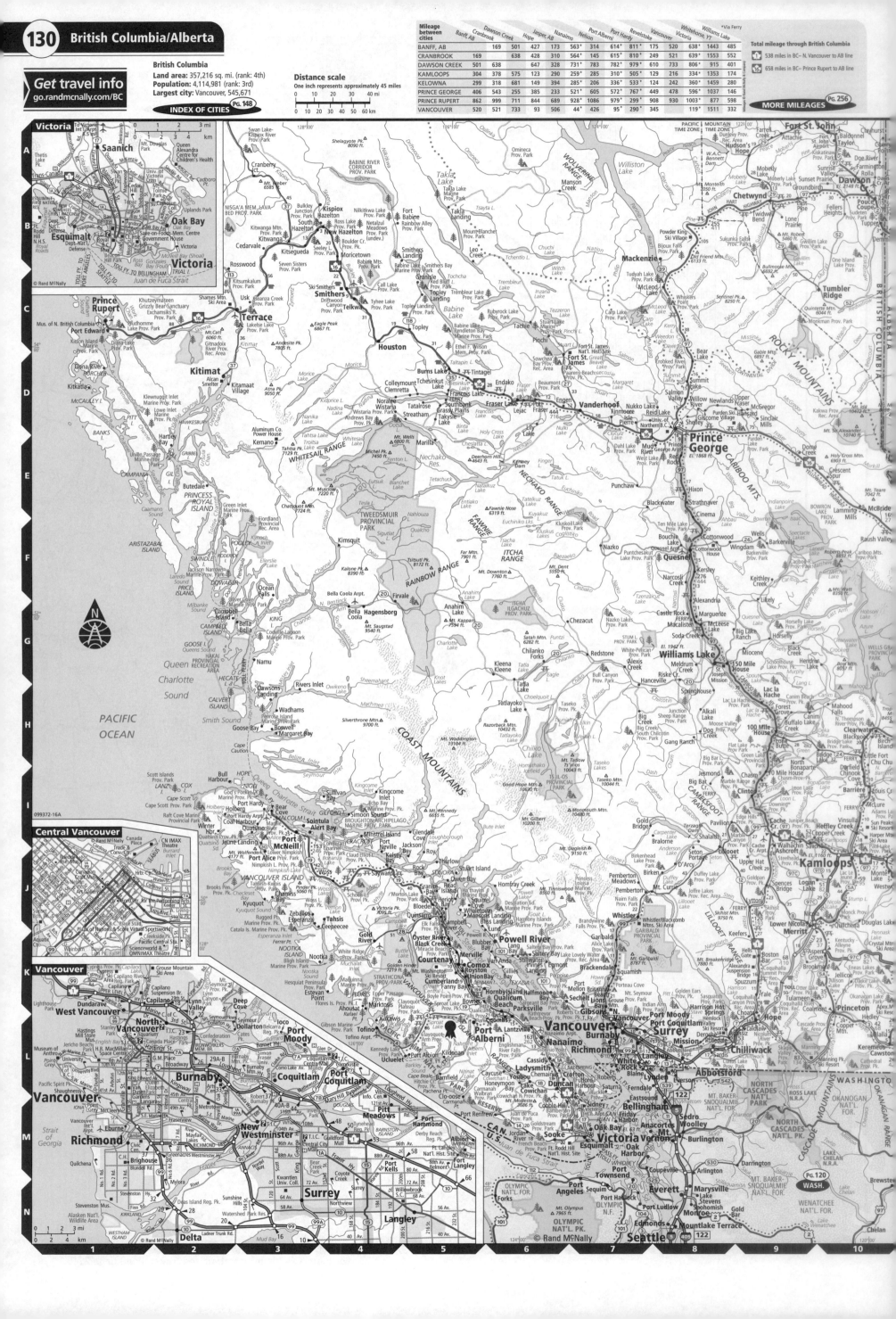

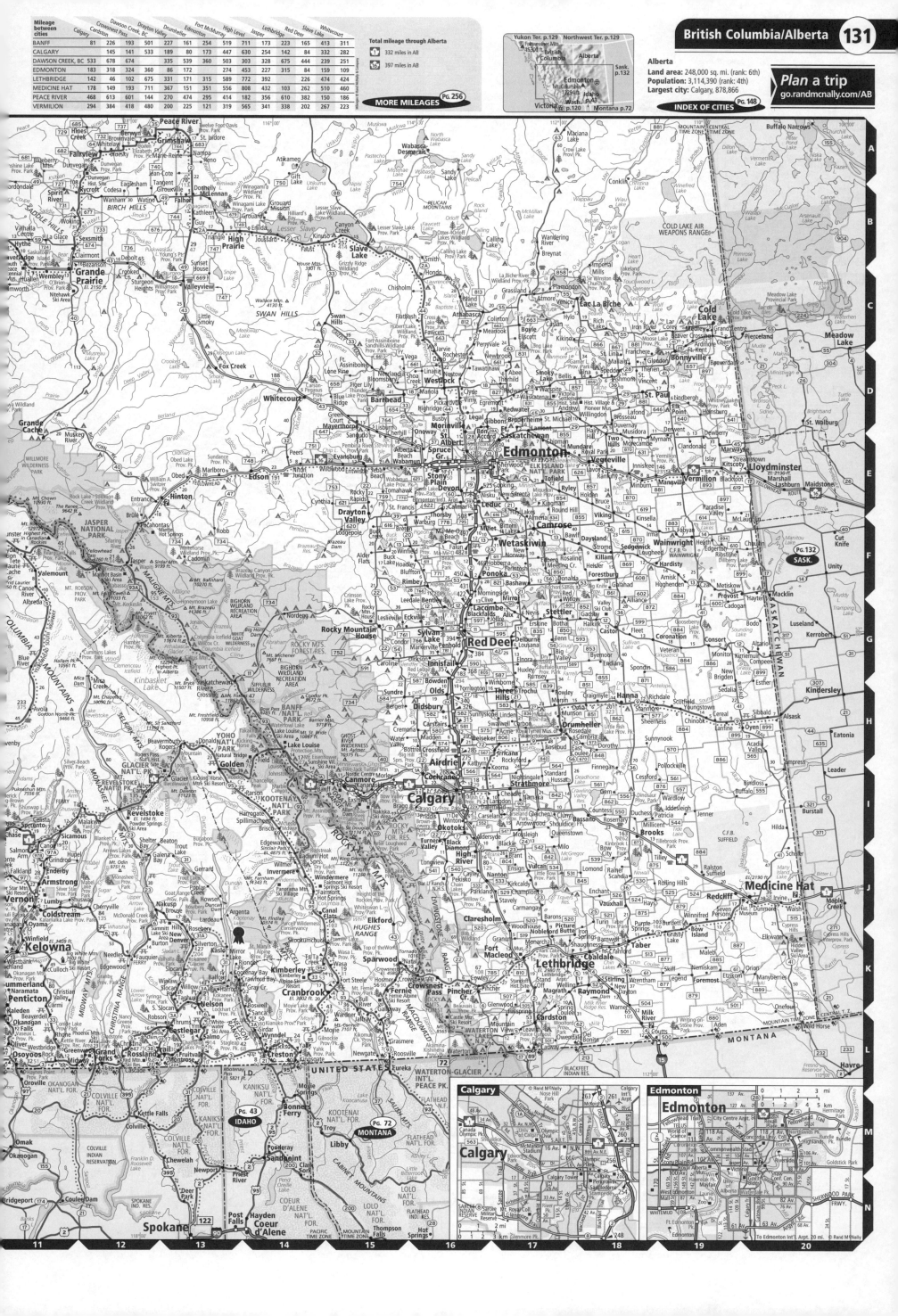

Mileage between cities

	Calgary	Cardston	Crowsnest Pass	Dawson Creek, BC	Drayton Valley	Drumheller	Edmonton	Fort McMurray	High Level	Jasper	Lethbridge	Red Deer	Slave Lake	Whitecourt
BANFF	81	226	193	501	227	161	254	519	711	173	223	165	413	311
CALGARY		145	141	533	189	80	173	447	630	254	142	84	332	282
DAWSON CREEK, BC	533	678	674		335	539	360	503	303	328	675	444	239	251
EDMONTON	183	318	324	360	86	172		274	453	227	315	84	159	109
LETHBRIDGE	142	46	102	675	331	171	315	589	772	392		226	474	424
MEDICINE HAT	178	149	193	711	367	151	351	556	808	432	103	262	510	460
PEACE RIVER	468	613	601	144	270	474	295	414	182	356	610	382	150	186
VERMILION	294	384	418	480	200	225	121	319	565	341	338	202	267	223

Total mileage through Alberta
① 332 miles in AB
⑯ 397 miles in AB

MORE MILEAGES Pg. 256

Alberta
Land area: 248,000 sq. mi. (rank: 6th)
Population: 3,114,390 (rank: 4th)
Largest city: Calgary, 878,866

INDEX OF CITIES Pg. 148

Plan a trip go.randmcnally.com/AB

Calgary

Edmonton

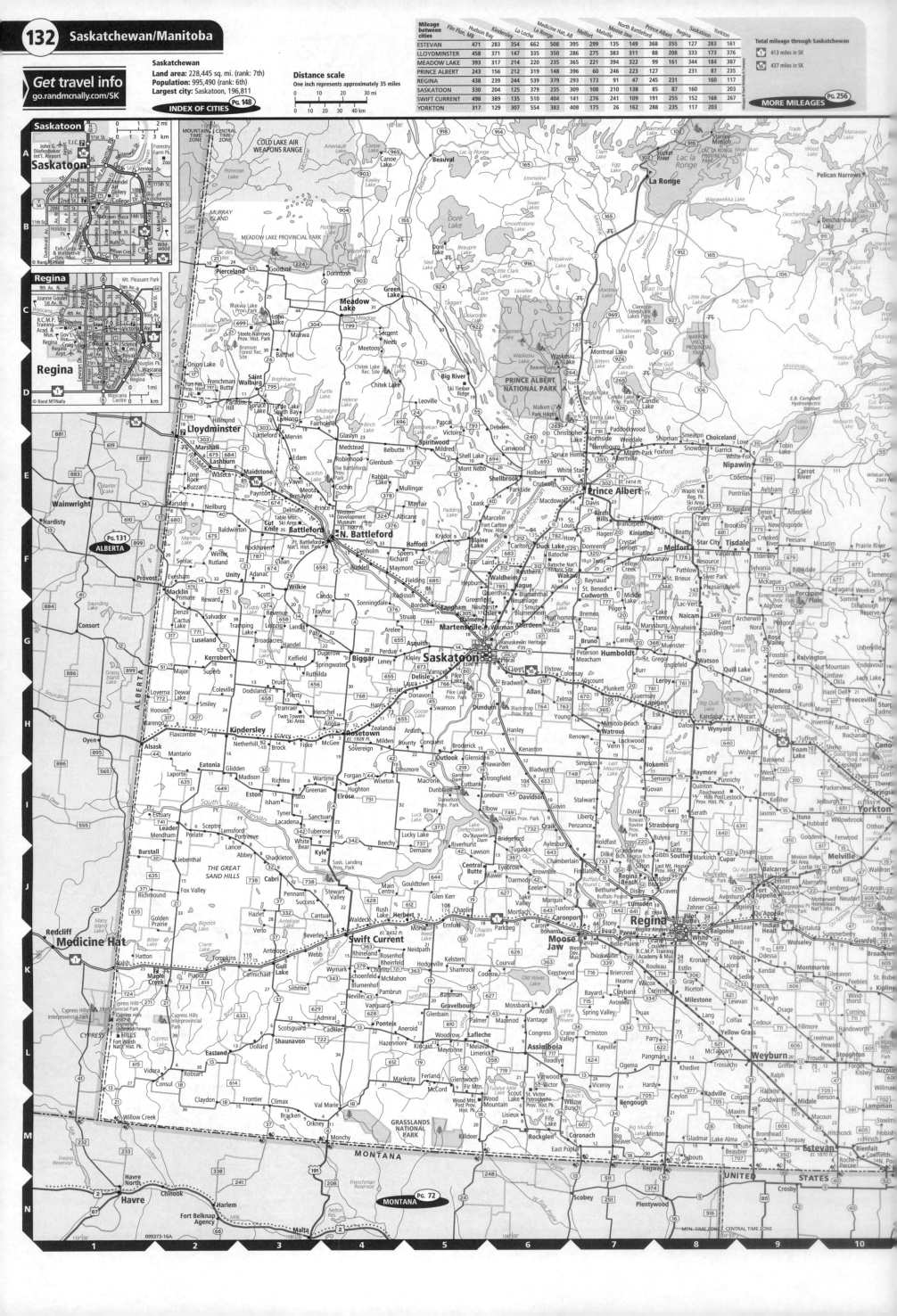

Get travel info
go.randmcnally.com/SK

INDEX OF CITIES PG. 148

Saskatchewan
Land area: 228,445 sq. mi. (rank: 7th)
Population: 995,490 (rank: 6th)
Largest city: Saskatoon, 196,811

Distance scale
One inch represents approximately 35 miles

MORE MILEAGES PG. 256

Mileage between cities	Flin Flon, MB	Hudson Bay	Kindersley	La Loche	La Ronge	Medicine Hat, AB	Melfort	Moose Jaw	North Battleford	Prince Albert	Regina	Saskatoon	Yorkton
ESTEVAN	471	283	354	662	508	395	299	135	449	368	355	127	283	161
LLOYDMINSTER	458	371	147	335	350	286	275	383	311	88	200	333	173	376
MEADOW LAKE	393	317	214	220	235	365	221	394	322	99	161	344	184	387
PRINCE ALBERT	243	156	212	319	148	396	60	246	223	127		231	87	235
REGINA	438	239	244	539	293	173	91	47	245	231		160	117	
SASKATOON	330	204	125	379	235	309	108	210	138	85	87		160	203
SWIFT CURRENT	498	389	135	510	404	141	276	241	109	191	255	152	168	267
YORKTON	317	129	307	554	383	408	175	26	162	288	235	117	203	

Total mileage through Saskatchewan
413 miles in SK
437 miles in SK

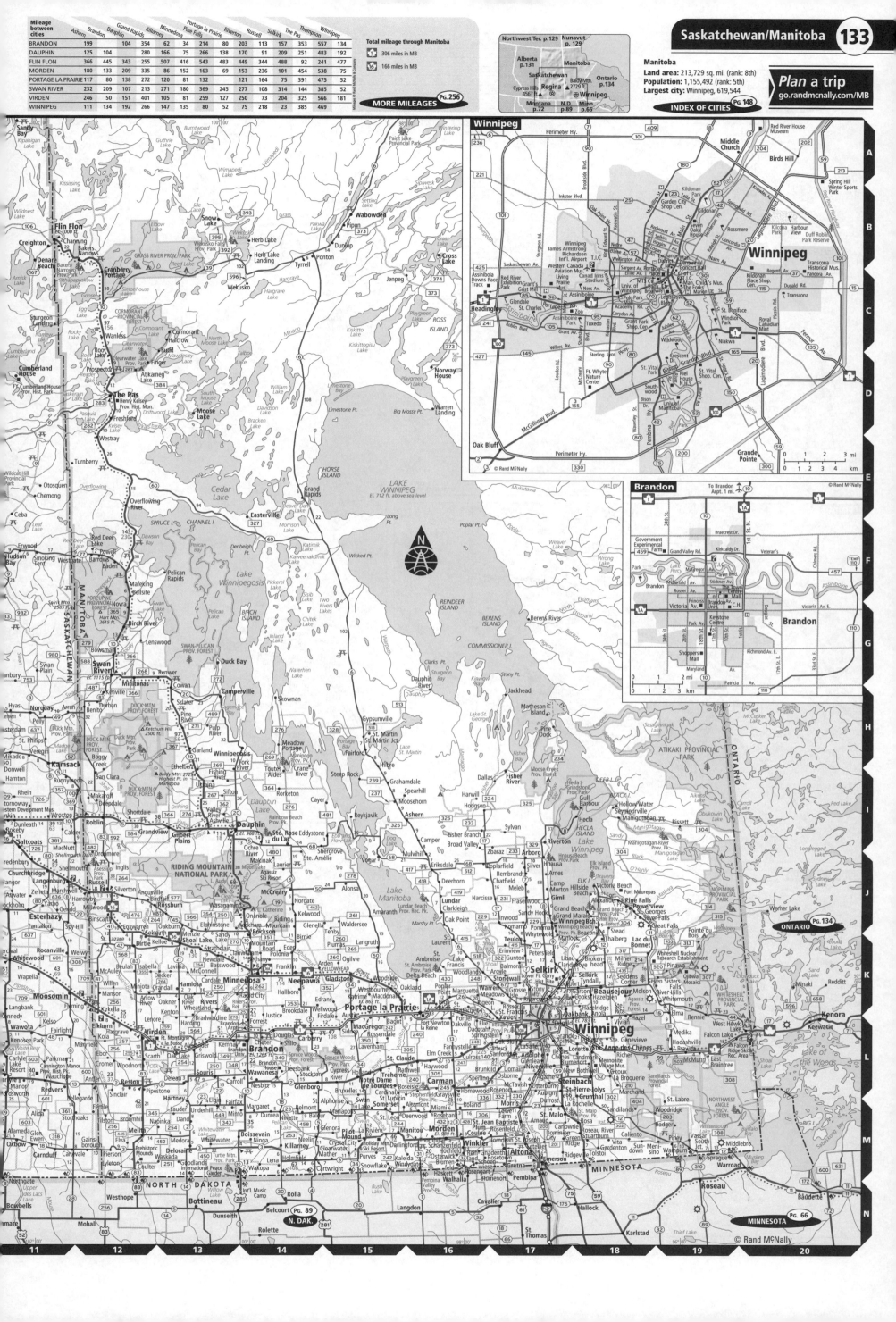

Land area: 354,342 sq. mi. (rank: 5th)
Population: 12,096,627 (rank: 1st)
Largest city: Toronto, 2,481,494

INDEX OF CITIES **Pg. 148**

For a glossary of common French terms, see page 129.

Mileage between cities	Barrie	Hamilton	Kenora	Kingston	London	Montreal QC	Niagara Falls	Ottawa	Owen Sound	Pembroke	Peterborough	Sault Ste. Marie	Sudbury	Thunder Bay	Timmins	Toronto	Windsor
KINGSTON	210	206	1304		275	187	247	117	285	156	122	341	557	380	997	516	161	387
LONDON	160	85	1274	275		456	138	363	144	361	196	71	527	350	967	533	125	120
NIAGARA FALLS	132	48	1246	247	138	428		335	163	333	168	204	499	322	939	505	88	250
OTTAWA	269	294	1225	117	363	335	335		343	95	171	429	494	308	918	455	249	475
SUDBURY	189	281	930	380	350	441	322	308	253	208	258	416	183		623	181	252	462
THUNDER BAY	806	898	307	997	967	1002	939	918	870	818	875	1033	440	623		519	869	1079
TORONTO	62	47	1176	161	125	342	88	249	121	247	82	191	429	252	869		435	237
WINDSOR	272	197	1386	387	120	568	250	475	275	473	308	90	639	462	1079	645	237	

Total mileage through Ontario
- 🛣 417 · 17 · 1358 miles
- 🛣 400 · 69 · 235 miles
- 🛣 401 · 513 miles

MORE MILEAGES **Pg. 256**

136 Québec

Land area: 527,079 sq. mi. (rank: 2nd)
Population: 7,443,491 (rank: 2nd)
Largest city: Montréal, 1,812,723

INDEX OF CITIES PG. 148

For a glossary of common French terms, see page 129.

MORE MILEAGES PG. 256

Mileage between cities	Baie-Comeau	Burlington, VT	Gaspé	Mont-Laurier	Montmagny	Montréal	North Bay, ON	Ottawa, ON	Québec	Rimouski	Rivière-du-Loup	Rouyn-Noranda	Saguenay	Salaberry-de-Valleyfield	Sept-Îles	Sherbrooke	Thetford Mines	Trois-Rivières
MONTRÉAL	412	102	568	148	186		362	133	158	327	264	391	283	59	530	95	144	95
OTTAWA, ON	539	227	695	123	313	133	229		285	454	391	326	410	98	657	220	271	216
QUÉBEC	274	244*	430	302	48	158	514	285		189	126	545	129	211	392		69	77
ROUYN-NORANDA	801*	494	957	243	575	391	174	326	545	716	653		670	420	919	487	533	469
SAGUENAY	195	369*	391	427	173	283		419	129	150*	251	670		336	336	271	194	202
SEPT-ÎLES	141	616*	328	676	345	530	886	657		203	265	919	336	583		518	144	457
SHERBROOKE	400	115	556	244	174	95	449	220	146	315	252	487	271	146	518		62	99
TROIS-RIVIÈRES	339	195	495	226	113	95	445	116	77	254	191	469	202	142*	457	99	83	

*Via Ferry

Total mileage through Québec

Route	Miles
20 / 132	937 miles
15 / 117	412 miles
40 / 138	765 miles

Mileage between cities	Amherst, NS	Bathurst, NB	Campbellton, NB	Charlottetown, PE	Corner Brook, NL	Edmundston, NB	Fredericton, NB	Gander, NL	Grand Falls, NL	Halifax, NS	Moncton, NB	New Glasgow, NS	Saint John, NB	St. John's, NL	St. Stephen, NB	Sydney, NS	Truro, NS	Yarmouth, NS	*Via Ferry
CHARLOTTETOWN, PE	93	249	319		482*	422	241	688*	384	164	119	67	218	597*	321	247	104	326	
EDMUNDSTON, NB	336	193	129	417*	860*		177	1080*	37	471	294	446	246	1281*	220	599	409	356	
FREDERICTON, NB	158	158	238	239*	682*	177		902*	139	293	116	268	70	1103*	79	421	231	180	
HALIFAX, NS	135	306	386	157*	519*	471	293	739*	433		105	271	940*	341	258	64	186		
MONCTON, NB	38	131	211	119	562*	294	116	782*	256	173		148	94	983*	164	301	111	365	
SAINT JOHN, NB	136	229	309	218	622*	246	70	880*	208	271	94	246		1081*	70	399	209	110	
ST. JOHN'S, NL	945*	1116*	1196*	597*	427	1281*	1103*	201	1243*	940*	983*	837*	1081*		1151*	688*	878*	1132*	
SYDNEY, NS	263	434	514	247	267*	599	421	487*	561	258	301	155	399	688*	469		196	450	

Total mileage through Atlantic Provinces		
2 308 miles (NB)		2 565 miles (NL)
1 101 miles (PE)	102 & 105 287 miles (NS)	

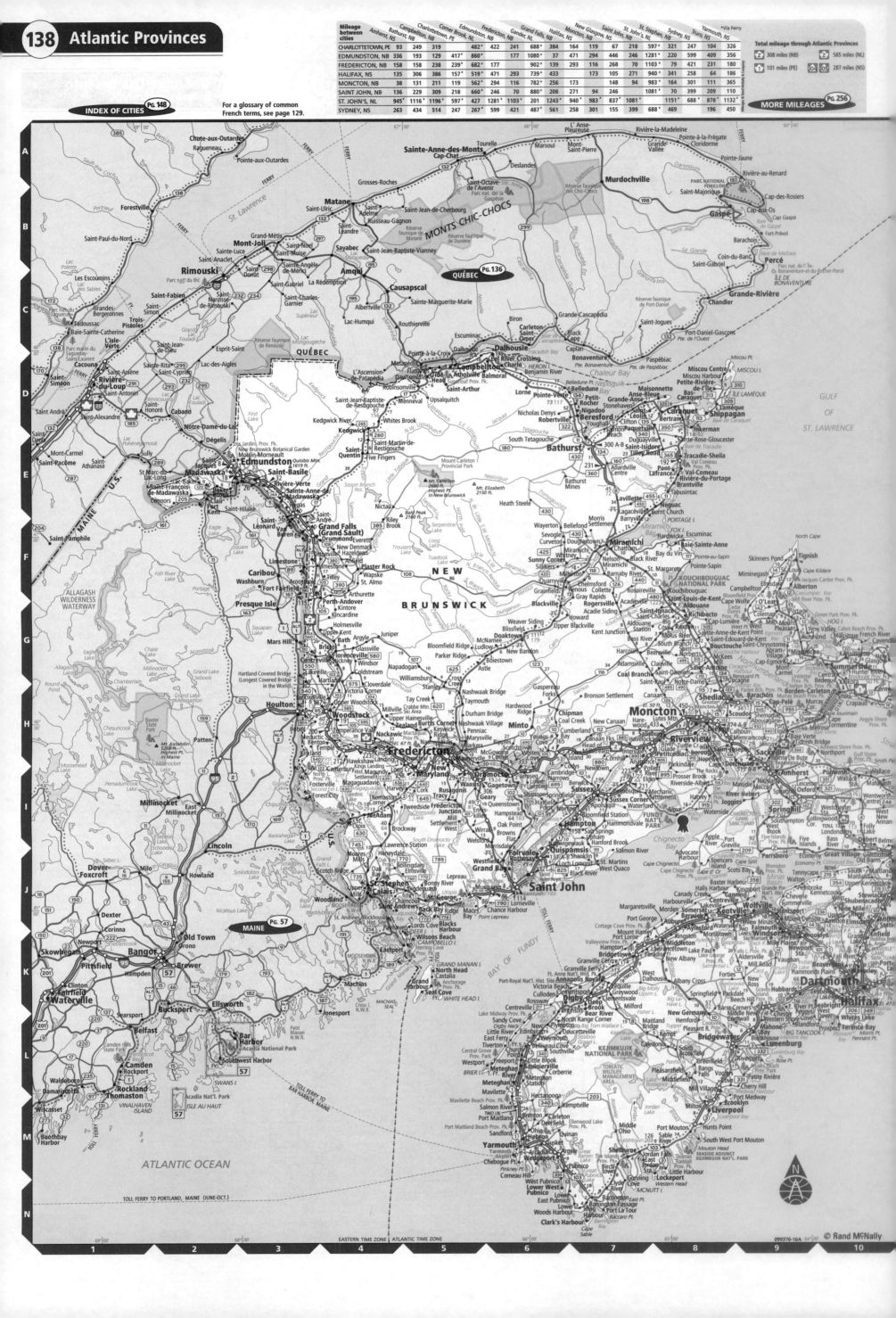

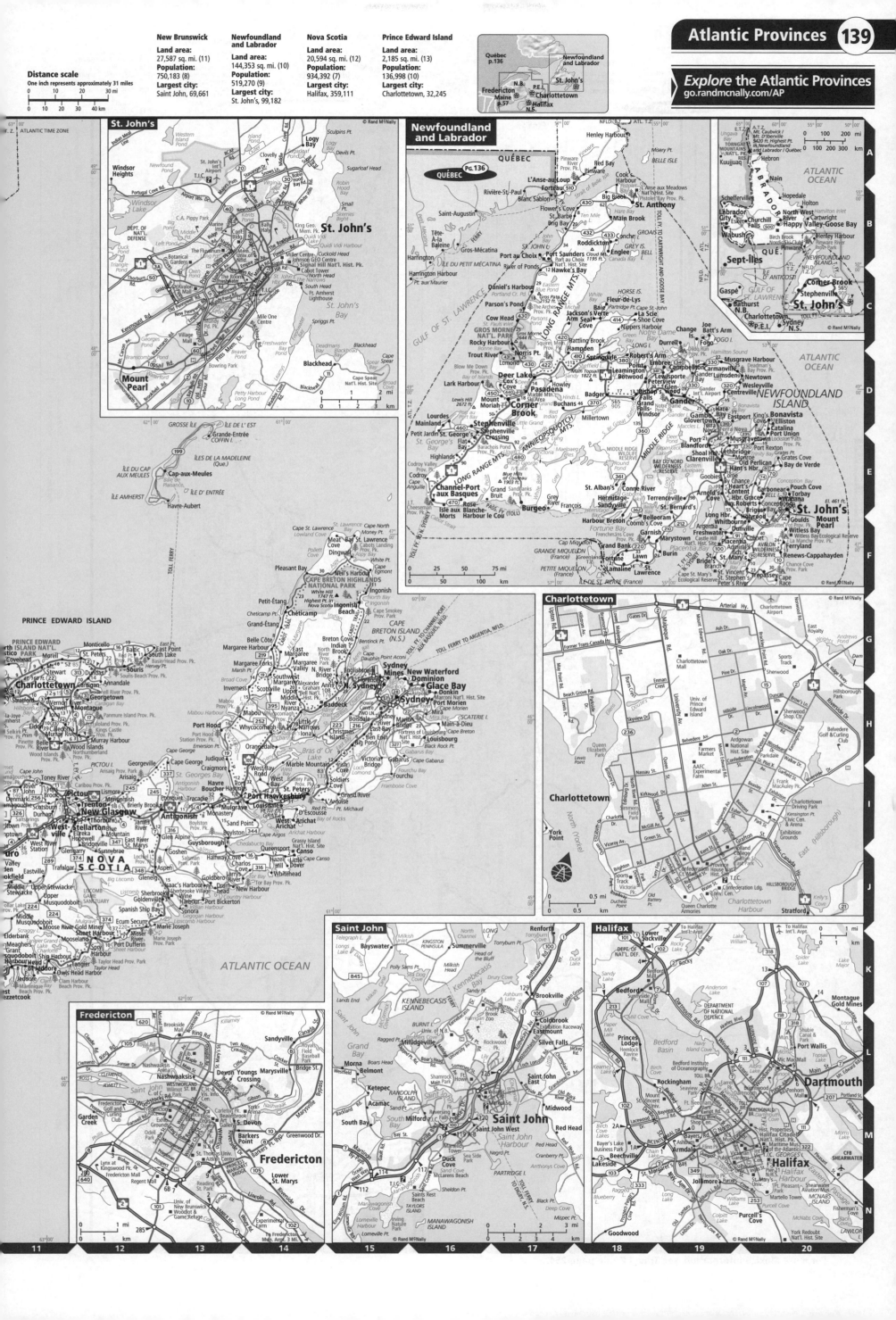

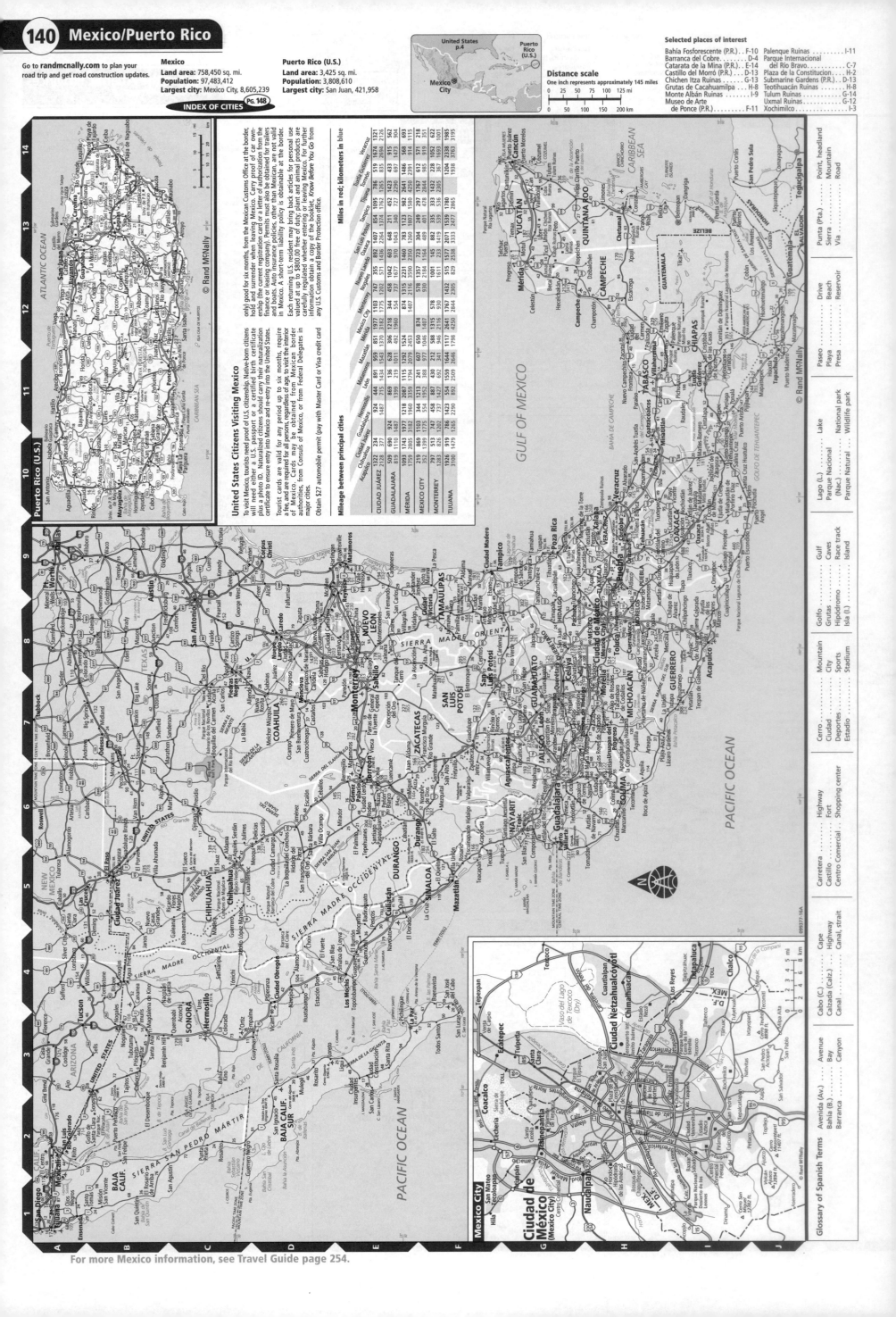

United States Counties, Cities and Towns

2000 Census populations or latest available estimates
Index to Canada and Mexico cities and towns, page 148

Alabama
Map pp. 16–17

Arizona
Map pp. 20–21

*City keyed to p. 19

Arkansas
Map pp. 22–23

California
Map pp. 24–27

Index keys NA to NN refer to Northern CA, pp. 24–25, SA to SN refer to Southern CA, pp. 26–27
*City keyed to p. 28
†City keyed to p. 29
‡City keyed to pp. 30–31

Alaska
Map p. 18

Colorado
Map pp. 32–33

*City keyed to p. 34

Connecticut
Map p. 35

Delaware
Map p. 36

Iowa
Map pp. 50–51

Kansas
Map pp. 52–53
*City keyed to p. 70

Kentucky
Map pp. 54–55

Louisiana
Map p. 56

Maine
Map p. 57

Maryland
Map pp. 58–59
* City keyed to p. 123
† Independent city; not listed in body of index.

Massachusetts
Map pp. 60–61

Michigan
Map pp. 62–63

Minnesota
Map pp. 66–67

Mississippi
Map p. 68

Missouri
Map pp. 70–71

Montana
Map pp. 72–73

Nebraska
Map pp. 74–75

Nevada
Map p. 76

New Hampshire
Map p. 77

New Jersey
Map pp. 78–79

* City keyed to pp. 84–85
‡ City keyed to p. 102

New Mexico
Map p. 80

New York
Map pp. 81–83

Index keys SA to SJ refer to Southern NY; p. 81. NA to NN refer to Northern NY; pp. 82–83
* City keyed to pp. 84–85

North Dakota
Map p. 89

North Carolina
Map pp. 86–87

* City keyed to p. 88

Ohio
Map pp. 90–93

Index keys NA to NN refer to Northern OH; pp. 90–91; SA to SN refer to Southern OH, pp. 92–93

*, †, ‡, See explanation under state title in this index.   County names are listed in capital letters and in boldface type.

Texas
Map pp. 110–113

Index keys WA to WT refer to Western TX, pp. 110–111, EA to ET refer to Eastern TX, pp. 112–113
* City keyed to p. 108
† City keyed to p. 109

Utah
Map pp. 114–115

Vermont
Map p. 116

Virginia
Map pp. 118–119

* City keyed to p. 117
† City keyed to p. 123
‡ City keyed to p. 122; Note: not included in any county.

Washington
Map pp. 120–121

* City keyed to p. 122

West Virginia
Map p. 124

West Virginia

Benwood, 1496 ..... A-6
BERKELEY CO., 93394 ... B-13
Berkeley Sprs., 703 ..... B-13
Bethany, 985 ..... B-2
Bethlehem, 2547 ..... A-6
Big Chimney, 650 ..... D-4
Blair, 500 ..... J-3
Blennerhassett, 3225 ..... C-4
Bluefield, 11119 ..... J-5
Bolivar, 1080 ..... C-14
Boomer, 600 ..... G-4
BOONE CO., 25703 ..... H-4
Bradshaw, 2371 ..... K-5
Bramwell, 412 ..... J-5
BRAXTON CO., 14851 ..... E-6
Brenton, 700 ..... J-4
Bridgeport, 7486 ..... C-7
BROOKE CO., 24515 ..... B-2
Buckhannon, 5687 ..... D-7
CABELL CO., 94031 ..... F-2
CALHOUN CO., 7387 ..... E-5
Cameron, 1142 ..... A-7
Caretta, 600 ..... J-4
Cedar Gr., 823 ..... G-4
Cedar Gr., 350 ..... C-4
Ceredo, 1621 ..... F-1
Chapmanville, 1145 ..... H-3
Charleston, 51176 ..... F-4
Charles Town, 3704 ..... C-14
Charmco, 150 ..... G-6
Chattaroy, 1136 ..... J-2
Chesapeake, 1567 ..... G-4
Chester, 2436 ..... A-2
Clarksburg, 16439 ..... C-7
CLAY CO., 10356 ..... F-5
Clay, 580 ..... F-5
Clearview, 563 ..... A-6
Clendenin, 1056 ..... F-4
Clothier, 270 ..... H-4
Coalwood, 700 ..... J-4
Cool Ridge, 600 ..... H-5
Cowen, 506 ..... F-6
Crab Orchard, 2761 ..... H-5
Craigsville, 2204 ..... F-6
Cross Lanes, 10353 ..... F-3
Culloden, 2940 ..... F-2
Daniels, 1846 ..... H-5
Danville, 540 ..... G-3
Davis, 577 ..... D-9
Delbarton, 442 ..... J-2
Despard, 1039 ..... C-7
DODDRIDGE CO., 7476 ..... C-6
Dunbar, 7740 ..... F-3
E. Bank, 896 ..... G-4
Eccles, 900 ..... H-5
Eleanor, 1491 ..... F-3
Elizabeth, 972 ..... D-4
Elk Forest, 600 ..... G-4
Elkins, 7109 ..... D-8
Elkview, 1182 ..... F-4

Elm Gr. J-11
Enterprise, 939 ..... C-7
Fairmont, 19049 ..... C-8
Fairview, 436 ..... B-7
FAYETTE CO., 46823 ..... H-5
Fayetteville, 2657 ..... G-5
Follansbee, 2971 ..... B-2
Ft. Ashby, 1354 ..... B-11
Ft. Gay, 818 ..... G-1
Franklin, 824 ..... E-10
Gary, 801 ..... J-4
Gassaway, 884 ..... E-6
Gauley Bridge, 706 ..... G-5
GILMER CO., 6950 ..... D-6
Glasgow, 743 ..... G-4
Glen Dale, 1475 ..... A-6
Glen Ft., 450 ..... G-4
Glenville, 1482 ..... D-6
Grafton, 5407 ..... C-8
GRANT CO., 11673 ..... D-10
Grantsville, 546 ..... D-5
Granville, 651 ..... B-8
GREENBRIER CO., 35027 ..... G-7
Guthrie, 600 ..... F-4
Hamlin, 1100 ..... G-2
HAMPSHIRE CO., 22025 ..... C-11
HANCOCK CO., 31350 ..... A-2
HARDY CO., 13287 ..... D-11
HARRISON CO., 68369 ..... C-7
Harrisville, 1861 ..... D-5
Henderson, 315 ..... F-2
Henlawson, 600 ..... H-3
Hico, 900 ..... G-5
Hinton, 2696 ..... H-6
Hometown, 350 ..... F-3
Huntington, 49198 ..... F-1
Hurricane, 5968 ..... F-3
Iaeger, 314 ..... J-3
Institute, 1800 ..... F-3
Inwood, 2084 ..... C-13
JACKSON CO., 28403 ..... E-4
JEFFERSON CO., 49206 ..... C-14
Jeffrey, 500 ..... H-3
Junior, 448 ..... D-8

KANAWHA CO.

Kenova, 3391 ..... F-1
Keyser, 5410 ..... C-11
Keystone, 395 ..... J-5
Kimball, 360 ..... J-4
Kistler, 900 ..... H-3
Kincaid, 450 ..... G-5
Kingwood, 2926 ..... C-9
Lavalette, 1100 ..... F-2
Leon, 120 ..... E-3
LEWIS CO., 17199 ..... D-7
Lewisburg, 3595 ..... H-7
LINCOLN CO., 22374 ..... G-2
LOGAN CO., 36237 ..... H-2
Lumberport, 959 ..... C-7
Mabscott, 1364 ..... H-5
Madison, 2634 ..... G-3
Mannington, 2082 ..... B-7
Marlinton, 1100 ..... F-7
Marlowe, 700 ..... B-14
Marmet, 1626 ..... G-4
MARSHALL CO., 34337 ..... A-6
Martinsburg, 15996 ..... C-13
MASON CO., 25761 ..... E-3
Masontown, 649 ..... B-9
Matewan, 501 ..... J-2
Maybeury, 300 ..... J-5
McDOWELL CO., 24273 ..... J-4
McMechen, 1821 ..... A-6
Middlebourne, 853 ..... C-6
Milton, 2262 ..... F-2
Minden, 1000 ..... G-5
MINERAL CO., 27028 ..... C-11
Mineral Wells, 2100 ..... D-4
Monongah, 912 ..... C-7
MONONGALIA CO., 84386 ..... B-8
MONROE CO., 13507 ..... J-6
Montcalm, 885 ..... J-5
Montgomery, 2030 ..... G-5
Moorefield, 2408 ..... D-11
MORGAN CO., 16022 ..... B-12
Morgantown, 28292 ..... B-8
Moundsville, 9472 ..... A-6
Mt. Gay, 700 ..... H-3
Mt. Hope, 1411 ..... H-5
Nettie, 500 ..... G-6
New Cumberland, 1043 ..... A-2
New Haven, 1528 ..... D-3
New Martinsville, 5791 ..... B-6
NICHOLAS CO., 26464 ..... F-6
Northfork, 454 ..... J-5
Nutter Ft., 1649 ..... C-7
Oak Hill, 7312 ..... G-5
Oceana, 1478 ..... J-4

Odd, 200 ..... J-5
OHIO CO., 45112 ..... A-7
Omar, 600 ..... H-3
Paden City, 2737 ..... B-6
Parkersburg, 32020 ..... C-4
Parsons, 1400 ..... D-8
Paw Paw, 507 ..... B-12
Pea Ridge, 6363 ..... F-2
PENDLETON CO., 7844 ..... E-10
Pennsboro, 1196 ..... C-6
Petersburg, 2534 ..... D-10
Peterstown, 497 ..... J-6
Philippi, 2826 ..... C-8
Pinch, 2811 ..... F-4
Pine Grove, 543 ..... B-6
Pineville, 676 ..... J-4
Pleasant Valley, 3119 ..... C-8
PLEASANTS CO., 7376 ..... C-5
Poca, 1017 ..... F-3
Pocatalico, 1500 ..... F-4
Pt. Pleasant, 4481 ..... E-3
Powellton, 1796 ..... G-5
Prosperity, 1310 ..... H-5
PRESTON CO., 30115 ..... B-9
Princeton, 6222 ..... J-5
Prosperity, 1310 ..... H-5
Quinwood, 450 ..... G-6
Racine, 450 ..... G-4
Rainelle, 1569 ..... G-6
RALEIGH CO., 79167 ..... H-5
Ramage, 200 ..... H-3
Rand, 2200 ..... G-4
RANDOLPH CO., 28571 ..... E-8
Ranson, 3703 ..... C-14
Ravenswood, 3991 ..... D-3
Reader, 500 ..... B-6
Red Jacket, 728 ..... J-2
Richwood, 2363 ..... F-6
Ridgeley, 709 ..... C-11
Ripley, 3266 ..... E-4
RITCHIE CO., 10540 ..... D-5
ROANE CO., 15407 ..... E-4
Rock Cave, 200 ..... E-6
Roderfield, 1000 ..... J-4
Romney, 1975 ..... C-11
Ronceverte, 1544 ..... H-7
Rowlesburg, 620 ..... C-9
Rupert, 944 ..... H-6
Ruth, 175 ..... H-4
St. Albans, 11105 ..... F-3
St. Marys, 1764 ..... C-5
Salem, 1586 ..... C-6
Shady Spr., 2078 ..... H-5
Shepherdstown, 1158 ..... C-14
Shinnston, 2240 ..... C-7
Sissonville, 4399 ..... F-4

Sistersville, 1512 ..... B-5
Smithers, 858 ..... G-5
Sophia, 1260 ..... H-5
S. Charleston, 12700 ..... F-4
Spencer, 2258 ..... E-4
Spring Valley, 900 ..... G-1
Star City, 1369 ..... B-8
SUMMERS CO., 13740 ..... H-6
Summersville, 3369 ..... G-6
Sutton, 993 ..... E-6
TAYLOR CO., 16291 ..... C-8
Terra Alta, 1496 ..... C-9
Thomas, 411 ..... D-9
TUCKER CO., 6943 ..... D-9
TYLER CO., 9340 ..... C-6
Union, 550 ..... J-6
UPSHUR CO., 23712 ..... E-7
Valley Gr., 405 ..... B-7
Verdunville, 500 ..... H-3
Vienna, 10770 ..... C-4
War, 692 ..... K-4
WAYNE CO., 42091 ..... G-2
Weirton, 19746 ..... B-2
Welch, 2371 ..... J-4
Wellsburg, 2727 ..... B-2
W. Liberty, 1203 ..... A-7
W. Logan, 397 ..... H-3
W. Union, 821 ..... C-6
Westover, 3926 ..... B-8
W. Pea Ridge, 2000 ..... G-14
Weston, 4041 ..... D-7
Wheeling, 29311 ..... A-6
White Sulphur Sprs., 2315 ..... H-7
Whitman, 450 ..... H-3
Williamson, 3181 ..... J-2
Williamstown, 2955 ..... C-4
Winfield, 2031 ..... F-3
WIRT CO., 5896 ..... D-4
WOOD CO., 87047 ..... D-4
WYOMING CO., 24479 ..... J-4

[This page is a dense geographic place-name index containing thousands of entries organized by U.S. state and Canadian/Mexican region. Representative section headings and map references follow.]

Travel Guide

United States
- Cities
- Scenery
- Heritage
- Outdoors
- Statewide travel info

Canada and Mexico
- Insider's tips
- Border crossing info

Oak trees surround the Bragg-Mitchell Mansion, built in 1855 near Mobile.

CITIES

Birmingham (F-6)

Located in central Alabama, Birmingham is bursting with classic Southern charm and hospitality. The history-filled city is nestled in the foothills of the Appalachian Mountains and offers visitors dining, shopping, attractions, events, and entertainment. Founded in 1871, Birmingham was at the crossing of two main railroad lines, making it one of the South's important industrial areas. It was once a major iron and steel production center, earning it the nickname the "Pittsburgh of the South." Some don't-miss stops include the Arlington Antebellum Home and Garden (dating from the 1840s), the Museum of Art, the Birmingham Civil Rights Institute, Riverchase Galleria (200-plus specialty stores and restaurants), Talladega Superspeedway, and Tannehill Ironworks Historical State Park.

Riverchase Galleria

Greater Birmingham Convention & Visitors Bureau: (800) 458-8085; www.birminghamal.org

Huntsville (B-7)

Seeing Alabama firsthand

Northern Alabama is home to the high-tech city of Huntsville, well-known space research center for both the U.S. Army and NASA. The U.S. Space and Rocket Center, home of the popular Space Camp, touches on the past, present, and future of space exploration and includes hands-on exhibits, actual spacecraft, demonstrations, movies, and flight simulators. The city is also known as Alabama's birthplace, and several attractions examine the heritage of the state's first English-speaking city and of the Civil War. Huntsville highlights include Alabama Constitution Village, Twickenham Historic District, Huntsville Botanical Garden, Museum of Art, North Alabama Railroad Museum, and Historic Huntsville Depot. Golfers won't want to miss 54-hole Hampton Cove Golf Course, the beginning of the legendary Robert Trent Jones Golf Trail, which includes 24 courses in nine cities in Alabama.

Huntsville/Madison County Convention & Visitors Bureau: (256) 551-2230; www.huntsville.org

Mobile (P-2)

Situated at the head of 27-mile-long Mobile Bay on the Gulf of Mexico, Mobile is a leading U.S. seaport. The city was founded in 1702 by the French and served as the original capital of the Louisiana Territory. The French heritage remains strong today and includes two weeks of family-friendly Mardi Gras festivities annually. The area is also known for lush foliage and blooming flowers — most notably azaleas — like those at Bellingrath Gardens. Other worthy stops include the Cathedral of the Immaculate Conception, Mobile Museum of Art, Fort Condé, and the Phoenix Fire Museum. From waterfront fun to the USS *Alabama* and scrumptious seafood creations, visitors find a variety of activities and attractions in "Mobeel."

Mobile Bay Convention & Visitors Bureau: (800) 566-2453; www.mobile.org

Fort Condé guard

✪ Montgomery (State Capital) (J-8)

The capital of Alabama and the birthplace of the modern civil rights movement, Montgomery was once the capital of the Confederate States of America. The Civil Rights Memorial on Washington Avenue stands as a testament to those who gave their lives in the struggle for justice and equality. The Rosa Parks Library and Museum contains interactive exhibits depicting the history of the movement and the bus boycott that began its period of nonviolent civil disobedience. The city's earlier history is retold at the First White House of the Confederacy, where period furnishings and the personal effects of Jefferson Davis are displayed. The restored buildings at Old Alabama Town depict 19th-century life from slave quarters to townhomes. Theatergoers enjoy the Alabama Shakespeare Festival in Blount Cultural Park. Fans of popular music trek to the Hank Williams Museum to see his costumes and listen to his timeless country ballads and upbeat tunes.

Montgomery Area Chamber of Commerce/ Convention & Visitors Bureau: (800) 240-9452; www.visitingmontgomery.com

SCENERY

Natchez Trace Parkway (A-3)

The 32-mile segment in the northwest corner of Alabama is the middle leg of a scenic byway that runs the entire length of the Natchez Trace, from Natchez, Mississippi in the south to Nashville, Tennessee in the north. This two-lane parkway follows the historic trail of people on the move: Native Americans, post riders, soldiers, and others. Today the tree-lined route takes travelers through woods and fields and past pioneer history sites, including Colbert Ferry Park, Freedom Hills, and Buzzard Roost Springs. Enjoy especially beautiful views midway through the drive when crossing the Tennessee River.

Selma to Montgomery March Byway (J-6)

This National Scenic Byway and Historic Trail travels 43 miles past some of the most important spots in the Civil Rights movement. From the quiet streets of Selma, the road winds up and down the rolling hills of Lowndes County to Montgomery. It is most famous for Dr. Martin Luther King, Jr.'s historic Selma-to-Montgomery march in 1965, which helped African-Americans gain voting rights in the South. Noteworthy stops on the route include the National Voting Rights Museum and Institute, Edmund Pettus Bridge, Brown Chapel (the starting point for the march), and the Alabama State Capitol.

Talladega Scenic Drive (F-9)

Climb to Alabama's highest point, Cheaha Mountain at 2,407 feet above sea level, during this drive in the east-central part of the state. The 26-mile route treats drivers to views of the Appalachian Mountains, deep green trees lining ridges and valleys, rock outcroppings, small rural towns, and on a clear day, plenty of blue sky.

Bellingrath

- ### Bellingrath Gardens & Home (Q-2)

  Located on a bluff overlooking the Isle-aux-Oies River near Mobile Bay, the renowned gardens and home of Walter and Bessie Bellingrath include 65 acres of more than 50,000 bulbs and dozens of varieties of flowers, native and exotic plants, and trees.

- ### Lookout Mountain Parkway (D-9)

  Green signs show the way along this 93-mile scenic trip from Gadsden, Alabama to Chattanooga, Tennessee. See waterfalls, rolling hills, farmland, mountains, and glimpses of wildlife.

- ### Natural Bridge (D-4)

  Located near the town of Natural Bridge in northwest Alabama, the sandstone and iron ore Natural Bridge measures 60 feet high and 148 feet long and dates back some 200 million years. It is the longest natural bridge east of the Rockies.

- ### William Bankhead National Forest (C-4)

  This forest is home to unexpected natural beauty. The turn-off from Highway 33 down to Caney Creek Falls reveals one of the forest's tallest and most-visited waterfalls. The drive around the Sipsey Wilderness — the largest wilderness area east of the Mississippi — also offers visitors glimpses of ridges, canyons, and flowing waters.

HERITAGE

Civil Rights Memorial (T-4)

The men and women who gave their lives for the Civil Rights movement are honored at this downtown Montgomery memorial. Engraved into the simple black granite memorial are the names of 40 men, women, and children who lost their lives from 1954 to 1968, along with key dates and events of the movement. The Memorial was built in 1989 and was designed by Maya Lin, also the architect of the Vietnam Veterans Memorial in Washington, D.C. The Memorial sits just blocks away from the church where Dr. Martin Luther King, Jr. preached and is adjacent to the new Civil Rights Memorial Center. This is the only U.S. monument honoring those who died fighting for racial equality.

www.tolerance.org/memorial/

Moundville Archaeological Park (H-4)

More than 800 years ago, Moundville was a large Mississippian settlement along the bluffs of the Black Warrior River in central Alabama. At its peak, the community was a 300-acre village and the largest North American city of the time. Today, the University of Alabama oversees the park and museum, both of which are open daily to the public. Visitors can take self-guided tours or call ahead for guided tours. A complete tour takes about 2-3 hours and includes the Jones Archaeological Museum, Indian Village, Crafts Pavilions, Douglass Nature Trail (a half-mile trail in the woodlands), several of the remaining 26 earthen mounds, and other sites showing evidence of a thousand years of human life at Moundville. The park is located 14 miles south of Tuscaloosa on Highway 69.

(205) 371-2234; moundville.ua.edu/home.html

Tuskegee Institute National Historic Site (J-10)

Located on the campus of Tuskegee University in east central Alabama, this noteworthy site became part of the National Park System in 1974. Tuskegee Normal School was a state-funded school that was established to educate newly freed slaves and their children. The Normal School later became the Institute, which officially opened on July 4, 1881 under the leadership of Booker T. Washington. The young principal — he was 26 when he started — hired individuals such as George Washington Carver and Robert Taylor to help develop the institute and earn its world-renowned status. See the legacy of Washington, Carver, and many others at this historic site whose original buildings were all student-built. The site includes the George Washington Carver Museum, which features exhibits, programs, and two films about Carver and Washington; the "Oaks," Booker T. Washington's home; and the Tuskegee Campus, a designated Historic District designed by Taylor, the first African-American graduate of MIT.

(334) 727-3200; www.nps.gov/tuin

USS *Alabama* Battleship Memorial Park (S-8)

USS Alabama

Some of Mobile's military might can be found at Battleship Memorial Park, home to the USS *Alabama* battleship, the USS *Drum* submarine, and 24 combat aircraft. The USS *Alabama* served in the Atlantic for a year before steaming to the Pacific in mid-1943. The "Mighty A" earned nine WWII Battle Stars and was the proud leader of the American fleet that entered Tokyo Bay after the Japanese surrender in September 1945. Visitors can climb inside the *Drum* and experience submarine life firsthand. The park also displays a B-52 Stratofortress named "Calamity Jane," an A-12 "Blackbird" spy plane, and an Aircraft Pavilion containing WWII fighter planes and aircraft from the Korean and Vietnam wars and Desert Storm.

(251) 433-2703; www.ussalabama.com

OUTDOORS

Conecuh National Forest (O-6)

Among these hardwood swamps, carnivorous pitcher plants, and southern coastal plain pine forests hides a maze of winding creeks and ponds great for a variety of outdoor activities. For example, 30-acre Open Pond is stocked with bass, catfish, bluegill, and other species that can be hooked from two fishing piers. There's also a swimming beach at Blue Lake and plenty of campsites. From this area there is easy access to the 20-mile Conecuh Hiking Trail, which meanders through magnolia, cypress, dogwood, and holly trees. Or take to the waters and canoe almost 50 miles of the shallow, sandy-bottomed Blackwater River. The river's dark water moves slowly at five miles per hour and eventually flows through Florida's Blackwater State Forest.

(334) 222-2555; www.fs.fed.us/r8/alabama

Getting ready to sail

Joe Wheeler State Park (A-5)

The Tennessee River empties into Wheeler Lake, which provides many water-related recreation opportunities. Visitors have access to a full-service marina, beach space, swimming, lakeside campgrounds, an 18-hole golf course, and picnic tables, all located near the park's main lodge. The Wheeler Dam area of the park also has a boat launch, along with both brick and wood cabins and a recreation area with tennis courts, and it's a prime fishing spot. All sorts of boats ply the lake's calm waters, including sailboats, motorboats, canoes, fishing boats, and pontoon boats.

(256) 247-5466; www.joewheelerstatepark.com

Little River Canyon National Preserve (B-10)

In the northeast corner of the state near the Georgia border, Little River flows down Lookout Mountain to form one of the South's most impressive river and canyon systems. This free-flowing river (no dam controls its flow) is divided into four different sections, ranging from nice and easy gentle ripples to rip-roaring rapids that offer wild rides. The preserve's white water is some of the best in the region and makes for challenging Class III to VI whitewater rafting and kayaking. The preserve offers stunning Appalachian Plateau landscapes year-round, and overlooks along the Canyon Rim Parkway are perfect spots to take in some of the area's forests, waterfalls, canyon rims, bluffs, streams, pools, boulders, and sandstone cliffs. This great variety of outdoor offerings also makes for first-rate hiking, biking, rock climbing, picnicking, wading, canoeing, hunting, and fishing.

First-rate hiking

(256) 845-9605; www.nps.gov/liri

Talladega National Forest (H-4, G-9, E-10)

This National Forest is divided into three ranger districts spread across central Alabama. Northwest of Montgomery is the Oakmulgee District. Here visitors will find plenty of water fun at Payne Lake Recreational Area, as well as a 1.5-mile nature trail along the lake that offers views of the ferns, forests, wetlands, and the remains of an early settler's home. To the northeast, the Talladega Ranger Unit occupies the southern half of the other large tract of forest. The Lake Shore Trail, Cave Creek Trail, Skyway Loop Trail, and other hiking trails of varying lengths crisscross the land. To the north, the Shoal Creek District contains several recreation areas and campgrounds along with the Pinhoti Trail system, which winds through mountains and valleys rich with hardwood forests, streams, and Cherokee history.

(256) 362-2909; www.fs.fed.us/r8/alabama

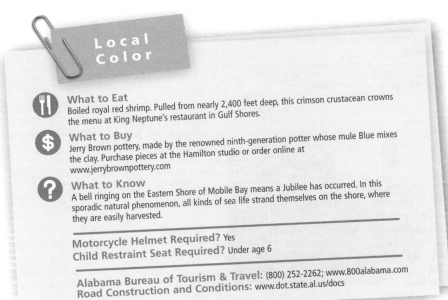

Local Color

What to Eat
Boiled royal red shrimp. Pulled from nearly 2,400 feet deep, this crimson crustacean crowns the menu at King Neptune's restaurant in Gulf Shores.

What to Buy
Jerry Brown pottery, made by the renowned ninth-generation potter whose mule Blue mixes the clay. Purchase pieces at the Hamilton studio or order online at www.jerrybrownpottery.com

What to Know
A bell ringing on the Eastern Shore of Mobile Bay means a Jubilee has occurred. In this sporadic natural phenomenon, all kinds of sea life strand themselves on the shore, where they are easily harvested.

Motorcycle Helmet Required? Yes
Child Restraint Seat Required? Under age 6

Alabama Bureau of Tourism & Travel: (800) 252-2262; www.800alabama.com
Road Construction and Conditions: www.dot.state.al.us/docs

A camper enjoys vistas on the Kenai Peninsula.

CITIES

Anchorage (G-8)
Alaska's largest city is bordered on three sides by Cook Inlet and on the east by the Chugach Mountains. It serves as a melting pot for all the various tribes of Alaska Natives in the state, and is the seat of power for the business community. But its biggest claim to fame is the Iditarod Trail sled dog race, which starts here the first Saturday in March and finishes in Nome. Visitors will find sophisticated dining and shopping in Anchorage, as well as easy access to downhill skiing, hiking, rafting, kayaking, wildlife viewing excursions, glacier cruises or white-water rafting and salmon-fishing trips. The city's Tony Knowles Coastal Trail, stretching 11 miles along Cook Inlet, offers scenic views for cyclists and walkers alike. Alaska's most comprehensive museums are also here: the Anchorage Museum of History and Art, the Anchorage Heritage Library and Museum, and the Alaska Aviation Heritage Museum.

Anchorage Convention & Visitors Bureau: (907) 276-4118; www.anchorage.net

Dutch Harbor/Unalaska (J-10)
Situated near the head of the Aleutian Islands, Unalaska and the port of Dutch Harbor are home to the world's most productive commercial fishery. Pollock, salmon, and king crab are bountiful here where the Pacific Ocean meets the Bering Sea. Lesser known is Dutch Harbor's connection to WWII as the only U.S. location bombed besides Pearl Harbor. Today, bunkers, Quonset huts, and other WWII relics sit side-by-side with archaeological remains that trace the area's history of human habitation at least 9,000 years. The Holy Ascension Russian Orthodox Cathedral offers picturesque evidence of Unalaska's history as a crossroads for the Russian fur trade from the mid-1700s through the early 1900s. Visitors also enjoy taking part in local archaeological dig programs and sport fishing.

Unalaska/Port of Dutch Harbor Convention & Visitors Bureau: (877) 581-2612; www.unalaska.info

Juneau

Trans-Alaska pipeline

Fairbanks (E-8)
Founded as a gold rush town at the beginning of the 20th century, Fairbanks prospered with the coming of the railroad in 1923 and construction of the trans-Alaska pipeline in the 1970s. Today, business leaders, politicians, do-it-yourself miners, dog mushers, artists, and construction workers rub elbows in this city perched on the edge of wilderness. Residents ride bikes to work at temperatures below zero and golf at 2 a.m. during long summer nights when the sun barely dips beneath the horizon. Although Fairbanks gets only 3.5 hours of dim sunlight on the winter solstice, the Northern Lights can be spectacular here from late September to early April. Learn about the state's history and culture at the University of Alaska Museum of the North, the Museum in Pioneer Park, or on a Chena River sternwheel riverboat ride.

Fairbanks Convention & Visitors Bureau: (800) 327-5774; www.explorefairbanks.com

☆ Juneau (State Capital) (H-12)
Gold, government, and an accessible glacier identify Alaska's capital city. Juneau is the only capital city in the U.S. with no road access, but it is served daily by air and marine ferry systems. Founded in 1880, when gold was discovered in the creek that flows through the present-day downtown, Juneau is Alaska's third-largest city. At the height of the rush, $158 million in gold was extracted from the rich ore lodes in the surrounding mountains. Before the mines closed in the early 1940s, Juneau boasted one of the largest gold mines in the world. You can visit the gold-domed St. Nicholas Russian Orthodox church; the Capitol; the Alaska State Museum; and a quaint and well-preserved historic district. Juneau serves as the gateway to Glacier Bay National Park.

Juneau Convention & Visitors Bureau: (800) 587-2201; www.traveljuneau.com

SCENERY

Arctic Circle Drive/Dalton Highway (B-8)
Outside Fairbanks, head to the tip of Alaska's far north (the End of the Road) and cross the Arctic Circle on Dalton Highway. The mostly gravel highway passes through undeveloped land with unusual scenery and seldom-seen wildlife. Paralleling the Trans-Alaska Pipeline System, the highway crosses the Yukon River and Brooks Mountain Range on its way to the Arctic Ocean. Four-wheel drive is not required, but emergency services are extremely limited.

Denali National Park/Mt. McKinley (E-7)

Dall's sheep ram

The highest peak in North America, Mt. McKinley also boasts one of the steepest rises in the world. For stunning views of the mountain and the park's ecosystems and abundant wildlife — caribou, moose, Dall's sheep, grizzly bears, birds and wildflowers — take the Tundra Wilderness bus tour from the visitor center to the Toklat River. Tours mid-May through mid-September.

● Alaska Marine Highway (J-4)

Alaska Marine Highway

A state-owned fleet of ferries travels more than 8,000 miles of scenic coastal routes from the famed Inside Passage to the windswept Aleutian Islands.

● Glacier Bay National Park and Preserve (H-11)
The bay's finger-like inlets are a wonderland of floating, natural ice sculptures that can somersault and crash into the water from as high as 200 feet at any given moment.

Moose

● Glenn Highway (F-9)
Head northeast from Anchorage to Glennallen to see snow-capped mountains, ancient forests, and summer fields of wild irises. Eagles and falcons circle above the road leading toward spectacular Wrangell-St. Elias National Park and Preserve.

● Seward Highway (G-8)
This 127-mile road linking Anchorage with Seward winds past saltwater bays, icy blue glaciers, knife-edged ridges, and alpine valleys. Look for whales at the Beluga Point Scenic Overlook turnout.

● Taylor Highway (E-10)
This summer-only road begins at Tetlin Junction on the Alaska Highway and twists through the rivers and hills of Fortymile Country, where several gold deposits were once struck.

HERITAGE

Alaska Native Heritage Center *(H-3)*

Learn traditional Native dancing, participate in an ancient ceremony, and discover the tricks of Arctic survival at one of Anchorage's most popular cultural attractions. Not only are visitors introduced to past and present Native traditions and customs, but

they also get to try their hand at some during workshops and demonstrations. Inside, the center's Welcome House exhibits celebrate Alaska's many different Native cultures. Outside, visitors are guided through five traditional village sites that circle a lake and a talking circle, where Native games are played. Open year-round.

Native traditional dress

(800) 315-6608;
www.alaskanative.net

Holy Ascension Russian Orthodox Cathedral *(I-11)*

This cathedral's onion-shaped domes and colorful ornate icons bear witness to the influence of some of Alaska's earliest settlers — Russian trappers and fur traders. Orthodox Christianity still plays a major role in the lives of many Alaska residents. In the town of Unalaska visitors can see beautiful artwork and learn about Russian architecture and history on a guided tour of Holy Ascension, one of the oldest cruciform-style Russian churches in the country. It is a National Historic Landmark and includes one of Alaska's largest and richest collections of Russian artifacts and religious icons. Public tours are offered year-round by reservation.

(907) 581-1456

Klondike Gold Rush National Historic Park *(G-12)*

Before George Carmack, Skookum Jim, and Dawson Charlie discovered gold along Bonanza Creek, a tributary of the Yukon River, the Alaskan town of Skagway consisted of one cabin. Once news of the strike reached

Seattle, stampeders wasted no time in flocking to Alaska on their way to the Yukon gold fields. By 1898, Skagway swelled with thousands of fortune-seekers. The park's visitor center, located in the restored White Pass and Yukon Railroad Depot, is a great place to begin a tour of the Skagway Historic District. Guided walking tours are available, as well

Yukon Railroad

as interpretive programs, film and slide presentations, and trail information. Coach tours leave from the depot and offer riders a spectacular view of the rugged countryside. The visitor center is open May through September. For information on off-season hours and programs, contact the park office.

(907) 983-2921; www.nps.gov/klgo

Northern lights

OUTDOORS

Iditarod Trail sled dog race

Dog Mushing Experiences *(E-8)*

Visitors travel from around the world to witness Alaska's famous sled dog races: the Iditarod Trail Sled Dog Race, sprint races held during Anchorage's Fur Rendezvous, the Kuskokwim 300, and the Yukon Quest International Sled Dog Race. But dog mushing is no longer just a spectator sport in Alaska. Visitors can try it in nearly every Alaskan city — even in

the summer. Tours range from half-hour rides to weeklong excursions into remote areas. In summer, tour companies in Juneau transport visitors by helicopter to

Helicopter transport

a dog-mushing camp on a nearby glacier, where they can learn the commands and take a short run. More serious adventurers should try a weeklong sled dog trip in and around Denali National Park or Fairbanks. These backcountry trips give visitors a chance to drive the sled and care for the dogs while winter camping or staying at a remote lodge.

For tours: (800) 862-5275 or the Alaska Dog Mushers
Association, (907) 457-6874

Kayaking next to an iceberg

Kachemak Bay/Alaska Maritime National Wildlife Refuge *(H-7)*

The mountain-ringed coast of Kachemak Bay, one of the most scenic bodies of water in the state, carves a 40-mile-long indentation in the southwestern edge of the Kenai Peninsula. The bay is a nature-lover's paradise whose mild climate attracts visitors year-round. Sea otters, seals, bald eagles, puffins, and countless other seabird species congregate here, making this estuary the perfect place for kayakers to experience a wildlife encounter. In Homer, various outfitters offer guided or unguided paddling tours in the bay's protected waters, which are part of the Alaska Maritime National Wildlife Refuge. Visitors can learn even more about the area's animals and environment at the Alaska Islands & Ocean Visitors Center in Homer.

(907) 235-6961; www.islandsandocean.org
For kayaking: (907) 235-7740; www.homeralaska.org

Mt. McKinley in Denali National Park

Stan Stephens Glacier & Wildlife Cruises *(G-8)*

The only way to see some of Alaska's most memorable geographic features and wildlife is by boat. Whale-watching and glacier cruises are popular throughout southeast and south-central Alaska, but one of the best places to climb aboard a charter is in the stunning Prince William Sound. Since 1971 Stan Stephens Glacier & Wildlife Cruises has operated out of Valdez, offering visitors a chance to see glaciers, whales, a huge sea lion haul-out area, puffins, sea otters, seals, bears, and more. The captain and crew also tell stories about the area's history - from the Alaskan Natives to gold and copper mining to the 1989 Exxon Valdez oil spill. Vessels feature plenty of heated indoor seating as well as outdoor viewing areas.

(866) 867-1297; www.stanstephenscruises.com

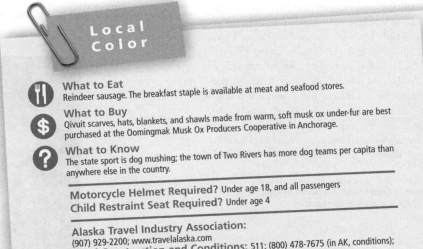

Local Color

🍴 **What to Eat**
Reindeer sausage. The breakfast staple is available at meat and seafood stores.

💲 **What to Buy**
Qiviut scarves, hats, blankets, and shawls made from warm, soft musk ox under-fur are best purchased at the Oomingmak Musk Ox Producers Cooperative in Anchorage.

❓ **What to Know**
The state sport is dog mushing; the town of Two Rivers has more dog teams per capita than anywhere else in the country.

Motorcycle Helmet Required? Under age 18, and all passengers
Child Restraint Seat Required? Under age 4

Alaska Travel Industry Association:
(907) 929-2200; www.travelalaska.com
Road Construction and Conditions: 511; (800) 478-7675 (in AK, conditions);
(866) 282-7577; (907) 456-7623 (conditions); www.dot.state.ak.us;
(907) 269-0450 (construction); 511.alaska.gov

TRAVEL GUIDE   Alaska

Surrounded by the towering red sandstone cliffs of Oak Creek Canyon, Sedona is a breathtaking day trip from Phoenix.

CITIES

Flagstaff (F-8)
A slow-paced town imbued with natural beauty, Flagstaff is a hub for sightseeing, hiking, biking, fishing in mountain lakes, and, in the winter, downhill and cross-country skiing. Stroll through the Arboretum, spread over 200 acres of ponderosa pine forest. See sky shows and enjoy interactive exhibits at Lowell Observatory on Mars Hill, near downtown. In the center of town is Riordan State Historic Park, a preserved mansion that was once the home of a wealthy frontier family. Some of the state's most spectacular sites are all within a short drive — the Grand Canyon, Oak Creek Canyon, Sedona's red rocks, Native American reservations, and a string of national monuments.

Flagstaff Convention & Visitors Bureau: (800) 842-7293; www.flagstaffarizona.org

Phoenix skyline

⭐ Phoenix (State Capital) (J-7)
Arizona's capital city sprawls across the Valley of the Sun on the northern edge of the Sonoran Desert. The Old West mingles with thriving metropolitan culture, luxurious resorts, and rugged outdoor recreation. Explore Phoenix's Native American art and history at the Pueblo Grande Museum and Archaeological Park, the Heard Museum, and the Pioneer Living History Museum. Locals and visitors alike take full advantage of the 325 days of annual sunshine here — the perfect forecast for adventures like horseback riding, hot-air balloon rides, river rafting, sailing, rock climbing, desert tours by jeep or covered wagon, and golfing. The city's numerous picturesque golf courses have earned Phoenix its moniker "Golf Capital of the World."

Greater Phoenix Convention & Visitors Bureau: (877) 225-5749; www.visitphoenix.com

Tucson (M-10)
It's easy to have a sunny disposition in Tucson, where bright daylight is rarely ever marred by cloudy skies and cactus forests cast long afternoon shadows on the desert floor. This resort city of golf courses and guest ranches is known for its natural wonders, university-supported museums, and excellent restaurants specializing in local varieties of Southwestern cuisine. The best place for a close-up look at Gila monsters, scorpions, and other desert creepers is the Arizona-Sonora Desert Museum. Mission San Xavier del Bac, considered one of the most exquisite examples of Spanish mission architecture in the country, is a must-see for anyone interested in the Spanish heritage of the Southwest desert.

Metropolitan Tucson Convention & Visitors Bureau: (800) 638-8350; www.visittucson.org

Yuma (L-2)
Nestled in the Yuma and Gila valleys of southern Arizona along the Colorado River, Yuma is an oasis for water lovers. Each year thousands of visitors beat the desert heat with houseboat stays, boat cruises through the Imperial National Wildlife Refuge, and water sports galore. The city's numerous historic sites are the other big draw. The Yuma Territorial Prison tops the list, giving visitors a

Yuma Crossing

glimpse of the harsh realities of frontier justice. Nearby, you'll find the Yuma Crossing State Historic Park, which includes the U.S. Army Quartermaster Depot. The Sanguinetti House Museum, in one of Yuma's oldest buildings, has artifacts and exhibits of Yuma's pioneer days.

Yuma Convention & Visitors Bureau: (800) 293-0071; www.visityuma.com

SCENERY

Grand Canyon National Park/ Yavapai Observation Station (p.19, M-8)
Huge windows offer visitors panoramic views of the canyon, including Phantom Ranch and the Colorado River below. The station, located one mile east of Market Plaza, also displays interesting exhibits about the canyon's fossil record.

Organ Pipe Cactus National Monument

Organ Pipe Cactus National Monument (M-6)
The monument preserves the largest habitat of its namesake, the organ pipe cactus, whose thick arms radiate from the ground, not from a central trunk. The cactus grows on sunny south-facing slopes and blooms after sunset only during May, June, and July.

- **Chiricahua National Monument (N-13)**
  Wind and weather have worked their magic on the 27-million-year-old volcanic rocks of this monument, leaving a forest of spires, hoodoos, and balanced boulders.

- **Horseshoe Bend (p. 19, J-10)**
  From a 1,700-foot cliff near Lake Powell, visitors can see the Colorado River make a dramatic 180-degree switchback around sandstone.

- **Lake Havasu's London Bridge (G-3)**
  More than 10,000 pieces of the original London Bridge were transported and rebuilt over the waters of the Bridgewater Channel of the Colorado River in this city's English village area.

- **Monument Valley Navajo Tribal Park (A-11)**
  Navajo guides introduce visitors to the buttes, mesas, and cultural traditions of the park, which is a small part of the 16-million-acre Navajo reservation.

- **Sedona - Oak Creek Canyon Scenic Road (F-8)**
  See the majesty of purple mountains, red rocks, a bubbling creek, and mile-high forests on this 14.5-mile route between Sedona and Flagstaff.

Folklorica dancers

HERITAGE

Mission San Xavier del Bac (T-2)

Built in 1783, this striking mission is known as the "white dove of the desert." Its white exterior gleams against the desert backdrop. Inside, high-rising domes and arches are ornately adorned in frescos. Behind the altar a dazzling array of color and gilding spans from the floor to the ceiling. It is an elegant blend of Moorish, Byzantine, and late Mexico Renaissance architecture. A restoration project in the church's interior uncovered vibrant colors and surprising levels of craftsmanship. Since the discovery, the church is being called the "Sistine Chapel of North America." Native crafts and food are sold daily outside the mission.

Mission San Xavier del Bac

(520) 294-2624; www.sanxaviermission.org

Montezuma Castle National Monument (G-8)

Montezuma Castle is actually a misnomer for this dwelling, situated about 100 feet up on a limestone cliff. When the ruins were first noted by 19th-century settlers, it was thought that they had been built by the Aztecs. But the Sinagua Indians were the actual architects of these five-story high-rise apartments, which were built sometime around 1150. The castle itself is not accessible due to its fragility, but a one-third mile round-trip interpretive trail leads to good viewpoints of the structure. The visitor center contains exhibits of intricate textiles, jewelry, and farming tools that have been found within the ruins. Other exhibits feature the flora and fauna of the Verde Valley or depict scenes from everyday life of the Sinagua tribe.

(928) 567-3322; www.nps.gov/moca

Queen Mine Tour (O-12)

Tucked away in the Mule Mountains at the base of Mule Pass Gulch is the old town of Bisbee, home of one of the richest copper mines in history: Queen Mine. Shops selling crafts and Western wares have long since replaced the city's saloons and brothels, but visitors can still tour the 1877 mine that was closed in the 1970s. Old miners, each with their own story to tell, often lead the underground tours. Once visitors are outfitted with a slicker, helmet, and miner's headlamp, they climb aboard the mine train and descend to the caverns and shafts below. Across the street is the Bisbee Mining & Historical Museum, a Smithsonian museum.

(866) 432-2071;
www.cityofbisbee.com/queenminetours.htm

Yuma Territorial Prison State Historic Park (p. 19, G-6)

This old cell prison, Arizona's most-visited state historic park, was actually built by the first seven inmates booked into the penitentiary in 1876. The prison operated for 33 years and housed more than 3,000 convicts, including many of Arizona's most dangerous and notorious criminals. Over the last century the prison earned an infamous reputation that has been played out in literature, movies, and television. Today visitors can step inside a prison cell or see the main gate and guard tower, which are all that remain of this example of frontier justice.

Yuma Territorial Prison gate

(928) 783-4771;
www.azstateparks.com/Parks/parkhtml/yuma.html

OUTDOORS

Family fun in the snow

Arizona Snowbowl (E-8)

Snowbowl is one of Arizona's coolest spots for outdoor adventure. Literally. With a summit elevation of 11,500 feet, this ski resort in the San Francisco Peaks is about 30 degrees cooler than most of the Arizona deserts. In summer it's the best place to beat the heat - taking a scenic chairlift ride up the mountain, horseback riding through ponderosa pines in the Coconino National Forest, or hiking a woodsy meadow. Come winter, skiers and snowboarders enjoy the mountain's varied terrain and beautiful snow-blanketed vistas. Snowbowl has a 2,300-foot vertical drop and 32 runs for beginners and experts alike.

(928) 779-1951; www.arizonasnowbowl.com

Colorado River Boat Cruises (L-2)

A jet boat ride on the Colorado River near the town of Yuma reveals an interesting slice of southwest Arizona history and wildlife. Narrated day trips with the Yuma River Tours boat captains cover 32 miles of the river. Cruises glide through the Imperial National Wildlife Refuge, where visitors get excellent opportunities for bird watching and spotting bighorn sheep, burros, and deer. American Indian petroglyphs are also part of the tour. Other highlights: an old miner's cabin and at Norton's Landing, a historic steamboat site that was once a thriving mining town.

(928) 783-4400; www.yumarivertours.com

Grand Canyon National Park (p. 19, M-8)

A mile deep and up to 18 miles across, this awe-inspiring gorge cuts across 277 miles of northern Arizona. Far below the rim, the mighty Colorado River twists and turns, alternating stretches of tranquil water with some of the world's most exciting rapids. This is prime white-water rafting. Expect breathtaking scenery and more than 200 miles of rapids and white water. Lava Falls, east of Lake Mead National Recreation Area, is the ultimate in rafting excitement. Trips vary from three to 21 days and run May through September. Contact the park for a list of tour operators.

(928) 638-7888;
www.nps.gov/grca/planyourvisit/
whitewater-rafting.htm

Kartchner Caverns State Park (N-11)

Not all of Arizona's natural wonders rise up from the desert floor. This one is underneath it. Kartchner Caverns boasts a variety of underground formations and colors that have earned the cave notoriety among spelunkers from around the world. Tour guides point out everything from the tiniest formation to the largest column in Arizona and explain the science behind the processes at work. Learn about the cave's history and earliest inhabitants in the park's Discovery Center. Guided tours are approximately 1½ hours and run year-round. Reservations are required.

Kartchner Caverns

(520) 586-2283;
www.azstateparks.com/Parks/parkhtml/
kartchner.html

Local Color

What to Eat
Native American fry bread. Excellent fry bread can be had at the Fry Bread House in Phoenix.

What to Buy
Cosanti bells. Made of ceramic or bronze, these windbells have won design awards for their creator, Paolo Soleri, and provide funding for his ongoing experiment in urban architecture, Arcosanti (located in the high desert north of Phoenix).

What to Know
Distance measurements on signs along I-19 in Arizona are given in kilometers. (Speed limits are posted in miles-per-hour.)

Motorcycle Helmet Required? Under age 18
Child Restraint Seat Required? Under age 5

Arizona Office of Tourism: (866) 239-9712; www.arizonaguide.com
Road Construction and Conditions: 511; (888) 411-7623; www.az511.com

Whitaker Point in Ozark National Forest looks out over the Upper Buffalo River valley.

CITIES

Eureka Springs (B-3)

Eureka Springs

Once known for its healing waters, Eureka Springs is now renowned for its well-preserved Victorian character. Narrow streets are lined with 1890s limestone-construction buildings while residential areas showcase gingerbread-ornamented homes and "painted ladies," houses that have been elaborately painted in period style. The entire downtown has been recognized by the National Register of Historic Places. In addition to modern spa retreats, the town hosts arts and music festivals and features boutique shopping. Visitors are a short drive away from outdoor adventures in the Ozarks such as canoeing and cave tours.

Eureka Springs Advertising and Promotion Commission: (866) 566-9387; www.eurekasprings.org

Fort Smith (E-1)

Known for its gritty frontier past, Fort Smith was the home of "hanging judge" Isaac C. Parker. His legacy can be seen at Fort Smith National Historic site, which features Judge Parker's courthouse, the restored gallows, and the old jail, so crowded it was known as "Hell on the Border." Fort Smith's past wasn't all grit, though. The 22-block Belle Grove Historic District is comprised of a variety of buildings representing 130 years of regional architecture. Visitors may ride a vintage streetcar from the Fort Smith Trolley Museum to the Fort Smith Museum of History, where a restored soda fountain awaits and exhibits chronicle the city's history from Indian days to the present. For different views of the city and surrounding region, try a carriage ride through the city, or chug into the Ozarks on a vintage train excursion.

Fort Smith Convention & Visitors Bureau: (800) 637-1477; www.fortsmith.org

Fort Smith Trolley Museum

Hot Springs (H-5)

The 147°F water that flows from the base of Hot Springs Mountain has attracted humans to this site for many hundreds of years. Local legend has it that American Indians met here in peace to experience the therapeutic benefits of the springs, and, as soon as American settlers began moving west, Hot Springs

Bathhouse Row

came to be known as the "National Spa." The city of Hot Springs boasts the only national park entirely within a city's limits, and people still flock here to "take the waters." The historic Bathhouse Row district, most of which has been restored to its original opulence, contains a wealth of art galleries and fine shops, as well as the Buckstaff, the last historic bathhouse to still operate as a spa, and the elegant Fordyce, now the visitor center for Hot Springs National Park.

Hot Springs Convention & Visitor's Bureau: (800) 772-2489; www.hotsprings.org

⭐ Little Rock (State Capital) (H-7)

Old State House Museum

Little Rock's historic homes and museums are what visitors write home about, but in the dead heat of summer, the city's lakes and river are nearly irresistible. The Old State House Museum holds some of the city's most interesting collections, including Confederate battle flags, First Ladies' gowns, and African-American quilts. The Historic Arkansas Museum includes original buildings from early Little Rock, including the circa 1826 Hinderliter Grog Shop and circa 1848 Federal-style Brownlee House. The Arkansas Arts Center is located in the MacArthur Park Historic District, a neighborhood of antebellum homes anchored by MacArthur Park, 36 acres first set aside in 1837 as an arsenal. Recent history is reviewed at the William J. Clinton Presidential Center, which includes a library housed in a building cantilevered out over the Arkansas River. After a tour of the historic Quapaw Quarter, grab a fishing pole and a picnic basket for a perfect respite on the banks of the Arkansas River.

Little Rock Convention & Visitors Bureau: (800) 844-4781; www.littlerock.com

OUTDOORS

Buffalo National River (C-6)

You don't need a canoe to enjoy the Buffalo River. One of the few unaltered rivers left in the United States, it runs through hilly, tree-covered country. Day hikers may choose from several trails, some with strenuous segments. The Rush trail (2.2 miles) leads through a complex of Morning Star Mine buildings, built in the 1880s to extract zinc ore. At the end of the Lost Valley trail (2.1 miles), hikers can

Hiking in the Buffalo National River area

crawl through a 200-foot cave to see a 35-foot waterfall. One loop of the Indian Rockhouse trail (3.5 miles) leads to Bat Cave. There are more than 100 miles of trails to explore in addition to backcountry trekking.

(870) 741-5443; www.nps.gov/buff

Lake Chicot State Park (M-11)

During spring and fall bird migration seasons, visitors to this park have the opportunity to check off several species on their birding lists. Waterfowl types include pelicans, anhingas, and loons (to name only a few), all attracted by the expanse of water and shoreline along this 20-mile-long oxbow lake. Formed when the Mississippi River changed course and cut off a section of the river, the lake is the largest natural oxbow in Arkansas and a well-populated stop along the famed Mississippi Flyway. Watercraft and bicycles are available to rent so you can get closer to where the birds are. Park staff lead interpretive lake tours.

(870) 265-5480; www.arkansasstateparks.com/lakechicot

Ouachita River (H-2)

Kayaking on the Ouachita River

Winding its way from the confluence of two streams to Lake Ouachita, this river (pronounced "WASH-i-taw") offers family-friendly floating fun. It's Class I for most of this 70-mile stretch, though in spots it can be Class II. There are plenty of access points along the river, many maintained by the Forest Service, in addition to picnic areas and campgrounds. Because much of this stretch is within the Ouachita National Forest, there aren't many houses along the riverbank. This ensures a quiet solitude in which to enjoy the trees and several bluffs. Bring along your fishing gear, as the river is known for its sunfish population as well as seasonal bass spawning runs.

(501) 321-5202; www.fs.fed.us/oonf/

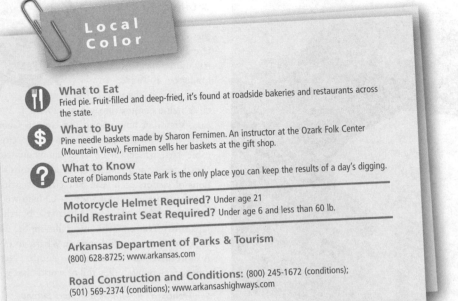

HERITAGE

Arkansas Post National Memorial

Arkansas Post National Memorial (J-10)

In 1686, long before Arkansas was even a U.S. territory, French traders established a settlement on the bank of the Arkansas River. What became known as the Arkansas Post was a critical link in the trade system between the western Great Lakes region and the Gulf of Mexico. The settlement's location shifted as the Arkansas River changed course, but today the site is located on a peninsula formed by the Arkansas and two backwaters. Visitors may view a film at the visitor center and tour the townsite, which includes remnants of Confederate earthworks built in 1863. Several trails pass through forest and along the water, where several migrating species of birds can be spotted as they follow the Mississippi Flyway.

(870) 548-2207; www.nps.gov/arpo

Historic Washington State Park (K-3)

Founded in 1824 and named after the first U.S. president, Washington served as the Confederate capital of Arkansas from 1863 to 1865. Today this state historic park features 30 restored public buildings and homes, many of them open for self-guided tours. Costumed docents greet visitors as they stroll along the unpaved streets reminiscent of the town's early-19th-century beginnings. The park features splendid examples of architectural styles such as Italianate and Greek Revival as well as humbler brace-frame structures. Among more popular exhibits are the collections of guns and knives. Between 11 a.m. and 3 p.m., lunch is served at the circa 1832 Williams' Tavern Restaurant.

(870) 983-2684;
www.historicwashingtonstatepark.com

Historic Washington State Park

Toltec Mounds Archeological State Park (H-8)

Between A.D. 600 and 1050 the Plum Bayou people of the Lower Mississippi Valley built a complex of mounds and earthenworks. Now the 110-acre site is a state park offering self-guided tours of the remaining mounds along two trails, one 0.8 miles and the other 1.6 miles long. Mound A is fully 49 feet high, though most rise much less high from the surrounding lowlands. Archaeologists postulate that several mounds once had houses atop them, while on top of others were religious structures. One is a formal burial mound. Workshops are held on-site to demonstrate ancient skills such as primitive pottery making and flint-knapping. Visitors also learn that the name of the park is a misnomer: The site's first owner thought the mound builders had been Toltecs, but the Toltecs lived only in Mexico.

Toltec Mounds

(501) 961-9442; www.arkansasstateparks.com/ toltecmounds/

Toltec Mounds

SCENERY

Twin Falls, Richland Creek, Ozarks

Boston Mountains Scenic Loop (E-1)

Two roads — older US 71 and newer I-540 — create a loop that traverses the Boston Mountains between Alma and Fayetteville. Drive US 71 for a twisty, curvy, up-close view of the rugged, green landscape. The interstate runs just west of 71 but offers soaring treetop views from several bridges. Through telescopes at the Artist Point observation deck, you can see White Rock Mountain and Lake Shepherd Springs.

Talimena Scenic Byway (H-1)

Gaze over the Ouachita Mountains from high points along the Talimena Scenic Byway. Stretching 54 miles between Mena, Arkansas and Talihina, Oklahoma, the Talimena Byway (SR 88) winds up and over to Rich Mountain (2,681 feet), the second highest peak in Arkansas. Look up for glimpses of hawks, eagles, and vultures soaring on updrafts. Near the mountaintops, the trees are twisted and gnarled from exposure to strong southerly winds and frequent winter freezings. Several turnouts afford panoramic views as well as glimpses into the past through interpretive signs.

Talimena Scenic Byway

● Crowley's Ridge Parkway (C-12)

Arkansas State Routes 141 and 163 in northeast Arkansas follow Crowley's Ridge, a crescent-shaped landform that rises 100-200 feet above the Mississippi delta. From this height drivers see across low, rolling tree-covered topography.

● Great River Road (D-14)

Silhouettes of bridges, shimmering floodwaters, and riparian wildlife are all to be seen as the Great River Road, a National Scenic Byway, winds along the Mississippi. It's noted with a captain's wheel in the *Road Atlas*.

● Magazine Mountain (F-3)

Switchbacks and hairpin turns along SR 309 lead to a view from the top of Magazine Mountain of treetops, bluffs, and myriad lakes. From this peak, the highest in Arkansas at 2,753 feet, lakes look like small puddles.

● Sylamore Scenic Byway (B-7)

A drive along SR 5, SR 14, and Forest Road 1110 affords views of limestone bluffs and cedar glade outcroppings.

● Scenic 7 Byway (B-5)

Arkansas State Route 7 winds through the Ouachita and Ozark mountains, replete with rich fall colors in autumn and lush green forest views in spring and summer.

TRAVEL GUIDE Arkansas

A natural arch in the Alabama Hills frames Lone Pine Peak.

San Francisco *(NM-5)*

Perched on a hilly peninsula overlooking the craggy shores of the Pacific Ocean and its namesake bay, San Francisco is unlike any other place in the world. The city's name conjures images of cable cars, Victorian houses, and the Golden Gate Bridge. Early birds usually get the seats on the city's famed cable cars, which fill up fast. San Francisco's exceptional beauty and endless list of attractions draw millions of visitors each year. The city's diversity is most evident in its neighborhoods — Chinatown, Haight-Ashbury, the Mission District, North Beach, Japantown/Nihonmachi, and Fillmore St. Also, don't miss Union Square, Fisherman's Wharf, and Nob Hill. A short drive north leads to wine country: Napa Valley, a tiny, remarkable valley full of world-class wineries.

San Francisco Convention & Visitors Bureau:
(415) 391-2000; www.onlyinsanfrancisco.com

San Francisco wharf

CITIES

Los Angeles *(SJ-11)*

Entertainment is this city's lifeblood. The Technicolor opulence of Los Angeles belongs only on the big screen — which is where many of this city's residents would rather be, anyway. Live the backlot Hollywood magic on tours of Paramount and Universal Studios, try to fit your fingers into handprints of celebs outside

Hollywood

Grauman's Chinese Theatre, or see the Walk of Fame. Visitors hoping for a star sighting can cruise by celebrity homes in Beverly Hills, while kids can meet their animated idols at Disneyland in nearby Anaheim. Explore the roots of Los Angeles in the sidewalk cafés and Mexican shops of Olvera Street, or travel further back in time with a stop at La Brea Tar Pits.

Los Angeles Convention & Visitors Bureau:
(800) 228-2452 or (213) 624-7300;
www.greaterlosangeles.com

✪ Sacramento *(State Capital) (NK-7)*

The Gold Rush paved the way to Sacramento, and that same spirit of discovery fuels this capital city today. Catch '49er fever by navigating downtown's Old Sacramento Historic District, whose Discovery Museum's Gold Rush History Center houses a large collection of gold specimens. Cobblestone streets and wooden sidewalks hug the riverfront at Old Sacramento State Historic Park, with its historic Hastings Building, western terminus of the Pony Express, and the Eagle Theatre. Another Old Sacramento treat is the California State Railroad Museum, with exhibits of the actual locomotives that revolutionized the western frontier. The State Indian

Delta King

Museum showcases artifacts and arts and crafts from 400 years of native Northern California cultures.

Sacramento Convention & Visitors Bureau:
(800) 292-2334; www.sacramentocvb.org

San Diego

San Diego *(SN-13)*

In San Diego a Mediterranean climate presides over a sun-kissed coast with majestic views of the Pacific. Spanish influences can be found at the Mission San Luis Rey de Francia; remnants of the Old West abound in Old Town. In the winter at Point Loma, California gray whales migrate from the chilly Alaskan seas to the warm shores of the Baja coast. For wildlife watching, check out the famous San Diego Zoo, the zoo's Wild Animal Park, or SeaWorld San Diego. Replenish with upscale dining at any of the Gaslamp Quarter's restaurants, or head south to Tijuana for a taste of Mexico.

San Diego Zoo

San Diego Convention & Visitors Bureau: (619) 236-1212;
www.sandiego.org

Santa Barbara *(SI-7)*

With its adobe walls and red-tile roofs, the peaceful, sunny coastal city of Santa Barbara is steeped in its Spanish past. Stroll the downtown's collection of Spanish adobe dwellings and El Paseo, a Spanish arts and crafts, shopping, and restaurant plaza built around the original Casa de la Guerra. The tilework and murals at the County Courthouse can be seen during a climb up the El Mirador bell tower, which offers a sweeping view of the city. Just to the east, the architecturally unique Mission Santa Barbara overlooks the sea. In nearby Mission Canyon visit the lush Botanic Garden and the Museum of Natural History with exhibits on the Chumash Indian tribe.

Mission Santa Barbara

El Presidio de Santa Barbara State Historic Park was one of the last Spanish military outposts in the Americas. Also of note are the Museum of Art and the Historical Museum. More than 60 wineries in the surrounding countryside offer tours and tastings.

Santa Barbara Conference & Visitors Bureau:
(805) 966-9222; www.santabarbaraca.com

Golden Gate Bridge

Anza-Borrego Desert State Park

Anza-Borrego Desert State Park (SM-16)

East of San Diego is an arid wonderland of mountains, canyons, washes, and badlands: Anza-Borrego. Encompassing about 1,000 square miles of the Colorado Desert, the park is nearly as large as Rhode Island. Some 500 miles of dirt roads and 110 miles of hiking and riding trails crisscross Anza-Borrego, but the most popular hike is the Borrego-Palm Canyon Trail. A mile-and-a-half scramble over rocky, sun-baked terrain dotted with cholla, agave, and barrel cactuses leads to a green, shady oasis where hundreds of fan palms tower over a tumbling stream. "Borrego" is a Spanish word for bighorn sheep; sharp-eyed hikers often spot these shy, graceful creatures along the trail.

(760) 767-5311; www.parks.ca.gov

Enjoying the beach

Huntington Beach (SK-11)

Internationally known as Surf City, Huntington Beach has been the center of the Southern California surfing scene since the 1920s. This is where Duke Kahanamoku introduced the sport from Hawaii and where the city is reputed to have some of the best surfing beaches in the state. In summer, countless vacationers gear up with local surf schools and learn to ride. Bolsa Chica State Beach's mild breaking waves make this spot enormously popular among beginning surfers. Huntington Beach is home to the U.S. Open of Surfing (every July), the International Surfing Museum, and the Walk of Fame near Municipal Pier. The city's 8.5 miles of beaches provide plenty of opportunities for sunning, swimming, and volleyball.

(714) 969-3492, (800) 729-6232; www.hbvisit.com

Lake Tahoe (NI-10)

A center for gamblers, beachcombers, hikers, and skiers, this resort area on the California-Nevada border is saturated with hotels, restaurants, and casinos. Numerous ski slopes on the surrounding mountains help make this region a year-round vacation area. In summer, folks linger on the public beaches or go parasailing, kayaking, boating, or jet skiing. For spectacular views of the glacier-formed lake and its surrounding mountain peaks, visitors can also hike, bike, or horseback ride the famed national recreation trail, Tahoe Rim Trail. The 165-mile trail winds through two states, six counties, and three national forests.

(775) 588-5900 or (800) 288-2463; www.bluelaketahoe.com

Lake Tahoe

Shasta Lake (ND-5)

This northern California destination in the Shasta Cascades — far from crowds and Hollywood hype — is one of the state's best spots for swimming, fishing, waterskiing, and jet skiing adventures. Majestic mountains and towering evergreens surround the photogenic lake. The hottest accommodations here are houseboat rentals, which may be the best way to explore the lake's 370 miles of shoreline. Don't miss Shasta Dam or caving tours at Lake Shasta Caverns. Anglers will enjoy Lake Shasta's trophy-size bass and 3- to 10-pound trout, along with bluegills, salmon, crappie, catfish, and sturgeon.

Houseboat

(530) 365-7500, (800) 474-2782; www.shastacascade.com

Lower Falls in Yosemite National Park

Yosemite National Park (NL-11)

Groves of giant sequoias, wildflower meadows, and towering granite peaks leave no doubt that nature reigns in Yosemite National Park. More than 800 miles of hiking trails, including the John Muir and Pacific Crest National Scenic trails, lead through meadows, along the Merced River, past waterfalls, or to the base of any one of the mountain lookout areas. Climbing enthusiasts flock to the park to take advantage of the sheer granite walls that characterize Yosemite Valley.

Climbing

Half Dome, El Capitan, and Washington Column are among the most popular. Other favorite Yosemite activities include horseback riding and biking. Best bet: Visit in the fall, winter, or spring, when visitation is lower and you can enjoy the landscape without being jostled by crowds.

(209) 372-0200; www.nps.gov/yose

Huntington Beach pier

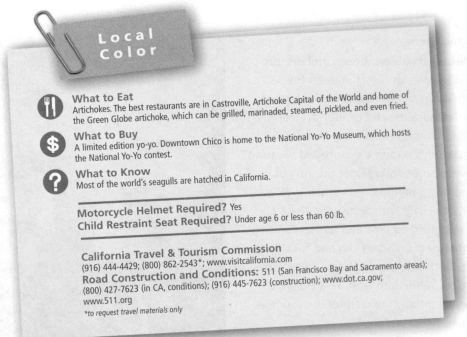

Local Color

🍴 **What to Eat**
Artichokes. The best restaurants are in Castroville, Artichoke Capital of the World and home of the Green Globe artichoke, which can be grilled, marinaded, steamed, pickled, and even fried.

$ **What to Buy**
A limited edition yo-yo. Downtown Chico is home to the National Yo-Yo Museum, which hosts the National Yo-Yo contest.

❓ **What to Know**
Most of the world's seagulls are hatched in California.

Motorcycle Helmet Required? Yes
Child Restraint Seat Required? Under age 6 or less than 60 lb.

California Travel & Tourism Commission
(916) 444-4429; (800) 862-2543*; www.visitcalifornia.com
Road Construction and Conditions: 511 (San Francisco Bay and Sacramento areas);
(800) 427-7623 (in CA, conditions); (916) 445-7623 (construction); www.dot.ca.gov;
www.511.org
to request travel materials only

SCENERY

Route 1, Big Sur Coast Highway

Big Sur Coast Highway (SD-3)

Follow coastal Route 1 from Carmel south to the San Luis Obispo County line to see rugged canyons and steep sea cliffs, windswept cypress trees, and towering redwood forests. Point Lobos is home to sea lions, harbor seals, and grey whales. The Overlook Trail at Julia Pfeiffer Burns State Park leads to McWay Falls, which plunge 80 feet directly into the Pacific.

Point Reyes National Seashore (NL-4)

Just north of San Francisco you'll find ocean-carved beaches, estuaries and salt marshes teeming with birds, deep forests of Douglas fir and Bishop pine, and lush meadows blanketed with wildflowers. Along the migratory paths of the gray whale and hundreds of birds, Point Reyes is also the habitat of sea lions, harbor seals, two herds of tule elk, and several species of deer.

- **Death Valley National Park (SB-13)**
  Drive the paved park road to Dante's View for a sweeping view of Death Valley and the snow-capped Panamint Range.

- **Del Norte Coast Redwoods State Park (NB-2)**
  Explore eight miles of wild coastline or lose yourself among dense stands of old redwoods in this Northern California park.

- **Half Dome, Yosemite National Park (NM-2)**
  This massive monolith rises more than 4,000 feet above the valley floor and can be seen throughout eastern Yosemite Valley and from Glacier Point.

Mt. Shasta

- **Mt. Shasta (NC-6)**
  Slumbering for the last 200 years, this immense volcano and the pristine lakes that surround it in Klamath National Forest are pure majestic beauty.

- **Mulholland Drive, Los Angeles (p. 30, E-1)**
  Ride the crest of the Santa Monica Mountains along the curves of legendary Mulholland Drive for spectacular views, day or night. On one side is the San Fernando Valley; on the other side lies Hollywood. On a clear day, you can see as far as the Pacific Ocean.

- **Salton Sea (SL-16)**
  Head south on SR 111 along the Salton Sea, a desert lake that is 235 feet below sea level and 25 percent saltier than the ocean.

HERITAGE

Alcatraz Island (NF-13)

One of the most visited sites in the Golden Gate National Recreation Area is Alcatraz Island, once a maximum-security prison known by inmates as "The Rock." Its reputation as a federal prison rested on its boast that no one ever escaped successfully, although some say the three men who made it off the island in 1962 beat the odds. Some of the bay's most beautiful views of San Francisco are to be savored from Alcatraz, but that was said to be part of the punishment. Guided tours give visitors a behind-the-scenes look at the cell house while they listen to recorded stories of former inmates and correctional officers remembering life on Alcatraz. Reservations are recommended for public tours.

(415) 561-4900; www.nps.gov/alcatraz

Alcatraz Island

El Camino Real & Spanish Missions (SL-12)

Twenty-one missions (all built before 1824) make up California's historic mission trail on the coastal Highway 101 from San Diego to Sonoma in the north. This route roughly traces El Camino Real (The Royal Road), named after the Spanish monarchy that funded expeditions into California to protect their empire. Most of the missions have been restored and continue to operate as active Catholic parishes. Some missions house a unique collection of artifacts and feature interesting architectural elements. San Juan Capistrano was fashioned out of stones into the shape of a cross. San Luis Obispo de Tolosa's roof is covered in tiles that replaced the original thatched roof. Visitors can pick up booklets for self-guided tours at most missions.

(800) 777-0369 or (916) 653-6995;
www.parks.ca.gov/default.asp?page_id=22722

Hearst Castle

Hearst Castle (SE-4)

Former estate of newspaper tycoon William Randolph Hearst, this opulent complex in San Simeon is one of the largest of approximately 5,000 historic house museums in the United States. On the grounds are a main castle, three surrounding guest houses, two swimming pools, and formal gardens. Tours take visitors back into time with stories about William Randolph Hearst and descriptions of the castle's precious art and antique collection, architecture, gardens and lifestyle. One sitting room is filled with Spanish antiques and Flemish tapestries, while the game room features two 1920s billiard tables. Outside is a magnificent Greco-Roman-style pool that gives visitors remarkable coastline views from the hilltop.

(800) 444-4445; www.hearstcastle.com

Marshall Gold Discovery State Historic Park (NJ-8)

The quiet little village of Coloma often supported a population of 10,000 as people streamed through the first California gold rush boomtown. It was here that James W. Marshall found glimmering flecks of gold in the tailrace of the sawmill he was building. His discovery on January 24, 1848 initiated the westward migration of countless others hoping to strike it rich. The park includes a reconstruction of Sutter's mill, Marshall's original 1860s cabin, an old schoolhouse, and a blacksmith shop. Visitors can pan for gold in the creek near the mill, hear stories of Gold Rush Days at the museum, or learn from a variety of living history programs in the village. The Gold Discovery Celebration in January marks the anniversary of Marshall's find with music, gold-panning demonstrations, and historical tours.

(530) 622-3470; www.parks.ca.gov

Marshall Gold Discovery State Historic Park

Colorado

Pikes Peak can be seen from the Garden of the Gods.

CITIES

Boulder (D-13)

This beautiful and eclectic town, set against the Flatiron Mountains at an altitude of 5,430 feet, attracts students, entrepreneurs, and outdoors lovers. Enjoy the boutiques, galleries, sidewalk cafés, vegetarian restaurants, and street musicians on the Pearl Street Mall. An excellent network of bike paths makes Boulder one of the most bike-friendly cities in the country. Visit the University of Colorado Natural History Museum and the National Center for Atmospheric Research, or tour the headquarters of tea-maker Celestial Seasonings. In summer, festivals are the main attraction. Annual favorites include the Shakespeare Festival, Colorado Music Festival, and Ragtime Festival. Venture just outside town for rock climbing in the Flatirons or fishing at Brainard Lake, Boulder Creek, and Boulder Reservoir.

Boulder Convention & Visitors Bureau: (800) 444-0447 or (303) 442-2911; www.bouldercoloradousa.com

Colorado Springs (H-14)

A sophisticated city with charming small-town ambiance, Colorado Springs is the gateway to Southern Colorado's outdoor adventures. It's a great vantage point from which to enjoy the rugged beauty of the Rockies, from Pikes Peak to the fanciful red sandstone formations of the Garden of the Gods. In town, visitors will find a fascinating collection of 7,000 giant and exotic insects from around the world at the May Natural History Museum. The Pro Rodeo Hall of Fame and Museum of the American Cowboy honors the greats of that sport with a presentation of rodeo and cowboy gear and personal memorabilia, multimedia shows, and Western art. At the U.S. Olympic Complex, visitors can tour the training center used by more than 15,000 athletes every year. Drive north of Colorado Springs and see the sleek buildings of the U.S. Air Force Academy spread against a backdrop of forests and mountains.

Colorado Springs Convention & Visitors Bureau: (800) 888-4748 or (719) 635-7506; www.coloradosprings-travel.com

Colorado Springs

⊛ Denver (State Capital) (E-13)

Sprawling on high, rolling plains at the base of the Rocky Mountains, Denver is a rapidly growing city that has become the cultural and tourist capital of the vast Rocky Mountain West. Denver's allure comes from the city's mix of cosmopolitan amenities and the spirit of the Old West. The Colorado History Museum exhibits some of the finest examples of pottery from the cliff dwellings at Mesa Verde, as well as detailed dioramas depicting old forts, American Indian buffalo hunts, and early gold mining methods. The U.S. Mint and Denver Zoo are other interesting stops (Mint tours must be arranged in advance.) Be sure to spend some time wandering LoDo, Denver's trendy and historic city center.

The Pepsi Center

Denver Metro Convention & Visitors Bureau: (800) 233-6837 or (303) 892-1505; www.denver.org

Durango (M-6)

Located in southwest Colorado's Four Corners region, Durango is steeped in its rich past. Visitors can explore the arts and crafts shops in this historic mining town's Victorian downtown or ride the Durango & Silverton Narrow Gauge Railroad. The train route winds through the rugged San Juan region to Silverton - an excursion over tracks that are a national civil engineering landmark. Outdoor adventurers will enjoy hiking, boating, fishing, swimming, mountain biking, and saddle and pack trips in the San Juan National Forest, or trout fishing, canoeing, and kayaking on the Animas River. Excellent downhill skiing and white-water rafting are also nearby.

Durango Area Tourism Office: (800) 525-8855; www.durango.org

Grand Junction (G-5)

At the edge of the Rockies and the desert mesas of the West, Grand Junction is the gateway to stunning natural wonders: Grand Mesa National Forest, Colorado National Monument, Gunnison Valley, and the western San Juan Mountains. The outdoor adventure begins here. Walk and bike along the Colorado Riverfront Trail System. Enjoy white-water rafting on the Colorado and Gunnison rivers, and hiking, mountain biking, hunting, fishing, and camping at Grand Mesa. In and around Grand Junction is Colorado's wine country, where 15 wineries offer visitors tasting and tour experiences. For indoor discoveries, try the Museum of Western Colorado in Grand Junction and the Dinosaur Journey Museum in nearby Fruita.

Grand Junction Visitor & Convention Bureau: (800) 962-2547; www.visitgrandjunction.com

SCENERY

Pikes Peak (H-13)

The view from the 14,110-foot summit of Pikes Peak just west of Colorado Springs inspired Katharine Lee Bates to write "America the Beautiful" after a visit in 1893. A toll road, a cog railway, or your own two feet will get you to the top.

Rocky Mountain National Park's Trail Ridge Road (p. 34, C-2)

At more than 12,000 feet above sea level, Trail Ridge Road is the highest continuous paved highway in the U.S. The 48-mile route between Estes Park and Grand Lake traverses magnificent alpine landscape in the heart of Rocky Mountain National Park. Watch for a dude ranch, lava cliffs, and forest canyon overlooks. Open mid-May through mid-October, depending on snow conditions.

Rocky Mountains

Santa Fe Trail (J-19)

The nation's oldest Western highway runs 188 miles in Colorado and includes the historic Bent's Old Fort trading post. Early American Indians, ranchers, and miners have left a distinctive mark on this historic trade route. Some say the shallow wagon wheel depressions in the prairie can still be seen on clear spring days.

- ● **Garden of the Gods** (H-14)
  Bizarre sandstone formations, balancing rocks, and eroded pinnacles dot this 1,350-acre preserve near Manitou Springs.

- ● **Grand Mesa Scenic and Historic Byway** (G-6)
  From the world's highest flat-topped mountain, take in 360-degree views of the Grand Valley's golden rubble and foliage below. One section of the 63-mile byway runs from Mesa to Cedaredge.

Grand Mesa in late summer

- ● **Lookout Mountain** (E-13)
  For a spectacular panoramic view of Denver, head west to Lookout Mountain, also home to the Buffalo Bill Memorial Museum and Grave.

- ● **Pawnee Pioneer Trails** (C-18)
  This route traverses an endless expanse of shortgrass prairie from Sterling to Ault. The frontier highway's Pawnee Buttes, 250-foot-high knobs, once guided American Indian and pioneer travelers.

- ● **Top of the Rockies Scenic Byway** (G-10)
  Leadville is the hub of the byway taking travelers across the Continental Divide, past the source of the Arkansas River, through a silver camp, and under Colorado's two highest mountains.

OUTDOORS

Arkansas River (G-10)

Colorado remains the largest river rafting destination in the United States, thanks to heavy springtime snow and 13 roaring river systems. Mid-May through August, river guides across the state lead paddlers on scenic, unforgettable waters. Expect all the adventure of world-class rapids coupled with fantastic mountain views, historic riverside trappers' cabins, and hawks circling overhead. The Arkansas River is the country's most popular rafting river with headwaters originating in the historic mining area around Leadville. It winds through the scenic mountain towns of Buena Vista and Salida and into the Royal Gorge. Other popular rivers include the Colorado, the Animas, and the Poudre.

Rafting the Arkansas River

Colorado River Outfitters Association: www.croa.org
Arkansas River Outfitters Association: www.aroa.org

Collegiate Peaks (H-10)

Colorado mountain climbing isn't for the fainthearted. But each year an increasing number of experienced hikers arrive here to conquer the state's Fourteeners (14,000-foot peaks). Colorado is home to 54 of the 61 Fourteeners in the continental U.S., and the Collegiate Peaks contain 11 Fourteeners, the largest concentration in the nation. The peaks come in many shapes with varying degrees of difficulty, but typically a very conditioned hiker can scale and descend one in a full day. The rewards along the way are plentiful: hidden lakes, white-water rivers, fields of wildflowers, wildlife, and endless camping opportunities.

Colorado Mountain Club: www.cmc.org/
CMC Boulder Group: (303) 554-7688;
www.cmcboulder.org

Colorado Trail (E-13)

This nearly 500-mile trail connects Denver to Durango, winding from wild and wooly terrain to serene settings. The Colorado Trail cuts through eight mountain ranges, seven national forests, six wilderness areas, and five major river systems. It serves backpackers and equestrians, but mountain bikers are the fastest growing group of trail users. For bikers it's the ultimate thigh-burning experience, rated among the most technical riding in the southern Rockies. The trail's many access points and variety of terrain cater to both novices and experts. Riders can tackle single sections or the entire trail (with the exception of wilderness areas), which is open for biking mid-June to August. Guidebooks and trail maps are available through the Colorado Trail Foundation.

(303) 384-3729; www.coloradotrail.org

Summit County (F-11)

Located between the Tenmile Range and the Continental Divide about an hour's drive west of Denver, Summit County consistently ranks as a premier ski and golf destination. Several of the state's ski resorts are here, including Breckenridge, Copper Mountain and Keystone. They promise visitors a long ski season (generally Thanksgiving through Easter or later) and some of the best powdery snow conditions around. In springtime, vacationers can spend the morning on the slopes and the afternoon on the resort golf course. Breckenridge boasts a 27-hole Jack Nicklaus-designed course,

Downhill skiing

and Keystone was recently ranked as one of the country's top resort golf courses by Golf Digest and Golf Magazine.

(800) 530-3099; summitchamber.org

HERITAGE

Durango & Silverton Narrow Gauge Railroad & Museum (M-6)

Relive history by traveling on tracks that once carried miners, cowboys, and Old West pioneers. The Silverton is a vintage 1880s coal-fired, steam-powered, narrow-gauge train that runs daily through the Animas Canyon of the San Juan Mountains, between Durango and Silverton. Registered as a National Historic Landmark, this ride is considered to be one of the last great train trips in North America. In summer, the train transports visitors 45 miles north to Silverton (traveling at a top speed of 18 mph) in 3 1/2 hours. After a two-hour layover, visitors are returned to Durango. Other shorter trips in the San Juan National Forest run throughout the summer and winter. A museum with 1880s railcars and locomotives is also on site. Reservations recommended.

(970) 247-2733, (877) 872-4607; www.durangotrain.com

The Ghost Town of St. Elmo (H-10)

The boom-and-bust cycle that characterized Colorado's mining industry more than 100 years ago left behind dozens of ghost towns. Aspen and Telluride transformed themselves into year-round resort towns. But St. Elmo, once a vibrant railroad thoroughfare with 50 mines in operation, wasn't as fortunate. One of Colorado's best-preserved ghost towns, St. Elmo boasts a general store, bank, saloon, and several other original buildings as well as a handful of year-round residents. This small gem of Americana is listed on the National Register of Historic Places. It is located just west of Nathrop on County Road 162.

(719) 395-6612; www.coloradoheadwaters.com

Mesa Verde National Park (M-5)

Mesa Verde, located 37 miles west of Durango, preserves and protects a variety of Ancestral Puebloan dwellings. More than 4,000 known archaeological sites lie within the park, ranging from pit houses built during the A.D. 500s to the cliff dwellings of the 1200s. These were once occupied by 24 different Native tribes, including all of the Pueblo Indians of New Mexico, the Hopi tribe in Arizona, and the Ute and Navajo peoples. Mesa Verde park rangers lead unforgettable archaeological tours of several sites. Cliff Palace, Balcony House, Long House, and Spruce Tree House are among the most popular. Also in the park, the Chapin Mesa Archaeological Museum boasts a great collection of American Indian pottery.

(970) 529-4465; www.nps.gov/meve

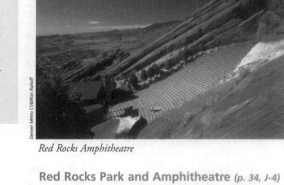

Red Rocks Amphitheatre

Red Rocks Park and Amphitheatre (p. 34, J-4)

Legendary bands, including The Beatles and U2, have played to sold-out crowds in this famous outdoor amphitheater formed millions of years ago by Mother Nature. The amphitheater's two 300-foot sandstone monoliths, Ship Rock and Creation Rock, are taller than Niagara Falls. In the surrounding park a well-marked trail winds through valleys and meadows and around spectacular rock formations. The Visitor Center at Red Rocks is filled with interactive educational displays featuring the geologic and musical history of Red Rocks.

(720) 865-2494; www.redrocksonline.com

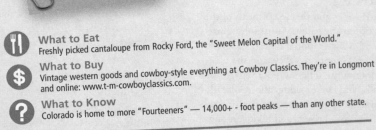

Local Color

🍴 **What to Eat**
Freshly picked cantaloupe from Rocky Ford, the "Sweet Melon Capital of the World."

💲 **What to Buy**
Vintage western goods and cowboy-style everything at Cowboy Classics. They're in Longmont and online: www.t-m-cowboyclassics.com.

❓ **What to Know**
Colorado is home to more "Fourteeners" — 14,000+ - foot peaks — than any other state.

Motorcycle Helmet Required? Under age 18 and for passengers
Child Restraint Seat Required? Under age 6 and less than 55 in.

Colorado Tourism Office: (800) 265-6723; www.colorado.com
Road Construction and Conditions: 511; (877) 315-7623 (in CO);
(303) 639-1111; www.cotrip.org

Connecticut

The re-created 19th-century seaside village of Mystic Seaport is the nation's leading maritime museum.

Connecticut River and Coast Tour (F-10)

The joy is in the journey along this drive up one side of the Connecticut River — a National Heritage River — and down the other. State parks and forests line the route. Start at Deep River, driving SR 154 *Connecticut River* north to Middletown, then head south again on SR 66, 151, 82, and 156. Of the many unspoiled areas in New England, this part of Connecticut or "land beside the long tidal river" is outstanding.

Connecticut Wine Trails (F-5)

Marked by blue signage, the Connecticut Wine Trails meander through country dotted with lakes, rolling countryside, and quaint towns. One of the two trails starts in the Housatonic Valley and continues via SR 25 and 34 to the Litchfield Hills. There are four vineyards along this route, each as picturesque as the others.

CITIES

✪ Hartford (State Capital) (C-9)

Situated on the Connecticut River, Hartford has played a central role in the cultural and industrial development of New England and the nation. The city was founded in 1636 by colonists from Massachusetts seeking a site for their utopian community. The nation's oldest newspaper, the Hartford Courant, was first published here in 1764, and the bustling town was the home of the Hartford Wits, a group of late-18th-century intellectuals. Today modern buildings loom over the Old State House, while the striking Legislative Office Building is adjacent to the gold-domed capitol building (1879). The Wadsworth Atheneum Museum of Art, established in 1842, is nation's oldest continually operating public museum. Displays at the Museum of Connecticut History in the State Library include the Colt Collection of Firearms and the Royal Charter, which was whisked away from agents of James II and hidden in an oak tree.

Central Regional Tourism: (800) 793-4480 or (860) 244-8181; www.enjoycentralct.com

Wadsworth Atheneum

New Haven (G-7)

Once an important manufacturing center, New Haven is now known almost exclusively as the home of Yale University. It's an Ivy League town with bustling blue-collar neighborhoods, and the heart of it all is the colonial-era New Haven Green with its stately trees and steepled churches. The university boasts the Beinecke Rare Book and Manuscript Library, the Yale Center for British Art, and the Peabody Museum of Natural History. The New Haven Museum & Historical Society exhibits antiques. The Creative Arts Workshop features crafts. Other nearby attractions include Shore Line Trolley Museum and Fort Nathan Hale. During the summer, many jazz and cultural festivals are held throughout the city.

Greater New Haven Convention & Visitors Bureau: (203) 777-8550, (800) 332-7829; www.newhavencvb.org

New London (F-12)

From whaling to sailing, New London has always looked to the sea for its livelihood. The city is home to the U.S. Coast Guard Academy and to Connecticut College, whose entire 725-acre campus overlooking Long Island Sound is maintained as an arboretum. American works of fine and decorative arts as well as paintings by the Impressionists are among the extensive collections at the Lyman Allyn Art Museum. Historic homes abound including the Shaw-Perkins Mansion, which served as the state's naval office during the American Revolution, and the restored Hempsted Houses, which contain original Colonial-era furnishings. Of more recent vintage, the Monte Cristo Cottage was the family home of Nobel Prize-winning playwright Eugene O'Neill and the setting for some of his greatest works. The city's recreation spots include Fort Trumbull State Park, the fine sandy beach at Ocean Beach Park, and a recently completed Waterfront Park offering improved access to the downtown harbor.

Connecticut East Convention & Visitors Bureau: (800) 863-6569; www.mysticmore.com, www.ci.new-london.ct.us

Waterbury (E-6)

The city bills itself the "Brass Capital," as the Waterbury Button Company began making brass buttons here in 1812. Several Waterbury buildings such as the red clock tower of the Waterbury Republican-American building or the spires of St. John's or St. Anne's churches rise above rooflines. Along Grand Street is a historic district featuring City Hall and other structures designed by American architect Cass Gilbert. The city also has two historic residential areas, Hillside and Overlook. Mattatuck Museum displays three centuries of local history and works from artists with a Connecticut connection. Fulton Park is not just for fans of the outdoors; the park is also on the National Register of Historic Places. Brass City Ballet, Seven Angels Theatre, and the Waterbury Symphony Orchestra round out Waterbury's cultural attractions.

Clock tower at Waterbury Republican-American building

Northwest Connecticut Convention & Visitors Bureau: (203) 597-9527, (888) 588-7880; www.waterburyregion.com

---

• **Hurd State Park** (E-9)
In autumn, it's hard to beat the panoramic view of the changing hardwood foliage bordering the Connecticut River along CT 151 near East Haddam.

• **Kent Falls** (C-4)
Feel the mist from the largest waterfall in Connecticut as it cascades 250 feet to join the Housatonic River in Kent Falls State Park.

• **Old New-Gate Prison & Copper Mine** (A-8)

Kent Falls

Located off SR 20 north of East Granby, the site of the 1705 copper mine (it temporarily became a Continental Congress prison) offers spectacular views of the lush Farmington Valley below.

• **Sleeping Giant State Park** (F-7)
Near Hamden on SR 10, between the Mill and Quinnipiac rivers, the lookout tower in this state park provides views of New Haven and Long Island Sound beyond.

• **West Cornwall Covered Bridge** (B-4)
Built in 1841 and still painted red, Connecticut's most photogenic bridge is located on CT 128 in West Cornwell.

West Cornwall Covered Bridge

TRAVEL GUIDE   Connecticut   Connecticut

OUTDOORS

Devil's Hopyard State Park (E-11)

Folklore says that the name Devil's Hopyard refers to an early settler named Dibble who grew hops. Another tale references sightings of devilish ghouls dancing among hop vines. In any case, early settlers knew beautiful country when they saw it. Today there are more than 15 miles of hiking trails. In the winter, cross-country skiers and snowshoers flock to these same trails. Paralleling the Eight-Mile River, the trails lead through hemlock forest and by marshlands. The Orange Trail leads to a scenic overlook of the valley, which is extraordinary for its fall foliage display. The 1,000-acre park is also home to Chapman Falls and serves as a stop on a flyway for migratory song birds.

Chapman Falls

(860) 873-8566;
www.dep.state.ct.us/stateparks/parks/
devilshopyard.htm

Housatonic Valley River Trail (D-4)

The northern portion of the Housatonic River Trail for canoeing or kayaking leaves quaint New Milford and winds by Bridgewater and through Brookfield and Newtown en route to Long Island Sound. Take a leisurely one-hour trip or plan a more adventurous half-day or multi-day itinerary to see the entire length. There are plenty of outfitters and marine supply houses in the river-

Canoeing

side towns. Some offer moonlight paddles. Along the trail, there are opportunities for viewing wildlife. A few bird-watching sanctuaries are located along the way as are nature trails and historic spots. Many communities sponsor weekend events and activities, from apple picking and concerts to popular local festivals. In all, the Housatonic River flows south 150 miles from its source in Massachusetts.

(203) 775-6256; www.hvceo.org/rivertrail.php

Little Pond Boardwalk

White Memorial Conservation Center (C-5)

Near Litchfield, the state's largest nature center and wildlife sanctuary covers 4,000 acres and features 35 miles of ungroomed carriage roads available as multi-use trails for hiking, horseback riding, cross-country skiing, and other seasonal outdoor activities. In addition to trails, there are campgrounds, boating facilities, and special areas for recreational gatherings. The center also operates a nature museum with programs that encourage visitors to interact with nature. Bird observation platforms have also been constructed. The center is west of town on CT 202.

(860) 567-0857; www.whitememorialcc.org

HERITAGE

Coventry (C-11)

Situated among rolling hills and farm country, Coventry was the birthplace of Revolutionary War hero Nathan Hale, who spoke the immortal words "I only regret I have but one life to lose for my country" as he was being hanged as a spy by the British. Visit the Nathan Hale Homestead, furnished with many of the Hale family's possessions, and nearby Nathan Hale State Park. The Strong-Porter House (ca. 1730), built by Nathan Hale's uncle, is also open for tours.

Nathan Hale Homestead

Coventry is also well known among home gardeners for the Caprilands Herb Farm, where more than 300 varieties of herbs are grown in 38 gardens. There are antique playthings set in imaginative re-creations of period rooms at the Special Joys Antique Doll Shop.

(860) 742-6324; www.coventryct.org

Mystic Seaport (F-13)

The country's largest living history maritime museum is located in Mystic, 10 miles east of New London on I-95. The indoor/outdoor maritime museum is a classic coastline stopover. Explore the re-created 19th-century whaling village with its extensive collection of ships, buildings, art, ship models, artifacts, and exhibit galleries. The preservation shipyard, where craftsmen apply traditional skills to maintain the museum's fleet of historic ships, was once a working shipyard and produced more than 600 vessels. The freedom schooner *Amistad* was reproduced at Mystic and now sails from New Haven as a floating classroom. *Amistad* serves as a goodwill ambassador for the state of Connecticut and, outside U.S. borders, for America.

(860) 572-5315, (888) 973-2767;
www.visitmysticseaport.com

Weir Farm National Historic Site (G-4)

Home of J. Alden Weir, an American Impressionist painter, this farm near Ridgefield has hosted three generations of artists. Weir used the farm as a summer retreat for 40 years, drawing inspiration from the landscape. Mahonri Young, who married one of Weir's daughters, was a noted sculptor who lived at the farm after Weir and built a second studio on the property. The New England surroundings became the subject of works by Childe Hassam, Albert Pinkham Ryder, and John Twachtman. In addition to the home and two studios, the 60-acre property includes a visitor center, outbuildings, and several barns. The site is located in Connecticut's Housatonic Valley; other famous former residents of this area were P. T. Barnum and Mark Twain.

(203) 834-1896; www.nps.gov/wefa

Weir Farm National Historic Site

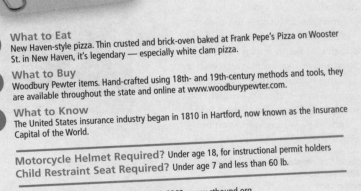

Local Color

🍴 **What to Eat**
New Haven-style pizza. Thin crusted and brick-oven baked at Frank Pepe's Pizza on Wooster St. in New Haven, it's legendary — especially white clam pizza.

$ **What to Buy**
Woodbury Pewter items. Hand-crafted using 18th- and 19th-century methods and tools, they are available throughout the state and online at www.woodburypewter.com.

❓ **What to Know**
The United States insurance industry began in 1810 in Hartford, now known as the Insurance Capital of the World.

Motorcycle Helmet Required? Under age 18, for instructional permit holders
Child Restraint Seat Required? Under age 7 and less than 60 lb.

Connecticut Tourism: (800) 282-6863; www.ctbound.org
Road Construction and Conditions: (800) 443-6817 (in CT);
(860) 594-2650 (conditions); www.ct.gov/dot (construction)

Delaware

A Federal fortress from 1859, Fort Delaware is located on Pea Patch Island.

CITIES

⭐ Dover *(State Capital) (G-3)*

Delaware's capital city, Dover is one of the smallest and oldest state capitals and has kept its original charm and beauty. Visitors can tour the 18th-century Old State House and admire the Colonial homes on the Green, which was laid out in 1722 in accordance with William Penn's 1683 orders. At the Hall of Records, the Royal Charter and Penn's founding order are on display. Six of the eight Delaware State Museums are in Dover, including the John Dickinson Plantation, home to the "Penman of the American Revolution." The Delaware Agricultural Museum and Village has restored and reconstructed buildings and a fine collection of agricultural equipment. Dover Downs features NASCAR races in the spring and fall and har-
ness racing in winter. Dover Air Force Base maintains a historical museum with vintage aircraft, including a B-17 Flying Fortress and an open-cockpit PT 17 bi-plane.

Old State House

Kent County Tourism Convention & Visitors Bureau: (800) 233-5368 or (302) 734-1736; www.visitdover.com

Newark *(C-1)*

This industrial town is the home of the University of Delaware. A lovely tree-lined mall graces the Old College, built in 1833. Nearby, you'll find the Battle of Cooch's Bridge Monument, which marks the site of Delaware's only Revolutionary War battle. According to legend, Betsy Ross' 13-star flag design, the Stars and Stripes, first flew here. A 90-foot tower in Iron Hill Park overlooks the battle site. You can also visit the Iron Hill Museum, which is housed in a former one-room schoolhouse and features the du Pont mineral collection, fossils, and other Delaware archaeological artifacts. White Clay Creek State Park offers an equestrian center, hunting, fishing, and interpretive pro-
grams. Hikers will find 20 miles of trails including a route that leads to the first point surveyed on the Mason-Dixon Line.

Delaware Tourism Office: (866) 284-7483; www.visitdelaware.net

Rehoboth Beach *(K-5)*

This family resort community has been called the "Nation's Summer Capital" because so many Washingtonians vacation here during the season. The central community of Delaware's 24 miles of Atlantic shoreline offers swimming, sunning, camping, water sports, and live-
ly nightlife. The Rehoboth Art League galleries and studios in Henlopen Acres are open to the public in summer. South of town is Delaware Seashore State Park, a seven-mile strip of land separating Rehoboth and Indian River bays from the Atlantic Ocean. Park visitors enjoy ocean or bay swimming, boating, fishing, camping, surfing, and horse and nature trails. The region hosts many autumn festivals, including the Sea Witch Halloween and Fiddler's Festival.

Rehoboth Beach

Rehoboth Beach-Dewey Beach Chamber of Commerce: (800) 441-1329 or (302) 227-2233; www.beach-fun.com

Wilmington *(C-3)*

Settled in the mid-17th century by Swedish immi-
grants, the port city of Wilmington prospered as a rail and industrial center. Visitors can learn more about this first Swedish settlement in North America at Fort Christina Historical Park, which marks the Swedes' 1638 landing site. Other Swedish sites include Holy Trinity (Old Swedes) Church, built in 1698, and the adjacent Hendrickson House (1690). Nearby, the Kalmar Nyckel Shipyard Museum, which focuses on the 17th and 18th centuries, commemorates the ships that brought these early arrivals. In Rodney Square a statue of Caesar Rodney memorializes the patriot who rode from Dover to Philadelphia on July 2, 1776 to break the Delaware delegation's deadlocked vote on approving the Declaration of Independence. Market Street pedestrian mall offers boutiques, sidewalk cafés, the Old Town Hall Museum, Willingtown Square's historic homes, the Playhouse, and the Grand Opera House with its classic Victorian wrought-iron facade.

Caesar Rodney Statue

(800) 489-6664 or (302) 295-2210; www.visitwilmingtonde.com

OUTDOORS

Cape Henlopen State Park *(J-5)*

Cape Henlopen, the largest of Delaware's state parks, is located where Delaware Bay and the Atlantic Ocean meet. It covers six miles of ocean shoreline and is a favorite spot for swimming, fishing, and recreation. Hikers can follow trails through the dunes or tackle the 80-foot Great Dune. Winds continually shift the sands, creating "walking dunes," so-called because they creep along. During World War II, guns and bunkers were hidden in the dunes, and concrete observa-
tion towers were built to scan for enemy vessels. Visitors today can climb an observation tower for a 360-degree view of the Cape. A Seaside Interpretive Trail leads visitors to various highlights. The Seaside Nature Center offers seasonal migratory bird-
watching programs, among others.

Cape Henlopen

(302) 645-8983; www.destateparks.com/chsp/chsp.htm

Prime Hook National Wildlife Refuge *(I-4)*

When horseshoe crabs spawn in late May, red knots, short-billed dowitch-
ers, sanderlings, and ruddy turnstones flock to this more than 10,000-acre wildlife preserve near Milton. Most of the refuge is marshland, both tidal and freshwater. Canoes can navigate streams and creeks in the refuge. Spot bald eagles during nesting season, peregrine falcons, hawks, and numerous waterfowl such as loons, herons, egrets, and pelicans. In the fall, migrating snow geese congre-
gate here. In all, 267 species of birds frequent the refuge.

(302) 684-8419; primehook.fws.gov

Trap Pond State Park *(L-3)*

Created in the late 1700s to power a sawmill that exploited the stands of bald cypress, Trap Pond lies within 3,200 acres that were designated a state park in 1951. The park encom-
passes the northern part of the Great Cypress Swamp. A wilderness canoe trail runs through it, passing through stands of bald cypress. Water floods the forest seasonally. Bird watchers may sight warblers, tanagers, and pee-wees. Rental canoes, kayaks, row-
boats, surf boats, and paddle boats are available for exploring 90-acre Trap Pond. It is open for fishing and canoeing, and summer weekend visi-
tors can take a guided pontoon boat tour on its waters.

(302) 875-5153; www.destateparks.com/tpsp/tpsp.htm

SCENERY

Assawoman Wildlife Area Trail (L-5)
Created from nine former farms on the Delaware coast, Assawoman Wildlife Area is managed by the U.S. Forest Service and is noted for migrating and wintering waterfowl. This auto trail on a dirt road through the wildlife area features numbered stakes that point out bat and purple martin boxes, bluebird and wood duck nest boxes, as well as other birds that frequent the area. Trees and plants in the area are also pointed out along the trail.

Brandywine

Brandywine Valley (B-8)
Several routes out of Wilmington travel through historic, wooded Brandywine Valley. Heading towards the Brandywine Battlefield and Chadds Ford in Pennsylvania, you'll pass Brandywine Creek State Park. The route goes over the Brandywine River with a hilltop view of the du Pont estate and through the Smith Bridge, a rebuilt 1839 wooden covered bridge. It winds past Keurner's Farm, once painted by Andrew Wyeth, and on to Brandywine Battlefield in Chadds Ford.

● **Abbott's Mill** (J-3)
Southwest of Milford on Route 620, view this historic gristmill owned by the Delaware Nature Society.

● **Cape May-Lewes Ferry** (J-5)
Drive aboard the Cape May-Lewes Ferry for a 17-mile, 80-minute ride through Delaware Bay to Cape May, NJ. Dolphins sometimes swim alongside the ferry.

● **Coastal Heritage Greenway Trail** (C-9)
Follow 90 miles of Delaware coastline from Fox Point State Park to Fenwick Island. The route travels along two-lane roads (primarily SR 9) through villages, coastal estuaries, marshes, meadows, and historic homes.

● **Fenwick Island Lighthouse** (M-5)
Visit the Fenwick Island Lighthouse, built in 1858 to warn ships away from the Fenwick shoal.

● **Millsboro Pond** (L-4)
A number of ponds surround Millsboro in south-central Delaware. Bald eagles roost at Millsboro Pond.

HERITAGE

Hagley Mill

The Hagley Museum and Library (C-8)
This museum depicts the world of 19th-century American industry. Located on the 235-acre site of the original du Pont black powder works, the museum complex features restored mills, an operating waterwheel and water turbine, and demonstrations of working machinery. The complex also includes Eleutherian Mills, the Georgian-style country house built by E.I. du Pont in 1803 and filled with five generations of the family's antiques. The Hagley Library continues to acquire numerous manuscripts and company records from the period, specializing in the Middle Atlantic region.

(302) 658-2400; www.hagley.org

John Dickinson Plantation (H-3)
Built in the mid-1700s, this plantation was the boyhood home of John Dickinson, the "penman of the American Revolution" and signer of the Constitution. Samuel Dickinson, a wealthy Quaker tobacco farmer and merchant, brought his family, including 8-year-old John, here in 1740. John eventually inherited the property. Quakers opposed slavery officially in 1776, so John freed his slaves the next year. Visitors can learn more about slavery and John Dickinson's life as a farmer, author, and politician at this historic brick home, outbuildings, and log dwelling.

(302) 739-3277; www.destatemuseums.org

Prime Hook National Wildlife Refuge (see pg. 165)

Johnson Victrola Museum (G-8)
Discover the men, machines, and recordings of the golden age of the phonograph at this Delaware State Museum. The museum honors Eldridge Reeves Johnson, Delaware native and inventor, who founded the Victor Talking Machine Company (predecessor of RCA) in 1901. The museum is patterned after a 1920s Victrola dealer's store and features one of the premier collections of talking machines, Victrolas, early records, and memorabilia.

(302) 739-4266; www.destatemuseums.org

Johnson Victrola Museum

Winterthur Museum and Gardens (B-8)
The former country estate of Henry Francis du Pont, Winterthur is a museum with more than 175 rooms filled with his collection of decorative arts made or used in America between 1640 and 1860. Take a stroll through the lush 60-acre garden that is colorful no matter what time of year you are visiting. You can also spend time in the research library dedicated to American and European decorative art and material culture — it contains more than 70,000 volumes and is open to the public. The surrounding 982-acre estate has several hundred acres open to the public, including gardens landscaped in the style of an 18th-century English park.

(800) 448-3883; www.winterthur.org

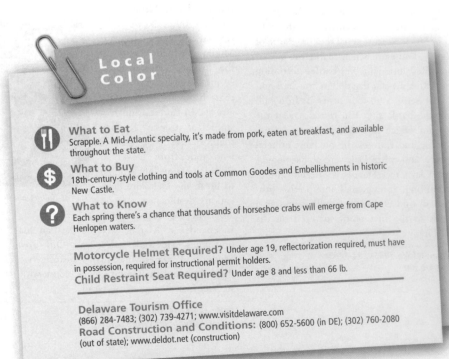

Local Color

🍴 **What to Eat**
Scrapple. A Mid-Atlantic specialty, it's made from pork, eaten at breakfast, and available throughout the state.

💲 **What to Buy**
18th-century-style clothing and tools at Common Goodes and Embellishments in historic New Castle.

❓ **What to Know**
Each spring there's a chance that thousands of horseshoe crabs will emerge from Cape Henlopen waters.

Motorcycle Helmet Required? Under age 19, reflectorization required, must have in possession, required for instructional permit holders.
Child Restraint Seat Required? Under age 8 and less than 66 lb.

Delaware Tourism Office
(866) 284-7483; (302) 739-4271; www.visitdelaware.com
Road Construction and Conditions: (800) 652-5600 (in DE); (302) 760-2080 (out of state); www.deldot.net (construction)

TRAVEL GUIDE

Delaware

Florida

The setting sun spills its last rays onto the beach at St. Petersburg/Clearwater.

CITIES

Jacksonville (C-9)

Named for Andrew Jackson, this city on the St. Johns River is one of Florida's largest metropolitan areas. Decorative art lovers gather to see the celebrated collection of Meissen porcelain at the Cummer Museum of Art and Gardens. Jacksonville Zoo and Gardens offers a walking safari to view its 800 rare and exotic animals. Families have fun at the Museum of Science and History and the Fort Caroline National Memorial. For boutique shopping, art galleries, antiques, and trendy restaurants, visit the San Marco district or the historic Riverside neighborhood. Jacksonville Landing, located downtown, is an enclosed shopping and entertainment center with many retail stores and restaurants under one roof. East of the city is Jacksonville Beach, an oceanfront resort with a boardwalk, a long sandy beach, a lighted fishing pier, and Pablo Historical Park.

Jacksonville and the Beaches Convention & Visitors Bureau: (904) 798-9111, (800) 733-2668; www.visitjacksonville.com

Key West (T-9)

Deep-sea fishing, reef cruises, conch tour trains, the restored Audubon House and Gardens, and Ernest Hemingway's home and museum await at the southernmost U.S. city. Located at the end of US 1, Key West is 150 miles from Miami, yet only 90 miles from Cuba. This tiny spot has a lot to offer, including the East Martello Museum and Gallery, which features exhibits of war relics. The Mallory Square district along the waterfront doubles as a meeting place to celebrate the key's fabled sunsets. Spend the day snorkeling or visiting the Aquarium, the Mel Fisher Maritime Museum, or the Wrecker's Museum. Dry Tortugas National Park and Fort Jefferson National Monument are only 70 miles away and are accessible by ferry service or chartered seaplane.

Key West Chamber of Commerce: (800) 352-5397; www.fla-keys.com

Conch train in Key West

Miami (Q-13)

Sea and sunshine, glittering luxury hotels, and an endless variety of activities have made this surf city on the Atlantic side of Florida an international favorite. Explore the Art Deco district of South Beach, experience Cuban culture on Calle Ocho (8th Street), or visit the Caribbean community centered around Little Haiti, where menus and music mix with American spirit. The Miami Seaquarium, Parrot Jungle Island, and Monkey Jungle are family favorites. The Miami Metro Zoo features animals in natural habitats. Nearby is the Miami Science Museum, which has science displays ranging from Florida wildlife to gemology and which offers sky shows in the planetarium. The splendor of the Vizcaya Museum and Gardens, an Italian Renaissance-style villa, should not be missed.

Greater Miami Convention & Visitors Bureau: (305) 539-3000, (800) 933-8448; www.gmcvb.com

Discovery Cove in Orlando

Orlando (H-10)

This city is synonymous with Florida's family entertainment industry. Disney World started the theme park phenomenon and there are now 95 just in the greater Orlando area. The Magic Kingdom, Epcot, and Disney's Animal Kingdom are internationally recognized venues. At SeaWorld, there's a walk-through shark exhibit and a killer whale and sea lion show. Universal Studios Florida has sound stages where movies and television programs are produced right next door to movie-related rides. Ditto at nearby Disney-MGM Studios. Off the set, there's more to do, like shopping at outlet centers, factory stores, or the state's largest enclosed mall, the Florida Mall. The Orlando Museum of Art features special exhibits in addition to a collection of American art, African art, and art of the ancient Americas.

Orlando/Orange County Convention & Visitors Bureau: (407) 363-5872 or (800) 972-3304; www.orlandoinfo.com

St. Augustine (D-10)

Founded by the Spanish in 1565 and reigning as the oldest European settlement in the United States, this resort city has a penchant for the past. A project called the Old St. Augustine Restoration has revived the Spanish Colonial section where historic homes are open to the public and craft shops are thriving. Among the most intriguing of the Spanish-period structures are the Castillo de San Marcos, the Basilica of St. Augustine, and the San Agustin Antiguo (Spanish Quarter), a re-creation of an 18th-century Spanish Colonial village. The Lightner Museum displays antiques and decorative arts on a massive scale. The Castillo de San Marcos, a national monument, is the oldest masonry fort in the country. South of the city on Anastasia Island is the St. Augustine Alligator Farm, with wildlife shows, a zoo, and a museum.

St. Augustine, Ponte Vedra & the Beaches: (800) 653-2489; www.getaway4florida.com

St. Augustine

⍟ Tallahassee (State Capital) (B-2)

A storybook southern city, Florida's capital is located in an area of the state called "the Big Bend" or "where the panhandle meets the peninsula." Famous for its canopied streets lined by moss-draped live oaks, Tallahassee is also the home of picturesque Florida State University and Florida A&M University. Stroll through the Park Avenue Historic District where a chain of seven parks encircles restored houses, many on the National Register of Historic Places. The Governor's Mansion, modeled after Andrew Jackson's home, The Hermitage, is open for tours as is the capitol building itself, one of only five tower capitols in the country. Tour the restored Old Capitol, too, along with the Museum of Florida History where a nine-foot mastodon and Spanish galleon treasures await.

Tallahassee Area Convention & Visitors Bureau: (850) 606-2305, or (800) 628-2866; www.seetallahassee.com

Tampa (J-7)

Skyscrapers and rich diversity reach out in this city by Tampa Bay. Marvel at the Moorish architecture of the University of Tampa. Busch Gardens features exotic gardens in addition to thrill rides and a world-class zoo. For nightlife, head toward Ybor City, a former cigar-manufacturing district. Often referred to as "a city within a city," this restored neighborhood is filled with quaint streets bursting with Hispanic entertainment, nightclubs, fine restaurants, bakeries, and shops. All provide a delightful glimpse into Cuban culture. Hyde Park Village is an upscale shopping area near Bayshore Boulevard with exclusive boutiques and cafés. The Florida Aquarium displays marine life in a three-story glass dome on the Tampa Bay waterfront. For spectator sports, there's horse racing, greyhound racing, and professional hockey and football.

Tampa Bay Convention & Visitors Bureau: (800) 448-2672 or (813) 223-1111; www.visittampabay.com

Ybor City nightlife

SCENERY

Sea oats and sand dunes

Cape San Blas (T-7)

Escape to the beach at St. Joseph Peninsula State Park on Cape San Blas. The sugar-white beach sand joins forces with sea oats to create towering free-form dunes, some reaching 30 to 40 feet high and arguably among the largest in Florida. With a background of crystal-clear aquamarine water from the Gulf of Mexico or St. Joseph's Bay, it's hard to turn away from the water to look at the forested areas of the park, but it is worth it. In August, monarch butterflies by the thousands rest in the trees; the Cape is a stopover on the annual monarch migration to Mexico. Bird sightings are common throughout the year on the Cape, as more than 200 species have been identified in residence.

Everglades National Park (Q-11)

The "River of Grass," a huge waterway 50 miles wide but only one to three feet deep, slowly creeps through the park. It is a freshwater slough disguised as a sawgrass prairie. In either case, it is critical to the ecosystem that sustains an interdependent chain of wildlife. Enjoy the views from SR 9336 between Homestead and Flamingo.

Florida Keys (S-13)

The 150 miles between Miami and Key West present horizons of blue as far as the eye can see — on either side of US 1. As the road meanders from key to key on its way to the southernmost point in the 48 contiguous states, the view changes only in the depth of the color in the sky reflecting off the blue of the water.

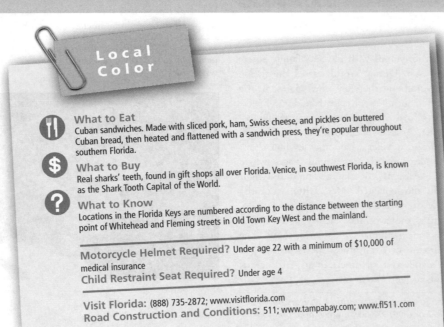

US 1 connects the Florida Keys

Ding Darling National Wildlife Refuge (O-8)

This refuge offers a four-mile, one-way scenic drive that meanders through a 7,000-acre mangrove estuary. It may not be the largest wildlife refuge, but it is one of the busiest, with significant numbers of wading birds, including woodstorks, white ibis, and yellow-crowned night herons, and migrating waterfowl. American alligators bask in the sun along Wildlife Drive. Open 7:30 a.m. to sunset every day except Friday.

● Fakahatchee Strand Preserve State Park (P-10)

Located on Janes Memorial Scenic Drive, just west of Copeland, the best time of the year to see the celebrated display of native orchids is November through February.

● Long Key (S-12)

Near mile marker 67.5 on the Overseas Highway, the remains of a 100,000-year-old coral reef stretch above sea level as evidence of a time when the water was as much as 30 feet higher than it is today.

● Mallory Square (P-6)

Residents and tourists alike gather each evening where Market Street meets the Gulf of Mexico on Key West to celebrate the setting of the sun.

Myakka River

● Myakka River State Park (p. 37, H-5)

Accessible by the only public subtropical forest canopy walkway in North America, the park's 74-foot observation tower affords views once enjoyed only by our fine feathered friends.

● Ponce de Leon Inlet Lighthouse (G-11)

The gallery at the top of the 175-foot-tall Ponce de Leon Inlet Lighthouse offers a panoramic view of the Atlantic Ocean. The lighthouse is at the end of South Peninsula Drive, 10 miles south of Daytona Beach.

● Tallahassee (p. 36, J-8)

Live oaks arch over historic streets like Old St. Augustine, Meridian, or Miccosukee Roads to form canopies of green throughout the capital.

HERITAGE

Amelia Island

American Beach (B-10)

In 1935, a man named A.L. Lewis established the first beach in Florida exclusively for African-Americans. Lewis, founder of Afro-American Life Insurance, became one of the country's first African-American millionaires. During the days of segregation, American Beach was a haven for African-American vacationers and their families, drawing thousands of visitors to Amelia Island, easily accessible from north of Jacksonville. No longer segregated, American Beach is still easy to find: Cross the Thomas J. Shave Bridge, turn right at the first traffic signal, and follow the signs. Over the years, Amelia Island evolved into an exclusive getaway for people from all over the world. MaVyne Betsch, the great-granddaughter of Mr. Lewis, offers tours to visitors, starting from her home at Gregg and Lewis Streets.

(800) 226-3542; www.islandchamber.com

Historical Museum of Southern Florida (p. 37, N-5)

Experience the last 10,000 years in a single afternoon visit to "Tropical Dreams: A People's History of South Florida," a state-of-the-art audio-visual retelling of the contributions of early settlers in Florida, including those of Cuban descent. This is only one of the many exhibits that chronicle the life and times of Cuban Americans, descendants of the colonists of the New World, those who relocated during the height of 1920s tourism, and the refugees of modern times. The museum, located in the Cultural Center Plaza, also schedules walking and biking tours through Miami's Little Havana neighborhood where Cuban American contributions in art, music, cuisine, architecture, and lifestyle can be experienced firsthand.

(305) 375-1492; www.historical-museum.org

Marjorie Kinnan Rawlings State Historic Site (E-8)

Located near Hawthorne, the home of the author and the inspiration for her Pulitzer Prize-winning novel *The Yearling* epitomizes Florida in the middle 1900s. Its location in the middle of huge growths of cypress and heart pine, the ambience of the orange groves and the marshes, and the Cracker-style architecture of her house are representative of rural Florida. The layout of the homestead also reflects the lifestyle of the ranchers (those that "cracked" the whip while herding cattle), growers, and farmers that settled in the interior of the state. Listed on the National Register of Historic Sites, the house is open to the public for tours October to July*. The grounds are open year-round.

(352) 466-3672;
www.floridastateparks.org/marjoriekinnanrawlings

Timucuan Ecological and Historic Preserve (B-10)

Just northeast of Jacksonville, the Timucuan preserve encompasses 46,000 acres of estuary and marine forest landscape situated between the St. Johns and Nassau rivers. It was named after the original American Indian inhabitants and includes several sites marking occupation by varying groups of American and European colonists. Among the historic ruins are Fort (de la) Caroline, established by sixteenth-century French Huguenots; Kingsley, a nineteenth-century sea island cotton plantation that illustrates antebellum life; and Yellow Bluff Fort, an earthen fortification used by both Union and Confederate forces during the Civil War. The 600-acre Theodore Roosevelt Area highlights the ecological importance of the preserve.

(904) 641-7155; www.nps.gov/timu

Local Color

🍴 **What to Eat**
Cuban sandwiches. Made with sliced pork, ham, Swiss cheese, and pickles on buttered Cuban bread, then heated and flattened with a sandwich press, they're popular throughout southern Florida.

💲 **What to Buy**
Real sharks' teeth, found in gift shops all over Florida. Venice, in southwest Florida, is known as the Shark Tooth Capital of the World.

❓ **What to Know**
Locations in the Florida Keys are numbered according to the distance between the starting point of Whitehead and Fleming streets in Old Town Key West and the mainland.

Motorcycle Helmet Required? Under age 22 with a minimum of $10,000 of medical insurance
Child Restraint Seat Required? Under age 4

Visit Florida: (888) 735-2872; www.visitflorida.com
Road Construction and Conditions: 511; www.tampabay.com; www.fl511.com

OUTDOORS

Snorkeling

Citrus County (G-7)

Snorkeling is an excellent way to observe manatees at close range. And there is no better place to see them than in the clear, spring-fed Crystal River. The river and the Crystal River National Wildlife Refuge provide a critical habitat for this endangered species.

Through joint conservation efforts, this area has the largest concentration of manatees in the world. Visitors can take guided swims to snorkel or scuba near the manatees or board boat cruises to observe them in the wild. Pack your own gear or arrangements can be made with local tour companies. Instructions are given on how to get close to a 13-foot, 3,000-pound manatee without frightening the shy herbivore.

*(800) 587-6667 or (352) 628-9305;
www.visitcitrus.com*

Manatee

Cocoa Beach (I-12)

Go horseback riding along the Canaveral National Seashore with the Kennedy Space Center in the background. Or explore a wooded trail along the banks of the Little Econ River under an impressive canopy of oak, sweet gum, and hickory trees. Rides vary in length from one hour to day trips that last up to 4 1/2 hours. Along these Florida horse trails, on the beach or inland, riders enjoy the beauty of the state, its wild flowers, memorable scenery, and glimpses of wildlife not available from the road.

Nature hike

*(877) 321-8474 or (321) 454-2022;
www.visitcocoabeach.com*

Everglades Backcountry (by land) (R-11)

Head toward Flamingo, located deep in Everglades National Park, where several of the park's longer hiking trails begin. Flamingo is at one end of the 99-mile Wilderness Waterway, a well-marked path through small islands, expanses of grasses, and saltwater estuaries. Hikers can spend a few hours on shorter trails, or pack gear for a backcountry overnight trip on trails ranging from two to 15 miles. Many visitors postpone leaving and stay at the campground.

(305) 242-7700; www.nps.gov/ever

Kayaking the Everglades

Everglades Backcountry (by water) (R-11)

Flamingo is also the stepping off point for kayaking the backcountry in Everglades National Park. Escorted day or overnight water tours travel through sun-dappled mangrove tunnels and across broad sawgrass prairies. On the water, visitors become one with nature as they explore irreplaceable ecosystems on any of the clearly marked water trails. Beginners may wish to take the two-mile Noble Hammock Trail; more experienced paddlers could spend two to six hours following the Hell's Bay Trail. Bird life is extraordinary here. Visitors may see endangered species such as the wood stork or manatee. At the very least, keep an eye out for crocodiles and alligators. This is the one spot in the world in which the two species coexist. Concessionaires outfit and deliver to and from trailheads. Kayaks and canoes are available for rental.

(305) 242-7700; www.nps.gov/ever

Key Largo (S-13)

John Pennekamp Coral Reef State Park, the first underwater sanctuary in the nation, protects part of the only living coral reef within the continental border of the United States. More than 60,000 acres of the park lie underwater. This is an ideal place for scuba divers and snorkelers, expert and novice alike. There are many different areas to dive, both depths and shallows, and all teem with colorful fish and coral. Concessionaires lead scuba and snorkeling classes and offer rental equipment. Popular underwater sites include the reconstructed wreck of a Spanish galleon, actual shipwrecks, sunken cannons that fascinate schools of parrot fish, and the famous Christ of the Deep statue, one of the most photographed underwater subjects in the world. (It's located in the adjacent Florida Keys National Marine Sanctuary.)

(305) 451-1202; www.pennekamppark.com

Suwannee River Canoe Trails (C-6)

Made famous in the song by Stephen Foster, the name Suwannee (which Foster shortened to "Swannee") comes from an ancient Native American word meaning "echo." The Suwannee flows through unspoiled river swamp with oaks, pines, palmettos, and tall cypress overhead. The surrounding area is home for a variety of wildlife on the ground and in the sky, including birds of prey such as redtailed hawk and osprey. With songbirds calling from the trees and long-legged great blue herons foraging in the shallow waters, the river is bucolic for most of its run from Georgia's Okefenokee Swamp to the Gulf of Mexico. However, there is a challenging strip called Big Shoals located above the town of White Springs. Paddlers can hear the roar of the rapids long before they are in sight. Big Shoals is the only Class III whitewater rapid in the state.

Osprey

*(850) 488-3701;
www.dep.state.fl.us/gwt/guide/regions/north/trails/
suwanne_lower.htm*

TRAVEL GUIDE | Florida

The sheer cliffs found in Black Rock Mountain State Park are hidden by the blue fog of early morning.

SCENERY

Okefenokee Swamp (O-10)

Cypress trees dripping with moss give the preserved wetlands of Okefenokee National Wildlife Refuge an air of mystery. Access the 650-square-mile refuge from US 1 at Waycross, US 441 at Fargo, or via SR 23 and Spur 121 at Folkston. One of the most primitive wilderness areas in the country, the refuge supports wildlife ranging from bears, bobcats, and alligators to marsh and wading birds, and a variety of unusual plant life. Visit the Interpretive Centers for films, live exhibits, and lectures, and explore the swamps on a guided boat tour.

Providence Canyon State Park (K-3)

Only seven miles west of Lumpkin on SR 39C, near the Alabama state line, massive gullies as deep as 150 feet help Providence Canyon State Park earn the nickname "Georgia's Little Grand Canyon." There are strata of canyon soil in pink, orange, red, even purple. With its kaleidoscope of colors and abundance of flowers including the rare plumleaf azalea, the site is a magnet for photographers and backpackers who hike the rim trail to get better views of the canyon.

● **Banks Lake National Wildlife Refuge** (N-8)
Two miles west of Lakeland along SR 122, Banks Lake provides a panorama of moss-draped cypress trees mirrored in the shallow still water of Georgia's largest pocosin or upland swamp.

● **Brasstown Bald** (B-6)
High Pointers rejoice at the view of the cloud forest and the Chattahoochee National Forest from the observation platform on Brasstown Bald, the highest point in Georgia, just south of Hiawassee off SR 180.

Brasstown Bald

● **Dungeness Ruins** (O-13)
Be among the 300 visitors allowed each day to visit Cumberland Island National Seashore via a 45-minute ferry ride from St. Marys. Walk through the haunting stone ruins of the Thomas Carnegie estate, which is slowly being taken over by the forest's overgrowth.

● **John's Mountain Overlook** (C-3)
Located on the Armuchee Ridges, this overlook off Pocket Road near Villanow offers outstanding views to Alabama and Tennessee. "Armuchee" is a Cherokee word meaing "land of flowers" — a description that is still accurate.

● **Marshes of Glynn Overlook Park** (N-12)
The coastal marshlands that inspired poet Sidney Lanier in 1870 to immortalize their mystery in his work still mesmerize visitors who now arrive by car via Gloucester St. from US 17.

● **Tybee Island Lighthouse** (K-14)
Climb 178 steps to the top of America's third-oldest working lighthouse and enjoy a spectacular view of Tybee Island framed by the Atlantic Ocean and the Intracoastal Waterway.

CITIES

✪ Atlanta (State Capital) (E-4)

Atlanta, the capital of Georgia, is often referred to as the capital of the New South. It is a major financial, industrial, and educational center. Architectural landmarks include the gold-domed state capitol building and Peachtree Street buildings like Peachtree Center and Woodruff Arts Center, home to opera, symphony, ballet, repertory, and the High Museum of Art. Regional history covering antebellum years to the present is the focus of the Atlanta History Center, and the Martin Luther King, Jr. National Historic Site is dedicated to nonviolent protest. The Jimmy Carter Library and Museum features a replica of the Oval Office. Tour CNN studios, shop, or be entertained at Underground Atlanta, then head next door to World of Coca-Cola. For great shopping and hot nightlife, check out the Buckhead neighborhood.

Modern metropolis of Atlanta

Atlanta Convention & Visitors Bureau: (404) 521-6600, (800) 285-2682; www.atlanta.net

Augusta (F-11)

A popular resort and vacation spot, Augusta is best known to golfers as the home of the Masters, the legendary tournament that marks the unofficial start of each new golfing season. Augusta National, where the Masters is played, is one of hundreds of golf courses in the area. Greats of the game are memorialized at Georgia Golf Hall of Fame and Botanical Gardens, a 17-acre site along the downtown Riverwalk with fountains, ponds, and formal flower beds. Nearby, the Morris Museum of Art is dedicated to Southern artists from the early 1800s to the present, and the National Science Center's Fort Discovery has nearly 300 hands-on activities exploring the wonders of the natural world. Augusta was founded in 1736 and boasts several historic districts. Information on walking tours is available at the Historic Cotton Exchange Welcome Center. The Augusta Canal National Heritage Area, one of the nation's oldest intact canal systems, is a prime spot for outdoor activities.

Augusta Golf and Gardens

Augusta Metropolitan Convention & Visitors Bureau: (706) 724-4067, (800) 726-0243; www.augustaga.org

The riverwalk in Columbus

Columbus (J-3)

Columbus, a busy riverfront city on the central part of the Chattahoochee River, is known as "the Center of the Sunbelt South." The downtown area of Georgia's third-largest city follows a grid system established during the colonial era. Columbus is the birthplace of the Coca-Cola formula, home of the Coca-Cola Space Science Center, and a top producer of denim fabric in the United States. Port Columbus Civil War Naval Museum houses hulls of the ironclad Civil War gunboats *Muscogee* and *Jackson*, rescued after 100 years on the bottom of the Chattahoochee. The National Infantry Museum at Fort Benning has a vast collection of military small arms. Visitors can tour five homes in the historic district, including Pemberton House, restored Victorian home of the inventor of Coca-Cola. Also visit the Columbus Museum and the Springer Opera House (the State Theatre of Georgia).

Columbus Convention & Visitors Bureau: (706) 322-1613, (800) 999-1613; www.visitcolumbusga.com

Savannah (K-13)

Founded in 1733 as a Crown colony, Savannah was designed with six public squares where townspeople could draw water from public wells. Though elaborate fountains have replaced the wells, people still gather in the 20-plus park-like settings now surrounded by landmark buildings. Georgia's oldest city retains its charm with mansions from the 18th and 19th centuries, cobblestone streets, impeccably kept gardens, and tree-shaded avenues. History reports that during Union General William Tecumseh Sherman's march to the sea, he was so taken with Savannah's beauty that he refused to burn it. Ships still glide past the Riverfront, where shops, restaurants, galleries, taverns, and museums are housed in restored cotton warehouses. City Market provides a plaza for boutiques, open-air concerts, more art galleries, and al fresco dining. Visitors usually encounter a festival in Savannah. The city hosts more than 200 each year.

Savannah Convention & Visitors Bureau: (877) 728-2662 or (912) 644-6401; www.savannahvisit.com

HERITAGE

Chickamauga and Chattanooga National Military Park (B-2)

Established in 1890, Chickamauga and Chattanooga National Military Park is the first, oldest, and, at 9,000 acres, the largest national military park. While the intrepid walk different areas of the battlefields, the park is so vast that most visitors opt for a driving tour. Both self-guided tours and guided auto-tours can be arranged at the visitors center. Located in the far northwestern part of Georgia, the park preserves the site of one of the most intense series of battles of the Civil War. More than 34,000 men lost their lives over the course of nearly three months in late 1863. The Union goal was to capture Chattanooga, a rail center considered to be the gateway to the Confederacy. In the spring of 1864, victorious Union General William Tecumseh Sherman established Chattanooga as the base for his march to Atlanta and the sea.

(706) 866-9241; www.nps.gov/chch

Historic District of Savannah (S-13)

Visit 18th- and 19th-century architectural masterpieces on a walking tour through the nation's largest National Historic Landmark District. Within a 2.5-square-mile area, 1,600-plus restored structures have been rated historically and architecturally significant. The Savannah Historic District is also important for its distinctive grid plan, which follows the original town plan designed in 1733 by Gen. James E. Oglethorpe, founder of the British colony of Georgia. Savannah maintains much of his plan based on divisions called wards, squares, and "trustee lots." Many of the original squares survive and are surrounded by fine examples of Georgian, Greek Revival, and Gothic styles. Notables include the Owens-Thomas House built in 1818 on Oglethorpe Square, the circa 1917 Beaux Arts-style Edmund Molyneux Mansion on Bull Street, and the 1853 Gothic Revival Greene House located on Madison Square.

(912) 944-0455; www.savannahvisit.com

Hofwyl-Broadfield Plantation (M-13)

Moss-draped live oaks line the drive to Hofwyl-Broadfield Plantation, now a Georgia state park. The trees are as old or older than the rice fields that once surrounded them. For more than 150 years, one family cultivated the marshes along the Altamaha River to grow rice and support a genteel, Low Country society way of life. William Brailsford started the rice plantation in the early 1800s. Despite great difficulty, the family managed to continue growing rice through the Civil War. The visitors center provides an overview of life at Hofwyl-Broadfield through a film and exhibits, including a model of the plantation in its prime. The center is a short walk from the estate's antebellum home, which is furnished with family heirlooms, 18th- and 19th-century furniture, and Cantonese china. There is also a nature trail that follows the edge of the marsh where rice once thrived.

(912) 264-7333, (800) 864-7275;
www.gastateparks.org/info/hofwyl/

Martin Luther King, Jr. National Historic Site (p. 42, C-10)

Established in 1980, the Martin Luther King, Jr. National Historic Site in Atlanta was created to protect the places where Dr. King was born, lived, worshipped, and is buried. A number of facilities are operated in tandem with the site including Ebenezer Baptist Church, where Dr. King worshipped as a young boy and later returned to as co-pastor, and The King Center, established in 1968 by his widow, Coretta Scott King. The King Center is dedicated to preserving Dr. King's legacy of nonviolent social change. It also includes exhibits on Dr. King, Mrs. King, and Mahatma Gandhi. Dr. King's birth home is part of the complex along with Fire Station #6, now a bookstore, and Peace Plaza. Visitors are invited to write their own thoughts at one of the testimony and response stations.

(404) 331-5190 or (404) 331-6922; www.nps.gov/malu

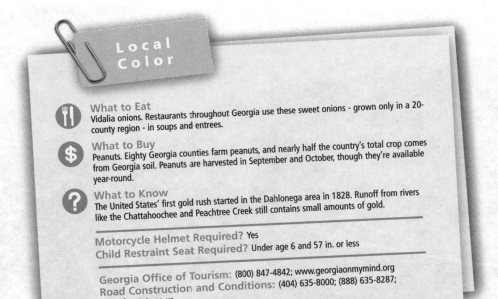

Local Color

🍴 **What to Eat**
Vidalia onions. Restaurants throughout Georgia use these sweet onions - grown only in a 20-county region - in soups and entrees.

💲 **What to Buy**
Peanuts. Eighty Georgia counties farm peanuts, and nearly half the country's total crop comes from Georgia soil. Peanuts are harvested in September and October, though they're available year-round.

❓ **What to Know**
The United States' first gold rush started in the Dahlonega area in 1828. Runoff from rivers like the Chattahoochee and Peachtree Creek still contains small amounts of gold.

Motorcycle Helmet Required? Yes
Child Restraint Seat Required? Under age 6 and 57 in. or less

Georgia Office of Tourism: (800) 847-4842; www.georgiaonmymind.org
Road Construction and Conditions: (404) 635-8000; (888) 635-8287; www.dot.state.ga.us

OUTDOORS

Altamaha River canoeing trail

Altamaha River (L-10)

Designated by the Nature Conservancy as one of the world's 75 last great places, the unspoiled Altamaha River is home to more than 120 rare and endangered species of animals and plants. Formed by the Oconee and Ocmulgee Rivers, it is crossed only seven times (six times by roads and twice by railroads) along its 137-mile route to the Atlantic. The Altamaha is the second-largest watershed on the eastern seaboard, totaling 1.2 million acres. It is one of Georgia's foremost canoeing trails. Canoeists, kayakers, and birdwatchers revel in the scenery along its route, which includes the only known example of old-growth, longleaf pine and black oak forest in the United States. Along the way watch for the gopher tortoise in the slow-moving water or flowering button bush, milk vine, or Georgia tickseed growing along the shores.

(912) 367-7731; www.baxley.org

Portaging

Black Rock Mountain State Park (B-7)

With an elevation of 3,640 feet, this is Georgia's highest state park. It boasts 1,502 acres of scenic land including Black Rock Mountain, which spans the Eastern Continental Divide. Named for the dark-colored sheer cliffs found within its boundaries, the park includes a summit visitor center, a 17-acre lake, and 11 miles of hiking trails. The trails pass fields of wildflowers, winding streams, and verdant forests. The Ada-Hi Falls Nature Trail is one quarter-mile long; the Tennessee Rock Trails is 2.2 miles long and follows the crest of the Eastern Continental Divide; and the James E. Edmonds Backcountry Trail is 7.2 miles long. All are well marked.

(706) 746-2141 or (800) 864-7275;
www.gastateparks.org/info/blackrock

Chattahoochee National Forest (B-5)

"The Chat" is an excellent example of the benefits of reclamation. Since this national forest was established in 1911, continuous efforts to reseed, replant, and reintroduce plants and wildlife have made it into Georgia's finest. At 749,689-some acres, it is also Georgia's largest and most popular attraction. There are 430 miles of trails designed to accommodate all levels of hikers, bikers, and equestrians; the 2,135-mile Appalachian Trail starts in the Chattahoochee. Within the forest's boundaries, trails wind past rushing rivers, graceful waterfalls, and meadows of wildflowers. Two trails near Bull Mountain and Jack Mountain are earmarked as shared trails for mountain biking and equestrian use. The forest has 10 wilderness areas and more than a thousand miles of trout streams.

Family-friendly Chattahoochee National Forest

(770) 297-3000; www.fs.fed.us/conf

Cliffs line the coast of the 'Big Island' (Hawai'i).

CITIES

⭐ Honolulu, O`ahu (State Capital) (N-4)

Crossroads of the Pacific and capital of a multi-island state, Honolulu is the port of entry for millions of visitors to Hawaii. While Waikīkī Beach with its towering resort hotels and restaurants is the undisputed center of action, plenty of other attractions await nearby. The Honolulu Zoo houses 1,230 mammals, birds and reptiles, while the Waikīkī Aquarium introduces visitors to more than 420 species of aquatic plants and animals. For an intimate look at tropical creatures, snorkeling remains very popular at Hanauma Bay Nature Reserve. Those who prefer freshwater thrills in a more structured setting can head to Hawaiian Waters Adventure Park where the slides, tube rides and waterfalls occupy 25 acres. 'Iolani Palace and the Bishop Museum are filled with the heirlooms of Hawaii's last ruling family. The USS *Arizona* Memorial provides sober reflection on the lives lost during the Pearl Harbor attack that brought the United States into World War II.

O`ahu Visitors Bureau: (877) 525-6248;
www.co.honolulu.hi.us/menu/visitors/

Hawai'i Convention Center

Līhu`e, Kaua`i (I-2)

The cultural and business center of Kaua'i, this small city is part sugar town, part shipping center, and — as the island's main port of entry at Nawiliwili Harbor — part tourist magnet. The Kaua'i Museum presents an excellent overview of the island's culture and history. Exhibits include seashell collections, Hawaiian quilts, and artifacts from Hawai'ian kings and queens. Nearby, you can visit the Grove Farm Homestead, a remarkably well-preserved early sugar plantation. Tours are by appointment only. Also of interest is the manor house at Kilohana Plantation, built in the English-Tudor style in 1935. Nawiliwili Bay mixes exceptional natural beauty with the more utilitarian necessities of the shipping industry. Kalapaki Beach is a fine spot for swimming and surfing.

Kaua`i Visitors Bureau: (808) 245-3971, (800) 262-1400;
www.kauaidiscovery.com

Hawai'ian children perform the traditional hula dance

Hilo, Hawai`i (M-10)

The main port of the "Big Island" (Hawai'i), Hilo is also the gateway to Hawai'i Volcanoes National Park and the many scenic and historic attractions on what is also called the Orchid Island. Hilo gardens and greenhouses (which welcome visitors) ship masses of orchids to the mainland. Lyman House Memorial Museum was the home of American missionaries in the 1800s; historical and geological exhibits are found here, as well as a display on the island's early inhabitants. Downtown, the Pacific Tsunami Museum chronicles the immense forces of earthquake-generated massive waves, some of which have hit Hilo directly. On Wednesdays and Saturdays, a downtown farmer's market features sarongs, T-shirts, and delicious fresh fruits and foods for sale. North of the city is 'Akaka Falls State Park, where the highest of several waterfalls drops 420 feet.

Rainbow Falls, Hilo

Hilo Downtown Improvement Association:
(808) 935-8850; www.downtownhilo.com

Lahaina, Maui (K-7)

A National Historic District and former royal capital, Lahaina also served as a whaling port and central location for missionaries. Many of the town's buildings reflect the 19th-century heritage. Stop for a guided tour of Baldwin House, a missionary doctor's 1830s home filled with period furniture and artifacts. The 100-year-old Pioneer Inn near Baldwin House still offers libations to thirsty customers. At the Old Lahaina Courthouse, markets and art shows are often conducted under the shade of an old banyan tree. The courthouse now serves as a visitor information center and houses an art gallery. Other attractions in town include many fine art galleries, boutiques, restaurants, shops, and Victorian-era inns. Visitors can ride the open-air coaches of the Lahaina-Kā'anapali & Pacific Railroad, also known as the "Sugar Cane Train," from Lahaina to the resorts of Kā'anapali.

LahainaTown Action Committee: (888) 310-1117
or (808) 667-9175; www.visitlahaina.com

SCENERY

Hawai`i Volcanoes National Park (Hawai`i) (M-9)

Entering the park, travel the 11-mile Crater Rim Drive to see steam vents and get a peek at the caldera at Kīlauea Overlook. Continue to the Jagger Museum to learn more about volcanoes and Hawaiian legends surrounding them before turning onto the 20-mile Chain of Craters Road. There are a number of pullouts on the 3,700-foot descent, ending at Holei Sea Arch. Lava has actually flowed over the road, so visitors park their cars and walk over the hardened lava and may be able to view the active flow as it pours, hissing, into the ocean. On the return out of the park, it's worth it to stop at the Thurston Lava Tube, a cavelike structure formed from lava.

Pali Lookout, O'ahu

The Road to Hāna (Maui) (K-8)

It takes three hours to make the 53-mile trip from Kahului airport to Hāna, as the road twists around 600 curves and over 54 bridges on the famed rugged, yet scenic drive. The road passes pineapple and taro fields (the vegetable used to make poi), waterfalls, and verdant rainforest vegetation. At the halfway point in Keanae, the main site is Keanae Arboretum, with a spot to swim and walk through the rainforest.

● `Iao Valley State Park (Maui) (K-7)
Take the 'Iao Valley Road from Wailuku along the 'Iao Stream, past tropical gardens and the curves of the black gorge to lush 'Iao ("supreme light" in Hawai'ian) Valley State Park.

● Laupāhoehoe Point Park (Hawai`i) (L-10)
Drive down to this beautiful small park off Hwy. 19, where a tsunami (massive harbor wave) came ashore in the late 1940s. Waves still crash on the rocks near a memorial to the victims of the tsunami.

● Nu`uanu Pali (O`ahu) (M-5)
Drive or hike up 1,000 feet to this windy point overlooking O'ahu's windward coast. King Kamehameha I drove warriors over these cliffs in a 1795 battle.

● Pepe`ekeo Scenic Drive (Hawai`i) (M-10)
Just north of Hilo, this four-mile drive winds along the ocean, past the Hawaii Tropical Botanical Garden as well as coves and waterfalls.

● Spouting Horn (Kaua`i) (I-2)
Off Lawa'i Road, the ocean rushes into a lava tube, creating a hissing sound as the water spurts up to 50 feet in the air. Best seen at sunrise and sunset.

Spouting Horn, Kaua'i

OUTDOORS

Haleakalā Volcano (Maui) (K-8)

Intrepid travelers awaken well before dawn for a sleepy trip by van up to the 10,023-foot summit of Haleakalā to watch the sun rise. The volcano's name actually means "house of the sun" in Hawaiian. Cyclists can then tour Haleakalā National Park and see the crater of this extinct volcano before heading downhill. The Crater Road twists through 28 switchbacks on the exhilarating 38-mile ride down by mountain bike. Various tour operators provide these sunrise trips, which include breakfast.

(800) 525-6284; www.visitmaui.com

Crater of Haleakala Volcano

Kilauea Point (Kaua`i) (I-2)

See a red-footed booby or watch for Hawaii's state bird, the nene, at the Kilauea Point National Wildlife Refuge. On this windy northernmost spot on Kaua`i, visitors can watch for humpback whales and dolphins or spot Hawaiian monk seals. The main attraction is the birds, however. Odd-looking giant frigate birds, albatross, brown boobies, and other seabirds flock here to nest in the cliffs. Another favored spot is the national historic landmark Kilauea Lighthouse, built in 1913.

(808) 828-1413;
pacificislands.fws.gov/wnwr/kkilaueanwr.html

Surfing, O'ahu

Mauna Kea (Hawai`i) (L-9)

Observatories on Mauna Kea

Touch the sky from atop Mauna Kea volcano. Visitors on this adventure trip start at sea level, riding in a van up to a base camp for dinner. The climb continues up the volcano to watch the sun set and the stars pop out of the sky. In the thin air thousands of feet above sea level, it's easy to see major constellations, planets, and other astronomical sights. Clouds float by below, and other islands can be seen in the distance. Eleven countries maintain giant telescopes on Mauna Kea. Tour groups use their own high-powered scopes, as visitors are not permitted in the observatories.

(808) 961-5797 or (800) 648-2441;
www.bigisland.org

Waikīkī Beach, Honolulu

Waikīkī (O`ahu) (H-9)

Of course, there are the monster-sized winter waves that make the North Shore beaches famous for extreme surfing. But the average Joe or Josephina can hop on a board on less-terrifying waves and learn to surf at Waikīkī Beach. Lifeguards provide free instruction at Haleiwa Surf Center, but most visitors may find it easiest to work with one of Waikīkī's famed "beach boys" at Canoes and tackle the gentle, rolling surf here.

(877) 525-6248; www.visit-oahu.com

HERITAGE

Preparation of poi, a traditional Hawai'ian food

Kalaupapa Hansen's Disease Settlement (Moloka`i) (J-6)

Mules carry visitors down a steep path at the base of the cliffs to this site. Established in 1866 as a place of forced isolation for those affected with Hansen's disease (leprosy), it remained so until 1969. There is still a Hansen's disease community here, though banishment is no longer practiced. Father Damien (Joseph de Veuster), a Belgian priest, served the people of Kalaupapa, contracting leprosy in 1885 and dying in 1889 after working with the residents for 16 years. Tours provide an overview of the colony's history and that of leprosy in the Hawai'ian Islands. Visitors may only visit the site on a commercial tour.

(808) 567-6802; www.nps.gov/kala

USS Arizona *Memorial, Pearl Harbor*

Pearl Harbor (O`ahu) (M-4)

On December 7, 1941, the Japanese launched a successful surprise air attack on the naval base at Pearl Harbor, killing 2,400 people and sinking or damaging 21 ships. Today, visitors take a Navy boat to the Arizona Memorial, which is situated above the sunken battleship USS *Arizona*, from which oil still leaks into the surrounding water drop by drop. Also at Pearl Harbor, visitors can climb aboard the battleship USS *Missouri* and the USS *Bowfin* submarine.

(808) 422-0561; www.nps.gov/usar

Place of Refuge (Hawai`i) (L-8)

Called Pu'uohonua o Hōnaunau in Hawaiian, this sacred spot was a place where those who broke a law (kapu) against the gods could be safe from the death penalty. The person had to paddle a canoe or swim to the Place of Refuge, usually hotly pursued by warriors. On arrival, a priest would absolve the law-breaker of their crime. Now a national park with water lapping three sides, the Place of Refuge has a reconstructed temple and thatched structures as well as the gravesites of royalty. A visitor center provides brochures on a self-guided trail, and artisans offer demonstrations of traditional Hawaiian arts and crafts such as canoe building.

Place of Refuge

(808) 328-2326 or (808) 328-2288; www.nps.gov/puho

Local Color

🍴 **What to Eat**
Manapua, a steamed bread bun stuffed with Chinese barbequed pork, can be found throughout the island at places like Libby's Manapua Shop in Honolulu.

💲 **What to Buy**
Niihau shell lei. The tiniest and most prized of Hawaiian shells, they wash up on the windward shore of Niihau, whence they're collected and strung. A large selection is at Hawaiian Trading Post in Lawai.

❓ **What to Know**
Hawaii's Big Island is the only place where you can visit a white, black, or green sand beach, all on one island.

Motorcycle Helmet Required? Under age 18, reflectorization required
Child Restraint Seat Required? Under age 8

Hawai'i Visitors & Convention Bureau: (800) 464-2924; www.gohawaii.com
Road Construction and Conditions: (808) 536-6566 (construction);
www.hawaii.gov/dot/publicaffairs/roadwork/ (construction)

Rafting is a favorite activity on the Salmon River.

CITIES

✪ Boise *(State Capital) (K-2)*

The capital of Idaho and its largest city, Boise lies in the shadow of the western edge of the Rocky Mountains. This valley city was once a respite along the Oregon Trail. Today, the 150 acres in Ann Morrison Park along with the pools and flowers of Platt Gardens are among the city's most beautiful and relaxing spots. In the Corinthian-style capitol building are displays on agriculture, forestry, and mining products and processes. St. Michael's Episcopal Cathedral has rare Tiffany glass windows. A weaponry museum is located inside the Old Idaho Penitentiary, with botanical gardens adjacent. Boise offers fishing enthusiasts plenty of good sport, and the city is also a gateway to Boise National Forest.

Capitol building

Boise Convention & Visitors Bureau: (800) 635-5240, (208) 344-7777; www.boise.org

Coeur d'Alene *(D-2)*

Originally a mining and timber town, Coeur d'Alene has become an internationally known resort destination on one of Idaho's most beautiful lakes. A long floating boardwalk surrounds the Coeur d'Alene Resort's marina, and excursion boats leave city docks daily for short trips along the north section of the 25-mile lake. Roads to the north and east of here lead to magnificent mountain scenery in the Coeur d'Alene National Forest. A short drive east of town is Cataldo Mission, built 1848-53 by Father Ravalli and by converted Coeur d'Alene Indians. It was restored in the 1980s as a historic monument.

Coeur d'Alene Visitor's Bureau: (877) 782-9232 or (208) 664-3194; www.coeurdalene.org

Cataldo Mission

Idaho Falls *(K-7)*

Green space is plentiful in Idaho Falls, home to 39 parks and the 14-mile Snake River Greenbelt. From River Parkway, you can see the broad, swift falls on the Snake River for which the city is named. This eastern Idaho town is considered the gateway to outdoor adventure amid natural grandeur, as it lies just west of the Teton Range, with Yellowstone and Grand Teton national parks a few hours' drive away. While in Idaho Falls, don't miss exhibits on local natural history at the Museum of Idaho. Visitors also enjoy shopping, restaurants, and the charm of Historic Downtown.

Idaho Falls skyline

Idaho Falls Convention & Visitors Bureau: (866) 365-6943; www.visitidahofalls.com

Lewiston *(F-1)*

On their journey westward, the Lewis and Clark Expedition passed through the site this little river town, set at the confluence of the Snake and Clearwater rivers. Consequently, Lewiston and its twin city Clarkston (just a bridge over the Snake River away) were named in honor of the renowned explorer duo. In the heart of the Lewis-Clark Valley, Lewiston attracts vacationers to the wonders of Hells Canyon, to the vast national forests and wilderness areas spreading through Lewis and Clark country, and to the Nez Percé Indian Reservation, its neighbor to the east. A drive up the famous Spiral Highway on Lewiston Hill north of town reveals breathtaking views of the region. For the adventurer, jet-boat excursions to Hells Canyon or overnight rafting and camping trips down the Snake River are a must.

Lewiston Chamber of Commerce: (208) 743-3531, (800) 473-3543; www.lewistonchamber.org

Twin Falls *(M-4)*

Here, visitors will discover geologic wonders on a grand scale. Located on the edge of the spectacular Snake River Canyon, Twin Falls was carved out of the rugged high desert. From walkways on the Perrine Bridge, which towers 486 feet over the Snake River Gorge, take in a dramatic view of the canyon. Twin Falls also lies at the heart of the Great Rift, a 635-square-mile geological phenomenon. The area's fissures, spatter cones, and lava tubes have been created by 60 different lava flows and more than 25 volcanic eruptions. East of the city, the "Niagara of the West," Shoshone Falls, plunges 212 feet displaying a wild, natural beauty.

Twin Falls Area Chamber of Commerce: (208) 733-3974, (866) 894-6325; www.twinfallschamber.com

SCENERY

Sawtooth National Recreation Area *(J-4)*

This 756,000-acre area contains more than 300 alpine lakes and the headwaters for five major Idaho rivers, including the Salmon. It's Rocky Mountain scenery at its best. Highlights along the Sawtooth Scenic Byway (Highway 75) include the Galena Summit and Redfish Lake. Pick up a free audio tape tour at a ranger station.

Sawtooth National Recreation Area

Teton Scenic Byway *(K-8)*

This route, beginning in eastern Idaho's Swan Valley, heads north on Highway 31 through the lush, rolling farmland of the famous Idaho potatoes to the sweeping Teton Valley rangelands. To the east, the snowy peaks of the Teton Range rise to 13,700 feet.

- ### Bruneau Dunes State Park & Observatory *(L-3)*
  These sand dunes peak at 470 feet, making them among the tallest dunes in North America. Look for lizard and rabbit tracks, or peer through a telescope at the night sky.

- ### Hells Canyon Scenic Byway *(H-2)*
  This narrow 22-mile road passes beneath towering cliffs of black and green basalt that form the canyon walls dividing Idaho and Oregon.

Priest Lake

- ### Priest Lake *(B-2)*
  The 23,000-acre lake is an uncrowded, unspoiled wilderness area nestled beneath the majestic Selkirk Mountains in Idaho's northern region.

- ### Snake River Birds of Prey National Conservation Area *(L-2)*
  Head 20 miles south of Boise along the Snake River to see North America's densest concentration of nesting birds of prey.

  Snake River

- ### Thousand Springs Scenic Byway *(L-4)*
  Thousands of springs, believed to be the reappearance of the Lost River that sinks into the lava fields near Arco, dapple the side of the Snake River Canyon off US 30.

OUTDOORS

Climbing at City of Rocks

City of Rocks National Reserve (N-5)

City of Rocks is considered one of the best technical rock-climbing areas in the nation, especially for face climbing. The reserve covers 14,100 acres of land renowned for its scenic, geologic, and historic significance. Magnificent granite columns and spires, some reaching 60 stories tall, are among the oldest rocks in North America, dating back 2.5 billion years. During the days of westward expansion, these spires served as a major landmark along the California Trail. The 100- to 300-foot spires provide most of the climbing opportunities, and, to date, about 700 routes have been described here. Pick up a climbing guide at the Reserve headquarters.

(208) 824-5519; www.nps.gov/ciro

Hells Canyon National Recreation Area (H-2)

Between Oregon's Wallowa Mountains and Idaho's Seven Devils Mountains, the Snake River cuts the deepest gorge in North America - several thousand feet deeper than the Grand Canyon. In Hells Canyon more than 900 miles of trails cross legendarily rough terrain, beckoning rugged hikers, backpackers, mountain bikers, and horseback riders. Watch for elk and mule deer as well as old mining buildings and American Indian petroglyphs. On the Snake River, expect excellent rafting with massive Class III & IV rapids. The fishing on the river is also outstanding. Trout, bass, and sturgeon are the three big catches. Jet boats run sightseeing cruises from Lewiston at the northern end and from Hells Canyon dam at the southern end.

(208) 628-3916; www.fs.fed.us/hellscanyon

Route of the Hiawatha Trail (D-3)

This old railroad track, now converted into a mountain biking trail, has been called one of the most scenic stretches of railroad in the country. Starting near the Lookout Pass Ski Area, bikers pass through 10 cavernous train tunnels and across towering train trestles as high as 230 feet. The route crosses the Bitterroot Range, leading riders past bubbling mountain creeks with deer, elk, moose, and spectacular mountain views. From the starting point it's all downhill, and a shuttle service will return you to the top. Bike rentals with helmets and flashlights are available. Open late May - early October.

(208) 744-1301; www.skilookout.com/hiaw

Biking across a trestle

Stanley Basin (J-4)

Idaho is a snowmobiler's playland with 7,000+ miles of groomed snowmobile trails, more than any other western state. The trails traverse some of the most spectacular scenery in North America, but perhaps the most magnificent views are in the Sawtooth Mountains surrounding the Stanley Basin. Massive amounts of snow, groomed trails (165 miles of them), and uncrowded off-trail riding draw snowmobilers each year. Miles of ungroomed trails lead enthusiasts off the main route to remote lakes and vast meadows. A favorite scenic route is the Stanley to Redfish Lake loop at the base of the Sawtooth Mountains.

(208) 737-3200; www.fs.fed.us/r4/sawtooth

HERITAGE

US Highway 12

Lewis and Clark Historic Trail (F-2)

Retrace the rugged expedition route Lewis and Clark and the Corps of Discovery traveled 200 years ago. The trail segment that cuts through the Orofino area represents one of the most difficult and demanding legs of their voyage to the Pacific Ocean — an 86-mile trek across the Bitterroot Range in what is now the Clearwater National Forest. U.S. Highway 12 follows part of the explorers' route along the Lochsa River and winds through a narrow canyon between forest and river. The Lolo Trail, an ancient travel route of the Nez Percé Indians, is another path Lewis and Clark followed westward. Several outfitters lead guided trips along the Lolo Trail across the Clearwater National Forest.

(402) 661-1804; www.nps.gov/lecl/

Oregon National Historic Trail Site (L-3)

When pioneers in covered wagons reached southern Idaho's Three Island ford, they faced a tough decision: Risk the dangerous crossing of the Snake River or endure the dry, rocky route along the south bank of the river. About half of the emigrants took the risk, but not all survived the swift, swirling river. An interpretive center at the Three Island Crossing State Park in Glenns Ferry, one of the Oregon Trail's most famous spots, tells the story. See replica wagons or dip a toe into the river crossing area. On the south side  *Replica wagon* of the Snake you can see the trail's wagon ruts and view the Three Islands from an overlook. Each year in August the park re-enacts the crossing.

(801) 741-1012; www.nps.gov/oreg/

The Silver Valley (D-3)

This northern Idaho valley, which includes the towns of Wallace and Kellogg, bills itself as the Silver Capital of the World. From the region's early mining days until 2000, the valley turned out more silver than any other mining area in the world. In Kellogg, visitors can dig into mining history at the Staff House *Crystal Gold Mine* Museum, once part of the Bunker Hill Mine. Take an underground tour of the Crystal Gold Mine to learn how miners tested the quartz veins and see some of the gold and wire silver they discovered. Eleven miles east in Wallace, an entire town on the National Register of Historic Places, you can visit the railroad and mining museums and take the Sierra Silver Mine tour.

Kellogg: (208) 784-0821;
www.historicsilvervalleychamberofcommerce.com
Wallace: (208) 753-7151, (800) 434-4204;
www.wallaceidahochamber.com

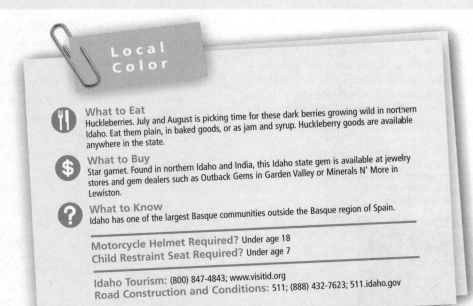

Local Color

What to Eat
Huckleberries. July and August is picking time for these dark berries growing wild in northern Idaho. Eat them plain, in baked goods, or as jam and syrup. Huckleberry goods are available anywhere in the state.

What to Buy
Star garnet. Found in northern Idaho and India, this Idaho state gem is available at jewelry stores and gem dealers such as Outback Gems in Garden Valley or Minerals N' More in Lewiston.

What to Know
Idaho has one of the largest Basque communities outside the Basque region of Spain.

Motorcycle Helmet Required? Under age 18
Child Restraint Seat Required? Under age 7

Idaho Tourism: (800) 847-4843; www.visitid.org
Road Construction and Conditions: 511; (888) 432-7623; 511.idaho.gov

A trolley ride in Galena takes passengers all around town.

CITIES

Chicago (C-13)

Chicago's Buckingham Fountain

After the Great Chicago Fire of 1871 left the city in ruins, architect Daniel Burnham devised Chicago's forward-thinking design, with a 29-mile-long lakefront park system, a handy numerical grid system for streets, and wide residential boulevards. Today the largest city in the Midwest is a sprawling mixture of innovative architecture, fine dining, outstanding accommodations, lively nightclubs and theaters, and world-class museums. The beautiful lakefront setting is what visitors notice first, but much of the city's character resides in its constantly evolving neighborhoods, like Chinatown, Andersonville with its Swedish heritage, the German influence in Lincoln Square, and the Mexican community of Pilsen. Famed for its modern sculpture by Picasso, Calder, Chagall, and Miro in monumental downtown plazas, Chicago is also distinguished by its symphony, opera, and professional sports teams, including the Bulls, Bears, Cubs, White Sox, and Blackhawks.

Chicago Convention & Tourism Bureau: (312) 567-8500 or (877) 244-2246; www.choosechicago.com
Chicago Office of Tourism: (312) 744-2400; www.ci.chi.il.us/tourism

Peoria (G-8)

Named for the Illini Indians who occupied the area, Peoria is one of the oldest settlements in the state. Glen Oak Park has a botanical garden, a zoo, a fishing lagoon, and amphitheater concerts in summer. Wildlife Prairie State Park features wild animals native to Illinois in large natural habitats accessible by nature trails, an orphan animal nursery, and pioneer buildings. Flanagan House (1837) is the oldest in the city; Pettengill-Morron House (1868) has mid-Victorian furnishings. See the world's largest accurately scaled model of the solar system at Lakeview Museum of Arts and Sciences, or vintage cars and engines at Wheels O'Time Museum. Abraham Lincoln practiced law at Metamora Courthouse in Metamora, Ill., about 15 miles northeast of Peoria. The Peoria RiverFront is home to plenty of restaurants and provides the dock for riverboat cruises and a riverboat casino.

Peoria Area Convention & Visitors Bureau:
(309) 676-0303, (800) 747-0302; www.peoria.org

Rockford (A-9)

A city based in manufacturing and distribution, Rockford grew from a stagecoach crossing on the Rock River. Many of the city's cultural attractions are grouped together in Riverfront Museum Park: the Burpee Museum of Natural History has exhibits of life-sized Native American dwellings and dinosaurs castings; Rockford Art Museum houses a collection of American paintings of the last 200 years; and the exhibits at the Discovery Center Museum include the outdoors WaterWorks area among its dozens of hands-on activities that encourage interest in the arts and sciences. Horticultural interests are represented at three major gardening attractions: Klehm Arboretum and Botanic Garden, the Sinnissippi Gardens, Greenhouse, and Lagoon, and the Anderson Japanese Gardens. An exceptional example of Victorian architectural exotica, the Tinker Swiss Cottage is filled with 19th-century treasures collected from around the

Anderson Japanese Gardens

world. Warm weather fun may be had at Magic Waters Waterpark with its 43 acres of slides, tubes, pools, and river rides.

Rockford Area Convention & Visitors Bureau:
(800) 521-0849 or (815) 963-8111; www.gorockford.com

⭐ Springfield (State Capital) (J-8)

Illinois' capital is a treasure trove of sites honoring Abraham Lincoln. Visit the only home Lincoln ever owned, which is now a national historic site; the Old State Capitol, where he delivered his "House Divided" speech; and Lincoln's Tomb, where he and his family are buried. The Abraham Lincoln Presidential Library and Museum is dedicated to telling his life story. In two buildings, it houses the world's largest collection of Lincoln-related documents and artifacts. To explore a more recent place and time, stop by the Dana-Thomas House, designed by Frank Lloyd Wright. Then visit the state capitol building to see today's government in action. Lucky enough to be in Springfield during August? Check out the Illinois State Fair.

Springfield Convention & Visitors Bureau:
(217) 789-2360; (800) 545-7300;
www.visit-springfieldillinois.com

Lincoln family home

OUTDOORS

Giant City State Park (R-9)

Located near Carbondale and named for its towering sandstone formations (some as tall as 80 feet), Giant City offers 18 miles of trails for hiking and horseback riding (the park stable rents horses for trail rides except in winter). There are ponds for fishing, and two areas of the park are open to rock climbers and rappellers with their own equipment. Hikers enjoy many trails including the Post Oak (designed to accommodate disabled visitors), Devil's Standtable, Trillium, and Arrowwood trails. The 12-mile Red Cedar Hiking Trail is a challenge to even dedicated backpackers. The Giant City Nature Trail is also known as the "Giant City Street," as it comprises gangways towering or giant-sized slabs of sandstone formed millions of years ago.

(618) 457-4836;
www.dnr.state.il.us/lands/landmgt/parks/r5/gc.htm

Giant City State Park

Illinois and Michigan (I&M) Canal National Heritage Corridor (E-11)

The I&M Canal State Trail follows the historic route of the I&M Canal, the final link in an all-water route between the East Coast and the Gulf of Mexico. Built between 1836 and 1848, it helped Illinois gain in prosperity and population. To gain perspective on its impact, hike the 62-mile trail that follows it from Rockdale to Peru. There is a 15-mile designated canoe trail between Channahon and Morris and a five-mile canoe trail between Utica and Peru. The I&M Commission office in Lockport has maps of driving tours as well. Due to the fragility of the trail and canal embankment, motorized vehicles and equestrian use are prohibited. From the trail there are connections to many of the natural and historic sites along the route.

(815) 727-2323; www.nps.gov/ilmi

Illinois Beach State Park (A-13)

Located in Zion, the sand dunes of Illinois Beach are unique to this 4,160-acre recreation area that includes six-and-a-half miles of both sandy and gravelly beaches. This park incorporates the only remaining beach ridge shoreline left in the state. Glacial advances and retreats and the ever-present wind from across Lake Michigan created its dunes, swales, and marshes. While the shoreline is intriguing, water sports lure most visitors. Enthusiasts can swim or bring their own personal watercraft for unparalleled runs on the lake swells. For a longer stay, pitch a tent at the park's campground; it is the only campground on the Lake Michigan shoreline between Chicago and Wisconsin.

(847) 662-4811;
www.dnr.state.il.us/lands/landmgt/parks/r2/
ilbeach.htm

Kankakee River State Park (F-13)

The Kankakee River runs through the 4,000-acre Kankakee River State Park near Bourbonnais and provides ample

Kankakee River State Park

opportunities for fishing, boating, and canoeing. Naturally channeled, the Kankakee is listed on the Federal Clean Streams Register and anchors the park's recreational activities. Kankakee River State Park also includes the Rock Creek Canyon area featuring a waterfall and limestone caves. The park offers 10 miles of bike trails, 15 miles of equestrian trails, hiking trails, an archery range, and 250 campsites. The most popular river trip is a 12-mile journey through sweeping river bends from Kankakee to the state park. Average paddling time: three to five hours.

(815) 933-1383;
www.dnr.state.il.us/lands/landmgt/parks/r2/
kankakee.htm

Kickapoo State Recreation Area (I-13)

The Middle Fork of the Vermilion River, a federal and state designated Scenic River, runs through this park near Danville. Kickapoo was the first state park to be built on strip-mined land. It has taken more than 50 years for the trees and vegetation to reclaim the sub-soil and for the stagnant mine ponds to clear. With the river, several lakes, and 22 deep ponds, Kickapoo is popular with water devotees. There are concession-aires for canoes, kayaks, paddleboats, and river tubes. Scuba divers with their own equipment are welcome. The dry acres of the park feature hiking trails, horseback riding, and mountain biking. The 2,843-acre park has plenty of hills left from its mining days. The trails are rated easy to very technical. If a challenging ride sounds intriguing, try the 11.5-mile run through wooded hills and reclaimed gorges.

(217) 442-4915; www.dnr.state.il.us/lands/
landmgt/parks/r3/kickapoo.htm

HERITAGE

Lincoln's New Salem home

Lincoln's New Salem State Historic Site (J-7)

Just south of Petersburg, this log cabin village has been painstakingly reconstructed to represent the 1830s, when Abraham Lincoln lived there for six years as a young adult. During that time he clerked in a store, split rails, acted as postmaster, failed in a business venture, worked as a deputy surveyor, and enlisted to serve in the Black Hawk War. He also ran for a seat in the Illinois General Assembly in 1832 and lost. He won the seat two years later. There are 23 buildings in this natural, unspoiled setting, and costumed interpreters bring the village to life. Set on 700 acres, New Salem includes several walking trails and two restaurants.

(217) 632-4000; www.lincolnsnewsalem.com

Tour of Bronzeville (p.47, E-13)

In a city of neighborhoods, Bronzeville represents both an area and an era in Chicago. This tour provides an opportunity to explore a historic district that is still rich in African-American heritage and to step into a time when Bronzeville was the center of Chicago's African-American culture. Tour the neighborhood of the restored and renovated homes representative of the lifestyle of the residents in the early 1940s. Stops include the incomparable DuSable Museum of African American History, with its retrospective on the evolution of black culture in the United States and visiting exhibits, and the Little Black Pearl Workshop, which offers an intriguing look at the role of art in the black community. The tour also visits Art Park, part of the CYC/Elliott Donnelley Youth Center with its arts initiative for African-American youth. Neighborhood Tours depart from the Chicago Cultural Center, 77 E. Randolph St. Refreshments are included on the tour.

(312) 742-1190; www.chgocitytours.com

Cahokia Mounds State Historic Site (p.69, E-8)

Near Collinsville are the remains of an ancient city founded by a Mississippian culture that flourished between A.D. 700 and 1400 and which then vanished. At 100 feet high, Monk's Mound is the largest prehistoric earthen mound in the New World. It covers 14

Cahokia Mounds

acres. Atop this mound would have been a massive building, perhaps another 50 feet in height. The engineering skills and the buildings that survived this civilization intrigue researchers and visitors today. This culture, based on an agricultural, chiefdom society, thrived and included an estimated 20,000 residents. It is listed by the United Nations Education, Scientific and Cultural Organization (UNESCO) as a World Heritage Site. An interpretive center provides an overview of the mounds and their builders.

(618) 346-5160: www.cahokiamounds.com

SCENERY

Shawnee National Forest (R-11)

Near Harrisburg, the picturesque Ozark and Shawnee Hills meet miles of rolling farmland in the Shawnee National Forest. Situated between the Mississippi and Ohio rivers and encompassing most of far-southern Illinois, the 278,000-acre national forest features five distinct ecosystems: prairie wetlands, hardwood forests, lakes, rivers, and small canyons. The impressive sandstone rock formation is in the northeastern section of the forest and is known as the "Garden of the Gods."

Starved Rock State Park (E-9)

Waterfalls, river bluffs, and canyons carved by the force of glaciers (and viewable now from six overlooks) vie for attention at Starved Rock State Park. The stream-fed canyons are particularly intriguing as each transforms into a waterfall after a rain. One of the most popular stops is a tree-covered 125-foot butte right outside the Starved Rock State Park Lodge. This is the butte of the Native American legend of retribution that gave the area its name.

● **Cache River State Natural Area** (S-9)
In Belknap, just south of Vienna off US 45, Sunflower Lane leads toward the recreational area where massive bald cypress trees have lived for more than 1,000 years.

● **Ferne Clyffe State Park** (R-9)
One mile south of Goreville on SR 37, the entrance road to the park heads toward Hawks' Cave, where a 150-foot long shelter bluff faces other impressive, fern-covered rock formations.

● **Giant City State Park** (R-9)
From any side of the 50-foot viewing platform on the 85-foot observation tower in the park, the Shawnee National Forest yawns across the landscape to meet the horizon.

● **McCune Sand Prairie** (E-7)
Five and one-half miles north of Mineral on Gold Township Road AA, 200 acres of blown sand produce fields of prickly pear cactus, native grasses, and wild flowers.

● **Mississippi Palisades State Park** (B-6)
At the confluence of the Mississippi and Apple rivers two miles north of Savanna on Route 84, erosion has carved unusual rock formations in the steep, soaring cliffs including Twin Sisters, Indian Head, and Sentinel.

● **Sears Tower** (p. 47, E-12)
From the Skydeck, 1,353 feet above the corner of Wacker and Adams, the view of Chicago's fabled architecture is rivaled by what lies beyond at the lakefront to Indiana, and on clear days, even Michigan and Wisconsin.

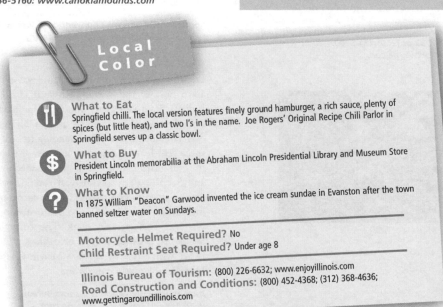

Local Color

🍴 **What to Eat**
Springfield chilli. The local version features finely ground hamburger, a rich sauce, plenty of spices (but little heat), and two l's in the name. Joe Rogers' Original Recipe Chili Parlor in Springfield serves up a classic bowl.

$ **What to Buy**
President Lincoln memorabilia at the Abraham Lincoln Presidential Library and Museum Store in Springfield.

❓ **What to Know**
In 1875 William "Deacon" Garwood invented the ice cream sundae in Evanston after the town banned seltzer water on Sundays.

Motorcycle Helmet Required? No
Child Restraint Seat Required? Under age 8

Illinois Bureau of Tourism: (800) 226-6632; www.enjoyillinois.com
Road Construction and Conditions: (800) 452-4368; (312) 368-4636;
www.gettingaroundillinois.com

The Indiana Convention Center and RCA Dome are located in Indianapolis.

CITIES

Evansville (S-3)

In the southwest corner of the state, Evansville was founded in 1847 and is Indiana's third-largest city. In prehistoric times, it was the center of a large settlement of Middle Mississippian peoples, and Angel Mounds State Historic Site reflects that history in the well-preserved site. Historic homes here include the French Second Empire-style Reitz Home Museum and the Georgian-style Willard Carpenter home. Downtown, visitors can stroll along the Ohio riverfront on a brick pathway or try casino gaming aboard the side-wheel Spirit of Evansville riverboat. Also downtown, the 100-year-old Evansville Museum of Arts, History, and Science features a planetarium, a permanent art collection and changing exhibits.

Evansville Convention & Visitors Bureau: (800) 433-3025 or (812) 421-2200; www.evansvillecvb.org

Fort Wayne (D-13)

Settled by people since prehistoric times, Fort Wayne derived its name from General "Mad" Anthony Wayne, who came to wrest it from the Northwest Indian Confederation in 1794. Three rivers converge here. Each year more than 500,000 people visit the 42-acre Children's Zoo, which features an Indonesian Rainforest, Australian Adventure area, and a chance to ride in a jeep through an African animal exhibit. The Fort Wayne Museum of Art's 1,300-piece collection emphasizes 19th- and 20th-century artwork and has a hands-on gallery for kids. Gardeners and plant lovers can stroll through three gardens at the Foellinger-Freimann Botanical Conservatory — the Sonoran Desert House, the Showcase Garden, and the Tropical Garden. History buffs will want to check out the Lincoln Museum, with 11 exhibit galleries and hundreds of artifacts from Lincoln's time.

Fort Wayne/Allen County Convention & Visitors Bureau: (800) 767-7752 or (260) 424-3700; www.visitfortwayne.com

Children's Museum of Indianapolis

✪ Indianapolis (State Capital) (J-9)

Founded in 1821, centrally located Indianapolis became the state capital in 1825. The Indianapolis 500 race has been drawing fans to the Indianapolis Motor Speedway since 1911. The city hosts a number of other major sports venues: Conseco Fieldhouse, home of the Indiana Pacers; RCA Dome, home of the Indianapolis Colts; the Major Taylor Velodrome; and the Indiana University Natatorium, where Olympic swimming and diving trials are held. The Children's Museum of Indianapolis, the world's largest children's museum, boasts a life-size *T. rex* model, two-story water clock, planetarium, working carousel (adults can ride, too), and toddler room with water play area, among other activities. The Eiteljorg Museum of American Indians and Western Art, the Indiana State Museum with natural history exhibits, and Circle Centre mall keep downtown visitors entertained.

Indianapolis Convention & Visitors Association: (800) 323-4639; www.indy.org

South Bend (A-8)

On the southern bend of the St. Joseph River, South Bend was established in 1835 and grew into a manufacturing city with businesses making wagons, plows, and eventually Studebaker autos, O'Brien paints, and Singer sewing machines. The College Football Hall of Fame encourages fans to cheer during the final seconds of an afternoon game in the 360-degree theater, test skills against a collegiate player, and pass footballs through targets. History buffs can tour the Copshaholm Mansion and Gardens, 38-room home to industrialist J.D. Oliver and his wife Anna in the late 1800s. At the Studebaker National Museum, learn about how the 1852 blacksmith shop-turned-wagon company began making autos in 1902, and see several historical vehicles, including one of Lincoln's carriages.

South Bend/Mishawaka Convention & Visitors Bureau: (800) 519-0577; www.livethelegends.org

Terre Haute (L-4)

French for "high land," Terre Haute was established in 1816 next to the Wabash River. It is the home of Indiana State University and Rose-Hulman Institute of Technology. Kids can play at the Children's Science & Technology Museum, pretending to be a pilot on a space vehicle or a newsroom anchor, or trying various musical instruments. The home of famed union leader and Socialist party presidential candidate Eugene V. Debs is open to visitors and features some of the original furnishing and artifacts. The three-story home is a National Historic Landmark. The collection of the Swope Art Museum focuses on 19th- and 20th-century art, with pieces by William Merritt Chase, Thomas Hart Benton, and Grant Wood.

Terre Haute Convention & Visitors Bureau: (800) 366-3043; www.terrehaute.com

SCENERY

Amish Country (A-10)

One of the largest Amish communities in the United States is centered in north-central Indiana in Elkhart and LaGrange Counties. At the edges of the area, visitors might notice the neat white farmhouses with clotheslines, but no electrical wires. Eventually, a black buggy, prominently marked with an orange triangle, will appear.

Brown County State Park

Brown County (M-8)

Begin the drive in the college town of Bloomington, heading east on SR 46. It's an area where artists such as T.C. Steele went for inspiration in the early 1900s, and log cabins and woodsy settings still capture the fancy of many visitors. A turn south on SR 135 winds through part of the Hoosier National Forest. Stop at tiny Story for a gourmet meal and to admire the chockablock antiques in the dining room of the Story Inn, a former grain mill.

- ### Indianapolis' North Meridian Street (p. 47, J-18)
  Elegant homes and the Governor's Mansion show off along the splendid main thoroughfare from 38th Street north.

- ### The National Road (J-12)
  Cutting across the middle of Indiana is the historic National Road, or US 40. Antique shops pack small towns like Cambridge City, and west of Indy is rolling prairie.

- ### Ohio River Route (O-12)
  Follow the river on SR 56 and SR 156, ogling the historic homes in 19th-century Madison through small river towns to the many church steeples of Aurora.

Covered bridge

- ### Parke County's Covered Bridges (J-5)
  Well, the Bridges of Madison County may be more famous, but here they're more numerous, centered around Rockville.

- ### Whitewater Canal (L-12)
  Watch the locks operate on the 1830s Whitewater Canal in Metamora, a quaint town northwest of Cincinnati.

TRAVEL GUIDE | Indiana

OUTDOORS

East Race Whitewater (p. 47, B-19)

East Race Whitewater

On summer weekends, bring your own kayak or canoe, or rent an inflatable "funyak" or a six-person raft on site to head down the East Race Waterway, a 1,500-foot artificial white-water course in South Bend. One of only six artificial courses in the world, the East Race Waterway uses water from the St. Joseph River to propel rafters through the course, which runs alongside South Bend's downtown. Because the course can be changed, it is also used for advanced rafters and races, such as Olympic trials for canoe and kayak slalom. When races are held, the public may watch from the lighted pathways along the riverfront. A fish ladder at the waterway allows seasonal viewing of chinook salmon and steelhead trout.

(574) 233-6121 or (574) 299-4768; www.sbpark.org/parks/erace.htm

Hoosier National Forest (N-8)

With 200,000 acres to explore, stretching through one-third of south-central Indiana, there's a lot of hiking to be done in Hoosier National Forest. The 13,000-acre Charles C. Deam Wilderness Area, near Monroe Lake in Monroe County, lets hikers explore many trails over ridges, through hollows, and along Hunter Creek. A stand of old-growth trees,

Patton Cave

with walnut trees 40 inches in diameter and 130 feet high, lies in the Pioneer Mothers Memorial Forest just outside Paoli. In the far southern section, just west of SR 37 and north of I-64, the sandstone outcrops and cliffs provide a beautiful nature walk through Hemlock Cliffs. Through much of the forest, rich with minerals, geodes can be found, and caves abound.

(812) 547-7051; www.fs.fed.us/r9/hoosier/

Indiana Dunes (A-5)

While most of northern Indiana is covered with farmlands, the far northwestern corner of the state borders the southern tip of Lake Michigan. Here, at Indiana Dunes National Lakeshore, visitors can scramble up a series of 200-foot-high sand dunes and roll down them in summer, trek through snow to spot winter wildlife, or join an interpretive bog walk from the Dorothy Buell Memorial Visitor Center. Many migratory birds stop to rest here, so it's a great spot for birding, too. At the visitor center, learn about the retreating glaciers that carved this part of Indiana some 14,000 years ago, find out how the dunes were formed, and sample some of the many programming activities offered.

(219) 926-7561; www.nps.gov/indu

Major Taylor Velodrome (p. 47, J-17)

Just over a dozen velodromes exist in the United States, and new cyclists at this banked oval outdoor track can take an orientation class and join in an hour-long ride on selected evenings each week. In the early summer, several eight-hour training sessions are held for more serious beginners. Named after Marshall "Major" Taylor, an African-American world champion bicycle racer of the early 1900s who was born and started his career in Indianapolis, the velodrome also holds inline skating competitions. From the bleachers adjacent to the track, visitors can watch races from collegiate level to professional, as well as practicing cyclists.

(317) 327-8356; www.majortaylorvelo.com

HERITAGE

Auburn Cord Duesenberg Museum

Auburn (B-13)

Early automobile enthusiasts flock to Auburn for the many antique car events and sites here. The Auburn Cord Duesenberg Museum features more than 100 vehicles from the early 1900s to World War II, focusing on Indiana-made cars. On display: the huge, custom-made Duesenberg Model J, made from 1928-1937, which was the most luxurious car made in the United States. The National Automotive and Truck Museum of the United States emphasizes post-World War II cars and trucks. See one of the original 1950 cars that raced in the Pan-American Highway road rally, La Carrera Panamerica. NATMUS is housed in two former Auburn Automobile Company factory production buildings.

(877) 833-3282 or (260) 927-1499; www.dekalbcvb.org

French Lick/West Baden Springs (P-7)

Home to former Boston Celtics star and Indiana Pacers president of basketball operations Larry Bird, French Lick and West Baden Springs are two tiny Indiana towns that drew health-seekers to the mineral-rich waters in the 1800s, and were the height of decadence during the roaring twenties. The famous and infamous, including Al Capone, would take a train into town to gamble and imbibe alcohol while local officials turned a blind eye. Today, visitors can "set a spell" in a rocking chair on the grand front porch of the French Lick Springs Resort & Casino. Next door sits the domed splendor of the West Baden Spring Hotel. A preservationist saved it from the wrecking ball in the mid-1990s; it's currently under renovation and scheduled to open as a hotel and casino in December 2007.

(877) 422-9925 or (812) 936-3418; www.orangecountyin.com

West Baden Springs Hotel

Historic New Harmony (R-2)

Two 19th-century utopian communities started in this one-stoplight town on the Wabash River, and many of the 32 buildings from those days are open for tours from March through December. In 1814, two years before Indiana became a state, German Lutheran Church separatist George Rapp founded a group called the Harmonie Society, which was best known for its emphasis on work and prayer. From Harmonist times, eight sites and 25 buildings remain, including log cabins, the granary, and a community house. Visitors are invited to walk and meditate on a reconstructed maze. Robert Owen brought intellectuals and social reformers in 1825 after the Harmonists left. Buildings from that period include Owen's 1830 home and Thrall's Opera House.

(800) 231-2168; www.newharmony.org

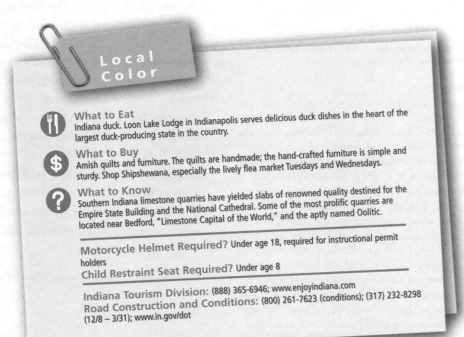

Local Color

🍴 **What to Eat**
Indiana duck. Loon Lake Lodge in Indianapolis serves delicious duck dishes in the heart of the largest duck-producing state in the country.

💲 **What to Buy**
Amish quilts and furniture. The quilts are handmade; the hand-crafted furniture is simple and sturdy. Shop Shipshewana, especially the lively flea market Tuesdays and Wednesdays.

❓ **What to Know**
Southern Indiana limestone quarries have yielded slabs of renowned quality destined for the Empire State Building and the National Cathedral. Some of the most prolific quarries are located near Bedford, "Limestone Capital of the World," and the aptly named Oolitic.

Motorcycle Helmet Required? Under age 18, required for instructional permit holders
Child Restraint Seat Required? Under age 8

Indiana Tourism Division: (888) 365-6946; www.enjoyindiana.com
Road Construction and Conditions: (800) 261-7623 (conditions); (317) 232-8298 (12/8 – 3/31); www.in.gov/dot

The last commercially built steam engine may have been built in Datong, China, but it found a home in Iowa where it steams its way over scenic bridges in the Des Moines River valley.

CITIES

Des Moines skyline

⭐ Des Moines *(State Capital) (I-10)*

Midwestern hospitality is plentiful in this political, economic, and cultural center of Iowa. The Des Moines metropolitan area has retained its charm and preserved its history while providing the amenities of a much larger city, like minor league baseball with the Triple-A Iowa Cubs, its own ballet company, and a symphony orchestra. Despite its development, driving across the entire city still takes less than 30 minutes. In the heart of Des Moines is a three-mile skywalk — where three 18-hole mini golf courses are set up each February for the annual Skywalk Open Golf Tournament. The Iowa State Fairgrounds hosts the Iowa State Fair, the largest tourist event in the state. The fairgrounds, listed on the National Register of Historic Places, are busy throughout the year with auto racing, concerts, and other events.

Greater Des Moines Convention & Visitors Bureau: (515) 286-4960, (800) 451-2625; www.seedesmoines.com

Dubuque *(E-18)*

Built on and below bluffs skirting the Mississippi, Dubuque first grew rich from lead mining. The city takes much of its character from the elegant homes and buildings that remain from this earlier period. For a unique travel experience, ride the Fenelon Place Elevator, built as a commuter route and now claimed to be the world's shortest and steepest scenic railway. In the harbor area, the new National Mississippi River Museum and Aquarium boasts a riverfront campus that includes the William Woodward River Discovery Center, the National Rivers Hall of Fame, and the Fred W. Woodward Riverboat Museum. Along with interactive displays, the museum's wide-ranging exhibits include a working boatyard and a wetlands area with boardwalk trail and natural history outposts. Sightseeing and dinner cruises aboard stately riverboats also leave from the harbor.

Dubuque Area Chamber of Commerce: (563) 556-4372, (800) 798-8844; www.dubuquechamber.com/

Quad Cities *(I-19)*

The Quad Cities cluster at the only place the Mississippi flows from east to west. Rock Island, on the Illinois side, offers access to Arsenal Island, the bit of land the river flows around at this point. Here you can tour the home of Colonel George Davenport, the area's first settler, and watch barges and towboats negotiate Lock and Dam No. 15 at the Mississippi River Visitor Center. In Moline, Illinois, the John Deere Pavilion looks back on the development of farm implements from simple plows to behemoth combines. On the Iowa side, Bettendorf offers the Family Museum, where interactive exhibits stimulate kids' interest in health, weather, music, and other subjects. And in Davenport, the Putnam Museum's natural history displays touch on Native Americans, the mysteries of Asia and Egypt, and the mammals of the world.

Quad-Cities Convention & Visitors Bureau: (563) 322-3911, (800) 747-7800; www.visitquadcities.com

Sioux City *(E-1)*

This tri-state agricultural processing and shipping center on the Missouri River was founded in 1854, 50 years after explorers Lewis and Clark passed through the area. Interactive exhibits at the Lewis & Clark Interpretive Center bring the adventurers' exploits to life by focusing on a single day in their travels. Displays on the Corps of Discovery and the development of the Siouxland area may also be seen at the nearby Sergeant Floyd River Museum. Architecture buffs should stroll along the Fourth Street Historic District for its concentration of Richardson Romanesque-style buildings. Another impressive Romanesque building houses the Sioux City Public Museum and its displays on life sciences, paleontology, and local American Indian tribes. The natural history of western Iowa's Loess Hills is the focus of the Dorothy Pecaut Nature Center. Across the Big Sioux River in southernmost South Dakota, the Adams House and Nature Preserve offers recreational trails and the remains of an 1870s farming community.

Sioux City Tourism Bureau: (712) 279-4800, (800) 593-2228; www.siouxcitytourism.com

Waterloo *(F-13)*

Commercial center for the northeast Iowa farming region, Waterloo is also home to the giant John Deere tractor works. The combination of urban and rural industries makes the city a natural choice as headquarters for the Silos and Smokestacks National Heritage Area, a collection of some 70 individual sites designed to tell the story of American agriculture. Touring the John Deere facilities requires a visit to four different factories to witness the entire tractor-making process. The Bluedorn Science Imaginarium offers interactive science exhibits on lasers, bubbles, and other fun physics. Take a guided tour of the Rensselaer Russell House, a restored 1861 Victorian mansion with original furnishings. Hike or bike along the Cedar Valley Nature Trail, a 52-mile linear park built on the former railroad line running from Waterloo to Cedar Rapids.

Waterloo Convention & Visitors Bureau: (319) 233-8350, (800) 728-8431; www.waterloocvb.org

OUTDOORS

Cedar Falls *(E-13)*

Trail riding, hiking, walking, skating, and wandering are so popular in this town that an annual Cedar Trails Festival is scheduled, including a "Light Up the Night" candlelit ride. Winding through the community are more than 30 miles of trails which, when added to the greater metro trail system, more than double the system's length to 65 miles. The trail in Cedar Falls, often called the "Gateway to the Trails," connects to the Cedar Valley Nature Trail, a linear park that follows a rail-to-trail conversion and continues through the valley for 52 miles. No motorized vehicles are allowed on the trails.

Candlelit ride

(800) 845-1955 or (319) 268-4266; www.cedarfallstourism.org

Maquoketa Caves State Park *(G-18)*

The park contains 13 caves, more than any other state park in Iowa. Located near Maquoketa, the caves were once rich with milk-white stalactites and stalagmites, and many have survived the onslaught of souvenir seekers. The caves vary in height from the very low Dugout cave to the 1,100-foot-high Dancehall cave. A trail system with limestone formations, bluffs, and overlooks links the caves. Wearing old clothes and sturdy shoes and carrying a flashlight are strongly suggested as some caves can be explored by foot, but others may require a bit of crawling. Trail highlights include the Natural Bridge, which spans nearly 50 feet above Raccoon Creek, and the 17-ton Balanced Rock.

(563) 652-5833: www.iowadnr/parks/

Yellow River Valley *(B-16)*

Located in Allamakee County, this valley is one of the most remote of the wild stream areas in the Midwest. Set aside at least eight hours to canoe from Volney to the mouth of the river. The stream has a steep gradient, ranging from a six-foot drop to nearly a 27-foot drop per mile. The gradient is one of the reasons the first saw mill in the state was built on the riverbank. All along the river there is evidence of former gristmills that once seeded its banks. Packing binoculars is a good idea. They will help spot any of the 291 bird species that make this area their home. These include bald eagles, turkeys, and turkey vultures. Mammals like it as well with black bears, bobcats, and river otters also in the valley.

(563) 568-2624; www.allamakeecounty.com/

HERITAGE

Brucemore

Brucemore (H-15)

A day at this estate in Cedar Rapids reveals the lifestyle of the rich and famous in the early 20th century as lived by the second owners of the house. Situated on 26 acres, the estate, built circa 1886, includes a 1915 Lord and Burnham greenhouse, a swimming pool installed in 1927, and a swan pond. The 21-room Queen Anne-style mansion is one of 21 properties of the National Trust for Historic Preservation. Made of wood, the grand staircase is the architectural jewel of the home. A mural of Richard Wagner's "The Ring of the Nibelung" graces one wall of the Great Hall where family portraits and a Skinner organ can be found. The house and visitors center now serve as a community arts center.

(319) 362-7375; www.brucemore.org

Dragoon Trail (I-10)

Follow the Dragoon Trail road markers from Des Moines through the state to Fort Dodge. It took the Dragoons, cavalry soldiers serving as scouts, three years to establish outposts between the two key locations in what would become the state of Iowa. Their main route followed the Des Moines River. Today travelers can explore the 200-mile greenbelt corridor along the Des Moines, Boone, and Raccoon rivers and discover it much like the Dragoons found it. The route traces the most scenic, undisturbed portion of their exploration. Points of interest along the way include Lake Red Rock, Ledges State Park, the Kate Shelley High Bridge, and Dolliver Memorial Park. The first signs for the Dragoon Trail appear in downtown Des Moines on the east side of the Des Moines River.

(888) 472-6035, (515) 242-4705; www.traveliowa.com

Capitol building

Iowa State Capitol (I-10)

On a sunny day, the gleam from the 23-karat-gold-leafed dome of the capitol building in Des Moines can be seen for miles. It should. It has been gilded four times in the last 120 years. Inside, legislative, judicial, and even executive offices are shown on tours along with a five-story law library, a scale model of Battleship *Iowa*, and a collection of First Lady dolls. On the 165-acre campus, memorials and monuments, such as the 1894 Soldiers and Sailors Monument of the Civil War, honor fallen heroes. Nearly 80,000 Iowa men served during the Civil War, the largest number of soldiers per capita of any state. There are also miniatures of the Statue of Liberty and the Liberty Bell. A statue of Abraham Lincoln reading to one of his sons, Tad, is the only known statue representing a United States president as a family man.

(515) 281-5591; www.legis.state.ia.us/Pubinfo/Tour

SCENERY

Loess Hills National Scenic Byway (I-3)

Located in western Iowa at the border with Nebraska, the Loess Hills region boasts a rugged range extending for 200 miles that rises from the prairie on one side and the flatland on the other. In Iowa, the yellow-brown hills follow the massive Missouri River Valley. Along the north-south route, parallel to Interstate 29, the byway presents a delicate environment rich in flora that thrives in the ancient soil thought to be deposited during the ice ages. An abundance of wildlife and pristine farms and villages make for a remarkable drive.

Loess Hills

Preparation Canyon State Park (H-3)

A drive along the park road affords views of the grassy mounds, flora, and wildlife in this canyon that was first reported by Lewis and Clark and the Corps of Discovery on their expedition to the Northwest. Later, it became a stopping-off point for wagon trains, especially Mormons en route to Idaho where the travelers could prepare for the rest of the journey and, for the devout, for the afterlife. The canyon is surrounded on three sides by ridges and rugged, windblown hills that aid in keeping the area secluded.

Western Skies Scenic Byway (I-7)

Elk Horn windmill

A 100-mile-plus drive along Highway 44 from Panora in the western part of Iowa to Logan offers a picturesque alternative to I-80. Watch for windmills along the way; many have been transported from Denmark. Along the way travelers experience colorful prairie sunsets, rolling meadows, and rivers.

Madison County bridge

● Bridges of Madison County (J-8)

Like the covered bridge that anchored the story in the best-selling novel, Winterset has a number of turn-of-the-century bridges to capture the imagination.

● Fenelon Place Elevator (E-18)

At the top of the world's shortest, steepest scenic railway, the view includes downtown Dubuque and the Mississippi River slicing between Iowa, Illinois, and Wisconsin.

● Grant Wood Scenic Byway (G-16)

Be as inspired as Iowa's native son Grant Wood at the Americana sites found along the route named in his honor between Anamosa and Stone City.

● Mosquito Park (L-17)

More of an overlook, this mini-park in Burlington provides one of the best views in southeastern Iowa of the Mississippi River and the limestone bluffs that frame it.

● Mt. Hosmer (B-16)

Fifty miles of the Mississippi Valley, including three states, can be seen from this 104-acre park located atop a 400-foot bluff in Lansing.

View of Mississippi River

Local Color

What to Eat
Trappistine creamy caramels. Soft and chewy, sometimes coated in chocolate, the locally famous caramels can be purchased in the Dubuque area and ordered from the Trappistine Nuns of Our Lady of the Mississippi: www.trappistine.com

What to Buy
Amana Woolen Mill blanket. Originally part of the Amana Colonies, the historic Amana Woolen Mill still weaves highly rated 100% wool products.

What to Know
Sergeant Charles Floyd, the only member of the Lewis and Clark expedition team to die during the journey, is buried near present-day Sioux City, Iowa.

Motorcycle Helmet Required? No
Child Restraint Seat Required? Under age 6

Iowa Tourism Office: (800) 345-4692*; (888) 472-6035; (515) 242-4705; www.traveliowa.com
Road Construction and Conditions: 511; (800) 288-1047; www.511ia.org
*to request travel materials only

Autumn bathes the Flint Hills in color.

CITIES

Kansas City (D-19)

All the action in Kansas City used to be on the Missouri side of the border, but now it's on the Kansas side, too. Sports enthusiasts line up for NASCAR action at the Kansas Speedway, while outdoors types head over to shop at the sportsman's paradise Cabela's, with its abundance of hunting, fishing, and outdoor paraphernalia. The Nebraska Furniture Mart with 700,000 square feet of display space attracts home décor shoppers. Just outside the city limits in Bonner Springs stands the National Agricultural Center and Hall of Fame with a re-created village consisting of a farm house, poultry hatchery, one-room schoolhouse, and blacksmith's shop. A barbed wire exhibit in the center shows the diverse designs of the fence that tamed the West. Also in Bonner Springs: Moon Marble, with bins full of marbles and games galore.

Kansas City, Kansas/Wyandotte County Convention & Visitors Bureau: (800) 264-1563 or (913) 321-5800; www.visitthedot.com

Spencer Museum of Art

Lawrence (E-18)

The University of Kansas dominates this town of 80,000. Founded by abolitionists determined to keep the Kansas Territory free of slavery, Lawrence was burned in 1863 by the pro-slavery Quantrill's Raiders and 150 citizens were killed. Now the historic buildings in the compact downtown feature restaurants and boutiques. One of the Underground Railroad sites in the city is Fire Station No. 4, once a stone barn where runaway slaves hid in the mid-1800s. At the University, on Mount Oread, the Spencer Museum of Art includes a 22,000-piece collection of paintings, sculptures, and photography. Also on campus, the Robert J. Dole Institute of Politics delves into the life of the senator, as well as Kansas' history and culture.

Lawrence Visitor Information Center: (888) 529-5267; www.visitlawrence.com

⭐ Topeka (State Capital) (D-17)

Topeka was founded in 1854; only seven years later it beat out several contenders in fierce competition to become the state capital. Tour the French Renaissance-style capitol building to view its beautifully detailed interiors and murals by John Steuart Curry. Topeka took center stage in the history of race relations in 1954 when the Supreme Court ruled against school segregation; the new Brown v. Board of Education National Historic Site & Museum in the restored Monroe School commemorates

Capitol building

the events surrounding that landmark decision. Also noteworthy: the Kansas Museum of History, whose exhibits include a locomotive from the Atchison, Topeka, and Santa Fe, a 1950s diner, covered wagon, and Cheyenne tipi. The Topeka Zoo in Gage Park has 300 animals displayed in an enclosed tropical rainforest and other settings. Gage Park is also the site of the Reinisch Rose Garden, a one-mile mini-railroad, and a restored 1908 carousel.

Topeka Convention and Visitors Bureau: (800) 235-1030 or (785) 234-1030; www.topekacvb.org

Wichita (I-13)

Kansas' largest city first found fame as a cattle town. Today, it is the state's main commercial center, supporting five major aircraft manufacturers among other industries. Flight and Design is one of the exhibit areas at Exploration Place, an interactive learning center for all ages. For a look back at the region's Native American heritage, visit the Mid-America All-Indian Center with its re-created Indian village and annual September powwow. The expanded Wichita Art Museum has added a new great hall to display works by contemporary glass artist Dale Chihuly, supplementing its collection of

Powwow

American works of the last 300 years. At Sedgwick County Zoo, the new Downing Gorilla Forest occupies its own island, where visitors are immersed in the wilds of equatorial Africa. Diners and shoppers enjoy clubs, shops and live performances at Old Town, the city's prime entertainment district.

Greater Wichita Convention & Visitors Bureau: (800) 288-9424 or (316) 265-2800; www.visitwichita.com

SCENERY

Gypsum Hills Scenic Byway (J-10)

Red shale and sandstone form the landscape here of deep canyons and high hills. The soil's iron leaches out to form a rusty color in the flat-topped buttes that are capped with white gypsum. On the route, Medicine Lodge is the site of a stockade built in 1874 to protect the territory from Osage and other tribal raids that occurred after an 1867 peace treaty between the U.S. and the Five Tribes of the Plains — Arapahoe, Comanche, Prairie Apache, Kiowa, and Cheyenne.

Stockade Museum in Medicine Lodge

Flint Hills Scenic Byway (F-15)

A 48-mile trip takes you through one of only four untouched tallgrass prairies in the world, and the only one in the United States. Named for the chert, or flint rock that covers the gentle slopes of 100-400 feet, the Flint Hills are primarily pasture land. Cattle roam the fields that stretch from Council Grove southwest of Topeka to Cassoday. The route passes a historic limestone mansion, schoolhouse, and barn, as well as the Chase County Courthouse, built in 1873.

● **Cimarron National Grassland** (J-2)
Self-guided scenic tour through the 180,000 reforested acres of what was windblown land in Dust Bowl times.

● **Feedlot Overlook** (H-6)
Just 2½ miles east of Dodge City off US 50/56, check out more than 20,000 cattle that are corralled in a feedlot.

● **Four State Lookout** (A-17)
On clear days visitors can see parts of Kansas, Missouri, Nebraska, and Iowa from up on a bluff outside White Cloud.

● **Frontier Military Scenic Byway** (H-19)
On this route learn about 19th-century military life at Fort Leavenworth (to the north) and Fort Scott (to the south). The U.S. Army used this trail to transport troops and supplies.

● **Route 66** (J-19)
It's only a half-marathon (13.2 miles) through southeastern Kansas, but worth visiting the Old Riverton Store and Marsh Arch Rainbow Bridge.

● **Sunflower Fields** (C-4)
This is the Sunflower State, so drive through the western part, near Colby and Goodland, to see these huge flowers in bloom.

Sunflower field

🍴 **What to Eat**
Beef and buffalo. Flint Hills tallgrass fattens up the animals, while restaurants across Kansas serve prime cuts. Buffalo is best had at Smoky Hill Bison Co. in Assaria.

💲 **What to Buy**
Wheat weavings. More than 10 million bushels of wheat harvested annually supply wheat shafts to be woven into Christmas ornaments, wall decor, wreaths, and other objects. Kansas Originals Market in Wilson features a large selection.

❓ **What to Know**
The only original, unplowed tallgrass prairie in North America is located in the Flint Hills, home of the Tallgrass Prairie National Preserve.

Motorcycle Helmet Required? Under age 18
Child Restraint Seat Required? Under age 8 and less than 80 lb. and less than 57 in.

Kansas Travel & Tourism: (800) 252-6727; www.travelks.com
Road Construction and Conditions: 511; (800) 585-7623; 511.ksdot.org

World's largest ball of twine, near Cawker City (C-10)

OUTDOORS

Windsurfing on the reservoir

Cheney Reservoir (H-12)

At the Cheney Reservoir in Cheney State Park, 18 miles west of Wichita, some come to fish for walleye. But many come to windsurf and sail, taking advantage of the strong prairie wind that blows across the 9,537-acre reservoir. The lake features two marinas, one of which is devoted strictly to wind-propelled watercraft. The lake turns into a flurry of colorful sails when national sailing regattas take place here.

(316) 542-3664; www.kdwp.state.ks.us

Quivira National Wildlife Refuge (G-10)

Named for the area's first human inhabitants, the Quivira Indians, this wildlife refuge encompasses 22,135 acres of grassland and salt marsh. It's located on the North American Flyway and provides rich opportunities for birders to spot common and endangered bird species. During spring and early summer, rare whooping cranes and piping plovers may be seen. But visitors are more likely to spot white-faced ibis, American avocets, and sandpipers, to name a handful of the 250-some species that stop over here. In autumn the marshes host thousands of migrating pintail and mallard ducks. An auto tour winds through the refuge, stopping at places such as spillways, which show how water is managed throughout the area. One stop is at the trailhead of the Migrant's Mile footpath. This trail becomes a boardwalk over the marsh, then heads into the grasslands (the refuge protects nearly 13,000 acres of them), where quail, meadowlarks, and hawks roam.

(620) 486-2393; quivira.fws.gov

Biking trails

Prairie Spirit Rail Trail (F-18)

Walk or ride a bike along the 33-mile converted rail trail from Ottawa to Welda. The route passes through areas of native tallgrass prairie and woodlands. The more adventurous bikers may want to join the eight-day, 400-mile Bike Across Kansas trip in June that travels the entire width of the state.

(785) 242-1411; www.visitottawakansas.com

Sailing

HERITAGE

Pawnee Indian Village Museum (B-11)

The state's very name comes from one of the Native American peoples that lived here: the Kanza Indians. Kansas' rich Native American history is evident throughout the state, not just in the name. In territory located in present-day Kansas and Nebraska, there were between 10,000 and 30,000 Pawnee divided into four bands. Smallpox and cholera decimated them, and a small group now lives south of Kansas in Pawnee, Oklahoma. At the Pawnee Indian Village Museum State Historic Site near Republic, view an excavated 1820s earth lodge dating from the height of Pawnee presence. Here is where Lt. Zebulon Pike visited in 1806, and 2,000 Pawnees once lived. A museum encloses the excavated lodge, where artifacts such as a Pawnee sacred bundle are on display. Walk the Kitkehahki Nature trail to see remains of other homes.

(785) 272-8681; www.kshs.org/places/pawneeindian/

Trail of Lewis and Clark (C-17)

Two hundred years ago, Meriwether Lewis, William Clark, and the Corps of Discovery explored the uncharted West of the United States, traveling through northeastern Kansas for two weeks along the Missouri River. Today, visitors can trace that path by following the Glacial Hills Scenic Byway, stopping in many of the same spots. At Fort Leavenworth, view unmarred river landscape from high atop the river banks. At Independence Creek just outside Atchison, the Corps celebrated their first July 4th. A new riverfront project includes a 10-mile biking and hiking trail from downtown to Independence Creek.

(800) 252-6727; www.lewisandclarkinkansas.com

The Underground Railroad (F-18)

The Adair family of Osawatomie welcomed abolitionist John Brown in the mid-1800s to help establish Underground Railroad sites. The cabin still stands under a stone pergola at the John Brown Museum State Historic Site. Bloody raids by both pro-slavery and anti-slavery contingents led to the moniker "Bleeding Kansas" for the territory until it was admitted in 1861 as a free state. Sites of the Underground Railroad can be found in Lawrence (the center of the free state movement), Quindaro (in present-day Kansas City), and a number of other spots. Nicodemus, a National Historic Site, is the only surviving all-African-American community (established 1877).

Greater Wichita Convention & Visitors Bureau:
(800) 288-9424 or (316) 265-2800; www.visitwichita.com

Exploring the outdoors

Horse farms proliferate in the Bluegrass region, near Lexington.

CITIES

Bowling Green (L-6)

Bowling Green is the chief commercial center for south central Kentucky. Sports car enthusiasts know it as the home of the Chevrolet Corvette. The National Corvette Museum displays some 75 mint condition models and prototypes, and the General Motors Corvette Assembly Plant may be toured throughout most of the year. The city is also the home of Western Kentucky University. The Kentucky Library and Museum on the university's pretty 200-acre campus

National Corvette Museum

houses a wealth of decorative objects, historical artifacts, books, and documents. More than 50 interactive exhibits spark curiosity at BRIMS, the Barren River Imaginative Museum of Science. Beech Bend Park and Splash Lagoon offers rides and games, miniature golf, and water slides. Take a 45-minute boat and walking tour of the Lost River Cave to discover the history of a natural wonder that has seen multiple human uses over the last 10,000 years.

Bowling Green Area Convention & Visitors Bureau: (800) 326-7465 or (270) 782-0800; www.visitbgky.com

✪ Frankfort (State Capital) (G-11)

When the bitter rivalry between Louisville and Lexington couldn't be settled to either city's satisfaction, Frankfort was chosen, in 1792, as a compromise candidate to be Kentucky's seat of government. Most of the city's attractions are of an historic nature. Tour both the Greek Revival-style Old State Capitol, with its self-supporting white stone staircase and 1850s artwork, and the present State Capitol building, constructed in 1910 and noted for the Parisian influence of its architectural details. Liberty Hall is the site of two elegant 19th-century homes with original furnishings and extensive formal gardens. Hand weapons, uniforms, and equipment are the focus of the Kentucky Military History Museum. The tomb of Daniel Boone and his wife, Rebecca, is in Frankfort Cemetery overlooking the city. For a break from the past, tour the area's distilleries and end your stay on a sweet note with a stop at the factory of Rebecca-Ruth Candies, where bourbon chocolates originated.

Frankfort/Franklin County Tourist & Convention Commission: (800) 960-7200 or (502) 875-8687; www.visitfrankfort.com

Keeneland Race Track

Lexington (H-12)

Founded in 1775, Lexington occupies the rolling limestone plateau at the heart of Bluegrass country. Legendary for the breeding of championship Thoroughbred horses, the region also bases its economy on tobacco, handicrafts, and various industrial interests. Miles and miles of white plank fencing run beside rural roads, delineating ranches, farms, and grazing pastures. Nearly 50 different breeds may be seen at the Kentucky Horse Park, where Man o' War lies at rest and the International Museum of the Horse offers exhibits on the 55 million years of interaction between humans and horses. The park features the American Saddlebred Museum, the Draft Horse Barn, and the show ring Parade of Breeds. Tour the area's historic homes, which include Ashland, home of statesman Henry Clay; the childhood home of Mary Todd Lincoln, and the estates of John Wesley Hunt, a prominent early businessman, and Joseph Bryan, grand-nephew of Daniel Boone.

Lexington Convention & Visitor's Bureau: (800) 845-3959 or (859) 244-7737; www.visitlex.com

Louisville (G-8)

Named in honor of French king Louis XVI, Louisville is Kentucky's largest city. Fortuitously located at the Falls of the Ohio, the city is an important transportation and manufacturing center, and the home of horse racing's most famous single event. The Kentucky Derby Museum offers tours of the barns at Churchill Downs and a 360-degree, high-definition video, "The Greatest Race." The collections at the Speed Art Museum cover 6,000 years from Egyptian antiquities to contemporary works. Visitors can tour Locust Grove, the home of George Rogers Clark, who established the first permanent settlement at Louisville. Costumed interpreters at the Frazier International History Museum demonstrate the uses of a vast collection of weaponry spanning 1,000 years. The new Muhammad Ali Center offers a non-traditional museum that tells the boxing legend's life story while encouraging viewers to find their own personal greatness. Board a steamboat as the calliope plays for a scenic dinner cruise along the Ohio.

Greater Louisville Convention & Visitors Bureau: (800) 626-5646; www.gotolouisville.com

SCENERY

Duncan Hines Scenic Road (L-6)

For a taste of rural Kentucky, take an 82-mile trip through small towns and past mansions, one-room schoolhouses, churches, and a Civil War battlefield. Begin in Bowling Green, where Duncan Hines was born in 1880, then head up through cave country, ending at Mammoth Cave National Park. Stop in the tiny burg of Smith's Grove, where great antiques shops line the main street and several fine local craftsmen create treasures from furniture and wooden bowls to hand-crafted knives.

US 68 Scenic Byway (H-12)

Head through the rolling hills of Kentucky horse country on this scenic highway between Lexington and Maysville. Travelers are mesmerized by the white wooden fences of horse farms that stretch for miles along this byway, which was once a buffalo trace, then a 19th-century Shaker road. Stops could include Shakertown at Pleasant Hill; Duncan Tavern in Paris, which hosted many historic figures including Daniel Boone; and the site of a Civil War battle at Blue Licks Battlefield State Park.

Shakertown at Pleasant Hill

● Boone Creek Scenic Byway (H-13)

Nine miles loop past horse farms and stone fences, as well as the 1813 limestone home of the Iroquois Hunt Club.

● Daniel Boone's Grave (B-12)

A stop at Daniel Boone's grave in the Frankfort Cemetery provides a beautiful panoramic view overlooking Kentucky's capital city.

● Great River Road (F-2)

Alongside this 40-mile stretch, watch the Mississippi River flow past a wildlife refuge and the Civil War site of Columbus Belmont State Park.

Ohio River

● Ohio River Overlook (B-7)

The arching bridge on I-65 that carries visitors from Indiana into Kentucky via Louisville provides an excellent overview of the Ohio River.

● Pine Mountain Road (L-16)

Drive to the crest of Pine Mountain (2,800 ft.) on this scenic trip through eastern Kentucky's rugged terrain.

OUTDOORS

Big South Fork National River and Recreation Area (N-12)

Class I to Class IV rafting

Straddling the border of Kentucky and Tennessee, this combined national river and national recreation area is filled with sandstone arches and spectacular gorges. While there are plenty of hiking and mountain biking opportunities, white-water rafting is the big attraction for many visitors. With rapids ranging from Class I to Class IV, fun rafting spans from easy to challenging. More than 80 miles of navigable river run through the recreation area, but the best known is the 11-mile stretch between Burnt Mill Bridge on the Clear Fork and Leatherwood Ford Bridge, where the Class III and Class IV rapids run. The big three rapids with names like Washing Machine, Double Falls, and the Ell have rafters anticipating the challenge.

(606) 376-5073; www.nps.gov/biso

Mammoth Cave National Park (K-17)

Explore part of the largest cave system in the world, with more than 350 miles of mapped passageways. The cave was declared a national park in 1941, and is home to many creatures such as cave

Mammoth Cave

crustaceans, blind cave beetles, cave crickets, but not many bats. Kentucky's number one attraction, Mammoth Cave offers 14 tours ranging in difficulty from easy, self-guided or guided tours to challenging ones that include crawls through spaces only nine inches high. Above ground, hikers can join a guided ranger hike or strike off on their own through one of the largest stands of old-growth timber in Kentucky (located in the north section of the park). Other options include the chance to fish or canoe along 31 miles of the Green and Nolin Rivers, or ride horses on the many miles of trails. In the spring, the park permits morel mushroom hunters to harvest small quantities of the delicacy.

(270) 758-2180; www.nps.gov/maca

Natural bridge

Red River Gorge Geological Area (I-15)

More than 100 natural arches and other geologic features such as cliffs and ridges impress hikers who venture into the 60 miles of trails in this section of the Daniel Boone National Forest. Many of these fantastic sites can be spotted from hiking trails, making it easy for the visitor to enjoy the features. The Sky Bridge arch, one of the most accessible, spans 75 feet and towers 23 feet high. Steep valleys carve through the 12,646-acre Clifty Wilderness within the geological area, with cliffs and arches throughout the forested terrain. A portion of the Red River, Kentucky's only nationally designated Wild and Scenic River, runs through the Clifty Wilderness. Part of the geological area is outside the national forest, in Natural Bridge State Park. The 900-ton natural bridge found there spans two ridges.

(606) 663-2852; www.redrivergorge.org

HERITAGE

Abraham Lincoln Birthplace National Historic Site (J-8)

Abraham Lincoln, the 16th president of the United States, was born on February 12, 1809 in a log cabin near Sinking Spring. An early 19th-century log cabin

Abraham Lincoln Birthplace

similar to the one Lincoln was born in is preserved in a Beaux Arts granite building here. A spring flowing over a granite ledge pours into a sinkhole near the memorial building. The historic site includes about ⅛ of the original 348.5-acre farm owned by Thomas and Nancy Lincoln. In 1811 the Lincolns moved a few miles away to Knob Creek due to a dispute over land rights at Sinking Spring. The rights for the Knob Creek land, too, were disputed, causing the Lincolns to move to Indiana when Abraham was seven. Also on the historic site is a visitor center covering Lincoln history and memorabilia.

(270) 358-3137; www.nps.gov/abli

Dr. Thomas Walker State Historic Site (M-14)

Seventeen years before Daniel Boone entered Kentucky (1767), physician and surveyor Dr. Thomas Walker took a group of explorers through what became known as the Cumberland Gap to find a suitable settlement spot for his employer, the Loyal Land Company. During his explorations he discovered a river and named it Cumberland, after the Duke of Cumberland. The historic site features a replica of a log cabin built in 1750, and is surrounded by 12 acres of parkland. The cabin is open year-round and admission is free. Every October the town of Barbourville, where the site is located, hosts a week-long Daniel Boone Festival celebrating Boone's search for a route through Kentucky.

(606) 546-4400; parks.ky.gov

Kentucky Horse Park

Kentucky Horse Park (H-12)

The Kentucky Horse Park lies in the heart of horse country. Visitors learn about and see 50 different breeds at the 1,200-acre working horse farm during a daily parade of the breeds. The International Museum of the Horse at the horse park features an art gallery with traveling exhibitions on equine artwork and permanent exhibitions devoted to topics such as the draft horse and sporting horses. The park's other museum is dedicated to the American Thoroughbred. In addition, visitors can watch a farrier make horseshoes, measure their own stride against Man o' War's 28-foot stride at the horse's memorial and grave, as well as see the final resting place of many other equine champions.

(800) 678-8813 or (859) 233-4303; www.kyhorsepark.com

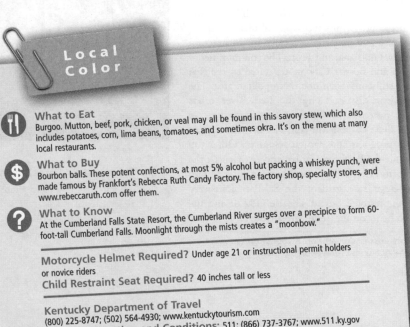

Local Color

🍴 **What to Eat**
Burgoo. Mutton, beef, pork, chicken, or veal may all be found in this savory stew, which also includes potatoes, corn, lima beans, tomatoes, and sometimes okra. It's on the menu at many local restaurants.

$ **What to Buy**
Bourbon balls. These potent confections, at most 5% alcohol but packing a whiskey punch, were made famous by Frankfort's Rebecca Ruth Candy Factory. The factory shop, specialty stores, and www.rebeccaruth.com offer them.

❓ **What to Know**
At the Cumberland Falls State Resort, the Cumberland River surges over a precipice to form 60-foot-tall Cumberland Falls. Moonlight through the mists creates a "moonbow."

Motorcycle Helmet Required? Under age 21 or instructional permit holders or novice riders
Child Restraint Seat Required? 40 inches tall or less

Kentucky Department of Travel
(800) 225-8747; (502) 564-4930; www.kentuckytourism.com
Road Construction and Conditions: 511; (866) 737-3767; www.511.ky.gov

Mardi Gras revelers toss "throws" during the annual New Orleans parade.

SCENERY

Creole Nature Trail
All-American Road (I-2)

During the 180-mile drive from Sulphur to Lake Charles, sections of this road hug the Gulf shore. In Hackberry, see the operations for commercial crabbing, fishing, and shrimping. As the route skirts marshland, drivers pass signs that warn of alligators that might wander on the road ahead. There are more than 3,000 alligator nests in Louisiana's outback, so spotting a gator is not rare. There are also more than 250 species of birds, including geese, ducks, and songbirds. Stop at the Peveto Woods Bird and Butterfly sanctuary to listen and see songbirds up close.

Creole Nature Trail

Mississippi River Road (H-7)

Between New Orleans and Baton Rouge, follow the winding roads on the east or the west bank of the Mississippi. You'll learn about the many cultures that have thrived here, from the Native Americans to the French, Germans, Spanish, and Cajuns, to the African slaves. There are loads of antebellum plantation homes to see, little river towns, local museums, prehistoric Indian sites, and of course, the mighty Mississippi.

- **Bienville Trace Scenic Byway** (B-7)
  This 450-mile byway in northwest Louisiana travels through rolling hills and pine forests.

- **Jean Lafitte National Historic Park and Preserve** (I-9)
  Take the short route to see the Chalmette Battlefield where General Andrew Jackson's troops defeated the British in 1815.

- **Longleaf Trail Scenic Byway** (A-3)
  See sandstone outcrops, mesas, and buttes along with longleaf pines on this 17-mile drive through the Kisatchie National Forest.

- **San Bernardo Scenic Byway** (H-10)
  Just outside New Orleans, St. Bernard Parish was founded by people from Spain's Canary Islands, and their descendants live there today. The main industries are charter fishing and seafood, and evidence of both abounds along the drive.

Toledo Bend

- **Toledo Bend Forest Scenic Byway** (E-2)
  Take a 160-mile drive along the Toledo Bend Reservoir to watch anglers vying for bass and crappie as well as golfers tackling the fairways, or stop to walk among the trees in Vernon Parish.

CITIES

⊛ Baton Rouge (State Capital) (G-7)

Hard-working Baton Rouge is both state capital and center of the petro-chemical industry with a busy port for ocean-going vessels on the Mississippi River. The 34-story New State Capitol was built at the direction of Governor Huey P. Long, who was assassinated there and is buried in its gardens. Called the "castle on the river" for its unique blend of Gothic and Victorian architecture, the Old State Capitol allows visitors to hear Governor Long "live" in an animatronic exhibit, "The Kingfish Speaks." On the waterfront, visitors can tour the restored World War II destroyer USS Kidd. The LSU Rural Life Museum offers a fascinating look back at a recreated 19th-century plantation and the vernacular homes of various settlers. Tour Magnolia Mound, a restored French Creole plantation dating from 1792. For a closer look at the Louisiana wilds, stroll nature trails through a magnolia-beech forest and cypress-tupelo wetlands at Bluebonnet Swamp.

Centroplex Fountain,
Old State Capitol

Baton Rouge Area Convention & Visitors Bureau: (800) 527-6843; www.bracvb.com

Lafayette (H-5)

Industrially, Lafayette is an administrative center for off-shore oil and gas drilling interests; culturally, it's the heart of Cajun country, offering myriad opportunities to sample Cajun music, food, and history. Stop at the Acadian Culture Center to discover the history of the Cajun way of life beginning with the expulsion of the Acadians from Nova Scotia and their resettlement in Louisiana. Acadian Village offers a collection of authentic Acadian houses, dating back to 1800, a general store, and blacksmith's. Cooking and crafts demonstrations are part of the fun at Vermilionville, a 23-acre Cajun/Creole heritage and folklife park recreating Acadiana during the years 1765 to 1890. Just outside Lafayette, Chretien Point Plantation features a French plantation home with a rich history encompassing the pirate Jean Lafitte, buried treasure, ghosts, and the Civil War. Lafayette Natural History Museum and Planetarium has exhibits on many other cultures of the bayou region including Native Americans, Creole, and African-American.

Lafayette Convention & Visitors Commission: (800) 346-1958; www.lafayettetravel.com

Preservation Hall

New Orleans (H-9)

Visitors to the Crescent City enter a timeless city laden with mystery and romance. The heart of the city, the French Quarter, dates back to 1718, its architecture reflecting 300 years of Spanish, French, and Caribbean influences. At Jackson Square, artists and street performers entertain near St. Louis Cathedral, one of the oldest Roman Catholic churches in the country. Riverwalk, a huge marketplace located on the Mississippi River, features unusual food and retail shops. Tour the Garden District with its colorful, older estates and lush vegetation. At the Audubon Zoo, exhibits like Jaguar Jungle and Reptile Encounter house 1,500 animals from all corners of the Earth. Head to Bourbon Street in the Vieux Carre to hear New Orleans-style jazz and savor New Orleans-style cooking.

New Orleans Tourism Marketing Corporation: (504) 524-4784; www.neworleansonline.com

Shreveport (B-2)

Named for steamboat captain Henry Miller Shreve, Shreveport is the commercial and cultural center for Ark-La-Tex, a 200-mile region formed by the junction of Arkansas, Louisiana, and Texas. The communities of Shreveport and Bossier City are separated by the Red River, yet still considered one metropolitan area. The entertainment district along the Red River offers museums, riverboat gambling, and street festivals. In town, the State Exhibit Museum displays dioramas of Louisiana products and natural resources. Other top sites include the Barnwell Garden and Art Center; the R. W. Norton Art Gallery; the American Rose Center with its huge rose garden; the Sci-Port Discovery Center; the restored Strand Theatre (1925); and the lasers and lights on the Texas Street Bridge.

Shreveport-Bossier Convention & Tourist Bureau: (888) 458-4748; www.shreveport-bossier.org

HERITAGE

Fort Jesup State Historic Site (E-3)

This site in northwestern Louisiana recalls the days right after the Louisiana Purchase when boundaries were not clearly defined between the United States and Spain. Before Fort Jesup was built in 1822, this was a no man's land of lawlessness. The restored kitchen/mess hall, the only remaining structure from the original complex, features a stone fireplace with a 7.5-foot opening. Also on site are reconstructed officers' quarters with a re-created officer's bedroom. Costumed guides conduct tours and demonstrate frontier skills daily. Both buildings house artifacts from the era, and the original butcher block still stands in the kitchen.

(888) 677-5378 or (318) 256-4117;
www.crt.state.la.us/parks/iFtjesup.aspx

Rural Life Museum

Rural Life Museum (B-13)

Probably the most iconic image of the South is a beautiful plantation home. Louisiana has loads of them, many open for tours. To learn about working life at a plantation, however, visit Louisiana State University's Rural Life Museum, which features 27 buildings, including a re-created working 19th-century plantation, with slave cottages and overseer's house filled with artifacts and tools. While there's no grand plantation mansion to tour at the Rural Life Museum, visitors will learn about how the huge sugar and cotton plantations were operated. Other buildings in the plantation area include a sick house, commissary, blacksmith's shop, sugar house, and grist mill.

(225) 765-2437; rurallife.lsu.edu

Vermilionville (H-14)

In the mid-18th century, French settlers in the area of eastern Canada known as Acadia were forced out by the British, and many of them came to Louisiana. Over time, the name Acadian was shortened to Cajun. French-speaking Cajuns still live in the southern part of the state, and a number of historical sites recognize their history, music, and culture. Early Cajun and Creole history is the focus of Vermilionville in Lafayette. Costumed guides at this living history museum cook, play music, and perform Cajun dances, covering Acadian life from 1765-1890. Located on the banks of Bayou Vermilion, the museum is a small village with 18 structures, including a trapper's cabin, a school (where children were forbidden to speak French), and a house constructed partly of mud and Spanish moss. There are six restored original homes.

(866) 992-2968 or (337) 233-4077;
www.vermilionville.org

OUTDOORS

Audubon State Historic Site (F-7)

Famous for his realistic depictions of birds, John James Audubon was inspired by Louisiana. He spent a few months in 1821 at Oakley Plantation as a tutor, during which time he worked on 32 paintings. The plantation is now the Audubon State Historic Site. The restored 1806 home features furnishings from the time when Audubon lived there and includes a detached plantation kitchen, a barn, and slave cottages. Guided tours begin in a 9,000-square-foot visitors center built in 2003 of antique cypress and pine to resemble a cotton press barn. The tours include an orientation film and history of the home. A walking path, the Cardinal Trail, winds through the 100-acre site.

(888) 677-2838; www.crt.state.la.us/parks/iaudubon.aspx

Fishing in Bogue Chitto National Wildlife Refuge

Bogue Chitto National Wildlife Refuge (G-10)

The Bogue Chitto River meanders through St. Tammany and Washington parishes in this national refuge established by President Jimmy Carter in 1980. The bottomland hardwood forest is home to deer, turkey, snakes, and birds. Waterways slice through the swampy land, and boaters paddle past bald cypress and tupelo gum trees as they glance overhead for a glimpse of an owl or Swainson's warbler. Visitors to the refuge can hike, fish, hunt, canoe, and bird watch. Many like to take a half-day or longer tubing down the Bogue Chitto River, or paddling a canoe or kayak. Outside of the refuge, several outfitters offer rentals and trip options.

(985) 882-2000; www.fws.gov/boguechitto

Honey Island Swamp (H-9)

As the tour boat quietly drifts past tendrils of Spanish moss hanging from cypress trees, it's easy to think of a swamp as a tranquil place. But especially during the warmer months, visitors are likely to spot alligators cruising for lunch, bringing the harsh reality of Louisiana's bayou country into focus. At Honey Island Swamp, an ecologist-led tour helps visitors identify birds such as egrets, herons, and ibis, and other wildlife like beavers. Fishermen angle for bluegill, bass, and crawfish. Honey Island Swamp is even rumored to have its own swamp creature. The trips provide a glimpse into the traditional Cajun way of life, when boats were the main method of transportation in this part of southern Louisiana.

(985) 641-1769; www.honeyislandswamp.com

Kisatchie National Forest (A-3)

Comprised of 604,000 acres spread over five districts and seven parishes (Louisiana's equivalant of counties) in the north-central part of the state, the Kisatchie is Louisiana's only national forest. There are four lakes for boating and fishing and 355 miles of trails to hike, mountain bike, or ride on horseback. Some trails are dedicated to motorized vehicles. Hunting is also permitted in the forest. Rangers work with the National Wild Turkey Federation to sustain the population of wild turkeys that roam here. The forest is also active in the red-cockaded woodpecker recovery project. For those seeking a more primitive environment, the 8,700- acre Kisatchie Hills Wilderness area features a few trails and steep terrain.

Kisatchie National Forest

(318) 473-7160; www.fs.fed.us/r8/kisatchie/

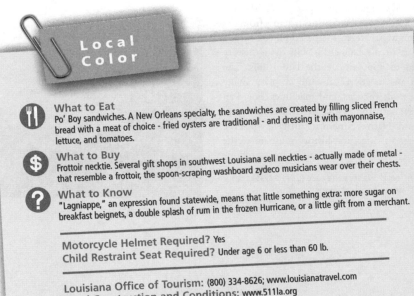

Local Color

What to Eat
Po' Boy sandwiches. A New Orleans specialty, the sandwiches are created by filling sliced French bread with a meat of choice - fried oysters are traditional - and dressing it with mayonnaise, lettuce, and tomatoes.

What to Buy
Frottoir necktie. Several gift shops in southwest Louisiana sell neckties - actually made of metal - that resemble a frottoir, the spoon-scraping washboard zydeco musicians wear over their chests.

What to Know
"Lagniappe," an expression found statewide, means that little something extra: more sugar on breakfast beignets, a double splash of rum in the frozen Hurricane, or a little gift from a merchant.

Motorcycle Helmet Required? Yes
Child Restraint Seat Required? Under age 6 or less than 60 lb.

Louisiana Office of Tourism: (800) 334-8626; www.louisianatravel.com
Road Construction and Conditions: www.511la.org

The sun's last rays play upon trees at the base of Mt. Katahdin in Baxter State Park.

CITIES

★ Augusta *(State Capital) (F-4)*

Maine's capital grew from the community surrounding Old Fort Western on the banks of the Kennebec River. Built in 1754, the fort has been restored and is the oldest surviving wooden fort in New England. You can visit the fort and see costumed interpreters performing military and domestic chores. The elegant state capitol building (1829) with its granite dome was designed by Charles Bulfinch, the architect of the U.S. Capitol in Washington. Self-guided tours are available. Nearby, the Maine State Museum offers displays ranging from archaeology to marine engineering. You can also tour Blaine House. Purchased in 1862 by one-time presidential candidate James G. Blaine, the mansion has served as the official residence of Maine's governors since 1919. The surrounding park-like grounds were designed by noted landscape architect Frederick Law Olmsted.

Kennebec Valley Chamber of Commerce: (207) 623-4559; www.augustamaine.com

"Whatever Festival" in Augusta

Bangor *(E-6)*

This city between the North Woods and the ocean is the perfect place to get outfitted for a trip to the rugged northcountry. Bangor's location on the Penobscot River at the edge of the woods helped it become the world's largest lumber port. See a 31-foot-high statue of lumberjack Paul Bunyan across from the Civic Center on Main Street. Maine Forest & Logging Museum is part of the Leonard's Mills living history site, re-created to approximate the late 1800s. The Cole Land Transportation Museum displays many trucks, buses, work vehicles, and machines. For even more history, see the Hudson Museum's pre-Columbian and Native American artifacts or Page Farm & Home, a living rural history museum of the early 1900s.

Bangor Convention & Visitors Bureau: (207) 947-5205; (800) 916-6673; www.bangorcvb.org

Bar Harbor *(F-8)*

In the mid-1800s artists Thomas Cole and Frederic Church traveled to this little-known fishing village to paint its seascapes and landscapes. Their art caught the attention of the East Coast moneyed elite, and soon these patrons arrived on the scene. A resort town was born. Saltwater swimming, magnificent stands of trees, sweeping landscapes, and refreshing summer weather have made Bar Harbor the focal point of a celebrated area. Nearby Acadia National Park offers dramatic views of the ocean and plentiful outdoor activities. In Bar Harbor, visitors can enjoy the Historical Society and Natural History museums and the nearby Wendell Gilley Bird Carving museum; the Oceanarium; whale-watching; and the ferry to Nova Scotia.

Bar Harbor Region Chamber of Commerce: (207) 288-5103; www.barharbormaine.com

Portland *(H-3)*

Maine's largest metropolis was established by the British in 1632 as a trading and fishing settlement. Situated on a peninsula in Casco Bay, Portland today boasts a busy waterfront with fisherman and ferries, sightseeing cruises and pleasure boats, and restaurants and shops. Visitors like to walk the historic streets, view the Casco Bay islands, and explore the Portland Museum of Art, the Children's Museum of Maine, the Maine Historical Society, and Wadsworth-Longfellow House, home of the poet. Also see Tate House (1755), Victoria Mansion (1858), the restored 19th-century Old Port Exchange with shops and restaurants, and Portland Head Light (1791), the oldest lighthouse in continuous use in the country. Scenic cruises are another popular tourist pastime.

Convention & Visitors Bureau of Greater Portland: (207) 772-5800; www.visitportland.com

Portland Head Light

SCENERY

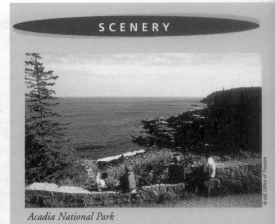

Acadia National Park

Acadia Byway *(F-8)*

Start just south of Trenton, pass through Bar Harbor, and loop around the eastern lobe of Acadia National Park. Craggy shorelines, colorful bobbing lobster buoys, tranquil forests, and granite-capped mountains are a few of the gems along this stretch.

Old Canada Road Scenic Byway *(D-4)*

Running from northwest Solon to the Canadian border, US 201 traces the path of generations of travelers between Maine and Quebec. The byway passes through historic villages and outposts in a remote and unspoiled section of Maine's sprawling forests. Stop for scenic viewpoints of the Kennebec River, Wyman Lake, and the Dead River.

Carrabassett River Valley

● Carrabassett River Valley *(D-3)*

Look for the Appalachian Trail crossing and many scenic turnouts that access the river on this route along SR 27 in Maine's western mountains.

● Million Dollar View *(B-8)*

This eastern Maine route on US 1 from Danforth to Orient gives travelers spectacular views of the Chiputneticook chain of lakes, rolling hayfields, and Peekaboo Mountain.

Vista from the top of Mt. Battie

● Mt. Battie *(G-6)*

This beautiful peak is the only one in Camden Hills State Park accessible by car. The one-mile Maiden Cliff Trail overlooking Lake Megunticook is another favorite spot.

● Rangeley Lakes Scenic Byway *(E-2)*

Watch for moose and eagles, and wild trout and salmon as you wind around mountains, rivers, and more than 100 lakes and ponds from Madrid to Byron.

● Schoodic Scenic Byway *(F-8)*

Historic lighthouses, blueberry fields, rocky islands, and mountain views highlight this loop around the dramatic lesser-known part of Acadia National Park.

OUTDOORS

Kayaking in Acadia National Park

Acadia National Park (F-8)

You'll need several days to explore even a sliver of this massive park on Mount Desert Island (pronounced "dessert"). For spectacular mountain and ocean views, hike the alligator-back rock formations to the summit of Bubble Rock. A tougher ascent is Acadia's highest peak: Cadillac Mountain, where the rays of the sun first hit the United States (Oct. - March). Here visitors can catch a sunrise, count the offshore islands, or watch storm clouds develop and edge closer. The best way to traverse remote areas and hear Acadia's history is on a horse-drawn carriage ride. John D. Rockefeller, Jr. built 57 miles of carriage roads so that visitors could take in the rocky beauty of coastal Maine at a leisurely, elegant pace.

(207) 288-3338; www.nps.gov/acad

Carriage ride

Baxter State Park/Mt. Katahdin (A-6)

This wilderness and forest preserve covers more than 204,733 acres of land surrounding Maine's highest peak, Mount Katahdin (Baxter Peak), which rises 5,268 feet in the northern portion of the state. This mountainous landscape — the park contains 46 peaks — provides the best rugged hiking in the state and marks the northern terminus of the Appalachian Trail. Many other scenic and challenging paths intersect the preserve including the Knife Edge Trail, which is notorious for the 2,000-foot vertical drop on either side of the trail. The Kidney and Daicey Ponds, Grassy Pond, Rocky Pond, and the Fowler Ponds give visitors excellent fishing opportunities and the chance to canoe with the scenic North Woods as a backdrop.

(207) 723-5140; www.baxterstateparkauthority.com

Mt. Katahdin in Baxter State Park

L.L. Bean's Outdoor Discovery Schools (H-3)

This may be the best way to explore Maine's splendid wilderness or pick up a new hobby. Classes in fly-fishing, kayaking, outdoor photography, cross-country skiing, and more are geared for all ages and abilities. Many short introductory classes take place in and around Freeport, while longer excursions lead visitors to locations as remote as the Allagash Wilderness Waterway in northern Maine. Experts (for example, state champions and ex-Navy SEALs) and certified instructors from around the country teach the year-round classes, which can last from one hour to five days and range in price from $12 to $1,300.

(888) 552-3261; www.llbean.com

Fly-fishing

HERITAGE

Abbe Museum (G-13)

With locations in downtown Bar Harbor and at Sieur de Monts Spring in Acadia National Park, the Abbe is the only museum devoted solely to Maine's American Indian heritage. The traditions of the Wabanaki ("People of the Dawn") are well preserved here through artifacts, workshops and demonstrations by American Indians, archaeology field schools, performances, lectures, and hands-on programs. More than 50,000 objects spanning 10,000 years are part of the Abbe's collections. Many of the oldest artifacts, such as stone and bone tools and pottery, were excavated by museum staff. The Abbe is known for its Native baskets of the Northeast, which date to the early 1800s.

Abbe Museum

(207) 288-3519; www.abbemuseum.org

Downeast Heritage Museum (C-10)

The town of Calais sits at the crux of the historic St. Croix River and the tidal waters of the Passamaquoddy Bay on the Canadian border. Here, the Downeast Heritage Museum interprets the area's history, beginning with the native Passamaquoddy people and the first European settlers on nearby St. Croix Island in 1604. Discover what life was like on St. Croix Island at that French settlement, the first settlement in North America. Interactive exhibits explain how the locals made their livelihoods from the area's natural resources, progressing from timber for shipbuilding to lumber and pulp for paper, and including fish farming and boatbuilding.

(207) 454-7878 or (877) 454-2500; www.downeastheritage.org

Maine Maritime Museum (H-4)

The town of Bath's 260-year history as a shipbuilding center is preserved at the Maine Maritime Museum. On the 20-acre museum grounds, you can tour the restored Percy & Small Shipyard (dating from the late 19th century), the museum's boatshop, where the craft of wooden boatbuilding is still practiced, and an active fishing schooner. Exhibits range from techniques of early fishing and navigation to ship models and the salvage of shipwrecks. Several excursions around the bay and up the coast are also available, and visitors can get snacks or lunch in the museum's Long Reach Hall, which overlooks the Kennebec. Fine older homes of ship captains and merchants can be seen in the city's historic district.

(207) 443-1316; www.mainemaritimemuseum.org

Sabbathday Lake Shaker Village (G-3)

This village in New Gloucester was founded by a group of Shaker missionaries in 1783. Today, Sabbathday Lake is the only active Shaker community in the world. The 1,800-acre village includes 18 buildings, a tree farm, an apple orchard, vegetable gardens, a commercial herb garden, hay fields, pastures, a flock of sheep, and a variety of other livestock. Guided tours give visitors a look inside the Maine Shaker heritage and culture of the past and present. One stop on the tour is the 1794 Meetinghouse, the architectural jewel of the village and the location for the Shakers' worship services today. The museum's reception center and Shaker store are open to the public and feature a unique selection of books, Shaker-made goods, and culinary herbs and medicinal teas, which are still packaged by the United Society of Shakers. Open Memorial Day through Columbus Day.

Early Shaker meeting

(207) 926-4597; www.shaker.lib.me.us

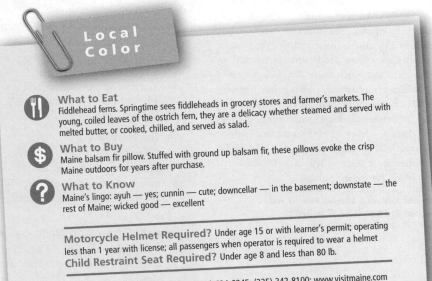

Local Color

What to Eat
Fiddlehead ferns. Springtime sees fiddleheads in grocery stores and farmer's markets. The young, coiled leaves of the ostrich fern, they are a delicacy whether steamed and served with melted butter, or cooked, chilled, and served as salad.

$ What to Buy
Maine balsam fir pillow. Stuffed with ground up balsam fir, these pillows evoke the crisp Maine outdoors for years after purchase.

? What to Know
Maine's lingo: ayuh — yes; cunnin — cute; downcellar — in the basement; downstate — the rest of Maine; wicked good — excellent

Motorcycle Helmet Required? Under age 15 or with learner's permit; operating less than 1 year with license; all passengers when operator is required to wear a helmet
Child Restraint Seat Required? Under age 8 and less than 80 lb.

Maine Office of Tourism: (888) 624-6345; (225) 342-8100; www.visitmaine.com
Road Construction and Conditions: 511; (207) 624-3595; (866) 282-7578
www.511maine.gov

Boats ply the waters of Baltimore's Inner Harbor.

CITIES

⭐ Annapolis *(State Capital) (E-14)*

Maryland's capital city and home of the U.S. Naval Academy, Annapolis is imbued with a deep sense of history, with structures that date back to the 1690s. The Old Senate Chamber in the State House and the

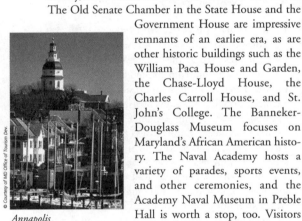

Annapolis

Government House are impressive remnants of an earlier era, as are other historic buildings such as the William Paca House and Garden, the Chase-Lloyd House, the Charles Carroll House, and St. John's College. The Banneker-Douglass Museum focuses on Maryland's African American history. The Naval Academy hosts a variety of parades, sports events, and other ceremonies, and the Academy Naval Museum in Preble Hall is worth a stop, too. Visitors can take guided walking tours of

Historic Annapolis and the U.S. Naval Academy. There are also narrated harbor cruises that depart regularly from the dock.

Annapolis and Anne Arundel County Conference & Visitors Bureau: (888) 302-2852; www.visit-annapolis.org

Baltimore *(C-13)*

This inland port and Atlantic seaboard city is located on the upper reaches of the Chesapeake Bay and is famous for its blue crabs, baseball at Camden Yards, and row houses with immaculate white marble stoops. Founded in 1729 as a customs house for the Virginia colony's tobacco farmers, Baltimore soon became one of the world's major seaports. Today the city bursts

Harborplace, Baltimore

with things to see and do. Start at the Fort McHenry National Monument and Historic Shrine, where Francis Scott Key penned the words of

the "Star-Spangled Banner." Another popular spot is the Inner Harbor with its many attractions: Harborplace, the National Aquarium, the Maryland Science Center, Pier Six Concert Pavilion, the USS *Constellation*, and the Baltimore Maritime Museum. Beyond the Inner Harbor, visit some of area's historic homes, like the Flag House and Star-Spangled Banner Museum and the Edgar Allan Poe House and Museum, and the Poe Grave site.

Baltimore Area Convention & Visitors Association: (877) 225-8466; www.baltimore.org

Frederick *(C-10)*

Home to Civil War heritage and historic sites, Frederick also boasts a number of terrific outdoor activities, restaurants, shopping, museums, and attractions. The city of Frederick, founded in 1745, has a 50-block downtown historic district that includes many gorgeous examples of 18th- and 19th-century architecture. The district is famed for its clustered spires. Other notable historic spots in the area include three covered bridges, Monocacy National Battlefield, the National Museum of Civil War Medicine, and the National Shrine of St. Elizabeth Ann Seton. Outdoor lovers have their choice of 90 parks, ranging from the municipal to state level, and visitors won't want to miss the Catoctin Wildlife Preserve & Zoo either. Shoppers can peruse an array of antique shops, art galleries, and orchard markets. With a wide a range of international restaurants, good food is never far.

Tourism Council of Frederick County: (800) 999-3613 or (301) 600-2888; www.fredericktourism.org

Ocean City's boardwalk

Ocean City *(I-20)*

Maryland's top beach resort is in full swing from April through October each year when sunny skies, warm temperatures, and low humidity draw millions of visitors. Many hotels and activities make it a perfect family vacation destination. Ten miles of white sandy beach are backed by dunes, and the three-mile picture-perfect boardwalk offers food, entertainment, an amusement park, and much more. Outdoor activities include swimming, sunbathing, walking, beach volleyball (the Dorchester Street Volleyball Park has ten courts and tournaments), bicycling, fishing, golfing, and inline skating. Other nearby attractions include Frontier Town, Jolly Rogers Park, and the Life-Saving Station Museum. Ocean City is also close to Assateague Island National Seashore.

Ocean City Convention & Visitors Bureau and Department of Tourism: (800) 626-2326 or (410) 213-0552; www.oceancity.org

SCENERY

Chesapeake Country Scenic Byway *(E-15)*

The 85.5-mile Chesapeake Country Scenic Byway shows off the surrounding area's natural beauty and takes visitors through more than a dozen small historic towns. The byway starts in Stevensville and snakes north to Chesapeake City. Rare and endangered species like the colonial water bird as well as more common migrating birds, hawks, eagles, and vultures may be spotted because the region is an important stopover on the Atlantic Flyway. Stops include Mt. Harmon Plantation, Betterton Beach, Kent Farm Museum, Church Hill Theater, C&D Canal Museum, Queen Anne's County Courthouse, and Christ Church.

Historic National Road

Historic National Road *(A-2)*

This road runs through Illinois, Indiana, Ohio, West Virginia, and Pennsylvania before entering western Maryland and ending in Baltimore. In the Old Line State, the 170-mile route primarily follows Alternate US 40 and SR 144, including a section of the state's Historic National Pike that runs from Baltimore to Cumberland. Drivers tour seven of the state's most historic and scenic counties. The offerings range from the Baltimore & Ohio Railroad Museum and the Barbara Fritchie House to the C&O Canal towpath and Eckhart Mines. This first federally funded road was a gateway to the West through the Allegheny Mountains for many 19th-century pioneers.

- #### Great Falls of the Potomac River *(E-11)*
  The overlook on Olmsted Island near the Great Falls Tavern Visitor Center in Potomac offers spectacular views of the falls.

Great Falls

- #### Green Ridge State Forest *(B-5)*
  Point Lookout, Banners, Warrior Mountain, and No Name Overlooks provide sweeping views of the Potomac River and 44,000 acres of oak and hickory forest.

- #### Janes Island State Park *(K-17)*
  Almost completely surrounded by the Chesapeake Bay and its inlets, this park is a peaceful natural paradise with miles of secluded shoreline, marsh areas, and few signs of civilization.

- #### The Narrows *(A-4)*
  Along the National Historic Road, drivers will pass through a natural 1,000-foot gap in the mountains with rock cliffs on Will's Mountain and dense forest lining the creek below.

- #### Baltimore World Trade Center *(M-11)*
  Take a ride up to the 27th-floor observation deck, the "Top of the World," for panoramic views of the Inner Harbor, Chesapeake Bay, and the downtown area. This is the nation's tallest pentagonal building.

HERITAGE

Antietam National Battlefield (B-8)

This Civil War site marks the endpoint of Confederate General Robert E. Lee's first invasion of the North. On September 17, 1862, more than 23,000 men were killed or wounded. This battle remains the bloodiest single-day battle in American history. On September 22, 1862, five days after a bloodbath that shocked the nation, President Lincoln published a preliminary Emancipation Proclamation. Today, the best way for visitors to view the expansive battlefield is to take the self-guided driving tour. The 8.5-mile route includes 11 stops, the story behind each of which is narrated on an audio tape available at the visitor center. (The tour can take two hours, even without getting out of the car.) Walking or biking the road is possible. A 26-minute film, "Antietam Visit," is shown every half-hour except at noon in the visitor center. The movie re-creates the battle and President Lincoln's visit to the Union commander General George B. McClellan.

(301) 432-5124; www.nps.gov/anti

Chesapeake Bay Maritime Museum

Chesapeake Bay Maritime Museum (F-15)

Since 1965, this museum has introduced visitors to the history and culture of the Chesapeake Bay. Located in the charming village of St. Michaels, the 18-acre museum campus is home to nine exhibit buildings and the Point Lookout Tower, which offers visitors spectacular vistas of the Miles River and surrounding area. At the Waterman's Wharf, a recreated crabber's shanty, visitors can check eel or crab pots for a recent catch or tong for oysters. The museum's Boat Yard demonstrates the traditions of a working waterfront. Shipwrights and apprentices restore boats or preserve and maintain the museum's floating fleet of historic Bay boats.

(410) 745-2916; www.cbmm.org

Fort McHenry National Monument & Historic Shrine (J-5)

One of Baltimore's most famous historic spots is this star-shaped fort, which earned its place in national lore after the British tried to attack the city during the War of 1812. During the Battle of Baltimore, the fort withstood 25 hours of British bombardment, but in the end strong artillery fire repulsed the British, thus saving a key port city. The battle, fought on September 13-14, 1814, was also the inspiration for Francis Scott Key to write the poem "The Star-Spangled Banner," which was later set to music and became the U.S. national anthem. Today, visitors can learn about Fort McHenry's history and the writing of the poem at the National Parks Service's only designated National Monument and Historic Shrine. Self-guided tour maps can be obtained at the visitor center, which is marked by a statue of Major George Armistead, the commander of the Fort during the 1814 bombardment.

(410) 962-4290; www.nps.gov/fomc

U.S. Naval Academy Museum (M-20)

In Annapolis, Preble Hall is home to the United States Naval Academy Museum, a museum dedicated to preserving artifacts related to the history and traditions of the U.S. Navy during the last 200 years. The museum sits on the grounds of the U.S. Naval Academy just inside the Maryland Avenue gate. Inside the main wrought iron door, visitors are surrounded by pink travertine marble panels in the entrance foyer. This is the beginning of an impressive collection displayed in four exhibition galleries, including artifacts such as ship models, paintings, prints, flags, uniforms, swords, firearms, medals, manuscripts, photos, and gear. Museum objects can also be seen in the Chapel crypt, Memorial Hall, the Yard, and many of the academic buildings.

(410) 293-2108; www.usna.edu/Museum/

OUTDOORS

Assateague Island State Park & National Seashore (J-20)

Assateague Island, a 37-mile-long barrier island, stretches from Maryland's Ocean City down across the Virginia border and has two NPS-run districts in addition to a state park. The island is constantly changing due to the area's gentle breezes and strong winds, as well as from the Atlantic Ocean's tossing waves and the bay's calmer waters. The National Seashore is known for its free-roaming wild horses. Visitors can enjoy a number of recreational activities by the seaside at both the state and national parks: hiking, biking, bird-watching, fishing, camping, swimming, sunbathing, and boating.

National Seashore: (410) 641-1441;
www.nps.gov/asis
State Park: (410) 641-2120;
www.dnr.state.md.us/publiclands/eastern/
assateague.html

Chesapeake and Ohio (C&O) Canal National Historical Park (B-6)

From Cumberland, Maryland down to Washington, D.C., the C&O Canal follows the Potomac River for 184.5 miles. The canal was in operation from 1828-1924 as a transportation route, mainly for hauling coal to the port of Georgetown in the nation's capital. Today, there are still many original structures — locks, lock houses, and aqueducts — that remind visitors of the canal's transportation history. This family-friendly park offers great historical, cultural, and recreational opportunities both on land and water. Millions of visitors hike or bike the historic canal's fairly flat, continuous trail through the scenic Potomac River Valley every year. Other fun activities include taking a mule-drawn canal boat ride at Georgetown, canoeing or kayaking watered sections of the canal, viewing exhibits at the six visitor centers, fishing, and camping.

(301) 739-4200; www.nps.gov/choh

Gunpowder Falls State Park (B-14)

Central Maryland's 18,000-acre Gunpowder Falls State Park is a haven for outdoors lovers. The park was established to protect the stream valleys of Big and Little Gunpowder Falls and the Gunpowder River. The area's topography offers visitors a mix of terrain from steep, rugged slopes to tidal marshes and wetland. The park has more than 100 miles of trails and offers hikers ample opportunity to explore on foot, while cyclists can enjoy the 21-mile Northern Central Railroad Trail. Water-lovers will enjoy swimming, boating, paddling, tubing, and fishing in both freshwater and tidal areas. There is exceptional trout fishing in a special trout management stream. Overnight getaway stays at Mill Pond Cottage, a charming and fully equipped house nestled in the Hereford Wildlands, offer visitors a relaxing escape that's also close to an array of recreational opportunities.

(410) 592-2897;
www.dnr.state.md.us/publiclands/central/
gunpowder.html

Wisp Mountain Resort (B-1)

Wisp Resort

Come winter or summer, Wisp Mountain Resort has plenty of outdoor adventure for all ages. For snow lovers, there are more than 20 runs to challenge skiers and snowboarders, while special parks and arena areas give snowboarders and snowtubers free rein to play. Snowmobiling and sleigh rides are offered if conditions permit. In the summer, the resort has an 18-hole golf course; a 20,000 square-foot paved and wood skate park for skateboarders, inline skaters, and bikers; great mountain biking and mountain boarding down the wooded nature trails or ski slopes; scenic chair lift rides for stunning views of nearby Deep Creek Lake; paintball; Frisbee golf; guided ATV tours; and fishing in Deep Creek Lake. The Sewickley Spa offers skin care services as well as massage and body therapies for relaxation and rejuvenation.

(800) 462-9477 or (301) 387-4911;
www.wispresort.com

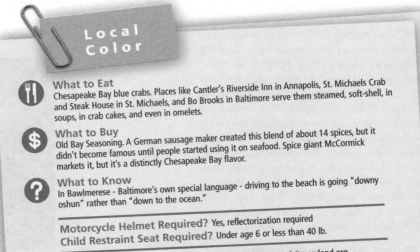

Local Color

What to Eat
Chesapeake Bay blue crabs. Places like Cantler's Riverside Inn in Annapolis, St. Michaels Crab and Steak House in St. Michaels, and Bo Brooks in Baltimore serve them steamed, soft-shell, in soups, in crab cakes, and even in omelets.

What to Buy
Old Bay Seasoning. A German sausage maker created this blend of about 14 spices, but it didn't become famous until people started using it on seafood. Spice giant McCormick markets it, but it's a distinctly Chesapeake Bay flavor.

What to Know
In Bawlmerese - Baltimore's own special language - driving to the beach is going "downy oshun" rather than "down to the ocean."

Motorcycle Helmet Required? Yes, reflectorization required
Child Restraint Seat Required? Under age 6 or less than 40 lb.

Maryland Office of Tourism: (800) 634-7386; www.visitmaryland.org
Road Construction and Conditions: (800) 327-3125 (conditions); (800) 541-9595 (conditions); (410) 582-5650; www.chart.state.md.us

A weathered house overlooks the windswept beach on Cape Cod.

CITIES

✪ Boston (State Capital) (E-14)

Boston Harbor

One of the major U.S. metropolitan centers, Boston is a rare combination of modern commercial city and Old World, colonial charm. Its importance in American history has earned it the nickname "Cradle of the Revolution," and one of the best places to explore its past is the famed Freedom Trail. This 2.5-mile walk through some of the oldest sections of town takes visitors past 16 historic locations. Faneuil Hall — meeting spot of Revolutionary leaders — also sits on the trail and is home to a lively mix of shops, restaurants, and entertainment. Boston Public Garden offers the chance to ride in a swan boat and, in season, thousands of flowers.

Greater Boston Convention & Visitors Bureau:
(888) 733-2678; www.bostonusa.com

Lowell

Lowell (C-13)

Located at the confluence of the Merrimack and Concord rivers, Lowell sits in the heart of the Merrimack Valley and is a former mill town where visitors can still experience the thundering beat of 80 looms working in a historic mill. Many of the mills, canals, and early housing of the textile era have been preserved and restored as part of Lowell National Historical Park. One notable stop is the Boott Cotton Mills Museum, where visitors can explore the Boott Mill boardinghouse and exhibits on working people. Other local draws include the New England Quilt Museum, which displays both contemporary and historic quilts, the American Textile History Museum, and the Whistler House Museum of Art, which houses works by American painter James Abbott McNeill Whistler and other American artists.

Greater Merrimack Valley Convention & Visitors Bureau:
(978) 459-6150; www.lowell.org

Springfield (G-5)

The state's third-largest city is best known for the manufacture of the Springfield rifle and the invention of basketball. Located on the banks of the Connecticut River, Springfield sits in a broad valley in western Massachusetts. Visitors can find all sorts of experiences here, from a quaint New England historic village to the thrills of Six Flags New England, the region's largest amusement park. Springfield Armory, established in 1779 and the oldest U.S. arsenal, is now a national historic site and contains the world's largest collection of American firearms. The Naismith Memorial Basketball Hall of Fame honors Dr. James Naismith, who founded the sport in 1891. Visitors can shoot baskets, watch films, and enjoy exhibits and memorabilia. Storrowton Village Museum in West Springfield is a collection of restored New England buildings including a meetinghouse, schoolhouse, and blacksmith shop.

Greater Springfield Convention & Visitors Bureau:
(800) 723-1548 or (413) 787-1548; www.valleyvisitor.com

Worcester (F-10)

This city's roots are in the Industrial Revolution, and it continues to be a center of manufacturing, research, and biotechnology today. Worcester is situated in the hill country of central Massachusetts at the headwaters of the Blackstone River. Downtown Worcester's DCU Center complex hosts numerous conventions, trade shows, performing artists, and sports events. Other notable points of interest include the Worcester Art Museum, one of New England's largest art museums, with a fine collection of European, Eastern, and American art; the Higgins Armory Museum, which displays an extensive collection of medieval and Renaissance armor; and the Salisbury Mansion, one of the best-documented historic houses in New England.

Central Massachusetts Convention & Visitors Bureau:
(800) 231-7557 or (508) 755-7400; www.worcester.org

SCENERY

Mohawk Trail (B-2)

The 65 miles that form this scenic byway from Greenfield to Williamstown along Route 2 run on one of the nation's oldest roads. The trail received its name when the Mohawk tribe battled and defeated the Pocumtucks who lived along the route. Visitors can still hike parts of this ancient path from the main road. The byway has more than 100 attractions to stop and see, from old churches and striking statues to Mt. Greylock (the tallest mountain in Massachusetts) and the Bridge of Flowers.

Old boats in Cape Cod Bay

Old King's Highway (J-18)

This Massachusetts State Scenic Byway runs for 34 miles along Route 6A, tracing the inner edge of Cape Cod Bay from Sandwich to Orleans. The road follows what was once an Indian trade route. Today, drivers can see anything from sea captain houses and pilgrim churches to cranberry and salt marshes. The byway passes through seven cape towns with gracious houses, well-manicured lawns, and plenty of restaurants and shops.

● **Chesterfield Gorge** (E-4)
Dramatic views of rock walls and the Westfield River are to be had from the half-mile foot trail that runs along the top of the deep gorge.

● **Martha's Vineyard** (L-17)
This triangular island possesses stunning scenery on all three sides, but the view from Gay Head on the southwest corner offers panoramas of Menemsha, Squibnocket Pond, Chilmark Woods, the shoreline, and on a clear day, the Elizabeth Islands.

● **Salisbury Beach State Reservation** (A-16)
Year-round the beach is pictureque, but in fall and winter, you'll see harbor seals sunning themselves on the jetty.

● **Scargo Hill Observation Tower** (J-19)
Gaze across Cape Cod Bay toward the summer resort of Provincetown.

● **Tanglewood** (E-1)
The Berkshires of western Massachusetts provide a splendidly verdant setting for the Boston Symphony Orchestra, which has made its summer home here for 60 years.

Cape Cod National Seashore

HERITAGE

Boston National Historical Park (J-2):

From the gold-domed Old State House to a historic burying ground to the Charlestown Navy Yard, visitors on the Freedom Trail encounter 16 sites that together tell the tale of how this country was "conceived in liberty" and wrested from the British in the Revolutionary War. The 2.5-mile self-guided Freedom Trail begins in Boston Common at the Old State House and is marked on the sidewalk by red paint or red bricks. Stops include the Old South Meeting House, Faneuil Hall, the Paul Revere House, and the Old North Church. Charlestown Navy Yard and the Bunker Hill Monument (intermittently closed for construction until spring 2007) are located across the Charles River. In the Yard the U.S. Navy leads tours of the USS *Constitution* — nicknamed "Old Ironsides" — the oldest commissioned warship afloat. Rangers conduct tours through the Yard itself and the USS *Cassin Young*, a World War II destroyer. A climb to the top of the 221-foot Bunker Hill Monument obelisk affords views of Boston and the Atlantic ocean. At Dorchester Heights (in South Boston and not on the Trail) the tale of the British evacuation of Boston is told.

(617) 242-5642; www.nps.gov/bost

Old Sturbridge Village (G-8)

Learn about everyday life in a small New England town from 1790 to 1840. Farmers, craftsmen, and shopkeepers in period dress work the 200-acre village to provide visitors a taste of New England's past through a variety of collections, exhibits, and programs. Experience all aspects of life, from spinning at Widow Fenno's, kitchen chores at the Fitch House, to milking a cow or watching a blacksmith work. Visitors can examine early mills where waterpower not only turned grain into flour, but also helped to saw logs into lumber and to prepare wool for spinning. Heirloom gardens, the Bullard Tavern, and specialty shops round out a full day's adventure.

(508) 347-3362; (800) 733-1830; www.osv.org

Plimoth Plantation (H-16)

Experience Plymouth much as it was in the 17th century at this living history museum. The museum has two separate locations: Plimoth Plantation, located three miles south of Plymouth, and the *Mayflower II*, located on the Plymouth waterfront. The plantation re-creates the Pilgrims' 1627 coastal village, and costumed interpreters demonstrate crafts and daily chores while speaking the Shakespearean English of that time. At the Crafts Center, watch period furnishings and clothing take form, or visit the Nye Barn to learn about the rare heritage breed livestock at the museum. A different perspective can be found at Hobbamock's (Wampanoag) Homesite, where modern-day American Indians practice and preserve the traditions, skills, and culture of the Wampanoag tribe. Back at the waterfront, visitors can board the *Mayflower II*, a full-scale reproduction of the vessel that brought 17th-century colonists to America.

Plimoth Plantation

(508) 746-1622; www.plimoth.org

Salem Maritime National Historic Site (H-10)

Salem may be best known for the witch trials of 1692, but it was also an important port city that helped develop maritime trade after the Revolution. Salem Maritime, the first National Historic Site in the national park system, was established in March 1938 to preserve the maritime history of New England. The site includes nine acres of waterfront land with 12 historic structures and a downtown visitor center. All of the sites help document the development of the colonial era's Atlantic triangular trade routes, the role of privateering during the Revolutionary War, and international trade with the Far East, which helped the fledgling nation gain its economic independence. Salem Maritime is also the central point of the Essex National Heritage Area, which includes thousands of historic places in Essex County.

(978) 740-1660; www.nps.gov/sama

OUTDOORS

Ashuwillticook Rail Trail (C-2)

In the northwestern corner of Massachusetts, from Adams to Lanesborough, visitors can bike the Berkshires along one of the state's newest paved rail trails. The trail follows the right-of-way of a former railroad and runs parallel to Route 8 for 11 miles through the towns of Cheshire, Lanesborough, and Adams. Along the route, there are several access points with parking lots and restrooms. "Ashuwillticook" comes from the Native American name for the south branch of the Hoosic River and means "the pleasant river in between the hills." Along the way, riders, skaters, and walkers will pass through the Hoosac River Valley, which sits between Mt. Greylock — the highest point in Massachusetts — and the Hoosic Range. Other noteworthy sights include the Cheshire Reservoir, the Hoosic River, and surrounding wetland areas that are home to a variety of wildlife.

(413) 442-8928;
www.mass.gov/dcr/parks/western/asrt.htm

Boston Harbor Islands National Recreation Area (K-9)

Thirty-four islands within Boston Harbor comprise this recreation area. The islands are managed by a special partnership including the National Park Service and several private and public organizations. Visitors enjoy exploring tide pools, hiking trails and salt marshes, walking through Fort Warren, biking, kayaking, camping, fishing, boating, picnicking, swimming, and climbing the lighthouse stairs. And it's all just a short distance from downtown Boston. Each island has its own history and outdoor opportunities, so plan ahead according to interests and availability. Access to the islands varies; most are reached by only boat (ferries, shuttles, and tour boats are all available), but a few are accessible by land. Some areas are open year-round, while most locations are open seasonally.

(617) 223-8666; www.nps.gov/boha

Cape Cod National Seashore (H-20)

More than 43,000 acres of shoreline and uplands form this national seashore between Cape Cod Bay and the Atlantic Ocean. The area boasts 40 miles of pristine ocean beaches with six swimming beaches, 11 self-guided nature trails, several spectacular cycling trails, dozens of clear freshwater ponds, and a variety of picnic areas and scenic overlooks. There are also a number of historic structures that can be toured including lighthouses, Cape Cod-style houses, and a lifesaving station. The park maintains three bike trails: Province Lands, a 5.45-mile hilly loop among the forests, sand dunes, and ponds; Head of the Meadow, a four-mile trail that follows the edge of a freshwater marsh; and Nauset, a 3.2-mile out-and-back trail that connects Salt Pond with Coast Guard Beach. Other favorite activities include bird watching, boating, fishing, hiking, kayaking, swimming, and nature walks on the trail or beach for wildlife viewing.

(508) 349-3785; www.nps.gov/caco

EcoTarium (B-20)

Treetop ecology is alive, well, and waiting to be explored at this Worcester nature center. Pull on a helmet, strap on a harness, and then take a walk on a series of platforms and rope bridges suspended 40 feet in the air among the treetops of a grove of hickory and oak trees. The ropes, ladders, and platforms replicate those used by scientists studying the diversity of life in tree canopies around the world. The Tree Canopy Walkway is open for guided one-hour programs only, and reservations are required. On the rest of the outdoor grounds, visitors can also enjoy three scenic nature trails — the Vibram, Timescape, and Meadow — which include stops at Lower Pond and a New England meadow. The EcoTarium's mission of environmental education also extends to an indoor museum with exhibits and a planetarium.

EcoTarium

(508) 929-2700; www.ecotarium.org

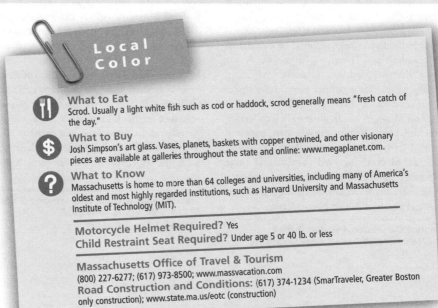

Local Color

What to Eat
Scrod. Usually a light white fish such as cod or haddock, scrod generally means "fresh catch of the day."

What to Buy
Josh Simpson's art glass. Vases, planets, baskets with copper entwined, and other visionary pieces are available at galleries throughout the state and online: www.megaplanet.com.

What to Know
Massachusetts is home to more than 64 colleges and universities, including many of America's oldest and most highly regarded institutions, such as Harvard University and Massachusetts Institute of Technology (MIT).

Motorcycle Helmet Required? Yes
Child Restraint Seat Required? Under age 5 or 40 lb. or less

Massachusetts Office of Travel & Tourism
(800) 227-6277; (617) 973-8500; www.massvacation.com
Road Construction and Conditions: (617) 374-1234 (SmarTraveler, Greater Boston only construction); www.state.ma.us/eotc (construction)

TRAVEL GUIDE   Massachusetts

Dense forest shades a road on the Keweenaw Peninsula.

CITIES

Detroit (R-13)

In 1701, Antoine de la Moche, Sieur de Cadillac, established a fort at a site the French called *le détroit*, "the strait." Thanks to its strategic location between lakes Huron and Erie, Detroit grew into an important trading post, then a major hub of shipping and man-ufacturing. In the early 20th century, it became the cen-ter of America's automobile indus-try. Visitors expect-ing to find a decay-ing Rust Belt city are pleasantly sur-prised by Detroit's abundant cultural offerings, such as the internationally renowned Detroit Institute of Arts, the Motown Historical Museum, and the sprawling complex of attractions known as The Henry Ford in neighboring Dearborn. The complex includes Greenfield Village, the Henry Ford Museum, and the Ford Rouge auto plant tour. The Detroit Zoo ranks as one of the world's finest. The downtown area, anchored by the seven-tower Renaissance Center, is steadily becoming revitalized, attracting visitors with new sports stadi-ums, restaurants, and shops.

Detroit Institute of Arts

Detroit Metro Convention & Visitors Bureau:
(313) 202-1800, (800) 338-7648; www.visitdetroit.com

✪ Lansing (State Capital) (Q-9)

Michigan's state capital combines a small-town feel with big-city sophistication. Home to Michigan State University, Lansing boasts a thriving performing arts scene, numerous golf courses, and a minor league baseball team called the Lugnuts. The neoclassical state capitol building has been restored to its original Victorian grandeur and is well worth a visit. A few blocks away sits the Michigan Historical Museum, whose highlights include a copper mine and a three-story-tall relief map of Michigan. The R.E. Olds Transportation Museum has an outstanding collection of Oldsmobile cars. Within the forested parkland along the Red Cedar River is Potter Park Zoo, where snow leopards, black rhinos, red pandas, and more than 400 other animals roam in natural habitats. South of the river, nature trails wind among the maples, oaks, pines, and ponds of Fenner Nature Center.

Greater Lansing Convention & Visitors Bureau:
(888) 252-6746 or (517) 487-6800; www.lansing.org

Cherries at Grand Traverse Bay

Traverse City (J-6)

Nicknamed "The Cherry Capital of the World," this popular four-season resort lies at the heart of Michigan's cherry-growing region. Each July it hosts the eight-day National Cherry Festival, one of the most popular annual events in the United States. But there's much more to Traverse City than cherries. Throughout the summer, visitors flock here to swim, fish, and boat on Lake Michigan's Grand Traverse Bay and the numerous smaller lakes in the area. Others come to tour local wineries, explore nearby Sleeping Bear Dunes National Lakeshore, take scenic drives around the Leelanau Peninsula, or attend concerts at the Interlochen Center for the Arts. In the winter, there's downhill skiing and snowboarding at half a dozen local ski areas as well as an excellent network of trails for cross-country skiing and snowmobiling.

Traverse City Convention & Visitors Bureau:
(800) 940-1120, (231) 947-1120;
www.visittraversecity.com

Grand Rapids (P-6)

The hometown of former President Gerald R. Ford is considered the primary cultural and business hub of western Michigan. A thriving arts scene includes Michigan's only professional ballet company as well as opera, theater, and symphonic concerts. At the Gerald R. Ford Museum, visitors can eavesdrop on a typical day in the Oval Office, view a re-creation of a White House State Dinner, and check out the actual tools used in the Watergate break-in. The Van Andel Museum Center features a huge collection that has been organized into an interactive exhibition called Collecting A to Z. At the Blandford Nature Center & Mixed Greens, hiking trails lead visitors through woodlands, fields, ravines, and marshes. Grand Rapids is also home to the Frederik Meijer Gardens & Sculpture Park, the largest tropical conservatory in the state.

Grand Rapids/Kent County Convention & Visitors Bureau:
(800) 678-9859 or (616) 459-8287;
www.visitgrandrapids.org

SCENERY

Black River National Scenic Byway (B-10)
Near the westernmost point of the Upper Peninsula, County Road 513 follows the Black River as it flows northward to Lake Superior through the pines, hemlocks, and hardwoods of the Ottawa National Forest. The 11-mile drive passes five waterfalls — Great Conglomerate, Potawatomi, Gorge, Sandstone, and Rainbow Falls — before reaching Black River Harbor, a popular recreation area.

The Tunnel of Trees (G-7)
This is the nickname for the 20-mile stretch of SR 119 between the towns of Harbor Springs and Cross Village near the northern tip of the Lower Peninsula. As the narrow road twists and curves along the Lake Michigan shoreline, trees crowd it on both sides, and their interlocking limbs create a tunnel effect. In autumn, as the leaves change to bright yellows, oranges, and reds, the drive is espe-cially beautiful.

● **Brockway Mountain Drive** (A-13)
This 10-mile drive runs along the spine of the Keweenaw Peninsula and links the Upper Peninsula towns of Copper Harbor and Eagle Harbor. A parking area at the drive's midpoint offers spectacular views of Lake Superior and the surrounding forested hills.

● **Mackinac Bridge** (F-8)
Arching 200 feet above the Straits of Mackinac, Michigan's most famous bridge treats I-75 trav-elers to a 360° vista of blue water, distant islands, and huge freighters.

Mackinac Bridge

● **Michigan's "Thumb"** (P-14)
Michigan Highway 25 hugs the Lake Huron coast between Port Huron and Bay City, a 150-mile stretch that boasts beautiful beaches, three state parks, numerous lighthouses, and charm-ing little harbor towns like Lexington and Port Austin.

● **Pierce Stocking Drive** (I-4)
A "must" for visitors to Sleeping Bear Dunes National Lakeshore, this seven-mile loop winds through "ghost forests," climbs to the summits of tow-ering coastal dunes, and provides views that stretch far up and down the Lake Michigan shoreline.

Sleeping Bear Dunes

● **River Road National Scenic Byway** (K-11)
River Road parallels the Au Sable River for 22 scenic miles through the pines, hemlocks, and maples of the Huron National Forest.

HERITAGE

Colonial Michilimackinac Historic State Park *(F-8)*

Located at the south end of the famous Mackinac Bridge, Colonial Michilimackinac is a reconstruction of a French and British military outpost and fur-trading village. The original fort was built by the French in 1715, then taken over by the British in 1761. It remained under British control until 1781. Today, visitors will find faithful reconstructions of 14 buildings, including Ste. Anne's Church, soldiers' barracks, and a powder magazine. An American Indian encampment sits just outside the fort's walls. Costumed interpreters bring the colonial period to life through reenactments of such events as a traditional French wedding and the arrival of voyageurs from Montreal. "Treasures From the Sand" is an underground archaeological exhibit of artifacts such as coins, rosary beads, and buttons from soldiers' uniforms.

(231) 436-4100; www.mackinacparks.com

Fort Michilimackinac and the Mackinac Bridge

The Henry Ford *(p.64, K-5)*

Formerly known as the Henry Ford Museum and Greenfield Village, the 12-acre Henry Ford complex in the Detroit suburb of Dearborn includes the Henry Ford Museum and its five exhibits of Americana. Among the exhibits are "The Automobile in American Life," a unique, in-depth look at the world the car has created, and the "Innovation Station" learning game. Autos on display range from early horseless carriages to fondly remembered family sedans. Visitors can also view a 1946 diner, a 1950 drive-in theater, and a Holiday Inn guest room from the 1960s. Greenfield Village, which adjoins the museum, features more than 80 historic structures, some built here and others moved here from their original locations around the country and grouped thematically. Spanning some 300 years, the structures include such treasures as Thomas Edison's laboratory, George Washington Carver's cabin, a 19th-century railroad roundhouse, and the Logan County Courthouse, where Abraham Lincoln practiced law. The Henry Ford also includes an IMAX Theater, the Benson Ford Research Center, and the Ford Rouge auto plant tour.

(313) 982-6001, (800) 835-5237; www.thehenryford.org

USS *Silversides (0-4)*

Credited with sinking 30 Japanese vessels, the USS *Silversides* is one of the most highly decorated WWII submarines. It was profiled on the silver screen in "Destination Tokyo" starring Cary Grant. Decommissioned in 1946, the sub has been berthed since 1987 in Muskegon's Pere Marquette Park, along the south side of the Muskegon Channel. Visitors can pick up an information sheet and climb down the hatchway for a fascinating guided tour (in season) or self-guided tour (off season) through the sub's narrow passageways and tiny rooms. It might seem hard to believe, but eight officers and 72 enlisted men once shared these close quarters for weeks at a time. The submarine is part of the Great Lakes Naval Memorial & Museum, which also includes a Prohibition-era Coast Guard cutter, the McLane W-146.

(231) 755-1230; www.glnmm.org

USS *Silversides*

OUTDOORS

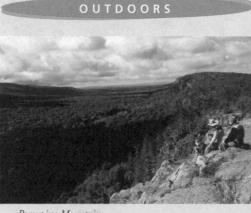

Porcupine Mountains

Porcupine Mountains Wilderness State Park *(B-10)*

Located on the Lake Superior shoreline of the Upper Peninsula, this 60,000-acre park is a realm of virgin northern hardwood forest, ancient mountains, wild rivers, and pristine lakes. Twenty trails crisscross the wilderness and cover 90 miles of ground, much of it rugged and steep. The longest single trail is the Lake Superior Trail, which hugs the shoreline for 17 miles of rigorous inclines. The four-mile Escarpment Trail, which runs along the top of high escarpment skirts, offers some of the most magnificent scenery in the park, including sheer cliffs, the Lake of the Clouds, and the vast blue expanse of Lake Superior. The park's highest point, appropriately named Summit Peak, has an observation deck providing views that stretch into Wisconsin and Minnesota.

(906) 885-5275; www.michigan.gov/dnr

Family camping

Sleeping Bear Dunes National Lakeshore *(I-4)*

This recreational paradise stretches for 35 miles along the eastern shore of Lake Michigan and also includes two uninhabited offshore islands, North Manitou and South Manitou. Prevailing westerly winds have created towering sand dunes, some of which slope steeply down to the lake. Many visitors come just to see the dunes or to attempt the Dune Climb, a 150-foot ascent that rewards climbers with a scenic view of Glen Lake. Canoeing and inner-tubing are popular activities on the placid Crystal and Platte rivers. Hikers will find a wide variety of trails both on the mainland and on the two islands, which are accessible by ferry. In winter, 55 miles of trails are available for cross-country skiers.

Dune Climb

(231) 326-5134; www.nps.gov/slbe

Vasa Pathway *(J-6)*

In a state full of great places to cross-country ski, this trail system near Traverse City ranks near the top. Loops of two, three, six, and sixteen miles wind through Pere Marquette State Forest beneath a canopy of snow-covered white pines. Several times a week, the trails are meticulously groomed for both classic and skate skiing. Intermediate and advanced skiers will find plenty of hills to challenge their skills, while beginners can stick to the flatter areas. The trailhead, located near the town of Acme, has a warming hut, restrooms, and plenty of parking. In February, the Vasa Pathway hosts one of the top Nordic events in the U.S.: the North American Vasa.

Cross-country skiing

(231) 941-4300; www.traversetrails.org

Local Color

🍴 **What to Eat**
Pasty. Pronounced PASS-tee, this all-in-one meal was devised by Cornish miners working the Upper Peninsula's coal and copper mines. A crust surrounds meat, root vegetables, and onions. Travelers find them in stores and restaurants.

$ **What to Buy**
Red flannels. In Cedar Springs, the Cedar Springs Red Flannel Company (www.redflannels.com) makes classic drop-seat long johns as well as other red flannelwear. October sees the Red Flannel Festival.

? **What to Know**
The Michigan Great Lakes shoreline has more lighthouses - 116 - than any other state.

Motorcycle Helmet Required? Yes
Child Restraint Seat Required? Under age 4

Travel Michigan: (888) 784-7328; www.michigan.org
Road Construction and Conditions: (800) 381-8477;
(888) 305-7283 (construction in West and Southwest Michigan); (800) 641-6368
(construction in Metro Detroit); www.michigan.gov/dot

Bluffs along the powerful Mississippi River are ablaze in color.

CITIES

Duluth (J-12)

This major inland port makes much of its busy waterfront. Harbor tours yield closeup views of ocean-going vessels, Great Lakes freighters, grain elevators, and the city's signature aerial lift bridge. In Canal Park, the Lake Superior Maritime Visitor Center has scale-model ships, full-scale cabin replicas, and videos on commercial shipping. Nearby, the freshwater tanks of the Great Lakes Aquarium give visitors a glimpse of life at the very considerable depths of Lake Superior. For more maritime adventure, tour the S.S. William A. Irvin Ore Boat, a retired freighter noted for her elegant state rooms. Railroads too are an important part of the city's past and present. The restored downtown terminus known as The Depot houses cultural facilities including the Lake Superior Railroad Museum with its beautifully restored engines and cars. Departing from The Depot, the North Shore Scenic Railroad offers excursions to points as far away as Two Harbors.

Duluth Convention & Visitors Bureau: (218) 722-4011, (800) 438-5884 or (218) 722-4011; www.visitduluth.com

Duluth harbor

Minneapolis (O-9)

Minneapolis is the most cosmopolitan city of the upper Midwest. One of the nation's finest regional theatres, the Guthrie, occupies an impressive new home on the banks of the Mississippi. Designed to complement its neighbors in the historic Mill District, the theater has three performance spaces ranging from 250 to 1,100 seats. Theatergoers can also head to Hennepin Avenue for the latest touring Broadway productions. The Walker Art Center, known for its 20th-century and contemporary collections, has undergone major expansion, as has the Minneapolis Institute of Arts, whose new wing (opening spring 2006) increases museum space by forty percent. The Turnblad Mansion, which houses the American Swedish Institute, will open a new wing in 2007. Serious shoppers flock to south suburban Bloomington to take in the myriad shops at Mall of America, the nation's largest shopping mall, which comes complete with its own theme park and other amusements.

Greater Minneapolis Convention & Visitors Association: (888) 676-6757 or (612) 767-8000; www.minneapolis.org

Rochester (S-11)

Often called one of the country's most livable cities, Rochester is a company town renowned for the presence of the Mayo Clinic. The medical center was founded in 1914, and its buildings still dominate the city skyline. Visitors can tour the research facilities and take the clinic's architecture and art tour. In its new home - stylishly clad in hammered zinc and copper - the Rochester Art Center offers changing installations by contemporary artists and a permanent collection of works by 20th-century painters and sculptors. At Mayowood, the estate of Dr. Charles W. Mayo, visitors will find a collection of antique treasures from around the world. The gardens and grounds surrounding the 49-room Tudor mansion once owned by Dr. Henry S. Plummer are open for year-round enjoyment; the interior of the estate may be toured during summer months. Displays at the Olmsted County History Center include a one-room schoolhouse and an 1860-era log cabin.

Rochester Convention & Visitors Bureau: (507) 288-4331, (800) 634-8277; www.rochestercvb.org

✪ Saint Paul (State Capital) (P-10)

Unlike its flasher twin, Minnesota's capital projects an image of solidity and thoughtful reserve. The city's roots may be explored at Historic Fort Snelling, where costumed interpreters capture the flavor of the 1820s frontier. The Alexander Ramsey House, once occupied by the first territorial governor, still boasts its original furnishings. Also reflective of the city's serious side are the state capitol, with one of world's largest unsupported marble domes, and the Renaissance architecture of the Cathedral of St. Paul. For lighthearted fare, try a sternwheeler or showboat excursion on the Mississippi. Como Park's Zoo and Conservatory burst with exotic animals and plants. Dinosaurs, mummies, and a plethora of interactive exhibits set the mind to wondering at the Science Museum of Minnesota. Opera, symphonies, and musicals are found at the elegant Ordway Center for the Performing Arts. Works by the great sculptors and painters of the last 200 years are displayed at the Minnesota Museum of American Art in its new home downtown.

Capitol building

Saint Paul Convention & Visitors Bureau: (651) 265-4900, (800) 627-6101; www.stpaulcvb.org

SCENERY

Minnesota River Valley National Scenic Byway (P-4)

Located in southwestern Minnesota, SR 67 and connecting roads (including a few gravel ones) comprise a 287-mile scenic byway that follows the Minnesota River from Granite Falls through Mankato. Along the way, the route meanders through rolling farmland and woodlands of oak, elm, and cottonwood. This is one of the state's premier fall color drives; in the summer, the area bursts with wildflowers.

North Shore Drive (J-12)

For 297 miles from Duluth to Grand Portage, five miles south of the border, SR 61 runs between the rocky coast of Lake Superior on one side and the slopes of the Sawtooth Mountains on the other. Be prepared to stop to smell the pine-scented air and to witness wilderness streams cascading over waterfalls. Old mining settlements dot the shoreline and cater to sports fishermen today as they did to the ore boats of years past. In Two Harbors, look for the *Edna G.*, a restored tugboat that is open for tours.

Waters of the Dancing Sky Scenic Byway (D-9)

This byway (SR 11) rolls through "big water" country along the Canadian border. The peaceful waters once transported French voyageurs in pelt-laden canoes. Today they provide a playground for outdoor enthusiasts, especially fishermen. The route continues through International Falls and beyond to Lake of the Woods. Look toward the night sky for the aurora borealis, whose curtains of colors crossing the sky give the byway its name.

● **Alexander Ramsey Park (O-6)**
Located in the town of Redwood Falls, Ramsey Falls is a stunning water cascade in the summer, and a curtain of white ice in winter.

● **Inspiration Peak (K-3)**
Off county road 38 in Ottertail County, this peak is the second-highest in Minnesota and offers exceptional views of maple hardwood forests and many of the county's 1,000 lakes.

Headwaters of the Mississippi River, Park Rapids

● **Itasca State Park (H-5)**
In Itasca State Park off US 71 near Bemidji, stepping stones lead across the narrow headwaters of the Mississippi River long before it earns its moniker "mighty."

● **Noerenberg Memorial Park (p. 65, F-1)**
A brick path leads through elegant formal gardens of daylilies and ornamental grasses to an overlook in Wayzata of Lake Minnetonka, the largest lake within the metropolitan Minneapolis area.

● **Pipestone National Monument (J-2)**
Just north of Pipestone off US 75, a three-quarter-mile trail through a tallgrass prairie leads to rosy-pink quartzite bluffs where Native Americans still gather the red stone to make ceremonial pipes.

● **Sugar Loaf Bluff (R-13)**
Illuminated at night, this 85-foot tower of quarried stone sits atop a 500-foot bluff providing a bird's-eye view of Winona, Lake Winona, the Mississippi River, and a broad swath of apple orchards.

OUTDOORS

Jay Cooke State Park (J-11)

There's Class I river rafting on the upper part of the St. Louis River, where bluffs and wooded hills loom over the tranquil water. But the lower part of the St. Louis is another story. As the river nears Carlton, it gains speed as it tumbles over slabs of ancient, exposed rock and charges through low-lying woods and bogs within Jay Cooke State Park. A suspension bridge spans the river within the park, providing an aerial view of the water rushing below. Yet, depending on the season and rainfall, the St. Louis can slow to a trickle.

(218) 384-4610;
www.dnr.state.mn.us/state_parks/jay_cooke

Root River State Trail (S-13)

Bike enthusiasts can follow the flow of the Root River for 42 miles on a black-top trail along the river bluffs between Fountain and Houston. In the winter, cross-country skiers can follow the same route in this scenic corner of southeastern Minnesota. The trail winds through a valley, passes a small dam, and continues over old railroad bridges. Along the way, sightings of hawks in the sky are as common as the sound of songbirds from the trees. Watch for wild turkeys on the trail. There are trail centers in Lanesboro, Rushford, and Houston, plus other rest areas.

(651) 296-5029; (888) 868-7476;
www.dnr.state.mn.us/state_trails/blufflands

Family biking

Hiking

Superior Hiking Trail (G-13)

Only foot travel is allowed on this 205-mile trail that wends its way along the ridgeline above Lake Superior from Two Harbors through seven state parks to the Canadian border. Along the way, enjoy breathtaking views of the Sawtooth Mountains, sparkling rivers and streams, rushing waterfalls like the Upper, Middle and Lower Falls of the Gooseberry River, and forests of fir, cedar, spruce, and northern hardwoods. At times the trail is steep and challenging, but the views it provides are extraordinary. With 30 access points — one every five to ten miles on SR 61 north of Duluth — there are any number of loop or out-and-back hikes possible. Lodge-to-lodge hikes can be arranged with a tour operator. Campsites are available every five to eight miles. The trail is known for excellent signage.

(218) 834-2700; www.shta.org

HERITAGE

Hibbing (H-10)

This area of Minnesota is the "iron ore capital of the world." Since ore shipping began in 1895, more than 1.4 billion tons of earth have been removed to form the largest open-pit iron mine anywhere. That's the equivalent of the amount of earth that would need to be removed if a small tunnel were dug from Minnesota through the center of the Earth and out the other side. Located just north of town on US 169, the Hull-Rust-Mahoning mine has been worked since 1895. The vast pit extends more than three miles in length and is up to two miles wide and nearly 600 feet deep. More on mining and the area can be found at the Minnesota Museum of Mining and at Ironworld Discovery Center. Hibbing is also the hometown of legendary songwriter and musician Bob Dylan.

(218) 262-3895; (800) 444-2246; www.hibbing.org

Historic Fort Snelling (p. 65, H-6)

Restored to its 1827 appearance, a stone fortress anchors Historic Fort Snelling and overlooks the confluence of the Mississippi and Minnesota rivers. The fort was built in 1825 as an outpost to control commercial traffic on the waterways. Daily life at the settlement is reenacted today through a living history program. Visitors can talk to soldiers, cooks, laundresses, storekeepers, and artisans about life on the frontier, even scrape a hide or shoulder a musket. A hospital, powder magazine, and the restored commandant's quarters — the oldest standing residence in the state — are also located at the fort.

Fort Snelling

(612) 726-1171; www.mnhs.org/places/sites/hfs

Split Rock Lighthouse State Historic Site (H-13)

At this landmark lighthouse, costumed interpreters introduce visitors to a keeper's life in the mid-1920s. The U.S. Lighthouse Service built Split Rock Lighthouse between 1907 and 1910 after a fierce gale in November 1905 damaged 29 ships and wrecked two off the rocky shore. Once the public could easily reach the picturesque lighthouse via the North Shore highway (built in 1924), Split Rock became a tourist destination as well as a critical Great Lakes navigational beacon. The light was decommissioned in 1969, and eleven years later the keeper's house was restored to its 1920s appearance. The visitor's center features a film about the Lake Superior iron ore shipping industry and exhibits on how lighthouses work. Guided tours of the fog signal building, lighthouse, and keeper's house are conducted daily. Every year on November 10, the beacon is lit in remembrance of the 29 men who perished aboard the *Edmund Fitzgerald*, a freighter lost in 1975 during another terrible November gale.

(218) 226-6372; www.mnhs.org/places/sites/srl/

New Ulm (R-7)

Founded in 1854 by German immigrants, New Ulm wears its heritage proudly, as evidenced by the Glockenspiel in the center of town. Probably the most German city in Minnesota (and possibly in the whole country), New Ulm has a distinctly European feel. Its wide streets, classic architecture, and overwhelming proportion of German-flavored restaurants and stores all celebrate the heritage of Bavaria and the impact German-Americans have had on the development of this area of Minnesota. Hermann's Monument, a memorial to the Teutonic hero, offers a commanding view of the surrounding countryside. Tours at the August Schell Brewery include the brewery's gardens and deer park.

New Ulm

(888) 463-9856 or (507) 233-4300; www.newulm.com

Local Color

What to Eat
Walleye. Fresh, thick, white walleye fillets are available in specialty groceries like Byerly's. Tavern on Grand in St. Paul serves a legendary fillet.

What to Buy
Jewelry set with thomsonite, a mineral found only on Lake Superior's shore and a few other locations worldwide. Gift shops along Lake Superior's north shore, from Duluth to Grand Marais, carry thomsonite jewelry.

What to Know
In the summer, most everyone leaves at noon Friday (or earlier) to "go to the lake" - any one of the 11,000-some in the state.

Motorcycle Helmet Required? Under age 18 or instructional permit holders
Child Restraint Seat Required? Under age 4

Minnesota Office of Tourism: (800) 657-3700; (651) 296-5029;
www.exploreminnesota.com
Road Construction and Conditions: 511; (800) 542-0220; www.511mn.org

TRAVEL GUIDE Minnesota

Shrimp boats crowd Biloxi's harbor.

CITIES

Biloxi (M-9)

The Gulf Coast's oldest town, Biloxi was founded by the French in 1699 and ruled during the following centuries by Spain, England, the West Florida Republic, the Confederate States, and the United States. It has been a popular vacation destination since the mid-1800s, and it continues to draw visitors with its combination of sunshine, beaches, sport fishing, casino gambling, and history, despite the devastation wrought by hurricanes in the summer of 2005. Beauvoir, the 52-acre estate where Confederate president Jefferson Davis spent his last 12 years, tops the list of historical attractions (having sustained heavy damage in 2005, it won't re-open until June 2008). Other spots where Biloxi's past is on display include the Old Biloxi Cemetery, where many of the original French settlers are buried, and the Old Biloxi Lighthouse (1848).

Mississippi Gulf Coast Convention & Visitors Bureau: (228) 896-6699, (888) 467-4853; www.gulfcoast.org

✪ Jackson (State Capital) (H-6)

Capitol building

From its earliest days as a stop on the Old Natchez Trace, Mississippi's capital and largest city has been a regional trading center and distribution point. Visitors can tour the imposing state capitol building. Living examples of more than 200 native species of fish may be seen in the aquariums at the Mississippi Museum of Natural Science along with other ecological displays. Small-town and farm life take center stage at the Mississippi Agriculture and Forestry Museum, where the National Agricultural Aviation Museum offers a collection of early crop-dusting planes. Programs at the Russell C. Davis Planetarium/Ronald McNair Space Theater range from stargazing to laser light shows and large format films. Exhibits at the Smith Robertson Museum and Cultural Center highlight the life and accomplishments of Mississippi's African-American community.

Jackson Convention & Visitors Bureau: (601) 960-1891, (800) 354-7695; www.visitjackson.com

Natchez (J-3)

When cotton was king on the land and steam ruled the river, Natchez was the greatest of the cotton ports. Thanks to cotton and shipping fortunes, this Mississippi River town boasts some of the South's most beautiful antebellum mansions, churches, and public buildings. Graceful white columns, tree-lined entranceways, and richly landscaped gardens reflect the genteel charm of mid-1800s Natchez. Among the great houses here are Rosalie (1820), Stanton Hall (1857), Longwood (1860), Melrose (1847), and Monmouth (1818). Nine mansions are open for touring year-round, and many others are open during the annual spring and fall pilgrimages. Natchez is also rich in Native American history, as visitors will learn at the Grand Village of the Natchez and Emerald Mound, two local archaeological sites that feature ceremonial mounds. Natchez Under-the-Hill, once called "The Barbary Coast of Mississippi," is today a quaint district of shops, riverboat gaming, and restaurants.

Natchez Convention & Visitors Bureau: (601) 446-6345, (800) 647-6724; www.visitnatchez.com

Vicksburg National Military Park

Vicksburg (H-4)

Nicknamed "The Gibraltar of the Confederacy," Vicksburg withstood powerful Union attacks in 1862, but in 1863 General Grant's army and Admiral Porter's ironclads drew a tight noose around the city. The siege lasted 47 days before the half-starved city surrendered. Visitors can learn about the siege and see monuments, trenches, and gun positions in the 1,800-acre Vicksburg National Military Park. Artifacts from a gunboat, which was raised from the bottom of the Mississippi River, are on display in the USS *Cairo* Museum. Cedar Grove antebellum home, now an inn, still has a cannonball lodged in the parlor wall. The Old Court House Museum also contains siege exhibits. Antebellum homes in the area include Anchuca, Balfour House, Duff Green Mansion, and Martha Vick House.

Vicksburg Convention & Visitors Bureau: (601) 636-9421, (800) 221-3536; www.vicksburgcvb.org

SCENERY

Great River Road (D-4)

The Mississippi segment of this National Scenic Byway parallels the Mississippi River from the Tennessee border south to the Louisiana border, alternating between US Highway 61 —"the Blues Highway" — and SR 1. High levees mean that glimpses of the river are rare, but the classic delta scenery and cultural history along the route more than compensate. Great River Road State Park, which sits high on bluffs near Rosedale, has a four-level observation tower that affords spectacular views of the river.

Natchez Trace Parkway (I-5)

Designed for leisurely travel, this 444-mile-long multi-state thoroughfare closely follows the historic Natchez Trace between its namesake town on the Mississippi River and Nashville, TN. From its starting point in Natchez, the parkway angles northeastward for 310 miles through Mississippi, passing Port Gibson, Jackson, Kosciusko, and Tupelo before crossing into Alabama. The numerous recreational spots, cultural attractions, and points of interest along the way include antebellum mansions, American Indian mounds, historic sites, Civil War battlefields, and the birthplaces of Elvis Presley and Oprah Winfrey. The parkway's visitor center at milepost 266 in Tupelo features exhibits and an audiovisual program about the trace and its importance to river trade and westward expansion.

Natchez Trace Parkway

● Arkabutla Lake (B-6)

Scenic Loop 304 makes a half circle around this lake in the state's northwestern corner. The route begins in Coldwater, passes through Arkabutla and Eudora, and ends in Hernando.

● Bell Road (G-5)

In the decades leading up to the Civil War, this narrow, winding road was the main route between Yazoo City and Vicksburg. Time and progress have obliterated most of the road, but a deeply rutted segment survives south of Yazoo City.

● De Soto National Forest (L-9)

Between Hattiesburg and Biloxi, state routes 29 and 15 take travelers through the heart of De Soto's piney woods.

● Hospitality Highway (M-8)

US 90 runs along the Gulf Coast for 22 miles between Bay St. Louis and Biloxi, passing long white beaches, glittering casinos, historic sites, and antebellum homes, most notably Jefferson Davis's Beauvoir.

● Mississippi River at Vicksburg (H-4)

An overlook at the State Welcome Center off I-20 offers a great view of the river and two huge highway bridges spanning it.

HERITAGE

Delta Blues Museum (C-5)

The corner of Issaquena Avenue and 4th Street in downtown Clarksdale was a blues mecca back in the day when juke joints lined the streets and sharecroppers would come to socialize and party on Saturday nights. In 1979, the Carnegie Public Library established the Delta Blues Museum to chronicle the important role this hard-working Cotton Belt town played in blues history. Given that trains figure so heavily in traditional blues, it is appropriate that the museum occupies the old freight depot of the Yazoo and Mississippi River Valley Railroad. Inside, visitors will find an extensive collection of recordings, videos, rare photographs, memorabilia, and books tracing the roots and development of the blues. The museum also offers regular seminars and programs. Its gift shop and bookstore are an incredible source of rare recordings and publications.

(662) 627-6820; www.deltabluesmuseum.org

Port Gibson (I-4)

After capturing Port Gibson during the Mississippi Campaign of 1863, Union General Ulysses S. Grant decided to spare the town, declaring it "too beautiful to burn." Thanks to Grant's clemency, Port Gibson today boasts an abundance of antebellum homes. Two of the most notable are Oak Square (1850) and Rosswood (1857), located 10 miles south of town. Both of these stately Greek Revival mansions were built for wealthy cotton plantation owners and today operate as inns. Windsor, the largest and most spectacular antebellum mansion in Mississippi and a landmark for riverboat pilots on the Mississippi, was destroyed by a fire in 1890. All that remains are 23 of the original Corinthian columns that lined the mansion's sides.

(601) 437-4351; www.portgibsononthemississippi.com

Rowan Oak (C-7)

From 1930 to 1962, this large primitive-Greek Revival house in Oxford was home to William Faulkner, one of the greatest literary voices of the 20th century. Built in 1844 by a Colonel Robert Shegog from Tennessee, it was originally known as the Shegog House and later as the Bailey Place. When Faulkner and his new wife and two stepchildren bought the then-decrepit house, they renamed it for the rowan tree of Scottish legend. During his 32 years at Rowan Oak, Faulkner wrote most of his greatest novels, including *Light in August, Absalom! Absalom!, The Unvanquished,* and *Go Down, Moses.* In 1972, 10 years after Faulkner's death, his daughter Jill Faulkner Summers sold the house to the University of Mississippi, which continues to oversee it today. Visitors can tour the house and see Faulkner's office, bedroom, original furnishings, and memorabilia.

(662) 234-3284;
www.olemiss.edu/depts/u_museum/rowan_oak/
interactive.html

Winterville Mounds State Historic Site (E-4)

Located six miles north of Greenville on Mississippi's western border, this site preserves the remains of a prehistoric Native American ceremonial center. Indians of the Mississippian civilization occupied the site from about A.D. 1000 to A.D. 1450 and constructed at least 23 large flat-topped mounds for religious purposes. Some of the mounds have been destroyed by farming, grazing, and highway construction, but 12 of the largest ones — including 55-foot-high Temple Mound — remain. Listed on the National Register of Historic Places, the Winterville Mounds are among the largest and best-preserved in the southeastern United States. Visitors can take a self-guided tour of the mounds and explore the park's museum, which displays archaeological artifacts recovered from the site and from elsewhere in the Mississippi Delta, including pottery, stone tools, and ornaments.

(662) 334-4684;
www.mdah.state.ms.us/hprop/winterville.html

OUTDOORS

Black Creek (K-8)

Black Creek flows lazily through the heart of southern Mississippi's De Soto National Forest, wrapping around numerous wide, white sandbars along the way. Contrary to its name, Black Creek isn't black — tannic acid from decaying leaves tints its waters a weak-coffee brown. Mississippians rank it as one of the state's most beautiful streams, and the National Park Service agrees: In 1986, the 21-mile stretch between Moody's Landing and Fairly Bridge was declared a National Wild and Scenic River. Not surprisingly, Black Creek is a popular spot for canoe trips. Outfitters in Brooklyn and Janice offer trips ranging from a few hours to few days and supply canoes, safety gear, and shuttle service.

(601) 528-6160;
www.fs.fed.us/r8/mississippi/desoto

Gulf Islands National Seashore (M-9)

The Mississippi portion of this national seashore is comprised of one mainland area — Davis Bayou — and five barrier islands: Horn, Petit Bois, East Ship, West Ship, and parts of Cat. The islands, which can only be reached by boat, offer visitors long expanses of white beaches, blue waters, and historic structures. Popular activities include hiking along the beaches, swimming, surf fishing, wilderness camping, bird watching, boating, and picnicking. Horn Island and Petit Bois Island are designated wilderness areas, and only private boats travel to them. Davis Bayou is a unique ecosystem of underwater grasses, shallow waters, and shoreline hardwood trees. Visitors can walk a half-mile self-guided nature trail, fish for blue crab, bike the Live Oak Bicycle Trail, and stop in to the William M. Colmer Visitor Center.

(228) 875-9057; www.nps.gov/guis

Hiking

Tishomingo State Park (B-10)

Steep hills, high cliffs, plunging waterfalls, and odd rock formations make for spectacular hiking at this 1,530-acre park in Mississippi's Hill Country. Lying along the Natchez Trace Parkway near the state's northeastern corner, Tishomingo was created in the 1930s by the Civilian Conservation Corps and named for a Chickasaw Indian chief. The highlight of its 13-mile trail system is the popular Bear Creek Outcropping Trail. After crossing bouldery Bear Creek on a 200-foot-long swinging bridge, the 3.5-mile trail follows the creek and treats hikers to some of the park's most remarkable cliffs, outcroppings, overlooks, and overhangs, including 60-foot-high Jean's Overhang. Not surprisingly, the park is a mecca for rock climbers.

(662) 438-6914; (800) 467-2757
www.home.mdwfp.com/parks.aspx

© National Park Service

Gulf Islands National Seashore

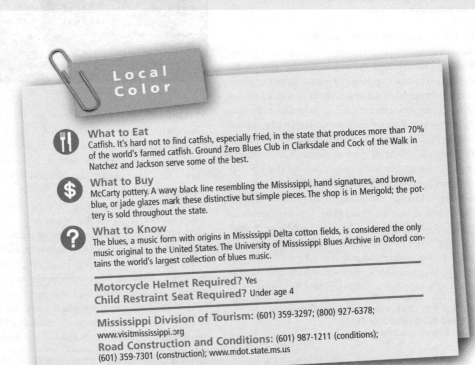

Local Color

🍴 **What to Eat**
Catfish. It's hard not to find catfish, especially fried, in the state that produces more than 70% of the world's farmed catfish. Ground Zero Blues Club in Clarksdale and Cock of the Walk in Natchez and Jackson serve some of the best.

💲 **What to Buy**
McCarty pottery. A wavy black line resembling the Mississippi, hand signatures, and brown, blue, or jade glazes mark these distinctive but simple pieces. The shop is in Merigold; the pottery is sold throughout the state.

❓ **What to Know**
The blues, a music form with origins in Mississippi Delta cotton fields, is considered the only music original to the United States. The University of Mississippi Blues Archive in Oxford contains the world's largest collection of blues music.

Motorcycle Helmet Required? Yes
Child Restraint Seat Required? Under age 4

Mississippi Division of Tourism: (601) 359-3297; (800) 927-6378;
www.visitmississippi.org
Road Construction and Conditions: (601) 987-1211 (conditions);
(601) 359-7301 (construction); www.mdot.state.ms.us

The sun rises over a misty landscape at Rocky Forks Conservation Area.

CITIES

Branson (L-12)

A settler named Rueben Branson gave this town its name, but writer Harold Bell Wright gets credit for starting its tourism industry. His popular 1907 book *The Shepherd of the Hills*, which celebrated the area's beauty and its people, drew visitors from around the country. With the creation of two lakes at its doorstep — Taneycomo in 1913 and Table Rock in 1959 — Branson evolved into a resort community catering to growing numbers of vacationers. The Baldknobbers Hillbilly Jamboree, Branson's first music show, opened in 1959 and was soon followed by shows featuring the Presley Family, the Plummer Family, and the Foggy River Boys. Today this town of just 6,050 people is home to more than 40 music theaters which together offer more seats than Broadway. Branson also lures visitors with attractions like Silver Dollar City theme park, the Branson Scenic Railway, and the Shepherd of the Hills Homestead.

Craftsman at Silver Dollar City

Branson/Lakes Area Chamber of Commerce & Convention & Visitors Bureau: (800) 296-0463; www.bransonchamber.com

✪ Jefferson City (State Capital) (G-14)

Missouri's capital spreads along the south bank of the Missouri River near the center of the state. Appropriately, the city takes its name from the president who brought this part of North America into the United States through the Louisiana Purchase. Its centerpiece is the Roman renaissance-style state capitol building, which overlooks the river and the city from high atop a bluff. At the foot of the bluff lies Jefferson Landing, a state historic site comprising three buildings from the city's original river landing: the Lohman Building (1839), the Christopher Maus House (1854), and the Union Hotel (1855). Two other interesting stops in Jefferson City are the Missouri State Highway Patrol Education Center, which displays historic policing equipment and vintage patrol cars, and the Missouri Veterinary Museum, which offers a collection of more than 2,500 veterinary instruments.

Jefferson City Convention & Visitors Bureau: (573) 632-2820, (800) 769-4183; www.visitjeffersoncity.com

Kansas City (E-9)

Renowned for its fine steaks, barbecue, and jazz, Missouri's largest city boasts more fountains than any other city outside Rome. Country Club Plaza, built in the 1920s and noted for its graceful Spanish architecture and chic shops, began the trend towards civic-minded commercial development. More recently, Union Station has seen extensive restoration and the addition of theaters, a science museum, and restaurants. Crown Center, another top entertainment and shopping complex, includes the visitor center for Hallmark Cards. Kansas City is home to one of the country's top general art museums, the Nelson-Atkins Museum of Art. The adjacent Kansas City Sculpture Park provides a setting for mammoth pieces by Henry Moore and other 20th-century sculptors. The Museums at 18th and Vine include the American Jazz Museum and the Negro Leagues Baseball Museum, each with memorabilia plus audio and video presentations. The Arabia Steamboat Museum displays items recovered from the ill-fated vessel that sank in the Missouri River in 1856.

Convention & Visitors Bureau of Greater Kansas City: (816) 221-5242, (800) 767-7700; www.visitkc.com

Nelson-Atkins Museum of Art in Kansas City

St. Louis (G-18)

Ride the elevator cars to the top for expansive views and visit the below-ground museum that explains the physics of this engineering marvel. Many of the city's finest cultural venues are found in and around the vast expanse of Forest Park. At the St. Louis Zoo, the African river scene attracts hippos, elephants, and cheetahs. The St. Louis Art Museum has a collection of 30,000 works spanning all eras of artistic endeavor. Hundreds of fun interactive exhibits make up the St. Louis Science Center. In the Loop neighborhood, the St. Louis Walk of Fame commemorates musicians, writers, and others with St. Louis roots. For nightlife, head back to the riverfront and the high-energy dance clubs of Laclede's Landing, a restored 19th-century warehouse district in the shadow of the Arch.

St. Louis Convention & Visitors Commission: (314) 421-1023, (800) 916-8938; www.explorestlouis.com

SCENERY

Missouri's Rhineland (G-16)

Between St. Charles and Jefferson City, SR 94 follows a twisting course along the Missouri River through a scenic landscape of farmland, vineyards, bluffs, and quaint towns. The area bracketed by Hermann in the west and Washington in the east is often called Missouri's Rhineland due to its abundance of wineries and the strong German culture evident in places like Hermann, Marthasville, and Washington.

Missouri's Rhineland

St. Louis to Van Buren (G-18)

This long loop drive winds through one of the most rugged and beautiful parts of the Ozark Mountains. From St. Louis it follows SR 21 southeast past three of the state's best-known parks: Elephant Rocks, Taum Sauk Mountain, and Johnson's Shut-Ins. Reaching US 60, the route heads west through Van Buren, gateway to the Big Spring area and the Ozark National Scenic Riverways. At Winona, it turns north and follows SR 19 on a meandering route to Cuba, and then returns to St. Louis via I-44.

● **Branson and Table Rock Lake (L-12)**

This loop drive heads south out of Branson on US 65, then west on SR 86 to the junction with SR 13, just north of Blue Eye. Turning north, the drive passes through the resort town of Kimberling City, then returns to Branson on a stretch of SR 76 highlighted by the Shepherd of the Hills Homestead and Inspiration Point Tower.

● **The Great River Road (D-16)**

Between Hannibal and St. Peters, the Great River Road (SR 79) takes travelers along an especially scenic stretch of the Mississippi River, with views of thickly wooded islands and towering limestone bluffs.

● **King Hill Overlook (D-8)**

Located at the southern end of St. Joseph, this overlook provides great views of the Missouri River and the northeastern corner of Kansas.

● **Lanagan to Noel (L-9)**

SR 59 winds along Indian Creek beneath spectacular overhanging limestone bluffs in the five-mile stretch between these two towns in the southwestern corner of the state.

● **Old Route 66 through Devils Elbow (I-14)**

Named for a sharp bend in the Big Piney River, Devils Elbow boasts a number of classic buildings from the heyday of Route 66. Devils Elbow Bridge, constructed in 1923, offers an excellent view of 200-foot-high bluffs of Gasconade dolomite that were once touted as "one of the seven scenic wonders of Missouri."

Devils Elbow Bridge

HERITAGE

Mark Twain Birthplace State Historic Site (D-15)

Samuel Langhorne Clemens, whom the world would come to know as Mark Twain, was born in Florida, Missouri, on November 30, 1835, in a modest two-room cabin. The home is now enshrined within an ultramodern museum a quarter of a mile south of where it once stood. A red granite monument marks the original site of this humble abode, of which Twain himself wrote "Recently someone in Missouri has sent me a picture of the house I was born in. Heretofore I always stated that it was a palace, but I will be more guarded now." In addition to the cabin, the museum houses first editions of Twain's books, a manuscript of *The Adventures of Tom Sawyer* rendered in Clemens' own hand, and an impressive collection of contemporary newspaper articles about the famous author.

(573) 565-3449; www.mostateparks.com/twainsite.htm

Festival in Ste. Genevieve

Ste. Genevieve (H-19)

The oldest town in Missouri and one of the most charming, Ste. Genevieve dates back to the late 1740s when a group of French-Canadians arrived to farm the fertile alluvial soils of the Mississippi floodplain. Following a disastrous flood in 1785, Ste. Genevieve's residents moved their town to higher ground three miles to the north. A surprising number of homes and buildings from the late 18th and early 19th centuries survive today, and the town's National Landmark Historic District offers visitors a remarkable window into Missouri's French Colonial past. The Felix Vallé State Historic Site preserves several of the most notable structures, including the Dr. Benjamin Shaw House (1819); the American Federal-style Felix Vallé House (1818); and the Amoureux House (1792), with its characteristic *poteaux en terre* walls.

(800) 334-6946, (573) 883-7102; www.mostateparks.com/felixvalle.htm

Truman House (E-9)

Located in the Kansas City suburb of Independence, this roomy Victorian home is the centerpiece of the Harry S. Truman National Historic Site. Truman, the 33rd President of the United States and the only Missourian ever to hold that office, moved to the house in 1919 when he married Bess Wallace and lived there until his death in 1972. During his administration (1945-1953), it was known as the "Summer White House." The house has been preserved to look as it did during the Trumans' lives, and contains many family heirlooms. Guided tours are offered daily.

(816) 254-9929, (816) 254-2720; www.nps.gov/hstr

Truman House

OUTDOORS

Ozark Trail: Middle Fork (I-16)

With the completion of the Middle Fork section in December 2005, the Ozark Trail winds for 200 continuous miles through the southeast section of the state. This 23-mile section begins at county road DD, just north of SR 32, and wends its way south through a spring-, stream-, and seep-filled area. Hikers are in the upper basin of the Middle Fork of the Black River, and will cross many streams that form the headwaters of the Middle Fork. Small savannahs break up the hardwood forest and occasional pine stands. Barton Fen, a sensitive wetland area, shelters breeding populations of the endangered Hines Emerald dragonfly. A foot-traffic-only portion of the trail has been built especially to preserve this habitat; bike and horseback riders should take the bypass along county road 79. The Middle Fork section ends near Oates, on county road J.

Ozark Trail: (573) 468-5427; www.ozarktrail.com/middlefork.htm

Middle Fork waterfall

Katy Trail (F-18)

This recreational trail stretches nearly the entire width of Missouri, from St. Charles in the east to Clinton in the west. For most of its 225-mile length, it follows the old right-of-way of the Missouri-Kansas-Texas (MKT) Railroad — nicknamed "the Katy" — along the Missouri River. Trailside scenery ranges from rolling farmland and bucolic valleys to wetlands, bottomland forests, and high limestone bluffs. The eastern section of the trail passes through "Missouri's Rhineland," an area where the German culture brought by 19th-century settlers remains strong. Although the Katy Trail runs through hilly terrain, the trail itself is generally level and therefore ideal for casual bikers and families. More than two dozen trailheads spaced at intervals along the trail provide parking and amenities.

Bicycling the Katy Trail

(800) 334-6946; www.mostateparks.com/katytrail.htm

Ozark National Scenic Riverways (J-16)

When the Army Corps of Engineers proposed damming the Current River, public outcry was so great that the federal government stepped in to save this stream and its tributary, Jacks Fork. In 1964, 134 miles of the Current and Jacks Fork rivers were designated the Ozark National Scenic Riverways. The rivers wind serenely through an Ozark landscape of hardwood forests and limestone mountains honeycombed with caves. They are fed by more than 100 natural springs, most notably Big Springs, which discharges an astonishing 278 million gallons of water each day. Gentle and free-flowing, the Current and Jacks Fork are ideal for canoeing and tubing and offer numerous riverside caves, springs, and waterfalls to explore. Concessionaires rent both canoes and tubes and will arrange trips that last from several hours to more than a week.

(573) 323-4236; www.nps.gov/ozar

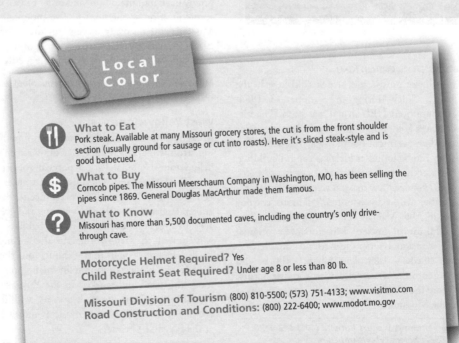

Local Color

What to Eat
Pork steak. Available at many Missouri grocery stores, the cut is from the front shoulder section (usually ground for sausage or cut into roasts). Here it's sliced steak-style and is good barbecued.

What to Buy
Corncob pipes. The Missouri Meerschaum Company in Washington, MO, has been selling the pipes since 1869. General Douglas MacArthur made them famous.

What to Know
Missouri has more than 5,500 documented caves, including the country's only drive-through cave.

Motorcycle Helmet Required? Yes
Child Restraint Seat Required? Under age 8 or less than 80 lb.

Missouri Division of Tourism (800) 810-5500; (573) 751-4133; www.visitmo.com
Road Construction and Conditions: (800) 222-6400; www.modot.mo.gov

TRAVEL GUIDE Missouri

Autumn colors surround a traditional red barn.

CITIES

Billings (I-13)

The coming of the Northern Pacific Railroad in 1882 established this Montana city bordered by rim rocks. The state's largest city is a gateway to several historic and recreational gems: Little Bighorn Battlefield National Monument, Bighorn Canyon National Recreation Area, Yellowstone Park, and Absaroka-Beartooth Wilderness. Take in scenic views of five mountain ranges and visit Boothill Cemetery on Black Otter Trail. Pictograph Cave State Park, about seven miles from town, has American Indian pictographs dating back more than 4,500 years. At Pompey's Pillar, a sandstone butte along the Yellowstone River 25 miles east off I-94, you'll find more pictographs as well as initials carved by explorer William Clark as he passed through on the celebrated Lewis and Clark Expedition.

Billings Area Chamber of Commerce Convention & Visitors Council: (406) 245-4111, (800) 711-2630; billingscvb.visitmt.com

Helena

⊛ Helena (State Capital) (G-7)

When four lucky prospectors struck gold here in the Last Chance Gulch during the summer of 1864, Helena (pronounced HEL-ah-na) was born. The discovery of placer gold, quartz gold, and silver, as well as lead, created an overnight boom town. Traces of other state history can be found at Helena's capitol building, which is graced by the huge painting *Lewis and Clark Meeting the Flatheads*, a masterpiece by Charles M. Russell. Other works by Montana's famous cowboy artist are in the Mackay Gallery, located in the Montana Historical Society Museum. The original governor's mansion is open year-round. St. Helena's Cathedral, Reeder's Alley, Last Chance Gulch, and Holter Museum of Art are also worth a visit. Cruise boats explore the Missouri River's cliffs and canyons at Gates of the Mountains Wilderness Area.

Helena Convention & Visitors Bureau: (406) 442-4120, (800) 743-5362; helenacvb.visitmt.com

Kalispell (C-4)

Nestled in the beautiful Flathead Valley, this small, hip town has plenty of history, culture, and outdoor recreation. Take a walking tour of the city's historic buildings, which include the Conrad Mansion, the former home of Kalispell's founder, Charles E. Conrad. The 26-room Victorian mansion features original furnishings and three acres of gardens and grounds. In Woodland Park, you'll find attractive lagoons and formal gardens. Flathead Lake is popular for boating, and the branches of the Flathead River offer excellent fly fishing, white-water rafting, and canoeing. In the Flathead National Forest, you can explore wilderness areas and glaciers. Glacier National Park and the Big Mountain Resort are also nearby.

Flathead Convention & Visitor Bureau: (406) 756-9091, (800) 543-3105; www.fcvb.org

Missoula (F-4)

The home of the University of Montana is an eclectic mix of students, ranchers, foresters, nature lovers, and writers. Missoula is the site of the largest smokejumpers firefighting base in the country. In addition to exhibits on the behavior of wildland fires, the Smokejumper Visitor Center offers a look at a 1930s firetower and the loft where the jumpers stay when not engaged in their demanding work. The Historical Museum at Fort Missoula preserves thirteen of the fort's original buildings with displays on the exploration and development of western Montana. Visit the Rocky Mountain Elk Foundation Wildlife Visitor Center to view the collection of full-sized mounts of grizzly bear, mountain lion, and other beasts. Given its scenic location at the head of five mountain valleys, Missoula offers ready access to the Clark Fork, Blackfoot, and Bitterroot rivers for vigorous kayaking and white-water rafting or a day of serene fly fishing.

Missoula Convention & Visitors Bureau: (406) 532-3250, (800) 526-3465; www.missoulacvb.org

West Yellowstone (K-8)

Miles of snowmobile and ski trails and fine trout-fishing streams make this village at the west entrance to Yellowstone National Park a popular tourist stop all year. The Grizzly and Wolf Discovery Center will give you a close-up look at these magnificent, dangerous, and endangered animals. Brown bears and grey wolves also live in the center's natural habitats. At the Museum of the Yellowstone, in the former Union Pacific Depot, you'll find exhibits on the Native Americans, pioneers, mountain men, and railroad men who lived and worked in the Yellowstone area plus displays about the park and its wildlife. In the evenings (May-Sept.), catch musicals and melodramas at the Playmill Theatre.

West Yellowstone Chamber of Commerce and Visitors Information Center: (406) 646-7701; westyellowstonecvb.visitmt.com

SCENERY

Beartooth Highway

Beartooth Highway (K-11)

Glaciers cap 20 mountain peaks in the Beartooth area, one of the highest and most rugged areas in the country. This scenic drive starts in Cooke City on US 212, dips into Wyoming, and ends in Red Lodge, MT. Expect possible road closures from fall through early spring.

Kings Hill Scenic Byway (F-9)

Just south of Great Falls, US 89 meanders through the Lewis and Clark National Forest and Little Belt Mountains. Stretching 71 miles, the route offers spectacular views of pristine mountain lakes and streams. Gravel roads that intersect the main highway connect to trailheads, campgrounds, and old mines.

- ● **Big Sheep Creek Back Country Byway (K-6)**
  This isolated gravel road, leading from Dell into the canyons of Beaverhead-Deer Lodge National Forest, is an excellent place to spot bighorn sheep in the evenings.

- ● **Lake Koocanusa Scenic Byway (B-2)**
  In the state's northwest corner, SR 37 hugs the eastern edge of Lake Koocanusa, which cuts a narrow fjord-like gorge between mountains.

- ● **Missouri Breaks Back Country Byway (D-12)**
  Loop east out of Winifred to overlook the Upper Missouri National Wild & Scenic River and cross rugged landscape first described by Lewis and Clark as "the Deserts of America."

Missouri Breaks

- ● **Pioneer Mountains Scenic Byway (I-5)**
  In the Beaverhead-Deerlodge National Forest, you'll see lofty granite peaks, mountain meadows, and lodgepole pine forests on Route 484 from Polaris to Wise River.

- ● **St. Regis-Paradise Scenic Byway (E-2)**
  Pass from wide-open rolling flats to steep canyon walls in the Lolo National Forest. Follow Route 135 east of St. Regis near the Idaho border.

OUTDOORS

Big Sky

Big Sky Resort (J-8)

This year-round resort near Yellowstone National Park has some of the best skiing and snowboarding around. *Skiing* magazine recently named Big Sky the eighth-best resort in North America. It gets 400 inches of snowfall each year, boasts 85 miles of runs, and features a half-pipe and two terrain parks. The big difference is elbow room. Unlike at Colorado resorts, lift lines are basically non-existent here. In winter, take an old-fashioned sleigh ride, trek through the woods on snowshoes, or crisscross breathtaking trails on a snowmobile. In summer, golf the Arnold Palmer course, explore the area on horseback, or spend a day white-water rafting.

*(406) 995-5000, (800) 548-4486;
www.bigskyresort.com*

Flyfishing the Gallatin River

Gallatin and Yellowstone Rivers and Fort Peck Lake (D-15)

The sun slants through tall trees and dances on gurgling mountain streams abundant in trophy-sized trout ... just like in the movie *A River Runs Through It* (1992). The popular fly-fishing movie set in Montana was filmed here along the Gallatin and Yellowstone rivers. Those spots, as well as the Madison River, are some of the state's best bets for big catches. If lake fishing is your thing, head to Fort Peck Lake, the most popular spot for trolling or shore fishing for walleye. Surrounding the reservoir are one million acres of protected wild lands, the Charles M. Russell Wildlife Refuge, where you'll likely see deer, waterfowl, raptors, and, in season, the nation's largest remaining herd of prairie elk.

*(406) 841-2870, (800) 847-4868;
visitmt.com/tripplanner/thingstodo/fishdetail.htm*

St. Marys Lake in Glacier National Park

Glacier National Park (B-5)

Throughout the ice ages, the monumental movement of glaciers carved sharp peaks out of the Continental Divide and gouged deep valleys where hundreds of lakes now glisten. If you have time and stamina, the best way to experience the beauty, scale, and power of Glacier National Park's mountains is to hike them. Seven hundred miles of maintained trails lead deep into this huge ecosystem, and park visitor centers  supply free hiking maps for some of the more popular trails: Lake McDonald Trail, Many Glacier Trails, and Logan Pass. Many of the glacier-fed lakes within the park are open for swimming and boating. Several outfitters offer rafting trips along the pristine drainage of the Flathead River.

(406) 888-7800; www.nps.gov/glac

HERITAGE

Grant-Kohrs Ranch

Grant-Kohrs Ranch National Historic Site (G-6)

In the second half of the 19th century, western plains cattle ranching was, literally, a huge business. At its peak, this 30,000-acre ranch was the headquarters of a ten-million-acre cattle empire scattered over four states and two Canadian provinces. Today the working ranch comprises 1,500 acres and 90 structures that span the evolving cattle industry. Rangers lead tours of the original 23-room house adorned with luxurious furnishings. After you've seen the house, experience ranch life by walking through buildings like the cowboys' bunkhouses, the Draft Horse Barn, and the Blacksmith Shop. During summertime, be sure to taste chuck wagon cooking and watch other demonstrations of typical ranch activities.

(406) 846-2070; www.nps.gov/grko

Custer National Cemetery

Little Bighorn Battlefield National Monument (I-15)

This historic battlefield, the site of "Custer's Last Stand," is located along the banks of the Little Bighorn River on the Crow Reservation in southern Montana. Historical records show that Custer and the more than 200 soldiers in his regiment died here on June 25 and 26, 1876. Visitors can walk through the battle sites and the Custer National Cemetery or take a one-hour guided bus tour. The visitor center features interpretive exhibits and programs. Rangers are also on hand to give talks about the history of the site and the Plains tribes. In August, the reservation holds an annual tribal celebration, which includes a craft fair, traditional dancing, and a rodeo.

(406) 638-2621; www.nps.gov/libi

National Bison Range (E-4)

Established in 1908, the National Bison Range is one of the oldest wildlife refuges in the nation. More than 350 bison roam this 18,500-acre range, located just north of Missoula between the Rocky Mountains and Bitterroot Range. Watch these hulking 2,000-pound animals graze peacefully on the prairie under the big Montana sky. Stop in at the visitor center and learn about the connection between bison and Native Americans that reaches far beyond a source of food.  *National Bison Range*

Elk, deer, pronghorn, black bear, coyote, and ground squirrels are some of the other animals you could see here. Also watch for more than 200 species of birds, including eagles, hawks, meadowlarks, bluebirds, ducks, and geese.

(406) 644-2211; www.fws.gov/bisonrange/nbr

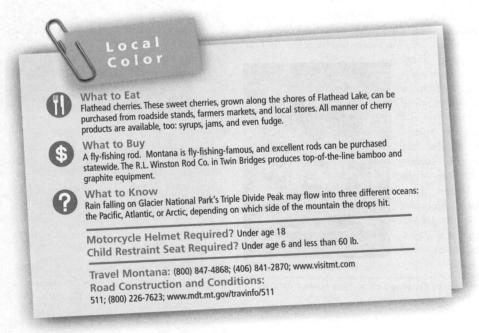

Local Color

🍴 **What to Eat**
Flathead cherries. These sweet cherries, grown along the shores of Flathead Lake, can be purchased from roadside stands, farmers markets, and local stores. All manner of cherry products are available, too: syrups, jams, and even fudge.

💲 **What to Buy**
A fly-fishing rod. Montana is fly-fishing-famous, and excellent rods can be purchased statewide. The R.L. Winston Rod Co. in Twin Bridges produces top-of-the-line bamboo and graphite equipment.

❓ **What to Know**
Rain falling on Glacier National Park's Triple Divide Peak may flow into three different oceans: the Pacific, Atlantic, or Arctic, depending on which side of the mountain the drops hit.

Motorcycle Helmet Required? Under age 18
Child Restraint Seat Required? Under age 6 and less than 60 lb.

Travel Montana: (800) 847-4868; (406) 841-2870; www.visitmt.com
Road Construction and Conditions:
511; (800) 226-7623; www.mdt.mt.gov/travinfo/511

TRAVEL GUIDE Montana

Wagon trains following the Oregon Trail and the Mormon Trail passed through the hills and plains of Nebraska.

CITIES

North Platte (J-8)

North Platte's location has made it a center of cross-country transportation, whether by covered wagon, rail, truck or automobile, for 150 years. The world's largest railroad classification yard is located here. Railroading enthusiasts can watch from the Golden Spike Tower as freight cars are continuously sorted at Bailey Yards and sent to different parts of the country. Cody Park Railroad Museum displays the Union Pacific's Challenger 3977, one of the largest steam locomotives ever constructed. North Platte was once the home of Buffalo Bill Cody, the legendary frontiersman and inventor of the Wild West Show. His ranch is the centerpiece of a state park where the great showman's memorabilia is on display. The Lincoln County Historical Museum has more historic relics, wagons, and buildings from the pioneering era, in addition to an exhibit featuring WWII canteen memorabilia. In June, North Platte hosts Nebraskaland Days, which include the four-night PRCA Buffalo Bill Rodeo, musical performances, and parades.

North Platte/Lincoln County Convention & Visitors Bureau: (308) 532-4729, (800) 955-4528; www.visitnorthplatte.com

Stuhr Museum of the Prairie Pioneer

Grand Island (K-13)

The county seat of Hall County and the fourth largest city in Nebraska, Grand Island offers some subtle yet spectacular scenery and plenty of recreational diversion. At the Stuhr Museum of the Prairie Pioneer there are pioneer displays, a museum shop, and a replica of an 1890s railroad town, complete with costumed historical interpreters. Fonner Park has thoroughbred racing from February through mid-May, with simulcast racing the rest of the year. Every July, Grand Island hosts the Central Nebraska Ethnic Festival, where you might hear Scottish bagpipes while noshing on an enchilada and watching Native American dancers.

Grand Island/Hall County Convention & Visitors Bureau: (308) 382-4400; www.visitgrandisland.com

⭐ Lincoln (State Capital) (K-17)

Spurred on by the presence of the University of Nebraska, Lincoln is one of the state's main cultural centers as well as the seat of state government. The university's influence is especially felt on fall Saturdays when the entire city seems to turn out to cheer on the Cornhusker's legendary football team. The capitol building, which houses the country's only unicameral legislature, towers over the city as an architectural tour-de-force, its interior ornamented with thousands of carvings, paintings, sculptures, mosaics, and inlaid wood. Exhibits at the Museum of Nebraska History trace the state's development since prehistoric times with an in-depth look at the cultures of the Plains Indians. The University of Nebraska State Museum offers an excellent collection of elephant and mammoth fossils along with displays of Southwest pottery and state wildlife. Boutiques, restaurants, and entertainment spots are found in the Haymarket District, an area of redeveloped 19th-century warehouses.

Lincoln Convention & Visitors Bureau: (402) 434-5335, (800) 423-8212; www.lincoln.org

Omaha (J-19)

The building of the Union Pacific Railroad gave Omaha its first push towards larger success. Today, it's Nebraska's largest city, a center for agriculture and the insurance industry. The city's most important cultural asset, the Joslyn Art Museum, is recognized for a wide-ranging collection that includes ancient Greek, Renaissance, modern European, and American 19th- and 20th-century artworks. The Durham Western Heritage Museum in the restored Union Station offers displays of Indian and settlers dwellings, railroadiana, and rare coins. The Mormon Trail Center at Historic Winter Quarters details the Mormon's tragic winter of 1846-47 when almost 600 died in the extreme mid-continent cold. The top-rated Henry Doorly Zoo includes a large indoor rainforest and an underwater shark tunnel along with many rare and endangered species from around the world. The cobble-stoned streets of the Old Market guide shoppers through a quaint district of antiques shops, boutiques, pubs, and restaurants.

Joslyn Art Museum in Omaha

Greater Omaha Convention & Visitors Bureau: (866) 937-6624; www.visitomaha.com

SCENERY

Sandhills Journey Scenic Byway (K-13)

Sandhills, remote farms, marshes and lakes, winding rivers, and the Nebraska National Forest, which is hand-planted, combine to make Nebraska Highway 2 one of the top scenic routes in the country. Between Grand Island and Alliance, there are sightings in the endless sky of migrating sandhill cranes. At different segments of the drive, there are views from the road of vast fields of wildflowers and segments of 20,000 square miles of grass-covered sand dunes, the largest sand dune formation in the Western Hemisphere.

Sandhill crane migration

Scotts Bluff National Monument (H-1)

Located near Gering, Scotts Bluff was a prominent natural landmark for emigrants on the Oregon Trail. Today, it preserves the memory of that trail as well as of the California and Mormon Trails. Summit Road allows visitors to drive to the top for an awe-inspiring view of the terrain that the pioneers crossed. The Oregon Trail Pathway leads from the visitor center to the remnants of the Oregon Trail, where ruts from the wagons are still visible.

● **Arbor Lodge State Historical Park** (K-19)
J. Sterling Morton, founder of Arbor Day, lived in the 52-room Victorian house here with a porch overlooking acres of trees, now an arboretum near Nebraska City.

● **Buttes** (F-3)
Pine-studded buttes break the endless horizon of Nebraska's western panhandle with stark, oblique silhouettes.

● **Lillian Annette Rowe Sanctuary** (K-12)
This sanctuary is located in the heart of the sandhill crane staging area near Gibbon where near 500,000 cranes pass on their northward migration.

● **Old Baldy** (E-13)
Near Lynch, a lookout area frames the hill flanked by a 10-mile stretch of undisturbed Missouri River just as it is described and named in the journal of Lewis and Clark.

Old Baldy

● **Pine Ridge** (E-2)
The hills in northwest Nebraska near Crawford round off at 4,700 feet and closely resemble the fabled Black Hills of neighboring South Dakota.

● **Smith Falls** (E-9)
Located near Valentine, an historic bridge across the Niobrara River provides access to a 70-foot waterfall, the highest in the state.

HERITAGE

Ashfall Fossil Beds
State Historical Park (F-14)

Twelve million years ago, a massive volcanic eruption in southwest Idaho produced so much powdered volcanic ash that one to two feet of it traveled and fell on northeastern Nebraska near Royal. While most life survived the initial ashfall, the animals and birds continued to graze on ash-covered grass and breathe the ash-filled air. Within days, the smaller species, like birds, died. For larger mammals, like rhinos, it took five weeks. All carcasses were covered by the drifting ash, and the skeletons remain today. The excavation center is staffed by visiting paleontologists who can field questions before visitors tour the park. The Rhino Barn holds the excavation of many of the 17 species that have been identified. These include horses, camels, rhinoceroses, and deer, in addition to crowned cranes and giant tortoises. Open May through October.

(402) 893-2000; www.ashfall.unl.edu

Ashfall Fossil Beds

Dancing Leaf Earth Lodge and Cultural Learning Center (K-8)

A recreated earth lodge provides the setting for an experience in Native American life along Medicine Creek near the town of Wellfleet. The local Native Americans were farmers and believed to be of the Upper Republic Culture, which preceded the Pawnee tribe. Learn to tan hides, taste a bowl of bison stew, listen to oral history, and walk the grounds surrounded by prairie and little else. A small museum exhibits fossils and artifacts from the area. Medicine Creek is internationally famous as the site of many archaeological digs. Established hiking trails and canoeing are available, as are overnight accommodations in earth and log lodges styled after those used by the Pawnee.

(308) 963-4233; www.dancingleaf.com

Fort Atkinson State Historical Park (I-19)

Life-size bronze sculptures of the participants honor the site where members of the Corps of Discovery first met Native Americans, a delegation of the Otoe-Missouria tribe. Expedition members wore full-dress for the occasion. In their journal, Lewis and Clark chronicled the meeting and referred to the meeting place as "Councile Bluff." They also added that the location would be an excellent site for a fort. Fort Atkinson was established within two years. It was the first U.S. fort west of the Missouri River and it played a major role in western expansion and in fur trade. The grounds are open year-round, while the visitors center is open only during summer months, when living history demonstrations and reenactments are scheduled.

(402) 468-5611; www.outdoornebraska.org

Great Platte River Road Archway Monument (K-12)

Conceived as a monument to the western movement, The Great Platte River Road Archway straddles I-80, the busiest transcontinental highway in the interstate system. At eight stories high, it also towers over the highway. Designed like a log cabin, the monument's interactive exhibits follow a timeline starting with the Oregon, Mormon, and California Trails to the advent of the Lincoln Highway, from the beginning of a national communications network to the use of fiber optics. Stories of the trails, the Pony Express, the Iron Horse, even drive-in movies are recounted as visitors stroll through the exhibits on a "trail" of their own. The Archway Monument includes a restaurant and gift shop featuring foods and merchandise made in Nebraska.

(877) 511-2724; www.archway.org

OUTDOORS

Chadron State Park (E-3)

Located among the rolling hills of the Pine Ridge Forest, Chadron is Nebraska's first state park. Fish for trout in Chadron Creek or ride a paddleboat on the lagoon. Hiking, horseback, and jeep rides take visitors through the park. But it is the miles of hiking/nature trails in the park and more miles of trails that lace forestlands that bring the bikers. While Nebraska isn't known for mountains, it does have rugged "hills" that rise to 5,000 feet in the Pine Ridge area within Chadron State Park. With its ponderosa pine forests, rimrock ridges, deep canyons, and open grasslands, "the Ridge" boasts more than 170,000 acres of public land.

(308) 432-6167; www.chadron.com

Chadron State Park

Cowboy State Recreational and Nature Trail (E-9)

When the 321 miles of the Cowboy Trail are finished, it will be the longest rail-to-trail conversion in the United States. It crosses the state in the north from Norfolk to Chadron. Of the 136 miles that have been completed, the 18-mile stretch at Valentine gives many visitors pause because it crosses the Niobrara River on a bridge built 148 feet above the water, just as the Chicago & North Western Railroad's Cowboy Line did many years ago. Other segments include 102 miles between Norfolk and Stuart and another 16-mile stretch from Bassett to Ainsworth. The trail is open to hiking, biking, and horseback riding. Bicycle rentals available at two locations: at Andrew Bicycle & Fitness in Norfolk and at Yucca Dune in Valentine.

(402) 471-5511; www.outdoornebraska.org

Lake McConaughy (J-6)

Surrounded by white sandy beaches and cottonwood trees, with 36,000 acres of water and 5,500 acres of land, Lake McConaughy is the largest reservoir in Nebraska. More Nebraskans vacation at Lake McConaughy (fondly called "Big Mac") than at any other place in the state. It boasts 100 miles of white-sand beaches. For water enthusiasts there is scuba diving, sailing, wind surfing, even wakeboarding. Concessionaires offer equipment rentals and lessons. For a break from the sun and water, head over to the Lake McConaughy Visitor/Water Interpretive Center, which features two 1,500-gallon aquariums, a computerized theater, and an interactive learning center focusing on the significance of water in Nebraska.

(308) 284-8800, (800) 658-4390; www.lakemcconaughy.com, www.visitogallala.com

Niobrara National Scenic River (E-9)

The 76 miles of the Niobrara designated as a Wild and Scenic River provide outstanding canoeing opportunities for tens of thousands of paddling enthusiasts every year. Waters run swiftly through a shallow course cut through Great Plains bedrock. The 12,600-square-mile watershed includes hundreds of springs, which contribute clear, cold water to the river, often tumbling over waterfalls directly into the main watercourse. Canoers paddle through landscape that varies between ranchland, canyons, cliffs, and forests. A great variety of plant and animal life occupy the area due to this region hosting the intersection of six different ecosystems. Ponderosa pines, deciduous species common in the eastern United States, and northern boreal species mix with three kinds of prairie: tallgrass, mixed grass, and shortgrass.

Canoeing on the Niobrara National Scenic River

(800) 658-4024; www.nps.gov/niob

Snowcapped Sierra Nevada surround Lake Tahoe.

CITIES

⊛ Carson City (State Capital) (F-2)

History museums and well-preserved architecture remind visitors of Carson City's rustic frontier town beginnings. Follow the Kit Carson Trail through downtown's historic district to see mansions, courthouses, a depot, and a former brewery-turned-art center. As befits the Silver State, the sandstone capitol is topped by a silver-colored dome. The State Museum, in the Old Mint Building, contains historical objects and mineral specimens. In the State Railroad Museum you'll find the Virginia & Truckee Railroad Collection, which includes restored steam engines and railroad equipment. Bowers Mansion, ten miles to the north, was built by a Comstock Lode millionaire and is now a museum. Just south of Carson City is Genoa, a quaint village settled by Mormon traders in the 1850s.

Carson City Convention & Visitors Bureau:
(775) 687-7410, (800) 638-2321; www.visitcarsoncity.com

Elko (C-7)

This northeastern Nevada town lies in the heart of cowboy country. Dude ranches, cattle drives, and Western cultural events thrive here at one of the last outposts of the real American West. Elko is home of the Western Folklife Center, the annual Basque Festival, and National Cowboy Poetry Gathering. At the Northeastern Nevada Museum, see historical and nature exhibits, art, films, and pioneer vehicles on the grounds. Nearby, the Wild Horse and South Fork state recreation areas, the Jarbidge Wilderness, and the majestic Ruby Mountains provide outstanding hunting, fishing, camping, hiking, cross-country skiing, and snowmobiling.

Skiing near Elko

Elko Convention & Visitors Authority: (775) 738-4091,
(800) 248-3556; www.exploreelko.com

Las Vegas

Las Vegas (L-8)

Lush desert oasis, glittering gambler's paradise, and fabulous resort town all in one, Las Vegas draws millions of visitors each year to a flashing spectacle of casinos, stage shows, and elaborate theme park hotels. While the famous Las Vegas Strip continues to sprout ever more astounding architectural wonders, downtown casinos have huddled together under the extraordinary Fremont Street Experience, a massive canopy of dancing lights covering five city blocks. Revel in the exotic memorabilia at the Liberace Museum or view the Imperial Palace Auto Collection and its hundreds of classic autos. For a glimpse of the city's past, head to Old Las Vegas Mormon Fort, a refurbished 1850s fort containing antiques and displays on local history. Clark County Heritage Museum has items from early mining and railroad days and an unrestored ghost town.

Las Vegas Convention & Visitors Authority:
(702) 892-0711, (800) 332-5333; www.visitlasvegas.com

Stateline (G-1)

Combine the breathtaking scenic beauty of Lake Tahoe and its surrounding mountains with round-the-clock casino action and you get one of the country's top vacation destinations. Exquisite resorts speckle the Lake Tahoe area, offering visitors countless activities. The skiing here is exceptional, especially when you catch a view of Lake Tahoe from the slopes or gondolas. Hike or mountain bike around the lake on the 165-mile Tahoe Rim Trail, a loop with amazing panoramic views. Play a round of golf at a lush local course designed by Robert Trent Jones, Jack Nicklaus, or Arnold Palmer. Big-name entertainers, cabaret acts, and casinos make for lively nightlife.

Reno/Sparks Convention & Visitors Authority:
(775) 827-7600, (800) 367-7366;
www.visitrenotahoe.com

SCENERY

Great Basin National Park/ Lehman Caves (G-10)

One of this park's natural wonders is not above ground, but below. Take a ranger-led tour of the small underground cavern to see an array of stalactites, stalagmites, flowstone, and columns. Lehman is famous for rare formations called "shields," two circular halves that resemble clam shells. Above-ground vistas include the Lexington Arch and the glacier at Wheeler Peak.

Valley of Fire State Park (K-9)

For more than 150 million years, wind and rain have sculpted the park's fiery red sandstone into spectacular domes, spirals, and towers. As the sun moves slowly across the sky, these bizarre formations seem to change color. Some even begin to take on shapes that resemble other things — animals, humans, even a beehive.

- ● **Angel Lake Scenic Byway** (C-8)
  Sometimes called the "Highway to Heaven," this stretch of SR 231 rises several thousand feet through pine, mahogany, and aspen trees to Angel Lake.

- ● **Extraterrestrial Highway** (I-7)
  Watch for signs warning of alien encounters and "Warp 7" speed limits along the desolate SR 375, known for the many UFO sightings and for the top-secret Area 51.

- ● **Lake Tahoe Scenic Byway** (F-2)
  Thousands of forested acres climb upward from the beaches that stretch along the east shore. At Cave Rock, the road burrows through 25 yards of rock.

- ● **Las Vegas Strip** (p. 77, L-2)
  Neon lights and spouting volcanoes help make Vegas' main drag one of the world's only byways that is more scenic at night than by day.

- ● **Red Rock Canyon Road** (L-8)
  Outside of Las Vegas, SR 159 winds through the Red Rock Canyon National Conservation Area, known for its stunning red and cream-colored sandstone formations.

Red Rock Canyon

OUTDOORS

Lake Mead National Recreation Area (L-10)

This oasis lies at the junction of the Mojave, Great Basin, and Sonoran Deserts in one of the hottest and driest places on Earth. The horizon here looks limitless and is framed by striated stone, mountains, colorful wildflowers, and open sky. Even in the sweltering summertime, the waters of Lake Mead are blue and cool, beckoning vacationers. Within the park you can rent a houseboat or powerboat or head to a beach for swimming and sunbathing. The lake is stocked with bass, catfish, crappie, bluegill, and other species waiting for the well-cast lure. Sail or windsurf here against a backdrop of mountain ranges and desert expanses. Rafting and boating excursions, Hoover Dam tours, and scuba diving are other popular options.

Sailing on Lake Mead

(702) 293-8990; www.nps.gov/lame

Ruby Mountains Wilderness (D-8)

Near Elko, the scenic Lamoille Canyon Road takes hikers, backpackers, and equestrians into the heart of Ruby Mountain Wilderness. Here you'll find impressive views on the most popular (yet still uncrowded) route: Ruby Crest National Recreation Trail. Considered by many to be the preeminent Nevada trail, the Ruby Crest winds 40 miles around glacial lakes and through a across a series of rugged peaks and valleys. A two- to three-day backpacking trip will lead adventurers to such high-elevation gems as 10,893-foot Wines peak. Watch for one of the largest herds of mule deer in Nevada, mountain goats, bighorn sheep, and streams teeming with trout. Himalayan snow cocks and Hungarian partridges have been introduced into this wilderness area.

(775) 752-3357; www.fs.fed.us/htnf

Sand Mountain Recreation Area (F-4)

This huge stretch of dunes just north of "the loneliest road in America" (US 50) and east of Fallon was formed thousands of years ago. Quartz particles from ancient glaciers ground away Sierra granite, and the basin below (where the recreation area is today) created a natural trap for the airborne sand particles. The dunes are quickly becoming a haven for sandboarders who crave extreme thrills on the razorbacks and steep runs. While carving the nearly 600-foot-tall dunes, you can hear the booming sounds of the shifting sands. The area is also a favorite spot for off-road vehicles.

(775) 885-6000; www.nv.blm.gov/carson/Recreation/ Rec_SandMtn.htm

Mountain biking

Tahoe Rim Trail (G-1)

Expect lofty views of granite peaks, vibrant green meadows, and Lake Tahoe's blue waters on this 165-mile trail for hikers, bikers, and horseback riders. The Tahoe Rim Trail, which loops through six counties around Lake Tahoe on the basin's ridge tops, offers a good mix of easy and challenging terrain for mountain bikers. Check trail maps online or at the Tahoe Rim Trail Association since some sections of the trail are closed to bikers or allow biking only on even-numbered days. Start your ride at the Spooner Summit trailhead (off US 50) and head south through broad meadows and dense woods of ancient firs and across the volcanic flanks of South Camp Peak.

(775) 298-0012; www.tahoerimtrail.org

HERITAGE

Hoover Dam (L-9)

During the Great Depression, thousands of men and their families came to the harsh and barren Black Canyon to build the largest dam of its time. It took less than five years and more than 3.25 million cubic yards of concrete. At the enormous Hoover Dam facility, now a National Historic Landmark, you can take a guided tour of the inner workings and walk along the upper decks of this engineering miracle. Large elevators drop visitors 500 feet down into the wall of Black Canyon to see the power plant and its eight giant generators. Visitor center films, photos, and other displays explain the dam's history and construction.

Hoover Dam

(702) 494-2517, www.usbr.gov/lc/hooverdam/

Nevada Northern Railway Museum (F-9)

Northwest of Great Basin National Park, numerous ghost towns dot in the sagebrush valleys surrounding Ely. The historic mining town of Ely is home to the Nevada Northern Railway Museum, where visitors can experience the sights and sounds of old-time railroading. Maintained by former railroad employees, the museum's 56-acre complex with 49 historic structures is considered a National Historic District in itself. See several authentic steam, electric, and first-generation diesel locomotives as well as freight and passenger cars. During the summer you can ride train cars Number 93 and Number 40 — The Ghost Train of Old Ely. For the ultimate railroad experience, visitors can rent one of the museum locomotives and operate it on the mainline track.

(866) 407-8326, (775) 289-2085; www.nevadanorthernrailway.net

Nevada Northern Railway Museum

Virginia City (F-2)

After silver was discovered on nearby Mount Davidson, Virginia City quickly grew into Nevada's preeminent town. It was settled in 1859, and by 1861, when the Nevada Territory was established, the city held three-quarters of the territory's population. Nearly 30,000 people lived here during the 1860s and 1870s, the "Bonanza" years when the Comstock Lode yielded silver ore. By the 1880s, however, the lode began to dry up, and the city did, too. It was nearly a ghost town by the turn of the 20th century. Today the entire city is a national historic district. Many beautiful buildings, including the schoolhouse, courthouse, opera house, and several mansions still stand. The Way It Was Museum chronicles Virginia City's rise and decline. Ride the historic V&T (Virginia & Truckee) railroad to Gold Hill and back, or take a walking or trolley tour to see many of the best-preserved structures and get a feel for 19th-century boomtown life.

(775) 847-7500; www.virginiacity-nv.org

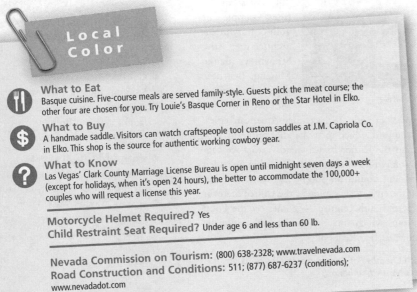

Local Color

What to Eat
Basque cuisine. Five-course meals are served family-style. Guests pick the meat course; the other four are chosen for you. Try Louie's Basque Corner in Reno or the Star Hotel in Elko.

What to Buy
A handmade saddle. Visitors can watch craftspeople tool custom saddles at J.M. Capriola Co. in Elko. This shop is the source for authentic working cowboy gear.

What to Know
Las Vegas' Clark County Marriage License Bureau is open until midnight seven days a week (except for holidays, when it's open 24 hours), the better to accommodate the 100,000+ couples who will request a license this year.

Motorcycle Helmet Required? Yes
Child Restraint Seat Required? Under age 6 and less than 60 lb.

Nevada Commission on Tourism: (800) 638-2328; www.travelnevada.com
Road Construction and Conditions: 511; (877) 687-6237 (conditions); www.nevadadot.com

Birch and maple trees show their fall colors in White Mountain National Forest.

CITIES

✪ **Concord** *(State Capital) (K-7)*

New Hampshire's capital was first settled by Massachusetts colonists who ventured north along the Merrimack River in 1725. When the Industrial Revolution washed over New England, the Merrimack was harnessed to power mills. Later in the 19th century the Concord Coach, a stage coach manufactured by the town's most well-known concern, Abbott Dawning, became an icon of westward expansion. Today this small city thrives as the center of state politics as well as a locus of state history. The state capitol building, known here as the State House, was built in 1819 using locally quarried granite (this is, after all, the Granite State). Visitors can see a prime example of a Concord Coach in the Museum of New Hampshire History. The city is also home to the oldest two-story dwelling located between Massachusetts and Canada: the Reverend Timothy Walker House, 263 years old.

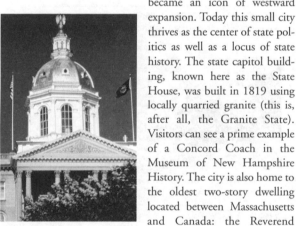

Capitol building dome

Greater Concord Chamber of Commerce: (603) 224-2508; www.concordnhchamber.com

Hanover *(I-5)*

Hanover anchors the Upper Valley region of the Connecticut River where it forms the state line between Vermont and New Hampshire. Hanover is a classic New England town, with white steepled churches, a traditional downtown area, and vibrant cultural life. Dartmouth College, founded in 1769, is located here and contributes venues such as the Hopkins Center for the Performing Arts and the Hood Museum of Art as well as a continually refreshed stream of talented young people to Hanover's lively arts scene. The League of New Hampshire Craftsmen (a group created during the Great Depression, whose mission is to preserve artisanal heritage) has one of its retail stores downtown. Hanover visitors are very close to outdoor recreation with Vermont's Green Mountains and New Hampshire's White Mountains an hour or two's drive away. In fact, the Appalachian Trail runs right through Hanover on Main Street.

Hanover Area Chamber of Commerce: (603) 643-3115; www.hanoverchamber.org

Currier Museum of Art

Manchester *(L-8)*

Located at the Amoskeag Falls of the Merrimack River, Manchester has grown to be the state's largest city and industrial metropolis. Along the river rise the brick buildings of the Amoskeag Mills, which began manufacturing textiles in 1838. When the company closed in 1936, Manchester citizens bought the mill and guided it back to profit, also bringing other diversified industry to the city. Today the buildings have been reborn as an acclaimed office and residential complex. Architecture buffs enjoy the range of styles, from industrial-era rowhouses downtown to 18th-century homes in nearby communities to a special treat, the Zimmerman House. Part of the renowned Currier Museum of Art, this home is the only example of Frank Lloyd Wright's work on the East Coast that is open to the public. In May and June, visitors may watch salmon make their way up the fish ladder at Amoskeag Fishways, which offers other programs year-round.

Greater Manchester Chamber of Commerce: (603) 666-6600; www.manchester-chamber.org

Portsmouth *(L-10)*

Located at the mouth of the Piscataqua River and New Hampshire's only sea outlet, Portsmouth was designated the first of six U.S. naval shipyards in 1800. Perhaps the best way to encounter Portsmouth is via the Portsmouth Harbour Trail. The oldest stop on this self-guided tour is the 1664 Richard Jackson House. Other highlights include the 1718 Warner-MacPhaedris House, occupied by the same family for 200 years and a fine example of 18th-century urban architecture; the Strawbery Banke Museum (see next page); streets lined with five-story rowhouses typical of early 19th-century American cities; the naval shipyard, which today handles primarily submarines; and the harbor itself, where visitors see tugboats and sometimes piles of road salt freshly unloaded from ships and bound for snowy highways. Another glimpse of the city — ale capital of the United States at the turn of the 20th century — comes on the Local Brewery Tour, which includes locally and nationally known brews such as Redhook.

Portsmouth Harbor

Portsmouth Chamber of Commerce: (603) 436-3988; www.portsmouthchamber.org

SCENERY

Connecticut River Trail *(K-4)*

Follow the Connecticut River along the Vermont/New Hampshire border as it meanders through small New England communities punctuated by white church steeples, farmlands, and valleys. Near Claremont, it passes the solitary mount, or monadnock, of Mt. Ascutney. It also crisscrosses the Connecticut River Birding Trail, where sharp-eyed spotters can sight warblers, swallows, and scarlet tanagers, among other species.

Great North Woods *(C-7)*

You're within a stone's throw of Québec, Maine, and Vermont in this far northern corner of the state, a land of tall pines and moose. Follow US 3 from Colebrook, the largest town in the area although its population is less than 2,000, right up to the Canadian border.

Moose

Kancamagus Highway *(G-8)*

Named for an American Indian chief, the Kancamagus follows Native footpaths and old logging trails as it slices through the middle of the state and the White Mountains National Forest along SR 112. The route passes a covered bridge and climbs nearly 3,000 feet as it twists through Kancamagus Pass. It's known for spectacular fall foliage and the Rocky Gorge Scenic Area, where the Swift River has carved a path through granite.

● **America's Stonehenge** *(M-8)*

In Salem off SR 111 east, view rock structures built about 4,000 years ago. A wooded path leads to the site, with chambers and ceremonial rooms designed around the astrologic calendar.

● **Arts and Antiquing** *(L-6)*

Beginning at President Franklin Pierce's homestead in Hillsborough, head southwest via US 202 and SR 137 to Peterborough and Jaffrey, stopping at arts and antiques shops in quaint villages along the way.

Hampton Beach, coastline

● **Ocean Shore** *(M-10)*

Stop at one of five state parks along the Atlantic Ocean shore by following Route 1A from Hampton Beach to Portsmouth.

● **White Mountains** *(F-8)*

Travel on SR 16 through ski areas and past ravines along the eight-mile auto route to the peak of Mount Washington. The entire route runs from West Ossipee to Gorham and skirts the Appalachian Trail.

OUTDOORS

Beaver Brook

Beaver Brook (N-7)

Started more than 40 years ago on just 12 acres, Beaver Brook has grown to 2,000 acres and 35 miles of trails in southern New Hampshire. The Beaver Brook Association emphasizes conservation and nature, and educational programs and workshops are offered throughout the year on topics such as organic gardening, wildlife tracking, and snowshoeing. The landscape at Beaver Brook is diverse, with several ponds and wetlands areas as well as northern hardwood forests. Trails wind along ridges and past meadows, swamps, ponds, and of course, Beaver Brook. Some trails are open to biking and horseback riding. Volunteers design and maintain 12 theme gardens at Maple Hill Farm, which also features a restored farmhouse, barn, and cooperage. Beaver Brook is located about six miles from Nashua.

(603) 465-7787; www.beaverbrook.org

Mount Washington (F-8)

A hike to the summit of Mount Washington ranks as a lifetime achievement. It's the highest peak in the Presidential Range (6,288 feet) and notorious for its bad weather. The planet's highest wind speeds have been recorded here, including the world record of 231 m.p.h. in 1934. One of the standard routes to the top begins at Pinkham Notch Visitor Center in the White Mountain National Forest. The Appalachian Mountain Club maintains this facility, which offers meals and lodging in addition to invaluable trail and weather information. Once on the trail,

intrepid hikers encounter rough, rocky sections, sometimes steep and treacherous, while moving through hardwood forests, then stunted tree growth, then the beauty of the alpine zone above tree level (covered in blooms mid-June). At the summit, a visitor center maintained by the state park system offers food and shelter. If the weather is good, the views stretch to Canada, the Atlantic, Massachusetts, and the Adirondacks.

Appalachian Mountain Club: (603) 466-2721; www.outdoors.org

Odiorne Point State Park

Odiorne Point State Park (L-10)

With only 18 miles of beaches on the Atlantic Ocean, New Hampshire is not known as a beach destination. But Odiorne Point State Park offers both Atlantic beaches and tidepools as well as freshwater ponds and marshes to explore. The park features the largest undeveloped stretch of seacoast in the state. It is the site of the first European settlement in New Hampshire (1623). One of those early settlers was John Odiorne, for whom the park is named. Military bunkers were buried here during World War II, with gun battery sights trained on the sea. Visitors like to hike, ride a paved bike trail, picnic, and learn about the environment and tidepools at the Seacoast Science Center. Naturalists take groups on hikes into seven coastal habitats. In winter, skiers take to the cross-country trails, while in summer, band concerts are held on the science center lawn.

(603) 436-1552; www.nhstateparks.com/odiorne.html Seacoast Science Center: (603) 436-8043; www.seacentr.org

HERITAGE

Fort at No. 4 (K-4)

This outdoor museum demonstrates life on the northern frontier between the years 1744 and 1760. The fort was built when the Massachusetts colony designated four new "plantations" in the Connecticut River valley and the Farnsworth brothers headed north to claim Number 4 (the plantations were known by number, not name). Fort buildings have been reconstructed according to contemporary accounts, drawings, and archaeological excavations. Inside the walls, visitors may tour a watchtower, lean-tos, houses, and the great hall. Outside the walls, typical buildings such as a corn barn and blacksmithy are also open. At the different structures, costumed interpreters tell about often-perilous 18th-century life. Annual events such as the Militia Muster bring this turbulent era to life. The fort is open early June through late October.

(888) 367-8284; www.fortat4.com

Saint-Gaudens National Historic Site (J-4)

Tucked away in the Connecticut River valley, the home, garden, and studio of Augustus Saint-Gaudens (1848-1907) harbor present-day artists and preserves a chapter of the nation's art history. Saint-Gaudens was the United States' premier sculptor in the late 19th century, famous for works such as the serenely sad memorial to Henry Adams' wife Marian (known as Clover). The original is in Rock Creek Cemetery, Washington, D.C., but a bronze recast is here. Visitors may tour the home, named Aspet, or take guided walking tours of the grounds. Monuments, galleries, and studios are located throughout the site, which spreads over 150 acres, many of them forest and wetlands. Along the two-mile Blow-Me-Down Trail or the quarter-mile Ravine Trail, hikers may see beaver, ducks, warblers, or newts among the many kinds of animals present. A boardwalk at Blow-Me-Down Pond now allows visitors to get that much closer to the water's edge.

Saint-Gaudens National Historic Site

(603) 675-2175; www.nps.gov/saga

Strawbery Banke Museum (L-10)

When the English sailed into the mouth of the Piscataqua River in 1630, they noticed thickets of wild berry bushes on the riverbank and established their settlement, Strawbery Banke, at that spot. The commercial outpost became a thriving seaport (the name was changed to Portsmouth in 1653) and then suffered slow decline after the Revolutionary War disrupted Atlantic trade patterns. In the early 19th century, immigrants began to make their homes here, and the neighborhood became known as Puddle Dock. Today the museum encompasses 10 acres filled with more than 20 original buildings, some hundreds of years old, that trace life in Portsmouth from the late 1600s to the 1950s. Some buildings are furnished to period, while others are shops in which artisans ply traditional crafts. An herb garden is filled with plants such as bee balm, bedstraw, and bugleweed that would have been used medicinally, in the kitchen, or for various textile dyes.

(603) 433-1100; www.strawberybanke.org

Herb garden at Strawbery Banke

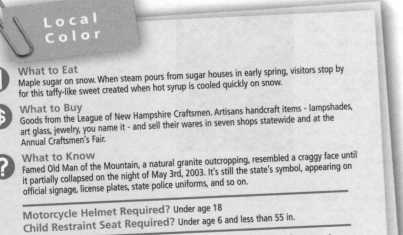

Walking trails wind through Island Beach State Park, home to New Jersey's largest osprey colony.

CITIES

Atlantic City (Q-10)

Boardwalk at Atlantic City

There's a lot more in the cards than just casinos for Atlantic City visitors. Relax on the sandy beaches, stroll the four-and-a-half-mile boardwalk for plenty of amusement and beach cuisine, or explore the more cultural side of this tinsel town. The family-friendly Atlantic City Aquarium — Ocean Life Center offers aquariums, touch tanks, and interactive exhibits. For even more marine schooling, visit the Brigantine Sea Life Museum and Marine Mammal Stranding Center, a hospital and refuge that offer visitors a closer look at rescued whales, dolphins, seals, and sea turtles. For a taste of the bizarre, don't miss Ripley's Believe It or Not! Museum on the Boardwalk. Atlantic City Outlets – The Walk offers dining and high-end outlet shopping on a multi-block stretch of Michigan Avenue. Fine art is housed at the Noyes Museum of Art in Oceanville and at the Atlantic City Art Center where national and regional artists have exhibited work for more than 40 years.

Atlantic City Convention & Visitors Authority: (888) 228-4748; www.atlanticcitynj.com

Cape May (T-7)

A beach resort since 1766, this seaside town is a National Historic Landmark and the oldest seashore resort in the nation. New Jersey's southernmost town was a favorite retreat of several 19th-century presidents and continues to be a top vacation spot today. Swim at pristine beaches, fish, tour the more than 600 restored Victorian homes, or climb nearby Cape May Lighthouse.

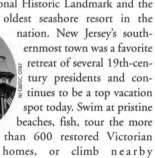
Queen Victoria Bed & Breakfast

Beachcombers have long enjoyed searching for "Cape May diamonds," sea-washed-and-worn clear beach pebbles. Non-beach stops should include the Mid-Atlantic Center for the Arts, Emlen Physick Estate, Historic Cold Spring Village, or a ride on the ferry to Lewes, Delaware. See the Cape May Zoo, and the Cape May Courthouse and historic Cold Springs Village.

Chamber of Commerce of Greater Cape May: (609) 884-5508; www.capemaychamber.com

Newark (F-12)

Newark, the state's largest city, is much more than Newark Liberty International Airport, one of the world's busiest commercial airports. The city is a major commercial, financial, and educational center and a gateway to the culture, history, sports, and industry of the state. The Newark Museum offers a large, impressive collection of American, Tibetan, African, and American

New Jersey Performing Arts Center

Indian art and artifacts. Second only to Mount Rushmore, Newark is also the site of sculptor Gutzon Borglum's most important works, including the great bronze group, Wars of America, and his famous Abraham Lincoln. Don't miss the huge Cathedral Basilica of the Sacred Heart, a vast French Gothic structure complete with soaring spires, Carrara marble, and hundreds of stained glass windows. One of the state's cultural hotspots is the New Jersey Performing Arts Center, which regularly features some of the best performers in music, dance, and theater.

City of Newark: www.gonewark.com

✪ Trenton (State Capital) (J-8)

1790 marks the year that Trenton became New Jersey's state capital. The city was once projected to become the capital of the United States, too. The State House was built two years later in 1792 and is the second oldest in continuous use. The complex also includes the State Museum and the Old Barracks Museum where Hessian troops were housed when Washington crossed the Delaware River. Nearby, Washington Crossing State Park includes the Ferry House (where the Colonials briefly took shelter) and the Swan Collection of Revolutionary War memorabilia.

Washington Crossing State Park

Trenton Downtown Assn.: (609) 393-8998; www.trenton-downtown.com

SCENERY

Delaware River Scenic Byway (J-8)

From Trenton, the capital city, Route 29 follows the Delaware River for 35 miles up to Frenchtown, passing through charming historic communities such as Titusville, Lambertville, and Stockton, agricultural landscapes, and recreation areas (e.g. Bull's Island Recreation Area). The byway parallels the Delaware & Raritan (D&R) Canal much of the way, and there are several access points to the towpath for walking and biking. Fantastic views of the river, wooded hills, and sheer cliffs are a small part of the natural beauty.

Pinelands National Reserve (O-8)

The Pinelands — a 1.1-million-acre region that includes wilderness areas — is the largest tract of open space east of the Mississippi River and 22% of the state's total land area. Visitors are treated to a variety of flora and fauna, historic towns and villages, and scenic settings. One unusual feature is the pygmy forest, a mature but dwarf forest consisting of pine and oak tress less than 11 feet tall. Serene woodland surroundings, scenic sandy trails, and clean, clear waters allow visitors to enjoy a special part of New Jersey's past.

● **Absecon Lighthouse** (Q-11)
Visitors who climb to the top of this 1857 lighthouse are rewarded with singular views of Atlantic City.

● **Barnegat Lighthouse** (N-12)
This 165-foot structure stands tall on Long Beach Island and treats visitors to excellent views of the island, Barnegat Bay, and Island Beach State Park, one of the state's last stretches of barrier island ecosystem.

High Point State Park

● **High Point State Park** (B-9)
Superior sights are found at this park, which rises to 1,803 feet and marks the state's highest point. The view from the top encompasses the Kittatinny Mountains and part of New York.

● **Paterson Falls** (D-12)
New Jersey's largest waterfall, nestled in the northeastern corner of the state on the Passaic River, measures 77 feet high and 280 feet across. The three-to-six million gallons of water that go over the falls each minute generate electricity for the public grid.
Paterson Falls

● **Twin Lights of Navesink** (H-13)
From 200 feet above sea level in Highlands, New Jersey, this state historic site overlooks the Shrewsbury River, Sandy Hook, Raritan Bay, New York Harbor and skyline, and the Atlantic Ocean.

HERITAGE

Sandy Hook Lighthouse (H-13)

Sandy Hook Lighthouse

The country's oldest operating lighthouse can be found at the tip of the Gateway National Recreation Area in the Sandy Hook Unit. This historic lighthouse was designed by Isaac Conro and built in 1764. It was originally constructed to help mariners enter the southern side of the New York Harbor and boasts the first siren fog signal, which was installed in 1868. Sandy Hook Lighthouse has survived the British occupation during the Revolutionary War and constant exposure to harsh elements due to its location and was restored in spring 2000. The grounds are open daily, and tours of the tower are offered on weekends (except in winter) by the New Jersey Lighthouse Society.

*(732) 872-5970;
www.cr.nps.gov/maritime/park/sandyhk.htm,
www.nps.gov/gate*

Edison National Historic Site* (E-12)

West Orange, New Jersey is home to one of the most influential inventors in U.S. history, Thomas Alva Edison. For more than 40 years, Edison's laboratory — built in 1887 — was the creative home of life-changing inventions such as the motion picture camera, the nickel-iron alkaline electric storage battery, greatly improved phonographs, and sound recording. Today, the Edison National Historic Site includes the inventor's extensive laboratory, library, and home, Glenmont. Visitors can enjoy displays of the first light bulb, phonograph, motion picture equipment, Edison's records, and many other historic exhibits. This educational and entertaining place offers insight into important aspects of America's industrial past and Edison's influence on life and the economy.

(973) 736-0551; www.nps.gov/edis
This site is temporarily closed for renovation and expansion through 2006.

Washington Crossing State Park (I-8)

The site of this state park was the setting of one of the pivotal battles in the American Revolution. General George Washington and 2,400 men crossed the rough, icy waters of the Delaware River on Christmas Day in 1776 and landed at Johnson's Ferry, what is now Washington Crossing State Park, after nightfall. They began their march to Trenton early the next morning and defeated the Hessian troops in an unexpected attack at dawn. Although the park is known for its historical significance, it also offers many other activities. There are numerous trails for hiking and cross-country skiing and ample opportunity for nature and wildlife viewing. A wide variety of birds winter in the park, and wildlife species include whitetail deer, fox, racoons, owls, and hawks. The park also supports an assortment of hardwoods, red cedars, Eastern white pines, Norway spruces, and many other plants and wildflowers.

*(609) 737-0623; www.state.nj.us/dep/parksandforests/
parks/washcros.html*

OUTDOORS

Delaware Water Gap National Recreation Area (C-8)

Almost 70,000 acres of land along the shores of the Delaware River at the Pennsylvania-New Jersey border form this impressive outdoor haven. The name says it all: a mile-wide gaping hole in the Appalachians through which the Delaware River flows. With water and woods within easy access, this area is bursting with recreation opportunities. Thick forests and wooded hills make for splendid hiking and mountain biking. The Delaware River and numerous streams and ponds offer plenty of boat launches for canoeing, kayaking, rafting, and boating; beaches for shore-side fun; fishing; and swimming. Horseback riding and cross-country skiing are also possible. Set foot on the famed Appalachian Trail on the park's New Jersey side off Route 206, one mile south of Millbrook Village. The trail climbs 300 feet over the span of one mile to a fire tower and wide vistas.

(570) 426-2452; www.nps.gov/dewa

Island Beach State Park (M-13)

Visitors can enjoy sunbathing, swimming, surf fishing, strolling, scuba diving, hiking nature trails, crabbing, or scoping out birds at this Atlantic Coast beach park. Birders especially will be delighted by this waterside gem, home to the one

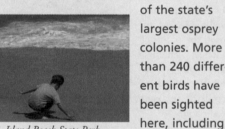
Island Beach State Park

of the state's largest osprey colonies. More than 240 different birds have been sighted here, including the brown pelican, blue heron, black skimmer, and least tern. Island Beach State Park remains one of the few natural barrier beaches along the coast, and its 10-mile stretch of striking white sand makes it a perfect place to sit and enjoy the sights and sounds of the surf.

*(732) 793-0506;
www.njparksandforests.org/parks/island.html*

Ringwood State Park (C-12)

Mountain bikers from the North Jersey area are almost sure to recommend the same place for some of the state's best singletrack action: Ringwood State Park, which sits along the New York state border. The park features both carriage roads with some steep, rocky

Mountain biking

sections and singletrack trails for miles and miles of hilly cycling terrain. Other highlights of the park include the State Botanical Garden and Shepherd Lake, which offers swimming, boating, fishing, and picnicking on the shore.

*(973) 962-7031;
www.njparksandforests.org/parks/ringwood.html*

Schooner A.J. Meerwald (R-7)

Sail away on New Jersey's official tall ship, an authentically restored Delaware Bay oyster schooner which measures 115 feet long. The ship was launched in 1928 and outfitted for surf clamming in the late 1950s, after the oyster industry crashed. Retired in the late 1970s, it was donated to the Delaware Bay Schooner Project in 1989 and now serves as a sailing classroom that promotes ecological and historical awareness of

A.J. Meerwald

the Delaware Bay region. Sailors learn about the southern shore region's land and sea life firsthand on a variety of sailing trips. The Meerwald's home port is in Bivalve, NJ, but the ship also docks at numerous other New Jersey cities, including Cape May. It sails April through October, and visitors are advised to call ahead for reservations.

(856) 785-2060; www.ajmeerwald.org

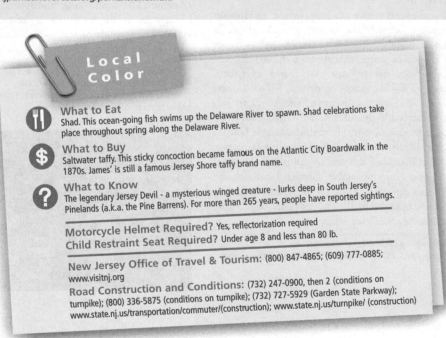

Local Color

What to Eat
Shad. This ocean-going fish swims up the Delaware River to spawn. Shad celebrations take place throughout spring along the Delaware River.

What to Buy
Saltwater taffy. This sticky concoction became famous on the Atlantic City Boardwalk in the 1870s. James' is still a famous Jersey Shore taffy brand name.

What to Know
The legendary Jersey Devil - a mysterious winged creature - lurks deep in South Jersey's Pinelands (a.k.a. the Pine Barrens). For more than 265 years, people have reported sightings.

Motorcycle Helmet Required? Yes, reflectorization required
Child Restraint Seat Required? Under age 8 and less than 80 lb.

New Jersey Office of Travel & Tourism: (800) 847-4865; (609) 777-0885;
www.visitnj.org
Road Construction and Conditions: (732) 247-0900, then 2 (conditions on turnpike); (800) 336-5875 (conditions on turnpike); (732) 727-5929 (Garden State Parkway); www.state.nj.us/transportation/commuter/(construction); www.state.nj.us/turnpike/ (construction)

A home in Santa Fe displays characteristic adobe and wood architecture.

CITIES

Old Town in Albuquerque

Albuquerque (E-5)

The largest city in New Mexico sprawls along the Rio Grande below the precipitous Sandia Mountains. Many visitors head straight to Old Town, the remarkably well-preserved area of the original settlement. It's a great place to shop for turquoise jewelry, sample Southwestern cuisine, and soak up history. But Albuquerque has plenty of other attractions. The Indian Pueblo Cultural Center explores the history and traditions of New Mexico's 19 pueblos. At Rio Grande Nature Center State Park, trails wind through the bosque, a riverine forest of cottonwoods, willows, tamarisk, and Russian olive trees. Old Route 66 (Central Avenue) is lined with architectural gems dating from the heyday of the "Mother Road," including classic motor courts from the 1930s and 40s.

Albuquerque Convention & Visitors Bureau:
(800) 284-2282; www.itsatrip.org

Ruidoso (H-6)

This year-round resort sits high in the Sacramento Mountains beneath the towering peak of Sierra Blanca. Its name — Spanish for "very noisy" — comes from the alpine stream that tumbles through its center, not from the throngs that crowd its streets. Catering to a wide variety of visitors, Ruidoso offers top-notch golf courses, dozens of shops and art galleries along Sudderth and Mechem Drives, and horse racing at Ruidoso Downs. In the surrounding Lincoln National Forest, outdoor enthusiasts can hike, camp, mountain bike, and fish among tall ponderosa pines and aspens. From November through March, there's world-class downhill skiing at Ski Apache, which is owned and operated by the Indians of the neighboring Mescalero Apache Reservation.

Ruidoso Valley Chamber of Commerce:
(505) 257-7395, (877) 784-3676; www.ruidosonow.com

⭐ Santa Fe (State Capital) (D-6)

Located at the base of the Sangre de Cristo Mountains and surrounded by 1 million acres of National Forest, New Mexico's capital city enjoys a spectacular setting, proximity to great spots for outdoor recreation, and a climate that's sunny and mild. Its history stretches back nearly four centuries, and its culture is a rich stew of Spanish, Indian, and American influences. A major culinary and art capital, this city of 65,000 boasts more than 200 restaurants, 250 galleries, and numerous excellent museums. And Santa Fe is eminently walk-able: Many of its top points of interest, galleries, and shops lie within a short stroll of the central plaza.

Santa Fe

Santa Fe Convention & Visitors Bureau:
(505) 955-6200, (800) 777-2489; www.santafe.org

Taos (C-6)

In many ways, this town of 6,000 people is much like the Santa Fe of 50 years ago. Like the capital 55 miles to the south, Taos nestles up against the Sangre de Cristos and offers abundant opportunities for outdoor sports. Taos Ski Valley, with its challenging "black diamond" runs, consistently ranks among the top ten North American ski resorts. Taos also boasts a robust arts scene and top-notch museums such as the Harwood Museum of Art and the Millicent Rogers Museum. The town's long history and polycultural heritage are on display at places like the Kit Carson Home, La Hacienda de los Martinez, and the 1,000-year-old Taos Pueblo.

Taos County Chamber of Commerce & Visitor Center:
(800) 732-8267; www.taoschamber.com
Taos Ski Valley Chamber of Commerce: (505) 776-2291;
www.taosskivalley.com

Sangre de Cristo Mountains near Santa Fe

SCENERY

Cedar Crest to Sandia Crest (E-5)

Hiking the La Luz Trail isn't the only way to get to the top of the Sandia Mountains: You can also drive there. The Sandia Crest National Scenic Byway, which begins near the town of Cedar Crest, climbs the mountains' western flank, gaining 4,000 feet in elevation over the course of 14 twisty miles. At the summit, an observation deck provides panoramic views that can extend 100 miles in every direction.

View of the Brazos Cliffs

Taos to Chama (B-6)

Heading northwest from Taos, US Hwy 64 crosses the 650-foot-deep Rio Grande Gorge, then continues across the Taos Plateau, a quintessentially Western landscape of rabbitbrush and ranches. The terrain and vegetation abruptly change at the town of Tres Piedras, and the highway begins to climb into the Brazos Mountains, where tall stands of fir and aspen alternate with lush meadows (keep an eye out for elk). Near the 10,000-foot crest there are several roadside pullouts with sweeping views of the broad Chama River Valley and the chiseled quartzite face of the 2,000-foot Brazos Cliffs.

● **The High Road to Taos** (C-6)
This less-traveled route between Espanola and Taos crosses barren badlands, ascends forested mountains, and passes through a number of fascinating little towns, including Chimayo, site of the famous Santuario de Chimayo, and Truchas, where Robert Redford filmed "The Milagro Beanfield War."

● **Jemez Country** (C-5)
West of Los Alamos, SR 4 traverses the steep Jemez Mountains, then drops down into the Valles Caldera, a shallow, 16-mile-wide bowl created by the collapse of a massive volcano more than a million years ago.

● **Old Mesilla Plaza** (J-4)
Lined with trees and ancient adobe buildings, this plaza is one of the loveliest in New Mexico.

● **Trail of the Mountain Spirits** (I-2)
This 110-mile-long National Scenic Byway follows SR 15 from Silver City north to Gila Cliff Dwellings National Monument; the return trip loops through Mimbres on SR 35, then returns to Silver City via Santa Clara. The drive is breathtaking, but it's not for the fainthearted: In many places the road is tortuous and narrow, making for white knuckles.

OUTDOORS

Capulin Volcano rim

Capulin Volcano National Monument (B-9)

The big draw here is the chance to walk down into a dormant volcano. More than 1,000 feet high and nearly perfect in its conical symmetry, Capulin Volcano rises dramatically from the plains of northeastern New Mexico. The Volcano Road spirals up from the volcano's base to a parking area near the rim. From there, a short trail leads down into the crater, where visitors can get a close look at the volcano's vent. The one-mile-long Crater Rim Trail circles the crater and provides panoramic views of the surrounding volcanic landscape and parts of three neighboring states: Colorado, Oklahoma, and Texas. The visitor center at the base of the volcano offers exhibits about the area's geology, wildlife, and human history, and a ten-minute film about volcanoes.

Frogs are often seen along the trail

(505) 278-2201; www.nps.gov/cavo

Road leading to Capulin Volcano rim

Cloudcroft Rim Trail (I-6)

The charming village of Cloudcroft is perched at the lofty elevation of 9,000 feet in the Sacramento Mountains and encircled by the 1.2-million-acre Lincoln National Forest. The vistas and the mountain biking are unbeatable. The Rim Trail, which consistently ranks as one of the top ten trails in the United States, runs for 18 miles along the spine of the Sacramentos and offers views of the San Andres Mountains 30 miles to the west and the gypsum dunes of White Sands National Monument. Other popular trails include Pumphouse Canyon, Willie White, La Luz Canyon, and Silver Springs Loop. For road bikers, there are hundreds of miles of forest roads that wind peacefully through tall stands of aspen, pine, and spruce trees.

(505) 682-2733, (866) 874-4447; www.cloudcroft.net
(505) 434-7200, (505) 682-2551
www.fs.fed.us/r3/lincoln/

Sandia Mountains (E-5)

Hundreds of miles of trails lace the Sandias, which shoot up abruptly and steeply from Albuquerque's eastern edge. One of the best-known trails is called La Luz, Spanish for "The Light." Starting in the foothills at an elevation of roughly 7,000 feet, La Luz ascends through several different climate and vegetation zones before reaching 10,678-foot Sandia Crest. It's a strenuous, eight-mile climb, but hikers are rewarded with knockout views of the city, the Rio Grande Valley, and if the timing is right, the spectacular light at sunset — when the sky and mountains glow in warm shades of orange and pink — that gives this trail its name. Some hardy souls hike back down the trail, but most people hop on the Sandia Peak Aerial Tramway.

(505) 281-3304;
www.fs.fed.us/r3/cibola/districts/sandia.shtml

HERITAGE

Chaco Culture National Historical Park (C-3)

From roughly A.D. 850 to A.D. 1250, Chaco Canyon was the hub of a sophisticated pre-Columbian Indian civilization. The Chacoan people, ancestors of the Pueblo Indians, built monumental structures, complex irrigation systems, and an extensive network of well-engineered roads. This remote park, which was named a World Heritage Site in 1987, preserves ruins at 13 major sites and more than a hundred smaller ones. Pueblo Bonito, the most impressive structure, was originally four stories high and contained 600 rooms and 40 kivas. The visitor center offers films and exhibits explaining the Chaco culture. A paved road loops through the canyon, and short trails lead from the road to the individual sites. In summer, rangers offer informative walks, interpretive programs, and campfire talks.

(505) 786-7014; www.nps.gov/chcu

Chaco Culture National Historical Park

Hacienda de los Martinez (C-6)

Built in the years 1804-1827, the fort-like *casa mayor* (great house) of Antonio Severino Martinez — farmer, rancher, trader, merchant, and Taos mayor — has been carefully restored to reflect life in Spanish Colonial New Mexico. Visitors can walk through nearly all of the 21 rooms — including the *cocina* (kitchen), *sala* (living room), *granero* (grainery), blacksmith's shop, servants' quarters, and chapel — and imagine themselves back in the 19th century. It's the details that bring the hacienda to life: Seeing the foods and spices arranged on the kitchen table, or the saddles, hides, and sombreros displayed in the trade room, you feel as if Antonio and his family are still present and going about their daily routines.

(505) 758-1000; www.taoshistoricmuseums.org

Las Vegas (D-7)

Located at the point where the eastern plains meet the Sangre de Cristo Mountains, Las Vegas was founded in 1835 as Nuestra Señora de los Dolores de las Vegas Grande ("Our Lady of Sorrows of the Great Meadows"). It thrived in the mid-1800s as a major stop on the Santa Fe Trail, but its true heyday began with the arrival of the railroad in 1879. Awash in prosperity, its residents built hundreds of elegant buildings and homes. Today, more than 900 structures in Las Vegas are listed on the National Register of Historic Places. Many of them — including the Plaza Hotel, a landmark since 1882 — have been restored to their 19th-century appearance. The Chamber of Commerce and the Plaza Hotel offer free pamphlets that map out walking and driving tours.

(505) 425-8631, (800) 832-5947; www.lasvegasnm.org
(505) 425-3591, (800) 328-1882;
www.plazahotel-nm.com

Mogollon Ghost Town (H-1)

Of the dozens of ghost towns scattered around New Mexico, Mogollon is one of the most interesting and best-preserved. The town sits in narrow Silver Creek Canyon, hemmed in by the canyon walls and bisected by the creek. It was born in the 1890s as a camp for miners working claims in the Mogollon Mountains and soon became known for its violence and lawlessness. The mountains yielded millions of dollars in silver and gold, but when the mines began to play out in the 1940s Mogollon was all but abandoned. Today its adobe, brick, and wooden buildings survive in varying states of dilapidation, but the growing stream of visitors has encouraged the town's few remaining residents to preserve and restore this colorful piece of New Mexico's history.

(800) 733-6396; www.newmexico.org

Local Color

What to Eat
Christmas chile sauce. Both red and green chiles are grown in abundance; the resulting sauce made with both is a state specialty obtainable at Albuquerque's Chili Pepper Emporium.

What to Buy
Authentic Indian bracelets. Twenty-two Native American tribes live in the state. Each produces a distinctive style of jewelry. Skip Maisel's Wholesale/Retail jewelry and crafts shop in Albuquerque has a huge selection.

What to Know
In Santa Rosa, an underground river feeds an 81-foot-deep crystal-clear artesian spring called the Blue Hole. Visibilities range from 50-100 feet, and it's a constant 64°F, ideal for snorkeling and scuba.

Motorcycle Helmet Required? Under age 18, reflectorization required
Child Restraint Seat Required? Under age 7 or less than 60 lb.

New Mexico Department of Tourism: (800) 733-6396; www.newmexico.org
Road Construction and Conditions: (800) 432-4269; www.nmshtd.state.nm.us

Water thunders over the edge of Niagara Falls.

CITIES

⊛ Albany *(State Capital) (NK-19)*

In addition to being the state capital, Albany has a rich heritage of its own. American Indians inhabited the area for hundreds of years and were joined in 1624 by the Dutch, who wanted to trade for furs. The Dutch heritage is still reflected in many street names, the architecture of several buildings such as the Quackenbush House, and the annual Tulip Festival each May. The city's charter dates to July 22, 1686. Albany's location near the confluence of the Mohawk and Hudson Rivers has long made it an important hub for transportation. The city was also the site of the first railroad in America, which ran for 16 miles between Albany and Schenectady. Today, visitors will find colonial homes, historic churches, museums, and modern performing arts centers.

Albany County Convention & Visitors Bureau:
(800) 258-3582; www.albany.org

Buffalo *(NJ-3)*

Located on the eastern shore of Lake Erie, Buffalo is New York's second-largest city, a major railroad center, and one of the most active Great Lakes ports. The heart of the city is Niagara Square, dominated by a monument to President William McKinley, who was assassinated here in 1901. The Theodore Roosevelt Inaugural National Historic Site also makes its home in this town. For a panoramic view of western New York, ride up to the 25th-floor observatory in City Hall. Museums are aplenty in this town and highlights include the Albright-Knox Art Gallery and Buffalo Museum of Science. Explore the waters of the area by taking a sightseeing cruise of the harbor, the Niagara River, and Lake Erie; boats depart from the Erie Basin Marina daily. Architecture buffs can tour Frank Lloyd Wright's recently restored Darwin Martin House, just one of many masterworks built in Buffalo by Wright, H.H. Richardson, and Louis Sullivan.

Buffalo Niagara Convention & Visitors Bureau:
(800) 283-3256; www.visitbuffaloniagara.com

Rockefeller Plaza

New York *(SG-6)*

Economic capital, media capital, publishing capital, theater capital, art world capital: New York City is by many standards the most powerful and important city in the world. Visitors encounter an unforgettable array of sights and sounds and a pace that never slows much below a quick jog. The bright lights of Broadway draw those looking for splashy new musicals and prize-winning plays. Reinvented Times Square, ringed with evermore astounding displays of advertising, bursts with family-oriented attractions. Art lovers can see the Museum of Modern Art, the grand Metropolitan Museum, or trek to Soho to look for truth and beauty there. Most visitors stick to Manhattan, but the Bronx has its famous zoo and Brooklyn its noble Brooklyn Bridge (a fine place for a stroll). And in New York's harbor, the Statue of Liberty still lifts her lamp, welcoming all who "yearn to breathe free."

New York City & Company:
(212) 484-1200; www.nycvisit.com

Rochester *(NI-7)*

This city located on the Genesee River is the third largest urban area in New York. The area's first gristmill was built here in 1789, and by the 1820s there were so many flour mills lining the riverbanks that Rochester was known as the "Flour City." Today, visitors will find plenty of cultural options along with great antique shopping, sporting events, and scenic Erie Canal cruises. The summer Lilac Festival draws thousands; history buffs enjoy the Susan B. Anthony House and the George Eastman House. Don't miss a stop in Rochester's Public Market, too — it was established in 1827 and is still a year-round center for fresh local produce and other goods.

Visit Rochester: (800) 677-7282; www.visitrochester.com

Syracuse *(NI-12)*

The geographic center of the state, Syracuse is also located within 350 miles of all major metropolitan areas in the Northeast. Syracuse owes much of its development to the Erie Canal, which provided the transportation that the city needed to grow. The Erie Canal Museum, located in the 1850 Weighlock Building, relates the history of Syracuse through presentations and interactive exhibits and also includes the *Frank Buchanan Thomson*, a full-size canal boat. Syracuse University offers a public art gallery, sports, concerts, and many other events. Other highlights include the 1905 Carnegie Library Building, Everson Museum of Art, and Alliance Bank Stadium, home of the Syracuse SkyChiefs minor league baseball team. Downtown Armory Square, once a warehouse district, is now a chic area offering nightlife, restaurants, and shopping.

Syracuse Convention & Visitors Bureau: (800) 234-4797;
www.visitsyracuse.org

SCENERY

Lakes to Locks Scenic Passage *(SK-5)*

This scenic byway is also referred to as "The Great Northeast Journey." The route begins in the Albany area, in Waterford, where the Erie Canal meets the Hudson River. The drive heads north on US 4, SR 22, and US 9 for 234 miles along the edge of the Adirondacks, paralleling Lake Champlain all the way up to Rouses Point, NY, which is situated along the Canadian border. This road takes drivers through small villages and charming hamlets while showcasing the region's rich history and natural beauty.

Seaway Trail

Seaway Trail *(NA-16)*

The Seaway Trail's 454 miles parallel the St. Lawrence River, Lake Ontario, the Niagara River, and Lake Erie. Well marked by official byway signs, this nationally recognized drive begins east of Massena on the St. Lawrence River and ends near Ripley at the New York-Pennsylvania border. The byway takes visitors across a variety of landscapes and along several bodies of water, with harbors, cityscapes, quaint villages, and rural communities along the way. (The Seaway Trail continues 50 miles through Pennsylvania to the Ohio border).

● Catskill Mountains *(NM-17)*

The Adirondacks aren't the only mountains worth seeing in the state. There are 35 summits higher than 3,500 feet in the Catskills and plenty of lofty waterfalls, sheer cliffs, deep gorges, and mountain vistas.

Canoeing

● Niagara Falls *(NI-3)*

See the famous falls from the U.S. side. Prospect Park is a prime place for viewing the American Falls and upper rapids, and visitors might even catch a rainbow in the mist.

● Prospect Mountain Veterans Memorial Highway *(NG-19)*

This scenic highway is accessible via I-87 and treats visitors to spectacular views of Vermont's Green Mountains, New Hampshire's White Mountains, the Adirondacks' High Peaks, and Lake George.

● Seneca Lake Wine Trail *(NJ-9)*

This trail in the Finger Lakes region meanders along the shores of Seneca Lake past some of the most diverse wine producers in the eastern United States as well as some of New York's most picturesque and serene settings.

HERITAGE

Home of Franklin D. Roosevelt

Home of Franklin D. Roosevelt National Historic Site (SA-6)

About 90 miles north of New York City in the beautiful Hudson River Valley is Springwood, the home of four-term President Franklin D. Roosevelt. This 300-acre National Historic Site is located in Hyde Park, New York and includes FDR's lifelong home, the Presidential Library and Museum, a rose garden, the gravesite of President and Mrs. Roosevelt, an ice house, stables, and miles of trails. Visitors can take self-guided tours of the museum, but visits to the home are by guided tour only (regularly scheduled guided tours are given throughout the day).

(845) 229-9115; www.nps.gov/hofr

National Baseball Hall of Fame and Museum (NJ-15)

Antique game ticket

Baseball reigns in Cooperstown. It is believed (though no one knows for certain) that baseball's roots can be traced back to Cooperstown in 1839 when Abner Doubleday introduced a diamond-shaped field, a pitcher and catcher, and bases to the popular game "Town Ball," which thus earned the sport's current name. This central New York museum houses and preserves all sorts of baseball memorabilia, artifacts (like the bat Sammy Sosa used to hit his 500th career home run on April 4, 2003), works of art, literature, photographs, and more. The museum also oversees the election of National Baseball Hall of Famers and honors those individuals and their careers.

(888) 425-5633; www.baseballhalloffame.org

Sagamore Hill National Historic Site (p. 85, D-20)

Theodore Roosevelt's home from 1885-1919 sits 45 miles east of New York City in Oyster Bay, Long Island. The 23-room home is built in the Queen Anne style and is furnished as it was during Roosevelt's lifetime. During the 26th president's term from 1901-1909, Sagamore Hill became known as his "Summer White House" and was the center of a lot of public attention. This historic site includes three components: Sagamore Hill, a visitor center, and the Old Orchard Museum, which features exhibits about President Roosevelt's life from childhood to post-Presidency. Admission to Theodore Roosevelt's home is by guided tour only.

(516) 922-4788; www.nps.gov/sahi

Statue of Liberty National Monument & Ellis Island (p. 84, I-9)

There is no better symbol of American freedom and democracy than the Statue of Liberty. Majestic views of New York Harbor and the statue awe visitors during the ferry ride to Liberty Island and Ellis Island. The statue was a gift of friendship from the French that was dedicated on October 28, 1886 and has since become one of the most widely recognized monuments in the world. Ellis Island was incorporated as part of the national monument in May 1965. Ellis Island served as New York's port of entry from 1892-1954 and as the first stop for millions of immigrants. Today, the museum on Ellis Island examines the history of immigration and the island's key role in the mass migration of the late 19th and early 20th centuries.

(212) 363-3200; www.nps.gov/stli or www.nps.gov/elis

OUTDOORS

Adirondack Mountains (NE/NF-16)

The Adirondack Mountains hide an abundance of unspoiled streams and lakes seemingly made for peaceful canoe rides. Canoe country extends from the Old Forge area northwest through numerous bodies of water to Tupper Lake and Saranac Lake. Nick's Lake, located two miles from Old Forge, is a good starting place for beginning paddlers. It's small and manageable with unspoiled beaches and forested shores. Another favorite spot is Lake Lila, where visitors can navigate to and around five islands and also enjoy great birding, thanks to a large loon population and active ospreys. For those who prefer to stay on land, the Adirondacks are also home to some of the state's best hiking. Check out the High Peaks region for everything from a fun family walk to a weeklong backcountry-backpacking trek.

(518) 846-8016; www.visitadirondacks.com

Central Park (p. 84, B-4)

Catching the best of city life doesn't mean leaving the great outdoors behind. Central Park's 843 acres located in the heart of Manhattan offer a wide variety of activities. Visitors and native New Yorkers alike enjoy running, walking, bicycling, skating, horseback riding, tennis, basketball, baseball/softball, soccer, football, swimming, row boating, fishing, birding, lawn bowling, croquet, and ice skating. Bikes, boats, ice skates, and other equipment can be rented on site for reasonable rates. The park also hosts a number of different events for adults and children, so check before heading out.

(212) 310-6600; www.centralparknyc.org

Central Park

Finger Lakes Region (NK-10)

The Finger Lakes region, which borders Lake Ontario in west-central New York, is home to 11 huge lakes and the former Erie Canal, now the New York State Barge Canal. The area was carved by ancient glaciers, which left deep, narrow lakes, rocky gorges, waterfalls, and rolling hills. Outdoor activities abound year-round, but winter sports reign with ample opportunity for downhill or cross-country skiing, snowboarding, snowmobiling, and ice-fishing. Bristol Mountain and Greek Peak offer top-notch skiing, and Finger Lakes National Forest has more than 30 miles of interconnecting trails for cross-country skiing and snowmobiling, including the 12-mile Interloken Trail, and two miles of the North Country Trail, a National Scenic Trail.

Skiing at Bristol Mountain

(800) 548-4386; www.fingerlakes.org

Hudson Valley (SA/SB-6)

Bikers will delight in the riding opportunities in the Hudson Valley. It's beautiful countryside, with river scenes, local farms, and many stopworthy attractions. The 60-mile round-trip through the Hyde Park Historic Sites is a challenging but rewarding route. It starts and finishes at the Hyde Park Town Hall and along the way passes by several historic points of interest such as the Vanderbilt and Mills mansions, the Old Rhinebeck Aerodrome, and the Franklin D. Roosevelt National Historic Site. The hills and valleys on this route take visitors through the heart of the Hudson River Historic District and uncover some of the great history, natural beauty, art, and culture of the region.

(800) 232-4782; www.travelhudsonvalley.org; www.hvnet.com

TRAVEL GUIDE | New York

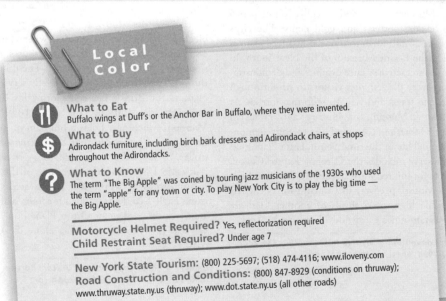

Local Color

🍴 **What to Eat**
Buffalo wings at Duff's or the Anchor Bar in Buffalo, where they were invented.

💲 **What to Buy**
Adirondack furniture, including birch bark dressers and Adirondack chairs, at shops throughout the Adirondacks.

❓ **What to Know**
The term "The Big Apple" was coined by touring jazz musicians of the 1930s who used the term "apple" for any town or city. To play New York City is to play the big time — the Big Apple.

Motorcycle Helmet Required? Yes, reflectorization required
Child Restraint Seat Required? Under age 7

New York State Tourism: (800) 225-5697; (518) 474-4116; www.iloveny.com
Road Construction and Conditions: (800) 847-8929 (conditions on thruway); www.thruway.state.ny.us (thruway); www.dot.state.ny.us (all other roads)

The beaches seem endless at Cape Hatteras National Seashore.

CITIES

Asheville (E-1)

Nestled 2,216 feet high in the Blue Ridge Mountains at the confluence of the French Broad and Swannanoa Rivers, Asheville offers an unusual combination of Appalachian charm and cosmopolitan sophistication. Its most famous attraction is Biltmore Estate, the 8,000-acre country estate of George W. Vanderbilt. Each year nearly one million people visit the estate and tour its magnificent 250-room château. Asheville's charming and vibrant downtown is filled with eclectic shops, great restaurants, and Art Deco buildings that date back to the city's Gilded Age heyday. The Grove Arcade reopened in 2002 after a six-decade hiatus, with 50 owner-operated businesses selling "the best of western North Carolina." Several downtown sites honor the writer Thomas Wolfe, Asheville's most famous native son. The Blue Ridge Parkway hugs the city's southern and eastern edges.

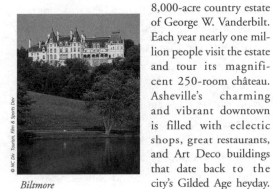

Biltmore

Asheville Area Chamber of Commerce Convention & Visitors Bureau: (888) 247-9811, (800) 280-0005; www.exploreasheville.com

Charlotte (F-5)

The number two banking center in the nation, Charlotte's reputation for fiscal responsibility dates to the early 1800s when a branch of the U.S. mint operated here. Today, that former treasury building houses the Mint Museum of Art and its collection of paintings, porcelains, pottery, and gold coins. The city's transition from mill town to modern financial giant is outlined at the Levine Museum of the New South. In addition to interactive science exhibits and demonstrations, Discovery Place invites visitors to stroll through a tropical rain forest and view large-format movies. At the Charlotte Museum of History and Hezekiah Alexander Homesite, costumed interpreters demonstrate Colonial life in the rural South. Latta Plantation Nature Preserve includes the Carolina Raptor Center, a sanctuary for injured birds of prey. Racing fans head to Lowe's Motor Speedway in Concord for NASCAR events, while high-speed thrills of another kind are found at Paramount's Carowinds theme park.

Charlotte Convention & Visitors Bureau: (704) 334-2282, (800) 722-1994; www.visitcharlotte.com

⊛ Raleigh-Durham-Chapel Hill
(Raleigh, State Capital) (E-12)

These neighboring cities in central North Carolina form the Research Triangle, home to some of the nation's largest corporations and to numerous institutions of higher learning, including Duke University, North Carolina State University, and the University of North Carolina. Raleigh's top attractions include the Greek Revival-style state capitol building and three state museums: the Museum of Art, the Museum of Natural Sciences, and the Museum of History. President Andrew Johnson's cabin birthplace has been preserved and moved to Mordecai Historic Park along with other 19th-century structures. In Durham, a huge interactive science technology center called the North Carolina Museum of Life and Science makes science interesting and fun. Bennett Place State Historic Site commemorates the site where Confederate General Joseph E. Johnston yielded his army to Union General William T. Sherman at the end of the Civil War. In Chapel Hill, the UNC campus holds the outstanding Ackland Art Museum and the 600-acre North Carolina Botanical Garden.

Greater Raleigh Convention & Visitors Bureau: (919) 834-5900, (800) 849-8499; www.visitraleigh.com Durham Convention and Visitors Bureau: (919) 687-0288, (800) 446-8604; www.durham-nc.com Chapel Hill/Orange County Visitors Bureau: (919) 968-2060, (800) 968-2060; www.CHOCVB.org

Wilmington (J-14)

Wedged between the Atlantic Ocean and the Cape Fear River, Wilmington has been an important port city since the mid-1700s. Chief among its charms is the 230-block riverfront historic district, where hundreds of

USS North Carolina

18th- and 19th-century buildings, houses, and mansions have been carefully restored. These include the Burgwin-Wright House, which briefly served as headquarters for British General Cornwallis during the American Revolution, and the 1859 Bellamy Mansion, which now holds a museum of history and design arts. Visitors can tour the district on foot, by trolley, by horse-drawn carriage, or by riverboat. The Battleship USS *North Carolina*, one of the mightiest fighting ships of World War II, sits across the river along Eagle Island and is open for tours daily. Nearby are the great gardens of Orton Plantation and Airlie Gardens as well as fine beaches along the Cape Fear coast.

Cape Fear Coast Convention & Visitors Bureau: (800) 222-4757; www.capefearcoast.com

SCENERY

Linn Cove Viaduct

Blue Ridge Parkway (D-2)

America's most famous scenic drive rides the crest of the Blue Ridge and Black Mountains for nearly 250 miles through western North Carolina, with numerous overlooks and pull-outs along the way. The parkway reaches its highest elevation — 6,047 feet — at Richland Balsam Overlook, but the views are equally spectacular at places like Craggy Gardens and Linville Falls. Probably the most-photographed stretch of the parkway is the Linn Cove Viaduct, a triumph of engineering that snakes around Grandfather Mountain in the shape of a double S.

Cherohala Scenic Skyway (p. 88, L-1)

Completed in 1996 after more than 30 years of planning and construction work, this all-but-undiscovered highway connects Robbinsville and the Tennessee town of Tellico Plains. True to its name, it climbs more than 5,400 feet into the sky as it twists along high mountain crests. More than two dozen overlooks — with names like Hooper Bald, East Rattlesnake Rock, and Spirit Ridge — provide views of forest-blanketed valleys and ranks of blue mountain ridges receding into the distance.

The Outer Banks (F-20)

Highway 12 runs for roughly 100 miles along this arc of long, narrow barrier islands that separate Albemarle and Pamlico Sounds from the Atlantic Ocean. From Corolla in the north to Ocracoke in the south, the highway traverses a sparsely populated landscape of low dunes lined with sandy beaches on the ocean side and lagoons and marshes on the inland side. Much of the drive falls within Cape Hatteras National Seashore.

- ### Cullasaja River Gorge (M-3)
  Between the western North Carolina towns of Highlands and Franklin, US 64 descends through the gorge that the Cullasaja River has carved through granite gneiss. Clinging tightly to the tumbling river, the highway provides access to Bridal Veil Falls, Dry Falls, and Cullasaja Falls.

- ### Greenfield Park and Gardens (M-18)
  A five-mile scenic drive winds through gardens of azaleas, camellias, and roses as it makes a loop around cypress-ringed Greenfield Lake in Wilmington.

- ### Newfound Gap Road (p. 88, I-5)
  From its starting point near the town of Cherokee, the main road through Great Smoky Mountains National Park follows the Oconaluftee River, then climbs steeply up the Thomas Divide before reaching an overlook at 5,048-foot Newfound Gap.

- ### Sandhills Scenic Drive (F-7)
  In the 50-mile stretch between Carthage and Albemarle, SR 24/27 crosses a landscape of low, rolling sandhills, fertile farmland, and pine forest.

OUTDOORS

Carolina Beach State Park (K-14)

This 761-acre park is located on Pleasure Island, a triangle of land between the Atlantic Ocean and the Cape Fear River. It's one of the few places in the world where the infamous venus flytrap can be found growing wild. This carnivorous plant — one of five insect-eating plants found here — is native only within a 60- to 75-mile radius of Wilmington. Hikers can easily spot the plants, with their lethal, jaw-like leaves, along the park's half-mile Flytrap Trail. The three-mile Sugarloaf Trail travels along the Cape Fear River for one mile to Sugarloaf Dune, an excellent place to observe water birds. Boardwalks along the way cross tidal marshes, and fiddler crabs can often be seen scurrying over the mud flats. From Sugarloaf, the trail continues past lime sink ponds and returns to its starting point through a mixed pine and hardwood forest.

(910) 458-8206;
www.ils.unc.edu/parkproject/visit/cabe/home.html

Max Patch (K-5)

Few places in the eastern United States can match the beauty of the grassy bald known as Max Patch Mountain. Located near the Tennessee border just northeast of Great Smoky Mountains National Park, the 4,629-foot mountain is domed by 350 acres of open grassland. From the summit, the surrounding Appalachian mountainscape — Great Smokies, Blue Ridges, Blacks, Balds — unfolds in a 360-degree panorama. On clear nights, "the Patch" becomes a natural planetarium that offers unbeatable stargazing, thanks to its openness, elevation, and the absence of competing light sources. Max Patch and adjoining Buckeye Ridge are magnets for horseback riders, and local stables offer trips ranging from a few hours to a few days. Another popular way to enjoy the area is by llama trek, with woolly 400-pound beasts of

burden carrying all of the food and equipment.

Appalachian Ranger District/French Broad Station,
Pisgah National Forest: (828) 622-3202;
www.cs.unca.edu/nfsnc

Nantahala River (p. 88, J-4)

The Nantahala hasn't flowed freely since construction of the Nantahala Dam in 1942. However, the river regains something of its wild character every day

Rafting on the Nantahala River

when Duke Power opens the dam's Tainter gates and cold lake-bottom water races through the Nantahala Gorge. This predictable water flow and the scenic beauty of the 1,600-foot-deep gorge have made the Nantahala one of North Carolina's most popular recreational rivers. Rated as Class II-III, the river tumbles over some 20 rapids — with names like The Bump and Whirlpool — on its 8.5-mile trip through the gorge. Nantahala Outdoor Center and other local outfitters provide rafts, canoes, kayaks, "duckies" (inflatable kayaks), and safety equipment as well as transportation. U.S. Forest Service regulations require that rafters weigh at least 60 pounds.

(828) 524-6441;
www.cs.unca.edu/nfsnc/recreation/nantahala.htm

Llama trekking to Max Patch

HERITAGE

Cradle of Forestry (L-5)

In 1895, George W. Vanderbilt acquired an 80,000-acre tract of land that stretched some 20 miles south of his famous Biltmore Estate. Much of "Pisgah Forest," as he called it, was in an unhealthy condition due to

Cradle of Forestry

fires, wholesale and careless logging, and erosion. Vanderbilt was determined to restore the forest to robust health through forestry, which was then a new concept. To this end, he hired professional foresters — first Gifford Pinchot, then Dr. Carl Alwin Schenck. In 1898, Schenck established Biltmore Forest School, the first school in America to teach scientific approaches to forest management. The school's site is commemorated as the Cradle of Forestry. Visitors can tour original buildings, watch an 18-minute film in the Forest Discovery Center, climb onto a 1915 logging train, and stroll along two miles of paved forest trails.

(828) 884-5713; www.cradleofforestry.com

Old Salem (p. 88, G-8)

The town of Salem — now part of Winston-Salem — was founded in 1766 by Moravians, Protestants from Germany. Thanks to the skill and industriousness of its citizens, Salem quickly became a center of trade and culture in the Piedmont region. The

Old Salem

original settlement is preserved as Old Salem, a historic district encompassing roughly 90 acres just south of downtown Winston-Salem. More than 100 homes, shops, and buildings have been restored to their 18th-century appearance and appointed with original or period furnishings. Many of the homes and buildings are privately owned, but twelve are open for tours. Costumed interpreters answer visitors' questions, provide historical background, and demonstrate crafts and skills. The historic district also offers museum shopping, dining, and lodging.

(888) 653-7253; www.oldsalem.org

Portsmouth (G-19)

Founded in 1753, this village on Portsmouth Island in the Outer Banks thrived as a seaport for roughly 100 years, thanks to its location on busy Ocracoke Inlet. Portsmouth served mainly as a "lightering" point — a place where cargo was transferred from large oceangoing vessels to lighter shallow-draft boats. However, in the mid-1800s, the inlet began to shoal, a hurricane cut a deeper inlet at Hatteras, and shipping traffic drifted away. Portsmouth survived as a fishing village, but its population declined until the last two residents left in 1971. Today the abandoned village is part of Cape Lookout National Seashore. Visitors can learn about life in a typical Outer Banks village by walking the streets and trails, exploring exhibits in the visitor center, and touring several buildings, including the post office/general store, the school, and the U.S. Life Saving Station. Portsmouth can be reached by ferry from Ocracoke.

(252) 728-2250; www.nps.gov/calo

Outer Banks

Local Color

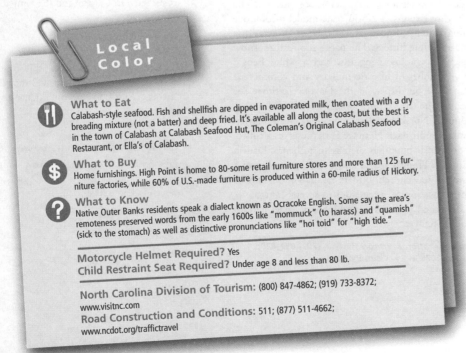

🍴 **What to Eat**
Calabash-style seafood. Fish and shellfish are dipped in evaporated milk, then coated with a dry breading mixture (not a batter) and deep fried. It's available all along the coast, but the best is in the town of Calabash at Calabash Seafood Hut, The Coleman's Original Calabash Seafood Restaurant, or Ella's of Calabash.

💲 **What to Buy**
Home furnishings. High Point is home to 80-some retail furniture stores and more than 125 furniture factories, while 60% of U.S.-made furniture is produced within a 60-mile radius of Hickory.

❓ **What to Know**
Native Outer Banks residents speak a dialect known as Ocracoke English. Some say the area's remoteness preserved words from the early 1600s like "mommuck" (to harass) and "quamish" (sick to the stomach) as well as distinctive pronunciations like "hoi toid" for "high tide."

Motorcycle Helmet Required? Yes
Child Restraint Seat Required? Under age 8 and less than 80 lb.

North Carolina Division of Tourism: (800) 847-4862; (919) 733-8372;
www.visitnc.com
Road Construction and Conditions: 511; (877) 511-4662;
www.ncdot.org/traffictravel

North Dakota has many scenic rivers that provide great kayaking adventures.

Little Missouri National Grasslands (D-2)

Totaling more than one million acres, this area is the largest of any grasslands found in the western United States. With open prairies, high plains, and badlands, it is one of the last places where visitors can experience the wide-open spaces as early American Indians and the first European settlers saw them.

Painted Canyon (E-2)

The Visitor Center at Theodore Roosevelt National Park provides a spectacular view of the canyon with its rolling hills and colors. A 36-mile loop leads to several overlooks and hiking trails. There are also historic buildings along the way including Peaceful Valley Ranch, which was a cattle and horse ranch during the late 1800s.

Theodore Roosevelt National Park

Theodore Roosevelt National Park (D-2)

A 14-mile drive through the North Unit of the 70,000-acre national park takes visitors by multi-colored corrugated cliffs and domes in the badlands. Despite the forboding name, a variety of plants and animals thrive here in the open grasslands and barren rock. In spring, acres of colorful wildflowers cover the prairie. Mule deer graze on the open plains with elk, bison herds, and wild horses, while white-tailed deer find refuge in the woodlands.

● **Des Lacs National Wildlife Refuge Backway** (B-5)
This 19-mile drive south of Kenmare offers an excellent opportunity to view wildlife and migratory birds.

● **Enchanted Highway** (F-4)
Giant metal sculptures of critters and caricatures flank Route 22 between Dickinson and Regent.

● **International Peace Garden** (A-8)
Located near Dunseith, this horticultural showcase was created as a tribute to the peace that exists between Canada and the United States.

● **Standing Rock Historical Scenic Byway** (F-7)
Located south of Mandan, this route winds through areas that look much as they did when Sitting Bull lived on Standing Rock Reservation.

● **Turtle Mountain Scenic Byway** (B-8)
This 53-mile byway in Rolette County passes pastoral landscapes as it climbs and then descends Turtle Mountain.

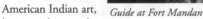

CITIES

✪ Bismarck (State Capital) (F-7)

Railroad builders, hoping to attract German capital, named this town for the late 19th-century chancellor of Germany, Otto von Bismarck. The Missouri River port and rail crossing first became the capital of the territory and then of the state. Visit the restored Governor's Mansion, the North Dakota Heritage Center Museum, and the state's largest zoo, the Dakota Zoo. Camp Hancock Museum, once the campsite of the men who built the Northern Pacific Railroad, has displays showing the role played by the railroads in Bismarck's early days. To the visitor from a large metropolis where streets are walled by high-rises, the 19-story Art Deco skyscraper capitol building might seem misnamed. But, looming above the plains, its white limestone and black granite mark a dramatic exclamation point on the horizon. From its rooftop gallery, view the wide-open spaces, the modern city below, and the historic frontier town of Mandan across the Missouri River.

Bismarck-Mandan Convention & Visitors Bureau:
(701) 222-4308, (800) 767-3555;
www.discoverbismarckmandan.com

Fargo (F-13)

Along with Moorhead, its sister city in Minnesota across the Red River, this area forms a commercial and agricultural center for both states. The Wells Fargo Express was such an important factor to development during the railroad-building era that Fargo was named after its founder. It is the largest city in the state, and it is the largest city on the map between the twin cities of Minneapolis-Saint Paul, MN and Spokane, WA. Though progressive, Fargo values its past. This reverence is reflected in its historic downtown business area and on residential streets, such as 8th Street South where a cluster of Victorian mansions are complimented by original, ornate street lighting. The Plains Art Museum's permanent collection includes regional, Native American, folk, and contemporary artwork.

Fargo-Moorhead Convention & Visitors Bureau:
(701) 282-3653, (800) 235-7654;
www.fargomoorhead.org

Grand Forks (D-12)

The University of North Dakota is located here in the heart of the Red River Valley. On its campus are the North Dakota Museum of Art and the high-tech Center for Aerospace Sciences. The Grand Forks County Historical Society maintains several historic buildings including the Myra Museum, which has exhibits on pioneer life in the valley, and Campbell House (1879), an original log cabin with pioneer furnishings. At Engelstad Arena the Fighting Sioux challenge other WCHA hockey rivals. At the city's Visitor Center, a 12-minute film chronicles the devastating 1997 flood. Since the flood, the Town Square has come back to life with shops, restaurants, free outdoor concepts, and a summer Saturday farmers' market.

Grand Forks Convention & Visitors Bureau:
(701) 746-0444, (800) 866-4566;
www.visitgrandforks.com

Mandan (F-7)

Stroll down Main Street between 2nd and 4th Avenues for a taste of Western shopping at its best: Western wear, American Indian art, homemade candy, and a real old-fashioned drugstore soda fountain. The Five Nations Arts Depot is located in the historic Burlington Northern Railroad Depot and is a primary outlet for arts and crafts from North Dakota American Indian artists. General George Custer's home is restored at Fort Lincoln State Park. A replica of Fort Mandan, the winter headquarters for Lewis and Clark's Corps of Discovery and built by the Expedition, is located a few miles downstream on the Missouri River.

Guide at Fort Mandan

Bismarck-Mandan Convention & Visitors Bureau:
(701) 222-4308, (800) 767-3555;
www.discoverbismarckmandan.com

Minot (C-6)

Founded as a railroad town in 1887, Minot is a commercial center for northern plains agriculture with additional connections to the aerospace industry. The Magic City Express, a 2/5ths scale-model locomotive running through Roosevelt Park, helps preserve the city's railroading history. The park's zoo features snow leopards, kangaroos, penguins, and a white Bengal tiger. A number of historic military and commercial airplanes are on display at the Dakota Territory Air Museum. The city's ethnic roots are celebrated during the annual Norsk Hostfest, a five-day Scandinavian festival. Scandinavian Heritage Park preserves a collection of historic buildings such as an authentic Danish windmill, a Finnish sauna, and a full-size replica of a Norwegian stav church. Birders are drawn to Minot as a central location for excursions to several sanctuaries including the Upper Souris and J. Clark Sayler national wildlife refuges.

Minot Convention & Visitors Bureau: (701) 857-8206,
(800) 264-2626, www.visitminot.org

HERITAGE

Knife River Indian Villages National Historic Site (E-6)

Knife River Indian Villages

For a glimpse of life on the northern plains before the advent of explorers, fur traders, and settlers, spend a day visiting the three villages of the Hidatsa Indian tribe. The Hidatsa may have arrived at Knife River as early as the early 1300s. Today, these three villages are a National Historic Site. An Earthlodge people, the Hidatsa were farmers, hunters, and great traders, in both goods and in knowledge. Traditional oral histories helped to preserve the culture of the people that, through increased Western contact, was slowly losing its way. In the end, the smallpox epidemic of 1837 greatly reduced the populations of this and other Indian nations. Within 40 years, the Hidatsa and other groups were relocated and finally moved to the Fort Berthold Reservation. Today, the nation is known as the Three Affiliated Tribes.

(701) 745-3300; www.nps.gov/knri

Lewis and Clark Trail (F-7)

Lewis and Clark Interpretive Center at Washburn

Starting at Mandan, the road on the east side of the Missouri River is numbered ND 1804, marking the year the Corps of Discovery arrived in the Red River Valley. On the west side of the river, ND 1806 commemorates the expedition's return. Between Mandan and Williston, the road passes by 12 historic landmarks including Knife River Indian Villages National Historic Site, the Cross Ranch State Park with its pristine waterscapes, and Fort Union Trading Post National Historic Site, once an impressive trading post with 18-foot high cottonwood walls and stone bastions. There's also plenty of scenery including the Missouri River as it meanders north and west, rugged hills on the horizon, and towering bluffs near the shores of Lake Sakakawea.

(800) 435-5663; www.ndtourism.com

Fort Abraham Lincoln

Trail of the 7th Cavalry (F-7)

Rich in both military and early Native American history, Fort Abraham Lincoln was once an important infantry and cavalry post. It was from this fort that Lt. Col. George Armstrong Custer and the 7th Cavalry rode out on their ill-fated expedition against the Sioux at Little Big Horn. Portions of the military post, including the lieutenant colonel's home (called Custer House), have been reconstructed. Nearby On-A-Slant Indian Village features reconstructed earthlodges depicting the lifestyle of the Mandan Indians, who occupied this site between 1575 and 1781. A modern campground is located in a scenic wooded area adjacent to the Heart River with picnic sites and playground equipment. Walking along the gently sloping hills, visitors have a panoramic view of the Missouri River.

(701) 667-6340; www.ndtourism.com; www.ndparks.com/parks/FLSP.htm

OUTDOORS

Lake Sakakawea

Lake Sakakawea (D-6)

At 178 miles in length, Lake Sakakawea has more shoreline than the California coast. It is one of the three largest man-made reservoirs in the United States. Named for the Shoshone/Hidatsa woman who accompanied Lewis and Clark and the Corps of Discovery on their quest for a route to the Pacific Ocean, the lake resulted from the construction of Garrison Dam in the 1950s. At any time of the day, there are water activities on this massive lake. Besides fishing for walleye, northern pike (the official state fish that can exceed 20 pounds), and chinook salmon in the lower harbors, there's swimming, water skiing, sailing, and general boating. Several outfitters rent pontoons, canoes, kayaks, and motor boats.

(701) 328-2525; www.parkrec.nd.gov/parks/parks9-z.htm

The Maah Daah Hey Trail

The Maah Daah Hey Trail (F-3)

The name for this trail comes from the Mandan Indians and means "an area that has been or will be around for a long time." Rolling prairie and stark, sand-colored buttes surround hikers, bikers, and horseback riders, who all share the trail. It's signed by a turtle, an appropriate symbol of steadfast perseverance. For 96 miles this multi-use single track follows a route that connects the Theodore Roosevelt National Park South Unit with the North Unit. It starts in Sully Creek State Park, then heads north, continuing through the Little Missouri National Grasslands as well as state and private land until the trail ends at the TRNP North Unit. Bikers should know that bicycles are not allowed on sections of the trail within Theodore Roosevelt National Park.

(701) 225-5151; www.nps.gov/thro/tr_mdh.htm

Pembina River (A-12)

Biking the trails at Pembina River

Miles of lush, unbroken forest now grow in the space left by a wide, ancient river fed by meltwater from glaciers in Canada. The forests are bordered by a range of hills and mountains that extends to the international border. There are many trails for hiking and biking and even a road for a scenic drive, but the best way to experience the Pembina Delta and the Pembina Gorge is from a canoe. The only white water found in North Dakota is on today's narrower Pembina River and, except for the spring, it is a Class I easy float. Spring weather often brings increased flow from its source in La Riviere, Manitoba, that can cause the rapids to increase in intensity for a short period of time.

(701) 328-2525; nd.water.usgs.gov/photos/resources/pembinariver.html

Red River Valley (C-13)

There are many birding sites in this area of the valley including Turtle River State Park, Kellys Slough National Wildlife Refuge, the Prairie Chicken Management Area, and the Oakville Prairie. North Dakota has more national wildlife refuges than any other state. A number were created by refilling marshes and reseeding the barren plains with native grasses. The sight of tens of thousands of birds flocking to these refuges during migration is extraordinary. More than 300 species have been documented in the Red River Valley alone, including the short-eared owl and the greater prairie chicken. In the winter, the snowy owl, snow buntings, and common redpoll have been observed.

(701) 250-4418; www.ndtourism.com; mountain-prairie.fws.gov/refuges/nd

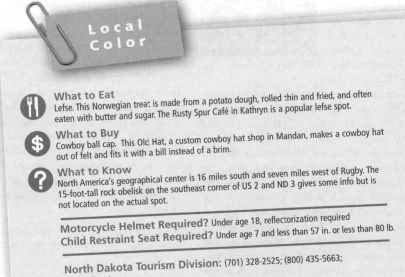

Local Color

What to Eat
Lefse. This Norwegian treat is made from a potato dough, rolled thin and fried, and often eaten with butter and sugar. The Rusty Spur Café in Kathryn is a popular lefse spot.

What to Buy
Cowboy ball cap. This Old Hat, a custom cowboy hat shop in Mandan, makes a cowboy hat out of felt and fits it with a bill instead of a brim.

What to Know
North America's geographical center is 16 miles south and seven miles west of Rugby. The 15-foot-tall rock obelisk on the southeast corner of US 2 and ND 3 gives some info but is not located on the actual spot.

Motorcycle Helmet Required? Under age 18, reflectorization required
Child Restraint Seat Required? Under age 7 and less than 57 in. or less than 80 lb.

North Dakota Tourism Division: (701) 328-2525; (800) 435-5663; www.ndtourism.com
Road Construction and Conditions: 511; (866) 696-3511; www.dot.nd.gov/divisions/maintenance/511_nd.html

Biking country roads in Ohio includes rolling farmland views.

CITIES

Cincinnati (SG-2)

A major transportation and industrial center, Cincinnati took root where canals and railroads met and crossed the Ohio River. Along the redeveloped waterfront, barges and showboats ply the waters, although most visitors are likely to be watching games at the new Great American Ball Park or Paul Brown Stadium, where the Reds and Bengals play. Among the latest riverfront additions, the National Underground Railroad Freedom Center offers interactive exhibits on the universal impulse towards freedom. The Taft Museum of Art, housed in a Federal-period mansion, has reopened after extensive renovations, allowing the public to again view its outstanding collection of porcelains and Old Masters paintings. The Cincinnati Art Museum in Eden Park exhibits works spanning the entire history of art, while the Museum Center at Union Terminal houses several worthwhile facilities including the Museum of Natural History and Science, the Cinergy Children's Museum, and the Cincinnati History Museum. Family fun can also be had at the first-rate Cincinnati Zoo.

Cincinnati Zoo

(800) 344-3445; www.cincinnatiusa.com

Cleveland (NF-15)

A city historically based on shipping and heavy industry, Cleveland has benefited from redevelopment of its Lake Erie waterfront and the banks of the Cuyahoga. The high-tech energy of the remarkable Rock and Roll Hall of Fame garners worldwide attention. Next door, the Great Lakes Science Center offers hundreds of brain-stimulating exhibits on the environment, technology, and scientific phenomena. In the University Circle area, visit the Cleveland Museum of Art, Cleveland Botanical Garden, Museum of Natural History, and Western Reserve Historical Society. Animals and visitors at Cleveland Metroparks Zoo can roam through 168 rolling, woodland acres as well as a two-acre indoor rainforest. On Euclid Avenue, Playhouse Square, a complex of renovated 1920s movie palaces, offers a wide array of theatrical entertainments including ballet and opera. For more nightlife, explore downtown's East Fourth Street or the Warehouse district with restaurants, bars, live music, and comedy.

The Flats, Cleveland

*Convention & Visitors Bureau of Greater Cleveland:
(800) 321-1004; www.travelcleveland.com*

⊛ Columbus (State Capital) (SB-9)

Ohio's capital city, Columbus is the home of Ohio State University and a center of technological innovation. At COSI Columbus, families can enjoy a planetarium and hands-on science exhibits dealing with the human body, space, oceans, and other subjects. The Columbus Zoo, which is noted for its unprecedented success in raising three generations of gorillas, also offers reptiles, manatees, and a coral reef on its 100 acres of habitats and displays. Near the zoo, Zoombezi Bay Water Park is filled with amusements, rides, and water park features. Climb aboard a replica of Christopher Columbus's flagship, the *Santa Maria*, at Battelle Park. German Village, south of downtown, offers interesting shops and products in a quaint neighborhood of restored 19th-century homes. Dozens of galleries, boutiques, nightclubs, cafés, and bistros line the streets of the Short North Arts District.

*Experience Columbus: (866) 397-2657;
www.experiencecolumbus.com*

U.S. Air Force Museum

Dayton (SC-4)

Ever since the days of the Wright Brothers, Dayton has been known as a center of invention. Numerous high-tech firms are located in the city called the Birthplace of Aviation. Tour the multiple sites comprising the Dayton Aviation Heritage National Historical Park, including the Huffman Prairie Flying Field. The city is home to Wright-Patterson Air Force Base, where the National Museum of the U.S. Air Force displays more than 300 aircraft and missiles. One of the nation's finest midsize museums, the Dayton Art Institute offers a substantial collection of African, European, Asian, and American art. SunWatch Indian Village is an archaeological park preserving the site of a planned native village of the 13th century. Explore the interactive science exhibits at Boonshoft Museum of Discovery, and visit Carriage Hill Farm, a living history farm of the 1880s with live animals, blacksmith shop, and country store.

*Dayton/Montgomery County Convention & Visitors
Bureau: (800) 221-8235; www.daytoncvb.com*

SCENERY

CanalWay Ohio (NI-15)

This 110-mile scenic byway follows the path of the historic Ohio and Erie Canal from Cleveland to Dover. Sites along the way include the Canal Visitor Center, the restored German immigrant town of Zoar, and the Cuyahoga Valley Scenic Railroad. Shops and restaurants are in Canal Fulton, a canal port in the 1840s and 1850s.

Cuyahoga Valley Railroad

Ohio River Scenic Route (NK-20)

Running for 303 miles along the banks of the Ohio River, this was the first nationally designated scenic byway in Ohio. It stretches from East Liverpool in the east to Cincinnati in the west, and continues into Indiana and Illinois. The route passes through many small river towns. Stops could include the town of Steubenville, with its 1787 Old Fort Steuben reconstruction; the Ohio River Museum in Marietta; and the Ulysses S. Grant birthplace and boyhood home in Point Pleasant.

Gallipolis

● Amish Country Byway (NK-15)

Check out the Amish and Mennonite Heritage Center, one-room schools, and Amish farms along a 76-mile route in central Ohio.

Amish buggies

● Land of the Cross-tipped Churches (NL-3)

For 38 miles through rural farming region of western Ohio, look for the many churches capped with spires and crosses.

● Ledges Overlook (NG-16)

One-half mile from the Ledges Trail parking lot in Cuyahoga Valley National Park, flat rocks provide an excellent vantage point for viewing the wooded park.

● Jefferson County Southern Scenic Byway (NM-19)

Take a 15-mile meander through eastern Ohio's Jefferson County. Stop in Mt. Pleasant, a historic Quaker town that includes a number of sites listed on the National Register of Historic Places.

● Maumee Valley Scenic Byway (NE-6)

Pass the 1794 site of the Battle of Fallen Timbers on this route along the Maumee River.

● Scenic Olentangy Heritage Corridor (NM-9)

North of Columbus, this 10.5-mile route parallels the Olentangy River, passing historic homes, schoolhouses, and the scenic mill district.

OUTDOORS

Cuyahoga Valley National Park (NG-15)

Hills and valleys carved by prehistoric glaciers set the stage for this scenic park between Cleveland and Akron. Begin a bike trip along the Ohio & Erie Canal trail at the Canal Visitor Center, a former canal boat passenger station at Lock 38. Costumed guides conduct canal lock demonstrations in summer. In winter, go snowshoeing, cross-country skiing, sledding, or tubing at the Kendall Lake Winter Sports Center. Cuyahoga, a Native American word for crooked, describes the meandering river that cuts through the park. It's a place to watch for wild turkey and deer as well as beavers and painted turtles. Listen for songbirds that migrate through here each spring and fall, among the 194 bird species found in the park.

(216) 524-1497; www.nps.gov/cuva

Hocking Hills State Park (SE-11)

With 25 miles of hiking trails that traverse rugged hills and pass streams, waterfalls, and caves in beautiful south-

Old Man's Cave

eastern Ohio, this park packs a lot of adventure opportunities. Eastern hemlocks line the popular one-mile Old Man's Cave trail, which goes past Blackhand sandstone and Upper Falls. The 2.5-mile Conkle's Hollow Rim Trail follows the edge of a gorge named after W.J. Conkle, who carved his name in the sandstone wall. Naturalists lead hikes and conduct programs throughout the year, including fall color and snow hikes, maple syrup boiling demonstrations, photography workshops, history walks, and Christmas cave tours. The park features cottages, cabins, and camping, as well as a dining lodge.

(740) 385-6841; www.hockinghillspark.com

John Bryan State Park and Clifton Gorge State Nature Reserve (SC-5)

Adjacent to each other, these two picturesque spots along the Little Miami State and National Scenic River in western Ohio lure hikers and rock climbers. The 269-acre Clifton Gorge preserves dolomite and limestone gorges, with great overlook spots. At the 752-acre John Bryan State Park, go sledding or cross-country skiing in the winter, and try rappelling and rock climbing in a specially designated area. The gorges of these areas were formed by retreating glaciers. In shaded spots, find Canada yew and mountain maple; oaks and maples throughout the park create spectacular fall color. Wildflowers grow in abundance: There are more than 340 species, including bluebells, wild columbine, Jack-in-the-pulpit, and wild ginger.

(937) 767-1274;
www.dnr.state.oh.us/parks/parks/jhnbryan.htm or
www.dnr.state.oh.us/dnap/location/clifton.html

Lake Erie Islands State Park (NE-10)

Take a car ferry or just bring a bike to one of the five state parks comprising Lake Erie Islands State Park: Kelleys Island, Catawba Island, Oak Point, South Bass Island, and Middle Bass Island. (Middle Bass Island State Park is curently under development.) The parks on Kelleys and South Bass islands feature campgrounds, while the other parks maintain day-use areas. Climb to the top of Marblehead Lighthouse, built in 1822 and the oldest continuously operating Great Lakes lighthouse and a state park. Enjoy fishing, boating, picnicking, bike riding, or just watching the waters of Lake Erie.

(419) 797-4530;
www.dnr.state.oh.us/parks/parks/lakeerie.htm

HERITAGE

Buckeye Furnace State Memorial (SG-12)

In the mid to late 1800s, Ohio's Hanging Rock Iron Region bustled with charcoal-fired blast furnaces producing iron for the expansion of the railroads, machinery, and even Civil War cannons. The region was the second-largest producer of iron in the U.S. As many as 100 men and 50 teams of oxen produced 12 tons of iron a day at this furnace, which has been restored with the original stack. Built in 1852, it went out of blast in 1894. The former charging house and engine house are open. Also on the 270-acre site is a replica company store and office that provide visitor information, as well as two nature trails that pass abandoned ore pits. The grounds are open year-round; the store and office are open by appointment only.

(800) 860-0144; www.ohiohistory.org/places/buckeye/

Fort Meigs (NC-1)

In the late 1700s and early 1800s, Ohio was the wild western edge of the United States. The young nation was still battling American Indians and the British for survival. This fort was built in 1813 to protect the state from a British invasion and successfully endured two attacks. The 10-acre site in Perrysburg, enclosed by a stockade wall, features the largest reconstructed log fort in the country. There are seven blockhouses and five cannon batteries to see. A number of events during the year feature reenactments and costumed interpreters.

Interpreter at Fort Meigs State Memorial

(800) 283-8916; www.fortmeigs.org

National Underground Railroad Freedom Center (SM-3)

In its five history galleries, Cincinnati's National Underground Railroad Freedom Center helps explain the dangerous path slaves took to gain freedom in the decades preceding the Civil War. The critical role played by abolitionists and freedmen is explored as well. The 158,000-square-foot facility features the Underground Railroad Children's Exhibit, a slave jail donated by a Kentucky farmer, and a story theater. The center also emphasizes research and the continuing struggle for freedom.

(513) 333-7500; www.undergroundrailroad.org

Freedom Center

Yoder's Amish Home (NK-15)

Located between Trail and Walnut Creek, this 116-acre working farm allows visitors to learn more about Amish life. The farm is located in Holmes County, site of the largest Amish community in the world. The property is owned by Eli Yoder, a member of the Old Order Amish community until he was 21, and his wife Gloria, who was also raised as Amish. A visit includes tours of two homes and the barn, with guides discussing Amish customs and life. Guests can take buggy rides and touch farm animals at a petting zoo. Open April through October.

(330) 893-2541; www.yodersamishhome.com

Local Color

What to Eat
Buckeyes. The sweet version, that is - Harry London Candies makes sugary peanut butter balls dipped in chocolate to look like buckeye tree nuts. There are stores throughout the state, and a huge factory and store in North Canton.

What to Buy
Metal whistle. The American Whistle Company in Columbus is the only manufacturer of metal whistles in the country.

What to Know
At 15 feet deep and 35 feet wide, the glacial grooves on Kelleys Island are believed to be the largest glacial striations in the world. A section was cut away and shipped to the Smithsonian Institution in Washington, D.C.

Motorcycle Helmet Required? Under age 18, novice riders, and passengers if driver is required to wear helmet
Child Restraint Seat Required? Under age 4 or less than 40 lb.

Ohio Division of Travel & Tourism: (800) 282-5393; www.discoverohio.com
Road Construction and Conditions: 511, (513) 333-3333 (Cincinnati/northern Kentucky area); (888) 264-7623 (in OH); (614) 644-7031 (conditions); (440) 234-2030 (conditions on turnpike); (888) 876-7453 (construction on turnpike); www.buckeyetraffic.org; www.ohioturnpike.org; www.artimis.org (Cincinnati/northern KY area)

The "Gates of Time" memorialize the minutes before and after the 9:02 a.m. bombing of the Alfred P. Murrah Federal Building on April 19, 1995, in Oklahoma City.

CITIES

Bartlesville (C-17)

Located in northeastern Oklahoma, this bustling small city is sometimes called "the town that oil built." The Nellie Johnstone No. 1, the first commercially successful well drilled in Oklahoma, is in Johnstone Park, kept as it was when it struck oil. It isn't the city's only landmark. Price Tower is a 19-story art gallery and hotel designed for Great Plains living by Frank Lloyd Wright. At Woolaroc Ranch, Museum, and Wildlife Refuge, the development of western America is traced through artifacts and art by Frederic Remington, Charles Russell, and other famous artists. Visit the Frank Phillips Home and, in nearby Dewey, the Victorian Dewey Hotel, the Tom Mix Museum, and an 1800s frontier village replica, Prairie Song. Lucky enough to be in Bartlesville in June? Enjoy the OK Mozart International Festival and listen to his work performed by classical music legends such as Itzhak Perlman.

Bartlesville Area Convention & Visitors Bureau: (918) 336-8708, (877) 273-2007; www.visitbartlesville.com

Guthrie (E-13)

Guthrie sprang out of the prairie overnight during the Land Rush of 1889, a brand new city of 10,000 people, then languished, unchanged by time, when the state capital was removed to Oklahoma City in 1910. Today, it is one of the largest historic districts in the country with thousands of well-preserved Victorian-era commercial buildings and homes lining its brick-sidewalk streets. A charming downtown offers boutiques, galleries, and antique shops. The enormous Scottish Rite Temple on Old Capitol Square boasts decorative features recalling ancient Egyptian, Assyrian, Greek, and Roman civilizations. For a look at the state's settlement, visit the Oklahoma Territorial Museum. The State Capital Publishing Museum features early printing equipment and interesting architectural details. Musicians will want to see the vintage banjo collection at the National 4-String Banjo Hall of Fame Museum. The city hosts the Guthrie Jazz Banjo Festival on Memorial Day weekend and the Oklahoma International Bluegrass Festival in October.

Guthrie Chamber of Commerce: (800) 299-1889; www.guthrieok.com

✪ Oklahoma City (State Capital) (F-13)

A little more than a million people live in the metro area of Oklahoma's capital city, nearly a third of the state's entire population. The state capitol building boasts an oil well on its lawn. It wasn't until 2002 that the dome of the capitol building was added to the structure, even though the dome was part of the original 1910 design. Before the dome was built, its design was altered to include a 17-foot statue of an American Indian called "The Guardian," which now graces the top. Stop by the Omniplex, which houses several museums and a planetarium, and the Oklahoma City Museum of Art at its downtown location. The National Cowboy and Western Heritage Museum boasts an extraordinary collection of Western art. Catch a water taxi to Bricktown, an entertainment district or browse the Paseo art quarter or Stockyards City where livestock auctions are held and cowboys are part of the neighborhood. Western Avenue is a treasure trove of boutiques, clubs, and fine dining.

Oklahoma City Convention & Visitors Bureau: (405) 297-8912, (800) 225-5652; www.visitokc.com

Jazz Hall of Fame, Tulsa

Tulsa (D-17)

An oil boomtown in the 1930s, Tulsa is Oklahoma's second-largest city and leading cultural center. In addition to companies offering opera, symphony, and ballet, Tulsa is home to exceptional museums including the Philbrook Museum of Art, an Italian-style villa with an extensive collection of Renaissance and Native American art, and the Gilcrease Museum, a comprehensive collection of fine art, artifacts, and archives related to the American West. Self-guided tours are available of the downtown Art Deco District, another legacy of the boom years of the 1920s and 1930s. The Oklahoma Aquarium allows visitors to view hundreds of denizens of the deep and a unique collection of fishing equipment. Stroll through the acres of woodlands and gorgeous blooms at Woodward Park and the Tulsa Garden Center. At the Tulsa Air and Space Museum, the ESky™ Theater provides an extraordinary planetarium experience. For after-hours entertainment, try the trendy nightspots of Brookside and the Brady District.

Tulsa Chamber of Commerce: (800) 558-3311; www.visittulsa.com

SCENERY

Chickasaw National Recreation Area (I-14)

Lushly foliated eastern woodlands give way to sweeping mixed grass prairie at this 10,000-acre recreational area. Underneath the surface, water rushes down a subterranean formation, then bubbles to the surface, creating freshwater springs and, where it passes through mineral-rich rocks, mineral springs. For at least 7,000 years Native Americans have lived near these curative waters.

Talimena Scenic Byway (H-19)

Named for the two cities that it connects — Talihina in Oklahoma and Mena, Arkansas — this National Forest Scenic Byway follows the ridge over the Winding Stair and Rich mountains chains, the highest ranges between the Appalachians and the Rockies. It provides views of forested mountaintops and, thanks to the loblolly pine and hardwood growth, one green glen after another.

Rodeo rider

● **Black Mesa State Park** (B-1)
Unique rock formations and an abundance of desert plant life such as cholla cactus flowers provide a xeric landscape in the Panhandle.

● **The "Breaks"** (G-8)
Just south of Erick, this area of broken mesas, or what locals call the Breaks, offers great bird-watching.

● **Honor Heights Park** (E-18)
Famous for its azaleas, this 122-acre park in Muskogee was built as a tribute to World War I veterans and includes a well-marked rose garden, trails, ponds, and an arboretum.

● **Myriad Botanical Gardens** (K-2)
The Myriad features a 224-foot-long glass tropical conservatory called the Crystal Bridge that offers terrific views of downtown Oklahoma City and contains an extensive collection of prized plants.

● **Tallgrass Prairie Preserve** (B-16)
Known for its herd of free-roaming bison and wildflowers blooming in the middle of prairie grasses, the 38,600 acres of the Tallgrass Prairie Preserve near Pawhuska provide an opportunity to experience the beauty of the Great Plains.

● **Turner Falls** (I-14)
Honey Creek winds its way through the Arbuckle Mountains South of Davis and cascades 77 feet to form the highest waterfall in the state.

Native American child

HERITAGE

Cherokee Heritage Center *(E-19)*

Located at the end of the Trail of Tears — the 1,000-mile forced march of the Eastern Cherokee Indians — the town of Tahlequah has been the capital of the Cherokee Nation since 1841. The street signs are printed in Cherokee as well as in English. The Cherokee Heritage Center, considered the finest example of a tribally specific educational facility, includes the Cherokee National Museum, Adams Corner Rural Village, the Ancient Village, and the Tsa La Gi Amphitheater. The center preserves Cherokee history and culture through more than 50 annual events. It also provides assistance for genealogy searches at the Cherokee Family Research Center.

(918) 456-6007; www.cherokeeheritage.org

National Cowboy and Western Heritage Museum *(J-3)*

This Oklahoma City museum covers the full spectrum of the Old West, with 8 galleries displaying contributions of Native Americans, pioneers, and cowboys.

There is fine art from Charles Russell and Frederic Remington as well as the famous 18-foot sculpture created for the San Francisco 1915 Panama-Pacific International Exposition by James Earle Fraser, *The End of the Trail.* Another of Fraser's works — a statue of Abraham Lincoln — is also in the museum. Visitors can walk through a recreated cattle town called

*End of the Trail
by James Earle Fraser*

Prosperity Junction or watch an early Western-genre movie. The museum features displays celebrating rodeo heroes, Wild West performers, and cowboys.

(405) 478-2250; www.nationalcowboymuseum.org

Oklahoma City National Memorial *(K-2)*

The Oklahoma City National Memorial remembers those who lost their lives in the bombing of the Alfred P. Murrah Building on April 19, 1995. The grounds include the Survivor Tree (an American elm that was disfigured by the bombing), the Field of Empty Chairs, a Reflecting Pool, the Rescuers' Orchard, a children's area, and the monumental bronze-clad Gates of Time where visitors are invited to leave their handprints. An adjacent museum exhibits powerful video programs, poignant oral histories, and bomb-damaged artifacts. The outdoor memorial is open 24 hours a day throughout the year.

*(405) 235-3313;
www.oklahomacitynationalmemorial.org*

Route 66 Museum *(F-10)*

Nearly 400 of the 2,400 miles of Route 66 cross the state of Oklahoma. That's more than any other state on its run through eight states and three time zones. Cyrus Avery, the road's architect, was born in Oklahoma and lived in Tulsa.

Route 66 devotees say there's no better way to cruise the "Main Street of America" than by visiting the diners, drive-in theaters, and mom-and-pop gas stations within Oklahoma's borders. In Clinton, the Route 66 Museum houses memorabilia and artifacts gathered from the small towns that the legendary route connects.

(580) 323-7866; www.route66.org

OUTDOORS

Grand Lake O' the Cherokees *(C-19)*

Reportedly the best bass fishing lake in Oklahoma, Grand Lake is also considered the crappie capital of the world. It is also the largest in a chain of lakes nestled in the foothills of the Ozarks in northeastern Oklahoma. Created in 1940 as part of the Pensacola Dam project, Grand Lake is now bordered by 10 state parks, with 1,300 miles of shoreline and 46,500 surface acres of water. In addition to fishing, it supports boating, cruising, sailing, parasailing, water skiing, and personal watercraft activities. Because the lake is oriented in a southwest to northeast direction, sailors can take full advantage of prevailing winds. Rental boats and equipment are available at any of the 30 full-service marinas.

(918) 786-2289; www.grda.com/water/grand.html

Roman Nose State Resort Park *(E-11)*

Located in the canyon where the Cheyenne overwintered, Roman Nose

*Entrance to Roman Nose
State Park*

State Resort Park features bluffs that overlook ancient mesas and freshwater lakes in west-central Oklahoma. The Spring of Everlasting Waters, a confluence of subterranean rivers, produces water at the rate of 600 gallons per minute, which supports the park and its wildlife. Roman Nose offers a variety of activities for outdoor enthusiasts, even golf. For golfers, there is an 18-hole course with a practice putting green. Cedar-lined canyons lure visitors to the equestrian trails. One-, two-, and three-hour interpretive rides are available; a three-hour dinner ride includes a trip through the canyon and across the lakes to a dinner prepared over an open fire. Buffalo grass and wild blue sage add to the beauty of the park named for the last chief of the Cheyenne.

(580) 623-4215; www.oklahomaparks.com

Buffalo

Wichita Mountains Wildlife Refuge *(H-10)*

Not far from Lawton in southwestern Oklahoma, the Wichita Mountain National Wildlife Refuge encompasses 60,000 acres of land and 13 lakes. It is an open range for buffalo, elk, deer, and Texas longhorn cattle. Visitors enjoy hiking, biking, and rock climbing. Nine hiking trails are outlined on a trail map that is available online or at the Visitors Center. In all, there are 15 miles of marked trails, open during daylight only. Hikers can go up Elk Mountain in less than an hour. Motorized vehicles and bicycles are allowed on the 3.5 miles up to Mount Scott. Climbing — from boulder-hopping to highly technical — is permitted in the public-use day area.

(580) 429-3222; wichitamountains.fws.gov

Hiking

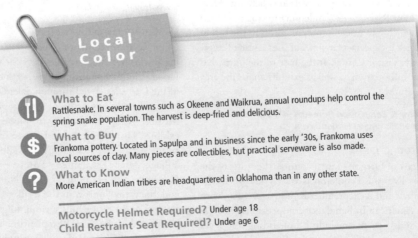

Local Color

What to Eat
Rattlesnake. In several towns such as Okeene and Waikrua, annual roundups help control the spring snake population. The harvest is deep-fried and delicious.

What to Buy
Frankoma pottery. Located in Sapulpa and in business since the early '30s, Frankoma uses local sources of clay. Many pieces are collectibles, but practical serveware is also made.

What to Know
More American Indian tribes are headquartered in Oklahoma than in any other state.

Motorcycle Helmet Required? Under age 18
Child Restraint Seat Required? Under age 6

Oklahoma Tourism & Recreation Department:
(800) 652-6552; www.travelok.com
Road Construction and Conditions:
(405) 425-2385, (888) 425-2385 (conditions); www.okladot.state.ok.us

Low tide at Ecola State Park's Crescent Beach exposes monoliths.

CITIES

Ashland (M-4)

Nestled between the Siskiyou and Cascade ranges, Ashland is home to one of the nation's premier cultural events, the Oregon Shakespeare Festival. You'll find the festival grounds in Lithia Park, a 93-acre retreat of winding paths and beautiful trees, where three theaters run productions from late February to the end of October. Mineral waters from Lithia Springs are piped to fountains in the plaza. Outdoor recreational opportunities abound in and around Ashland. Mt. Ashland, the highest point in southern Oregon west of the Cascades, offers skiing in winter and hiking in summer. Several outfitters lead white-water rafting excursions on the Rogue and other nearby rivers.

Oregon Shakespeare Festival

Ashland Oregon Chamber of Commerce: (541) 482-3486; www.ashlandchamber.com

Bend (H-8)

With pine forests to the west and the high desert of the intermountain region to the east, Bend is a year-round center of recreation, the gateway to Deschutes National Forest. Before heading into the wilderness, visit the indoor and outdoor exhibits at the High Desert Museum for a first-hand look at the area's wildlife plus exhibits on its history and various cultures. Deschutes National Forest is a popular recreation area with skiing, hiking, fishing, rafting, and almost everything else. Within the forest, Newberry National Volcanic Monument offers a chance to explore many strange and wonderful remnants of past volcanic activity. Hike through Lava River Cave, a mile-long uncollapsed tube through which lava once flowed, or climb to the top of Paulina Peak for spectacular views of the Cascade Range. Lava Lands Visitor Center, at the base of the butte, has maps and information as well as exhibits about the area and its features.

Bend Visitor & Convention Bureau: (541) 382-8048, (800) 949-6086; www.visitbend.com

Pendleton (C-13)

In the heart of Oregon's ranch country the spirit of the Old West lives on. Pendleton is widely known for its fine woolens and its September Round-Up rodeo, with parades, American Indian dance competitions, and traditional rodeo events including bull riding and steer roping. Interesting displays at the Round-Up Hall of Fame tell the stories of the people, animals, and history of the event. See another side of this cowboy town by touring the downtown historic district, including Pendleton Underground, tunnels, erstwhile bordellos,

Chinese living quarters, the Heritage Station Museum, and Pendleton Woolen Mills. At the Confederated Tribes of the Umatilla Indian Reservation, five miles east, see dance performances and visit Tamástslikt Cultural Institute Museum, Crow's Shadow Institute of the Arts and Wildhorse Gaming Facility.

Pendleton Chamber of Commerce: (541) 276-7411, (800) 547-8911; www.pendleton-chamber.com

Portland (C-5)

This river city, located at the junction of the Willamette and Columbia rivers, offers everything expected of a major city except rush hour traffic jams. Portland boasts a sophisticated fine dining and arts-and-culture scene along with endless recreational activities. Styled on a European model, Portland is a city designed for pedestrian and bicycle traffic, with the landscape dominated by 37,000 acres of open space containing parks and miles of nature trails. In Washington Park you will find Hoyt Arboretum, the International Rose Test Garden, the Japanese Garden, the Forest Discovery Center, and the Oregon Zoo, featuring chimpanzees and Asian elephants. Don't miss the excellent collections at the Portland Art Museum and the Oregon Historical Society. The Oregon Museum of Science and Industry and Crystal Springs Rhododendron Garden are other visitor favorites.

Japanese Garden

Portland Visitors Association: (503) 275-8355; www.travelportland.com

⭐ Salem (State Capital) (E-4)

Climb to the rotunda of Oregon's state capitol building in this Willamette Valley city for views of Mount Hood, Mount Jefferson, and other snowcapped peaks of the Cascades. Pedal through Salem's parks on miles of excellent biking trails or visit popular attractions: Mission Mill Museum, with pioneer woolen mill exhibits; Historic Deepwood Estate; Bush House and Bush Barn Art Center; A.C. Gilbert's Discovery Village; the Enchanted Forest; the Riverfront Carousel; and Thrill-ville U.S.A. Numerous wineries and vineyards flourish in the fertile volcanic soils and microclimates of the hills surrounding Salem. Produce stands and iris fields are also plentiful here. To the east, at Silver Falls State Park, hike around and behind 10 dramatic waterfalls, or bike or ride horses through old-growth forests and quaking aspens.

Salem Convention & Visitors Association: (800) 874-7012, (503) 581-4325; www.travelsalem.com

SCENERY

Historic Columbia River Highway (C-6)

This road, with its detailed stonework, arched bridges, tunnels and viaducts, snakes through nearly 50 miles of the Columbia River Gorge. Stop at Multnomah Falls, the most visited natural site in Oregon, and don't miss the route's various clifftop views from as high as 900 feet above the river.

Pacific Coast Scenic Byway (M-1)

Along US 101, the Pacific Ocean is rarely out of sight. The road winds and dips and takes you by such places as Cape Foulweather and Cape Perpetua, high cliffs overlooking the ocean. Stop at coastal lighthouses, watch shrimp boats come in at Newport, or experience the dunes and sea lion rookery at Florence.

● **Elkhorn Scenic Byway** (E-15)
This loop west of Baker City (SR 7, Forest Road 73, and US 30) winds around gold mining ghost towns, the Elkhorn Mountains, and stunning lakes and rivers.

● **Hells Canyon Scenic Byway** (C-15)
Pass cattle country, lush valleys and basalt cliffs, the majestic Snake River, and the Oregon Trail. Follow SR 86 and SR 82 around the Wallowa Mountains.

● **McKenzie Pass - Santiam Pass Scenic Byway** (G-8)
Circle snowcapped volcanoes, lofty waterfalls, and ancient lava fields on the SR 242 - SR 126 loop just northwest of Bend. Sections closed in winter.

Sahallie Falls in McKenzie River

● **Outback Scenic Byway** (I-7)
Head south on SR 31 from La Pine to Lakeview to experience south-central Oregon's vast, rugged, and remote plains, reminiscent of the Australian Outback.

● **Volcanic Legacy Scenic Byway** (K-6)
See wavy lava flows and lava tube caves in this dramatic landscape, stretching from Crater Lake to the east side of Upper Klamath Lake and into California.

Oregon Coast

OUTDOORS

Columbia River Gorge

Columbia River Gorge National Scenic Area (C-8)

At 80 miles long and up to 4,000 feet deep, this river canyon isn't just picturesque, it's also a spectacular wind tunnel. Gusts whip up quickly here when pressure differences between weather east and west of the Cascades collide. It's an ideal scene for windsurfers and kiteboarders, who rank this one of the best spots in the country. Amateurs come from around the world for racing and freestyle events throughout the summer. The best place to rent a board or take a lesson is one of the numerous shops in Hood River or The Dalles, which are near beginner areas on the river.

*(541) 308-1700;
www.fs.fed.us/r6/columbia/forest*

White-water rafting

Paradise Wilderness Lodge (L-1)

For outdoorsy types in search of a remote retreat, Paradise Wilderness Lodge is the place. Surrounded by southern Oregon's forested mountains, the rustic lodge lies on the rugged, boulder-lined banks of the Rogue River, which has been designated a National Wild and Scenic River. And the only way to get there is by foot or by boat. It's an undisturbed natural setting, home to black bears, bald eagles, and a river full of steelhead and salmon. Guests stay in simple cabins without phones or televisions and eat family-style in the dining room. The lodge arranges nearly any type of guided adventure: white-water rafting, fishing, kayaking, hiking, and more.

*(888) 667-6483, (541) 247-6968;
www.paradise-lodge.com*

Windsurfing

Portland River Tours (L-19)

Hop aboard any of Portland's tour boats for a unique perspective of this river city. Various historic boats, such as the sternwheeler *Rose*, cruise the Willamette and Columbia rivers. The most exciting adventures, though, are offered by Willamette Jetboat Excursions, a tour company that warns passengers that they might get wet and to dress accordingly. The two-hour tours (a one-hour version is offered in July and August) cover 37 miles of scenic beauty. See giant ships up close, elegant riverfront homes, historic sites, the magnificent Willamette Falls, and maybe an eagle or osprey. May through October, boats depart daily from the Oregon Museum of Science and Industry dock.

*(503) 231-1532, (888) 538-2628;
www.willamettejet.com*

HERITAGE

Fort Clatsop National Memorial (A-2)

After a grueling journey through previously uncharted lands of the Louisiana Purchase and Oregon Territory, the Lewis and Clark expedition reached the Pacific Ocean in mid-November of 1805. After constructing Fort Clatsop, the weary group spent about three months preparing for the return trip. Located at the mouth of the Columbia River, this 125-acre park includes the spring, canoe landing, and most importantly a reconstruction of the fort in which the expedition wintered. Costumed interpreters demonstrate candle making and gun firing each summer and tell stories of events that occurred there. Year-round, visitors can tour the fort or exhibits and see replicas of dugout canoes. Eagles occasionally make an appearance at the canoe landing.

(503) 861-2471; www.nps.gov/focl

John Day Fossil Beds National Monument (F-11)

Named for the John Day River in north-central Oregon, the fossil beds provide a nearly continuous geologic history dating back six million to 54 million years. Three-toed horses and saber-toothed cats are a couple of the 2,000-plus species of plant and animal fossils identified here. In the monument's Painted Hills Unit, hiking trails lead through red claystone hills formed millions of years ago by volcanic activity. The Clarno Unit formations contain fossilized remains of a near-tropical forest and the Clarno Arch. The Sheep Rock Unit has nature trails and is the location of the National Park Service headquarters and visitor center.

(541) 987-2333; www.nps.gov/joda

John Day Fossil Beds National Monument

Lighthouse Tours (G-2)

The view from Heceta Head Lighthouse, or from any of Oregon's lighthouses for that matter, is what Oregon guidebooks are made of. Climb to the lantern or tower watch rooms for 360-degree vistas and learn how the lights work. Hear captivating stories about what life was like for the light keepers who lit the way for mariners off Oregon's perilous coastline. All of this state's nine lighthouses have been listed on the National Register of Historic Places and are open for tours in summer: Cape Blanco, Heceta Head, Umpqua River, Yaquina Bay, Yaquina Head, Cape Meares, Cape Arago, Tillamook Rock, and Coquille River.

Yaquina Head Lighthouse

(800) 551-6949; www.oregonstateparks.org

National Historic Oregon Trail Interpretive Center (E-15)

This center, just east of Baker City, sits atop the summit of Flagstaff Hill on one of the major wagon routes of the great westward migration, the Oregon Trail. It preserves 0.6 miles of wagon ruts marking the trail over which thousands of pioneer wagon wheels turned. Learn about the hardships of the journey through displays of pioneer artifacts and living history exhibits. Center staff and volunteers dress in period clothing and portray pioneers through plays, demonstrations, and musical performances. Stop in at the center's outdoor wagon encampment, lode mine sites, and amphitheater. Hike the four-mile trail system that loops around Flagstaff Hill and leads to viewpoints and historic sites, including Oregon Trail ruts.

(541) 523-1843; oregontrail.blm.gov/Index.htm

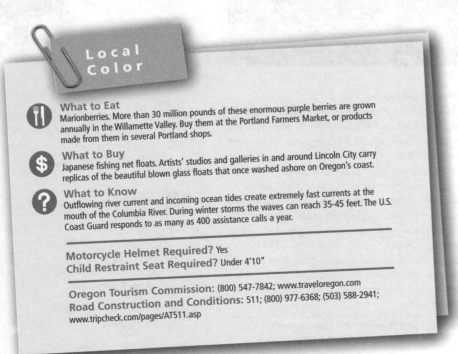

Local Color

What to Eat
Marionberries. More than 30 million pounds of these enormous purple berries are grown annually in the Willamette Valley. Buy them at the Portland Farmers Market, or products made from them in several Portland shops.

What to Buy
Japanese fishing net floats. Artists' studios and galleries in and around Lincoln City carry replicas of the beautiful blown glass floats that once washed ashore on Oregon's coast.

What to Know
Outflowing river current and incoming ocean tides create extremely fast currents at the mouth of the Columbia River. During winter storms the waves can reach 35-45 feet. The U.S. Coast Guard responds to as many as 400 assistance calls a year.

Motorcycle Helmet Required? Yes
Child Restraint Seat Required? Under 4'10"

Oregon Tourism Commission: (800) 547-7842; www.traveloregon.com
Road Construction and Conditions: 511; (800) 977-6368; (503) 588-2941; www.tripcheck.com/pages/AT511.asp

A leisurely drive through the Pocono Mountains during autumn reveals gorgeous vistas.

CITIES

Erie (WC-3)

Pennsylvania's only port on the Great Lakes is an industrial and shipping center for an agricultural region where fruit-growing thrives thanks to the tempering influence of Lake Erie. Visitors and locals take to the waters along seven miles of sandy beaches at Presque Isle State Park. Boating, swimming, and picnicking are the park's most popular activities, though there are ample opportunities for fishing, sailing, hiking, taking a scenic drive, and bird watching among other activities. Wet fun is available year-round at Splash Lagoon, an indoor water park featuring the unpredictable antics of the giant tipping Tiki bucket. More family-oriented entertainment is on hand at Waldameer Park & Water World with its 75 rides, slides, and attractions. The Erie Maritime Museum is

Swimming in Lake Erie

home to the U.S. Brig *Niagara*, a reconstruction of Commodore Perry's relief flagship that won the Battle of Lake Erie during the War of 1812.

Erie Convention & Visitors Bureau: (800) 524-3743; www.visiteriepa.com

⭐ Harrisburg (State Capital) (EN-4)

Location was key in the selection of Pennsylvania's capital city in 1812. The Susquehanna River marks Harrisburg's western boundary, and the city has long been an important transportation/distribution center, as well as a scenic riverfront home for the state capitol. Venture over water to family-friendly City Island where visitors will find two restaurants, mini-golf, a restored carousel, train and carriage rides, Commerce Bank Park (home of the Harrisburg Senators AA minor league baseball team), and much more. Small town charm and capital city charisma make Harrisburg a perennial Pennsylvania favorite.

Hershey Harrisburg Regional Visitors Bureau: (800) 995-0969; www.hersheyharrisburg.org

Philadelphia (EP-12)

Pennsylvania's largest city may be best known as the home of the Liberty Bell, but the "City of Brotherly Love," founded in 1682 by William Penn himself, has lots more to offer. This history starts in Old City, where Independence National Historic Park, the Betsy Ross House, and a variety of restaurants and shops offer a taste of the

Tour guide

colonial period. South Philly is home to the bustling Italian Market and two of the town's signature Philly steak sandwich operations, Pat's King of Steaks and Geno's Steaks. A swinging arts scene thrives along the Avenue of the Arts, which serves as the creative heart of theater, dance, and music in the city. The Academy of Music and the Kimmel Center for the Performing Arts are found here. Stroll through beautiful Fairmount Park, the largest landscaped U.S. city park, for a peaceful outdoor break.

Greater Philadelphia Tourism Marketing Corporation: (215) 599-0776; www.gophila.com
Philadelphia Convention & Visitors Bureau: (215) 636-3300; www.pcvb.org

Pittsburgh

Pittsburgh (WM-4)

This former steel town surprises visitors with its natural beauty and cultural offerings. The Golden Triangle — where the Allegheny and Monongahela Rivers meet to form the Ohio — is marked by picturesque Point State Park (currently undergoing renovation), which offers great riverfront views of Heinz Field (home of the Steelers) and the North Shore. Don't miss one of the country's premier single-artist museums, the Andy Warhol Museum, with funky and fun pieces including the famous Campbell's soup label prints. No trip to Pittsburgh would be complete without a ride up to Mt. Washington on the Monongahela or Duquesne Inclines for breathtaking views of the downtown skyline day or night.

Greater Pittsburgh Convention & Visitors Bureau: (877) 568-3744; www.visitpittsburgh.com

SCENERY

Historic National Road (WQ-6)

This National Scenic Byway spans six states, originating in Maryland before heading west through West Virginia, Pennsylvania, Ohio, Indiana, and Illinois. This historic corridor was one of the first routes used by early settlers, and the 90-mile stretch that passes through southwestern Pennsylvania shows off natural beauty and historic highlights including Summit Mountain, Youghiogheny River Lake, Fort Necessity National Battlefield, and many historic homes, barns, toll houses, and bridges.

Longhouse National Scenic Byway (WE-8)

This scenic route boasts some of the most breathtaking views of the water and woods of Pennsylvania, showcasing unforgettable sights of the Kinzua Dam and Allegheny Reservoir, as well as traveling deep into the half-million-acre Allegheny National Forest. The 60 miles pass quickly with easy driving, multiple overlooks, and plenty of picnicking stops.

- ### Brady's Bend Overlook (WJ-5)
  Located five miles east of East Brady in west-central Pennsylvania, this overlook provides a 1,500-foot panoramic view of a U-shaped bend in the Allegheny River.

Brady's Bend

- ### Delaware Water Gap National Recreation Area (EI-13)
  Three scenic overlooks dot SR 611 along the Pennsylvania-New Jersey border, but the 40-mile middle stretch of the Delaware River and its surrounding 70,000 acres in New Jersey and Pennsylvania offer even more natural beauty.

- ### Lancaster County (EP-7)

  It's a beloved Pennsylvania picture: Amish country's gentle rolling hills, rich green fields, red barns, horses and buggies, and the absence of power lines crisscrossing the land.

Amish horse and buggy

- ### Grand Canyon of Pennsylvania (EF-2)
  The spectacular sights of the canyon, more than 1,000 feet deep, stretch for nearly 50 miles along the Pine Creek Gorge.

- ### Mt. Davis (WQ-7)
  Views from the observation tower at the highest point in the state (3,213 feet) are particularly pretty during the fall foliage season and offer a birds-eye perspective of the Appalachian Mountains and surrounding 581 acres of the Mt. Davis Natural Area.

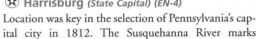

HERITAGE

Ephrata Cloister (EO-7)

Founded in 1732 by German settlers, Ephrata Cloister is one of America's earliest religious/communal societies. Conrad Beissel, the community's founder

Book from the Ephrata Cloister

and a German pietist mystic, and his followers pursued spiritual goals, not earthly rewards, and gathered in central Pennsylvania to form a community of celibate brothers and sisters and a married congregation of families. They became well-known for their hymns, songbooks, calligraphy, and printing. The last celibate member died in 1813, but the married congregation continued to live and worship at this Lancaster County National Historic Landmark until 1934. Today, the 9 restored Germanic-style buildings on the 28-acre reservation are not only architectural treasures from a bygone era, but also a window into the world of one of the two pietist groups that have played an important part in Pennsylvania's history.

(717) 733-6600; www.ephratacloister.org

Gettysburg National Military Park (EQ-3)

In south-central Pennsylvania, near the Maryland border, the site of the largest Civil War battle is preserved in nearly 6,000 acres. Portions of the battlefield have been maintained much as they were when the fighting began on July 1, 1863. This was the bloodiest battle of the war, with more than 51,000 wounded, killed, or captured, and it was a turning point in the Civil War. President Abraham Lincoln delivered the Gettysburg Address here in November 1863. View more than 1,400 monuments, markers, memorials, and plaques and 400 cannon along 26 miles of scenic roadways. The self-guided tour can take two to three hours.

(717) 334-1124; www.nps.gov/gett

Civil War re-enactment at Gettysburg

Pioneer Tunnel Coal Mine (EK-7)

One of Pennsylvania's most prized natural possessions is located in a 500-square-mile region in the northeast corner of the state. Anthracite, a special coal that is purer, harder, and yields a higher carbon content than other types of coal, is abundant in this region, which is the source of more than 95 percent of the Western Hemisphere's supply. Experience part of the region's anthracite history at the Pioneer Tunnel Coal Mine, a working coal mine that closed in 1931 but was reopened to the public in 1963. Visitors ride mine cars into the tunnel where experienced miners explain how anthracite coal is mined while pointing out interesting underground details such as veins of coal, gangways, manways, and chutes.

(570) 875-3850; www.pioneertunnel.com

Senator John Heinz Pittsburgh Regional History Center (L-4)

Located in Pittsburgh's historic Strip District, this 200,000-square-foot center run by the Historical Society of Western Pennsylvania has shared a special affiliation with the Smithsonian Institution since 2000. On the center's five floors visitors will find a 1790s log cabin, a 1940s trolley, tons of Heinz memorabilia, locally produced glass that at one time earned Pittsburgh the nickname "Glass City," and many other artifacts. The permanent exhibits look at life and history-shaping events and people of western Pennsylvania during the last 250 years, while traveling exhibits from the Smithsonian offer some of the country's best temporary displays. Open daily, the center features a fun play area called Kidsburgh.

(412) 454-6000; www.pghhistory.org

OUTDOORS

Hawk Mountain Sanctuary (EL-8)

Central-eastern Pennsylvania is home to the first refuge for birds of prey (also known as raptors). This 2,600-acre raptor sanctuary enjoys thousands of hawk, eagle, and falcon sightings during the birds' biannual intercontinental migrations and is one of the best places to observe raptors in the United States. Between August 15 and December 15, an average of 20,000 raptors may be counted. A rugged one-mile trail leads to the North Lookout, which rises 300 feet to a rocky outcrop on the Kittatinny Ridge for eye-level observation of bald eagles, red-tailed hawks, osprey, American kestrels, and many other species. The sanctuary's eight-mile trail

Raptor at Hawk Mountain Sanctuary

system offers a range of outdoor experiences, from an easy 100-yard stroll to the South Lookout to a four-mile trek around the River of Rocks boulder field. The sanctuary includes a visitor center with a bookstore, gallery, and gift shop, and free educational programs are offered most weekends from April through November.

(610) 756-6961; www.hawkmountain.org

Poconos winter fun

Ohiopyle State Park (WQ-6)

Some of the best white-water rafting in the eastern United States can be found in the Youghiogheny (yaw-ki-GAY-nee) River Gorge that runs for more than 14 miles through the heart of this popular park. Ohiopyle's 19,052 acres of rugged terrain make it an outdoor recreationist's paradise, offering adrenaline-filled white-water rafting, 27 miles of crushed-limestone bicycling trails, 79 miles of hiking trails, horseback riding, mountain biking, fishing, hunting, camping, snowmobiling, cross-country

White-water rafting in Ohiopyle State Park

skiing, and more. Several picturesque waterfalls, including 20-foot Ohiopyle Falls, and spectacular scenery round out this Fayette County favorite. The Falls Day Use Area near Ohiopyle Falls offers parking, restrooms, a gift shop, a snack bar, and scenic overlook platforms.

(724) 329-8591; www.dcnr.state.pa.us/stateparks/parks/ohiopyle.aspx

Pocono Mountains (EI-11)

The Pocono Mountains area consists of much more than romance and resorts. The surrounding region offers seven state parks, large stretches of state forest, and the 70,000-acre Delaware Water Gap National Recreation Area for plenty of outdoor adventure. Winter weather shouldn't keep anyone inside, either. The area offers more than 146 ski slopes and trails and plenty of opportunity to try out other cold-weather activities such as snow tubing, snowshoeing, snowboarding, ice skating, and ice fishing. Beginners and experts alike can sample a variety of downhill skiing resorts, including Alpine Mountain, Blue Mountain, and Camelback Ski Area, to name just a few. Summer visitors can enjoy scenic hiking, biking, fishing, and swimming.

(800) 762-6667; www.800poconos.com

Castle Hill Lighthouse overlooks the eastern entrance to Narragansett Bay.

CITIES

Bristol (F-8)

Settled in 1669 on a good harbor, Bristol thrived on shipping and shipbuilding. This trade produced so many fine houses that Hope Street is virtually an architectural museum. The Haffenreffer Museum of Anthropology features North and South American Indian objects and a collection of Eskimo art. The Herreshoff Marine Museum & America's Cup Hall of Fame tells the stories of the Herreshoff Boatyard, where many of the America's Cup-winning yachts were built. Blithewold Mansion & Gardens is a turn-of-the-20th-century estate overlooking Narragansett Bay and includes beautiful grounds and gardens and a 45-room mansion. In Colt State Park, the Coggeshall Farm Museum is a living history museum illustrating farm life of the 18th and 19th centuries. Restored Linden Place, a Federal-style mansion, has a carriage barn, some original furnishings, an art museum, and rose gardens for visitors to explore.

Bristol

East Bay Tourism Council: (888) 278-9948; www.eastbayritourism.com

Newport (H-7)

Newport's reputation as a prosperous port town dates back to the 1720s when wealthy planters from the Carolinas and West Indies escaped from the heat of their home towns to Rhode Island's gentle sea breezes and cultural offerings. Today, the town is still a favorite of well-heeled sailing enthusiasts and also has a large trove of 17th- and 18th-century buildings. Mansions representative of Gilded Age life line Bellevue Avenue and include opulent homes like The Elms, Rosecliff, Marble House, and Belcourt Castle. The Breakers, on Ochre Point Avenue, is Cornelius Vanderbilt's 70-room mansion and considered the most splendid of these summer homes. Other popular attractions include the International Tennis Hall of Fame, the Newport Art Museum, the Touro Synagogue National Historic Site, and Cliff Walk, a 3.5-mile path that runs along a cliff between the Atlantic and the sprawling yards of Newport mansions.

Newport County Convention & Visitors Bureau: (800) 976-5122; www.gonewport.com

⭐ Providence (State Capital) (D-7)

Roger Williams founded Providence in 1636, basing his community on religious tolerance and American Indian rights, principles that neighboring Massachusetts Puritans didn't hold. This liberal aura remains today, especially in the intellectual pursuits of area universities and the attitude of the city's various ethnic groups.

Providence

History runs deep in Rhode Island's largest city, especially on Benefit Street, one of the largest concentrations of restored houses in the country. Sites include the John Brown House, Governor Stephen Hopkins House, and the Nightingale-Brown House. Brown University sits at the top of College Hill, too. The Rhode Island School of Design has an excellent small art museum featuring the Pendleton Collection of American furniture and decorative arts. The state capitol building is a lovely marble-domed structure that includes several historical treasures, like a full-length portrait of George Washington by Gilbert Stuart and the colony's charter from England's King Charles II. Prospect Terrace, a landscaped park with scenic views of the city, is also the site of Williams' burial place and memorial.

Providence Warwick Convention & Visitors Bureau: (800) 233-1636; www.providencenightandday.com

Warwick (E-7)

South of Providence on Narragansett Bay, Warwick is the state's second largest city and is known as Rhode Island's retail capital with a plethora of shopping opportunities and restaurants. Its central location also makes it an ideal base for exploring the state. The city is composed of more than 30 unique villages, and historic houses line the streets of these diverse neighborhoods. Visitors can take walking tours through two of the villages — Apponaug and Pawtuxet — to learn about local lore and history. Warwick also offers visitors more than 39 miles of coast with freshwater and saltwater beaches, 12 marinas (more boat slips and moorings than any other city in the state), waterfront dining, and two historic lighthouses. Other notable attractions include Pontiac Mills, the Warwick Museum in the Kentish Artillery Armory, and the Warwick Historical Society, a restored 19th-century home with period rooms.

City of Warwick: (401) 738-2000; www.visitwarwickri.com
Providence Warwick Convention & Visitors Bureau: (800) 233-1636

SCENERY

Shannock Road (H-4)

This short but scenic road runs for 1.7 miles through southern Rhode Island from Route 112 to Route 2 through the towns of Charlestown and Richmond. Scenes range from woodlands, marshes, farm fields, and stone walls to the road's highlight, Historic Shannock Village. The village was listed in the National Register of Historic Places in 1983 and is a small, well-preserved, mid-19th-century rural textile mill village. Many other small mills like this one were built on waterways in Southern Rhode Island around the same time. As a result of the mills, villages were established and houses were built for the mill workers and their families. Shannock Village is a remnant of this era.

Veterans Memorial Highway (L-9)

This Rhode Island State Scenic Byway lies entirely within an urban area but offers drivers impressive views of the Providence skyline as well as beautiful natural settings and landmarks. The 2.4-mile stretch of road from Second Street to Route 103 in East Providence follows the Providence River and is also lined with maples, oaks, black pines, and sycamores. The route runs through heavily wooded areas with the nearby urban cityscape in the background and takes visitors by Squantum Woods, Watchemoket Cove, and Fort Hill Overlook.

● **Beavertail State Park** (H-6)
This park in Jamestown is known for some of the most beautiful vistas along the New England coastline. Drivers can visit the park's four overlooks by car or explore the rocky coastline on foot.

Blithewold Mansion

● **Blithewold Mansion Gardens & Arboretum** (F-8)
This impressive 45-room mansion dating from the 1890s and its 33 acres of beautifully landscaped grounds, gardens, and arboretum overlook Narragansett Bay and Bristol Harbor.

● **Ell Pond** (G-3)
Part of Rhode Island's only National Natural Landmark, this pond is nestled deep in a hollow and ringed by concentric circles of quaking bog, white cedar swamp, and red maple swamp.

Mohegan Bluffs in background

● **Mohegan Bluffs Scenic Natural Area** (L-5)
Located on Block Island, the 200-foot bluffs offer spectacular views of the Atlantic Ocean, the island's dramatic southern coastline, crashing surf, and the historic Southeast Lighthouse.

HERITAGE

International Tennis Hall of Fame (M-2)

This complex of buildings was completed in 1880 and was originally a private club for wealthy summer Newport residents. In 1881, it was also the site of the first U.S. National Lawn Tennis Championships (it later moved to Forest Hills, N.Y. and is now known as the U.S. Open). In 1954, the Newport Casino was designated the site of the International Tennis Hall of Fame. The museum was established by James Van Alen to preserve the sport's legacy, but it was not until 1986 that the hall of fame and museum was recognized by the International Tennis Federation. Today, the hall of fame is the world's largest tennis museum and houses an extensive library as well as the largest collection of memorabilia with more than 7,000 objects such as historic tennis equipment and clothing. Visitors can also swing away on the world's oldest continuously used competition grass courts, the only ones open for public play.

(401) 849-3990, (800) 457-1144; www.tennisfame.com

Linden Place Museum (F-8)

Located in the heart of Bristol at 500 Hope Street, Linden Place is a Federal-period mansion designed by Rhode Island architect Russell Warren in 1810 for General George DeWolf, one of the members of the famous seafaring DeWolf family. DeWolf's grandson, Colonel Samuel Pomeroy Colt, who eventually owned the property, too, was the founder and first president of the Industrial Trust Company (Fleet Bank) and the U.S. Rubber Company (Uniroyal). This historic mansion has been touched by fame: It's been visited by four U.S. presidents, was home to the actress Ethel Barrymore, and was also featured in the film *The Great Gatsby*. The mansion's interior showcases a dramatic Honduran mahogany spiral staircase and furniture as well as the 1906 Linden Place ballroom. The grounds include rose gardens, 19th-century sculptures, gazebos, and several other historic outbuildings.

(401) 253-0390; www.lindenplace.org

Roger Williams National Memorial (K-9)

This memorial honors Rhode Island's founder, Roger Williams, who strongly believed in religious freedom. He was banished from Massachusetts for his fervently held beliefs and in 1636 founded Providence. His colony served as a refuge where people of all backgrounds and religions could come and worship freely without fear of interference from the state. The Roger Williams National Memorial is located on a common area of the original Providence settlement and includes a visitor center and 4.5 acres of landscaped park. The visitor center highlights Williams' contributions to religion freedom through several exhibits and videos. Walking tours and ranger-led programs are also throughout the year.

(401) 521-7266; www.nps.gov/rowi

Slater Mill Historic Site (J-9)

Slater Mill Historic Site

Experience the lives of New England villagers and artisans who helped drive the Industrial Revolution at this living history museum in Pawtucket.

Authentic 18th- and 19th-century buildings and costumed guides explain and demonstrate what American life was like when people first moved from the farm to the factory in the 1830s. The site includes several stops: the Sylvanus Brown House, Historic Garden, Wilkinson Mill, and Old Slater Mill. The Brown House, a gambrel-roofed red cottage, was built in 1758 and shows a family's daily activities necessary to secure food, shelter, and clothing. A variety of crops are grown in the Historic Garden, from flax for linen and vegetables for eating to beautiful flowers. The Wilkinson Mill is a machine shop that helped make important machine tools for the textile industry. The Old Slater Mill represents the spinning and weaving mills that lined the banks of the Blackstone River and shows the progression of textile machinery.

(401) 725-8638; www.slatermill.org

OUTDOORS

Blackstone River Valley National Heritage Corridor (A-5)

The Blackstone River Valley region is known as the birthplace of the Industrial Revolution in America. The Blackstone River provided waterpower for industry with its 438-foot drop over the course of 46 miles. Today, this area administered by the National Park Service encompasses 24 communities and more than 400,000 acres from Worcester, MA to Providence, RI. The river provides excellent recreational opportunities as well as a chance to experience the area's living landscape. There are dozens of access points along the water for canoeing or kayaking; for those who prefer the land, there are plenty of picnic sites and walking trails. Dams, mills, canals, locks, and other structures related to waterpower and transportation are numerous along the Blackstone riverscape. For advanced paddlers, the river also has sections of more rigorous Class II and III rapids, created by dams and a highly variable stream flow.

(401) 762-0250; www.nps.gov/blac

Block Island (L-5)

In the Atlantic Ocean 12 miles south of the Rhode Island coast, Block Island is a seven-mile-long by three-mile-wide island named after Dutch navigator Adrian Block, who stumbled upon it in 1614. The island's exceptional terrain includes hills, numerous freshwater ponds (365 to be exact), and conglomerations of rocks and soil. Its 17 miles of beaches and 32 miles of nature trails make it a perfect outdoor getaway. It's become a popular destination for boating, sailing, surfcasting, fishing, swimming, picnicking, bicycling, beachcombing, kayaking, canoeing, and especially bird-watching. The island enjoys cool summer breezes, but is pounded by harsh winter storms, and more than 250 miles of ancient stone walls line the island to help battle the elements. Year-round ferry service is provided from

Point Judith, RI, and seasonal ferries run from Newport, RI, New London, CT, and Montauk, NY.

(800) 383-2474; www.blockislandchamber.com

East Bay Bike Path (L-10)

East Bay Bike Path

This popular and scenic bike path takes riders about 15 miles through the heart of Bristol County. The 10-foot-wide paved path starts in Providence's India Point Park and runs south through the towns of Riverside, Barrington, and Warren before arriving in Bristol. Riders are surrounded by woods one second and then, around the next turn, they might see sailboats in the harbor or ducks and other birds swimming in a tidal pond. The route follows the old Penn Central rail line and is never far from the water's edge. It crosses saltwater rivers twice over rebuilt trestles, and it's a flat, easy ride fit for all bikers of all levels. There are plenty of rest points along the way, including scenic spots and shopping/food stops.

www.riparks.com/eastbay.htm

North South Trail (I-4)

This multi-use trail meanders for 72 miles through mainly rural areas along the entire length of western Rhode Island. The trail takes users through eight towns and passes through seven state-owned forest management areas, too. While most stretches of the trail are open to hikers, mountain bikers, and equestrians, some segments are restricted to hiking only. The majority of the trail is off-road in picturesque forests, though certain sections run on low-traffic scenic town roads. Along the way, the North South Trail also takes visitors through historic villages and past quaint family farms, one-room school houses, old cemeteries, and small country churches. South end access is in Charlestown at Blue Shutters Beach, and north end access is in the Buck Hill Management Area.

www.visitrhodeisland.com/recreation/hiking.aspx

Local Color

What to Eat
Quahog. Pronounced KO-hog, it's a native clam served stuffed on the half shell (a "stuffie"), in chowder, or raw as "little necks." Almost all seafood restaurants offer their version of the stuffie statewide.

What to Buy
A boat. There are no taxes on boats sold in Rhode Island. Plenty of craftsmen build affordable boats as well as custom yachts.

What to Know
Locals often don't pronounce the letter "r," and they add it when others would not: "lobsta" (lobster), "pahster" (pasta), "chowda" (chowder), "wata" (water).

Motorcycle Helmet Required? Under age 21, drivers during first year, all passengers
Child Restraint Seat Required? Under age 7 and less than 54 in. and less than 80 lb.

Rhode Island Tourism Division: (800) 556-2484; (888) 886-9463; (401) 222-2601; www.visitrhodeisland.com
Road Construction and Conditions: 511; (888) 401-4511 (outside RI); www2.tmc.state.ri.us

Waves lap at the foundations of a Grand Strand pier.

CITIES

Charleston (H-10)

Steeped in history, Charleston represents the romance of the Old South and welcomes visitors with true Southern hospitality. From centuries-old aristocratic

Charleston

homes and graceful gardens of roses, camellias, and magnolias, to sunny beaches and several museums, the area is rich in a variety of unique experiences for Lowcountry guests. Charleston, founded in 1670, played a significant role in both the Revolutionary and Civil Wars. The Charleston Historic District, which covers much of the southern end of the peninsula, includes lovely landmarks that can be seen from horse-drawn carriage tours, boat tours, walking tours, house tours, or by wandering the narrow 300-year-old streets on your own. Famous house museums include the Nathaniel Russell House and Edmonston-Alston House, and picturesque plantation properties such as Drayton Hall, Magnolia Plantation, and Middleton Place show off sweeping estates, grounds, and gardens.

Charleston Area Convention & Visitors Bureau:
(800) 868-8118; www.charlestoncvb.com

⊛ Columbia (State Capital) (D-7)

The state's centrally located capital city is home to the University of South Carolina, making it a hub of education and state government. The Columbia Riverbanks Region also carries with it a rich history, and historic highlights include the Lexington County Museum's living history complex, Historic Columbia's House Museums, Fort Jackson, and the South Carolina State Museum. Riverbanks Zoo & Garden is one of the top zoos in the country, with more than 2,000 animals from rain forest, desert, undersea, and farm environments. Other notable stops include the Columbia Museum of Art and EdVenture Children's Museum as well as outdoor attractions including Lake Murray, Congaree National Park, and the Three Rivers Greenway.

Columbia Metropolitan Convention & Visitors Bureau:
(800) 264-4884; www.columbiacvb.com

Greenville/Spartanburg (B-4/5)

These neighboring Upstate towns situated at the foothills of the Blue Ridge Mountains in northwest South Carolina are historic centers of culture and community. The area serves as an industrial hub and economic center for the state and is the location of large international firms such as BMW and Michelin. Greenville was founded in the 1770s as a mill town on the Reedy River. Falls Park on the Reedy preserves the downtown area where the first mills were built and includes nature trails, gardens, and the Liberty Bridge, a 355-foot pedestrian bridge over the waterfall. Other highlights include the new Upcountry History Museum (which focuses on oral history), the Greenville County Museum of Art, the Zoo, and seven historic districts. Spartanburg was named after the Spartan Rifles, a Revolutionary War militia that teamed with troops to defeat the British in the Battle of Cowpens. Today, the city is home to several colleges, elegant antebellum plantations, rustic cabins, and more than a dozen registered historic landmarks.

Greenville Convention & Visitors Bureau:
(800) 351-7180; www.greatergreenville.com
Spartanburg Convention & Visitors Bureau:
(800) 374-8326; www.visitspartanburg.com

Myrtle Beach (E-13)

This beach town is an enormous playground filled with wide, sandy beaches and plenty of activities for the family. Beyond the sun and surf, the Grand Strand offers a plethora of boardwalks, amusement parks, nightlife, shopping, restaurants, golfing, and fishing. The Family Kingdom Water Park is home to the state's largest Ferris wheel. Other popular water parks include Myrtle Waves and the Wild Water and Race Theme Park. Alligator Adventure is an alligator park and research center where 'gators, Galapagos tortoises, birds, snakes, and other creatures can be spotted in a natural wetland habitat. Two state parks are nearby: Myrtle Beach State Park and Huntington Beach State Park. Those with a taste for speed should check out the NASCAR SpeedPark, where families can test their driving skills on eight tracks.

Myrtle Beach Area Convention & Visitors
Bureau/Chamber of Commerce: (800) 488-8998;
www.VisitMyBeach.com

Family Kingdom amusement park

SCENERY

Ashley River Road (A-12)

Journey into South Carolina's Lowcountry along this 11-mile road for a taste of the area's history, culture, and natural beauty. This route, which follows the Ashley River, passes old live oak trees with Spanish moss swaying in the breeze and brick gates marking the entrances to stately homes from days past. Historic plantation mansions like Drayton Hall and landmark churches paint a vivid picture of a former time. Slave labor made development of the area possible; African-American history can be found in many of the old Baptist churches along this route.

Cherokee Foothills Scenic Highway (A-6)

This National Scenic Byway takes drivers along the South Carolina/North Carolina/Georgia borders for a 130-mile arc through peach orchards, quaint villages, historic sites, state parks, lakes, and terrific scenery. The two-lane road (SR 11) follows an ancient Cherokee path whose heritage is still evident

Wildcat Falls

in many of the area's place and river names, such as Seneca, Keowee, Tamassee, and Oconee. The Blue Ridge Mountains loom majestically beyond the Piedmont hills. The byway can be accessed off of I-85 at Gaffney in the north or near Fair Play on the Georgia/South Carolina border in the south.

● Boone Hall Plantation (H-10)

Boone Hall Plantation

This historic plantation's famous avenue of oaks, a three-quarter-mile drive lined with massive, Spanish moss-draped live oaks, shouldn't be missed, nor should its beautiful grounds, gardens, or Colonial-Revival style mansion.

● Caesar's Head Overlook & Visitors Center (A-3)

At 3,266 feet, this overlook in Caesar's Head State Park is a great place for breathtaking views of the bordering Blue Ridge Mountains.

● Lake Moultrie Loop (F-10)

The 70-mile trip around the edge of Lake Moultrie from Pinopolis to Diversion Canal is full of natural beauty and sights of canals, history, and neighboring Francis Marion National Forest to the east.

● Old Sheldon Church Ruins (I-8)

Outside of the historic town of Beaufort, this serene spot was once the majestic Prince William Parish Church, first built in the mid-1700s of brick and tabby. The church was destroyed in May 1779 by British troops, rebuilt, then destroyed again by General Sherman's troops in 1865. Today it is a popular site for special ceremonies and picturesque picnics.

OUTDOORS

Chattooga National Wild & Scenic River (B-2)

Top-notch white-water rafting can be found on the first river in the South to be designated a National Wild & Scenic River, back in 1974. The Chattooga River, one of the region's foremost white-water rivers, forms the boundary between South Carolina and Georgia, and originates in the high mountains of North Carolina. The Chattooga remains one of the longest and largest undeveloped free-flowing mountain rivers in the Southeast, and its 56.9 miles can be broken into three segments: 39.8 miles that are designated wild, 2.5 miles that are scenic, and 14.6 miles that are recreational. The river provides a wide variety of scenery, from thundering waterfalls and cliff-enclosed deep pools to thick forests and undisturbed shorelines. Access to the river in South Carolina is in Sumter National Forest.

(864) 638-9568; www.fs.fed.us/R8/fms

The Grand Strand (E-13)

Practically every water sport is doable along the 60 miles of Atlantic Oceanfront that include Myrtle Beach's Grand Strand. The area's blue waters are perfect for saltwater fishing, boating, surfing, kayaking, scuba diving, jet skiing, parasailing, windsurfing, or just sunning and playing on the beach. This outdoor playground is supplemented with inland rivers, creeks, and marshes, as well as the Intracoastal Waterway, all of which offer calmer waters for those looking for quieter exploration or just a leisurely sight-seeing cruise. Plenty of local outfitters are available for equipment rental, guided tours, or instruction. At several family-friendly water parks (Wild Water and Family Kingdom Water Park to name a couple) kids and adults can slide, twist, turn, swim, and float down speed slides, lazy rivers, and wave pools.

www.myrtlebeachinfo.com/cvb/watersports/default.asp

Magnolia Plantation and Its Gardens (H-10)

This world-famous 300-year-old plantation may be best known for its beautiful, well-manicured gardens, but several active opportunities are available for visitors as well. The plantation, which is on the National Register of Historic Places, has been in the Drayton family since Thomas Drayton first arrived from Barbados in 1671. The grounds sit on the historic Ashley River Road and include the country's oldest public garden and a Reconstruction-era plantation house. In the garden, guests can hike or bike the nature trails, and canoe trips are also available. There is also a 45-minute nature boat tour that takes visitors around the 125 acres of rice fields for excellent wildlife viewing and a history lesson on the rice and river culture.

(800) 367-3517; www.magnoliaplantation.com

Table Rock State Park (A-3)

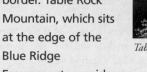

Some of the Palmetto State's most challenging hiking trails can be found at this 3,083-acre state park located in the northwest corner along the North Carolina border. Table Rock Mountain, which sits at the edge of the Blue Ridge

Table Rock Mountain

Escarpment, provides an awe-inspiring backdrop for hikers and visitors, who see the natural area much as it was when the Cherokee Indians lived here. The park's 12 miles of trails show off the area's streams, woods, and waterfalls, but only the Table Rock National Recreation Trail ascends 2,000 feet to Table Rock Mountain's granite-domed summit at 3,157 feet. Other treks include the Mill Creek Pass Trail, 4.1-mile Pinnacle Mountain Trail, Carrick Creek Trail, and wooded Ridge Trail. Besides an extensive trail system, the park has two lakes for fishing and boating, campgrounds, rustic cabins, and other recreational opportunities.

(864) 878-9813; www.southcarolinaparks.com

HERITAGE

Drayton Hall (H-10)

Located on the historic Ashley River Road in Charleston, Drayton Hall is America's oldest preserved plantation house that is open to the public. A National Historic Landmark dating back to 1742, the Georgian Palladian-style main house sits majestically on 630 acres that include gardens, walking trails, and lovely live oak trees along the Ashley River. Visitors can experience a different time period when they enter a house that still has no running water, electric lights, or central heat. Docent-led house tours are given on the hour and last 30-60 minutes. The tour includes all three levels of the house and examines the architecture, preservation, and family life in the house. Visitors may participate in a 45-minute interactive program, "Connections: From Africa to America," to gain a better understanding of African-American contributions to the Lowcountry way of life.

(843) 769-2600; www.draytonhall.org

Fort Sumter National Monument (B-14)

The Civil War began at this historic site. America's struggle to define itself as a nation included social, economic, and political conflict that eventually ignited into civil war at this famous fort on April 12, 1861. Issues of states' rights, federal authority, and slavery were at the forefront of the disagreement, and when South

Fort Sumter National Monument

Carolina seceded in protest of Lincoln's election, the impending war become a reality. Today, Fort Sumter remains a powerful memorial to both the South and North. Located in the middle of Charleston Harbor, Fort Sumter is only accessible by boat. There are two ferry departure sites for access to the fort, and the Fort Sumter Visitor Education Center at Liberty Square in downtown Charleston is the primary departure facility for visitors. The center's interpretive exhibits and rangers help explain the causes and events of the Civil War and why it began at this historic spot. The national monument also includes Fort Moultrie, located on Sullivan's Island.

(843) 883-3123; www.nps.gov/fosu

Historic Brattonsville (B-7)

Just outside McConnells, South Carolina, in southern York County, this 775-acre living history village provides a taste of life in the South during the late 18th and early 19th centuries. Brattonsville was once a major plantation in the area and remained a significant site in the Carolina Piedmont until the end of the 19th century. The Bratton family, a typical Scotch-Irish family settling in the colonies, founded the settlement around 1766. Today, the site gives visitors a glimpse of three generations of the family and of plantation life. It includes more than 30 structures, all of which can be toured. The Heritage Breed Farm Program, which preserves rare breeds of animals like Gulf Coast sheep, Devon cattle, and Dominique chickens, is another unique aspect of the site. There are eight miles of nature paths for biking, hiking, or horseback riding through the area's forest, wetland, and prairie.

(803) 684-2327; www.chmuseums.org

South Carolina State House (J-2)

One of the state's most splendid and architecturally significant buildings is in the heart of downtown Columbia. The South Carolina State House was originally designed by John R. Niernsee, who patterned it after grand European structures, but his death prevented him from finishing it and later architects strayed from his detailed plans. The building has several special architectural features including massive columns along the front portico (each cut from one solid piece of stone), hand-carved marble axes on both sides of the front door, bas-relief carvings, and a striking copper dome. There is also an impressive art gallery containing portraits, paintings, plaques, and other works of art that honor important people and events in South Carolina and U.S. history. The grounds include numerous monuments and statues, as well as the Gresette (Senate offices) and Blatt (House of Representative offices) Buildings.

(803) 734-2430; www.scstatehouse.net

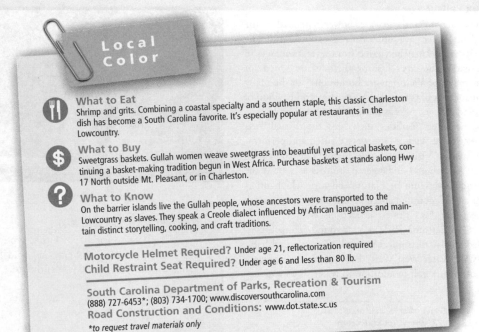

Local Color

🍴 **What to Eat**
Shrimp and grits. Combining a coastal specialty and a southern staple, this classic Charleston dish has become a South Carolina favorite. It's especially popular at restaurants in the Lowcountry.

💲 **What to Buy**
Sweetgrass baskets. Gullah women weave sweetgrass into beautiful yet practical baskets, continuing a basket-making tradition begun in West Africa. Purchase baskets at stands along Hwy 17 North outside Mt. Pleasant, or in Charleston.

❓ **What to Know**
On the barrier islands live the Gullah people, whose ancestors were transported to the Lowcountry as slaves. They speak a Creole dialect influenced by African languages and maintain distinct storytelling, cooking, and craft traditions.

Motorcycle Helmet Required? Under age 21, reflectorization required
Child Restraint Seat Required? Under age 6 and less than 80 lb.

South Carolina Department of Parks, Recreation & Tourism
(888) 727-6453*; (803) 734-1700; www.discoversouthcarolina.com
Road Construction and Conditions: www.dot.state.sc.us
*to request travel materials only

Scenic overlooks provide stunning views of eroded pinnacles and buttes in Badlands National Park.

CITIES

Aberdeen (B-10)

A commercial and industrial center in the state's northeast corner, Aberdeen is the home of Northern State University and Presentation College. The

Storybook Land, Aberdeen

Dacotah Prairie Museum tells the story of the development of the area; permanent exhibits touch on wildlife, the Hutterite community, and the Lakota Sioux. Aberdeen was once home to L. Frank Baum, the author of The Wizard of Oz books; his legacy is remembered in the annual Oz Festival at Wylie Park. The festivities include strolling storytellers, Oz characters, an arts festival, and memorabilia. Wylie Park's Storybook Land recreates the settings of children's tales like Peter Pan and Sleeping Beauty with a special Land of Oz devoted to Baum's timeless characters. Outdoors enthusiasts can enjoy a range of water sports at Mina Lake State Recreation Area. At Richmond Lake State Recreation Area, try hiking or horseback riding on prairie trails, or angling for walleye, bass, and catfish.

Aberdeen Convention & Visitors Bureau: (605) 225-2414; www.aberdeencvb.com

✪ Pierre (State Capital) (D-9)

The capital of South Dakota is pronounced "peer." A small town in the heart of an agricultural area, Pierre became the state capital in 1889. It is the second-smallest state capital in the U.S. (Montpelier, VT is smaller). You can tour the beautifully restored state capitol building, which features murals, historical displays, and marble staircases in the rotunda. The South Dakota Cultural Heritage Center has displays on the development of the state including the pioneer era, American Indian culture before the coming of white men, and life in the 20th century. The Discovery Center and Aquarium has hands-on exhibits and native fish displays. Nearby Lake Oahe, formed by the Oahe Dam on the Missouri River, offers fishing and other outdoor recreation. Tours of the dam and its power plants are given daily during summer.

Capitol building

Pierre Area Chamber of Commerce: (800) 962-2034; www.pierre.org

Rapid City (E-3)

Once a center of gold-mining operations, Rapid City has become the chief staging area for sightseeing excursions into the scenic Black Hills. Visit the Museum of Geology on the campus of the South Dakota School of Mines and Technology to see fossilized skeletons of gigantic invertebrates recovered from the Black Hills region. At the Journey Museum, exhibits tell the story of the area through interactive displays on geology, the Sioux Indians, industrial development, and other subjects. Reptile Gardens offers live animal shows featuring parrots, alligators, snakes and the ever-popular herd of giant tortoises, all in a setting of tropical splendor. More creatures of the wild may be encountered along the drive-through and walk-through areas at Bear Country USA. Area caves inviting exploration include Black Hills Caverns and Sitting Bull Crystal Caverns. Head to the Circle B Ranch Chuckwagon or the Flying T Chuckwagon for comedy, music, and a tinplate dinner.

Rapid City Convention & Visitors Bureau: (800) 487-3223 or (605) 343-1744; www.visitrapidcity.com

Falls Park, Sioux Falls

Sioux Falls (F-13)

Stone quarrying and the water power generated by the Big Sioux River gave Sioux Falls its early success. The impressive falls may be viewed from several vantages in Falls Park. The city's historic districts are noted for their wealth of Victorian-era homes built in the many popular styles of the time. The Washington Pavilion of Arts and Science houses numerous cultural and interactive learning facilities including the Visual Arts Center, Kirby Science Discovery Center, and performance spaces. Visit the Great Plains Zoo to see 70 species of rare and endangered animals as well as the Delbridge Museum of Natural History which offers dioramas of mounted species from all over the world. Among the city's newest attractions is the Butterfly House in Sertoma Park, a year-round, climate-controlled display of tropical butterflies in a natural habitat. Wild Water West Water Park offers go-cart racing and miniature golf in addition to water slides and lazy river rides.

Sioux Falls Convention & Visitors Bureau: (800) 333-2072; www.siouxfalls.com

SCENERY

Native American National Scenic Byway (E-9)

Begin a 101-mile drive through the prairie grass country of South Dakota in Chamberlain, passing through the Crow Creek and Lower Brule Sioux reservations. Along the way in little "villages," prairie dogs pop up their heads and call to each other. Watch for herds of bison and elk owned by some of the tribes, as well as pronghorn and deer. The drive ends in Fort Pierre, which once served as a trading center between native peoples and Europeans.

Iron Mountain Road, Black Hills National Forest

Peter Norbeck National Scenic Byway (F-3)

Big RVs can't squeeze through the sharp turns of Needles Highway (SR 87) and the narrow tunnels of granite that frame Mount Rushmore on Iron Mountain Road (US 16A). Norbeck, the conservationist and former South Dakota governor and senator who called the area home, said, "You're not supposed to drive here at 60 miles an hour. To do the scenery half justice, people should drive 20 or under. To do it full justice they should get out and walk." The drive traverses Black Hills National Forest and Custer State Park, winding past the pine-covered hills and rock formations, as well as several 1930s "pigtail bridges" that wind like a pig's tail.

● **Badlands Loop State Scenic Byway (E-4)**
For 30 miles along SR 240, see the badland formations up close.

● **Oahe Dam (D-7)**
North of Pierre, drive over one of the world's largest earth-rolled dams.

● **Sand Lake National Wildlife Refuge (A-10)**
Through the plains and the James River Valley, this refuge near Aberdeen is a flyway stopover for migratory birds in the spring and fall.

● **Spearfish Canyon (D-2)**
Along 22 miles of US 14A, see limestone cliffs and Bridal Veil and Roughlock Falls.

US 14A, Spearfish Canyon

● **Wildlife Loop Road (F-3)**
In Custer State Park, spot bison, pronghorn, bighorn sheep, prairie dogs, and wild burros that may stop in the middle of the road.

OUTDOORS

Black Hills

Black Hills *(E-3)*

Most of the rock climbing opportunities in this prairie state lie in the Black Hills area. There, the granite faces of the fingerlike rock pinnacles known as the Needles and even spots near Mount Rushmore National Memorial are challenging climbs. There are other climbable limestone and granite formations, including spots in Rapid City. Outfitters abound in the Black Hills area and are based in Rapid City, Hill City, and nearby Devils Tower, WY. The bravest souls attempt ice climbs in winter. In southeastern South Dakota, near Sioux Falls in Garretson, Palisades State Park features pink-hued quartzite cliffs, with a range of difficulty. No fixtures are attached to the rock. For the technically challenged, there are even a set of natural rock stairs to get you to the top of King and Queen Rock.

(800) 732-5682; www.travelsd.com

Canoeing

Missouri River *(G-10)*

The Missouri River cuts a wide swath right through the middle of South Dakota. Follow in the tracks of Lewis and Clark and the Corps of Discovery by kayaking this great route. While much

of the river has been changed by dams, two stretches along the Nebraska/South Dakota border remain much as they were in the day of the famous explorers. The first section flows 39 miles from the Fort Randall Dam near Pickstown to Running Water. The second section, 59 miles long, flows from Gavins Point Dam near Yankton to Ponca State Park, NE. These two stretches have been designated the Missouri National Recreational River. Trips pass islands, sand beaches, a wildlife refuge, and bluffs of sandstone, limestone, and chalk. Outfitters use sea kayaks, a stable boat that's easy to paddle in the flat but sometimes fast-flowing stretches.

(402) 667-2550; www.nps.gov/mnrr

Wind Cave National Park

Wind Cave National Park *(F-3)*

With a constant temperature of 53 degrees Fahrenheit year-round, Wind Cave makes a cool retreat in summer and a warm spot for winter exploring. There are several daily cave tours, ranging from a moderate walk though the natural entrance to a strenuous, crawl-along-on-your-hands-and-knees adventure. There's even a candlelight tour in a less-developed part of the cave. Located near Hot Springs, the cave is especially known for boxwork, a type of lacy, honeycomb-like calcite formation, and frostwork, another calcite formation that looks like frost. Above ground, go biking, birding, or horseback riding along the many trails of the 28,000-acre prairie and pine forest park. Wildlife include bison, elk, pronghorn, and the ubiquitous prairie dog.

(605) 745-4600; www.nps.gov/wica

HERITAGE

Akta Lakota Museum *(E-9)*

Akta Lakota Museum

South Dakota is home to several reservations, and more than 62,000 American Indians live here. The state offers a number of American Indian sites, but a good place to get a sense of history is the Akta Lakota Museum in Chamberlain. Akta Lakota means "to honor the people" and this museum at St. Joseph's Indian School does just that with exhibits of fancy beadwork of the Dakota, Lakota, and Nakota peoples (known collectively as Sioux) as well as other artifacts. Other exhibits cover weaponry and tools, and a doll exhibit shows authentic dress of American Indians of the 1800s. A 36-foot diorama shows what the prairies were like, with scenes of a buffalo hunt and everyday life. A gift shop sells Sioux artwork and crafts.

(800) 798-3452; www.aktalakota.org

Deadwood *(D-2)*

Historic Deadwood

Relive the wild, lawless days of a gold rush town at Deadwood. In the 1870s, the town was rife with saloons, betting parlors, and brothels. A reenactment of Wild Bill Hickok's fatal shooting occurs at the Old Style Saloon #10. Both Wild Bill Hickok and Calamity Jane are buried at the Mount Moriah Cemetery, a National Historic Landmark. Their headstones delve further into the tragic times of the early days. Learn about two founding families and see 19th-century artifacts, photos, and furnishings at the Adams Museum and House. To experience gold fever, the Broken Boot Gold Mine allows visitors to follow ore car rails into a 100-year-old mine. You can even try your hand at panning for gold here.

(800) 999-1876; www.deadwood.com

Laura Ingalls Wilder Homestead *(D-11)*

Laura Ingalls Wilder, author of the *Little House on the Prairie* book series, lived in De Smet (in the central-eastern portion of the state) in the late 1800s. On several summer weekends, the town presents an annual pageant portraying stories from the Wilder books. The home where Laura and her family spent their first winter in Dakota, the Surveyors' House, as well as the house that Pa Ingalls built in 1887, are open for tours. Both feature memorabilia and family artifacts. Take a ride in a covered wagon on the Ingalls Homestead, one mile east of De Smet. The homestead has a native grass prairie and hands-on activities. The family cemetery is also in De Smet.

(800) 776-3594; www.ingallshomestead.com

Prairie Village *(E-12)*

Fifty buildings make up this re-creation of an 1890s prairie town near Madison. The buildings include a church, one-room schoolhouse, store, bank, jail, log home, farm homes, and a claim shanty. There's even an opera house in which Lawrence Welk played his first performances. An 1893 carousel features hand-carved horses and is powered by a steam engine. Members of the Prairie Historical Society demonstrate old farming techniques and allow kids to try their hand at the tools as well. History buffs flock to the Annual Steam Threshing Jamboree on the last weekend in August, when oats are threshed by the antique machines and a steam sawmill whirs into action.

(800) 693-3644; www.prairievillage.org

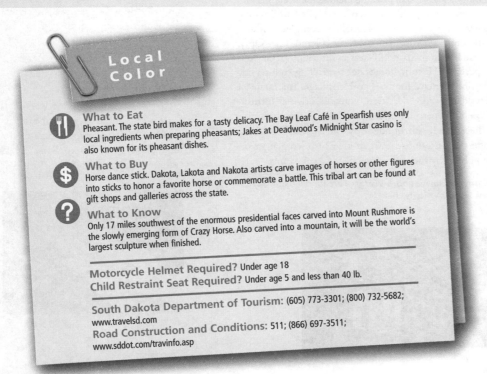

Local Color

What to Eat
Pheasant. The state bird makes for a tasty delicacy. The Bay Leaf Café in Spearfish uses only local ingredients when preparing pheasants; Jakes at Deadwood's Midnight Star casino is also known for its pheasant dishes.

What to Buy
Horse dance stick. Dakota, Lakota and Nakota artists carve images of horses or other figures into sticks to honor a favorite horse or commemorate a battle. This tribal art can be found at gift shops and galleries across the state.

What to Know
Only 17 miles southwest of the enormous presidential faces carved into Mount Rushmore is the slowly emerging form of Crazy Horse. Also carved into a mountain, it will be the world's largest sculpture when finished.

Motorcycle Helmet Required? Under age 18
Child Restraint Seat Required? Under age 5 and less than 40 lb.

South Dakota Department of Tourism: (605) 773-3301; (800) 732-5682; www.travelsd.com
Road Construction and Conditions: 511; (866) 697-3511; www.sddot.com/travinfo.asp

Cherohala Scenic Skyway rewards travelers with one spectacular vista after another.

CITIES

Chattanooga (G-15)

Nestled in a valley surrounded by steep ridges, Chattanooga is rich in family attractions, Civil War history, and magnificent scenery. Many visitors begin their explorations at Ross's Landing Park & Plaza, home to the excellent Tennessee Aquarium, where some 9,000 animals swim and cavort in naturalistic settings. Nearby is the

Tennessee Aquarium, Chattanooga

Creative Discovery Museum, a state-of-the-art children's museum and exploration center. The Hunter Museum of Art, which overlooks the Tennessee River, has one of the finest art collections in this part of the country. Railroad buffs flock to the Chattanooga Choo Choo Complex, which boasts the world's largest HO-gauge model railroad. The Lookout Mountain Incline Railway takes visitors on a steep ride to the top of the 2,120-foot mountain that overlooks the city. Point Park, located atop the mountain, commemorates the Civil War's "Battle above the Clouds."

Chattanooga Area Convention & Visitors Bureau: (423) 756-8687, (800) 322-3344; www.chattanoogafun.com

Gatlinburg (E-20)

Traditional folk art

All manner of amusements, shops, hotels, and motels line the streets of this popular resort town at the northern entrance to Great Smoky Mountains National Park. Visitors can explore the Guinness World Records Museum, catch a show at the Sweet Fanny Adams Theatre, see the life-sized religious dioramas at Christus Gardens, and take in a wide variety of rides, sights, and attractions. North of town, an eight-mile drive loops through the Great Smoky Arts and Crafts Community, home to more than 80 artisans working in traditional folk arts such as basketry, leathermaking, and doll making. Ober Gatlinburg, the year-round resort high on Mount Harrison, offers skiing, indoor ice skating, an alpine slide, and other recreational opportunities. A narrow road climbs the mountain, but the best way up is via the scenic aerial tramway.

Gatlinburg Department of Tourism & Convention Center: (800) 343-1475; www.gatlinburg.com

Memphis (F-1)

Located near the northern end of the Mississippi Delta, Tennessee's largest city takes its name from the ancient Egyptian city on the Nile Delta. Memphis' rich music history is one of its biggest draws. Graceland, Elvis Presley's home, attracts millions of visitors from around the world each year. Many of them also make a pilgrimage to the legendary Sun Studio where Elvis and other music greats such as Johnny Cash, Roy Orbison, and Jerry Lee Lewis recorded their first records. The home of W.C. Handy, "Father of the Blues," sits on Beale Street, a thriving downtown entertainment district. But

there's more to Memphis than music. The National Civil Rights Museum at the Lorraine Motel, site of Martin Luther King, Jr.'s assassination, tells the story of the American civil rights movement. Memphis' zoo and aquarium are adjacent to the fine Brooks Museum of Art in Overton Park.

Beale Street

Memphis Convention & Visitors Bureau: (901) 543-5300; www.memphistravel.com

★ Nashville (State Capital) (C-11)

Nashville, capital of the state of Tennessee, is also universally recognized as the capital of the country music recording industry. Devotees from all over the world arrive in June to attend the CMA Music Festival for concerts, banquets, and a fleeting chance to mingle with the stars. The exhibits at the home of the Country Music Hall of Fame include memorabilia and costumes along with interactive exhibits and listening posts. No music trip to Nashville is complete without attending a performance of the Grand Ole Opry, broadcast from its 4,400-seat auditorium at Gaylord Opryland. Historic homes dot the rolling countryside beyond the city limits: The Hermitage, the estate of President Andrew Jackson, contains original furnishings and personal effects of the Jackson family. Cheekwood, surrounded by well-tended gardens, offers American artworks in a 1920s Georgian mansion built by the coffee-merchant Cheek family.

Nashville Convention & Visitors Bureau: (800) 657-6910; www.visitmusiccity.com

Ryman Auditorium, Nashville

SCENERY

Cades Cove (p. 76, H-2)

Lying near the western edge of Great Smoky Mountains National Park, Cades Cove is a small, flat-bottomed valley hemmed in by 5,000-foot mountains. Scattered around its pastures and woodlands are dozens of old structures — homes, barns, schools, churches, stores, and a mill — that tell the story of what life was like for the valley's inhabitants in the 19th and early 20th centuries. An 11-mile loop drive takes visitors around the cove and past the many of the historic structures.

Cades Cove

Clingmans Dome Road (H-4)

This seven-mile-long road runs along the crest of the Great Smokies between Newfound Gap Road (US 441) and a parking area near the 6,643-foot summit of Clingmans Dome, Tennessee's highest point. A half-mile paved trail leads to an observation platform providing spectacular 360-degree views that on clear days can extend 100 miles and include parts of seven states.

Trail of Tears National Historic Route (G-16)

Historically enlightening and beautifully scenic, this drive follows the route of the forced march of some 16,000 Cherokee Indians in 1838. The 260-mile Tennessee segment begins at Red Clay State Park east of Chattanooga and heads northeast through Cleveland, and Charleston, then northwest through Dayton, Murfreesboro, and Nashville.

● **Cherohala Scenic Skyway** (F-18)
Stretching 50 mountainous miles between Tellico Plains, TN and Robbinsville, NC, this lightly traveled highway offers vistas that rival those of the Blue Ridge Parkway.

● **Lookout Mountain Scenic Highway** (K-1)
This steep drive climbs to the top of the 2,120-foot ridge that looms over Chattanooga. On a clear day, the view extends into Alabama, Georgia, and North Carolina.

● **Natchez Trace Parkway** (G-8)
Following the historic Natchez Trace for 445 miles between Nashville and Natchez, MS, this tree-shaded parkway allows travelers to take a leisurely trip into America's past. Highlights of the Tennessee segment include the Laurel Hill Wildlife Management Area, the Meriwether Lewis Monument, and Jackson Falls.

● **Tellico River Road** (F-18)
From its junction with the Cherohala Scenic Skyway in the state's southeastern corner, Tellico River Road (Forest Service Road 210) follows the rocky Tellico River for 5.6 miles before reaching the 100-foot Bald River Falls.

Tellico River

HERITAGE

The Hermitage (C-12)

Located on the eastern outskirts of Nashville, this two-story antebellum mansion was the home of Andrew Jackson, seventh president of the United States. The mansion was originally built as a brick Federal-style structure in the years 1819-21, then greatly expanded in 1831. Following an upstairs fire in 1834, it was rebuilt in the Greek Revival style, with six massive Corinthian columns lining the front. After leaving the presidency in 1837, "Old Hickory" returned to the Hermitage and lived there until his death in 1845. This National Historic Landmark is now maintained to look much as it did in 1837. Costumed guides lead visitors through room after room furnished with original Jackson family pieces. On the 1,120 acres of grounds surrounding the mansion are the humble log homes where Jackson and his wife Rachel lived before the mansion was built and the formal gardens where the two are buried. The visitor center displays changing exhibits from across the country and offers a café.

(615) 889-2941; www.thehermitage.com

Museum of Appalachia (C-19)

This 65-acre outdoor museum recreates an Appalachian pioneer village and working farm. Founder John Rice Irwin spent years crisscrossing the mountains in search of relics from the 18th and early 19th centuries. When he opened the museum in the late 1960s, it consisted of just one log cabin, but today it has grown to include more than 30 structures — including smokehouses, barns, a church, a schoolhouse, and numerous cabins — transported from their original locations. Every effort is made to create the feeling of an actual village: Interiors are filled with authentic period furnishings, gardens are enclosed by split-rail fences, and the pastures are filled with grazing cattle, mules, goats, and sheep. The museum also features exhibits of more than 250,000 artifacts, a Hall of Fame commemorating peoples' lives, and a gift and craft shop.

Museum of Appalachia

(865) 494-7680, (865) 494-0514;
www.museumofappalachia.com

Shiloh National Military Park (G-6)

Spread over 4,000 acres adjacent to the Tennessee River, this park preserves the site of the first major Civil War battle in the Western theater. The battle took place on April 6 and 7, 1862, when Confederate troops surprised General Ulysses S. Grant's Union army, which was encamped at Shiloh Church. The fighting raged until fresh Union troops turned the tide in Grant's favor. The park's visitor center features battlefield artifacts and a 25-minute orientation film. It's also the starting point for a 9.5-mile self-guided tour route that takes visitors past 14 wayside exhibits. During summertime, the battlefield comes alive with rangers offering interpretive programs and answering visitors' questions. More than 3,500 Union soldiers — most of them unidentified — are interred at the Shiloh National Cemetery. Confederate dead rest in a series of large burial trenches spread across the battlefield. Several American Indian mounds from farther back in history also dot the landscape.

Shiloh National Military Park

(731) 689-5696; www.nps.gov/shil

OUTDOORS

Ocoee River (G-18)

The Cherokee National Forest in Tennessee's southeastern corner holds one of the most popular white-water rivers in the United States. Each year roughly 300,000 rafters take the thrilling two-hour trip down the Middle Ocoee, a five-mile stretch of nearly continuous Class III and IV rapids with names like Gonzo Shoals, Double Trouble, Slingshot, and Hell's Hole. Controlled releases from upstream TVA dams guarantee ample water flow even during late-summer dry periods. Rafters can choose from some 25 local outfitters offering rafts, experienced guides, safety equipment, and transportation. Most of the outfitters also offer trips on the Upper Ocoee, a world-class watercourse that gained fame as the site of the 1996 Olympic white-water slalom competitions. The U.S. Forest Service's Ocoee Whitewater Center near Ducktown offers information on outfitters, water-release schedules, and other local recreation, including hiking and mountain biking.

(423) 496-5197, (877) 692-6050;
www.fs.fed.us/R8/ocoee

Ocoee River rafting

Reelfoot Lake (B-4)

Lying in the northwestern corner of the state just a few miles from the Mississippi River, Tennessee's largest natural lake was formed in 1811-12 when a series of violent earthquakes dramatically altered the local landscape. Reelfoot Lake soon became a major stopover point and wintering ground for birds migrating along the Mississippi Flyway, and in 1941 the northern third of the lake was designated a National Wildlife Refuge. Roughly 240 bird species have

been documented at the shallow, 18-mile-long lake, and winter visitors include some 400,000 mallards, 100,000 Canada geese, and up to 200 bald eagles. At the

Reelfoot Lake

Refuge, visitors can view the birds from two observation towers, a 2.75-mile auto tour route, or several primitive hiking trails. Reelfoot Lake State Park offers hiking trails, boardwalks, and guided pontoon-boat cruises. In season, park naturalists lead daily eagle-watching tours. With giant cypress trees ringing its perimeter and lily pads carpeting huge areas of its surface, the lake itself is exceptionally scenic.

(731) 253-7756; reelfoot.fws.gov

South Cumberland State Park (F-14)

Some of Tennessee's best hiking and most dramatic scenery can be found within this park atop the Cumberland Plateau. Comprised of 10 separate districts in four southeastern counties, South Cumberland encompasses 16,000 forested acres of tumbling streams, unusual rock formations, deep valleys, and 2,000-foot tablelands. Grundy Forest State Natural Area, the best-known of the 10 districts, offers two main trails. The relatively easy two-mile Grundy Forest Day Loop takes hikers through old-growth forest and past numerous waterfalls and a plunge pool. The Fiery Gizzard Trail, considered one of the top backpacking trails in the United States, represents the other extreme: This steep, difficult, and sometimes treacherous 17-mile trek descends into and climbs out of the deep, narrow Fiery Gizzard Gorge. The South Cumberland visitor center east of Monteagle offers detailed trail maps for all 10 districts.

South Cumberland State Park

(931) 924-2980; www.state.tn.us/environment/parks/SouthCumberland

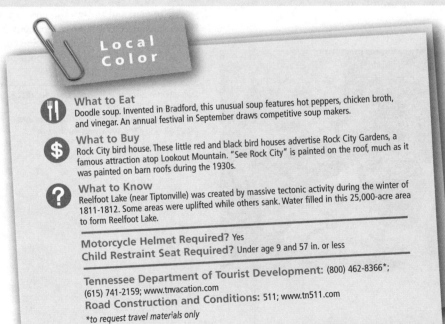

Local Color

What to Eat
Doodle soup. Invented in Bradford, this unusual soup features hot peppers, chicken broth, and vinegar. An annual festival in September draws competitive soup makers.

What to Buy
Rock City bird house. These little red and black bird houses advertise Rock City Gardens, a famous attraction atop Lookout Mountain. "See Rock City" is painted on the roof, much as it was painted on barn roofs during the 1930s.

What to Know
Reelfoot Lake (near Tiptonville) was created by massive tectonic activity during the winter of 1811-1812. Some areas were uplifted while others sank. Water filled in this 25,000-acre area to form Reelfoot Lake.

Motorcycle Helmet Required? Yes
Child Restraint Seat Required? Under age 9 and 57 in. or less

Tennessee Department of Tourist Development: (800) 462-8366*;
(615) 741-2159; www.tnvacation.com
Road Construction and Conditions: 511; www.tn511.com

to request travel materials only

The Alamo is where Davy Crockett, Jim Bowie, and other Texas defenders died under siege in 1836.

CITIES

⊛ Austin (State Capital) (EJ-6)

Austin has been dubbed "the playground of Texas," and rightfully so. This centrally located city is home to an eclectic environment that has been created in large part by the state capital and the University of Texas. On top of that, many musicians reside here — it calls itself the live music capital of the world — along with artists who create a thriving cultural setting. More than 300 sunny days each year make it easy to enjoy some of Austin's outdoor offerings, too. Nature trails, the Zilker Botanical Gardens, and Town Lake all are close to the heart of the city and provide hours of outdoor entertainment. Don't miss the city's most unusual natural attraction: 1.5 million bats live under the Congress Avenue Bridge and take flight every night at dusk from March through October.

Austin Convention & Visitors Bureau: (866) 462-8784; www.austintexas.org

Corpus Christi (EO-7)

The Corpus Christi area boasts 113 miles of beaches including the barrier islands along the Gulf of Mexico. The city sits on Corpus Christi Bay and serves as the gateway to Mustang Island and Padre Island National Seashore. With all that water within an easy drive, the opportunities for swimming, sunning, and outdoor sports are extensive. Spectacular sights are waiting at the Texas State Aquarium, the USS *Lexington* Museum on the Bay, the Texas State Museum of Asian Cultures, and the Bayfront Arts and Science Park. Birdwatchers won't want to miss Hans A. Suter Wildlife Refuge, where hundreds of birds representing more than a dozen species can often be counted in a single day.

Corpus Christi Convention & Visitors Bureau: (800) 766-2322; www.corpuschristicvb.com

Dallas

Dallas/Fort Worth (ED-7)

Dallas is a ritzy, glitzy, fashionable city where glass-walled buildings sparkle in the sun and big corporations flourish. The arts sparkle here, too. The city's busy downtown arts district is home to the Dallas Symphony, Museum of Art, Nasher Sculpture Center, and the Crow Collection of Asian Art museum. For a taste of the city's best, try the Deep Ellum Historic District's restaurant row for Texas treats or ethnic eats.

Fort Worth is Dallas' flip side. The arts and culture still run deep, but Fort Worth is best known for its "cow town" image, left over from the days when it was a stop on the Chisholm Trail. Poke around the Stockyards Historic District, home to western shops, Texas steakhouses, weekly rodeos, and stockyards. The Fort Worth Herd is a daily cattle drive of Texas longhorns in the stockyards. The town is no stranger to fine art, either, with one of the most renowned collections of museums in the nation.

Longhorn

Dallas Convention & Visitors Bureau: (800) 232-5527; www.visitdallas.com
Fort Worth Convention & Visitors Bureau: (800) 433-5747; www.fortworth.com

El Paso (WK-2)

El Paso stands alone on the far West Texas desert at the intersection of Texas, New Mexico, and Mexico. The town takes its name from a narrow mountain pass that an early explorer called "El Paso del Norte" or "the Pass of the North." The city's exceptionally rich and multicultural history is evident in its buildings, such as the El Paso Museum of Art and three stately historic missions. Visitors experience a historic and architectural rarity at the Plaza Theatre, one of the few remaining theaters from the 1930s. Local residents and visitors move easily across the Rio Grande via busy bridges connecting El Paso with its Mexican sister city, Ciudad Juárez.

El Paso Convention & Visitors Bureau: (800) 351-6024; www.visitelpaso.com

Space Center Houston exhibit

Houston (EK-10)

The state's largest and the country's fourth largest city is home to an amazing variety of top-notch restaurants, world-class shopping, distinctive museums, professional sports teams, a downtown theater district boasting almost 13,000 seats, and plenty of recreational attractions. Highlights include Space Center Houston, NASA's official visitors center; Kemah Boardwalk; the Menil Collection; and the San Jacinto Battleground State Historical Park, home to the Battleship USS *Texas*, a monument, and a museum. This important seaport city is also a hub for petroleum, natural gas, steel, cotton, shipbuilding, and other industries, often earning it the nickname "Energy Capital of the World." From high culture to honky-tonk, Houston has it all.

Greater Houston Convention & Visitors Bureau: (800) 446-8786; www.visithoustontexas.com

San Antonio (EL-4)

San Antonio is a fiesta city of mariachis and marketplaces, Mexican food and Spanish-Colonial courtyards. The city is a cultural link to the days when Texas was part of Old Mexico. Start at the Paseo del Rio, or River Walk, a picturesque and festive cobblestone riverside walkway 20 feet below street level with plenty of opportunity to eat, shop, dance the night away, or just cruise up and down the river. The Alamo, famed site of the tragic 1836 Texan holdout against the Mexican Army, remains the prime symbol of Texas' renegade spirit and a must-see spot. For a souvenir with flair, stop by El Mercado (Market Square) for more than 30 shops selling everything from postcards and Mexican dresses to painted papier-mâché vegetables and pottery.

San Antonio Convention & Visitors Bureau: (800) 447-3372; www.visitsanantonio.com

River Walk

Planning the day in Corpus Christi

OUTDOORS

Armand Bayou Nature Center (p. 108, G-8)

This nature center is one of the country's largest urban wildlife and wilderness preserves and is home to bison, raptors, reptiles, mammals, and much more. Located near Clear Lake, midway between Houston and Galveston, the center offers several active options for visitors, including birding activities, guided and self-guided hikes, various pontoon boat cruises, and guided canoe trips. More than 370 species of animals and birds make their home in the three ecosystems found in the more than 2,500 acres of coastal salt marsh, hardwood forest, and coastal prairie land in the preserve. Reservations are required for pontoon boat and canoe trips.

(281) 474-2551; www.abnc.org

Big Bend National Park

Big Bend National Park (WQ-7)

This West Texas park offers a full roster of short and long trails that wind through dramatic landscapes for some of the state's best hiking. The well-known South Rim Trail provides a magnificent panorama overlooking the desert 2,500 feet below as well as peaks 80 miles to the south in Mexico. The park, which sits along the Mexican border inside a sharp turn in the Rio Grande (hence the name Big Bend), is a meeting point of countries, cultures, and environments. Here, where the desert meets the mountains, visitors will find a biologically diverse group of plants, animals, and spectacular scenery that's still best discovered on foot.

(432) 477-2251; www.nps.gov/bibe

Corpus Christi Water Sports (EO-7)

With an average temperature of 71.2° and plenty of wind and waves, Corpus Christi is a water sport hot spot year-round. Those looking to hit the Gulf might try their hand at windsurfing, sailing, or kiteboarding. The city hosts the annual U.S. Open Windsurfing Regatta, and weekly sailboat regattas are held on Wednesday evenings all year. A variety of waterways ranging from open Gulf of Mexico waters to more calm and protected coves makes it easy for beginners and experts alike to find their match in the water. Lessons and equipment rental options are numerous.

*www.texasoutside.com/corpusframes/
watersports.htm*

Guadalupe River (EK-4)

Tube (or toob, as it's referred to in the local vernacular), raft, kayak, or canoe your way down the Guadalupe River, one of the most popular and well-known rivers in Texas. The Guadalupe's clear, cool waters make it a perfect summertime spot. Enjoying the river's crystal waters is a favorite activity of both locals and tourists, and plenty of outfitters rent tubes, rafts, and kayaks for fun rides at reasonable rates. There's usually a shuttle service to take you back to your starting point, or get a lift upstream and work downstream to the finish. There are numerous access points along the river. The most popular spots are in the Hill Country and south-central Texas, including Guadalupe River State Park and New Braunfels.

(830) 438-2656; www.tpwd.state.tx.us/park/guadalup/

Hueco Tanks State Historic Site (WK-2)

Climbers just can't keep their hands off the rock at this well-known site. Located 32 miles east of El Paso, the 860-acre park is named after the large natural rock basins, or "huecos," that have supplied trapped rainwater to the arid West Texas region for millions of years. Non-climbers can hike out to the "tanks," where they'll see a variety of pictographs left by prehistoric hunters, Apaches, and other American Indian peoples over the years. Mythological designs depicting human and animal figures remain visible on these rocks, and the most noted pictographs include more than 200 faces or "masks" by the prehistoric Jornada Mogollon culture.

(915) 857-1135; www.tpwd.state.tx.us/park/hueco

Horseback riding

Mayan Ranch (EK-3)

After a hearty, delicious chuck wagon breakfast, saddle up at the Mayan Ranch, one of the many dude/guest ranches in Bandera, the "Cowboy Capital of the World." There are two trail rides a day, one in the morning and one in the afternoon, and each lasts about 50 minutes and is lead by a cowboy guide. Those wishing to keep their feet closer to the ground can enjoy some of the ranch's other activities including horseshoes, tennis, fishing, swimming, hay rides, dancing, and more.

(830) 796-3312; www.mayanranch.com

HERITAGE

Bishop's Palace (EO-11)

This landmark Victorian home is one of Galveston's top attractions and the state's only structure on the American Institute of Architects' 100 outstanding buildings list. The limestone and granite "Palace" was built in 1886 for Colonel Walter Gresham and features 11 rare stone and wood mantels (including one that was a first-prize winner at the 1876 World's Fair in Philadelphia), a Venetian crystal chandelier, period wall coverings, and a staircase made of rosewood, satinwood, and mahogany that took 61 craftsmen to carve. The mansion-turned-museum is owned and run by the Catholic Diocese of Galveston-Houston and has tours seven days a week.

(409) 762-2475; www.galveston.com/historichomes

Gruene National Historic District (EK-5)

Saunter back in time at this warm Texas town named Gruene (pronounced "green"). Historic Gruene is located just upriver from downtown New Braunfels, which sits about halfway between San Antonio and Austin. This small town rests on a bluff overlooking the Guadalupe River and shares many of the same German roots as New Braunfels. Ernst Gruene first settled the area in 1845, and his second son Henry Gruene ran a successful cotton business that brought more families and buildings to Gruene's land. Many of these houses, built in various styles, still exist today, including Gruene Hall, which is the oldest dance hall in the state, and the Gristmill River Restaurant & Bar which is located in the ruins of the 100-year-old cotton gin. Gruene was placed on the National Register of Historic Places in the 1970s, and today it offers visitors a relaxing and rich look at Texas history.

Gruene Hall

(800) 572-2626; www.nbcham.org, www.gruenehall.com

National Museum of the Pacific War/ Admiral Nimitz State Historic Site (EJ-4)

This nine-acre historic site complex is one of the top institutions dedicated to preserving the history of World War II in the Pacific. The museum and site includes multiple stops. Inside the Admiral Nimitz Museum, learn about the history of Fredericksburg and Chester Nimitz, who was born here and became a 5-star fleet admiral and commander-in-chief of the Pacific Theater. The George Bush Gallery includes chronological exhibits and walk-through dioramas featuring the personal effects of veterans, aircraft and battleship remnants, art, and other pieces. The Pacific Combat Zone is the newest exhibit and transports visitors through various combat locations. The outdoor Japanese Garden of Peace was a gift from Japan in honor of Nimitz and incorporates stone, plants, and water in a traditional Japanese garden. The Plaza of Presidents features stone monuments for each president who served in WWII. The Veterans' Walk of Honor is a memorial wall honoring individuals, units, and ships from the war.

(830) 997-4379; www.nimitz-museum.org

National Museum of the Pacific War

▶ **The Petroleum Museum** (WK-10)

This Midland museum is interesting to out-of-staters and native Texans alike. Learn all about the oil industry and the history of petroleum through a variety of collections, exhibits, and dioramas, both inside and out. The museum is divided into four wings, each examining a different aspect of the history of petroleum production: geology, technology, culture, and transportation's relationship with petroleum. Exhibits include historic photos of a West Texas boomtown, 3-D models of oil strata, a collection of antique oil drilling rigs and equipment, and many other artifacts and works related to the production of petroleum and the life of oil workers.

Petroleum Museum

(432) 683-4403; www.petroleummuseum.org

President John F. Kennedy Sites in Dallas *(p. 109, B-4)*

The Sixth Floor Museum is located in the old Texas School Book Depository overlooking Dealey Plaza and marks the infamous window area where Lee Harvey Oswald fired his fatal shots at President John F. Kennedy. The museum's exhibits chronicle the assassination as well as the legacy of JFK. The John F. Kennedy Memorial stands nearby in the Dallas County Historical Plaza along with several other historical monuments and buildings and has thousands of visitors every year.

(214) 747-6660; www.jfk.org

Ranching Heritage Center *(WE-2)*

Learn about the history of ranching, pioneer life, and the livestock industry as you visit more than 36 authentic structures on this 30-acre site located on the edge of the Texas Tech campus in Lubbock. Stops include a bunkhouse, barn, dugout, windmills, ranch houses, corrals and pens, a one-room school, blacksmith shop, locomotive, stock cars, depot, Spanish compound, and other authentically restored and furnished ranch buildings. The center shows the development of ranch life from the 1780s to the 1930s. Docents dressed in period attire give tours to visitors on Sunday afternoons.

1837 ranch house

(806) 742-0498; www.ttu.edu/ranchhc

Relaxing

SCENERY

Hill Country

Devil's Backbone Scenic Drive *(EK-5)*

Cruise through the heart of Hill Country on one of Texas's most picturesque routes. FM 32, nicknamed the "Devil's Backbone," snakes along a high, razorbacked ridge that rises to an elevation of 1,274 feet and gives drivers a glimpse of the Blanco River during various stretches of the drive. Several pull-off vistas allow drivers to stretch their legs and scope out the surrounding scenery. Cedar, juniper, and live oak trees line both sides of this hilly drive and paint a lush picture not often associated with Texas, and from March to May, the wildflowers' beautiful blooms add bursts of color to the shades of green and brown. The road begins off FM 12 just south of the artsy town of Wimberley and runs west about 24 miles toward the town of Blanco.

El Camino del Rio *(WQ-6)*

Spanish for "The River Road," El Camino del Rio is a don't-miss drive in southwest Texas. From Lajitas, FM 170 heads northwest to Presidio (and beyond) and provides views unlike any other in the state. The paved route runs right through magnificent Big Bend Ranch State Park, plunging down mountains and meandering through canyons along the Rio Grande. Drivers should be aware that the route includes steep grades, sharp curves, and low-water crossings and therefore may not be suitable for large RVs or vehicles pulling large trailers.

● **Canadian River Wagon Bridge** *(WC-13)*

Tucked in the northeast corner of the state's panhandle, the steel span was built in 1916 over the Canadian River. Hikers and bikers now cross the bridge, which is a great platform for viewing wildlife and the area's abundant hills and valleys, cottonwoods and hackberries, all a sharp contrast to the neighboring treeless plains.

● **Daingerfield State Park** *(ED-11)*

Though eastern Texas is known for its pines, this park is home to dogwoods, redbuds, and wisteria vines that make for colorful springs, and the leaves of sweetgums, oaks, and maples lining Lake Daingerfield produce bright reds and golds in the fall.

● **McDonald Observatory** *(WN-6)*

Catch out-of-this-world views as well as magnificent mountain landscapes from one of the leading astronomical research centers in the country, perched high atop Mount Locke in the Davis Mountains of West Texas.

● **Mount Bonnell** *(WS-9)*

Beautiful views of Lake Austin and the surrounding Texas Hill Country are worth climbing 100 steps to the highest point in Austin (785 feet).

● **Palo Duro Canyon** *(WE-11)*

Steep bluffs plunge nearly 1,000 feet to the bottom of the nation's second-largest canyon. An array of intense colors make for impressive photographs.

Palo Duro Canyon

● **Wyler Aerial Tramway** *(WS-2)*

In Franklin Mountains State Park, it's a four-minute ride to the top of Ranger Peak, from which you'll see 7,000 square miles of canyons, cacti, wildlife, and rock formations in three states and two countries. A platform at the tramway's base provides equally stunning views.

Wildflower Watch

Motorists looking for the best wildflower locations along Texas roads can get tips on the state's best viewing spots by calling the Texas Department of Transportation's wildflower hotline. March to May is peak wildflower season, with April being the prime blooming month. The hotline is available daily during those months from 8 a.m. to 6 p.m., and callers can request information by region. (800) 452-9292

Indian paintbrushes and Texas bluebonnets

Local Color

🍴 **What to Eat**
Barbecue. Every region has its own style of barbecue. In Texas, the meat is slow-smoked over wood coals. Several family-owned BBQ pits in Elgin, Lockhart, Luling, Round Rock, and Taylor serve an authentic plateful.

💲 **What to Buy**
Custom cowboy boots and hats. Seems like every town has a boot- and hatmaker. One of the best known is Texas Hatters in Austin and Buda, run by the Gammage family.

❓ **What to Know**
Dance halls are the center of social activity in small towns throughout the state. The one in Gruene, built in 1878, has an open-air dance floor, a wood-burning stove, and antique advertisements in the rafters.

Motorcycle Helmet Required? Under age 21 and those without proof of $10,000 of medical insurance or who have not completed a training course
Child Restraint Seat Required? Under age 5 and less than 36 in.

Texas Tourism Division: (800) 888-8839*; www.traveltex.com
Road Construction and Conditions: (800) 452-9292; www.dot.state.tx.us

*to request travel materials only

Utah

Hoodoos crowd horseshoe-shaped natural ampitheaters at Bryce Canyon National Park.

CITIES

Logan (B-8)

This quaint northern university town lies in the heart of the Cache Valley. Logan's skyline is dominated by its Mormon Temple (1884) and Tabernacle, now a genealogical research site and concert venue where people can hear one of the country's few pipe organs. On the university campus, you can visit the Nora Eccles Harrison Museum of Art. Visit with docents dressed in period costumes as American Indians, mountain men, and pioneers at the American West Heritage Center. At the Daughters of Utah Pioneers Museum, see early Mormon historical artifacts. Logan Canyon Scenic Byway, northeast of the city, offers a scenic drive to Bear Lake State Park.

Cache Valley Tourist Council: (435) 755-1890, (800) 882-4433; www.tourcachevalley.com

Moab (J-13)

Scrub jay at Canyonlands National Park

Eons of geologic upheaval have created a red rock landscape here in southeastern Utah that must be seen to be believed. Moab is a great base for exploring the surrounding spectacular natural areas: dense alpine aspen groves, snow-capped peaks, Arches and Canyonlands national parks, the Dead Horse Point State Park, and thousands of miles of mountain bike and off-highway vehicle trails. Outfitters offer guided tours by mountain bike, horseback, river raft, cross-country ski, jeep, or plane. For dinosaur lovers, Moab Museum has exhibits on the archaeology and paleontology of the region. To the north off US 191, check out the Mill Canyon Dinosaur Trail, Sauropod Dinosaur Tracksite, and Potash Road Dinosaur Track.

Moab Area Travel Council: (435) 259-8825, (800) 635-6622; www.discovermoab.com

Park City (E-8)

Park City boomed with the discovery of silver in 1868. After being almost deserted, the town realized its second life with the ski resort boom of the late 20th century. The town sits at the foot of Park City Mountain Resort, the most prominent year-round resort in the state. Park City has become familiar to movie fans as the site of the Sundance Film Festival, held in mid-January, which highlights the work of independent moviemakers. Located in the old city hall, the Park City Museum includes the Territorial Jail and displays on the town's silver-mining days. For family activities and jaw-dropping events, visit the two nearby Olympic venues: Olympic Park and Soldier Hollow.

Park City Chamber of Commerce and Visitors Bureau: (800) 453-1360, www.parkcityinfo.com

St. George (N-4)

Brigham Young, who spent his winters here, chose St. George for Utah's first-to-be-completed Mormon Temple in the West. St. George is still popular in winter for people craving warmth and sunshine. It's southwestern Utah's gateway to the red rock canyons, pinnacles, arches, and spires of Zion National Park. The city is also known for its abundant golf courses and spas, including one that incorporates southern Utah's red rock locations in its aggressive outdoor fitness program. Learn about Mormon history in St. George at the Mormon Temple, the Brigham Young Winter Home (1873), and the Daughters of Utah Pioneers Museum. Snow Canyon State Park, northwest of the city, does not have snow but it does have interesting volcanic features, including lava caves and cinder cones.

St. George Area Convention & Visitors Bureau: (435) 634-5747 or (800) 869-6635, www.utahstgeorge.com

✪ Salt Lake City (State Capital) (D-8)

Located at the foot of the Wasatch Mountains, Salt Lake City possesses urban vibrancy with a rugged edge reminiscent of the old-time American West. Visitors can explore the city's Mormon roots at the 10-acre historic Temple Square, the Beehive House (former home of Brigham Young), and the Pioneer Memorial Museum. In 2002, the city hosted the Olympic Winter Games and revealed its transformation from pioneer town to sophisticated metropolis. A short drive from the city is the Great Salt Lake, where you can sail, swim, and bird-watch. Year-round mountain resorts abound in the surrounding Wasatch Mountains and their canyons.

Salt Lake Convention & Visitors Bureau: (801) 521-2822, (800) 541-4955; www.visitsaltlake.com

SCENERY

National Park (I-13)

Located in southeastern Utah near Moab, this park's claim to fame is its 2,000-plus arches, one of the greatest concentrations on Earth. The all-time best view here is Delicate Arch, accessible by a couple of trails varying in difficulty. The formations are at their most beautiful when morning or evening shadows play about them, causing dazzling color changes.

Delicate Arch

Highway 12 (L-9)

This 124-mile All-American Road connects Bryce Canyon National Park with Capitol Reef National Park. Drive through the Red Canyon Tunnel formation. Don't miss excellent views of red rock cliffs, the Grand Staircase, and, on a clear day, the La Sal Mountains south of Moab.

- **Dead Horse Point State Park (J-12)**
  Called Utah's most spectacular state park, Dead Horse Point towers 2,000 feet directly above the Colorado River, providing a breathtaking panorama of sculpted pinnacles and buttes.

- **Logan Canyon National Scenic Byway (B-8)**
  On US 89 from Logan to Bear Lake, stop at Bear Lake Overlook for a classic Utah alpine scene with a turquoise lake shimmering in the valley below.

- **Mirror Lake Scenic Byway (E-10)**
  At the summit of SR 150 from Kamas to the Wyoming border, see Moosehorn Lake, Hayden Peak, and the High Uinta mountains in one glance.

- **Monument Valley (N-12)**
  Jagged peaks and towering buttes help make the otherworldly landscape of Monument Valley along US 163 one of the most dramatic areas in the West.

Virgin River in Zion National Park

- **Zion National Park (M-6)**
  The Zion-Mt. Carmel Highway intersects with the Zion Canyon Scenic Drive, which takes you past colorful, sheer cliffs (almost 3,000 feet high) forming the narrow canyon (visitors must ride the shuttle on the Zion Canyon Scenic Drive).

▶ HERITAGE

American West Heritage Center (N-17)

For an in-depth yet entertaining view of the area's history, visit this 160-acre living history site in northern Utah's Cache Valley. View 100 years of Utah history in one stop at the center, which showcases the lives of the Shoshone people, 19th-century Utahan pioneers, and early 20th-century Mormon farmers. Open Memorial Day through Labor Day, the center depicts the history and culture of the West from 1820 to 1920. Visitors can wander through a historic farm, Native American village, pioneer settlement, blacksmith shop, ox barn, and other buildings. Storytelling and demonstrations bring the Old West to life. The center is best known for its Festival of the American West, an annual event staged from late July into early August.

(435) 245-6050, (800) 225-3378; www.awhc.org

Dinosaur National Monument

Dinosaur National Monument (E-13)

A rugged landscape of steep canyon walls and rushing rivers greets the eyes of visitors to this 325-square-mile area. Located in the northwest corner of Colorado and spilling over into Utah, the park is famous for its dinosaur quarry near Jensen, UT. Thousands of bones have been excavated from the quarry since Earl Douglass first unearthed eight apatosaurus tailbones in 1909. The quarry holds at least 1,500 dinosaur bones. Visitors can watch paleontologists work with these fossils through a large lab window. Don't miss the fossil-bearing layer forming one wall. In the eight-to-twelve-foot layer, some bones are exposed, allowing you to see them jumbled about just as they were laid down in the river 150 million years ago. After the wall, walk through several exhibits explaining a paleontologist's methods and presenting the kinds of dinosaurs found in the rocks.

(970) 374-3000; www.nps.gov/dino

Edge of the Cedars State Park & Museum (L-13)

The earliest inhabitants in the Four Corners area were the nomadic Ancestral Puebloans, who lived here from about A.D. 1 to A.D. 1300. They left behind remnants of their civilization throughout the region, and the Edge of the Cedars State Park & Museum has become the primary repository for the archaeological finds. Behind the museum visitors can climb into a Pueblo village ruin that still stands today. The museum showcases a vast collection of artifacts, including the largest display of prehistoric Puebloan pottery in the Four Corners region. Special events feature storytelling and craft workshops. The museum is one of the stops along the Trail of the Ancients, a multi-state route that accesses numerous archaeological, cultural, and historic sites in the Four Corners.

(435) 678-2238; www.stateparks.utah.gov/

Temple Square (D-15)

At the center of Salt Lake City is Temple Square, home to some of the most important monuments and buildings of the Mormon religion. While the gleaming white Mormon temple is not open to the public, many of the other buildings are. The Tabernacle, home to the world-renowned Mormon Tabernacle Choir, has an 11,623-pipe organ. Visitors can enjoy choir rehearsals or organ recitals. To find out more about early church leaders and the immigration of Mormons to Salt Lake City, visit the Joseph Smith Memorial Building and the Museum of Church History and Art. Meet at the flagpole for one of several daily guided tours of the square.

(801) 240-1000; www.ldschurch.org

Delicate Arch/Arches

OUTDOORS

Canyonlands National Park

Moab (J-13)

No doubt, Moab is Utah's adventure hub. Moab and the Colorado River are the center of the red rock universe for mountain biking, four-wheeling, and river rafting as well as extreme versions of these sports. Competitors come from around the country and world for mountain biking and off-road jeep events. The Moab Slickrock Bike Trail, one of the nation's best, offers a challenging loop ride amid outstanding scenery. The Kokopelli Mountain Bike Trail covers 140 miles between Moab and Grand Junction, Colorado. Nearby Dead Horse Point State Park, Arches National Park, and Canyonlands National Park offer countless other rugged adventures. Get suggestions and gear from Moab guides and outfitters.

Moab Area Travel Council: (435) 259-1370; www.discovermoab.com.

Mountain Resorts (E-9)

Utah claims to have the "Greatest Snow on Earth." The headquarters for both the U.S. ski and snowboard associations are here, and Utah's mountains hosted the 2002 Olympic Winter Games. Nine of the state's 12 mountain resorts, including Park City, Deer Valley, Alta, Snowbird, Snowbasin, and Sundance, are considered destination resorts. They've earned great reputations for their ski and snowboard terrain and summer activities (think extreme luge-like alpine slides and zip lines or biking, horseback riding, and hot-air ballooning). Pampering guests is a year-round activity in resort spas, restaurants, and accommodations.

(801) 534-1779; www.skiutah.com

Salt Lake City (D-8)

The Olympic spirit lives on in Salt Lake City and nearby Park City, home of the 2002 Winter Games. Guided tours lead visitors through Olympic competition sites that feature the world's highest altitude ski jumps and the fastest bobsled and luge track. Take in the incredible panoramic views of the Snyderville Basin from atop the ski jump. Year-round, visitors can watch competitions and demonstrations as well as aspiring youth and Olympic athletes in training at three

Learn to bobsled

different sites. Watch freestyle aerialists soar 40 feet in the air off the ski jump or take a class and learn to do it yourself. Try bobsledding on the Olympic track and travel 80 miles per hour with the equivalent of a 40-story drop in a minute. Cross-country ski or go snow tubing at Soldier Hollow, or take a class in skating, hockey, or curling at Olympic Oval.

Utah Athletic Foundation: (435) 658-4247; www.utahathleticfoundation.com

Snowboarding

Local Color

What to Eat
Fry sauce. Usually a ketchup and mayonnaise combo, this condiment is served throughout the state as a dipping sauce for fries. Some restaurants have their own secret recipes.

What to Buy
Handcrafted buckaroo-style saddles. This type of saddle reflects the traditions of Spanish-speaking vaqueros, or buckaroos. The only place to get one is at Bob Ray Saddles in Parowan.

What to Know
Slickrock is misleadingly named. When dry and free of blowing sand, this hard and smooth petrified sandstone found throughout southern Utah offers terrific grip for hiking shoes and mountain bike tires.

Motorcycle Helmet Required? Under age 18
Child Restraint Seat Required? Under age 5

Utah Travel Council: (801) 538-1030; (800) 200-1160; www.utah.com
Road Construction and Conditions: 511; (800) 492-2400; (866) 511-8824; www.utahcommuterlink.com

Vermont

A road and short hike lead to spectacular views from Owl's Head Mountain in Groton State Forest.

CITIES

Bennington (L-3)

Tucked away in the southwest corner of the state, Bennington is Vermont's fifth-largest community and only a few miles away from both New York and Massachusetts. The area is packed with things to see and do both indoors and out. Climb 412 steps or ride the elevator to the top of the Bennington Battle Monument. Other historical landmarks include the Old First Church, Robert Frost's gravesite, the Park-McCullough Historic Estate, and covered bridges. The Benning-ton Museum has a collection of Americana art and a Grandma Moses gallery, and in nearby Arlington the Norman Rock-well Exhibition displays Rockwell's work in his hometown. The town's ideal location between the Taconic and Green Mountains makes for plentiful outdoor recreation. The Green Mountain National Forest has hiking trails for all levels, and in the winter, snowmobiling, cross-country skiing, and snowshoeing are popular pastimes. Bennington College also makes its home here.

Bennington Monument

Bennington Area Chamber of Commerce: (800) 229-0252; www.bennington.com/

Burlington (D-3)

The state's largest city rises from the forested hills along the eastern shores of Lake Champlain. In Greenmount Cemetery, a monument topped by a statue of Ethan

Church Street, Burlington

Allen marks the grave of the fiery patriot. His homestead has been preserved north of town. The Robert Hull Fleming Museum, Vermont's most comprehensive collection of art and anthropology, is affiliated with the University of Vermont and has exhibits on Vermont history and art, American Indian relics, and Oriental art. The Vermont State Craft Center is at the Church Street Marketplace, and in nearby Shelburne, the Shelburne Museum features fine and decorative arts. The area is also a natural playground with great golfing, tennis, sailing, hiking, biking, and skiing in the winter. Cross Lake Champlain to Port Kent, New York on the Burlington Ferry, or take a cruise aboard the *Spirit of Ethan Allen* and the *Northern Lights*.

Lake Champlain Regional Chamber of Commerce: (877) 686-5253; www.vermont.org

Capitol building

⊛ Montpelier (State Capital) (E-5)

Montpelier, the smallest capital city in America, is situated in the picturesque valley along the Winooski River. A statue of Ceres, Roman goddess of agriculture, tops the glittering gold-leafed dome of Vermont's state house, a Greek Revival building located in the heart of downtown Montpelier. The capitol building's interior is appointed with gleaming marble floors, spiral staircases, and intricate wood trim. The building is home to the House and Senate chambers, the country's oldest legislative chambers in original condition. The centrally located city is also known for its many institutions of higher education and its key position in the heart of Vermont ski country. Other noteworthy stops include the Vermont Historical Society Museum, the Thomas Waterman Wood Art Gallery, and Hubbard Park and Tower. For a sweet treat, visit Morse Farm Maple Sugarworks — run by Vermont's oldest maple family — for free sugarhouse tours, and tastings.

City of Montpelier: (802) 828-3237; www.montpelier-vt.org

Rutland (H-3)

Once an important headquarters of the marble industry, the state's third-largest city is now known for its central location amidst middle Vermont's ski resorts. Killington, one of New England's top ski destinations, is just 15 miles east of Rutland. For summer visitors, mountain biking and alpine slides are just a couple of offerings. In Rutland, the Chaffee Center for the Visual Arts has 10 galleries displaying and selling the works of local and regional artists as well as hosting occasional live performances. At the Norman Rockwell Museum of Vermont, more than 2,500 works — including all of the artists' famous *Saturday Evening Post* magazine covers — are on display. The Wilson Castle, noted for its fortress-like architecture, is another popular spot. The residence's 32 rooms feature 84 stained-glass windows, 13 fireplaces, and antique and museum-piece furnishings.

Rutland Region Chamber of Commerce: (802) 773-2747; www.rutlandvermont.com

---

SCENERY

Middlebury Gap (G-4)

Route 125, the Middlebury Gap Road, was established as a Vermont State Scenic Byway in 1987 and is a favorite driving route in fall, when the surrounding Green Mountain National Forest begins to change to its multi-hued coat. The drive from Hancock on the eastern edge of the national forest through the woods and wildness to the quaint town of Middlebury may be short, but it's packed with breathtaking scenery and lots to do.

Smuggler's Notch (D-4)

Smuggler's Notch Road, an 18-mile stretch of Route 108 from Stowe to Jeffersonville, takes drivers through part of Smuggler's Notch State Park and Mt. Mansfield State Forest's lush forests and large rock outcroppings. There are multiple scenic pullouts and parking areas along this state-designated byway, which, as with many of Vermont's scenic routes, is especially dramatic in fall when the leaves take on bivrant colors. During the winter, this steep, winding road isn't plowed and becomes impassable for vehicles, but skiers come via alternate routes to cross-country and downhill ski at Smuggler's Notch Resort.

Vermont 100 (M-3)

Tucked along the eastern side of the Green Mountains is SR 100, a winding two-lane road that has evolved from cow paths and coach roads. This 210-mile route winds back and forth from Stamford on the Vermont-Massachusetts border all the way up to Newport on the U.S.-Canada border. The road passes farms and churches and travels through villages, orchards, mountain gaps, and some of the state's most picturesque scenes. Making this trip during the first two weeks in October gives drivers a front-row seat for fall foliage.

- **Cavendish Road** (I-5)

  Drive the seven miles of Cavendish Road (Route 131) and follow along the Black River and Hawks Mountain for views from numerous pullouts and great fishing along the riverbanks.

- **Elmore State Park** (D-5)

  From atop the 55-foot fire tower on Elmore Mountain (2,608 feet), visitors can view all 500 acres of Lake Elmore below and, in the distance, Mt. Mansfield and the Green Mountains. The view is worth the family-friendly 1.25-mile hike to the tower.

- **Groton State Forest** (E-6)

  Though you can't drive to the summit, the view from atop Owl's Head Mountain in this state forest is one of the most-photographed in central Vermont. The short but steep hike to the top shows off scenes of Spruce Peak, Camel's Hump, Kettle Pond, and other natural features.

- **Hubbard Park & Tower** (G-8)

  Views of Montpelier are to be had from atop the 54-foot observation tower in Hubbard Park, a 185-acre park that includes seven miles of hiking trails, picnic areas, and a pond.

- **Mt. Philo** (E-3)

  Awe-inspiring views of the Lake Champlain Valley and the Adirondack Mountains unfold from the mountaintop overlook in Mt. Philo State Park, Vermont's oldest. The overlook is accessible by car via a narrow, steep road (not suitable for campers and trailers).

Mt. Philo

▶ **HERITAGE**

Bennington Battle Monument (L-2)

Every year on August 16th, Vermont celebrates a holiday honoring the Revolutionary War Battle of Bennington. Near this site in 1777 Brigadier General John Stark and American troops defeated two British detachments in a key victory. Today, the battle is commemorated by a 306-foot blue-gray magnesian limestone monument, which was completed and dedicated in 1891. Visitors can ride an elevator up to the observation deck for views of the valleys and hills of Vermont, New York, and Massachusetts. The monument grounds are also home to several other statues and monuments, including a granite statue of Seth Warner, commander of the Green Mountain Boys, and a large granite boulder and bronze table dedicated to General Stark and the 1,400 New Hampshire men involved in the battle. Open mid-April through October.

(802) 447-0550;
www.dhca.state.vt.us/HistoricSites/html/
bennington.html

Hildene (K-3)

The summer home of Abraham Lincoln's oldest son, Robert Todd Lincoln, Hildene is a 412-acre estate with a 24-room Georgian manor house that was held in the family until 1975. The estate, which is located just off Vermont's historic Route 7A, also includes a carriage barn, formal gardens, and nature trails. The Georgian Revival-style home was completed in 1905, and Lincoln lived there for 21 years. Lincoln named his new home Hildene, meaning "hill" and "valley." The residence's elegant rooms contain many of the family's original furnishing, eight fireplaces, superb architectural details, and a 1,000-pipe organ, installed in the entrance hall as a gift to Lincoln's wife Mary in 1908 (today it's played for every tour). Visitors can take house tours of Hildene from May through the end of October and cross-country ski the walking trails during the winter months.

(802) 362-1788; www.hildene.org

President Calvin Coolidge State Historic Site/Plymouth Notch Historic District (I-4)

This rural Vermont village has remained practically unchanged since 1923 and is the birthplace and boyhood home of Calvin Coolidge, the 30th president of the United States. It was here that Coolidge received word of the death of President Harding and was sworn in by his father, a notary public, in the family homestead at 2:47 a.m. on August 3, 1923. The site includes the homes of Coolidge's family and neighbors, the community church, a cheese factory, a one-room schoolhouse, and a general store. All structures have been carefully preserved, many with their original furnishings. The president is one of seven generations of Coolidges buried in the town cemetery. The homestead and Plymouth Notch are open late May to October. The site's office, located in the Aldrich House, is open year-round and has exhibits for winter visitors.

(802) 672-3773; www.historicvermont.org/coolidge

Shelburne Museum (D-2)

Located just south of Burlington, the Shelburne Museum is Vermont's largest museum and home to one the nation's leading collections of American folk art, tools, toys, decorative arts, quilts, textiles, and paintings (by Degas, Manet, and Monet to name a few). The museum's 37 galleries and historic exhibition buildings span four centuries of history and are set up like a village on 45 acres of land. Special structures include a lighthouse, round barn, two-lane covered bridge, steam locomotive, vintage 1920s carousel, general store, and the restored 220-foot steamboat *Ticonderoga*, a National Historic Landmark. There are also five heritage gardens, a café, and a store. Daily hands-on craft workshops for the kids are offered in the summer. The museum is open early May through October.

Shelburne Museum

(802) 985-3346; www.shelburnemuseum.org

OUTDOORS

Green Mountain National Forest (G-4)

This expansive national forest's almost 400,000 acres run from the Massachusetts border north for 100 miles up to the Appalachian Gap, stretching nearly two-thirds of the length of Vermont. The national forest was established in 1932 after uncontrolled logging, fire, and flooding began to destroy the state's forests. Today, more than 70 million people live within a day's drive of this natural treasure, which offers multiple outdoor recreation activities in all seasons. Hike along the same forest paths that Native Americans and French-Canadian fur trappers traveled, mountain bike the rock- and root-covered 19th-century carriage paths, ski some of the state's finest slopes and cross-country trails, fish the forest's many ponds and brooks, or just enjoy a leisurely scenic drive. Wildlife viewing, picnicking, camping, canoeing, and fall foliage-viewing are also popular pastimes.

Camping

(802) 747-6700; www.fs.fed.us/r9/gmfl/

Killington (H-4)

Vermont has more ski resorts than any other New England state. This premier destination offers seven mountains, 200 trails, 31 lifts, and 87 miles to ski, snowboard, snowshoe, snowmobile, and snowtube. The season is long, usually running from mid-November to Memorial Day, so there's plenty of time to explore all those trails. The average snow base ranges from 18-52 inches from both the resort's extensive snow-making system — one of the country's best because of a connection to the Woodward Reservoir — and more than 250 inches of annual snowfall. Non-

skiers find plenty to do between ice skating, sleigh rides, snowmobile tours, indoor rock climbing, shopping, and movies.

(800) 621-6867; www.killington.com

Lake Champlain Bikeways (C-2)

This 1,400-mile network of bicycle routes in the Lake Champlain Valley of Vermont and parts of New York and Québec is a cyclist's haven. There are 35 loops and tours ranging from 10 to 60 miles in addition to the main 363-mile Champlain Bikeway, a route encircling the lake. The routes take riders past a rich array of natural, cultural, and historic sites while meandering along peaceful back roads and through quaint villages. There are plenty of places to stop and refuel or relax, whether it's for a couple of hours or for the night. There are also convenient access points to and from the route via passenger rail lines and ferry crossings. Some of North America's best biking can be done in this region.

www.champlainbikeways.org

Underhill State Park (D-4)

Hiking up to the state's highest point is no small feat. From the forests of Underhill State Park, the Halfway House Trail climbs 3.5 miles up to the Long Trail, which takes hikers a steep 1.2 miles up to "The Chin," the official summit of Mount Mansfield and Vermont's highest spot at 4,393 feet. From the top, enjoy excellent views of Vermont's Green Mountain range, Canada's Belvidere Mountain and Jay Peak to the north, New Hampshire's White Mountains to the east, and New York's Adirondack Mountains across Lake Champlain to the west. For a change of pace, take the 4.3-mile Sunset Ridge Trail down for spectacular views of the valley. There are four trails to the summit, and maps are available at the ranger station. Underhill State Park lies within Vermont's 34,000-acre Mt. Mansfield State Forest on the headwaters of Brown's River and near the Stowe ski area.

(802) 899-3022;
www.vtstateparks.com/htm/underhill.cfm

Local Color

🍴 **What to Eat**
Chicken pie. This simple dish of biscuits, chicken, and gravy, a standard feature of community suppers, is well-loved by Vermonters.

💲 **What to Buy**
Johnson woolen clothing. Icemen used to buy the pants because the weave is virtually waterproof. Clothes from Johnson Woolen Mills are still renowned for durability and practicality. A signature pattern is the red and black plaid.

❓ **What to Know**
Town meetings are still common in Vermont villages. Vermonters gather in their community halls and other places to hash out town issues.

Motorcycle Helmet Required? Yes, reflectorization required
Child Restraint Seat Required? Under age 8

Vermont Department of Tourism and Marketing: (800) 837-6668;
www.vermontvacation.com
Road Construction and Conditions: 511; (800) 429-7623;
www.aot.state.vt.us/travelinfo.htm; www.511vt.com

Virginia

Replicas of the Discovery, Godspeed, *and* Susan Constant *are moored at Jamestown.*

CITIES

Arlington *(D-15)*

Anchoring the west side of Memorial Bridge over the Potomac River from Washington, D.C., Arlington is located in the country's smallest county (Arlington Co.). Stroll through any of its five urban villages and discover multi-cultural neighborhoods, businesses, and museums.

Arlington National Cemetery

The county is most famous for Arlington National Cemetery, a military cemetery since the mid-1800s. The Tomb of the Unknowns and the gravesites for President John F. Kennedy, his wife Jacqueline Kennedy Onassis, and his brother Robert F. Kennedy are found here. There are more than 260,000 people buried at Arlington. It is also the site of Robert E. Lee's home of 30 years, Arlington House.

Arlington County Visitors Center: (703) 416-0784, (800) 677-6267; www.stayarlington.com

Charlottesville *(H-10)*

Established in 1762, Charlottesville was incorporated as an independent city in 1888. The 10.4 square miles that comprise the home of the University of Virginia remain independent of any county or other political subdivision. The city's downtown pedestrian mall features boutiques, restaurants, and lively outdoor entertainment like the Fridays After Five concerts. The university

University of Virginia rotunda

was founded by Thomas Jefferson, who laid out the grounds and designed its first building. Jefferson's home, Monticello, is nearby. It is the only house in the United States that is on the United Nations' World Heritage List. Close by are Ash Lawn-Highland, the 550-acre estate and home of his friend James Monroe; Michie Tavern (circa 1784) where Jefferson and Monroe would meet other friends; and Montpelier, James Madison's home. Children love the Virginia Discovery Museum. Adults can tour any number of nearby wineries.

Charlottesville/Albemarle Convention & Visitors Bureau: (434) 977-1783, (877) 386-1102; www.pursuecharlottesville.com

✪ Richmond *(State Capital) (J-14)*

Skyscrapers, antebellum homes, and the state capitol building stand together in graceful compatibility in this legendary city of the South. Its role as the capital of the Confederacy is commemorated at the White House of the Confederacy and the local home of Jefferson Davis. Among the area's many historical houses is Agecroft Hall, built in the late 15th century in England and moved in 1925 to Richmond. Valentine Richmond History Center contains an outstanding display of decorative arts depicting the life and styles of Richmond over the past 400 years. At Petersburg National

White House of the Confederacy

Battlefield, the longest siege in U.S. history took place when the Union Army surrounded the town for more than nine months in 1864-65.

Richmond Metropolitan Convention & Visitors Bureau: (888) 742-4666; www.visit.richmond.com

Roanoke *(K-6)*

Roanoke, nestled in the foothills of the Blue Ridge Mountains, is the chief industrial and commercial center of the southern Shenandoah Valley. The heart of the city is Market Square and the Roanoke Farmers' Market, which has been in operation since 1882. A restored warehouse on Market Square houses numerous cultural facilities including museums dedicated to art, history, and science. The city's long connection with railroading is celebrated at the Virginia Museum of Transportation. In addition to more than 40 pieces of rolling stock, the museum exhibits cars, carriages, and a large O-gauge model train layout. The O. Winston Link Museum exhibits Link's powerful photographs documenting the end of the steam railroad era. From the top of Mill Mountain, the illuminated Roanoke Star is visible from all over the city. Visit the Star's overlook for sweeping views of the entire Roanoke Valley.

Roanoke Valley Convention & Visitors Bureau: (800) 635-5535; www.visitroanokeva.com

SCENERY

Breaks Interstate Park *(B-5)*

This remote area near Breaks boasts a ravine so large it is called the "Grand Canyon of the South." Formed by the Russell Fork of the Big Sandy River, it is five miles long and one-quarter of a mile deep. The 4,600-acre park is shared with Kentucky and also offers spectacular views of its sister state.

Great Falls Park *(p. 123, E-3)*

Near McLean, visitors watch in awe as the Potomac River plunges over a series of precipices, descending 76 feet over the course of 3,500 feet. The Potomac flows through a series of vertical, jagged rocks and continues through a narrow gorge, named Great Falls by early colonists, creating a spectacular natural environment only 14 miles from Washington, D.C.

Skyline Drive

Skyline Drive *(F-11)*

Straddling the Blue Ridge Mountains, this drive winds through 105 miles of Shenandoah National Park. The 35-mile-per-hour speed limit affords opportunity to see many sights along the road. Seventy-five overlooks offer views of the Shenandoah Valley to the west of and the rolling Piedmont country to the east.

- ● **Albemarle County** *(G-10)*
  Mountain ranges in this part of Virginia's horse country are so blue they look unreal.

- ● **Belle Isle State Park** *(I-17)*
  Near Lively, scan the skies for tundra swans and a variety of other migratory birds.

- ● **Great Dismal Swamp National Wildlife Refuge** *(M-17)*
  One of the last large wilderness areas on the eastern seaboard is found near Suffolk.

- ● **Grundland Creek Park** *(L-17)*
  Visitors often get lost in the heavens at one of the Hampton Park District's stargazing programs.

- ● **Virginia Beach** *(p. 117, L-10)*
  Considered a terrific bathing beach, this is also a whale-watcher's wonderland, with common sightings of juvenile humpback whales and fin whales.

Virginia Beach

HERITAGE

America's Historic Triangle (K-16)

This triangle of historically significant sites (Williamsburg, Jamestown, and Yorktown) explores four centuries of history in the United States. At Williamsburg, once the fashionable capital of England's Virginia Colony, it is possible to see and explore colonial Virginia by walking among recreated shops and restored homes, riding in carriages, and even visiting the Governor's Palace, all staffed by costumed interpreters. The first settlement on the mainland has been reconstructed in Jamestown, with replicas of the three ships *Discovery, Godspeed*, and *Susan Constant*, which carried colonists to the New World. The triangle also includes Yorktown Battlefield, where Lord Cornwallis surrendered to General George Washington in 1781.

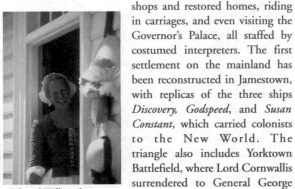
Colonial Williamsburg

(800) 368-6511; www.visitwilliamsburg.com, www.nps.gov/colo

Central Virginia Trail (G-14)

Trace historic campaigns of the Civil War by following any of five dedicated driving routes found throughout Virginia. In all, there are more than 250 sites to see, each telling stories through photographs, battle maps, and re-enactors. The Central Virginia Trail, for example, heeds the Yankee battle cry "On to Richmond." Portions of four major battlefields are maintained at Fredericksburg and Spotsylvania National Military Park, located west of I-95 on SR 3. The trail also passes close by Marye's Heights in Chancellorsville and through the Wilderness, where many believe the Union's Overland Campaign began in earnest. Other trails include the Northern Virginia Trail, the Southside Trail, the Valley & Mountains Trail, and the Tidewater Civil War Trail, which includes an account of the battle of the ironclads. Each site is car-accessible.

(804) 786-2051, (888) 248-4592; www.civilwartraveler.com, www.virginia.org

Monticello (H-11)

Walk the grounds lovingly cultivated by Thomas Jefferson at his mountaintop plantation. Jefferson, author of the Declaration of Independence and the Statute of Virginia for Religious Freedom, third president of the United States, and founder of the University of Virginia, served his country for more than five decades. Jefferson never completed Monticello, though he worked on it for more than 50 years until his death on July 4, 1826. The Roman neo-classic 43-room house with 11,000 square feet of living space is often referred to as "an essay in architecture." Sixty percent of the furnishings are original to the house; the remainder is of the same period. The eight acres of fruit trees and fruit-bearing shrubs in the garden are still called "the fruitery," just as Jefferson named it.

(434) 984-9822; www.monticello.org

Monticello

OUTDOORS

Appalachian Trail

Appalachian Trail (G-10)

More than 100 miles of the historic Appalachian Trail cut through Shenandoah National Park, many of them riding the crest of the Blue Ridge Mountains. At every point along the way, visitors are reminded of the majesty of the nation's great hardwood forests. Hikers refer to the trail as the "A.T" and it challenges short-term hikers, section-hikers, and through-hikers alike. The A.T. crosses the serpentine Skyline Drive 28 times, providing links to other areas and to supplies. The scenery is rewarding, with mountain streams, shimmering cascades, and great valleys like Big Meadows, which is filled with native grasses and plants. There are also views of a few of the remaining structures of the old mountain families.

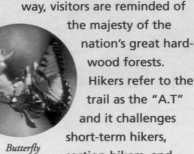
Butterfly

(304) 535-6331; www.nps.gov/appa

Scenic overlook

Assateague Island National Seashore (H-20)

For the uninitiated, surf fishing on this barrier island starts with demonstrations by National Park Service rangers (in summer months). The NPS provides the necessary gear or visitors can bring their own. It is one of the many interpretive programs offered on this island, which is famous for the annual wild pony swim to its sister island, Chincoteague. While summer flounder may be the catch of the inlets, on the beaches, surf fishing snares striped bass and red drum. Four-wheel drive vehicles with an off-road permit are allowed on the beach. With a fishing permit from the Visitor Center, visitors and their cars can stay on the beach overnight.

Assateague Island

Wild ponies

(757) 336-6577; www.nps.gov/asis

Virginia Creeper National Recreation Trail (D-6)

A rail-to-trail conversion near Abingdon, the Virginia Creeper got its name from locomotives that once strained along the area's steep grades. Visitors can walk, bike, or ride horses through 34 miles of breathtaking scenery. Nothing motorized is allowed on the trail. Originally a Native American footpath, the trail was used by early pioneers and reportedly by Daniel Boone as he forged trails to the west. Often referred to as one of the most beautiful trails in North America, the trail features 100 trestles and bridges, sharp curves, and scenery that surprises at each turn.

(276) 676-2282, (800) 435-3440; www.abingdon.com/tourism

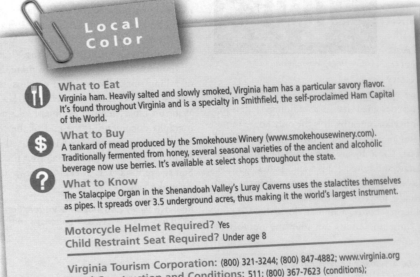

Local Color

What to Eat
Virginia ham. Heavily salted and slowly smoked, Virginia ham has a particular savory flavor. It's found throughout Virginia and is a specialty in Smithfield, the self-proclaimed Ham Capital of the World.

What to Buy
A tankard of mead produced by the Smokehouse Winery (www.smokehousewinery.com). Traditionally fermented from honey, several seasonal varieties of the ancient and alcoholic beverage now use berries. It's available at select shops throughout the state.

What to Know
The Stalacpipe Organ in the Shenandoah Valley's Luray Caverns uses the stalactites themselves as pipes. It spreads over 3.5 underground acres, thus making it the world's largest instrument.

Motorcycle Helmet Required? Yes
Child Restraint Seat Required? Under age 8

Virginia Tourism Corporation: (800) 321-3244; (800) 847-4882; www.virginia.org
Road Construction and Conditions: 511; (800) 367-7623 (conditions); (800) 578-4111; www.511virginia.org

Washington

North Cascades National Park preserves a rugged landscape.

CITIES

⊛ Olympia *(State Capital) (H-6)*

One of the most beautiful state capitals, Olympia sits on an arm of Puget Sound, with views of Mount Rainier and the Olympic Mountains. A stop at the impressive legislative building on the 35-acre Capitol Campus is a must. Stroll among Japanese cherry trees and flower gardens that include a reproduction of Copenhagen's famous Tivoli fountain, or visit the state conservatory. Exhibits of Washington history, forestry, and art are found displayed in the State Capital Museum. Visit Percival Landing boardwalk at Budd Inlet and the farmers' market. Run, bike, sail, and swim at Capitol Lake Park.

Olympia, Lacey, Tumwater Visitor & Convention Bureau: (360) 704-7544, (877) 704-7500; www.visitolympia.com

San Juan Islands Archipelago *(C-5)*

This collection of 172 named islands, and hundreds more unnamed, in the Salish Sea just north of Puget Sound is a wonderland of sailing, kayaking, whale watching, sport fishing and golf. The San Juans are home to hundreds of great scuba diving spots including the underwater marine reserves of Fort Casey and Deception Pass state parks. At San Juan Island National Historical Park on San Juan Island there are two partially reconstructed 1860s camps, one American and one English, with scenic hiking trails. Visit the information center and Whale Museum in Friday Harbor. Lopez Island is slow and friendly, with a great Perimeter Loop 32-mile road and whale viewing. Orcas Island has a charming village, arts and crafts galleries, views, lakes, waterfalls, campgrounds, a nature sanctuary, and excellent sea kayaking.

San Juan Islands Visitors Bureau: (888) 468-3701; www.visitsanjuans.com

Seattle *(F-7)*

This lively, cosmopolitan city, with its incomparable panorama of mountains, forests, and the islands of Puget Sound, is known for its espresso, brewpubs, seafood, and outdoor adventure. Shake off the morning fog with a hot latte, then descend below the city streets for a Seattle Underground Tour. Pike Place Market is famous for its fishmongers, who toss around the catch of the day for cheering spectators, but local vendors selling fresh produce and gift items like all-natural handmade soap also draw crowds. Seattle is equidistant from London and Tokyo. Influences from both and points in between can be found in the city's architecture, arts, and international attitude.

Seattle's Convention & Visitors Bureau: (206) 461-5888; www.visitseattle.org

Spokane *(F-19)*

Originally a fur trading center, Spokane was settled in 1872 and suffered a devastating fire not long afterward. Today its charm is evident in the fact that it is the smallest city to have ever hosted a World's Fair. The event took place in the 100-acre Riverfront Park, where visitors can now take a gondola ride high above Spokane Falls, ride the original 1909 Looff Carousel, or catch the latest IMAX feature. Those with a green thumb will be partial to the gardens in Manito Park or the annual Lilac Festival. The Spokane River Centennial Trail, which begins at the confluence of the Spokane and Little Spokane Rivers, is a haven for runners, walkers, and cyclists. Numerous fine wineries dot the surrounding countryside.

Spokane Regional Convention & Visitors Bureau: (509) 747-3230; www.visitspokane.com

Downtown Spokane

Walla Walla *(K-17)*

This pleasant college town takes its euphonious name from a Native American word meaning "many waters." Enhanced by well-cultivated parks and trees, Walla Walla offers a welcome respite from the monotonous landscape of much of eastern Washington. It's set against the backdrop of the Blue Mountains and surrounded by vineyards, wheat fields, and horse ranches. Stroll through the beautifully restored historic downtown or visit the Fort Walla Walla Museum Complex, which preserves original and reconstructed pioneer buildings and historic agricultural tools and machinery. Kirkman House (1880) has period furnishings and interesting architectural details. West of the city, the Whitman Mission National Historic Site presents the story of Marcus and Narcissa Whitman, who operated a mission on the Oregon Trail from 1836 to 1847.

Tourism Walla Walla: (877) 998-4748; www.wallawalla.org

SCENERY

Cascade Loop Scenic Highway *(B-8)*

This 440-mile loop in north-central Washington (SR 20, SR 525, US 2, and US 97) traverses magnificent areas: the San Juan Islands of Puget Sound, the green foot-hills and icy glaciers of Cascade Mountains Park, and the vast Upper Columbia River Valley. Some mountain passes are closed in winter.

Dry Falls Dam *(F-14)*

Before the last ice age, the Columbia River thundered over the giant Dry Falls with 40 times the volume of Niagara Falls. Powerful glacial meltwaters slowly etched out the patterns that make up the three-and-a-half-mile expanse of 400-foot-plus cliffs in Coulee City.

● **Columbia River Gorge Scenic Byway** *(M-9)*
This stretch along the Washington-Oregon border traverses thick forests and has spectacular viewpoints of sparkling waterfalls and Columbia River windsurfers.

● **Mount Baker Highway** *(B-7)*
Route 542 begins just east of Bellingham and climbs to Artist Point, the photogenic sight of Mount Shuksan reflected in the still waters of Picture Lake.

Mount St. Helens

● **Mount St. Helens National Volcanic Monument** *(J-7)*
Since its dramatic 1980 eruption, Mount St. Helens has been one of America's most famous volcanoes. Great viewpoint: Coldwater Ridge Visitor Center off SR 504.

● **Olympic National Park/ Hurricane Ridge** *(E-5)*
Named for its sometimes severe winter weather, Hurricane Ridge offers an incredible view of distant peaks and glaciers, even Vancouver Island on a clear day.

● **Steptoe Butte** *(H-19)*
This thimble-shaped natural monument of quartzite soars 3,612 feet above southeast Washington's flat lands.

Palouse Hills near Steptoe Butte

HERITAGE

Fort Vancouver National Historic Site (M-6)

The state's oldest non-American Indian settlement, Fort Vancouver was the western headquarters of the Hudson's Bay Company. The site was developed by the British trading company in 1825 along the banks of the Columbia River, and was overseen by Dr. John McLoughlin. Today the site contains several reconstructed buildings, including a fur warehouse, the bakehouse, and a Native American trade shop, all enclosed by a 15-foot-high palisade. The buildings have been furnished with period pieces and arranged to look as they did in the mid-1800s. Special events honoring the fort's British origins are held year-round. To commemorate Queen Victoria's birthday in May, volunteers and staff dress in period costume, fly the Union Jack over the fort, dance, and play music. Throughout the year park staff lead hourly guided tours.

(360) 816-6230; www.nps.gov/fova

Fort Vancouver National Historic Site

Seattle Underground Tours (p. 122, K-2)

This fun 90-minute tour is led by an informative guide seven days a week and provides a history of a three-block area where the street level was raised from eight to 35 feet after the Seattle fire of 1889. The tour travels along today's sidewalks in Seattle's old Pioneer Square, a 30-block National Historic District, to the 1890s sidewalks below where many storefronts and some interiors remain intact. The guide entertains visitors with punchy historical commentary about the more colorful events and characters that shaped Seattle's history. Discover why the invention of the modern toilet was a particularly big deal in Seattle. Find out the story behind the term Skid Road (Skid Row), which was coined in this neighborhood.

(206) 682-4646; www.undergroundtour.com

Yakama Nation Cultural Heritage Center (J-12)

Located on the ancestral grounds of the Yakama's 1.4 million-acre reservation in south-central Washington, this museum and cultural center tells the story of the Plateau People — the Yakamas. Learn how these Native Americans are both preserving their culture and adapting to current society. Explore various history and art exhibits or attend a Yakama cultural event at the center, a place that has become a major focal point of activity for the Yakama people. Less than five miles away in the town of Toppenish, visitors can investigate other Old West history on a tour of downtown's 55 murals depicting scenes of railroading, rodeos, farming, aviation events, and various historical events.

(509) 865-2800; www.yakamamuseum.com

OUTDOORS

Lake Chelan Ferry to Stehekin (E-13)

About three hours east of Seattle, board the *Lady of the Lake* passenger ferry near Chelan to escape the eastern Washington desert terrain and enter the gateway to

Mountain biking

densely forested and abundantly glaciated North Cascades National Park. The bustling small town of Stehekin sits at the head of Lake Chelan, which is 50.5 miles long and occupies the deepest gorge in the United States. Trails accommodate day-hikers, two-mile-loop enthusiasts, and backcountry experts. Mountain bikers, horseback riders, and cross-country skiers head up the Stehekin Valley, while anglers and rafters take to the streams and the big lake itself. In Stehekin, rent equipment or find an outfitter to guide your trip.

(800) 424-3526; www.lakechelan.com

Mt. Rainier National Park (H-9)

Mount Rainier, the tallest mountain in Washington's Cascade Range, dominates the horizon from as far away as 100  miles. Glaciers flow downward from Columbia Crest, spilling over rocks and cliffs. Old-growth forests cover the valley below, and alpine meadow flowers bloom in summer. The park offers about 240 miles of

Hiking in Mt. Rainier National Park

trails that lead into the wilderness. Serious trekkers can tackle the 93-mile Wonderland Trail. It circles the mountain, passing through every major life-zone in the park. A shorter, 18-mile section of the Wonderland Trail between Stevens Canyon Road and the White River entrance appeals to those who want to experience the same variety of terrain without spending two weeks on the trail. In winter, snowshoeing and cross-country skiing are popular.

(360) 569-2211; www.nps.gov/mora

San Juan Islands (C-6)

The San Juan Islands, accessible by ferry off Washington's northwest coast, are home to three resident pods of orcas (killer whales). Numerous charter companies in Friday Harbor give visitors close-up views of some of these 88 or 89 whales, which are most likely to be spotted from May through September. Another terrific way to experience the Pacific Northwest water and shoreline is by kayak. Various outfitters in Friday Harbor rent kayaks and lead tours, where paddlers might see bald eagles, seals, and the occasional whale. Washington State Ferries run from Anacortes to the San Juan Islands. Other ferry services depart from Seattle, Bellingham, Port Angeles, Port Townsend and Everett.

(888) 468-3701; www.visitsanjuans.com

Hiking along the coast

Local Color

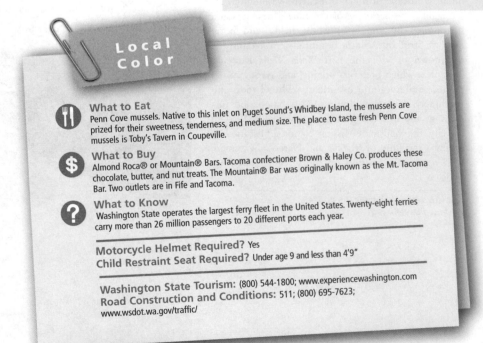

What to Eat
Penn Cove mussels. Native to this inlet on Puget Sound's Whidbey Island, the mussels are prized for their sweetness, tenderness, and medium size. The place to taste fresh Penn Cove mussels is Toby's Tavern in Coupeville.

What to Buy
Almond Roca® or Mountain® Bars. Tacoma confectioner Brown & Haley Co. produces these chocolate, butter, and nut treats. The Mountain® Bar was originally known as the Mt. Tacoma Bar. Two outlets are in Fife and Tacoma.

What to Know
Washington State operates the largest ferry fleet in the United States. Twenty-eight ferries carry more than 26 million passengers to 20 different ports each year.

Motorcycle Helmet Required? Yes
Child Restraint Seat Required? Under age 9 and less than 4'9"

Washington State Tourism: (800) 544-1800; www.experiencewashington.com
Road Construction and Conditions: 511; (800) 695-7623; www.wsdot.wa.gov/traffic/

West Virginia

This mile-long steel bridge spans the New River Gorge.

TRAVEL GUIDE | West Virginia

CITIES

Beckley (H-5)

In a state where proximity to rivers and rafting is paramount, Beckley is in the heart of it all, close to put-in sites for the New and Gauley rivers. It's also close to a number of state parks and resorts. Before river rafting, Beckley was known for its production of "smokeless" bituminous coal. Learn about the coal miner's life at the Exhibition Coal Mine, with "man-car" trips through 1,500 feet of underground passages in a former coal mine as well as tours of the coal miner's and superintendent's houses. Tamarack: The Best of West Virginia features a 200-seat theater; homestyle foods at a restaurant managed by the Greenbrier Resort; retail space with shops selling glass, handcrafted furniture and quilts; and craftspeople demonstrating fiber art, pottery, and blacksmithing. Hiking trails surround the center.

Tamarack Art Center

Southern West Virginia Convention & Visitors Bureau:
(304) 252-2244, (800) 847-4898; www.visitwv.com

✪ Charleston (State Capital) (F-4)

The state capital bills itself as the most northern of Southern cities and the most southern of Northern cities. It is also the state's cultural center with art galleries, theaters, a symphony, and a children's museum. The area is a center of glassmaking; factories offer tours daily. One of the largest enclosed downtown shopping malls, Charleston Town Center sells quilts, outdoor gear, and West Virginia items. At Avampato Discovery Museum, visitors can see a daily planetarium show, check out the traveling exhibits at the Art Museum, and try one or more of the 50-plus interactive exhibitions in the Science Gallery. The South Charleston Mound, a first-century Adena Indian mound, stands 175 feet high and 35 feet wide. It was first excavated by the Smithsonian Institution in 1883.

Charleston Convention & Visitors Bureau:
(800) 733-5469; www.charlestonwv.com

Huntington (F-2)

On the banks of the Ohio River at the borders of Kentucky, Ohio, and West Virginia, Huntington was established as a railroad hub between the East Coast and Midwest. The city's restored Victorian railroad depot now contains shops. Sternwheelers still ply the river on sightseeing excursions. Vintage radios from the '20s through the '50s as well as hi-fi sets, ham radios, and antique computers are on display at the Museum of Radio & Technology. For a fast ride on one of two wooden roller coasters or 16 other major thrill rides, Camden Park, West Virginia's only amusement park, is just the ticket. Slow up the pace to experience Appalachian farm life at Heritage Farm Museum and Village, a museum and re-created village of 12 buildings, a steam tractor display, sawmill, and blacksmith shop.

Cabell-Huntington Convention & Visitors Bureau:
(800) 635-6329; www.wvvisit.org

Wheeling (A-6)

The first capital of West Virginia extended the right to vote to Confederate General Thomas "Stonewall" Jackson's men. That decision cost Wheeling its capital status, as West Virginia was a Union state. Today, the city retains a Victorian-era look and offers shopping and various entertainment venues. To check out demonstrations of weaving and other crafts, visit the Wheeling Artisan Center, where local craftspeople display glass, pottery, and paintings and offer shows of their work. Just north of downtown, the streets of Victorian Old Town's national historic district are lined with grand Victorian homes. Many are open for tours from May through December. Trace the history of West Virginia — the only state that was created out of the Civil War — at Independence Hall Civil War Historic Site and Museum.

Wheeling Convention & Visitors Bureau: (800) 828-3097;
www.wheelingcvb.com

Charleston

SCENERY

Highland Scenic Highway (G-7)

Cutting through the Monongahela National Forest west from Richwood on SR 39 east to US 219, the 43 miles of this scenic road through the Allegheny Highlands rise in elevation from 2,325 feet to more than 4,500 feet. At the junction of Route 39/55 and Route 150, the Cranberry Mountain Nature Center features programs on topics such as birds of prey and forest ecology. Continuing on SR 150, the drive passes by the bogs of Cranberry Glades Botanical Area and the black bear sanctuary of Cranberry Wilderness.

Highland Scenic Highway

The New River Gorge (G-5)

Begin a loop tour at Canyon Rim Visitor Center on US 19 just north of Fayetteville to learn how nature carved this beautiful gorge. A boardwalk descends into the gorge with platforms offering views of the area's best-known landmark: the mile-long steel arch bridge that spans the gorge. Continue south on US 19 to Glen Jean exit to the Grandview Visitor Center, the highest point in the park at 1,400 feet above the river. At the Sandstone Falls Overlook on Route 20 you'll see an excellent view of the river-wide falls.

● **Coopers Rock State Forest** (B-9)
Popular with mountain bikers and hikers, the forest offers a beautiful overlook of the Cheat River Gorge. It's located off I-68 near Morgantown.

● **Harpers Ferry** (C-14)
Catch spectacular views of the Potomac and Shenandoah rivers.

Harpers Ferry

● **Hawks Nest State Park** (G-5)
Off US 60, near Ansted, view the New River from the edge of the gorge.

● **Point Pleasant** (E-2)
This scenic little town at the confluence of the Kanawha and Ohio rivers was the setting for the film *The Mothman Prophecies.*

● **Wheeling Suspension Bridge** (I-10)
Painted red, white, and blue, this was the first bridge over the Ohio River.

TRAVEL GUIDE | West Virginia

HERITAGE

Appalachian Crafts and Music (H-5)

Music and crafts are a major part of Appalachian heritage. In West Virginia, there are plenty of opportunities to sample the state's cultural history. One place to see it all is Tamarack: The Best of West Virginia, near Beckley. Here, local artisans demonstrate their crafts, such as textiles, stained glass, painting, woodworking, jewelry, and pottery. Six artists work on site every day. A fine arts gallery also displays artwork of West Virginians. At the Gov. Hulett C. Smith theater, performances are held every Sunday afternoon, often including mountain music. A food court operated by the West Virginia Greenbrier Resort features local cuisine.

(888) 262-7225; www.tamarackwv.com

Blenko Glass Factory and Museum (F-2)

More than 500 glass companies have operated in West Virginia. Several companies are still open and offer tours of their facilities. Here you'll find paperweights, sculptures, marbles, and glass beads, among other treasures. At Blenko Glass in Milton, a museum and a tour feature the hand-blown bottles, containers, vases, and mouth-blown sheet glass used in stained glass that are the 100-year-old company's specialties. A factory outlet occupies one floor of the Visitor Center, and another floor features specially designed stained glass. From an observation deck, visitors can view the artisans at work, from furnace to glass blower to finishing and cooling in special ovens.

Blenko Glass pitcher

(304) 743-9081; www.blenkoglass.com

Exhibition Coal Mine (H-5)

After the Civil War, railroads were built through the state to the Ohio River, and coal mining boomed. In 1913, a miner owed most of his average annual $737.62 wage to the coal company for housing, food, health care, and his own blasting powder. Miners labored in wet, dark, and dangerous conditions. The center of the former mining area is between Beckley and Bluefield. Former miners take visitors back 1500 feet along a real coal seam into a former mine at the Beckley Exhibition Coal Mine. A coal miner's home, superintendent's home, coal camp school, and coal camp church are also open for tours. Artifacts and vintage photos from early mining days are on exhibit in the museum. A gift shop on site sells coal jewelry and coal candy.

(304) 256-1747; www.beckleymine.com

Harpers Ferry (C-14)

Born as a Union state during the Civil War, West Virginia harbored many Confederate supporters, making it ripe for conflict. Historic sites are scattered across the state, but one of the most notable is Harpers Ferry. This is where John Brown seized the arsenal in an effort to free the slaves in 1859, a skirmish that fueled tensions in the years before the Civil War. It was also the site of the largest surrender of Union forces, in 1862. Learn more about Harpers Ferry history by taking a ranger-guided tour that focuses on themes such as John Brown's Raid, stories of Camp Hill, and Guns of Harpers Ferry. Visitors can tour the various museums at the national historic site, watch encampment groups that are often held here on weekends, hike the grounds, and listen to military band concerts.

(304) 535-6298; www.nps.gov/hafe

OUTDOORS

Greenbrier River Trail (F-8)

Hike, bike, or cross-country ski some or all of the 80 miles of the Greenbrier River Trail, a former track of the C&O Railway in the Greenbrier Valley. It runs adjacent to the Greenbrier River and is surrounded by the Allegheny Mountains, offering beautiful views all along. The trail begins at Cass Scenic Railroad State Park, passing by Seneca State Forest and Watoga State Park before ending in North Caldwell near Lewisburg. The trip runs through a number of small towns, such as Stony Bottom and Cloverlick, site of a restored depot. It also passes over numerous bridges and through the 511-foot Sharp's Tunnel, which dates from 1899, and the 402-foot Droop Mountain Tunnel, built in 1900. Services such as food and lodging are available along the route.

(800) 336-7009; www.greenbrierrivertrail.com

New and Gauley Rivers (I-6)

Rafting on the New River

Rapids that run from easy Class I and II to high-voltage Class V and V+ can be found on these two great rivers. Each season offers advantages, from the high spring flow through warm summer white water to the fully charged six-week fall drawdown of the Summersville Lake into the Gauley River. No wonder the International Rafting Federation held world white-water rafting championships here a few years ago. There are more than 20 rafting companies offering trips from half a day to three days. Despite its name, the New River is quite old, cutting a deep gorge that offers beautiful scenery and Class I-V rapids. The Gauley River, with rapids that range from Class II-V+ in spring and fall, invites thrill-seekers.

(800) 847-4898; www.visitwv.com

Oakhurst Links

Oakhurst Museum of Golf History (H-7)

Be really authentic and pick up a hickory-shafted club to swing at a gutta percha ball on the first organized golf club in the U.S., Oakhurst Links in White Sulphur Springs. Opened in 1884 by Russell Montague and several friends, it was played until about 1910, then restored and reopened to the public in 1994. Today, as then, a flock of sheep trims the course greens. Montague's home is now the Oakhurst Museum of Golf History, which features exhibits on the golf club and the famous Sam Snead, who hailed from the area. Golfers may reserve tee times from May to October on the historic course. Enthusiasts can even purchase a set of hickory-shafted clubs or replica gutta percha balls at the clubhouse.

(304) 536-1884; www.oakhurstlinks.com

Hikers take a break

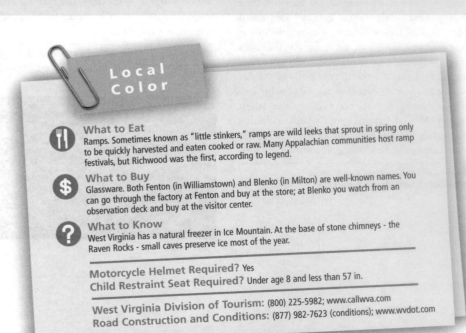

Local Color

What to Eat
Ramps. Sometimes known as "little stinkers," ramps are wild leeks that sprout in spring only to be quickly harvested and eaten cooked or raw. Many Appalachian communities host ramp festivals, but Richwood was the first, according to legend.

What to Buy
Glassware. Both Fenton (in Williamstown) and Blenko (in Milton) are well-known names. You can go through the factory at Fenton and buy at the store; at Blenko you watch from an observation deck and buy at the visitor center.

What to Know
West Virginia has a natural freezer in Ice Mountain. At the base of stone chimneys - the Raven Rocks - small caves preserve ice most of the year.

Motorcycle Helmet Required? Yes
Child Restraint Seat Required? Under age 8 and less than 57 in.

West Virginia Division of Tourism: (800) 225-5982; www.callwva.com
Road Construction and Conditions: (877) 982-7623 (conditions); www.wvdot.com

Wisconsin

The Quadracci Pavilion graces the Milwaukee Art Museum.

CITIES

Green Bay (J-13)

French explorer Jean Nicolet landed here in 1634 and established a trading post that came to be known as LaBaye. The British renamed the growing settlement Green Bay in the early 19th century. Today this port city, Wisconsin's oldest community, focuses on industry, wholesale distribution, and protecting the legacy of its heritage. Many visitors enjoy a few hours touring exhibits at the Oneida Nation Museum. The highlight is a walk through a reconstructed, full-size longhouse. At Heritage Hill State Historical Park, northeast Wisconsin's pioneer days are recalled by historic buildings representing four time periods spanning 1672-1905. No trip to Green Bay is complete without visiting the professional football shrine of Lambeau Field and the Packers Hall of Fame.

Lambeau Field, Green Bay

Packer Country Regional Tourism Office: (920) 494-9507, (888) 867-3342; www.packercountry.com

La Crosse (L-5)

After French explorers established a trading post at this spot where the Black and La Crosse rivers empty into the Mississippi, a settlement thrived as it became an important link to downriver ports. Now the city of La Crosse is known for the scenic bluffs and palisades that surround it. Enjoy the panorama from Grandad Bluff, 540 feet above the city, or cruise the river on the *La Crosse Queen*, the *Julia Belle Swain* (both double-deck sternwheelers), or the modern cruiser *Island Girl*. Hixon House, a 15-room mansion built in 1859, is furnished with many original Victorian and Oriental pieces. Many visitors take the tour at The City Brewery, whose water towers are painted to resemble a six-pack of beer.

Grandad Bluff, La Crosse

La Crosse Area Convention & Visitor's Bureau: (800) 658-9424; www.explorelacrosse.com

⊛ Madison (State Capital) (N-10)

Located on an isthmus between two lakes, the Wisconsin capital is a hub of culture, government, recreation, and industry. The white granite state capitol building, patterned after the national capitol, features a classic dome offering a view of surrounding countryside from an outdoor observation platform. Connected to the capital square by State Street, a vibrant pedestrian mall lined with cafés, restaurants, boutiques, and galleries. The flagship University of Wisconsin campus sprawls on hills overlooking Lake Mendota. A stop at the Memorial Union or Babcock Hall is rewarded with locally famous Babcock ice cream, produced on campus. Many area buildings were designed or inspired by Frank Lloyd Wright, such as the First Unitarian Church and the Monona Terrace Community & Convention Center. Visual and performing arts have a spacious home in the 400,000-square-foot Overture Center for the Arts.

Greater Madison Convention & Visitors Bureau: (800) 373-6376; www.visitmadison.com

Milwaukee (N-13)

Wisconsin's largest city, Milwaukee has a reputation for bratwurst and beer, but its German heritage is only one flavor in a complex metropolitan brew. The city has been a port of entry for many ethnicities and showcases its multicultural heritage with more than a dozen festivals, many held at lakeside Henry Maier Festival Park. These include Festa Italiana and Irish Fest, to name only two. (Summerfest is the biggest, but its focus is music.) Two popular tours, at the Harley-Davidson plant in Wauwatosa and the Allen-Edmonds shoe factory in Port Washington, highlight Milwaukee's manufacturing history. Cultural Milwaukee focuses on the soaring Santiago Calatrava-designed Quadracci Pavilion of the Milwaukee Art Museum but doesn't ignore the Betty Brinn Children's Museum, the Milwaukee Public Museum with its re-creation of streetscapes, and the Pabst Mansion. Visitors still intent upon sampling things German should stop by the Usinger's store, dine at Mader's (both located on Old World Third Street), or take one of three local brewery tours: Miller Brewing, Sprecher Brewing, or Lakefront Brewery.

Cinco de Mayo Festival, Milwaukee

Greater Milwaukee Convention & Visitors Bureau: (414) 273-3950, (800) 554-1448; www.visitmilwaukee.org

SCENERY

Lake Michigan Shoreline (B-13)

Door County

Door County is laced with country roads that show off the peninsula's natural beauty. One such road is Glidden Drive (County T) between Brauer and Whitefish Bay roads. The drive runs along the Lake Michigan shore, affording changing views of deep forest, sand dunes, and streams. One panoramic outlook over Lake Michigan includes a sand beach.

Trempealeau (K-5)

North of La Crosse, SR 35 curves west to the Mississippi river town of Trempealeau. While driving through this village perched high on rolling riverbank, look across the water for tree-covered Trempealeau Mountain. The meandering river is temporarily tamed by Lock and Dam No. 6. East of town, enjoy the prairie vistas. The drive around Trempealeau is one short section of the legendary Great River Road.

- ● **Bell Mound Overlook** (J-6)
  Between Black River Falls and Millston, Rest Area 54 off westbound I-94 provides a boardwalk up to a viewing platform from which you can see for miles out over rock towers and treetops in the Black River State Forest.

- ● **Blue Mound** (N-8)
  Drive out to Blue Mound State Park for vistas overlooking southwest Wisconsin's Driftless Area. Classic Wisconsin farmland ripples across rolling countryside at the foot of Blue Mound, the tallest hill in the southern half of the state.

- ● **Cranberry Marshes** (D-8)
  In the Manitowish Waters area, follow road signs to cranberry companies' marshes. The roads burst from beneath tree canopy to surprisingly wide-open expanses of marshland. Look closely for the cranberries.

Lake Superior

- ● **Lake Superior** (B-5)
  When paralleling the Lake Superior coast on SR 13, stop at the wayside west of Port Wing to walk right up to the wide expanse of water.

- ● **Mississippi Confluence** (O-5)
  From the Wisconsin Ridge campground in Wyalusing State Park, 500 feet above the surrounding countryside, watch the Wisconsin River flow into the Mississippi.

TRAVEL GUIDE Wisconsin

HERITAGE

George W. Brown Jr. Ojibwe Museum (E-8)

Ojibwe Indians have lived in northern Wisconsin since 1745. The Lac du Flambeau area (so-called by French fur traders who observed Ojibwe fishing at night by torchlight) is the center of Ojibwe culture and boasts two museums dedicated to teaching the heritage of this people. At the George W. Brown Jr. museum, a large diorama depicts Ojibwe life during the four seasons. A 22-foot dugout canoe, found underwater in 1980 and thought to be 180-280 years old, is on display, along with a seven-foot one-inch sturgeon speared in 1981. Visitors may participate in classes that teach Ojibwe arts and crafts such as making moccasins and birch bark baskets. Just outside the town of Lac du Flambeau, a recreated 18th-century Ojibwe village named Waswagoning occupies 20 acres on Moving Cloud Lake. By walking among the different structures, which include fish drying racks and a smokehouse, a vivid image of this way of life emerges.

Museum: (715) 588-3333
Waswagoning: (715) 588-2615; www.waswagoning.org;
www.ojibwe.com

Madeline Island Historical Museum

Madeline Island Historical Museum (B-6)

Board the ferry in Bayfield for a trip to the town of LaPointe, three miles offshore on Madeline Island. The largest isle of the Apostle Islands archipelago, it was named for the Ojibwe wife of prominent fur trader Michel Cadotte (her Ojibwe name was Equaysayway). Voyageurs, commercial fishermen, lighthouse keepers, missionaries, and vacationers have all lived on the Apostle Islands and left cultural legacies. The historical museum, which opened in 1958, preserves their history with permanent exhibits of Ojibwe artifacts, tools from the lumbering and maritime industries, and household and personal articles brought by missionaries. A more recent addition (finished in 1991) expands the presentation of island history with special temporary exhibits and a theater.

(715) 747-2415;
www.wisconsinhistory.org/madelineisland

New Glarus (O-9)

In 1845, 108 Swiss immigrants chose the rolling countryside of southern Wisconsin Territory for their new settlement because it closely resembled their old home in the canton of Glarus. Today New Glarus preserves Swiss traditions in its architecture, festivals, beer, and foods. Myriad shops line the chalet-crowded streets. Visitors sample baked goods, cheese, chocolates, and at the New Glarus Brewery, several seasonal brews. At the Swiss Historical Village, 14 buildings such as a Swiss bee house, settler's cabin, and one-room school house show how Swiss immigrants and pioneers settled the area. The Chalet of the Golden Fleece Museum, located in a mountain chalet, collects a farrago of items, Swiss and otherwise. Exhibits include Etruscan earrings and manuscripts of Gregorian chants as well as Swiss woodcarvings and an 18th-century tile stove. The town hosts annual celebrations such as Heidi Festival and Roger Bright Memorial Music Fest year-round.

New Glarus Chamber of Commerce & Tourist
Information: (608) 527-2095, (800) 527-6838;
www.swisstown.com

OUTDOORS

Door County (A-13)

Trails within Peninsula State Park and quiet farm roads provide bikers with miles of two-wheeled fun. For an easier ride, try the state park's Sunset Trail. Its 5.1 miles are covered with smooth gravel, and it remains fairly flat as it turns through several types of landscape, including marsh and hardwood forest. A quick .75-mile spur leads to Hidden Bluff and a nature center. More adventurous riders take on some 9 miles of off-road ruggedness. These trails hook up with back roads connecting the park with the town of Fish Creek. Outside the park, more back roads crisscross the peninsula and allow you to avoid traffic on SR 57 and SR 42. They roll past farms, cottages, and stands of trees that blaze brilliantly in autumn.

(920) 868-3258; www.wiparks.net

Northern Highland/American Legion State Forest (D-8)

In 1925 the state of Wisconsin set aside 225,000-some acres to protect the headwaters of the Flambeau, Wisconsin, and Manitowish rivers. The forest has become a haven hosting nearly two million people annually. Visitors come to swim, boat, and fish in nearly 900 lakes; bike 47 miles of mountain bike trails or hundreds of miles of logging roads; camp in developed sites or in the backcountry; and hike 39 miles of trails beneath the trees. Birders take note: nearly 73% of Wisconsin's total species count resides in this forest — 244 species total. Nesting pairs of loons are common. Watchful eyes may also spot rare wood turtles on the forest floor, Cooper's hawks in the sky, and otters or beavers in the swamps and streams. Winter visitors bring snowmobiles and cross-country skis.

(715) 385-2727; www.wiparks.net

Northwoods (D-5)

When the Northwoods lie hushed beneath a layer of snow, it's time to skim through the quiet on cross-country skis. The small town of Cable sits at the doorstep of the Chequamegon (shuh-WAH-muh-gun) – Nicolet National Forest, through which wind trails ranging from flat, short loops to longer, more challenging adventures, some as long as 42 kilometers. The Forest Service grooms the trails, usually for both skate and classic skiing. Several Cable ski shops offer rental equipment, and nearby towns such as Drummond also have gear available. Close by Cable is the Telemark Resort, which maintains 65 km of trails in 16 loops. One of North America's most prestigious ski marathons takes place here: the American Birkebeiner, 51 grueling kilometers between Cable and Hayward. When the race isn't running, anyone can ski the trails, which are punctuated by steep downhill stretches that test even the best skiers.

Cable Chamber of Commerce: (715) 798-3833,
(800) 533-7454; www.cable4fun.com
Cross Country Ski Northwest Wisconsin:
www.norwiski.com

Cross-country skiing

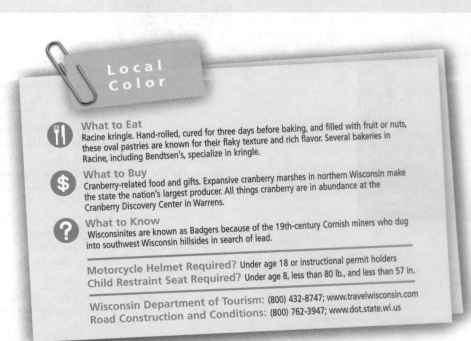

Wyoming

Pioneers headed west through Wyoming in the 1800s.

Casper (E-10)

Dinosaurs once roamed the center of Wyoming. In the mid-1800s, pioneer trails converged here, and Casper was established on the banks of the Platte River in the late 1800s. It is now Wyoming's second-largest city. The National Historic Trail Interpretive Center covers the history of the Oregon-California-Mormon-Pony Express Trails. About 40 miles outside Casper, pioneers carved their names into the granite of Independence Rock, marking their passage. Fort Caspar, a reconstructed site and museum, welcomed the pioneers, along with trappers and Native Americans. The town is named for Lt. Caspar Collins, who was killed during a battle near Ft. Caspar. Going back farther in time, step into the paths of giants at the Cottonwood Beach Dinosaur Trail footpath. North of the city lies the world's largest light oil field at the Teapot Dome Reserve. The North Platte River provides world-famous trout fishing holes, most notably Gray Reef.

Casper Area Convention & Visitors Bureau: (800) 852-1889; www.casperwyoming.info

Dancers at Cheyenne Frontier Days

✪ Cheyenne (State Capital) (H-13)

The capital of Wyoming, Cheyenne was first settled by men working on the Union Pacific Railroad and cattlemen. It's Wyoming's biggest city at just a tad more than 53,000 people. Every July, it hosts the largest outdoor rodeo, Cheyenne Frontier Days, dubbed the "Daddy of 'em All," with a Native American village featuring dancing, food and goods for sale, an old-fashioned Midway, parades, and music. The Old West Museum has exhibits from frontier days celebrations, as well as an impressive wagon collection. The Wyoming state capitol building shines with marble floors, carved woodwork throughout, stained glass, and wildlife displays. Other sites include the Cheyenne Depot Museum in Cheyenne Depot Square and the "Big Boy" steam engine, the world's largest steam locomotive.

Cheyenne Area Convention & Visitors Bureau: (800) 426-5009; www.cheyenne.org

Cody (B-7)

Founded by William "Buffalo Bill" Cody as a tourist town in 1895, the city of Cody lies just east of Yellowstone National Park. Frederic Remington,

Old Trail Town

Ulysses S. Grant, Annie Oakley, and Calamity Jane all stayed at Buffalo Bill's downtown Irma Hotel, named for his daughter. Mock gunfights are held nightly in the summer just outside the hotel, and there's a nightly rodeo in the summer at the city's edge. A one-hour Cody Trolley Tour provides a historic overview. The main attraction is the Buffalo Bill Historical Center, with five museums under one roof that encompasses 300,000 square feet. The five are the Cody Firearms Museum; the Whitney Gallery of Western Art; the Buffalo Bill Museum; the Plains Indian Museum; and the Draper Museum of Natural History. Other sights include Old Trail Town and western shops and restaurants in the quaint downtown.

Cody Country Chamber of Commerce: (307) 587-2777; www.codychamber.org

Jackson Hole (D-5)

Named both for an early fur trapper and for the valley bordered by mountain ranges known as a hole, this now-trendy town didn't have a permanent population until the 1890s when cattle ranchers arrived. The main business now is tourism. Jackson Hole lies at the doorstep of Grand Teton National Park with its abundance of wildlife, especially moose and elk. Hike around Jenny Lake, or camp, backpack, or climb one of the park's three peaks. There are also three major ski areas here that draw winter crowds to town. In fall and winter, the National Elk Refuge at the city limits is home to herds of the majestic animal. Many visitors pose under the famed antler

National Elk Refuge

arch in downtown Jackson Hole, made from the magnificent horns that the creatures shed. Outdoor enthusiasts can schedule float trips, pack trips, wagon rides, and fishing trips right here.

Jackson Hole Chamber of Commerce: (307) 733-3316; www.jacksonholechamber.com

Chief Joseph Scenic Highway (B-7)

Named for the 1880s-era Nez Percé chief, the 47-mile highway heads out of Cody up to the 8,048-foot-high Dead Indian Pass. It continues into Sunlight Basin through a series of switchbacks that provide beautiful views of the basin and Clarks Fork Canyon. The Clarks Fork River, which runs through the canyon, has been designated a Wild and Scenic River. At Sunlight Creek Bridge, you can stop for a view of the gorge.

Wind River Canyon (D-8)

The twelve miles of US 20 through the Wind River Canyon carve through eons of geologic time. Markers on the roadside date the cliffs on either side. The route snakes through the canyon floor, alongside the Wind River. The Crow people named the river, but when Lewis and Clark came in 1803, they named it Bighorn River. Thus, about one half-mile from the northern edge of the canyon, the river name officially changes to Bighorn River at a place called the Wedding of the Waters.

Wind River

Thunder Basin National Grassland (B-12)

A few miles north of Douglas on SR 59, the road stretches straight and flat, seemingly forever, into the grasslands. The horizon stretches so far that drivers can see rain approaching as darkened clouds move towards their vehicles. It's pure grass and sky.

● Pilot Butte Wild Horse Scenic Loop (L-6)

Start the 50-mile drive in either Green River off I-80 or Rock Springs at US 191. Some of the nearly 3,000 wild mustangs that still roam free in Wyoming may be spotted here.

Wild horses

● Signal Mountain Summit Road (D-5)

View the Grand Tetons, the valley, and Antelope Flats, and most of Grand Teton National Park from the 800-foot lookout.

● Snowy Range Scenic Byway (H-10)

Crossing the Medicine Bow Mountains in southeastern Wyoming, this two-lane road begins in sagebrush and quickly climbs until it runs next to the snow-covered 10,847-foot Snowy Range Pass and 12,013-foot Medicine Bow Peak. (The road is closed in winter.)

Snowy Range Scenic Byway

● Yellowstone Loop (B-2)

Numerous pullouts by geysers, mud pots, hot springs, and other thermal features, as well as the chance to spot bison, pronghorn, and elk, make the main national park road a scenic feast.

HERITAGE

Fort Laramie (F-13)

Fort Laramie symbolizes the history of westward expansion, serving first as a fur trading post, then as a supply point for Oregon Trail travelers, and finally as a military fort in the Great Sioux War. Costumed interpreters talk with visitors about the life of soldiers, women, trappers, and Native

Oregon Trail ruts

Americans who visited the fort. In Guernsey's trail ruts site, visitors can also follow in the footsteps and wagon wheel ruts of the estimated 300,000 pioneers who endured the Oregon Trail in the 1800s. At nearby Register Cliffs, pioneers carved their names and arrival dates in the sandstone.

(307) 777-6323; www.nps.gov/fola

Massacre Hill (B-10)

This site near Story commemorates the spot where Captain William J. Fetterman and 80 soldiers were killed in less than 30 minutes during an 1866 battle with a thousand Lakota, Cheyenne, and Arapahoe. The federal government was building a road in the middle of prime buffalo hunting territory, and a party that was cutting wood was attacked. Fetterman went to their rescue but was drawn into battle. Other nearby historic spots of the same era include the 1866 site of Fort Phil Kearny, the 1867 site of the Wagon Box fight, and Connor Battlefield historic site.

(307) 684-7629; www.philkearny.vcn.com

Petroglyph at Legend Rock

Thermopolis (D-8)

In 1993 dinosaur bones were found just outside Thermopolis. Visitors can join a dig, watch paleontologists at work in the lab, or just tour the museum at Wyoming Dinosaur Center. Hot Springs State Park, also in Thermopolis, was once a gathering spot for bison as well as American Indians. It features thermal pools where water springs forth at 135°F before emptying into cooling ponds. Boardwalks over the travertine terraces permit close-up views, and the state bathhouse features free 30-minute dips into a thermal pool. North of town near Hamilton Dome, climb next to Legend Rock petroglyphs carved into the red rock cliffs between A.D. 500 and the 19th century.

(307) 864-3192 or (877) 864-3192; www.thermopolis.com

OUTDOORS

Devils Tower National Monument (B-12)

Rock climbers have ascended this 1,267-foot-high granite monolith for 100 years. Climbers may ascend on their own or join a professional climbing outfit to tackle Devils Tower. Nonclimbers can watch or take a 1.3-mile hiking trail that curls around the monument. There are seven miles of trails throughout the park, all with opportunities for viewing birds, deer, and prairie dogs. At one time the rock was below the Earth's surface, but erosion left it exposed. Northern plains tribes called it Bear's Lodge, and American Indians consider it a sacred site. Out of respect for this tradition, the monument is closed to climbing during the month of June.

(307) 467-5283; www.nps.gov/deto

Devils Tower

Horsepack Trips

There's no shortage of horseback adventures in a quintessential Western state like Wyoming. Dude ranches dot the state, and outfitters in Grand Teton National Park and Yellowstone National Park can take equestrians out for an

Amazing vistas from the trails

hour, a day, or a week. The options in various towns like Jackson Hole and Cody include chuck wagon rides, covered wagon trips, mountain trails, and high desert paths. A typical expedition: Join a group from Dubois that packs through the range of Rocky Mountain bighorn sheep (visit the National Bighorn Sheep Interpretive Center) and up into grizzly bear territory at Togwotee Pass (9,658 feet high).

(307) 455-2556; www.duboiswyoming.org

Yellowstone National Park (B-5)

Join a Yellowstone Association Institute program for a day or a week to hike, view wildlife, and learn about the unique geology and ecology of the park. They

Old Faithful

are led by experts such as geologists, naturalists, and biologists who work in the park year-round and know where the wildlife roam. Lodging and Learning programs, geared towards adults and families, last about four days and cover topics such as animal tracking, exploring geysers and canyons, and watching for wolves, grizzlies, and other wildlife. In September, the Roosevelt Rendezvous covers four days of studying wildlife in the park with the experts.

(307) 344-2294;
www.yellowstoneassociation.org/institute/

Thermal pool

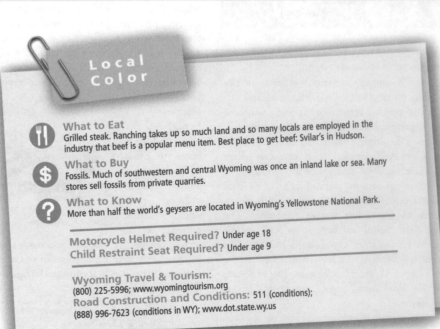

Local Color

🍴 **What to Eat**
Grilled steak. Ranching takes up so much land and so many locals are employed in the industry that beef is a popular menu item. Best place to get beef: Svilar's in Hudson.

$ **What to Buy**
Fossils. Much of southwestern and central Wyoming was once an inland lake or sea. Many stores sell fossils from private quarries.

? **What to Know**
More than half the world's geysers are located in Wyoming's Yellowstone National Park.

Motorcycle Helmet Required? Under age 18
Child Restraint Seat Required? Under age 9

Wyoming Travel & Tourism:
(800) 225-5996; www.wyomingtourism.org
Road Construction and Conditions: 511 (conditions);
(888) 996-7623 (conditions in WY); www.dot.state.wy.us

Washington, D.C.

A statue of George Washington is silhouetted in the rotunda of the U.S. Capitol.

There is little in any guidebook that prepares visitors for the grandeur that awaits in Washington, D.C. Located within the District of Columbia, it is a dynamic city with a penchant for change. As the capital of the United States, Washington is filled with government buildings, federal offices, and larger-than-life monuments.

The Thomas Jefferson Memorial, for example, shelters a bronze statue of the framer of the Declaration of Independence that is 19 feet high, sits on a six-foot pedestal, and weighs 10,000 pounds. The memorial itself is an open air design, a rotunda constructed of pillars and a dome. There is always a breeze at the Jefferson Memorial, a fitting tribute to a man who dedicated his life to the winds of change.

A stop at the Visitors Center in the Ronald Reagan Building will provide an overview of the city's history and help visitors get their bearings. Each season the nation's capital offers a different adventure for visitors.

AUTUMN

Exploring neighborhoods

Georgetown is one of the more famous of Washington's neighborhoods. Both escorted and self-guided tours are available of this 18th-century port that played an important role in the Underground Railroad. Today it is a fashionable address for many famous residents. Georgetown is filled with boutiques, restaurants, and with Georgetown University nearby, nightlife.

The Adams-Morgan neighborhood is an eclectic mix of international restaurants. Be sure to look up as many of the buildings are painted with murals.

Adams-Morgan neighborhood

Capitol tour?
Capital idea

The Capitol Guide Service provides guided tours of the Capitol that last only 45 minutes. Stops on the tour include the Rotunda, which is used for formal receptions and ceremonies, and the National Statuary Hall, which includes two statues of distinguished citizens from each state. Tours are free. Tickets can be picked up on the same day as the tour. Distribution begins at 9 AM at First St. and Independence Ave. Open 9 AM to 4:30 PM daily except for Thanksgiving and Christmas. For information, call (202) 225-6827.

Also in the autumn:

- Kennedy Center Prelude Festival
- Marine Corps Marathon

Action: See the monuments along the Tidal Basin from a paddleboat. Paddleboat rental information is available at the Visitors Center.

SPRING

National Cherry Blossom Festival

In 1912, First Lady Mrs. William Howard Taft and the Vicountess Chinda of Japan planted two cherry trees on the northern bank of the Tidal Basin. The trees still stand today, just west of the John Paul Jones statute. These trees were among the 3,020 cherry trees of 12 different varieties given to the United States by the citizens of Japan. Because of the mixture, there are cherry trees in bloom for nigh on three weeks, sometimes longer. Over the years, the profusion of pink and white blossoms has become the harbinger of spring for the entire country. A National Cherry

Cherry blossoms and Jefferson Memorial

Blossom Festival draws visitors from around the world. The festival includes many activities including arts, crafts, and culinary events. The National Park Service post predictions for blooms on their web site: www.nps.gov/nacc/cherry. For information on the festival, call (202) 547-1500, or visit www.nationalcherryblossomfestival.org

Also in the spring:

- The White House Easter Egg Roll
- The Smithsonian Kite Festival

Action: Many visitors opt for a bicycle ride along the National Mall and the Tidal Basin. A list of bicycle rental centers is available at the Visitors Center in the Ronald Reagan Building. A more unusual mode is on a Segway. Escorted group tours are offered using these personal transportation vehicles.

SUMMER

White House tour

Paperwork to tour the White House starts by contacting a member of Congress from your district at least one month (preferably six months) ahead of desired tour date. The self-guided tour, available to groups of 10 or more, includes public rooms such as the Map Room where FDR followed the events of World War II, and the State Dining Room that can seat 140 guests. Tours are offered 7:30 AM to 12:30 PM, Tuesday through Saturday. Lines form early as the tours are first-come, first-served. The White House Visitors Center offers lots of tips on how to make tours more memorable. For more information, call the White House Visitors Center, at (202) 456-7041 or visit www.whitehouse.gov.

Monumental sights

Tributes to moments of American history and to those who have led the country are depicted in monuments all around Washington. Several organizations offer tours at dusk when the long rays of the summer sun stretch along the landscape. Most monuments are illuminated. The dramatic lighting combined with the warm summer air provides breathtaking memories of Lincoln overlooking the Reflection Pool or of the shadows of the Depression depicted at the site of the FDR Memorial.

Other monuments include the African-American Civil War Memorial, the Korean War Veterans Memorial, the National World War II Memorial, the Vietnam Veterans Memorial, the Vietnam Women's Memorial, and the Washington Monument.

Also in the summer:

- Independence Day Celebration
- Arlington National Cemetery Tour

Action: If Washington's humidity gets too intense, relief can be found on board the air-conditioned DC Ducks. The tour on a 33-passenger amphibious vehicle includes live narration and a tour around the Mall before splashing down in the Potomac River for a mini-cruise.

WINTER

Photo junkies

Photographing Washington's building exteriors in winter is aided by a building-height restriction. Back in 1910, the U.S. Congress assured that no building would be taller than the U.S. Capitol. In the middle of winter, in the middle of the city, there's plenty of ambient light for photography.

Stay indoors

The Smithsonian Institution is really 15 different museums, many with retail shops. Other popular museums include:

- The Library of Congress, the largest library in the world
- International Spy Museum, with exhibits on the role of espionage
- National Gallery of Art for the permanent collection and touring exhibits

Also in winter:

- National Christmas Tree Lighting
- Washington Auto Show

Action: The National Gallery Ice Skating Rink is located next to the National Gallery of Art at 7th and Constitution Ave, NW. In the winter it is an outdoor rink set in a sculpture garden. In the spring, the rink is transformed into a fountain set in a flower garden. For information, visit www.dcchamber.org

Visitor information:
Washington, D.C. Convention and
Tourism Corporation
(202) 789-7000
www.washington.org

Musicians in Mexico City serenade visitors.

With advance planning, crossing the border to Mexico or Canada can be easier than you think.

Citizenship Documents

A U.S. passport or proof of citizenship, such as an original or certified birth certificate and photo identification (such as a driver's license) is required for entry into Mexico or Canada. Naturalized U.S. citizens should carry citizenship papers; permanent residents of the United States must bring proof of residency and photo identification.

Traveling with Kids

For children under the age of 18, parents should be prepared to provide evidence, such as a birth certificate or adoption decree, to prove they are indeed the parents. Single or divorced parents and parents traveling without spouses should carry a letter of consent from the absent parent or guardian to bring a child across either border. Mexico requires the letter to be original and notarized. Divorced parents should also bring copies of their custody decree. Adults who are not the parents or guardians of the children they are traveling with must have written permission from the parents or guardians to supervise the children.

Traveling with pets

Traveling with Pets

U.S. visitors may bring a dog or cat to Mexico with a pet health certificate signed by a registered veterinarian and issued within 72 hours of entry and a vaccination certificate for rabies, distemper, hepatitis, pip, and leptospirosis. A permit fee is charged at the time of entry. All dogs and cats three months and older are required to have a current rabies vaccination certificate that should identify the pet and indicate the trade name of the licensed rabies vaccine, serial number and duration of validity in order to enter Canada. Pit bulls are not permitted to enter Ontario.

Re-entry to the U.S.

Proof of both citizenship and identity is required for entry into the United States. Be able to provide proof of U.S. citizenship via a U.S. passport, or a certified copy of your birth certificate, a Certificate of Naturalization, a Certificate of Citizenship, or a Report of Birth Abroad of a U.S. citizen. To prove your identity, present either a valid driver's license, or a government identification card that includes a photo or physical description.

By January 1, 2008, the Western Hemisphere Travel Initiative will require all U.S. citizens to carry a passport or other secure document in order to enter or re-enter the United States. This initiative will be rolled out in two phases:

- December 31, 2006: Requirement applied to all air and sea travel to or from Canada, Mexico, Central and South America, the Caribbean, and Bermuda.

- December 31, 2007: Requirement extended to all land border crossings.

In 2006, the government began producing a secure, alternative passport card for U.S. citizens in border communities who frequently cross to Mexico or Canada. The biometric card will meet the requirement for this initiative and help expedite travel through ports of entry.

Border Crossing Waits

Allow plenty of time. The average time for customs clearance is 30 minutes, but this varies greatly depending on traffic flow and security issues.

MEXICO ONLY

Driving in Mexico

According to U.S. Department of State, tourists traveling beyond the border zone must obtain a temporary import permit or risk having their car confiscated by Mexican customs officials. To acquire a permit, you must submit evidence of citizenship, title for the car, a car registration certificate, driver's license, and a processing fee to either a Banjercito (Mexican Army Bank) branch located at a Mexican Customs office at the port of entry, or at one of the Mexican consulates in the U.S. Mexican law also requires posting a bond at a Banjercito office to guarantee departure of the car from Mexico within a period determined at the time of application. Carry proof of car ownership (the current registration card or a letter of authorization from the finance or leasing company). Auto insurance policies, other than Mexican, are not valid in Mexico. A short-term liability policy is obtainable at the border.

Tourist Cards

Tourist cards are valid up to six months, require a fee, and are required for all persons, regardless of age, to visit the interior of Mexico. Cards may be obtained from Mexican border authorities, Consuls of Mexico, or Federal Delegates in major cities. Cards are also distributed to passengers en route to Mexico by air.

For additional information on traveling in Mexico, contact the Mexican Embassy in Washington, D.C.: (202) 736-1000; www.embassyofmexico.org or go to the U.S. Department of State website, www.travel.state.gov/travel/tips/regional/regional_1174.html

CANADA ONLY

Driving in Canada

Drivers need proof of ownership of the vehicle or documentation of its rental, a valid U.S. driver's license, and automobile insurance.

Fast Pass for Frequent Travelers

For frequent travelers, the United States and Canada have instituted the NEXUS program, which allows pre-screened, low-risk travelers to be processed with little or no delay by U.S. and Canadian border officials. Approved applicants are issued photo identification and a proximity card, and they can quickly cross the border in a dedicated traffic lane without routine customs and immigration questioning (unless they are randomly selected).

For additional information on traveling in Canada, contact the Canadian Embassy in Washington, D.C.: (202) 682-1740; www.canadianembassy.org or go to the U.S. Department of State website, travel.state.gov/travel/tips/regional/regional_1170.html

DUTY-FREE DEFINED

Duty-free shops are shops where taxes on commercial goods are neither collected by a government, nor paid by an importer. For example, a Swiss watch purchased in a jewelry store in Mexico may cost you $250, a price that includes the duty and taxes that the importer paid to import it. The same watch purchased in a duty-free shop may only cost $175. That's because as long as the item stays in the duty-free shop, or exits the country with the purchaser, it has not been formally imported into the country. There has been no duty charged on it, and the duty-free shop owner has been able to pass on that savings. Its price is free of duty.

If you exceed your personal exemption, when you bring purchases home to the U.S from any shops, including those called duty-free, you will have to pay duty.

Source: U.S. Customs and Border Protection

FOOD POLICE

To protect community health and preserve domestic plant and animal life, many kinds of foods either are prohibited from entering the United States or require an import permit.

1. Every fruit or vegetable must be declared and presented for inspection, no matter how free of pests it appears to be. Failure to declare all food products can result in civil penalties.

2. Bakery goods and cured cheeses are generally admissible.

3. Permission to bring meats, livestock, poultry, and their by-products into the United States depends on the animal disease condition in the country of origin.

   - Fresh meat is generally prohibited from most countries.

   - Canned, cured, or dried meat is severely restricted from some countries.

Contact the U.S. Department of Agriculture, Animal Plant Health Inspection Services for more detailed information.

Source: U.S. Customs and Border Protection

HOTEL RESOURCES

Adam's Mark Hotels & Resorts
(800) 444-2326
www.adamsmark.com

America's Best Inns & Suites
(800) 237-8466
www.americasbestinns.com

AmericInn
(800) 396-5007

Baymont Inns & Suites
(877) 229-6668
www.baymontinn.com

Best Western
(800) 780-7234
www.bestwestern.com

Budget Host
(800) 283-4678
www.budgethost.com

Clarion Hotels
(877) 424-6423
www.clarioninn.com

Coast Hotels & Resorts
(800) 716-6199
www.coasthotels.com

Comfort Inns
(877) 424-6423
www.comfortinn.com

Comfort Suites
(877) 424-6423
www.comfortsuites.com

Courtyard by Marriott
(888) 236-2427
www.courtyard.com

Crowne Plaza Hotel & Resorts
(877) 227-6963
www.crowneplaza.com

Days Inn
(800) 329-7466
www.daysinn.com

Delta Hotels & Resorts
(888) 778-5050
(877) 814-7706
www.deltahotels.com

Doubletree Hotels & Guest Suites
(800) 222-8733
www.doubletree.com

Drury Hotels
(800) 378-7946
www.druryhotels.com

Econo Lodge
(877) 424-6423
www.econolodge.com

Embassy Suites Hotels
(800) 362-2779
www.embassysuites.com

Exel Inns of America
(800) 367-3935
www.exelinns.com

Extended StayAmerica
(800) 804-3724
www.extstay.com

Fairfield Inn by Marriott
(800) 228-2800
www.fairfieldinn.com

Fairmont Hotels & Resorts
(800) 257-7544
www.fairmont.com

Four Points Hotels by Sheraton
(800) 368-7764
www.fourpoints.com

Four Seasons Hotels & Resorts
(800) 819-5053
www.fourseasons.com

Hampton Inn
(800) 426-7866
www.hamptoninn.com

Hilton Hotels
(800) 445-8667
www.hilton.com

Holiday Inn Hotels & Resorts
(800) 465-4329
www.holidayinn.com

Homewood Suites
(800) 225-5466
www.homewood-suites.com

Howard Johnson Lodges
(800) 446-4656
www.hojo.com

Hyatt Hotels & Resorts
(888) 591-1234
www.hyatt.com

InterContinental Hotels & Resorts
(888) 424-6835
www.intercontinental.com

Jameson Inns
(800) 526-3766
www.jamesoninns.com

Knights Inn
(800) 843-5644
www.knightsinn.com

La Quinta Inn & Suites
(800) 642-4271
www.lq.com

Le Meridien Hotels
(800) 543-4300
www.lemeridien.com

Loews Hotels
(866) 563-9792
www.loewshotels.com

MainStay Suites
(877) 424-6423
www.mainstaysuites.com

Marriott International
(888) 236-2427
www.marriott.com

Microtel Inns & Suites
(800) 771-7171
www.microtelinn.com

Motel 6
(800) 466-8356
www.motel6.com

Omni Hotels
(888) 444-6664
www.omnihotels.com

Park Inn
(888) 201-1801
www.parkinn.com

Preferred Hotels & Resorts
(800) 323-7500
www.preferredhotels.com

Quality Inns & Suites
(877) 424-6423
www.qualityinn.com

Radisson Hotels & Resorts
(888) 201-1718
www.radisson.com

Ramada Inn/Ramada Limited/Ramada Plaza Hotels
(800) 272-6232
www.ramada.com

Red Lion Hotels
(800) 733-5466
www.redlion.com

Red Roof Inns
(800) 733-7663
www.redroof.com

Renaissance Hotels & Resorts
(800) 468-3571
www.renaissancehotels.com

Residence Inn by Marriott
(800) 331-3131
www.residenceinn.com

The Ritz-Carlton
(800) 241-3333
www.ritzcarlton.com

Rodeway Inn
(877) 424-6423
www.rodeway.com

Sheraton Hotels & Resorts
(800) 325-3535
www.sheraton.com

Signature Inns
(800) 526-3766
www.signatureinns.com

Sleep Inn
(877) 424-6423
www.sleepinn.com

Super 8 Motel
(800) 800-8000
www.super8.com

Travelodge Hotels
(800) 578-7878
www.travelodge.com

WestCoast Hotels
(800) 325-4000
www.westcoasthotels.com

Westin Hotels & Resorts
(800) 937-8461
www.westin.com

Wyndham Hotels & Resorts
(877) 999-3223
www.wyndham.com

RENTAL CAR RESOURCES

Take advantage of car rental opportunities

Advantage Rent-a-Car
(800) 777-5500
www.arac.com

Alamo
(800) 462-5266
www.alamo.com

Avis
(800) 331-1212
www.avis.com

Budget Rent-a-Car
(800) 527-0700 (U.S.)
www.budget.com

Enterprise Rent-a-Car
(800) 261-7331
www.enterprise.com

Hertz
(800) 654-3131 (U.S.)
(800) 654-3001 (International)
www.hertz.com

National Car Rental
(800) 227-7368
www.nationalcar.com

Payless Car Rental
(800) 729-5377
(U.S., Canada & Mexico)
www.800-payless.com

Thrifty Car Rental
(800) 847-4389
www.thrifty.com

CELL PHONE EMERGENCY NUMBERS

Alabama *47
Alaska 911
Arizona 911
Arkansas 911
California 911
Colorado 911; *277; (303) 329-4501
Connecticut 911
Delaware 911
D.C. 911
Florida 911
Georgia 911
Hawaii None
Idaho *477
Illinois 911
Indiana 911
Iowa 911; *55
Kansas *47

Kentucky (800) 222-5555 (in KY)
Louisiana 911; *577 (road emergencies)
Maine 911
Maryland 911
Massachusetts 911
Michigan 911
Minnesota 911
Mississippi 911
Missouri *55
Montana 911
Nebraska 911
Nevada *647
New Hampshire 911
New Jersey 911
New Mexico 911
New York 911
North Carolina 911

North Dakota *2121
Ohio 911
Oklahoma 911
Oregon 911
Pennsylvania 911
Rhode Island 911
South Carolina 911
South Dakota 911
Tennessee 911
Texas 911
Utah 911
Vermont 911
Virginia 911
Washington 911
West Virginia 911
Wisconsin 911
Wyoming 911

Checking out

To find a bed-and-breakfast at your destination, log on to bedandbreakfast.com®

NOTE: All toll-free reservation numbers are for the U.S. and Canada unless otherwise noted. These numbers were accurate at press time, but are subject to change. Find more listings or book a hotel online at randmcnally.com.

TRAVEL GUIDE On-the-road Resources

Mileage Chart

This handy chart offers more than 5,300 mileages covering 90 North American cities and U.S. National Parks. Want more mileages? Just visit **go.randmcnally.com/MC**, then type in any two cities or addresses.

	Albany NY	Albuquerque NM	Atlanta GA	Baltimore MD	Billings MT	Birmingham AL	Boise ID	Boston MA	Buffalo NY	Charleston SC	Charleston WV	Charlotte NC	Cheyenne WY	Chicago IL	Cleveland OH	Columbia SC	Columbus OH	Dallas TX	Denver CO	Des Moines IA	Detroit MI
Acadia N.P. ME	442	2523	1404	682	2516	1489	2949	292	737	1241	1062	1114	2215	1262	920	1190	1059	2072	2258	1580	1090
Albany NY		2081	1006	337	2075	1091	2507	164	295	896	664	768	1773	820	478	858	617	1674	1816	1138	648
Albuquerque NM	2081		1404	1926	994	1256	944	2245	1792	1725	1555	1630	539	1343	1606	1617	1465	647	439	977	1586
Amarillo TX	1796	285	1119	1641	970	971	1245	1960	1507	1440	1270	1345	515	1058	1321	1332	1180	362	430	798	1301
Atlanta GA	1006	1404		674	1831	149	2179	1098	896	321	503	244	1445	713	716	213	575	794	1419	899	726
Baltimore MD	337	1926	674		1960	783	2392	404	378	563	369	436	1658	705	380	512	416	1366	1696	1023	533
Big Bend N.P. TX	2239	591	1361	1931	1393	1216	1531	2331	1941	1682	1616	1605	938	1442	1755	1574	1614	565	838	1182	1685
Billings MT	2075	994	1831	1960		1779	620	2239	1786	2136	1739	1996	455	1246	1596	2027	1603	1428	555	943	1533
Birmingham AL	1091	1256	149	783	1779		2127	1183	905	470	570	393	1393	661	719	362	578	649	1339	847	729
Boise ID	2507	944	2179	2392	620	2127		2671	2218	2484	2134	2344	735	1702	2028	2375	2024	1703	830	1367	1965
Boston MA	164	2245	1098	404	2239	1183	2671		459	963	756	836	1937	984	642	912	781	1766	1980	1302	812
Brownsville TX	2116	993	1152	1808	1760	1026	2035	2208	1849	1468	1524	1396	1305	1480	1663	1360	1522	547	1220	1230	1673
Buffalo NY	295	1792	896	378	1786	905	2218	459		864	439	658	1484	531	189	748	328	1376	1527	849	359
Calgary AB	2460	1545	2357	2345	551	2305	755	2624	2171	2549	2124	2409	1006	1631	1981	2440	1988	1979	1106	1467	1918
Charleston SC	896	1725	321	563	2136	470	2484	963	864		471	208	1750	911	721	113	638	1115	1724	1207	839
Charleston WV	664	1555	503	369	1739	570	2134	756	439	471		265	1400	486	250	355	167	1051	1374	782	368
Charlotte NC	768	1630	244	436	1996	393	2344	836	658	208	265		1610	771	515	92	432	1038	1584	1067	633
Cheyenne WY	1773	539	1445	1658	455	1393	735	1937	1484	1750	1400	1610		968	1294	1641	1290	973	100	633	1231
Chicago IL	820	1343	713	705	1246	661	1702	984	531	911	486	771	968		341	802	350	933	1011	333	278
Cincinnati OH	727	1399	464	523	1546	467	1958	891	438	619	193	479	1224	293	252	510	111	938	1211	589	262
Cleveland OH	478	1606	716	380	1596	719	2028	642	189	721	250	515	1294	341		605	142	1190	1337	659	169
Columbia SC	858	1617	213	512	2027	362	2375	912	748	113	355	92	1641	802	605		522	1007	1615	1098	723
Columbus OH	617	1465	575	416	1603	578	2024	781	328	638	167	432	1290	350	142	522		1049	1277	655	202
Crater Lake N.P. OR	2917	1336	2589	2802	1033	2537	421	3081	2628	2894	2544	2754	1145	2112	2438	2785	2434	1983	1240	1777	2375
Dallas TX	1674	647	794	1366	1428	649	1703	1766	1376	1115	1051	1038	973	933	1190	1007	1049		882	683	1200
Denver CO	1816	439	1419	1696	555	1339	830	1980	1527	1724	1374	1584	100	1011	1337	1615	1277	882		676	1274
Des Moines IA	1138	977	899	1023	943	847	1367	1302	849	1207	782	1067	633	333	659	1098	655	683	676		596
Detroit MI	648	1586	726	533	1533	729	1965	812	359	839	368	633	1231	278	169	723	202	1200	1274	596	
El Paso TX	2307	267	1429	1999	1261	1284	1207	2399	1939	1750	1684	1673	806	1490	1753	1642	1612	633	706	1124	1733
Fargo ND	1472	1314	1369	1357	607	1317	1229	1636	1183	1561	1136	1421	791	643	993	1452	1000	1085	876	479	930
Grand Canyon N.P. AZ	2485	404	1808	2330	1073	1660	861	2649	2196	2129	1959	2034	779	1747	2010	2021	1869	1051	681	1355	1990
Grand Junction CO	2060	382	1665	1942	664	1585	625	2224	1771	1970	1620	1830	344	1255	1581	1861	1523	1128	246	920	1518
Great Smoky Mts. N.P.	839	1443	187	531	1809	300	2157	931	711	351	318	211	1423	584	544	242	403	883	1397	880	554
Hartford CT	109	2142	1001	307	2158	1086	2590	100	404	866	659	739	1856	903	578	815	678	1669	1899	1221	731
Houston TX	1761	890	797	1453	1675	671	1950	1853	1495	1113	1170	1041	1220	1089	1309	1005	1168	247	1035	948	1319
Indianapolis IN	789	1292	528	592	1434	476	1851	953	500	728	303	588	1117	181	314	619	173	882	1104	482	294
Jackson MS	1331	1055	386	1023	1688	241	2047	1423	1130	707	810	630	1317	747	944	599	803	408	1226	828	954
Jacksonville FL	1072	1648	346	739	2177	468	2525	1139	1040	239	647	384	1791	1059	897	289	814	1001	1765	1245	1015
Kansas City MO	1285	783	811	1088	1024	759	1372	1449	996	1116	766	976	638	529	810	1007	669	489	608	194	765
Las Vegas NV	2563	576	1980	2445	967	1832	632	2727	2274	2301	2123	2206	829	1758	2084	2193	2026	1223	749	1423	2021
Little Rock AR	1359	881	529	1051	1407	381	1785	1451	1061	850	736	755	1055	655	875	742	734	315	964	576	885
Los Angeles CA	2836	799	2203	2725	1240	2055	846	3000	2547	2524	2354	2429	1102	2031	2357	2416	2264	1439	1022	1696	2294
Louisville KY	830	1306	418	618	1537	366	1885	994	541	614	249	474	1151	299	355	505	214	837	1125	593	365
Memphis TN	1222	1014	391	914	1477	243	1825	1314	924	712	599	618	1091	536	738	604	597	454	1097	617	748
Mexico City MX	2725	1376	1761	2417	2257	1635	2316	2817	2527	2077	2202	2005	1802	2084	2341	1969	2200	1151	1717	1834	2351
Miami FL	1415	1963	661	1082	2492	783	2840	1482	1383	582	990	727	2106	1374	1240	632	1157	1316	2080	1560	1387
Milwaukee WI	921	1351	812	806	1175	760	1741	1085	632	1010	585	870	1007	92	442	901	449	1016	1050	372	379
Minneapolis MN	1235	1222	1132	1120	843	1080	1465	1399	946	1324	899	1184	878	406	756	1215	763	928	921	243	693
Mobile AL	1335	1245	329	1003	1874	261	2237	1427	1164	645	826	573	1507	920	978	537	837	598	1416	1014	988
Montpelier VT	169	2210	1180	509	2204	1265	2636	187	424	1068	838	942	1902	949	607	1017	746	1848	1945	1267	777
Montréal QC	226	2151	1222	562	2099	1307	2531	324	402	1121	835	984	1797	844	585	1074	724	1765	1840	1162	569
Nashville TN	1012	1223	243	704	1590	189	1938	1104	716	548	391	408	1204	472	530	439	389	663	1178	658	540
New Orleans LA	1432	1173	468	1124	1868	342	2228	1524	1243	784	911	712	1498	927	1057	676	916	526	1407	1008	1067
New York NY	159	2022	873	203	2066	982	2498	208	399	762	555	635	1764	811	486	711	554	1565	1807	1129	639
Norfolk VA	509	1910	558	234	2147	707	2544	576	576	431	410	320	1810	892	567	380	577	1350	1784	1192	720
Oklahoma City OK	1536	544	860	1382	1220	712	1495	1700	1247	1181	1010	1086	765	798	1061	1073	920	208	674	538	1041
Olympic N.P. WA	3017	1554	2773	2902	940	2721	615	3181	2728	3078	2681	2938	1345	2188	2538	2969	2545	2313	1440	1885	2475
Omaha NE	1278	869	995	1163	841	943	1233	1442	989	1300	950	1160	499	473	799	1191	795	672	542	138	736
Orlando FL	1214	1742	440	881	2271	562	2619	1281	1182	381	789	526	1885	1153	1039	431	956	1095	1859	1339	1166
Philadelphia PA	243	1941	772	102	2017	885	2449	310	388	661	476	534	1715	762	437	610	473	1468	1753	1080	590
Phoenix AZ	2544	463	1867	2389	1207	1719	922	2708	2255	2188	2018	2093	1002	1806	2069	2080	1928	1069	902	1440	2049
Pittsburgh PA	474	1651	686	251	1716	753	2148	586	216	654	229	448	1414	461	136	538	183	1228	1457	779	289
Portland ME	267	2348	1229	507	2342	1314	2774	117	562	1066	887	939	2040	1087	745	1015	884	1897	2083	1405	915
Portland OR	2927	1364	2599	2812	891	2547	425	3091	2638	2904	2554	2764	1155	2122	2448	2795	2444	2123	1250	1787	2385
Québec QC	373	2308	1379	709	2256	1464	2688	403	559	1268	992	1141	1954	1001	742	1231	881	1922	1997	1319	726
Raleigh NC	628	1759	407	295	2064	556	2473	695	637	280	325	169	1739	811	575	229	492	1199	1713	1107	693
Rapid City SD	1738	839	1514	1623	321	1462	943	1902	1449	1819	1410	1679	300	909	1259	1710	1266	1069	400	626	1196
Regina SK	2014	1282	1911	1899	475	1859	1097	2178	1725	2103	1678	1963	743	1185	1535	1994	1542	1520	843	1021	1472
Reno NV	2729	1021	2401	2614	959	2277	424	2893	2440	2706	2356	2566	957	1924	2250	2597	2246	1668	1052	1589	2187
St. Louis MO	1038	1043	557	841	1276	505	1624	1202	749	862	512	722	890	300	563	753	422	633	864	344	543
Salt Lake City UT	2206	605	1878	2091	552	1826	340	2370	1917	2183	1833	2043	434	1401	1727	2074	1723	1402	529	1066	1664
San Antonio TX	1956	715	992	1648	1482	866	1757	2048	1653	1308	1328	1236	1027	1210	1467	1200	1326	277	942	960	1477
San Diego CA	2896	816	2157	2742	1300	2012	965	3060	2607	2478	2371	2401	1162	2091	2417	2370	2281	1361	1082	1756	2354
San Francisco CA	2953	1097	2501	2838	1183	2353	648	3117	2664	2822	2580	2727	1181	2148	2474	2714	2470	1744	1276	1813	2411
Sault Ste. Marie ON	809	1784	1050	869	1282	1010	1904	944	519	1163	692	957	1422	469	505	1047	526	1374	1465	787	350
Savannah GA	938	1656	252	605	2083	401	2431	1005	906	105	513	250	1697	953	763	155	680	990	1671	1151	881
Seattle WA	2897	1434	2653	2782	820	2601	495	3061	2608	2958	2561	2818	1225	2068	2418	2849	2425	2193	1320	1765	2355
Shenandoah N.P. VA	462	1798	570	127	1952	655	2412	531	380	538	278	332	1678	697	372	422	408	1238	1652	1015	525
Shreveport LA	1553	833	608	1245	1613	463	1888	1645	1257	929	932	852	1158	851	1071	821	930	186	1067	736	1081
Spokane WA	2616	1327	2372	2501	539	2320	423	2780	2327	2677	2280	2537	996	1787	2137	2568	2144	1969	1096	1484	2074
Tampa FL	1270	1760	458	937	2289	580	2637	1337	1238	437	845	582	1903	1171	1095	487	1033	1113	1877	1357	1184
Thunder Bay ON	1189	1564	1378	1310	1049	1326	1671	1327	958	1570	1133	1398	1220	652	946	1461	967	1270	1263	585	791
Toronto ON	400	1818	958	490	1766	961	2198	564	110	974	549	768	1464	511	299	858	438	1432	1507	829	236
Tucson AZ	2532	451	1748	2318	1324	1603	1039	2718	2243	2069	2003	1992	990	1794	2057	1961	1916	952	890	1428	2037
Vancouver BC	3035	1572	2791	2920	958	2739	633	3199	2746	3096	2699	2956	1363	2206	2556	2987	2563	2331	1458	1903	2493
Washington DC	371	1886	636	38	1961	743	2393	438	389	525	366	398	1659	706	381	474	417	1326	1697	1024	534
Wichita KS	1475	593	970	1278	1063	822	1338	1639	1186	1291	956	1104	608	719	1000	1183	859	365	517	384	955
Winnipeg MB	1693	1533	1590	1578	723	1538	1345	1763	1404	1782	1357	1642	1010	864	1214	1673	1221	1304	1095	700	1151
Yellowstone N.P. WY	2251	975	2007	2136	174	1955	439	2415	1962	2312	1915	2172	520	1422	1772	2203	1779	1493	620	1119	1709
Yosemite N.P. CA	2823	989	2393	2708	1129	2245	594	2987	2534	2714	2450	2619	1051	2018	2344	2606	2340	1636	1048	1683	2281

	El Paso TX	Fargo ND	Grand Junction CO	Hartford CT	Houston TX	Indianapolis IN	Jackson MS	Jacksonville FL	Kansas City MO	Las Vegas NV	Little Rock AR	Los Angeles CA	Louisville KY	Memphis TN	Miami FL	Milwaukee WI	Minneapolis MN	Nashville TN
Acadia N.P. ME	2705	1913	2502	378	2159	1231	1729	1417	1727	3005	1757	3278	1272	1620	1760	1363	1676	1410
Albany NY	2307	1472	2060	109	1761	789	1331	1072	1285	2563	1359	2836	830	1222	1415	921	1235	1012
Albuquerque NM	267	1314	382	2142	890	1292	1055	1648	783	576	881	799	1306	1014	1963	1351	1222	1223
Amarillo TX	432	1011	674	1857	605	1007	770	1363	604	861	596	1084	1021	729	1678	1141	1043	938
Atlanta GA	1429	1369	1665	1001	797	528	386	346	811	1980	529	2203	418	391	661	812	1132	243
Baltimore MD	1999	1357	1942	307	1453	592	1023	739	1088	2445	1051	2725	618	914	1082	806	1120	704
Big Bend N.P. TX	324	1521	973	2234	641	1391	975	1512	988	1050	880	1130	1402	1019	1827	1525	1427	1228
Billings MT	1261	607	664	2158	1675	1434	1688	2177	1024	967	1407	1240	1537	1477	2492	1175	843	1590
Birmingham AL	1284	1317	1585	1086	671	476	241	468	759	1832	381	2055	366	243	783	760	1080	189
Boise ID	1207	1229	625	2590	1950	1851	2047	2525	1372	632	1785	846	1885	1825	2840	1741	1465	1938
Boston MA	2399	1636	2224	100	1853	953	1423	1139	1449	2727	1451	3000	994	1314	1482	1085	1399	1104
Brownsville TX	836	1620	1375	2111	355	1379	797	1230	1036	1562	788	1642	1310	927	1545	1563	1475	1136
Buffalo NY	1939	1183	1771	404	1495	500	1130	1040	996	2274	1061	2547	541	924	1383	632	946	716
Calgary AB	1812	992	1154	2543	2226	1819	2239	2703	1575	1284	1958	1557	1937	2028	3018	1560	1228	2116
Charleston SC	1750	1561	1970	866	1113	728	707	239	1116	2301	850	2524	614	712	582	1010	1324	548
Charleston WV	1684	1136	1620	659	1170	303	810	647	766	2123	736	2354	249	599	990	585	899	391
Charlotte NC	1673	1421	1830	739	1041	588	630	384	976	2206	755	2429	474	618	727	870	1184	408
Cheyenne WY	806	791	344	1856	1220	1117	1317	1791	638	829	1055	1102	1151	1091	2106	1007	878	1204
Chicago IL	1490	643	1255	903	1089	181	747	1059	529	1758	655	2031	299	536	1374	92	406	472
Cincinnati OH	1571	943	1457	788	1057	110	692	795	603	1960	623	2198	103	486	1125	392	706	278
Cleveland OH	1753	993	1581	578	1309	314	944	897	810	2084	875	2357	355	738	1240	442	756	530
Columbia SC	1642	1452	1861	815	1005	619	599	289	1007	2193	742	2416	505	604	632	901	1215	439
Columbus OH	1612	1000	1523	678	1168	173	803	814	669	2026	734	2264	214	597	1157	449	763	389
Crater Lake N.P. OR	1486	1642	991	3000	2226	2261	2391	2935	1782	760	2195	749	2295	2235	3250	2151	1878	2348
Dallas TX	633	1085	1128	1669	247	882	408	1001	489	1223	315	1439	837	454	1316	1016	928	663
Denver CO	706	876	246	1899	1035	1104	1226	1765	608	749	964	1022	1125	1097	2080	1050	921	1178
Des Moines IA	1124	479	920	1221	948	482	828	1245	194	1423	576	1696	593	617	1560	372	243	658
Detroit MI	1733	930	1518	731	1319	294	954	1015	765	2021	885	2294	365	748	1387	379	693	540
El Paso TX		1375	649	2302	753	1439	1043	1624	930	726	948	806	1470	1087	1939	1498	1369	1296
Fargo ND	1375		1120	1555	1332	831	1265	1715	601	1576	984	1849	949	1054	2030	572	240	1128
Grand Canyon N.P. AZ	653	1555	437	2546	1294	1696	1459	2052	1187	272	1285	495	1710	1418	2367	1729	1600	1627
Grand Junction CO	649	1120		2143	1279	1350	1472	2011	854	505	1210	778	1371	1343	2326	1294	1165	1424
Great Smoky Mts. N.P.	1516	1234	1643	834	970	401	540	527	789	2019	568	2242	287	431	870	683	997	221
Hartford CT	2302	1555	2143		1756	850	1326	1042	1346	2646	1354	2919	891	1217	1385	1004	1318	1007
Houston TX	753	1332	1279	1756		1025	442	875	732	1466	434	1559	956	573	1190	1163	1171	782
Indianapolis IN	1439	831	1350	850	1025		683	874	496	1853	591	2091	114	472	1189	280	594	287
Jackson MS	1043	1265	1472	1326	442	683		593	664	1631	262	1849	591	212	908	837	1062	417
Jacksonville FL	1624	1715	2011	1042	875	874	593		1157	2224	847	2430	764	709	343	1158	1478	589
Kansas City MO	930	601	854	1346	732	496	664	1157		1357	383	1630	517	453	1472	568	439	570
Las Vegas NV	726	1576	505	2646	1466	1853	1631	2224	1357		1457	275	1874	1590	2539	1797	1668	1799
Little Rock AR	948	984	1210	1354	434	591	262	847	383	1457		1680	522	139	1162	729	821	348
Los Angeles CA	806	1849	778	2919	1559	2091	1849	2430	1630	275	1680		2105	1813	2745	2070	1941	2022
Louisville KY	1470	949	1371	891	956	114	591	764	517	1874	522	2105		385	1079	398	712	177
Memphis TN	1087	1054	1343	1217	573	472	212	709	453	1590	139	1813	385		1024	626	851	211
Mexico City MX	1109	2224	1758	2720	964	2033	1406	1839	1640	1723	1466	1803	1988	1605	2154	2167	2079	1814
Miami FL	1939	2030	2326	1385	1190	1189	908	343	1472	2539	1162	2745	1079	1024		1473	1793	904
Milwaukee WI	1498	572	1294	1004	1163	280	837	1158	568	1797	729	2070	398	626	1473		335	571
Minneapolis MN	1369	240	1165	1318	1171	594	1062	1478	439	1668	821	1941	712	851	1793	335		891
Mobile AL	1221	1451	1662	1330	472	735	190	403	850	1821	452	2027	625	398	718	1019	1248	448
Montpelier VT	2481	1601	2189	202	1935	918	1505	1244	1414	2692	1533	2965	959	1396	1587	1050	1364	1186
Montréal QC	2298	1496	2084	335	1884	859	1547	1297	1331	2587	1450	2860	930	1313	1640	945	1259	1105
Nashville TN	1296	1128	1424	1007	782	287	417	589	570	1799	348	2022	177	211	904	571	891	
New Orleans LA	1100	1445	1653	1427	351	814	180	546	844	1749	423	1906	704	392	861	1017	1242	527
New York NY	2198	1463	2051	111	1652	730	1222	938	1226	2554	1250	2827	764	1113	1281	912	1226	903
Norfolk VA	1983	1544	2030	479	1355	713	944	607	1176	2486	1035	2709	659	898	950	993	1307	688
Oklahoma City OK	691	877	920	1597	455	747	615	1178	344	1120	337	1343	761	470	1493	881	783	679
Olympic N.P. WA	1817	1549	1235	3100	2560	2376	2657	3119	1966	1242	2395	1200	2479	2419	3434	2117	1785	2532
Omaha NE	1016	418	786	1361	919	622	852	1341	188	1289	571	1562	701	641	1656	512	383	754
Orlando FL	1718	1809	2105	1184	969	968	687	142	1251	2318	941	2524	858	803	229	1252	1572	683
Philadelphia PA	2101	1414	1999	213	1555	649	1125	837	1145	2502	1153	2740	683	1016	1180	863	1177	806
Phoenix AZ	436	1777	571	2605	1189	1755	1479	2060	1246	290	1344	370	1769	1477	2375	1814	1685	1686
Pittsburgh PA	1861	1113	1701	486	1347	359	993	830	855	2204	913	2450	393	776	1173	562	876	568
Portland ME	2530	1739	2327	203	1984	1056	1554	1242	1552	2830	1582	3103	1097	1445	1585	1188	1502	1235
Portland OR	1627	1500	1045	3010	2370	2271	2467	2945	1792	1021	2205	967	2305	2245	3260	2068	1736	2358
Québec QC	2455	1653	2241	430	2041	1016	1704	1444	1488	2744	1607	3017	1087	1470	1787	1102	1416	1262
Raleigh NC	1832	1461	1959	598	1204	628	793	456	1105	2335	884	2558	574	747	799	910	1224	537
Rapid City SD	1106	549	644	1821	1316	1110	1371	1860	707	1039	1090	1312	1220	1160	2175	838	609	1273
Regina SK	1549	546	1087	2097	1767	1373	1805	2257	1141	1444	1524	1717	1491	1594	2572	1114	782	1670
Reno NV	1171	1568	803	2812	1911	2073	2076	2747	1594	445	1902	473	2107	2035	3062	1963	1834	2160
St. Louis MO	1190	853	1110	1099	780	249	495	903	256	1613	346	1842	263	284	1218	383	578	316
Salt Lake City UT	868	1161	286	2289	1649	1550	1746	2224	1071	416	1484	689	1584	1524	2539	1440	1311	1637
San Antonio TX	558	1350	1097	1951	199	1159	637	1070	766	1284	592	1364	1114	731	1385	1293	1205	940
San Diego CA	728	1909	838	2958	1481	2108	1771	2352	1599	335	1676	124	2122	1830	2667	2130	2001	2039
San Francisco CA	1187	1792	1027	3036	1940	2297	2152	2745	1818	573	1978	381	2331	2111	3060	2187	2058	2320
Sault Ste. Marie ON	1931	679	1709	918	1527	538	1185	1339	956	2212	1093	2485	648	974	1711	404	550	821
Savannah GA	1625	1621	1917	908	972	770	582	140	1063	2232	781	2455	656	643	483	1052	1384	495
Seattle WA	1697	1429	1115	2980	2440	2256	2537	2999	1846	1122	2275	1142	2359	2299	3314	1997	1665	2412
Shenandoah N.P. VA	1871	1349	1898	434	1325	581	895	714	1044	2374	923	2597	527	786	1057	798	1112	576
Shreveport LA	821	1144	1313	1548	239	787	222	815	543	1409	196	1627	718	335	1130	925	981	544
Spokane WA	1590	1148	1008	2699	2216	1975	2229	2718	1565	1138	1948	1215	2078	2018	3033	1716	1384	2131
Tampa FL	1736	1827	2123	1240	987	986	705	202	1269	2336	959	2542	876	821	254	1270	1590	701
Thunder Bay ON	1711	446	1507	1298	1513	840	1364	1724	781	2010	1163	2283	958	1153	2039	581	345	1137
Toronto ON	1965	1163	1751	509	1551	526	1186	1150	998	2254	1117	2527	597	980	1493	612	926	772
Tucson AZ	319	1765	688	2621	1072	1743	1362	1943	1234	407	1267	487	1757	1406	2258	1802	1673	1615
Vancouver BC	1835	1567	1253	3118	2578	2394	2675	3137	1984	1260	2413	1285	2497	2437	3452	2135	1803	2550
Washington DC	1959	1358	1943	341	1413	593	983	701	1089	2462	1011	2685	615	874	1044	807	1121	664
Wichita KS	740	687	763	1536	612	686	709	1288	190	1169	447	1392	707	580	1603	758	629	698
Winnipeg MB	1594	221	1339	1776	1551	1052	1484	1936	820	1692	1203	1965	1170	1273	2251	793	461	1349
Yellowstone N.P. WY	1238	783	656	2334	1740	1610	1864	2353	1200	786	1575	1059	1713	1653	2668	1351	1019	1766
Yosemite N.P. CA	1111	1738	804	2906	1864	2167	2044	2637	1688	413	1870	305	2201	2003	2952	2057	1928	2212

	New Orleans LA	New York NY	Norfolk VA	Oklahoma City OK	Omaha NE	Orlando FL	Philadelphia PA	Phoenix AZ	Pittsburgh PA	Portland ME	Portland OR	Rapid City SD	Reno NV	St. Louis MO	Salt Lake City UT	San Antonio TX	San Diego CA	San Francisco CA	Seattle WA	Washington DC	Wichita KS
Acadia N.P. ME	1830	486	854	1978	1720	1559	588	2986	864	175	3368	2180	3171	1480	2648	2354	3338	3395	3338	716	1917
Albany NY	1432	159	509	1536	1278	1214	243	2544	474	267	2927	1738	2729	1038	2206	1956	2896	2953	2897	371	1475
Albuquerque NM	1173	2022	1910	544	869	1742	1941	463	1651	2348	1364	839	1021	1043	605	715	816	1097	1434	1886	593
Amarillo TX	888	1737	1625	259	652	1457	1656	748	1366	2063	1665	721	1306	758	944	512	1101	1382	1735	1601	417
Atlanta GA	468	873	558	860	995	440	772	1867	686	1229	2599	1514	2401	557	1878	992	2157	2501	2653	636	970
Baltimore MD	1124	203	234	1382	1163	881	102	2389	251	507	2812	1623	2614	841	2091	1648	2742	2838	2782	38	1278
Big Bend N.P. TX	988	2130	1915	643	1108	1606	2033	760	1793	2462	1951	1238	1495	1142	1192	446	1052	1511	2021	1891	801
Billings MT	1868	2066	2147	1220	841	2271	2017	1207	1716	2342	891	321	959	1276	552	1482	1300	1183	820	1961	1063
Birmingham AL	342	982	707	712	943	562	885	1719	753	1314	2547	1462	2277	505	1826	866	2012	2353	2601	743	822
Boise ID	2228	2498	2544	1495	1233	2619	2449	922	2148	2774	425	943	424	1624	340	1757	965	648	495	2393	1338
Boston MA	1524	208	576	1700	1442	1281	310	2708	586	117	3091	1902	2893	1202	2370	2048	3060	3117	3061	438	1639
Brownsville TX	706	2007	1710	743	1207	1324	1910	1272	1701	2339	2455	1604	2007	1180	1598	278	1564	2023	2525	1768	900
Buffalo NY	1243	399	576	1247	989	1182	388	2255	216	562	2638	1449	2440	749	1917	1653	2607	2664	2608	389	1186
Calgary AB	2419	2451	2532	1771	1392	2797	2402	1524	2101	2527	795	872	1276	1827	869	2033	1617	1500	675	2346	1614
Charleston SC	784	762	431	1181	1300	381	661	2188	654	1066	2904	1819	2706	862	2183	1308	2478	2822	2958	525	1291
Charleston WV	911	555	410	1010	950	789	476	2018	229	887	2554	1410	2356	512	1833	1328	2371	2580	2561	366	956
Charlotte NC	712	635	320	1086	1160	526	534	2093	448	939	2764	1679	2566	722	2043	1236	2401	2727	2818	398	1104
Cheyenne WY	1498	1764	1810	765	499	1885	1715	1002	1414	2040	1155	300	957	890	434	1027	1162	1181	1225	1659	608
Chicago IL	927	811	892	798	473	1153	762	1806	461	1087	2122	909	1924	300	1401	1210	2091	2148	2068	706	719
Cincinnati OH	805	661	603	854	729	904	580	1862	290	994	2378	1217	2180	356	1657	1215	2215	2404	2368	524	793
Cleveland OH	1057	486	567	1061	799	1039	437	2069	136	745	2448	1259	2250	563	1727	1467	2417	2474	2418	381	1000
Columbia SC	676	711	380	1073	1191	431	610	2080	538	1015	2795	1710	2597	753	2074	1200	2370	2714	2849	474	1183
Columbus OH	916	554	577	920	795	956	473	1928	183	884	2444	1266	2246	422	1723	1326	2281	2470	2425	417	859
Crater Lake N.P. OR	2509	2908	2954	1905	1643	3029	2859	1050	2558	3184	247	1356	317	2034	711	2044	873	418	422	2803	1748
Dallas TX	526	1565	1350	208	672	1095	1468	1069	1228	1897	2123	1069	1668	633	1402	277	1361	1744	2193	1326	365
Denver CO	1407	1807	1784	674	542	1859	1753	902	1457	2083	1250	400	1052	864	529	942	1082	1276	1320	1697	517
Des Moines IA	1008	1129	1192	538	138	1339	1080	1440	779	1405	1787	626	1589	344	1066	960	1756	1813	1765	1024	384
Detroit MI	1067	639	720	1041	736	1166	590	2049	289	915	2385	1196	2187	543	1664	1477	2354	2411	2355	534	955
El Paso TX	1100	2198	1983	691	1016	1718	2101	436	1861	2530	1627	1106	1171	1190	868	558	728	1187	1697	1959	740
Fargo ND	1445	1463	1544	877	418	1809	1414	1777	1113	1739	1500	549	1568	853	1161	1350	1909	1792	1429	1358	687
Grand Canyon N.P. AZ	1577	2426	2314	948	1221	2146	2345	217	2055	2752	1281	1079	717	1447	522	1119	555	793	1351	2290	997
Grand Junction CO	1653	2051	2030	920	786	2105	1999	571	1701	2327	1045	644	803	1110	286	1097	838	1027	1115	1943	763
Great Smoky Mts. N.P.	641	730	491	899	973	623	633	1906	501	1062	2577	1492	2379	535	1856	1165	2259	2540	2631	491	917
Hartford CT	1427	111	479	1597	1361	1184	213	2605	486	203	3010	1821	2812	1099	2289	1951	2958	3036	2980	341	1536
Houston TX	351	1652	1355	455	919	969	1555	1189	1347	1984	2370	1316	1911	780	1649	199	1481	1940	2440	1413	612
Indianapolis IN	814	730	713	747	622	968	649	1755	359	1056	2271	1110	2073	249	1550	1159	2108	2297	2256	593	686
Jackson MS	180	1222	944	615	852	687	1125	1479	993	1554	2467	1371	2076	495	1746	637	1771	2152	2537	983	709
Jacksonville FL	546	938	607	1178	1341	142	837	2060	830	1242	2945	1860	2747	903	2224	1070	2352	2745	2999	701	1288
Kansas City MO	844	1226	1176	344	188	1251	1145	1246	855	1552	1792	707	1594	256	1071	766	1599	1818	1846	1089	190
Las Vegas NV	1749	2554	2486	1120	1289	2318	2502	290	2204	2830	1021	1039	445	1613	416	1284	335	573	1122	2462	1169
Little Rock AR	423	1250	1035	337	571	941	1153	1344	913	1582	2205	1090	1902	346	1484	592	1676	1978	2275	1011	447
Los Angeles CA	1906	2827	2709	1343	1562	2524	2740	370	2450	3103	967	1312	473	1842	689	1364	124	381	1142	2685	1392
Louisville KY	704	764	659	761	701	858	683	1769	393	1097	2305	1220	2107	263	1584	1114	2122	2331	2359	615	707
Memphis TN	392	1113	898	470	641	803	1016	1477	776	1445	2245	1160	2035	284	1524	731	1830	2111	2299	874	580
Mexico City MX	1315	2616	2319	1347	1811	1933	2519	1433	2379	2948	2736	2008	2168	1784	1977	874	1725	2184	2806	2377	1504
Miami FL	861	1281	950	1493	1656	229	1180	2375	1173	1585	3260	2175	3062	1218	2539	1385	2667	3060	3314	1044	1603
Milwaukee WI	1017	912	993	881	512	1252	863	1814	562	1188	2068	838	1963	383	1440	1293	2130	2187	1997	807	758
Minneapolis MN	1242	1226	1307	783	383	1572	1177	1685	876	1502	1736	609	1834	578	1311	1205	2001	2058	1665	1121	629
Mobile AL	143	1202	887	805	1038	497	1101	1657	1009	1558	2657	1557	2266	681	1936	667	1949	2342	2727	965	899
Montpelier VT	1606	313	681	1665	1407	1386	415	2673	634	213	3056	1867	2858	1167	2335	2130	3025	3082	3026	543	1604
Montréal QC	1648	384	734	1606	1302	1439	468	2614	612	262	2951	1762	2753	1108	2230	2042	2920	2977	2921	596	1521
Nashville TN	527	903	688	679	754	683	806	1686	568	1235	2358	1273	2160	316	1637	940	2039	2320	2412	664	698
New Orleans LA		1323	1026	733	1032	640	1226	1536	1094	1655	2648	1551	2194	675	1927	546	1828	2270	2718	1084	890
New York NY	1323		375	1477	1269	1080	109	2485	389	311	2918	1729	2720	979	2197	1847	2838	2944	2888	237	1416
Norfolk VA	1026	375		1366	1360	749	278	2373	438	679	2964	1810	2766	922	2243	1550	2726	2990	2969	196	1366
Oklahoma City OK	733	1477	1366		464	1272	1396	1007	1106	1803	1915	861	1565	498	1194	473	1360	1641	1985	1342	157
Olympic N.P. WA	2838	3008	3089	2105	1783	3213	2959	1532	2658	3284	233	1263	811	2218	950	2367	1324	869	85	2903	1948
Omaha NE	1032	1269	1360	464		1435	1220	1332	919	1545	1653	524	1455	440	932	937	1622	1679	1663	1164	310
Orlando FL	640	1080	749	1272	1435		979	2154	972	1384	3039	1954	2841	997	2318	1164	2446	2839	3093	843	1382
Philadelphia PA	1226	109	278	1396	1220	979		2404	308	413	2869	1680	2671	898	2148	1750	2757	2895	2839	136	1335
Phoenix AZ	1536	2485	2373	1007	1332	2154	2404		2114	2811	1337	1302	735	1506	656	994	353	751	1412	2349	1056
Pittsburgh PA	1094	389	438	1106	919	972	308	2114		689	2568	1379	2370	608	1847	1505	2467	2594	2538	252	1045
Portland ME	1655	311	679	1803	1545	1384	413	2811	689		3194	2005	2996	1305	2473	2179	3163	3220	3164	541	1742
Portland OR	2648	2918	2964	1915	1653	3039	2869	1337	2568	3194		1214	578	2044	760	2177	1091	636	175	2813	1758
Québec QC	1805	531	881	1763	1459	1586	615	2771	769	276	3108	1919	2910	1265	2387	2199	3077	3134	3078	743	1678
Raleigh NC	875	494	177	1215	1289	598	393	2222	499	798	2893	1735	2695	851	2172	1399	2575	2856	2886	257	1233
Rapid City SD	1551	1729	1810	861	524	1954	1680	1302	1379	2005	1214		1167	959	644	1334	1372	1391	1143	1624	704
Regina SK	1985	2005	2086	1312	958	2351	1956	1684	1655	2058	1133	536	1436	1393	1029	1785	1777	1660	1062	1900	1155
Reno NV	2194	2720	2766	1565	1455	2841	2671	735	2370	2996	578	1167		1846	523	1729	565	224	753	2615	1560
St. Louis MO	675	979	922	498	440	997	898	1506	608	1305	2044	959	1846		1323	910	1859	2070	2098	878	446
Salt Lake City UT	1927	2197	2243	1194	932	2318	2148	656	1847	2473	760	644	523	1323		1320	749	747	830	2092	1037
San Antonio TX	546	1847	1550	473	937	1164	1750	994	1505	2179	2177	1334	1729	910	1320		1286	1745	2247	1608	630
San Diego CA	1828	2838	2726	1360	1622	2446	2757	353	2467	3163	1091	1372	565	1859	749	1286		505	1266	2702	1409
San Francisco CA	2270	2944	2990	1641	1679	2839	2895	751	2594	3220	636	1391	224	2070	747	1745	505		811	2839	1784
Sault Ste. Marie ON	1348	937	1056	1239	927	1490	926	2247	625	882	2175	1120	2378	741	1855	1651	2545	2602	2104	870	1146
Savannah GA	643	804	473	1112	1247	282	703	2119	696	1108	2851	1766	2653	809	2130	1167	2353	2753	2905	567	1222
Seattle WA	2718	2888	2969	1985	1663	3093	2839	1412	2538	3164	175	1143	753	2098	830	2247	1266	811		2783	1828
Shenandoah N.P. VA	996	330	205	1254	1155	856	229	2261	243	634	2832	1615	2634	790	2111	1520	2614	2858	2774	87	1234
Shreveport LA	344	1444	1166	393	731	909	1347	1257	1109	1776	2308	1250	1854	542	1587	409	1549	1930	2378	1205	550
Spokane WA	2409	2607	2688	1761	1382	2812	2558	1378	2257	2883	352	862	793	1817	723	2023	1471	885	281	2502	1604
Tampa FL	658	1136	805	1290	1453	83	1035	2172	1028	1440	3057	1972	2859	1015	2336	1182	2464	2857	3111	899	1400
Thunder Bay ON	1544	1343	1497	1125	725	1818	1332	2027	1066	1265	1942	951	2010	869	1653	1547	2343	2234	1871	1311	971
Toronto ON	1299	528	685	1273	969	1292	517	2281	326	592	2618	1429	2420	775	1897	1709	2587	2644	2588	499	1188
Tucson AZ	1419	2517	2302	995	1320	2037	2420	117	2102	2799	1454	1290	852	1494	773	877	409	868	1529	2278	1044
Vancouver BC	2856	3026	3107	2123	1801	3231	2977	1550	2676	3302	318	1281	896	2236	968	2385	1409	954	143	2921	1966
Washington DC	1084	237	196	1342	1164	843	136	2349	252	541	2813	1624	2615	878	2092	1608	2702	2839	2783		1279
Wichita KS	890	1416	1366	157	310	1382	1335	1056	1045	1742	1758	704	1560	446	1037	630	1409	1784	1828	1279	
Winnipeg MB	1664	1684	1765	1096	637	2030	1635	1996	1334	1701	1488	768	1684	1072	1277	1569	2025	1908	1417	1579	906
Yellowstone N.P. WY	2018	2242	2323	1285	1017	2447	2193	1026	1892	2518	835	497	778	1452	371	1547	1119	1002	764	2137	1128
Yosemite N.P. CA	2162	2944	[illegible]	[illegible]	[illegible]	[illegible]	[illegible]	[illegible]	[illegible]	[illegible]	[illegible]	[illegible]	[illegible]	[illegible]	[illegible]	[illegible]	[illegible]	[illegible]	[illegible]	[illegible]	[illegible]